THE NEW BIBLE SURVEY

THE
NEW BIBLE SURVEY

An Introduction to the Reading and Study
of the Bible

by

J. LAWRENCE EASON, M.A., Ph.D.

170 x

ZONDERVAN PUBLISHING HOUSE
GRAND RAPIDS   MICHIGAN

PREFACE

The New Bible Survey is designed for students who are beginning their first or introductory survey course in the basic contents of the Old and New Testaments. It is also well suited to the needs of the general adult reader, who wishes his reading and study of the Bible to be systematic and comprehensive.

This volume lays claim to usefulness on three main counts. One is the organization and arrangement of the total Bible into a few natural divisions. Another is the brief but substantial introduction to each of the books of the Bible. In addition, and by no means the least in importance, are the carefully chosen bibliographies.

The Bible is an ancient book and the beginning student faces certain problems in understanding its contents. The writer still remembers as a youth how puzzled he was trying to understand the big book which the family called the family Bible. It was not until some years afterward that he learned that the Bible was not one book, as he had supposed, but a whole library of sixty-six separate books, under as many separate titles.

Then there is the matter of *time* of origin of these different books. From the earliest to the latest, these sixty-six separate books extend well over a thousand years — from the books of Moses, about 1400 B.C., to the book of Revelation, about 96 A.D. Thus, a wide gulf of chronology lies between these ancient books themselves, and the times that produced them, as well as between the latest of them and the modern reader and the world as he knows it. Indeed, it requires imagination by the modern student to bridge this gulf.

Then, too, there are different kinds of compositions in this library of sixty-six different titles. Indeed, in this one library are contained all the types of great literature found outside the Bible. In the book of Psalms and in the books by the prophets in particular, the reader will find some of the world's greatest lyrics and rhapsodies; drama in the book of Job; short stories in Ruth, Jonah, and the book of Esther; orations in Deuteronomy; history and biography in the seventeen historical books of the Old Testament, and the four gospels and the book of Acts of the New; essays in Ecclesiastes and in the book of Proverbs; and letters by the apostles Paul, James, Peter, Jude, and John.

And this is not all. To add further to the reader's confusion, the books of the Bible frequently are not arranged chronologically as they were written. The most notable example of this in the Old Testament is the order of the books by the prophets, as they appear in our

Bible. For instance, the books of Isaiah and Jeremiah appear first and second respectively; whereas in point of time Isaiah probably appeared about *fifth* and Jeremiah about *ninth,* in order.

In the New Testament, the four gospels come first, whereas most of the great letters of the Apostle Paul were likely written before three of the gospels, Matthew, Luke, and John. Also, the letters of Paul are not arranged chronologically. For example the letter to the Romans appears first in our Bible, whereas it probably was *sixth* in the order of composition; and I and II Corinthians, which appear next after Romans, probably was preceded by at least three other important letters.

To simplify the approach of the introductory student to the books of Scripture, *The New Bible Survey* groups the sixty-six separate books into *eight natural divisions,* according to subject matter, thus: (1) The Seventeen Historical Books of the Old Testament; (2) the book of Psalms; (3) the Four books by the Wise Men of Israel; (4) the Seventeen Books by the Prophets; (5) the Four Gospels; (6) the Book of Acts; (7) the Letters of Paul; and (8) the Letters by the Apostles James, Peter, Jude, and John.

In addition, the groups and the individual titles within the groups, for study purposes, have been arranged chronologically according to the best opinion of their order, wherever such an arrangement worked to the advantage of the student.

There are other external matters which impede the student in his journey toward understanding his Bible. One is the format of the printed page. One student of the Bible declared, "The Bible is the worst printed book in the world." He was speaking of the older translations and versions. The *Berkeley Version of the Bible in Modern English* (1959) is here recommended to the student. It has met with wide acceptance among evangelicals and is published in the modern reader's format. It places the chapter and verse numerals in less conspicuous places on the page, paragraphs textual matter according to content, and generally presents poetry in verse form. The *King James Version* is also recommended here, if and when an acceptable edition of this beloved text appears in modern reader's format.

So far we have spoken of external matters. The introductory student of the Bible has other difficulties in understanding this ancient book of Hebrew origin. These relate to *internal* matters of interpretation and meaning. For one thing, ancient books are relatively short and brief. The authors doubtless were encouraged to make them so because of the scarcity of writing materials, and because of the mechanical difficulties in transcribing ideas upon papyrus, and upon parchment made from the skins of animals.

Such brevity often resulted in the absence of adequate introductions and transitions within the writer's composition, and often a corresponding obscurity and vagueness in his meaning for the modern reader. Nowhere else is this characteristic of style more noticeable than in the books by the Prophets, and more particularly in the so-called "Minor Prophets," who for the most part were *minor* only in the length of their compositions.

Thus, another aim of *The New Bible Survey* is to direct the student in understanding the content of the Bible text as it exists in our commonly used English versions. To this practical end, each book of the Bible has its own brief but substantial introduction. These introductions are designed specifically for the needs of first year students in the Bible survey. Thus, technical and theological problems of an advanced nature are not treated here. The extensive bibliographies throughout the book, however, will provide the student (who wishes to read further) with ample material on any topic or field, in which he may have special interest.

Fortunately, the understanding of the Bible has been greatly aided in recent years by the work of world famous archaeologists, linguists, historians, and other research scholars. The results of their discoveries and researches have been made available to the non-technical reader by the publication of such books as Dr. Werner Keller's *The Bible As History*, William Foxwell Albright's *Archaeology and the Religion of Israel* and *From the Stone Age to Christianity*, John Garstang's *The Foundations of Bible History*, Professor G. Ernest Wright's *Biblical Archaeology*, Merrill F. Unger's *Archaeology and the Old Testament* and *Archaeology and the New Testament*, and scores of others, not to mention the discovery and translation of the Dead Sea Scrolls at the ancient library of Qumran.

Finally, no survey course of the Bible is complete without introducing the student to adequate and workable bibliographies. The student here is introduced, not only to the newer works such as referred to in the paragraph above, but also to the whole world of scholarship in the Biblical field, and the supporting sciences. These bibliographies have been chosen with a view of their usefulness to the first year student, his present and future needs.

The writer wishes to acknowledge his indebtedness to others. A newcomer to the field is obligated to more people than he can name. He has received much help from the wide fraternity of Biblical scholars and writers during the more than thirty years he has taught the Bible, and during the preparation of this volume.

If he listed the hundred or more writers and the titles of books from which he has drawn help directly, what of the other hundreds that have influenced his work indirectly? However, the footnotes and bibliographies throughout this volume, and the General Bibliography with the names of the publishers and dates at the end, will indicate to the reader the main sources used in the preparation of this work.

Personal acknowledgment is here made to the following:

To Dr. Arnold B. Rhodes, Professor of Old Testament at the Louisville Presbyterian Seminary, for the outline of a basic bibliography in Old and New Testament scholarship and reference; to Dr. L. Nelson Bell, Executive Editor and founder of *Christianity Today*, for editorial and publication advice and assistance; to my former teachers: Henry Horace Williams, Professor of Philosophy at the University of North Carolina, for lectures and studies in Christianity and world religions; and to Dr. Edwin Greenlaw, Dean of the Graduate School of the University, for his seminars in graduate study; to Dr. L. R. Wilson, Librarian of the University, for personal favors and the facilities of a great library; to the librarians of the New Orleans Baptist Theological Seminary, for the use of its library and research facilities; to John W. Visser and the Rev. M. H. Faber, both of whom read the entire manuscript, for their constructive and critical suggestions on many technical and textual matters; to Dr. Richard L. Summers and to the Rev. Frank A. Brooks, Jr., my former and present pastors, both of whom read critically portions of the manuscript, for their suggestions and help; and finally, to my wife and daughter, both of whom are scholars in their own right, for encouragement and assistance.

CONTENTS

THE NEW BIBLE SURVEY

MAPS

PART ONE

ORIENTATION: GENERAL INTRODUCTION

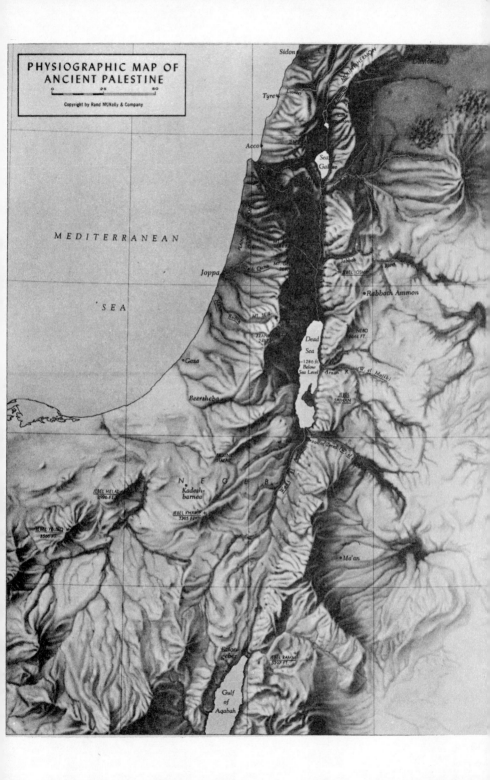

PHYSIOGRAPHIC MAP OF
ANCIENT PALESTINE

Copyright by Rand McNally & Company

MEDITERRANEAN

SEA

Sidon

Tyre

Acco

Joppa

Gaza

Beersheba

Sea of
Galilee

Rabbath Ammon

Dead
Sea
-1286 ft.
Below
Sea Level

Arnon R. (W. el Mojib)

NEGEB

Kadesh-
barnea

JEBEL HELAL

JEBEL YELLEG

JEBEL KHARM

Ma'an

Ezion-
geber

JEBEL RAMM

Gulf
of
Aqabah

Chapter 1

REASONS WHY PEOPLE READ THE BIBLE

William James, the first great American psychologist, once said that if man did not have a religion he would find it necessary to create one.[1]

Man was made with many curiosities and infinite yearnings. He wants to know where he came from; why he is here; and where he is going after he leaves here.

Thus, what William James is saying is that man is incurably religious.

It was Ralph Waldo Emerson who said that if the stars should appear one night in a thousand years, how man would believe and adore, and preserve for many generations the remembrance of the City of God which had been shown.

By nature man must worship a Power greater than himself, and must always be seeking answers to his questions, and the mysteries that surround his everyday existence.

Here is where the Bible comes in. It is conceded to be the most spiritual of all spiritual books; in short, to be the Word of God. Men differ, however, in what sense it is the Word of God. That has always made it an intriguing Book in man's quest for inner peace and happiness.

But the Bible has had many other attractions for its readers, and by these it has endeared itself to them. For one thing, the Bible contains the best of a great people's literature during some ten centuries of their national life. And in the Western world at least, it is regarded as the most important of the world's books.

That is to say, whether in religion or literature or life, the Bible tells the true story of man, and speaks a message so bold and convincing that all the world gradually is coming under its influence and leadership of ideas.

Suppose we now look briefly at some of the uses for which millions of readers, in varying degrees and purposes, have turned eagerly to their Bibles.

---

[1]See John Bright, *The Kingdom of God*, pp. 248-250, for a discussion of the idea. (Abingdon-Cokesbury, 1953.)

1. THE BIBLE AS LITERATURE

The Bible as literature has made a wide appeal to the literate of all ages; and today it is more highly esteemed than ever.

Peoples of all races and all cultures love a good story. And where else can the reader find a more charming short story than the idyllic story of Ruth, or a more adventurous short story than that of Jonah, or a more dramatic narrative than that contained in the story of Esther?

The poetic drama of Job is not surpassed by Sophocles' *Oedipus the King,* Shakespeare's *Hamlet,* or Ibsen's *Ghosts.* And Moses' Farewell Address to Israel in Deuteronomy has been read and pondered from the day it was delivered; whereas the great Philippics of Demosthenes and the orations of Cicero have all but been forgotten.

What historians of antiquity tell so much in so little space, and so well, as the books of I and II Samuel and I and II Kings, not to name the unrivaled epics of Jacob, Joseph, and Joshua, or the missionary journeys of Paul and his companions in Luke's Acts of the Apostles?

Or what letters in secular literature can match the fourteen Letters of Paul in the New Testament?

Philosophers of all ages have read and thought deeply upon the religion and the ethics of the prophets Amos and Isaiah and Jeremiah; of the wisdom of Proverbs and Job and Ecclesiastes; and especially upon the Way of Life revealed in the gospels of Matthew and Luke and John. Indeed, the governments and civilizations of the Western world have been revolutionized and made over by the ideals and ethics of these books.

If the philosophies of Plato and Aristotle are read as the starting point in modern thought and modern science, the philosophy and Gospel of the New Testament is the charter of the New Way of life, without which modern thought and science have no true meaning and no true destiny.

And perhaps the favorite of favorites in the Old Testament, is the matchless book of lyrics called the book of Psalms. All the world loves the Twenty-Third Psalm. And who has not been delighted and consoled with such other universal favorites as Psalms 8, 19, 24, 46, and 90, to name only a few?

Many readers, then, read the Bible as they read any other book: for its unrivaled stories, biographies, dramas, histories, essays, orations, poetry, and letters.

2. THE BIBLE AS HISTORY

It is a truism to say that the Bible is man's best book on religion. Indeed, for centuries it has been recognized as the revelation of man's salvation.

But only in recent years have discoveries by archaeologists, geologists, biologists, philologists, nuclear physicists, and other scientists proved to every one's satisfaction that the Book of Books is also magnificent history.

In his epoch-making book, *The Bible As History,* Dr. Werner Keller tells the romantic story of how archaeologists and other scientists have made their exciting discoveries, not only in Palestine, but in Egypt, Assyria, and Babylonia as well; in short, the author's story takes us wherever the political and economic struggles of these great powers involved the people of the Bible and the Bible story.

"In Palestine," says Dr. Keller, "places and towns that are frequently mentioned in the Bible are being brought back once more into the light of day. They look exactly as the Bible describes them and lie exactly where the Bible locates them."[2]

This is reassuring to the doubting Thomases. In fact, says Dr. Keller, "These breathtaking discoveries, whose significance it is impossible to grasp all at once, make it necessary for us to revise our views about the Bible. Many events that previously passed for pious tales must now be judged to be historical. Often the results of investigation correspond in detail with the Biblical narratives. They not only confirm but also illumine the historical situations out of which the Old Testament and the Gospels grew."

Sir Winston Churchill, who has both made more history and written more history than any of his contemporaries, is emphatic in his acceptance of the historical truth of the Bible.

Says Sir Winston, "We believe that the most scientific view, the most up-to-date and rational conception, will find its fullest satisfaction in taking the Bible story literally. We may be sure that all these things happened just as they are set out according to Holy Writ. We may believe they happened to people not so very different from ourselves, and that the impressions those people received were faithfully recorded, and have been transmitted across the centuries with far more accuracy than many of the telegraphed accounts we read of goings-on of today."

Sir Winston's view is shared by Thomas B. Costain, author of *The Silver Chalice* and many other distinguished novels. "The Bible," says Mr. Costain, in his cryptic comment, "*is* history in the *real* sense of the word."

Thus, from the changing outlook, we may confidently expect a new attitude toward the Bible, and more respect for it by all readers — and especially by the skeptics, who all too often have been *against* the Bible when they had no reason to be against it except the borrowed opinion of other doubters like themselves.

3. The Bible and Professional Writers

Professional writers go to the Bible for ideas, points of view, attitudes, character, and human interest. In particular, they seek the

2Introduction, p. xxii. (Morrow & Co., 1956)

vocabulary of simplicity, the phrase, the idiom, that which has made the translations and versions of the English Bible famous. The most celebrated of all the versions for language, the *King James Version,* is still a joy, not only to professional writers, but to all who read it.

Great poets like William Shakespeare, John Milton, William Wordsworth, Alfred Tennyson, and Robert Browning, of England, and our own Hawthorne and Longfellow and Whitman, to mention a few of the hundreds, have all been greatly influenced in their ideas, style, and philosophy of life, by their constant perusal of the English Bible.

Herman Wouk, author of *Caine Mutiny, Marjorie Morningstar,* and other popular novels, says that he has four main reference books: The *World Almanac,* Roget's *Thesaurus,* the English dictionary, and the Bible. "I read from my Bible every day," Wouk says.

"Whatever merit there is in anything that I have written," says John Ruskin, the English essayist and art critic, "is simply due to the fact that when I was a child my mother daily read me a part of the Bible and daily made me learn a part of it by heart."

Robert Louis Stevenson, author of *Treasure Island,* speaking of the books that influenced him in the different periods of his life, says, "The next book, in order of time, to influence me, was the New Testament, and in particular the Gospel according to Matthew."

The French philosopher and author, Jean Jacques Rousseau, testifies to the quality of language of the Bible, thus: "Peruse the books of philosophers with all their pomp of diction. How meager, how contemptible are they when compared with the Scriptures."

The Bible, then, from whatever angle we view it, is inexhaustible.

4. The Bible and Education

In every age since the time of Moses, the Bible has been used in the instruction of youth.

In his Farewell Address to Israel, Moses, speaking directly to parents, priests, and others whose duty it was to teach, charged them with these words:

> Hear, O Israel: The Lord our God is one Lord; and you shall love the Lord your God with all your heart, and with all your soul, and with all your might. And these words which I command you this day shall be upon your heart; and you shall teach them diligently to your children . . .   (Deuteronomy 6:4-9)

Thus, as soon as it was compiled, the Bible in its First Edition, called the Book of the Law of the Lord, was immediately put to work as the basic instruction of both old and young, and as their guide in the land to which they were going to possess, and which was to be their permanent home, Canaan.

Five hundred years later, Jehoshaphat, king of Judah about 876-852 B.C., continued his father King Asa's religious reforms in a singular way for his times. In the third year of his reign, he sent the royal princes, Ban-hail, Obadiah, Zechariah, Nathaniel, and Micaiah, to teach in the cities of Judah. With them, the princes took a company of Levites and priests. "And they taught in Judah," says the historian, "having the Book of the Law of the Lord with them; they went about through all the cities of Judah, and taught among the people" (II Chronicles 17:7-9).

Two other notable instances in which the Bible was used for the instruction of the whole people are, first, in the reign of King Josiah, and recorded in II Chronicles 34-35; the other, after the return of Israel from Exile, and recorded in the book of Nehemiah 8:3-18.

In its long educational history, the ancient Hebrew Bible had another tremendously fortunate thing happen to it of first importance in extending its educational influence. It was translated from the Hebrew into the Greek language by a large company of distinguished translators, *seventy,* in fact, according to tradition, from which it gets its traditional name, the *Septuagint* translation (285-150 B.C.). The world conquests of Alexander the Great, 336-323 B.C., caused the spread of the Greek language, ideas, and civilization throughout the known world, especially in such large cities as Alexandria, Egypt. In fact, Greek became the language of the world. That is why, a little later, the entire New Testament was written in Greek, and not in Hebrew, as was the Old Testament.

Ptolemy Philadelphus (285-247 B.C.) is usually given credit for inviting the Seventy Jewish scholars of Jerusalem to come to Alexandria for the work of translation. The population of Alexandria included many Greeks and Greek-speaking Jews, and so there was a demand for the Hebrew Scriptures to be translated into their language. Alexandria was also a great center of learning, with a library estimated at 200,000 volumes. Flavius Josephus, Jewish scholar and historian of the first century, relates that Demetrius Phalereus, librarian to Ptolemy, wished to add to his library a copy of the Hebrew Books in the Greek language.[3]

In the course of time, however, another great language was to compete with the Greek, and eventually was in turn to become the universal language. That was the language of the Roman people, Latin.

Julius Caesar, from the time he was made consul of Rome in 59 B.C. until his assassination in 44 B.C., succeeded in conquering the world much as Alexander the Great had done, less than three hundred years before him. So, by the fourth century A.D., Latin had become so predominantly the language of writing as well as the speech of the

---

[3]See John D. Davis, "Versions," *The Westminster Dictionary of the Bible,* Fifth Edition, pp. 621-628; Arthur Jeffery, "Text and Ancient Versions of the Old Testament," *The Interpreter's Bible,* Vol. I, pp. 46-62.

common people, that it became necessary once more to translate the Bible into the language of the day, Latin.

Damasus, bishop of Rome, urged Eusebius Hieronymus, or Saint Jerome as he was later called (340-420 A.D.), the most learned Christian scholar of his time, to produce a dignified and accurate version of the New Testament in Latin. Portions of the Scriptures had already appeared in old vernacular versions in Latin; but these were incomplete and often confusing.

By 384 A.D., Jerome had completed the gospels and certain portions of the Old Testament. But Rome did not seem the proper environment for his work; and he wished also to pursue his studies further in the Hebrew language with the aid of Jewish teachers. So, in 387 A.D., Jerome took up residence in the monastery at Bethlehem, the old city of David. By 405 A.D., his entire work was completed, and was called the *Latin Vulgate* translation, because it was in the language of the common people.

But Jerome's Bible was to come upon evil days. The vigorous faith of the Apostolic Age waned somewhat over the centuries, and in time the authority of the Scriptures was superseded by the authority of the Pope and the ecclesiastical orders of Rome. The main goal of education, it seemed, was to implant in the minds of the young a profound reverence for the Church and its authority. With such power in the Church and its leadership, all sorts of corruption and abuse developed. By the close of the Middle Ages, the Church had degenerated to a degree where priests were "selling indulgences" or pardons granted to sinners by the Pope to any who had the money to pay for them, regardless of their wrongdoing. There were many other abuses.

A young man by the name of Martin Luther (1483-1546) rediscovered the Bible and gave it back to the people, as the center of the Reform Movement which he initiated, in defiance of the Pope and the authority of Rome. Luther's discovery was that the Bible is its own authority, and that this authority is plainly written in the Bible itself: in the gospels, in the letters of Paul, and on every page of the New Testament, in fact.

The boldness and sincerity of Luther's preaching inspired confidence in the Reform Movement. One of his first important steps was to translate the New Testament into the German language (1522), so that it could be read and understood by the common people. Then he completed the translation of the entire Bible into German, and the people bought copies as fast as the presses could print them (1534). One writer says, "Church services were now also in the language of the people instead of in Latin as formerly, and the Bible became an important part of the service."

Luther's Reform Movement spread quickly to other lands, to Switzerland, the Netherlands, Scotland and England. Many outstanding leaders joined the movement, chief of whom was John Calvin (1509-1564), theologian and statesman, who fled from his native France and became leader of the Protestant Reformation at Geneva, Switzerland, and the West. In England, the Reformed Movement was stoutly supported by two noteworthy translators, William Tyndale (1492-1536) and Miles Coverdale (1488-1569), whose work stimulated others and gave the Bible wide circulation and influence among English-speaking peoples of the British Isles, and beyond.[4]

There is no way of adequately estimating the enormous and decisive educational influence of the Old and New Testament Scriptures on the nations over the centuries past. The Age of Enlightenment came with the religious Reform Movement. Autocracies and kingships were gradually changed into democracies throughout most of the Western world. The age of the dignity of the individual man, inspired by the teachings of the New Testament, was ushered in.

America was colonized with an open Bible. The founding fathers were a people of one Book, and that Book was the Bible. From the beginning, however, Americans have believed in the separation of Church and State, and wisely. But Americans of all creeds in the past have never been willing to be *separated* from the ethical and religious teachings of their Bible. But is it not true that the present generation of Christians is in danger of having just that happen to them? Cannot present day Americans find a way to use this Book, in public education, without violating the traditional principles of the separation of Church and State?[5]

5. The Bible and Eternal Life

Far and away the most important reason why readers read the Bible is that it contains the message of Eternal Life.

In a conversation with certain Jews of Jerusalem, Jesus Himself put His finger on the heart of the matter when He said to them: "You search the Scriptures, because you think that in them you have eternal life; and it is they that bear witness to me" (John 5:39).

This is why millions of readers in every generation read the Bible as they read no other book. It is the most spiritual, most religious book in the world. And it is the only book which gives man at all a satisfactory explanation of his present existence, his future, and his ultimate destiny.

Dr. George W. Truett, for forty-seven years the famous pastor of the First Baptist Church of Dallas, Texas, said: "God's first gift to the world is His Son Jesus Christ. His second best gift to the world is the Bible."

---

[4]For the story of later English translations, see *The Greater English Versions of Our Bible*, chapter 4, pp. 38-46.
[5]See John Paterson, "The Bible and Modern Life," *The Book That Is Alive*, pp. 169-183 (1954), for a most convincing chapter on how the influence of the Bible is disappearing from American life.

"We have suffered a heart-breaking disillusionment," said the late Dr. Charles E. Jefferson, New York pastor, in giving his view why people turn to the Bible when all else fails. "We expected great things from liberty and education, and have found they are broken reeds. Neither our wealth nor our science has given us either peace or joy."

The poet Walt Whitman, whom we ordinarily do not think of in connection with the Bible, gives this evaluation of what the Bible has meant to man in his struggle for the better life:

> How many ages and generations have brooded and wept and agonized over this book! What untellable joys and ecstasies, what support to martyrs at the stake, from it! To what myriads has it been the shore and rock of safety — the refuge from driving tempest and wreck! Translated in all languages, how it has united this diverse world! Of its thousands there is not a verse, not a word, but is thick-studded with human emotion.

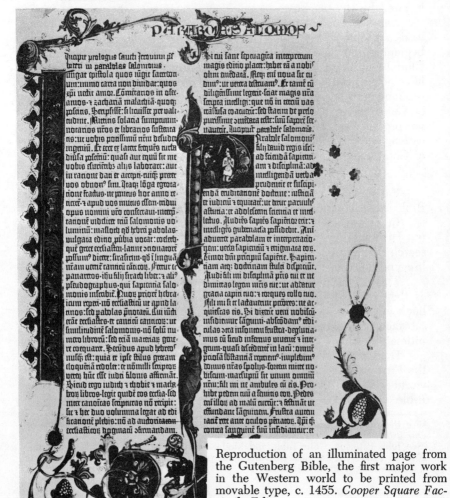

Reproduction of an illuminated page from the Gutenberg Bible, the first major work in the Western world to be printed from movable type, c. 1455. *Cooper Square Facsimile Edition.*

Chapter 2

THE INSPIRATION AND AUTHORITY OF THE BIBLE

The enduring popularity of the Bible throughout the generations amazes us, and yet we should not wonder that people read the Bible as they read no other book.

For the Bible is unique in that from the beginning it was recognized as God's own inspired Word to man, His revelation of Himself, and His divine plan for man's redemption and salvation.

The purpose of this chapter is to review briefly what devout Christians of all ages have steadfastly believed concerning the inspiration and authority of the Scriptures.

1. THE WITNESS OF THE BIBLE TO ITSELF

The Bible itself everywhere assumes that it is God's own Message delivered directly to the prophets and apostles by God Himself. For example, Moses introduced his recital of the Ten Commandments with these words, "And God spoke all these words, saying..." (Exodus 20). Then the record reads, "Moses came and told the people all the words of the Lord and all the ordinances; and all the people answered with one voice, and said, 'All the words which the Lord has spoken we will do.' And Moses wrote all the words of the Lord" (Exodus 24:3-4). Moses began his Farewell Address with these words, "The Lord our God said to us in Horeb, "You have stayed long enough at this mountain; turn and take your journey ... go in and take possession of the land which the Lord swore to your fathers, to Abraham, to Isaac, and to Jacob'" (Deuteronomy 1). And finally,

> When Moses had finished writing the words of this Law in a book, to the very end, Moses commanded the Levites who carried the ark of the covenant of the Lord, Take this book of the Law, and put it by the side of the ark of the covenant of the Lord your God, that it may be there for a witness against you (Deuteronomy 31:24-26).

In the books of the Old Testament after Moses, God speaks directly to the prophets. For instance, the book of Joshua opens with these words, "After the death of Moses the servant of the Lord, the Lord said to Joshua the son of Nun, Moses' minister ...." And in chapter 3:7, "And the Lord said to Joshua, 'This day I will begin to exalt you in the sight of Israel, that they may know that, as I was with Moses, so I will be with you.'" And the record concludes, "And

Joshua wrote these words in the book of the Law of God" (Joshua 24:25-26).

And so, all through the Old Testament, God's servants the prophets speak the words of the Lord. Of Samuel the historian says, "And Samuel grew, and the Lord was with him, and let none of his words fall to the ground. And all Israel from Dan to Beer-sheba knew that Samuel was established as a prophet of the Lord."

All the great writing prophets, from Joel to Malachi, introduce their messages with the simple testimony of the divine origin: "The word of the Lord that came to Joel"; Amos, "Thus says the Lord"; "The word of the Lord that came to Hosea"; "The vision of Isaiah"; "The words of Jeremiah . . . to whom the word of the Lord came"; "The oracle of the word of the Lord to Israel by Malachi," and so all the others.

Scholars for a long time have been impressed with the overwhelming testimony by the writers and speakers of the New Testament, including our Lord Himself, concerning the inspiration and authority of the Old Testament Scriptures. Indeed, with the exception of the books of Ezra, Nehemiah, Esther, Ecclesiastes, Song of Songs, Obadiah, Nahum, and Zephaniah, all the books of the Old Testament are directly quoted in the New Testament. The purpose of the quotations, and the circumstances under which they are given, is important. The written word is treated as the inspired and authoritative form in which the content of Divine revelation has been expressed and handed down. Indeed, as someone has well said, "If the Old Testament bears witness pre-eminently to the *One* who *is* to come, the New Testament bears witness to the One who *has* come." For He is the Word of God incarnate.

Jesus Himself emphasized not only that He had not come to destroy the Law and the Prophets but to fulfill them, but that "not an iota, not a dot, will pass from the Law until all is accomplished" (Matthew 5:17-18). On another occasion, after the Resurrection, Jesus' remarks to His disciples embraced the Old Testament Scriptures, and their Divine origin, when He said, "that everything written about me in the Law of Moses and the Prophets and the Psalms must be fulfilled" (Luke 24:44).

In one of his pastoral letters, the Apostle Paul testifies to the inspiration and authority of Scripture, in these comprehensive words: "All Scripture is inspired by God and profitable for teaching, for reproof, for correction, and for training in righteousness, that the man of God may be complete, equipped for every good work" (II Timothy 3:16-17).

In the letter to the Hebrews, which many believe was written by the Apostle Paul, the writer begins with this significant testimony to the Divine authoritativeness of Old Testament Scripture: "In many and various ways God spoke of old to our fathers by the prophets."

Peter, in II Peter 1:21, points out the all-important distinction between writings that come from "the impulse of man," and those that are true prophecies and are inspired by the Holy Spirit: "First of all you must understand this, that no prophecy of Scripture is a matter of one's own interpretation, because no prophecy ever came by the impulse of man, but men moved by the Holy Spirit spoke from God."

The testimony of the Apostle John was the keystone of the New Testament. What was this testimony? It was the promise to the apostles that the Holy Spirit would come and teach them all things, and lead them into all truth (John 14:26; 16:13). And then John's review of the contents and purpose of his book, in 20:30-31, indicates conclusively that he intends for his entire gospel to be his testimony that Jesus is the Christ, the Son of God, and that believing on Him all may have eternal life. Finally, he identifies himself as the author of the book, and asserts that "his testimony is true" (21:24).

2. The Testimony of History

By the middle of the first century A.D., or some twenty years after the Crucifixion, the early Christian Church already had in its possession the first of the inspired writings of the apostles. The letter from James appeared about A.D. 50, Paul's two letters to the Thessalonians about A.D. 51, and the gospel of Mark early in the 50's. And by A.D. 70, it is likely that all the great letters from Paul, three of the four gospels, the book of Acts, and the letters from Peter and Jude, were all in circulation. It is generally agreed that the gospel of John and the letters including the *Revelation* from John did not appear until late in the century.

What a heritage was that of first century Christians! It is evident from many sources that these inspired and authoritative documents were widely circulated and read aloud to countless gatherings of disciples. Also, it is noteworthy that by the time the Apostle Peter wrote II Peter 3:15-16, the Apostle Paul's letters were already recognized as inspired and authoritative, as is shown in Peter's reference to Paul:

> So also our beloved brother Paul wrote to you according to the wisdom given him, speaking of this as he does in all his letters. There are some things in them hard to understand, which the ignorant and unstable twist to their own destruction, as they do the other Scriptures.

New Testament history, however, begins with the *oral Gospel*, or with what has been called "the gospel behind the Gospels." Luke, in his book of Acts, gives us a stirring picture of the outpouring of the Holy Spirit at Pentecost and after, and the mighty preaching by Peter and the other leaders of the early Church. The story is continued with the evangelistic campaigns of Paul and his associates in the last two-thirds of Acts. It was out of this background of oral preaching, under the inspiration of the Holy Spirit, that the New Testament Scriptures were written.

It is worth noting also, in passing, that many gospels and letters which we do not now have were written before and during the years of the writing of the New Testament Scriptures. Luke, in the preface to his gospel, reminds us that "many have undertaken to compile a narrative of the things which have been accomplished among us." God, who always takes care of His own, saw to the preservation of His inspired Scriptures, but not to the protection of these other manuscripts which presumably were not essential for our divine instruction and guidance.

From the first half of the second century, Papias, bishop of Hierapolis, and others, indicate in their writings familiarity with the Four Gospels of the New Testament. In the words of Professor F. F. Bruce, "Irenaeus, bishop of Lyons in Gaul, writing about A.D. 180, regards the fourfold gospel as one of the axiomatic facts of the universe. There are four quarters of the world, he says, and four winds, and thus it is natural that the Church Universal should rest upon four pillars, and these pillars are the four Gospels."[1]

For one to write thus confidently about the number of the gospels, continues Professor Bruce, there must have been by his time general agreement in the churches throughout the world that these four were uniquely authoritative.

Although the Four Gospels were everywhere received from the beginning of the second century, not all of our 27 New Testament books were thought to be authoritative that early. However, the Apostolic Church received from the Jewish the belief in a written rule of faith, and so somewhat early there was a request for such a written rule for New Testament Scripture. The idea of a new canon is found from 180 to 200 A.D. in the writings of three great Church leaders: Irenaeus of Asia Minor and Gaul, Tertullian of North Africa, and Clement of Alexandria. One manuscript, the Muratorian fragment, gives us the canon of the Church at Rome about A.D. 200. According to this manuscript, seven books still lacked general recognition: Hebrews, James, II Peter, II and III John, Jude, and Revelation.

During the next hundred years or so, such devoted scholars as Origen and Eusebius, under Divine guidance, continued to study the Scriptures. Origen first approved the inclusion of Revelation, and was followed closely by Eusebius. Then came a period of official action by bishops of provincial churches, and later by councils or synods. In A.D. 367, Athanasius, bishop of Alexandria, proposed a list of 27

---

[1]*The New Bible Commentary,* rev. ed., 1954, p. 58.

New Testament books, which is the same as the present canon. At the synods of Hippo Regius (393 A.D.) and Carthage (397 A.D.), the New Testament canon of 27 books as we now have it was accepted. Saint Augustine (354-430 A.D.) approved the canon, and through the *Latin Vulgate Version* of the Scriptures (384-405 A.D.), it eventually came into vogue throughout the West. The canon of the Eastern Church in time was the same as that of the Western. Thus, the belief in a written rule of faith prevailed and the New Testament books were recognized as both unique and authoritative.

Before we go on to the next topic, let us see what the New Testament writers and speakers themselves had to say about a written rule of faith, and of the authority of their Scriptures.

First of all, Jesus Himself confirmed the belief in a written rule of faith by appealing to the Old Testament as the written Word of God (Matthew 5:17-18; Mark 12:36-37; John 5:37-47), and by instructing His disciples out of the Old Testament (Luke 24:44-48). The apostolic writers habitually refer to the Old Testament as authoritative (Romans 3:2, 21; 15:4; I Corinthians 4:6; II Timothy 3:15-17; II Peter 1:20-21). Also, these same apostles claimed for their own teaching, oral and written, like authority with the Old Testament (I Corinthians 2:7-13; 14:37; I Thessalonians 2:13; Revelation 1:1-3), and directed the public reading of their letters (I Thessalonians 5:27; Colossians 4:16; II Thessalonians 2:15; II Peter 1:15; 3:1-2), while revelations given to the Church through inspired prophets (Acts 11:27-28; 15:32; I Corinthians 14), were considered to form, with apostolic instruction, the foundation of the Church (Ephesians 2:19-21).

Thus, it was both natural and right that the inspired New Testament literature should be added to the inspired Scriptures of the Old Testament, and that therefore the written canon of faith be thus enlarged.

3. The Contemporary Witness

The history of the Holy Scriptures, as well as the history of the Church itself, from the fifth century to the Age of the Reformation, is a long and rugged story — a thousand years of faith and persecution, wherein the fortunes of the Bible rose and fell with the ever-changing times. As we have noted elsewhere, the vigorous faith of the Apostolic Age waned somewhat over the centuries, and in time the authority of the Scriptures was superseded by the authority of the Pope and the ecclesiastical orders of Rome. Thus, the so-called Dark Ages were "dark" for more reasons than secular history sometimes records.

But God never intended that His Word should be lost to His people, or that they should more than temporarily be separated from its Divine instruction and guidance. So, as in the days after Joshua, for example, God raised up a whole new school of prophets such as Martin Luther, John Calvin, and many other inspired leaders. The first thing they did was to "re-discover" the Bible and to give it back to the people, in translations which everyone could read, each in his own tongue. And the great number of translations and versions is one indication of how hungry the common people were for the Scriptures.

There have been more questions raised concerning the inspiration and authority of our Bible, or portions of the Bible, in the last one hundred years than in all the preceding centuries taken together. Why is this, we may ask?

The age of science did not reach its first peak in the Western world until about the time of the publication of Charles Darwin's famous book, *The Origin of Species by Natural Selection,* in 1859. Since that time, however, the spirit of inquiry has led men to investigate every department of human knowledge and experience. So, since the Bible deals with the chief interest with respect to man, his religion, it is but natural that it should be subjected to every kind of study and criticism. It has been. Although the great body of students of the Bible have had as their goal a sincere understanding of the Scriptures, the small minority, albeit a noisy minority, have often written with a "low view of the Bible," and as if they were presenting "a case *against* the Bible," rather than one *for* it. For that reason they have been classified as "liberals" and radicals of the critical school.

However, there is good reason to believe that the worst of the destructive criticism of the Scriptures belongs to our immediate past. This view is shared by the editor of a leading religious journal, in these words: "When liberalism was at its height two or more decades ago, evangelicalism inherited a significant role in American religious life. Championing the authority of the Scriptures it witnessed boldly against theological compromise."[2] R. K. Harrison, writing of the increasing respect for conservative views in English scholarly circles, says: "The last two decades have seen a resurgence of conservative evangelical scholarship, led . . . by such men as F. F. Bruce, H. L. Ellison, W. J. Martin, and D. J. Wiseman."[3]

Indeed, it is safe to say that, after all the Biblical "research" of liberal and radical scholars, and the great body of their publications, books and periodicals, the belief in the inspiration and authority of the Bible is now as firmly established in the minds and hearts of the Christian masses as at any time in the history of Christianity.

In the words of Ecclesiastes, God "has put eternity into man's mind," and He will never lack for witnesses. Speaking for the Old Testament, Professor Edward J. Young says,

[2]*Christianity Today,* January 5, 1962, p. 26.
[3]*Christianity Today,* February 13, 1961, p. 12.

. . . The Old Testament is the very Word of the God of truth. It is also the work of men. "Holy men of God spake as they were moved by the Holy Ghost" (II Peter 1:21b). In His inscrutable wisdom God chose and prepared for the task of writing those human agents whom He desired to speak His will. Then in mysterious fashion His Spirit wrought upon them, so that what they wrote, although in a very true sense their own, was nevertheless precisely what the Spirit of God desired. The Bible, therefore, in one sense may be regarded as a human book. Basically, however, it is divine, and God Himself is its author.[4]

Another recent evangelical voice is that of Dr. Wick Broomall, who speaks out in these words:

But the decisive factor that differentiates Christianity as the only true and authoritative faith is found in the divine inspiration of its records. The Early Church Fathers knew instinctively that, in the writing of the inspired prophets and apostles, they were listening to the voice of God. It was this voice, vibrating and pulsating with divine life, that made the canonical Scriptures infinitely more than a bare recital of facts or precepts such as we find in the Koran, the bible of Islam. Basically it is the fact that Christianity has back of it an inspired Bible that puts it in a category all by itself among the so-called religions of mankind.[5]

Among the older witnesses should be named the well known Benjamin B. Warfield: "The Church, then, has held from the beginning that the Bible is the Word of God in such a sense that its words, though written by men and bearing indelibly impressed upon them the marks of their human origin, were written, nevertheless, under such an influence of the Holy Ghost as to be also the words of God, the adequate expression of His mind and will."[6]

In a more recent testimony on revelation and inspiration, the beloved J. Gresham Machen wrote these words:

The contents of the Bible, then, are unique. But another fact about the Bible is also important. The Bible might contain an account of a true revelation from God, and yet the account be full of error. Before the full authority of the Bible can be established, therefore, it is necessary to add to the Christian doctrine of revelation the Christian doctrine of inspiration. The latter doctrine means that the Bible not only is an account of important things, but that the account itself is true, the writers having been so preserved from error, despite a full maintenance of their habits of thought and expression, that the resulting Book is the "infallible rule of faith and practice!"[7]

Another significant testimony of our time is the words of the Very Reverend Dr. James Pitt-Watson, Moderator of the General Assembly of the Church of Scotland, given with the presentation of the

[4]*An Introduction to the Old Testament,* Second Ed., 1958, p. 29.
[5]*Biblical Criticism,* 1957, p. 12.
[6]*Revelation and Inspiration,* 1927, p. 175.
[7]"Christianity and Liberalism," *Presbyterian Guardian,* 1940.

Bible at the Coronation of Queen Elizabeth II, Westminster Abbey, June 2, 1953:

> To keep your Majesty ever mindful of the Law and the Gospel of God as the Rule for the whole life and government of Christian Princes, we present you with this Book, the most valuable thing that this world affords. Here is wisdom; This is the royal Law; These are the lively Oracles of God.[8]

More than ten years ago, the members of the faculty of Westminster Theological Seminary, Philadelphia, agreed to write a Symposium and publish a book containing their testimony and witness, under the significant title, *The Infallible Word*. The names of the contributors to the volume are John Murray, Edward J. Young, N. B. Stonehouse, John H. Skilton, Paul Woolley, R. B. Kuiper, and Cornelius Van Til. The keynote of the undertaking is stated in the first sentence of the book, and is contributed by the first writer, John Murray:

> Christians of varied and diverse theological standpoints aver that the Bible is the Word of God, that it is inspired by the Holy Spirit and that it occupies a unique place as the norm of Christian faith and life.[9]

What is more significant, this type performance could be duplicated in kind in scores of other theological seminaries and Bible colleges throughout the land, with a wide assortment of denominations and church affiliation.

Thus, the time has come again when a true conservative need not apologize for his belief in historic orthodox Protestantism, or for his belief in the inspiration and authority of the Scriptures.

William Tyndale translating the Bible (painting by Alexander Johnstone). © *Radio Times Hulton Picture Library, British Broadcasting Corporation, London*

---

[8]Quoted by F. F. Bruce, *The English Bible: A History of Translations*, 1961, pp. 146, 224.
[9]N. B. Stonehouse and Paul Woolley, Editors, 1946, p. 1.

Chapter 3

WAYS TO READ THE BIBLE

1. READING THE BIBLE BY WHOLE BOOKS

The most practical approach to the reading of the Bible is to read it not by fragments, but by whole books.

The Hebrew writer, let us say, like any other writer, had a theme or message he wished to put into writing. He made his plan, gathered his material, and composed the piece as one complete whole. If the reader is to comprehend the book, as the author understood and planned it, he must be willing to stay with the reading of the composition until he has finished the last paragraph of it.

"No masterpiece of world-literature," says the late Professor C. Alphonso Smith of the University of Virginia, "has suffered so much by piece-meal reading as the Bible.[1] On Sundays," Professor Smith reminds us, "it is read aloud by select chapters or parts of chapters, and expounded by select verses; in Sunday schools it is taught with an equal disregard of book divisions; and even in home study and private reading the same hop-skip-and-jump method is generally followed."

"Suppose we should read Shakespeare the same way," Professor Smith continues, "one day a few passages from *Romeo and Juliet*, the next day an act from *Hamlet*, the third day a scene from *The Merry Wives of Windsor*. It has been practically overlooked that each book of the Bible, like each play of Shakespeare, is a unit in itself."

Mr. George Bernard Shaw, a keen observer of men and a prolific writer himself during his almost ninety-five years, in an interview made this observation about Bible reading:

Although it is the most widely distributed book in English, it is unique among literary works in this respect, that it is seldom read in the way that any other book is read: that is to say, from the first word on the first page to the last word on the last page. Instead, it is read in bits and pieces, when it is read at all; and it is true to say that the number of men and women who have read it straight through is small.[2]

[1]C. Alphonso Smith, *What Can Literature Do for Me?* pp. 14-15. (Doubleday, 1924.)
[2]St. John Ervine, *Bernard Shaw, His Life, Work and Friends,* p. 524. (William Morrow & Co., 1956.)

31

One way to avoid the piece-meal or hop-skip-and-jump method of reading the Bible is to try reading each book at a single sitting, as we do a magazine story or article. In this way one can concentrate on the meaning of the composition as a whole.

2. READING THE ENTIRE BIBLE AS ONE UNIT

This section title has a simple meaning. God has revealed Himself and His Plan for the salvation of men and women in what the Church fathers have called the Old and New Testaments — in sixty-six separate writings.

A careful and thoughtful examination of the writings of these two "Testaments" reveals the fact that they are as closely related as the two halves or parts of any whole. Each complements the other; the Old Testament is the forerunner of the New Testament, and the New is the fulfillment of the Old.

Viewing the Bible as *one*, and not solely as sixty-six separate units, gives the reader a vision of grandeur, like viewing the stars on a clear night, or the magnitude of the universe through a telescope.

Such a view gives the reader proper perspective, and enables him to view each book of the Bible, the earliest written and the latest, as so much human, religious experience in response to God's revelation. He can see himself in all the religious and ethical levels of the past, which each man re-lives in his lifetime, and to match his spiritual aspirations with the hopes of the vast human family, of which he is a part. Most important, he will see that the Bible is divinely inspired, and authoritative; God's Word for man.

This is another way of saying that it takes sixty-six books to present the whole story; to develop the complete picture. Each has its place, and each belongs to the whole. It is no accident that David built the first Jerusalem in Judah, and that the Christ established the New Jerusalem in the hearts of men and women.

3. BIBLE READING ACCORDING TO A PLAN

Many Bible readers feel that they accomplish more by having a definite plan to follow.

William Lyon Phelps, for a long time Professor of English at Yale University, tells the story of how he as a youth adopted the familiar scheduled plan of reading three chapters of the Bible each week day, and five chapters on Sunday, by means of which he was assured that he could read the entire Bible in exactly fifty-two weeks, or one year.

The plan, he confessed, had its advantages and disadvantages. Its advantage is in the fact that by following this schedule we can be sure to cover the entire Bible in one single year. One of its disadvantages is that it places the emphasis upon reading chapters as units, rather than upon the reading of whole books as units.

George Bernard Shaw at age ten, on hearing a schoolmate boast that he had read John Locke's difficult book, *On Human Understanding*, decided to surpass him by "reading the Bible straight through."

John Quincy Adams, the sixth President of the United States, once said: "I have for many years made it a practice to read through the Bible once every year." He did not mention what method he followed.

George Muller, however, of the Bristol Orphanage, is winner of sweepstakes as a Bible reader. "I have read the Bible through one hundred times," he declared many years ago, "and always with increasing delight. Each time it seems like a new book to me."

Although each of these methods of reading the Bible as a whole is good in its own way, and certainly each is to be commended, yet there seems to be lacking in each of them a certain compelling purpose. Is there a better plan which the modern reader may follow in the mastery and understanding of the *contents* and *message* of his Bible, and at the same time will bring to him what George Muller calls "increasing delight" in his Bible reading?

I believe that such a plan is that recommended and outlined in the Table of Contents of this volume, which simply is to read and study the Bible chronologically, and by related groups of books, beginning with the Seventeen Historical Books and continuing with the remainder of the eight grand divisions of our Bible, as thus organized.

4. READING THE BIBLE ALOUD

Many present day readers of the Bible are discovering that reading the Bible aloud is one of the best ways of understanding and enjoying it.

Charles Laughton, the late Hollywood actor and reader, related how he discovered that his enthusiasm for reading aloud was shared by almost every one else. In fact, he said that reading out loud had flowered into a "great revival" in recent years. "I had always enjoyed reading the Bible and other great literature out loud," he said in one of his communications; "my wife and I had often spent our evenings that way."[3]

When the war ended, he said, "I began reading the Bible before audiences in cities all over the country. I was once invited to read the Bible to an audience of ministers at Occidental College. Afterward, one of the ministers told me, 'You know, we ministers make a fetish of the Bible. You turn it into a dramatic, earthly tale of real people.' "

And then, in his characteristic manner, Mr. Laughton made this appeal to his American audience: "I assure you that you can do the

---

[3]*This Week* magazine, December 8, 1957.

same thing if you will try reading the Bible out loud in your own living room, just as our ancestors used to do in their daily Bible readings."

Strange as it may seem to us of the modern age, originally the Bible was read aloud almost exclusively. This was the custom in Bible times, long before the age of the printing of books. "Blessed is he who *reads aloud* the words of this prophecy, and blessed are those who *hear,* and who keep what is written therein." When the Apostle John wrote these opening words in the book of Revelation, which was to be read aloud to the Seven Churches of Asia Minor, he was aware of the custom and expected his letter to be so read.

The letters of the Apostle Paul were read aloud to the churches to which they were addressed, as were the letters of the other apostles included in the New Testament. At the close of his letter to the Colossians, the Apostle Paul said, "And when this letter has been read among you, have it read also in the church of the Laodiceans; and see that you read also the letter from Laodicea" (Colossians 4:16).

In her book, *A Man Called Peter,* Catherine Marshall tells how that part of her husband's effectiveness as a preacher was due to his reading of Scripture to his congregation. "As he read," she says, "we listeners, were first of all impressed all over again with the timeless beauty of the Biblical narratives. Peter's fine voice," she continues, "his feeling for the rhythm of the King James Version, his almost perfect diction threw that beauty of language into sharp perspective."[4]

Catherine Marshall agrees with Charles Laughton, too, when she speaks of the enhanced value of the Bible when read aloud correctly: "To most moderns," she says, "the Bible is a closed book; it seems dry and unintelligible. But when Peter read it for us, somehow it lived and breathed — and throbbed with life."

5. BIBLE READING MARATHONS

A fleet-footed Greek messenger, by the name of Pheidippides, ran 26 miles from the battlefield at Marathon to Athens, in 490 B.C., bearing the good news of victory by 192 gallant Athenians, who gave their lives to preserve the city and all Greece from conquest by the Persian army of Darius the Great.

In the modern Olympic Games, the "Marathon Race" still 26 miles and 385 yards, the exact distance from Marathon to Athens, is one of the athletic events in these world-wide competitions. And, generally, the term has come to mean any similar long-distance race or contest.

Bible reading "marathons" began in Old Testament times. Moses gave his First Edition of the Bible orally, in what has been called the

---

[4]Catherine Marshall, *A Man Called Peter,* p. 133. (McGraw, 1951.)

Farewell Address, and published in its entirety in the book of Deuteronomy.

After the period of Exile and Return to Jerusalem (about 445-433 B.C.), there was a historic occasion at which Ezra the priest and scribe, together with his thirteen reading assistants, read the Scriptures aloud publicly to all the people, reading from early morning until midday for the full seven days of their holy feast, "And they read from the Book, from the Law of God, clearly; and they gave the sense, so that the people understood the reading" (Nehemiah 8).

In England in the sixteenth century, when copies of the Bible were scarce, the church authorities would fasten a copy of the big Bible to the pulpit with a chain, so that readers could come and read. Large groups would gather in the churches to hear the Scriptures read aloud, hour after hour, and day after day, for considerable periods of time.

A Bible reading marathon in our times to attract considerable national attention was that conducted recently in the First Baptist Church of Garber, Oklahoma, by its minister the Rev. Wilbur Nuckalls and members of his congregation.

Promptly at 9 o'clock on Wednesday night, Mr. Nuckalls stood up in his pulpit and read: "In the beginning God created the heavens and the earth . . . ." Thus he started his congregation's cover-to-cover Bible reading marathon. Fifteen minutes later, the pastor yielded the pulpit to a housewife, who continued the reading where he left off. Almost every fifteen minutes thereafter, for four nights and three days, someone else stepped up and continued the reading—Genesis, Exodus, and on through the Old Testament and the New, until the last book was read aloud to an ever-changing, volunteer audience.

In all, 89 people from all trades, occupations, and professions, men and women and youths, took part in this most unusual Bible reading marathon, nearly half of whom were from outside the congregation.

Exactly at 3:55 Sunday morning, a girl read the last words of the book of Revelation from the King James Version: "The Grace of our Lord Jesus Christ be with you all. Amen." Thus the marathon ended and the Rev. Mr. Nuckalls was satisfied that the 78-hour-55-minutes reading experiment had served a useful purpose. He had dramatized the importance of Bible reading, not only for his church and community, but also for the whole country and the millions of readers who read his story.

The American Bible Society, a non-profit organization supported by some fifty-five denominations as well as by private subscriptions of individuals, has for many years been first in the printing and distribution of Bibles. More recently the Society has assumed prominence also in directing Bible reading on a wide scale through its Daily Bible

Reading program. A list of Daily Readings for the entire year may now be obtained by writing to the Publicity Department, 450 Park Avenue, New York 22, N.Y.

Thus, the American Bible Society conducts its own perpetual Bible reading marathon, which, with the aid of foreign Bible Societies, covers not only the United States but the whole face of the earth as well.

6. THE MOST SATISFYING BIBLE READING WILL ALWAYS BE PERSONAL

Every reader has his favorite books; those books which have brought peace and comfort to him in some crisis or tragic moment, or sustained him or her over the rough places of a lifetime.

A woman who lay dying of cancer testified that the book of Job spoke to her need as no other book of the Bible.

The woman was not alone in her regard for the book of Job. "There was a time in my life," says Dr. George W. Truett, "when for days and days, the only book I wanted to read was the book of Job, and I read it through and through."[5]

Another reader, Thomas Carlyle, a prophet himself in his own right, put the book of Job at the head of his list:

> I call this book, apart from all theories about it, one of the grandest things ever written. Our first, oldest statement of the never-ending problem—Man's Destiny, and God's Ways with him in the earth.

Charles Dickens, the most popular English novelist of the nineteenth century, would include the whole of the New Testament. "The New Testament," says Dickens, "is the very best book that ever was or ever will be known in the world."

As we have seen, Robert Louis Stevenson named the gospel of Matthew as the book in the Bible that had influenced him most.

Rider Haggard, an English novelist to whom we ordinarily do not attribute too much influence from the Bible, preferred the book of Ecclesiastes.

With modern readers, the gospel of Luke is a great favorite, as is the gospel of Matthew. Usually ministers prefer the Apostle Paul's Letters, especially the letter to the Romans. Poets and persons of imaginative temperament prefer Isaiah and the Psalms. The Twenty-Third Psalm is a universal favorite.

7. BIBLE READING FOR DEVOTION

The most satisfying Bible reading, we have said, will always be intensely personal. It is more than that; it will be *devotional*.

Jesus, who taught His disciples how to pray and gave them the "Lord's Prayer," also taught them how to read the Scriptures in the spirit of devotion.

---

[5]George W. Truett, *A Quest for Souls*, p. 265. (Broadman Press, 1917.)

Luke, who was a most careful scholar and historian, gives us a brief summary of some of the things Jesus taught His disciples during the forty days between the Resurrection and the Ascension (Luke 24). One occasion was the walk to Emmaus, Jesus' appearance and what He taught them regarding the meaning of the Old Testament Scriptures, and the comment of the two disciples.

Seeing how little they understood the central meaning of the prophets, Jesus exclaimed to them, thus:

> O foolish men, and slow of heart to believe all that the Prophets have spoken! Was it not necessary that the Christ should suffer these things and enter into His Glory? And beginning with Moses and all the Prophets, he interpreted to them in all the Scriptures the things concerning himself.

When the two disciples were alone, they said one to the other, "Weren't our hearts *glowing* while he was with us on the road, and when he made the Scriptures so plain to us?" (J. B. Phillips).

This is the test of devotional Bible reading, that the reader's heart *glows* within him while he reads and listens to God speak to him through His Word.

A recent quotation from an old Eskimo woman, one of the Kuskokwin tribe who live along the Bering Sea, illustrates well the meaning of Bible reading for devotion. The New Testament had just been translated and published in her language by the American Bible Society. When the missionary visited her and presented her with a copy of the new book, she said, "Thank you, thank you; Now God speaks to my heart."

The mystery and glory of the Bible is its divine appeal to all sorts and conditions of readers, each in his own language. People come to the Bible for many reasons; but they come mainly because they are in search of that inner peace and happiness, which somehow they have not found elsewhere but which they are persuaded may be found in the pages of Scripture.

The opening verses of the book of Genesis from the first edition of the Authorized (King James) Version, 1611. From the British Museum. *Courtesy of the Trustees of the British Museum*

Chapter 4

THE GREATER ENGLISH VERSIONS OF OUR BIBLE

1. INTRODUCTION

Which Bible or Bibles shall we own for our daily reading?

Norman Vincent Peale, pastor of the Marble Collegiate Church on Fifth Avenue, advised the reader to buy the best Bible he can afford; one that is handsome on the outside, handsome on the inside. One that he will read often and enjoy.

Somehow a man with a handsome new suit, or a woman with a beautiful new dress, can lift his head a little higher, with permissible pride, so to speak. We are human that way. We should be proud also of the Bible we read.

There are other choices. What *version* or what edition shall we buy and own? These and other questions concern many discriminating Bible readers.

Our present day Bibles in English have had many distinguished ancestors. The Bible in English, or portions of it, have appeared ever since the days of King Alfred the Great, who induced the scholars of his day to translate portions of the Holy Bible into Old English as early as the ninth century A.D.

John Wycliffe and his disciple, John Purvey, brought forth their translation of large portions of the Bible from the Latin *Vulgate* into English as early as 1382-1383, and 1388. These early versions were the first extensive rendering of the Scriptures into any form of Modern English. Since the printing press had not yet appeared, these versions circulated in manuscript copies only.

The real history of our modern Bible, however, begins with the joint work of two great scholars and poetic translators — William Tyndale and Miles Coverdale. Tyndale excelled as a scholar; Coverdale as a poet. The two made an excellent team. These devout servants of God labored in the Luther and Calvin tradition of early Protestantism in the West.

William Tyndale's translation of the New Testament arrived in England about 1526 from abroad, where he had gone from his native England to escape persecution. It was published at Worms, Germany.

Tyndale's work was translated directly from the Greek, although he made use of Martin Luther's German translation of the New Testament and Jerome's Latin *Vulgate* also as aids.

In 1530, 1531, and 1534, Tyndale issued editions of the Pentateuch, the book of Jonah, as well as a fresh edition of the New Testament.

Before his martyrdom, in 1536, he had translated other portions of the Old Testament, probably the historical books, and possibly had made a start on the books of prophecy. But he did not live to publish them. He was arrested in May, 1535, and on October 6, 1536, he was strangled and burned as a heretic, because he dared publish a new translation of the Bible.

One writer pays him this singular tribute: "But his work remained. It fixed the English standard of Bible translation, and its diction and style still live in the English Version (King James Version) and lend it literary charm and character."

Miles Coverdale built on the noble work of William Tyndale and completed it. Both men were abroad from England and translating at the same time. Coverdale's distinctive work, which he translated independently, include the poetic works of Job, Psalms, Proverbs, Ecclesiastes, Song of Songs, and the seventeen books of prophecy from Isaiah to Malachi.

So superb was Coverdale's poetic version of the Psalms, that it, virtually unchanged, is still used by the Church of England and the Protestant Episcopal Church of America in *The Book of Common Prayer.*

Coverdale's Bible, like Tyndale's work, was published abroad, very likely at Zurich, Switzerland, in 1535. It was the first complete English Bible to be issued from the press. Its New Testament and the portions of the Old Testament translated by Tyndale underwent few changes from the form in which Tyndale left them.

After the translations of Tyndale and Coverdale, a number of other versions appeared in England in the next fifty years. They include Matthew's Bible (John Rogers) in 1537; Taverner's Bible in 1539; the Great Bible in 1539-1541; the Geneva Bible (The Puritan Bible) in 1560; the Bishop's Bible in 1568; and the Rheims and Douay Bible (Roman Catholic) in 1582, 1609-1610.

Except for the Roman Catholic Version, which was an English translation of Jerome's Latin *Vulgate,* these versions leaned heavily on the work and translations of Tyndale and Coverdale.

The Bible has not always been divided into *chapter* and *verses* as it appears in our Bibles of today. The Jewish scholars, called *Masoretes,* about 700 A.D. at Tiberias, Palestine, first divided the Old Testament into *verses* for reading on the Sabbaths of the year.

It is generally believed that Stephen Langton, Archbishop of Canterbury, who died in 1228, was the first to divide the Scriptures into *chapter* divisions.

The division of the New Testament into its present verses is due to Robert Stephens, who introduced them into the Greek and Latin New Testament which he published at Geneva in 1551; and they were first adopted in the English version of the New Testament printed at Geneva in 1557.

The whole Bible first appeared with its present *chapters* and *verses* in Stephens' edition of the Latin *Vulgate* in 1555.

The first whole English Bible to be divided into chapter and verse divisions was the Geneva or Puritan Bible of 1560.

2. THE KING JAMES VERSION OF 1611

For English speaking peoples, the most famous and the most popular of all the English versions is the *King James Version* of 1611.

The original suggestion and proposal for a new version of the Bible came from President John Reynolds of Corpus Christi College, Oxford, during the conference and discussion between the Anglicans and the Puritans on January 16, 1604, at Hampton Court Conference. King James I, who was present at the Conference, was pleased by the proposal, and on February 10, 1604, he ordered "that a translation be made of the whole Bible as consonant as can be to the original Hebrew and Greek."

By July of 1604, the King had appointed 54 translators, "learned men . . . having especial skill in the Hebrew and Greek tongues" to make the new translation. It is to the credit of the king that he named both Anglican Churchmen and Puritans on his commission of translators. Mr. John Reynolds was himself a Puritan, and this fact may have influenced the King's choices.

The task was completed and published in 1611. A careful comparison of the *King James Version* with its predecessors, especially with the translations of Tyndale and Coverdale, indicates that strictly speaking it was not a new translation, but a superb scholarly *revision*, resulting from a fresh study of the original languages of Scripture — the Hebrew and the Greek. For example, by actual count about nine-tenths of the language of the New Testament of 1611, is still the language of Tyndale.

Likewise, a comparison of Miles Coverdale's great poetic translations of the book of Psalms, and other poetic books of Scripture, with the *King James Version*, shows that the language and poetry of the 1611 version is largely the language and poetry of the Coverdale translation.

But even so, the contributions made by the 1611 revisers were both superb and significant. For they had the good sense and talent, to know how to *improve* on all the great translations that had preceded them. This they modestly confess on their title page:

> Truly (good Christian Reader) we never thought from the beginning, that we should need to make a new Translation, nor yet to make a bad one a good one . . . but to make a good one better.

Although it has been about 350 years since this great work first appeared, it is now estimated that about 90[1] per cent of those who

---

[1]Because of the recent wide acceptance of the *Revised Standard Version* of 1952, this estimate may already be out of date.

today read the Bible in English translations, read it in the *King James Version*. The reason for its popularity is to be found in its excellence, both in translation and as literary composition. It came as the culmination and summit of many good translations and versions. It was produced in the age and spirit of Elizabethan England, which was an age of great writers. In short, these scholars, in addition to all their other qualifications, brought also to their task the talent of great men of letters.

Although the Puritans brought to America with them the Geneva or Puritan Bible of 1560, it was not long until it was supplanted by the *King James Version*, which has remained the Bible of the people to this day.

3. The English Revised Version of 1881-1885

By the second half of the nineteenth century, notwithstanding the popularity of the *King James Version* of 1611, it was felt both in England and America that the time had come for a new version of our Bible in English. For one thing, the language had changed in the 250 years or so since the 1611 version appeared, and many felt that there was need for a new version of the Bible in the language of the people.

Then, too, in these two and a half centuries many manuscripts "more ancient than those upon which the *King James Version* was based," had been discovered. Also, Greek and Hebrew scholarship had made great advances during the same period. Likewise, the discoveries of archaeology had thrown much light on the Bible and Bible times.

In February, 1870, the Convocation of the Province of Canterbury planned and authorized a fresh revision of the *King James Version*. Two companies of scholars, 37 members for the Old Testament and 28 for the New Testament, were formed for the task. About two-thirds of these members were chosen from the Church of England.

Two groups of scholars in America cooperated with the English, fifteen for the Old Testament and nineteen for the New Testament, representing nine different Protestant Churches.

The work on the new version was begun on June 22, 1870. The New Testament was ready for publication in May, 1881; the work on the Old Testament was completed four years later and was published in 1885.

It is generally agreed that the *English Revised Version* as a work of exact scholarship was a distinct improvement on the *King James Version*. This was thought to be especially noticeable in the books of prophecy in the Old Testament, and in the Letters of the New Testament, where the true meaning is often more understandable in the Revised Version.

In the second place, a serious attempt was made to improve the format, by printing much of the poetry as poetry and prose as prose, whereas the *King James Version* did not distinguish poetry from prose on the printed page. The spelling of proper names was also improved.

On the negative side, it has been charged that the revisers of 1881-1885, in their somewhat unbridled enthusiasm for scientific accuracy, went too far afield from the idiomatic excellence and beauty of the *King James Version.*

4. THE AMERICAN STANDARD VERSION OF 1901

Inasmuch as two groups or committees of American scholars co-operated with the English scholars in producing the *English Revised Version* of 1881-1885, the *American Standard Version* of 1901 in many respects is similar to that of the English. However, the changes in the two are significant.

The American version included revisions preferred by the two American committees, in those cases in which they disagreed with the English scholars, and also some changes the need for which had become more apparent in the sixteen years between the appearances of the two works.

In the first place, the *American Standard Version* undertook to improve the quality of expression used in the English version of 1881-1885. The American scholars at one and the same time aimed to retain the scientific accuracy of the English version, and also to return to the beauty and excellence of the *King James.*

There are many other changes in the American version of 1901 as compared with the English of 1881-1885. For example, the American version makes use of the name *Holy Spirit,* instead of the English *Holy Ghost,* as more correctly expressing the idea of the Spirit of God. Also, it substitutes the name *Jehovah* for Lord and God, wherever YHWH (Jehovah) is found in the original Hebrew manuscript.

Finally, the American scholars, in the matter of page format, re-moved the *verse numbers* from the margin, placed them inconspicuously within the text itself, and paragraphed the reading matter, not according to verses, but to correspond with the content of the passage. They also went much further than the English scholars in arranging and printing poetry as poetry.

5. THE AMERICAN REVISED STANDARD VERSION OF 1952

As they approached the middle of the twentieth century, many American churchmen felt that the time had come to consider a thorough revision of the version of 1901.

So, as its first step, the International Council of Religious Education, which consisted of the churches of the United States and Canada, appointed a committee of scholars to make inquiry as to whether further revision was necessary.

After more than two years of investigation, the Committee decided that there was need for a thorough revision of the *American Standard Version* of 1901, and that the new revision should "stay as close to the Tyndale-King James tradition as it can in the light of our present knowledge of the Hebrew and Greek text."

In 1937, the revision was authorized by the Council, and thirty-two scholars were appointed as members of the Committee and charged with making the revision. In turn, the Committee secured the review and counsel of an Advisory Board of fifty representatives of the cooperating church denominations.

The *Revised Standard Version* of the New Testament was completed and published in 1946. The complete Bible, containing both Old and New Testaments, was finished and published in 1952. As the members of the Committee finished their notable work, and bowed out, they instructed their spokesman to say these words, in their Preface:

> The REVISED STANDARD VERSION is not a new translation in the language of today. It is not a paraphrase which aims at striking idioms. It is a revision which seeks to preserve all that is best in the English Bible as it has been known and used through the years. It is intended for use in public and private worship, not merely for reading and instruction.
>
> We . . . have sought to put the message of the Bible in simple, enduring words that are worthy to stand in the great Tyndale-King James tradition.

It is generally agreed that the revisers of the 1952 version made progress in three particulars. For one thing, in the fifty years or so between the versions of 1881-1885 and 1901, a number of more ancient manuscripts were discovered and became available, both in Scripture and in secular and historical fields. As a result, inaccuracies and errors discovered in former versions were corrected. Also, words that have changed in meaning and are therefore misleading, have been replaced by language intelligible to the modern reader.

In the second place, to use their own words, the authors of the 1952 version have sought to put the message of the Bible in simple, enduring words that are worthy to stand in the great Tyndale-King James tradition. That is, in addition to the quality of accuracy in translation and in diction, they have sought further to embody in their work the quality of beauty and excellence of the *King James Version*. In this they claim to have made progress beyond that of the revisers of the 1901 version.

Finally, the revisers of 1952 feel that they have made progress in the *form* in which Scripture appears for the modern reader. Poetry is printed as poetry, not merely in the book of Psalms, but generally wherever poetry occurs in all the books of Scripture. A good example is the way the songs of Elizabeth and Mary are printed in the first two chapters of the gospel of Luke.

Here, too, Hebrew verse in English translation is for the most part effectively arranged to bring out the rhythm and cadence of the original. That is, it presents the parallelism and verse structure and pattern of Hebrew poetry, with new clarity and beauty.

Likewise, the prose portions of the Bible are paragraphed according to content, as a modern book is paragraphed. The effect of this modern paragraphing is further enhanced by the removal of all chapter and verse numbers from the margin to less conspicuous positions within the text itself.

6. THE NEW ENGLISH BIBLE OF 1961

On March 14, 1961, the New Testament of *The New English Bible* was published simultaneously throughout the world, with the Cambridge University Press and the Oxford University Press as joint publishers.

The new translation was the work of a large body of British scholars and literary advisers, under the direction and sponsorship of duly appointed representatives of the Church of England, the Church of Scotland, the Presbyterian Church of England, the Free Churches of Britain, the Churches of Wales and Ireland, the British and Foreign Bible Society, the National Bible Society of Scotland, and others.

The main feature of the new work is that it is a completely new translation of the Bible from the original Hebrew and Greek, and not a revision or reworking of existing versions.

In Britain there was a question whether successive revisions of earlier revisions, as great as they were, were adequate for the needs of the present day. The feeling was that the new translation should make use of the most accurate and up-to-date findings in all the relevant fields of knowledge — linguistic, textual, and historical — "and carried out by men who themselves hear the voice of God speaking to them in Holy Scripture."[2] And with this same feeling, another English Churchman as long ago as 1940 spoke, "All serious Christians are fundamentally at one in needing a version of the Scriptures which is as truthful as human skill, aided by the divine grace, can make it."[3]

This New Testament translation of *The New English Bible* is the work of thirteen years, and represents the best in British Biblical scholarship. It reads like a true translation and an enduring one. It is not only in the language currently spoken and understood; but it is in the best tradition of that language and aspires to be ageless.

The early acceptance of this British translation has been amazing. So well was it received that within five months after its publication date more than 3,000,000 copies were issued. Meanwhile, work on the Old Testament goes forward, with its publication date to be announced later.

Here we have in hand, and in prospect, another great English translation of the Holy Scriptures, and another landmark in the history of English translations.

[2]F. F. Bruce, *The English Bible: A History of Translations*, Oxford, 1961, p. 224.
[3]Cecil John Cadoux, *The Bible in Its Ancient and English Versions*, p. 274.

7. SOME OTHER MODERN VERSIONS

Our story would not be complete without at least some brief mention of a few other modern versions which have been found extremely useful to large numbers of students and readers of the Bible. The aim of these translations and versions is the same as that of the more conventional and authorized versions: to present a great religious literature in language easily intelligible and acceptable to the large body of modern readers, and at the same time to do it with the dignity and seriousness worthy of the Holy Scriptures.

(1) THE MOFFATT TRANSLATION. One of the best known of the one-man translators is James Moffatt, a Glasgow Scotsman with Oxford degrees and honors, who in 1922 first brought out his *New Translation of the Bible*, and who issued a final Revised Edition of his work in 1935.

Eight years earlier, 1927, Dr. Moffatt had come to America to become Professor of Church History at Union Theological Seminary. He was also appointed a member of the Committee of thirty-two scholars in charge of making the *Revised Standard Version* of 1952. However, his death in 1944 cut short his services in this important task.

(2) THE GOODSPEED VERSION. *The Bible, an American Translation*, appeared in 1935 by two eminent scholars and professors of the University of Chicago, J. M. Powis Smith and Edgar J. Goodspeed. Dr. Smith, Professor of Semitic languages and Literature at the University, was responsible for the Old Testament translation; Professor Goodspeed, Greek Scholar and Biblical Translator, did the New Testament. Their American translation made wide use of American colloquialisms, so that the language of Scripture might be more intelligible to present day readers. A Revised Edition of their work appeared in 1939.

(3) THE MODERN READER'S BIBLE. Another American translation, *The Modern Reader's Bible* by Professor Richard G. Moulton of the University of Chicago, is not a translation at all in the true sense. His work is an adaptation and special arrangement of the *English Revised Version* of 1881-1885, according to literary form and content. For example, the book of Psalms is printed as lyric verse, the book of Job and the Song of Songs appear as drama, with characters and speeches indicated. So also, history, the essay, and other forms, appear according to type as in any modern book.

Professor Moulton was a pioneer in introducing the feature of printing poetry as poetry throughout the Bible, and prose as prose in paragraphs according to content, with chapter and verse numbers removed to inconspicuous positions on the printed page, as in any other book. The influence of his work, which first appeared in 1895, is seen in later versions, and especially in the *Revised Standard Version*, of 1952.

(4) J. B. PHILIPS' NEW TESTAMENT. Another translation, which

has had wide acceptance, is the Rev. J. B. Phillips' *New Testament in Modern English*, which appeared first in separate volumes as early as 1947 and 1952, and as the complete New Testament in 1958.

Mr. Phillips is an English scholar and Churchman, who on May 8, 1957, was installed as Canon of Chichester. His translation makes a fresh approach to the meaning of New Testament Scripture and is noted for its directness and simplicity of language. It is widely recommended.

(5) THE BERKELEY VERSION. Of this version the well known scholar of the New Testament, F. F. Bruce, said, "Among recent English translations of the whole Bible which have been sponsored by private groups none is more worthy of special mention than *The Holy Bible: The Berkeley Version in Modern English*."[4]

In 1945 a translation of the New Testament, the work of Dr. Gerrit Verkuyl, was published under the title *The Berkeley Version of the New Testament* (from Berkeley, California, where the translator lived). Soon a staff of twenty scholars was named to produce a similar translation of the Old Testament under Dr. Verkuyl's direction as editor-in-chief. In 1959, fourteen years after the appearance of the New Testament, the complete work was published.

The Berkeley Version of the Bible is the work of conservative evangelical scholars. In comparison with the translation of the *Revised Standard Version* for example, with which it is often compared, wherever there was a choice of meaning or word or method, the translators of the Berkeley Version have usually followed the principle of conservative interpretation.

(6) THE AMPLIFIED BIBLE. Of the several "expanded" versions of the Bible, one of the most useful is *The Amplified New Testament*, published in 1958. This is indicated in its wide acceptance, inasmuch as some 750,000 copies were distributed in its first three years of publication.

This version was produced by a committee of twelve editors, working under the Lockman Foundation of La Habra, California. It is a true rendering of Westcott & Hort's Greek text of the New Testament.

The translation is "amplified" or expanded in the sense that alternative renderings, additional words, phrases, synonyms, are given by way of exposition to bring out the *full meaning* of the passage translated. To further assist the reader, these added explanations are skillfully indicated by the use of curved and square brackets, dashes and italics, to bring out the various shades of thought and meaning.

The Amplified Old Testament, published in 1962, is the counterpart of *The Amplified New Testament* and follows the same principles of translation and purpose as the first work.

---

[4] *Op. cit.*, p. 420.

Chapter 5

THE LAND OF CANAAN

1. PALESTINE AND ITS NEIGHBORS

The study of the geography of Palestine has always been a fascinating subject. It has been a rewarding one, too. For the people who produced the holy books of the Old and New Testaments were influenced profoundly by the rugged land and environment which surrounded them and which shaped their lives and destiny.

A glance at the map of ancient civilizations in Bible times will show the small country of Palestine as a part of what has been aptly called the "Fertile Crescent."[1] This semi-circular area extended from the Persian Gulf up the Mesopotamian Valley, and south through Syria and Palestine, and on into Egypt and the Valley of the Nile. In fact, Palestine formed the connecting link, or land-bridge so to speak, between the ancient land of Egypt and the Assyrian and Babylonian Empires of the north.

This Fertile Crescent was the center of civilization from the Stone Age to the Golden Age of Greece in the fifth century B.C.

But Palestine was never the center of this civilization of the Fertile Crescent, except possibly during the brief reign of King Solomon. On the contrary, the economic and political power was centered at both ends of the semi-circle — first in Egypt in the era of the Pyramid Kings, and then with the Assyrian and Babylonian Empires of the Mesopotamian Valley.

The Nile river of Egypt, and the Tigris and Euphrates rivers of Mesopotamia, made irrigation and a stable economy possible in those regions. However, these natural advantages, for the most part, were lacking in Syria and Palestine.

Situated in the middle of the semi-circle, in a land less favored by nature, Israel in the Providence of God, was to be a people *rich in spirit* if not in worldly goods, as were the empires to the north and south of them.

There were other compensations, too. Although the armies of conquerors passed through the western borders of the land, and many battles were fought on the soil of Israel, there were also obvious com-

---

[1] See map on page 14.

47

mercial and cultural advantages. For the caravans of trade and the pilgrims of many lands passed over this ancient highway of the world.

Moreover, from the time of Abraham on, the prophets of Israel never forgot one of the three promises of the covenant, namely, that through Israel, all the nations of the earth should be blessed.

2. PALESTINE ITSELF

The geography of Palestine, as is often the case of the geography of other lands, has had a determining influence upon the lives of the Hebrew people, their occupations, their social and political, as well as their religious life.

In the first place, Palestine is a very small country, but it has had an influence in world history altogether out of proportion to its size and natural resources. In Biblical times, the portion of the country west of the Jordan river, which was the main portion, was no more than 6,000 square miles. If to this we add the portion east of the Jordan river, we have a total of only about 10,000 square miles, no larger than the state of Vermont or the state of New Jersey.

Patriotic Israelites often spoke of their country as extending all the way "from Dan to Beer-sheba," which is from the foot-hills of Mount Hermon on the north, to the beginning of the desert region below Beer-sheba, on the south. Thus the total length, north and south, is slightly less than 150 miles. The distances from east to west are much shorter, as a look at the map will show.

In a country so small one would expect considerable similarity in the lay of the land, and in climate; but such is not the case in Palestine. For instance, along the coastal plain on the west side one meets a mild climate, with an average annual temperature of 65-70° F. Agriculture was a common occupation.

Now if one goes some 30 miles east to Jerusalem, at an altitude of nearly 2,600 feet, he will find a temperate climate with an average annual temperature of 60-65° F. Grazing and herding was a common occupation in this hill country.

If one goes east from Jerusalem "down to Jericho," a distance of 15 miles, he has descended 3,300 feet below the level of Jerusalem, and nearly 700 feet below the sea level of the Mediterranean, where tropical palm trees are a common sight on the landscape. In fact, Jericho was called "the city of palms."

It will be easier for us to carry in our mind's eye these essential differences and contrasts in climate, and lay of the land, if we divide all Palestine into four natural divisions for a brief picture study of each.

Our divisions will cut north and south, and we shall use the words that describe each best, thus: (1) The Coastal Plain; (2) The Hill

Country; (3) The Jordan Valley; (4) The Plateau "Beyond Jordan" (Transjordan).[2]

A. THE COASTAL PLAIN

The Coastal Plain of Palestine extends from Phoenicia on the north to the beginning of the desert lands of the Negeb on the south. This coastal strip is never more than ten or fifteen miles in width, from the Mediterranean to the hills, and contains much of the fertile agricultural lands of Palestine.

This plain may be divided into three sections: the plain about the city of Accho, which extends from Phoenicia to Mount Carmel; the plain of Sharon, which lies between Mount Carmel and the old city of Joppa; and farthest south, the plain of Philistia, the home of the ancient enemies of Israel, the Philistines, who later gave their name to the whole country. The word *Palestine* is derived from the word *Philistia*. One of the famous characters of the Old Testament, Samson (*Judges*), made his daring sallies among the Philistines, first at the old city of Gaza, and then into the Valley of Sorek, where he met Delilah and his downfall.

Palestine had an almost unbroken coast line, with no important seaport city or natural advantages to encourage commerce on the Mediterranean Sea, like her neighbors to the north, Phoenicia, which had her seaports of Tyre and Sidon, and Byblos, from which came our word *Bible*, and other seaports not so famous. Israel therefore was forced to develop her inland occupations of farming and grazing, and caravan trading.

The student of the Bible who forms the habit of associating Biblical events with their geographical background will often find answers to questions which otherwise might puzzle him. For example, why did so many of the great battles in Bible times take place in Esdraelon or the Valley of Jezreel, in the vicinity of Megiddo, between Mount Carmel and Mount Gilboa?

The geography of the region is the first answer. The old road from Egypt north passes through the plains country near the Mediterranean, until it approaches Mount Carmel. Then, because of Carmel, it turns sharply northeasterly, in the direction of the Sea of Galilee and the old Syrian city of Damascus.

Esdraelon or Jezreel is a "gate" or *pass*, between the mountains, into the valley beyond, and can be guarded militarily speaking, in a manner similar to that of the pass of Thermopylae, in the battle of 480 B.C. between the Greeks and the Persians; so all ancient generals knew the tactical advantage of forcing a battle engagement at Esdraelon.

For the center of population and activity, we must turn from the

[2]See Wright and Filson, *The Westminster Historical Atlas to the Bible,* Revised Edition, pp. 17-21. (Westminster Press, 1956.)

coastal plains to the hill country, where Israel was better able to defend herself against the constant threat of her enemies from without, and where she was to develop a religion and a civilization peculiar to itself, and one which was to be the determining factor in the cultural and religious life of the world.

B. The Hill Country

The Hill Country of Palestine embraces the three famous districts or small states of Galilee, Samaria, and Judah, and extends from Syria on the north to the desert and lower country south of Judah, called the Negeb. An airplane flight over this Hill Country will reveal one continuous range of hills and their connecting valleys and caravan trails, for the entire length of Palestine.

(1) Galilee. The first of these districts, Galilee, embraces the foothills of Mount Lebanon, west of the upper Jordan Valley and of the Sea of Galilee. In the upper half of Galilee, the terrain is rugged and the elevation at one point reaches almost 4,000 feet with a number of lesser hills and mountains between 2,000 and 3,000 feet in elevation. The lower half of Galilee, however, is less hilly and the climate is somewhat milder. Much of the rolling land in south Galilee, including the plains above Nazareth and west of the Sea of Galilee, may be cultivated as farm lands.

The antiquity of Galilee is seen in its famous cities built in the Valley of Jezreel, and used in ancient times to guard the gate or pass against trading caravans or armies from the southern coastal plain as they entered the Valley. Megiddo, dating from about 3500 B.C., was one of the most ancient. Here fought Joshua, Barak, Saul, and Josiah; and here the Jews believed would be the final battle of God's hosts with Satan and the powers of evil, the Armageddon as the Apostle John used it in Revelation 16:16. Jezreel was another ancient city (Joshua 19:17-18).

In New Testament times, a considerable population occupied Galilee. Jesus' home was at one of its important cities, Nazareth, and He adopted another, Capernaum, as headquarters during two of His three years of public ministry. All but one or two of the twelve apostles were natives of Galilee. The old historic road, running from Egypt to Mesopotamia, passed through Nazareth, Capernaum, and other cities, in its route north, thus connecting the district with important caravan trade and armies of the world.

(2) Samaria. Samaria has been called the geographical center of Palestine, occupying as it does the territory between the Coastal Plain on the west and the Jordan Valley on the east, and between Galilee on the north and Judah on the south.

After leaving the great Valley of Jezreel on his way south, the traveler soon comes upon Mount Gilboa (1,698 feet) and the hills of Samaria, which rise abruptly and eventually reach their highest point (3,317 feet), at Baal-hazor. The two most conspicuous peaks, however, are Mount Ebal (3,077) and Mount Gerizim (2,849 feet), which stand at the very heart of the district of Samaria, and guard an important system of caravan routes and crossroads which lead in every direction.

Two places of great historic interest are in the vicinity of these peaks — one is the old town of Shechem, beside which Abraham pitched his tent and built his first altar to the Lord on his entrance into Canaan, and which became famous in Hebrew history. The other place was Jacob's Well, which became one of the landmarks of all Israel. It was at this well, eighteen hundred years later, that Jesus at noonday conversed with the Woman of Samaria on the subject of Living Water.

Two other ancient cities of the district of Samaria are of special historic interest. One of these is the city of Samaria itself, from which the district received its name, and which became the capital of the Northern Kingdom. Omri, the sixth king of the Northern Kingdom, bought a piece of land called the Hill of Shemer, fortified it, and called the name of the city *Samaria* after the name of Shemer, the owner of the hill.

The other of the two famous cities, Bethel, was a city in the days of Abraham, his grandson Jacob, and was captured by Joshua in the conquest of Canaan. It was the religious capital of Jeroboam I and Jeroboam II of the Divided Kingdom, and the scene of the prophet Amos' preaching in the reign of Jeroboam II. When the Assyrians carried most of the population of the district of Samaria into captivity, they brought in colonists from Babylonia, Hamath, and Arabia, to take their places. Four hundred years later, Alexander the Great also introduced Syrians and Macedonians into Samaria. Thus, by New Testament times Samaritans were a mongrel race of many nationalities and thoroughly hated by the Jewish Pharisees.

(3) JUDAH. The third division of the Hill Country gets its pre-eminence from the fact that it contains Jerusalem, the world famous Hebrew capital, and the Temple, the center of Hebrew worship.

The hills of Judah are not so lofty as those of Samaria. In fact, the traveler, as he approaches Jerusalem from the north, notices that the hills descend in elevation to about 2,600 feet above sea level, although they rise again as he proceeds south of Jerusalem, reaching their maximum of 3,370 feet near Hebron.

West of Jerusalem, however, the hills slope more gently toward the Mediterranean and receive from the clouds coming in from that direction adequate rainfall for the small farms and vineyards in that region. On the contrary, east of Jerusalem and east of this central watershed, is the dry and bleak wasteland, because the clouds have already lost their moisture as they passed over the western Judean hills from the Mediterranean. Moreover, the deeply cut valleys leading down to the Dead Sea drop down so sharply that there is little opportunity for agricultural development.

Thus, the population and history of Judah centered much more in the lower and more fertile region west of Jerusalem, in what was called the *Shephelah* or lowlands area, between the mountains and the coastal plains country near the Mediterranean.

The Shephelah was important to the Hebrews for two reasons. It was fertile and generally well-watered, and furnished farming valleys for grain and vineyards and olive groves. But also, and equally important in early times, the Shephelah was used for defensive reasons, against the would-be conqueror of Jerusalem, the capital.

Thus, in this region were built a number of fortified cities — Gath, Lachish, Jarmuth, Librah, Azekah, Beth-shemesh, Eglon, and many others we read about in Old Testament history. In his devastating campaigns against Judah, Sennacherib of Assyria boasted that he captured 46 of these fortified cities, and took away with him 200,000 inhabitants.

South of Jerusalem, and below Hebron, the hills gradually descend to the *Negeb,* the dry southland which embraces the large desert area between Beer-sheba and Kadesh-barnea. Here Moses and the Israelites spent most of the forty years in "the Wilderness."

The Hill Country of Judah became the center of population and activity of Israel for almost a thousand years. In addition to their physical advantages, these hills also symbolized strength and protection in quite another way. The poet, especially David, "the sweet singer of Israel," looked upon the hills surrounding Jerusalem as symbols of the protecting care of the Lord:

> I will lift up mine eyes unto the hills,
> From whence cometh my help.
> My help cometh from the Lord,
> Which made heaven and earth.

C. The Jordan Valley

The Jordan river and the Jordan Valley are about as world famous as the Hebrew capital city of Jerusalem.

In the Jordan river our Lord was baptized to conform to the pattern and mission which He came to earth to fulfill. And the Sea of Galilee is in the Jordan Valley, around which our Lord spent two-thirds of His earthly ministry.

Scientifically speaking, the Jordan Valley is part of a great physical rift or geological *fault* in the face of the earth. This rift comes down from the north through Syria, runs between and divides Mount Lebanon and Mount Hermon, continues on through the Sea of Galilee and the Jordan Valley, into the Dead Sea, through the Arabah south, and on into the Red Sea, and thence extends into Africa.

One of the features of this geological rift is the *Sea of Galilee.*

Although the Jordan river as it comes down from the north is considerably above sea level, it drops swiftly as it enters the Sea of Galilee, which is 685 feet below sea level. This fresh water lake, called a "sea" because of its size, is nearly thirteen miles in length and about eight miles wide. It abounds in fish, and in the days of Jesus fishing was a profitable industry. Previous to their call, four of the twelve apostles, James and John, Peter and Andrew, were professional fishermen on this lake.

Another feature of the Jordan Valley is the Jordan River itself. The Jordan carries the snow waters from Mount Hermon and Mount Lebanon in a rapid descent to the Sea of Galilee. Then, as it leaves the Sea of Galilee in a more leisurely manner, it meanders slowly, zig-zagging for 200 miles to the Dead Sea, which in a straight line as a crow flies is only 65 miles distant. Except in March and April when it overflows its banks, the Jordan winds back and forth over its river bed, sustaining a green line of vegetation through the otherwise desolate and barren hills.

Still another feature of the Jordan Valley is the *Dead Sea*. When the Jordan river enters the Dead Sea, it descends to 1,275 feet below sea level, the lowest point below sea anywhere on the face of the earth. Like the Great Salt Lake in Utah, the Dead Sea has no outlet; and like the Great Salt Lake, the water contains a high percentage of salt (in the case of the Dead Sea about 25 per cent).

The length of the Dead Sea from north to south is about 47 miles, and the breadth at several points about 9½ miles. The maximum depth of the water at several soundings has been found to be from 1,275 feet to 1,300 feet. Except on the north end, where the Jordan enters, the Dead Sea is practically surrounded by a ring of precipitous cliffs and mountains, ranging from about 1,400 feet above water at the north end, to 2,000 feet in the middle, and 2,500 feet near the south end. On the east side, the commanding cliffs of Moab reach an altitude of 2,500 to 3,000 feet above the shore line. It was upon this plateau in the "Plains of Moab" that Moses and all Israel were encamped while completing plans for the conquest of Canaan.

Originally the Dead Sea was only about two-thirds its present length, the lower one-third being a fertile valley upon which was located the famous cities of Sodom and Gomorrah, and some other cities not so well known. The ancient Hebrews called this fertile valley "the Vale of Siddim." The reader will recall that Lot, Abraham's nephew, when given a choice of grazing grounds, chose the territory including this rich Vale.

About the time of Abraham (about 2,000 B.C.), a great catastrophe occurred in the area, perhaps an earthquake, setting free certain gaseous matter, which when ignited, caused the terrible conflagration that followed. The whole neighborhood of the Dead Sea abounds in sulphur and bitumen, furnishing materials for such a holocaust. In the words of one commentator, "The use of natural agencies in the destruction of these cities makes that destruction no less the act of God." Indeed, few episodes have impressed human beings more than this one. The expression, "Sodom and Gomorrah," became a legend and a symbol of wickedness and its sure punishment to all succeeding generations, and especially in the messages of the prophets, and of our Lord Himself.

D. The Plateau Beyond Jordan (Transjordan)

The expression "beyond Jordan" is common in Biblical literature, indicating that most Hebrew writers, and editors, were on the *west side* of the River when they wrote, although some scholars claim that the term refers to both sides.

However, a number of Biblical events of the first order took place on the east side of the River. Moses encamped the hosts of Israel in the plains of Moab before the entrance into Canaan; and Moses himself died and was buried on the east side of the Jordan. John the Baptist, who preached on *both* sides of the Jordan, was preaching and baptizing on the east side, at "Bethany beyond the Jordan," the day Jesus came to him to be baptized (John 1:28-33). Some months of Jesus' ministry were performed on the east side of the Jordan, including the miracles east of the Sea of Galilee. In the allotment of territory to the Twelve Tribes of Israel under Moses and Joshua, the tribes of Reuben, Gad, and one-half tribe of Manasseh, were given lands as their inheritance on the east side.

The Plateau Beyond Jordan is divided naturally into five sections by four small rivers which flow in a westerly direction into the Jordan Valley: (1) Bashan, (2) Gilead, (3) Ammon, (4) Moab, and (5) Edom.

(1) BASHAN. The territory of Bashan extends from Syria on the north to the Yarmuk river. A look at the map shows its location to the east and northeast of the Sea of Galilee. Like most of the surface of Palestine, Bashan has its outcropping of common limestone. Here, too, are extinct craters, patches of lava, and black basalt, indications of prehistoric volcanic activity.

However, much of this plateau soil is fertile and well suited to grazing and grain production, in spite of its somewhat limited rainfall. In the days of Abraham, Bashan was occupied by a race of giants. The last king of the giants of Bashan, Og, was defeated and slain by the Israelites under Moses (Deuteronomy 3:1-11).

The land was celebrated for its large cattle — "strong bulls of Bashan," says the Psalmist (Psalm 22:12) — and for its breed of sheep. The prophet Amos, while preaching at Samaria and Bethel, could think of no better term of reproach for the wicked and pampered women of wealth than to shout at them, "You cows of Bashan!"

(2) GILEAD. The section of Gilead lies principally between the

River Yarmuk on the north, and the River Jabbok on the south. It possessed more streams and springs than Bashan, and thus was better watered and capable of supporting a larger population. Also, it was nearer the Hill Country and Jerusalem, the center of activity in Palestine.

One of the famous products of the region of Gilead was *balm*, which also became a symbol of spiritual healing. The caravan of Ishmaelite traders, who "bought" and carried Joseph to Egypt, were "bearing gum, balm, and myrrh" as their products.

The desirability of the land of Gilead is indicated in the application of the Reubenites and the Gadites, two large tribal families, to Moses for permission to settle permanently in Gilead.

(3) AMMON. The land of Ammon extended mainly from the River Jabbok on the north, to the River Arnon on the south. In the main, the geographical aspects of the land of the Ammonites were similar to those of Gilead, more trees in some northern areas, and fewer streams in others, and therefore less water.

The ancient Ammonites were descendants of Ben-ammi, Lot's second son. They had a long and tangled history of intrigue and enmity with Israel and Israel's enemies. As unceasing enemies of Israel, they were often denounced by the prophets (Jeremiah 49:1-6; Ezekiel 21:20; 25:1-7; Amos 1:13-15; Zephaniah 2:8-11). On the other hand, as a part of his policy of foreign alliances and marriages, Solomon took several Ammonite women as wives (I Kings 11:1).

(4) MOAB. The kingdom of Moab lay south of the river Arnon as far as the River Zered. It is chiefly a rolling plateau, about 3,200 feet above sea level, and like large bodies of the other sections of the Plateau Beyond Jordan, it is well suited to grazing and herding. The inhabitants of Moab, like the people of Ammon, were descended from one of the sons of Lot, Abraham's nephew, named *Moab*.

Moab doubtless is remembered best by readers of the Bible because of the story of Ruth, a Moabitess who clung to her mother-in-law, Naomi. According to Josephus the Jewish historian, John the Baptist was imprisoned and beheaded at Machaerus, in the land of Moab, east of the Dead Sea.

(5) EDOM. The last of the sections "Beyond Jordan," Edom, stretches south and southwest of the river Zered for about 100 miles, and extends on both sides of the Arabah to the Gulf of Akabah. Because of its rugged terrain and semi-desert climate, much of this land is resigned to sparse, extensive herding.

Edom, however, had two great advantages. First, it controlled the caravan trade from the desert of Arabia on the east, to the great caravan center of Gaza on the west, forming a crossroads with the heavy trade route from Egypt to the Mesopotamian Valley in the north. Second, it possessed large quantities of copper and iron ore, something Palestine proper lacked.

Edom, which is another name for *Esau*, was occupied by the descendants of Esau, who sold his birthright to his twin brother, Jacob. The region was originally called the land of Seir. The rulers and peoples of Edom were generally the enemies of Israel and were denounced by nearly all the prophets.

The infamous family of the Herods, frequently mentioned in New Testament history, came originally from Edom, or *Idumaea* as the Greeks called Edom. The first Herod was called Idumaean Antipas, or just Antipas, the procurator or administrative agent for the Roman emperor, who received revenues and turned them over to the government. His more infamous son, Herod the Great, was king of Judea, 37-4 B.C., and was the Herod who murdered the Innocents, all male children in Bethlehem and in all that region who were two years old or younger, in his mad attempt to destroy the child Jesus. Herod the Great's three sons, Archelaus of Judea, Antipas of Galilee, Philip of the region east of Galilee, and his grandson Agrippa I of Judea, are all familiar to readers of the gospel story.

How these Idumaean Herods managed, politically, to get these important public positions from official Rome, of "ruling" with the power of a king, is a long story. In their private lives, these men and women were guilty of every crime in the book: usurpation, murder, incest, suicide, and all the rest. Herod the Great had ten wives from first to last, two of them being his nieces.

A shepherd and his flock in the Shepherds Fields near Bethlehem. The city is visible in the distant hills. © *Matson Photo Service*

PART TWO
THE HISTORICAL BOOKS OF THE OLD TESTAMENT

PALESTINE
UNDER JOSHUA AND
THE JUDGES
(12th and 11th Cen. B.C.)

EPHRAIM   Hebrew Tribes
                    Roads
Indefinite   *Jerash* Arabic names
Boundaries   underlined

Scale 0   10   20   30 mile

Copyright by Rand McNally & Company

Chapter 1

INTRODUCTION

By "historical books" we mean the *seventeen books* of the Old Testament which contain practically the full length story of the Jews "from the beginning" down to the close of the book of Nehemiah, or about 432 B.C.

At the same time, this does not mean that there is no historical material in the other twenty-two books of the Old Testament. Indeed, there is historical matter of a sort in every one of them; but their main character is not that of historical narrative.

The reader who makes himself familiar with the contents of these seventeen books, will be in possession not only of a valuable historical background and framework, but will also have first-hand acquaintance with a great historical literature.

Moreover, he will have a proper introduction to and understanding of the people who produced the other great works of the Old Testament: the book of Psalms, the books by the wise men of Israel, and the seventeen books of prophecy.

And most of all, the reader will see unfolding before his very eyes the making of our Bible and its progressive revelation of God the Father, and His Master Plan for the salvation of the human family.

For the better understanding and convenience of the reader, the historical books are grouped and arranged chronologically, as follows:

1. The Five Books of Moses:
    GENESIS
    EXODUS
    LEVITICUS
    NUMBERS
    DEUTERONOMY
2. The Books of the Conquest of Canaan:
    JOSHUA
    JUDGES
    RUTH
3. The Books of the Kings and Kingdoms:
    I AND II SAMUEL
    I AND II KINGS
    I AND II CHRONICLES

59

4. The Books of the Return and Restoration:
EZRA
ESTHER
NEHEMIAH

SUGGESTIONS FOR ADDITIONAL READING[1]

I. *Books on the Bible As a Whole*

*Albright, William Foxwell: *The Archaeology of Palestine and the Bible.*

*Bright, John: *The Kingdom of God.*

Burrows, Millar: *An Outline of Biblical Theology.*

Buttrick, George Arthur and Others, General Editors: *The Interpreter's Bible;* Vol. I contains special articles on the Bible as a whole.

*Davidson, Francis, A. M. Stibbs, and E. F. Kevan, Editors: *The New Bible Commentary;* General articles; Second Edition, pp. 15-71.

*Davis, John D. and H. S. Gehman: *The Westminster Dictionary of the Bible.* Fifth Edition.

Dodd, C. H.: *The Bible Today.*

*Foreman, Kenneth J., Balmer H. Kelly, Arnold B. Rhodes, Bruce M. Metzger, Donald Miller: *Introduction to the Bible. The Layman's Bible Commentary,* Vol. 1.

*Hastings, James, Editor: *The Dictionary of the Bible.* 5 Vols.

International Standard Bible Encyclopedia. 5 vols.

Keller, Werner: *The Bible As History.*

Manley, G. T.: *The New Bible Handbook.*

*Miller, H. S.: *General Biblical Introduction.*

Rowley, H. H.: *The Unity of the Bible.*

*Wright, G. Ernest and Floyd V. Filson: *The Westminster Historical Atlas to the Bible.* Revised Edition.

II. *Readings on the Historical Books of the Old Testament*

*Aalders, G. Ch.: "The Historical Literature of the Old Testament," *The New Bible Commentary,* pp. 31-37.

*Albright, William Foxwell: *From Stone Age to Christianity.*

Anderson, Bernhard W.: ·*Understanding the Old Testament.*

Bright, John: *The History of Israel.*

Francisco, Clyde T.: *Introducing the Old Testament.*

*Paterson, John: *The Book That Is Alive.*

---

[1] It is not necessary that the student read all the books in a large and extensive bibliography. But it is important that he be acquainted with them and have a chance to become familiar with viewpoints other than his own. For this reason the above reading lists, and the others throughout the book, cover a wide range of interpretative thought and opinion, but with emphasis always on conservative and constructive values in Biblical study and scholarship. Titles with an asterisk (*) indicate a starting point for introductory students. See also the general Bibliography in the back of the book.

Rowley, H. H.: *The Growth of the Old Testament.*

Tenney, Merrill C., General Editor: *The Zondervan Pictorial Bible Dictionary.*

Wright, G. Ernest: "The Faith of Israel," *The Interpreter's Bible,* Vol. I, pp. 349-389.

Wright, G. Ernest: *The Old Testament Against Its Environment.*

*Young, Edward J.: *An Introduction to the Old Testament.*

The famous statue of Moses, by Michelangelo, at Rome. © *Radio Times Hulton Picture Library, British Broadcasting Corporation, London*

Chapter 2

THE FIVE BOOKS OF MOSES, OR THE PENTATEUCH
(Genesis, Exodus, Leviticus, Numbers, Deuteronomy)

1. THE LAW

Historically and spiritually, the five books of Moses, in the thirty-three centuries or so since their original composition, have assumed more universal prominence than any other portion of the Old Testament. And this is understandable, because of the very high moral and religious standards and values set in the books of Moses as compared with the religious books of all other ancient peoples, and because they are recognized as God's revelation.

In the words of Professor J. R. Dummelow of Cambridge University, "It is well nigh impossible to overestimate the religious value of the book of Exodus. Nowhere else save in the Christian revelation is there to be found so sublime a conception of the nature of God, or a loftier and purer idea of morality."[1] And the same may be said of the other four books of this five-volume work.

The five books originally were called "The Law," or "The Book of the Law" (Deuteronomy 31:24; 31:26). They were also called "The Law of the Lord" (II Chronicles 31:4), and "The Law of Moses" (I Kings 2:3).

In Hebrew manuscripts, The Law or the Books of the Law are divided into five main parts. The Septuagint Translators of the Hebrew Old Testament into Greek (between 285 and 150 B.C.) gave the five parts of the manuscript their separate Greek names, as listed at the head of this chapter. Our English spellings are taken from St. Jerome's *Vulgate Latin Version* (390-405 A.D.).

Since the third century A.D., scholars have used the word *Pentateuch*, a Greek word meaning "the five-volume book," or one volume in five parts, as a convenient name for the first five books of the Old Testament.

Although these books contain the historical narrative of the Hebrews "from the beginning" down to the death of Moses, about 1400 B.C., the central theme of the books is The Law and the Covenant relationship between them and God their Creator, Redeemer, and Counselor.

---

[1] *A Commentary on the Holy Bible*, p. 48. (Macmillan, 1936.)

In the first place, the Pentateuch contains the basic facts of the Divine revelation: man's creation as well as that of the universe; man's fall and the provision for his redemption and salvation; the Saviour is promised (the "seed of the woman" of Genesis 3:15).

One major result of man's sin was his *bondage*, the Egyptian bondage being typical and symbolic. But by the hand of Moses, God delivered His people from the house of bondage and made a New Covenant of grace with them at Mount Sinai. The written code of this Covenant is the Mosaic Law, recorded in the book of Exodus, beginning at chapter 20, and in revised form in the book of Deuteronomy.

The Law was for Israel's education and discipline, in religion and in civil relations, for the next thousand years, and longer. It was not their salvation; but in it there was preparation for, and a promise of, their salvation.

They must become like Abraham, who was both an example and a pattern of faith. He believed in the revelation that came to him; he believed in God's plan of salvation for him; and his belief worked salvation for him.

The Apostle Paul, in his letter to the Galatians and elsewhere, made it abundantly clear how The Law was never intended for salvation, but was only a forerunner and educator in the faith that looked forward to the coming of the All-sufficient Christ, the only Saviour.

In all the editions of their Bible, The Law and the Books of the Law always came first in all Hebrew manuscripts and collections. Later Jews, looking back at the composition of their Holy Book, referred to it as "The Law and the Prophets." As great as were the prophetic books of the greater prophets, they never took priority over The Law.

It was the lost Book of the Law which King Josiah found and used as the basis of his reforms of 621 B.C. It was the Book of the Law which the priest and scribe Ezra brought with him from exile in Babylon to Jerusalem in 457 B.C. and read aloud to the people for seven days. It was the Law of the Lord of which the Psalmist sings in Psalms 1, 19 and 119. Jesus, a short time before the Ascension, spoke these words to His disciples: "These are my words which I spoke to you, while I was still with you, that everything written about me in The Law of Moses and the Prophets and the Psalms must be fulfilled."

2. THE AUTHORSHIP AND DATE OF THE PENTATEUCH

Both Hebrew and Christian tradition from the earliest times ascribed the authorship of the five books of the Pentateuch to Moses. Present day opinion among conservative scholars also strongly favors Moses as the author.[2] And for at least a hundred years now the discoveries of archaeologists in Egypt, Palestine, and in the Mesopotamian Valley have tended to confirm this opinion.

These archaeological discoveries verify the fact that writing was common in the Mosaic era. And as for the book of Genesis, there are ancient inscriptions, monuments, tablets, and other records, which had come down from previous generations, available from which Moses under Divine inspiration could have constructed the great book.

For example, introductory statements such as, "This is the book of the generations of Adam" (Genesis 5:1), "These are the generations of Noah" (6:9), and including nine other similar headnotes, all indicate ancient "books" and written records from which materials were gathered for the composition of the book of Genesis.

As for the books of Exodus, Leviticus, Numbers, and Deuteronomy, Moses himself was the main actor in the events recorded there, and from the abundance of internal evidence, it is likely that he was their author. In fact, from the books themselves we learn that Moses was a writer. He kept a full diary of the itinerary from Egypt to the Plains of Moab, with the names of places, persons, tribes, as well as a historical record of the localities, incidents and events of the journey (Numbers 33:1-49).

In addition to these personal accounts, there is the voluminous material covering the Ten Commandments, other Divine statutes, judgments, and ordinances, not to mention songs, short speeches, and full length orations such as are found in Deuteronomy. Indeed, the whole of the book of Deuteronomy professes to be a verbatim transcript of Moses' Farewell Address to the people.

Moses' writings, occasions, and the contents are referred to specifically in these passages: Exodus 17:14; 24:4; 34:27; Numbers 17:2; 33:2; Deuteronomy 6:9; 24:1, 3; 27:3, 4; 31:9, 19, 22, 24.

The modern reader is impressed with the great amount of personal and factual detail in these books, material given from the viewpoint of an eye-witness. The writer is either an eye-witness him-

---

[2]The Mosaic authorship is strongly supported by Professor Oswald T. Allis, *The Five Books of Moses*, Second Edition; Edward J. Young, *An Introduction to the Old Testament*, Chapter 8; and others, including archaeologists. The modern critical view is that the Pentateuch is a composite work by prophets or priests, variously placed from the 9th to the 6th centuries B.C., in which several literary sources have been blended, usually represented by the symbols J, E, D, and P. This view is represented in a recent work by Bernhard W. Anderson, *Understanding the Old Testament*, Chapter 1 (pp. 12-13), Chapter 6 for J, Chapter 8 (pp. 225-227) for E, Chapter 10 for D, and Chapter 12 (pp. 381-393) for P. Others include R. H. Pfeiffer, *Introduction to the Old Testament;* G. Ernest Wright, who summarizes the view of the German scholar Gerhard von Rad, as well as his own, in *The Interpreter's Bible*, Vol. I, pp. 349 ff.

A slightly different, and to some more plausible view, from that of Professors Allis and Young, is that of Professor G. Ch. Aalders of Free University of Amsterdam, in his detailed work, *A Short Introduction to the Pentateuch*, and summarized in *The New Bible Commentary*, Part One, pp. 31-34.

self, or he is repeating an eye-witness account by someone else. From the context, it is presumed that Moses was the eye-witness, and that he composed the narratives.

It is not without significance that Joshua regarded Moses as the author of the Book of the Law. Upon assuming his duties as Israel's new leader, he quoted the words of the Lord to that effect, Joshua 1:7, 8. Then at the close of his career, Joshua spoke similar words in his Farewell Address to the people, as recorded in Joshua 23:6.

Then there is the testimony of the New Testament, the most important of which are the words of our Lord Himself. As recorded in the gospel of Mark 7:10, Jesus declared, "Moses said, 'Honor thy father and thy mother.'" Also, in Mark 12:26, Jesus remarked, "Have ye not read in the Book of Moses?" and then proceeded to quote from the book of Exodus 3:6. Again, in the gospel of Luke 20:37, Jesus pointed out "that the dead are raised, even as Moses showed" (Exodus 3:6).

Also, not only did our Lord during His earthly ministry in Palestine regard the Books of The Law as having been written by Moses, but also testified to this fact after His Resurrection. He talked with two of His disciples on the road to Emmaus, regarding the Scriptures: "And beginning with Moses and all the Prophets, he interpreted to them in all the Scriptures the things concerning Himself" (Luke 24:27). And, finally, just before His Ascension, He spoke these words before the larger group:

> These are my words which I spoke to you, while I was still with you, that everything written about me in the Law of Moses and the Prophets and the Psalms must be fulfilled.

Apparently *all* the writers of the New Testament believed that Moses wrote the first five books of the Old Testament, which they called "The Law." The Apostle Paul, who in his letters refers many times to these books, quotes from one of them, Leviticus (18:5), using the phrase "Moses writes" (Romans 10:5). Again, in Romans 10:19, Paul quotes from Deuteronomy 32:21b, using the words "Moses says." Also, in I Corinthians 9:9, Paul quoted from Deuteronomy 25:4 with the phrase, "It is written in the Law of Moses." In the book of Hebrews (12:21), which most readers believe was written by Paul, is a quotation from Deuteronomy 9:19, which begins, "Moses said."

The Apostle John is another New Testament writer who believed that Moses was the author of the books of the Law. In his gospel, John testifies that Moses wrote (Deuteronomy 18:15) concerning the coming Messiah, in these words, "We have found him of whom Moses in the Law and also the Prophets wrote" (John 1:45). Also, in the book of Revelation 15:3, John refers to the triumphant Song of Moses, composed and sung on the occasion of the crossing of the Red Sea (Exodus 15).

Is it at all likely that all these persons, both Old and New Testament writers, were wholly mistaken as to the authorship of these books?

The brief introductory and transition statements, and a phrase here and there to clarify some place name, as well as the whole of chapter 34, were added by some later scribe for the benefit of later readers. Indeed, it would be surprising if, during the thirty-three centuries or so since the composition of these books, some minor changes had not been made in the text.

SUGGESTIONS FOR ADDITIONAL READINGS ON THE PENTATEUCH[3]

Bible Readings: The Books of *Genesis, Exodus, Leviticus, Numbers,* and *Deuteronomy.*

Text: *The Revised Standard Version;* or *The New English Bible* (New Testament, 1961; complete Bible to be issued later); or *The King James Version,* preferably in modern reader's format.

*Allis, Oswald T.: *The Five Books of Moses.* Second Edition.

Anderson, Bernhard W.: *Understanding the Old Testament,* pp. 1-59; 154-182.

Chapman, A. T.: *An Introduction to the Pentateuch.*

Good, Edwin M.: *You Shall Be My People.*

Green, William Henry: *The Unity of the Book of Genesis.*

*Kevan, E. F.: "Genesis," *The New Bible Commentary,* pp. 75-105.

*Leupold, Herbert C.: *Exposition of Genesis.*

McNeile, A. H.: *Deuteronomy, Its Place in Revelation.*

*Manley, G. T.: *The Book of the Law — Deuteronomy.*

Rylaarsdam, J. Coert: "The Book of Exodus," *The Interpreter's Bible,* Vol. I, pp. 833-848.

Smith, J. M. Powis: *The Origin and History of Hebrew Law.*

Welch, Adam C.: *The Code of Deuteronomy.*

*Young, Edward J.: "The Law of Moses," and "The Literary Criticism of the Pentateuch," *An Introduction to the Old Testament,* pp. 43-114; 115-164.

---

[3]Early in his introductory study of the Bible, the student should become acquainted with the important tools of efficient study, such as Bible dictionaries, concordances, encyclopedias, atlases, the standard English versions of the Bible, and the outstanding commentaries in sets. To assist him, he will find at the end of the book the General Bibliography of classified reading references, including names of publishers, dates, and brief comments. And most of all, the student should not overlook the fact that his main task is to read and master the basic contents of the Bible itself.

Chapter 3

GENESIS

1. THE IMPORTANCE OF THE BOOK OF GENESIS[1]

The book of Genesis is easily one of the most important of the thirty-nine books of the Old Testament. It is because this book throws so much light on the greatest of all mysteries: How things came to be. More than that, it introduces all the questions and problems dealt with in the rest of the Bible, as well as all the matters human beings are interested in or have been interested in through the ages.

The Hebrew word with which the book opens was translated into the Greek word *Genesis,* which in English means *origin* or "in the beginning." It has been said that about everything *begins* in the book of Genesis.

At the outset, the book brings the reader face to face with the two main ideas of the Bible. In the first place, it reveals God the Creator and gives us a picture of the universe as the work of His hand. And then it introduces man, and God's Plan for his redemption and salvation.

The record of Creation in Genesis is unique, because it speaks for itself. It is God's inspired message to man. That is to say, it presents the Creator and the story of Creation in language so convincing that it is at once both authoritative and trustworthy, and is the only book of Creation to be so accepted.

In the story of creation in polytheistic religions, the deities are dependent on Chaos or some other mythical source, from which they were evolved. Their position in the universe is a confused and uncertain one.

In our Bible, on the contrary, there is the One God, free and independent, who is the Creator, and who was before all things. The book of Genesis places Him in the center of *revelation,* and what is revealed to the reader is not so much the doctrine of Creation as *the doctrine of the Creator.*[2]

---

[1]One of the best introductions to Genesis is still the older but able work, Oswald T. Allis, *The Five Books of Moses* (1915). See also the briefer introductions by Professors Edward J. Young and E. F. Kevan, both of which are listed at the end of chapter 2, p. 66. For a "liberal" interpretation, see G. Ernest Wright, "The Faith of Israel," *The Interpreter's Bible,* Vol. I, pp. 349-351; Bernhard W. Anderson, *Understanding the Old Testament,* pp. 1-37, and 154-182; B. Davie Napier, *From Faith to Faith,* Chapter 2.

[2]See E. F. Kevan, Principal of the London Bible College, *The New Bible Commentary,* pp. 76ff. (Second Edition, 1954.)

The book of Genesis is unique in quite another way, which is its second main purpose. It places man at the center as well as the climax of earthly creation. "For thou hast made him a little lower than the angels," or a little less than God, in the words of the Psalmist.

This should have produced in man, not overweening pride as we have so often seen, but humility. For it revealed divine kinship, and made man the only creature capable of divine inheritance!

It has been said that the first sentence in the book — "In the beginning God created the heavens and the earth" — is the most sublime statement ever uttered. Indeed, the Apostle John must have thought as much, when he began his gospel with the famous passage:

> In the beginning was the Word,
> And the Word was with God,
> And the Word was God.
> He was in the beginning with God;
> All things were made through Him,
> And without Him was not anything made that was made.

2. THE STORY OF CREATION IN GENESIS COMPARED WITH STORIES OF CREATION IN OTHER ANCIENT RELIGIONS

The hymn of Creation, given in the first chapter of Genesis, moves forward majestically and triumphantly like the processional of the ages. IN THE BEGINNING GOD . . . AND THE EVENING AND THE MORNING WERE THE FIRST DAY!

In the Genesis story there is one God the Creator. He creates and presides over the universe with dignity and supreme power. He is interested in the welfare of His creatures. And He enjoys the work of Creation. God is the center and axis of the universe: for all things are shown in their relation to Him and their dependence upon Him. Everywhere there is order, plan and purpose. His majesty is shown in His Creation. In the words of the Psalmist,

> O Lord, our Lord,
> How excellent is thy name in all the earth!

In contrast with this view of Deity in Genesis, what a sordid picture is presented in the stories and cosmography of the ancient heathen nations!

Their stories tell of many gods, often in conflict with one another, and to whom creation is a mere episode in a string of other events. In our Bible, on the contrary, creation occupies the center of the stage and is the first scene in the great drama of human history.

Here is a brief account of the ancient Babylonian creation story:[3]

In the beginning, according to the story of the ancient priests of Babylon, there were only two gods: Apsu, the god of fresh water, and the female dragon Tiamat, both of whose waters were floating in *Chaos*. From their marriage sprang the gods of heaven and earth, who

[3]See T. G. Pinches, Translation of the Babylonian Creation Epic.

rebelled against their forbears and sought to create an orderly universe out of Chaos, or confusion.

But their victory was not an easy one. After many engagements, the god Ea defeated his father Apsu and became the hero and deity of Chaos. But his mother, the female dragon Tiamat, was determined. In her desire to destroy two of her own rebelling offspring, the gods of light and order, Tiamat created eleven monsters and appointed her new husband, Kingu, their leader. These eleven monsters, plus one, were identified later with the constellations, and the twelve signs of the zodiac — Hydra, Leo, Scorpio, Taurus, Sagittarius, Virgo, etc., after they had been bound by Marduk and chained to the stars.

Tiamat was defeated finally by this Marduk, Ea's son and her grandson, after many battles. He slew her and split her body into halves. Then he proceeded to create the world. Out of one-half of Tiamat's body Marduk made the canopy of heaven, and with the other half the abode of the departed Apsu.

There are other episodes of primeval conflicts between the dragons of darkness, and the gods of light and order. One of these refers to Kingu and the dragons having been bound and cast into hell fire by Marduk, the ruler of Chaos and the patron deity of Babylon.

The story finally goes on to describe the creation of man by Ea, from the blood of the slain Kingu, and to the assigning of the various spheres of influence to the remaining gods.

The Assyrian version of the creation story is much like the Babylonian, one difference being the substitution of the god Ashur, the patron deity of Ninevah and Ashur, for the god Marduk.

If we should examine the creation stories of ancient Egypt, or ancient Greece, we should find many striking similarities in episodes and deities, always allowing of course for the different names of the same or corresponding deities in the different lands.

3. MODERN SCIENCE AND THE STORY OF CREATION IN GENESIS

There are those who feel that the story of Creation in Genesis is over-simplified. It reads as if it were written for a child, in language suited to a child's understanding, they say.

The answer of devoted Bible scholars is that this childlike characteristic is precisely its glory. It is this simplicity, they repeat, which makes us sure of its divine inspiration.

If the work of Creation had been described in the language of modern science, no one during the thirty-three centuries or so since its first appearance would have found it intelligible. It is clear that it was designed for a people in the childhood stage of their development, and to be intelligible to everyone since. Moreover, if it had been written according to scientific ideas of the present day, it would most certainly be out of date in another hundred years.

Then, too, the "seven-day period" of Creation is objected to by some. What of all this vast work of Creation to be accomplished in only just seven days!

In the first place, the term *day* has been used to point out varying lengths of time, even in the Bible itself. In the Creation story "day" has different meanings. In 2:4, the word "day" seems to embrace the whole period of Creation.

In Psalm 90:4, a thousand years with the Lord are but as a *day*. In these passages: Joel 3:18; John 16:23; Acts 2:20, the term "That day" seems to mean the whole Christian era. And the Apostle Paul, in II Timothy 1:12, evidently uses "That Day" to mean the whole period of time beyond the Lord's Second Coming.

So many modern readers, quite properly, feel that each of the "seven days" of Creation may well represent vast periods of Creation time.

Professor E. F. Kevan, of the London Bible College, calls the language of Creation "a picturesque narrative, affording a graphic representation of those things which could not be understood if described with the formal precision of science. It is in this pictorial," Professor Kevan thinks, "that the divine wisdom in the inspiration of the writing is so signally exhibited."[4]

It has been observed by others, too, that the *order* of Creation as given in the Genesis story is quite acceptable to veteran geologists, whose archaeological accounts in general correspond to the Biblical account — that is, vegetation first, followed by sea animals and birds, and finally by the land animals, and man.

Other scientists, especially the astronomers, have in recent years been overwhelmed by the vastness of Creation as it pertains to the universe beyond. Larger and more competent instruments, such as the 200-inch mirror set up on Palomar Mountain in southern California, and the West Virginia station, bring us and the "heavens" ever closer to one another. And discoveries of each passing year cause scientists to revise upward their estimates of age, size and vastness of the universe, as they photograph and measure its segments.

Scientific measurements and estimates such as these stagger the imagination of the layman:

The sun is the center of our solar system, around which our earth and the other planets and satellites revolve. The distance is so great around this solar system that it takes our earth a whole year to make the journey, traveling at the rate of 72,000 miles per hour.

And yet our sun and solar system is only one member of the vast Galaxy called the Milky Way, which according to the estimates of astronomers contains more than 30,000,000,000 suns, many of them immensely larger than our sun, which itself is 1,500,000 times larger than our earth.

Astronomers estimate that the Milky Way Galaxy in diameter is

---

[4]*Op. cit.*, p. 56.

200,000 light-years, a light-year being the distance that light travels in a year at the rate of 186,000 miles per second.

If these figures have not made the reader too dizzy to stand on both feet, he has yet to remember that there are perhaps 1,000,000 Galaxies like the Milky Way, some of them millions of light-years apart. "And all this," in the words of one writer, "may be only a tiny speck in what is beyond in the infinite, endless stretches of space."

Mr. Lincoln Barnett, in his recent book on the work of Albert Einstein,[5] presents these and other startling figures about the universe:

1. The earth, as everyone knows, rotates about its axis every twenty-four hours at the rate of 1,000 miles per hour. This is man's slowest speed.

2. The earth's annual revolution about the sun is at the rate of 72,000 miles per hour.

3. The whole solar system, our earth included, is moving within the local star system at the rate of 46,800 miles per hour.

4. The local star system, our sun and solar system included, is moving within the Milky Way at the rate of 720,000 miles per hour.

5. And the whole Milky Way is revolving in harmony with the remote external Galaxies at the rate of 360,000 miles per hour — and all in different directions.

The wonders of Creation are again and again introduced by writers of the Scriptures to reveal the majesty and power of God the Creator. For example, the book of Job. To induce a spirit of humility in Job, the writer says,

> Hear this O Job;
> Stop and consider the wondrous
>   works of God . . .
> "Where were you when I laid
>   The foundation of the earth?" says the Lord.
> . . . "Or who laid its cornerstone,
> When the morning stars sang together,
>   And all the sons of God
>   shouted for joy?"   (Job 37, 38.)

Or Psalm 8:

> When I look at Thy heavens,
>   the work of Thy fingers,
> The moon and the stars which Thou
>   hast established;
> What is man that Thou art mindful
>   of him . . .?

3. The Contents of the Book of Genesis

The book of Genesis deals with the history and religion of the Hebrew people *before* their final settlement in Palestine (Canaan), which was to be their permanent home.

---

[5]See Lincoln Barnett, *The Universe and Dr. Einstein*, pp. 32ff. (William Sloane Associates, Second Revised Edition, 1957.)

In fact, about one-fifth of the book tells the story of the human family in their cradle, so to speak, in and about the Garden of Eden in the lower Mesopotamian Valley, not far from the ancient city of Babylon.

The contents of the book fall naturally into two main divisions: (1) The Beginnings of History, chapters 1 to 11; and (2) the Beginnings of the History of Israel, chapters 12 to 50.

A. The Beginnings of History, Chapters 1-11

The ancient world, before the coming of Abraham and the other patriarchs, is estimated variously by archaeologists and scientists as beginning with the Old Stone Age, and extending to about 2150 B.C.

(1) Creation and the Ancient World

The author of these first eleven chapters presents the beginnings of universal history as distinct from Hebrew history, which is his introduction to the book of Genesis and to the succeeding books of the Bible. No dates are given for these vast periods of time.

The first scene in the drama of human history begins with the creation of man, male and female, and in the image of God the Creator. Then follow in rapid succession the tragic events in the Garden of Eden, man's first disobedience and Fall. In Chapter 3, the author of the book of Genesis answers the question as to how evil came into the heart of man, who originally was created pure and loyal. His answer is that evil came from *without* man, through the cunning of the Serpent. Also, later Scripture indicates that it was Satan speaking through the Serpent (II Corinthians 11:3, 14; Revelation 12:9; 20:2).

Since evil did not originate within man, herein lies the hope of victory. Then the author, in chapter 3:14-15, prophesies the Covenant of Grace and man's eventual redemption through a promised Saviour. Meanwhile, man is expelled from the Garden, henceforth to make his own way in the world, under the penalty of his disobedience. Too, God's victory over the evil one is indicated in the curse placed upon the Serpent.

Indeed, we have in these first eleven chapters the epic story of all the generations of Adam, down to Noah, with prophetic emphasis on the Flood; the generations of Noah and his three sons, down to the appearance of Abraham. Like all writers of long ago, the author tells his story briefly, often covering whole epochs of time in a few sentences.

(2) Hebrew Style and the Modern Reader

Hebrew literature has its peculiarities of style. One of these is *repetition*.

This characteristic in its simplest form may be seen in the parallelism of Hebrew poetry. Examples of repetition are to be found in Hebrew literature as early as the Song of Moses, which the people sang after they escaped from the hand of Pharaoh across the Red Sea:

> I will sing to the Lord, for he has
> triumphed gloriously;
> The horse and his rider he has thrown
> into the sea.   (Exodus 15)

Every Bible reader is familiar with this type of repetition also in the book of Psalms.

But there is another form of repetition which is not so readily understood. In the Creation, for example, some readers and scholars have thought that the narratives of chapter 1, and of chapter 2, were two separate stories of Creation, originating from two different sources, and brought together here in sequence by the author or compiler.

A closer examination of the two chapters, however, will show their purposes to be different. In chapter 1, the writer *reveals* the creative work of God the Creator as an accomplished fact. In chapter 2, he is giving a brief *history* of the world as created, with special emphasis on man as the climax of earthly creation. In short, we have here an example of *parallel repetition,* and not two separate accounts of Creation.[6]

In this early method of writing, the composition proceeds by means of *progressive waves,* rather than in a straight line. The method is illustrated also in the repetition found in old English ballads, and in many of the older Mother Goose rhymes.

Other narratives in the book of Genesis which have bothered some readers are the Flood story, the story of how Joseph was carried to Egypt, and other stories which appear to have duplicate versions. These difficulties in interpretation of the text may be resolved in a manner similar to that of the Creation story.

For example, some readers are of the opinion that there are two separate accounts of the Flood story: one in which Noah is bidden to take *one pair* of each species of animals with him into the Ark, and the other in which he is instructed to take *seven.*

But on closer examination, it appears evident that Noah's general instructions are to take one pair of each species with him into the Ark. Then there were additional instructions, applying only to animals that were "clean," and of these Noah was bidden to take seven of each species. Here again, when rightly understood, we have another example of parallel repetition.

The reader will meet with other similar passages, especially in the

---

[6]Scholars who deny the Mosaic authorship of Genesis and the other books of the Pentateuch, and who hold to the so-called "documentary theory," claim to see "duplicate stories" in many of the Genesis narratives, beginning with the Creation story. For a different view, see the interpretation of Professor G. C. Aalders of the Free University of Amsterdam, *The New Bible Commentary,* Part One, pp. 32-34; Professor E. F. Kevan, *The New Bible Commentary,* Part Two, pp. 78ff. (Revised Edition, 1954.)

Old Testament, which appear to contain a duplication or consolidation of narratives. Often if he will examine them more closely, the difficulty will disappear. In fact, it is a good rule in the reading of Scripture to take the text at its face value.

B. The Beginnings of the History of Israel, Chapters 12-50

The story of the beginnings of the history of Israel is largely the stories of Abraham, his son Isaac, his grandsons Jacob and Esau, and his great-grandsons, the twelve sons of Jacob.

The approximate dates of the period are from about 2150 B.C., when Abraham and his father, Terah, and his nephew, Lot, left their native city of Ur, in Chaldea, to the close of the book of Genesis, about 1850 B.C.

(1) The Story of Abraham, Chapters 12-25

Although the narrative states that "Terah took Abram his son and Lot . . . and they went forth together from Ur of the Chaldeans to go into the land of Canaan," it is evident that Abraham is the central character of the story. With their families and servants and goods, they traveled up the Mesopotamian Valley in a northwesterly direction for a distance of 600 miles to the old city of Haran. Haran was a commercial center, even at this early date, being on one of the main trade routes between Babylonia, and the Mediterranean and Egypt.

Here at Haran the family established a second home, and waited no doubt for further directions from the Lord. For there were reasons for their migration from Chaldea, reasons which, we may be sure, were not thoroughly understood by Terah and Abraham, and which the writer does not state until later, when the call came to Abraham to go south into Canaan.

While we leave the family of Abraham at Haran, we may take a brief look at what had happened. Man, originally created in God's image and endowed with the ability to obey God, had disobeyed his Creator in the Garden of Eden and was cast out. Because of God's kindness, man did not die but was even enabled to discover things and to make inventions, and to reflect upon the life and the world that surrounded him.

Worst of all, he had drifted into idolatry, had become desperately wicked, until the day of the Flood came and overwhelmed him in catastrophe. Then Noah and his three sons were led by God toward what could have been a true life. But man's freedom was again too much for him to manage, and once more he became a worshiper of idols, and substituted other gods for the Creator who made him.

Would man never learn his lesson? Would he never learn to be loyal and obedient to his Creator, who had done so much for him?

Now Abraham, though he did not understand it, was being made ready for a new role. He would be God's prophet and spokesman for the true way of life. For the world of his day was in the grip of idolatry. Even his native Ur was an idolatrous city. So was Haran, his adopted home.

God's plan was to start all over. Abraham was to leave his people, including his father Terah, who himself was intent on going to Canaan. Abraham would face a new world, and with the aid of his Maker, he would establish the true religion in a new land. He must go on Faith, and what he needed to know would be revealed to him as he journeyed to the land where he would go.

So after his father's death at Haran, the call came to Abraham, thus:

> Go from your country and your kindred and your father's house to the land I will show you. And I will make of you a great nation, and I will bless you, and make your name great, so that you will be a blessing . . . And in thee shall all families of the earth be blessed.

In the next fourteen chapters of the book, the writer gives us the full length story of Abraham. First, there was the remaining 400 miles from Haran, down to Canaan. Abraham took with him Sarah his wife, and Lot his brother's son, and all their possessions, camels and cattle and slaves, and set forth.

In a world of idolatry, Abraham seems to have had one compelling idea, and that idea was that there is only One God. As his story unfolds, Abraham is seen devoting his entire life to the worship of Jehovah. It is therefore not surprising that when he arrived at Shechem, the first main stop on his journey south, the first thing he did was to build an altar to the Lord.

From Shechem, he went further southward on to Bethel for his next stop, where he pitched his tent. Here he built another altar and "called on the name of the Lord."

From Bethel, he journeyed on fifty or more miles further south, into the semi-desert region of the Negeb, where he came upon a severe drought and famine. And so Abraham and Sarah and Lot, and all that were with them, went down into Egypt, where because of the overflowing Nile, food was plentiful.

As soon as the famine was over, Abraham returned to Canaan. He returned by way of the Negeb, and then on to Bethel, where he had formerly set up his tent and built an altar. By this time, however, the flocks and herds of the two men had become so numerous "that the land could not support both of them dwelling together." There was also "strife" between the herdsmen of Abraham's cattle and the herdsmen of Lot's cattle.

So Abraham gave Lot his choice of territory and grazing lands. Lot chose the fertile Jordan Valley to the east, "and moved his tent as far as Sodom." Abraham took the hill country to the west.

The two choices, the writer would have us observe, were most important. Lot's choice was based on material advantage and self-interest, and a life in an environment of two notoriously wicked cities, Sodom and Gomorrah. Abraham's grazing territory, however, was the smallest part of his bargain. For from a herdsman's viewpoint, the hill country to the west could not be compared with the fertile valley of the Jordan and the wealth and prosperity of its cities.

But Abraham's faith and unselfish magnanimity proved once more his fitness for the great plans the Lord had for him, and his future:

> The Lord said to Abraham, after Lot had separated from him, "Lift up your eyes, and look from the place where you are, northward and southward and eastward and westward; for all the land which you see I will give to you and to your descendants for ever. I will make your descendants as the dust of the earth; so that if one can count the dust of the earth, your descendants also can be counted."

Abraham's "choice," and God's promise that went with it, was so important and far-reaching that it took all the rest of the Bible, both Old and New Testaments, to tell the story, and will take all future time to fulfill it!

Always, one thing leads to another. Lot, Abraham's nephew, got into trouble. There was a war between the four kings of Shinar (Babylonia) and the kings of Sodom and Gomorrah, and their allies, among whom Lot and his wife lived.

When the men of Sodom and Gomorrah fled in battle before the Shinars, they left their women and property, also Lot and his family and goods, in the hands of the victorious enemy.

Word of this came to Abraham where he dwelt by the Oaks of Mamre in his tent, and where he built an altar to the Lord. He led 318 of his trained young men, with their allies, in pursuit as far as Dan, surprised and routed the enemy at midnight, and brought back his nephew Lot and the captured men and women, and all their goods.

For this defeat of the common enemy, Abraham won a number of friends and allies, the most important of whom was Melchizedek, king of Salem (later Jerusalem) and priest of God Most High.

Melchizedek blessed Abraham, and God Most High, for delivering the enemy into his hand. And then he entertained Abraham royally with bread and wine. Most important of all, the two mighty patriarchs discovered that they served and worshiped the same God. So impressed was Abraham with his host, that he gave him a *tenth* of the spoils he had taken in battle, thus introducing *tithing* for the first time in our Bible.

Who was this Melchizedek?

Some have thought he was no more than a Canaanite chieftain, who ruled Salem before the coming of the Jebusites. Others, perhaps influenced by an old Hebrew tradition, think there is a probability that Melchizedek was Noah's oldest son Shem, who was still alive. If so, he was earth's oldest citizen, and now patriarchal priest of one-third of the human family.

At any rate, this Melchizedek is given a high rating in the Scriptures. For he is twice more referred to — by the author of Psalm 110, and by the writer of the book of Hebrews (chapters 5, 6, 7,), and each time as the type of the priesthood of Christ.

ABRAHAM IS CALLED "THE HEBREW"

What is the origin of the word *Hebrew?* Two explanations are usually given.

In the preceding story, when the Canaanite messenger came to tell Abraham what had happened to his nephew Lot, Abraham is referred to as "Abram the Hebrew." One explanation is that Abraham may have been so called from the name of his ancestor *Eber* (Genesis 11:14-16). The other explanation is that the Hebrew word means "of the country beyond," or to pass over as of a river, and contains an allusion to the crossing of the River Euphrates by Abraham and his family. The Septuagint version of the Hebrew into Greek translates the phrase, "Abraham the crosser."

In either case, it is a term used by foreigners to describe Abraham and the other newcomers among the Canaanites. A little later, beginning in the days of Jacob, the Jews called themselves "Israel," or "Israelites."

Abraham lived to be an old man. The Lord had blessed him in every way, except one. He was wealthy in cattle and riches beyond measure. But one thing was lacking. He had no son and heir to receive the inheritance and to bless the generations after him, as was contained in the Great Promise of his call.

To be sure, there was Ishmael; but Ishmael, because he was born of Sarah's Egyptian maid, Hagar, and a slave in Abraham's household, could not be the heir.

And so God appeared before Abraham, and said:

> I have made you the father of a multitude of nations. I will make you exceedingly fruitful; and I will make nations of you, and kings shall come forth from you. And I will establish my covenant between me and you and your descendants after you throughout their generations for an everlasting covenant, to be God to you and to your descendants after you.

As a sign of the covenant between God and Abraham and his descendants, *circumcision* was required of every male person. This sign and symbol was required until the fulfillment of the covenant in the coming of Christ, who, as the Apostle Paul explains in his Letter to the Galatians and elsewhere, became the All-sufficient Saviour, without the observance of circumcision and the Jewish ceremonial law.

The covenant also provided a son and heir for Abraham and his descendants:

And God said to Abraham, "As for Sarai your wife, you shall not call her name *Sarai*, but *Sarah* shall be her name. I will bless her, and moreover I will give you a son by her; I will bless her, and she shall be a mother of nations; kings of peoples shall come from her . . . And you shall call his name Isaac."

There was one other lesson which the Lord wished Abraham to learn. That was the lesson in sacrifice and worship.

The ancient custom among the Canaanites and other heathen tribes was to offer human sacrifice to their gods. To test Abraham's faith yet further, and to demonstrate that God preferred the worship and service of a *living son,* rather than that of a dead one, he "commanded" Abraham to go to the mountain to sacrifice his son Isaac.

Although this heathen custom was practiced, now and then, by later kings of Israel, such as Manasseh and others, ever after Abraham's experience it was described as "an abomination in the sight of the Lord."

Abraham is easily one of the greatest personalities in the religious history of the human race. One evidence of his position is that three great religions — the Jewish, the Mohammedan, and the Christian — regard him as one of their outstanding spiritual ancestors, and look to him as a type of perfect faith and true religion.

Rugged and homespun, Abraham like all great men, never imagined that he was important to God or man. Certainly, he never thought that he would be quoted by the Saviour, or that he himself would be remembered as long as the stars look down from heaven.

One of Abraham's last thoughts was a suitable wife for his son Isaac. Indeed, one of the most beautiful, as well as one of the most romantic stories in this wonderful book of Genesis, is the story of how Abraham sought a wife for his son Isaac, as told in chapter 24.

(2) THE STORY OF ISAAC, Chapters 25:19 to 26

And so with his marriage to the beautiful Rebekah, the story of Isaac begins.

But Isaac's story was to be neither a long, nor an eventful one. For in chapter 25, in which he tells of the death of Abraham, the writer also relates the story of the birth of Esau and Jacob. And from that point on, the twin-brothers "steal the show," so to speak, from their father Isaac, and the story is theirs for the next ten chapters.

Isaac was born in the south country, at Beer-sheba, in the semi-desert region of the Negeb, with which his story is largely identified. His father Abraham had doubtless moved southward from Hebron to Beer-sheba because of pressure from the stronger Canaanite tribes in the hill country, who had appropriated to themselves the better grazing lands.

Isaac, his son and successor as head of the tribe, was a peaceful patriarch, a man of retiring and contemplative disposition. To avoid strife with his neighbors, and to find broader pastures for his flocks and herds, Isaac and his herdsmen dwelt also as far south as the Well of Beer-lahairoi (Genesis 24:62).

And then the famine came. But the Lord directed him not to go to Egypt, as his father Abraham had done, but to go westward to Gerar, in the land of Abimelech king of the Philistines, near the Mediterranean . . .

> And the Lord appeared to him, "Sojourn in this land, and I will be with you, and will bless you; for to you and to your descendants I will give all these lands, and I will fulfill the oath which I swore to Abraham your father. I will multiply your descendants as the stars of heaven, and will give to your descendants all these lands; and by your descendants all the nations of the earth shall be blessed."

So the covenant promise to Abraham was renewed and extended to his son Isaac, and to his descendants for ever.

In the coastland country, Isaac became a successful farmer as well as herdsman. He sowed and reaped in the same year a hundred-fold. The Lord blessed him, and his flocks and herds increased beyond belief, until his riches and wealth were envied by all neighboring tribesmen . . .

> And Abimelech said to Isaac, "Go away from us; you are much mightier than we."

So Isaac, to avoid further strife between his herdsmen and the herdsmen of Abimelech, finally returned to Beer-sheba, the old home. Here he lived out the rest of his days and was obedient to the Lord as was his father Abraham.

(3) THE STORY OF JACOB AND ESAU, Chapters 27-36

The story of Jacob and Esau in the next ten chapters is largely the story of Jacob.

Isaac, as we have seen, was more than an uneventful, connecting link between his famous father Abraham, and his famous son Jacob, as some have called him, although he was that, too.

Isaac and Rebekah had two sons, twins, Esau and Jacob. In Jacob's case, a few minutes or even a few hours in birth, made much difference; for as second he was born without the family birthright. So Jacob's problem was to gain the birthright, somehow.

Esau was called the "hairy man." He was born that way. He appears to have inherited much of the characteristics of his more primitive ancestors. He was not only hairy, but he liked to hunt and to live in the wilderness. His ambition all lay in that direction. In later years, he was called the "wild ass man," in the wilderness country of Edom (Esau), where he and his tribe went to live, and for whom *Edom* was named.

Jacob, on the contrary, was called the "supplanter." What he wanted he proceeded to get, using whatever means the situation required. First of all, he wanted his brother's birthright; and with the aid of his mother, he deceived his aging and blind father Isaac. In this way he received the blessing that should have gone to Esau the firstborn.

Then, to escape the wrath of Esau, he fled for his life to the old homestead at Haran, in the Mesopotamian valley, where Abraham and his father Terah made their first stop on the way from Ur to Canaan. Here Jacob fell in love with the beautiful Rachel, his cousin, daughter of his Uncle Laban. Not having anything for dowry, Jacob agreed to work for Laban seven years for her in marriage.

But his uncle was a "crafty" man, and in bargaining, he often was more than a match for the wits of Jacob, although Jacob was not without craftiness himself, as he had proved in his unscrupulous dealings with his father Isaac and brother Esau.

So both uncle and nephew planned trickery, each against the other. Jacob's objective was to secure as much of Laban's property, cattle and sheep and goats, as possible, and then marry Rachel and leave for Canaan and Beer-sheba with all his family and property.

Laban's interests lay in another direction. He needed a herdsman desperately to look after his vast herds and flocks, and so by a delaying action, he aimed to keep Jacob on the job. Seven years passed and the wedding was held; but instead of Rachel, the homely and heavily veiled older sister Leah turned out to be Jacob's bride. And then, after some harsh words, Jacob agreed to work another seven years, for Rachel.

Meanwhile, Jacob was increasing the size of his flocks and herds, albeit at the expense of his Uncle Laban. For Jacob had his own ideas of bargaining, and of cross-breeding of livestock, and had not fared badly by his methods. Indeed, by simple strategy he had possessed himself of a large portion of his uncle's cattle.

Time passed, and Laban was still unwilling for Jacob to return to his home in Canaan.

Jacob had said to Laban,

> Send me away, that I may go to my own home and country. Give me my wives and my children for whom I have served you, and let me go.

But Laban said to him,

> If you will allow me to say so, I have learned by divination that the Lord has blessed me because of you; name your wages, and I will give it.

Finally, after twenty years, one day Jacob called for Rachel and Leah to come into the field where his flocks were, and said,

> I see your father does not regard me with favor as he did before . . . You know that I have served your father with all my strength; yet your father has cheated me and changed my wages ten times!

For one thing, Jacob was homesick. Too, his conscience was bothering him; for after all these years, he must soon face his brother Esau, whom he had wronged, and with whom he had not made peace. Meanwhile, he had already been punished in the death of his mother Rebekah, who had conspired with him to cheat Esau, and who had died in his absence.

But his discipline would become more severe, before he learned to put his reliance, not in scheming and trickery, but in simple faith in the love and blessing of the God of his grandfather Abraham and father Isaac.

Indeed, the life of Jacob is a parable of mankind. In the words of William Hazlitt, no young man thinks he shall ever die. In his youth, Jacob knew no handicap and balked at no scruple to gain what he wanted. But now his sins were fast coming home to him, and one day he would "wrestle with an angel," before he would be ready to inherit the Covenant Promise, and receive the new title of ISRAEL.

At length the day came for Jacob to return to the land of his fathers and to his kindred. Laban had gone to shear his sheep in the far field, and before he returned it would be three days . . .

> So Jacob arose, and set his sons and his wives on camels; and he drove away all his cattle, all his livestock which he had gained . . . to go to the land of Canaan to his father Isaac.

When Laban learned that Jacob with all his possessions had been gone three days, he took his kinsmen with him and pursued Jacob for seven days, until he caught up with him in the hill country of Gilead.

After many harsh words and charges on both sides, Laban finally lowered his voice, and said: "What can I do? . . . Come now, let us make a covenant, you and I; and let it be a witness between you and me."

So, at long last, Laban and Jacob concluded a covenant of friendship. Then they ate the covenant bread and tarried all night on the mountain.

Early in the morning Laban arose, kissed his grandchildren and his daughters, and blessed them; then he departed and returned home.

Jacob went on his way, and the angels of God met him. And when Jacob saw them, he said, "This is God's army!" He took the presence of the angels to mean that the Lord would bless him.

So Jacob, with an organized plan designed to impress his brother Esau, sent his herdsmen on ahead of him with a handsome present in cattle, which he had determined to give Esau as an offer of peace and friendship. Esau had long since moved from his father Isaac's home at Beer-sheba, to the hill country of Seir (Edom), the semi-desert lands south and east of the Dead Sea.

As his herdsmen were about to depart with the cattle selected for his present to his brother Esau, Jacob was afraid, and prayed to God. The prayer is still a pattern of humility, earnestness, and faith in God's promises:

> O God of my father Abraham and God of my father Isaac, O Lord who didst say to me, "Return to your country and to your kindred,

and I will do you good," I am not worthy of the least of all the steadfast love and all the faithfulness which thou hast shown to thy servant, for with only my staff I crossed this Jordan; and now I have become two companies. Deliver me, I pray thee, from the hand of my brother, from the hand of Esau, for I fear him, lest he come and slay us all, the mothers with the children. But thou didst say, "I will do you good, and make your descendants as the sand of the sea, which cannot be numbered for multitude" (Genesis 32:9-12).

The night before he was to face Esau, Jacob saw his wives and children safely across the little river Jabbok . . .

And Jacob was left alone; and a man wrestled with him until the breaking of the day.

Here we have a beautiful symbolic description, signifying a spiritual experience through which Jacob passed at the most critical moment in his life.

Jacob was wrestling with no less than the Spirit of God, and in this contest received the final lesson that humbled him and made him willing to take God's will for his own. It is a new Jacob we see hereafter.

Your name shall no more be called *Jacob,* but *Israel;* for you have striven with God and with men, and have prevailed.

Whatever plans for revenge Esau may have had before he met his brother, when he lifted up his eyes and saw Jacob, he dropped them. For, "Esau ran to meet him, and embraced him, and they wept."

The courtesies, according to custom, were long and extended, on both sides. At first Esau refused Jacob's great present, saying, "I have enough, my brother; keep what you have for yourself."

But Jacob urged him, and then Esau took it. Both men knew the custom. For Esau not to accept the gift, would indicate continuing hostility; and not until the present was accepted could Jacob be sure that all was well between them.

Afterwards, Esau turned and said to Jacob, "Let us journey on our way, and I will go before you," meaning that he wished his brother Jacob and his family to follow, and return with him to the land of Seir.

Jacob hesitated between *yes* and *no,* and finally excused himself, saying that his wives and children and cattle were tired from their long journey from Haran, and needed to camp and rest.

Jacob wished to please Esau, whose generosity was evident in all that had happened between them; but at the same time he knew it would be best to keep the two companies apart.

So, as Esau's company passed out of sight, Jacob and his people rested at Succoth, and then crossed the Jordan from the east side to the west, and journeyed on to the old camp at Shechem, where Abraham his grandfather made his first stop in Canaan.

At Shechem, Jacob's life followed the pattern of the *new* Jacob.

From the local Canaanite chieftain he bought a piece of land on which he pitched his tent. There he erected an altar to the Lord and worshiped. He also dug a well in the vicinity. This bears his name and has been famous in Hebrew history for nearly 4,000 years.

When trouble arose between the tribe of Jacob and the Canaanites, the Lord directed Jacob to move further south to Bethel, and there erect an altar.

Jacob remembered a vow he had made at Bethel, to the God who appeared to him when he fled from his brother Esau, on the night he dreamed of angels ascending and descending on a ladder let down from heaven.

So Jacob, before he departed from Shechem, said to his household, his wives and children and servants,

> Put away the foreign gods that are among you, and purify yourselves, and change your garments; then let us arise and go up to Bethel, that I may make there an altar to the God who answered me in the day of my distress and has been with me wherever I have gone.

Jacob's wives and servants were all from Haran, in Padan-aram, and were idolators. They brought with them their household gods, which included the teraphim which Rachel took with her from her father's house. At this point they gave to Jacob all the foreign gods and images, and also the earrings, worn superstitiously as charms, and Jacob hid them under the oak near Shechem.

Here Jacob started a crusade against false gods and idols, and other forms of idolatry, which was to be of the greatest importance in years to come. Indeed, it was to be a major issue in the religion of Israel for the next twelve centuries.

Moses, as we shall see, spent no small part of his time in teaching the people to obey and to be faithful to their God, and to put no other gods before him. The first two of the Ten Commandments expressly forbid the worship of other gods, and idols. The chief message of the prophets, from Moses to Malachi, was in opposition to idolatry. And it was chiefly because Israel and Judah forgot God, and took after other gods and idols, that they were later exiled and punished in a foreign land.

After the religious dedication at Bethel, Jacob and his large family journeyed on south to Hebron, to which his father Isaac had long since moved from Beer-sheba. On the way, Jacob's life was saddened by the sudden death of Rachel, at the birth of his twelfth and last son, Benjamin. She was buried near Bethlehem, and Rachel's Tomb may be seen there to this day.

Jacob finally rejoined his father Isaac, after a separation of thirty years. His mother Rebekah had died many years earlier, while he was in Haran.

Fortunately, he reached Hebron in time to see Isaac, who was now one hundred and eighty years old, and who died shortly after Jacob's arrival. He was buried near Hebron, at the old Machpelah Place, which Abraham bought from Ephron the Hittite for a family burying-place at the time of Sarah's death, and which became the most famous in the Old Testament. On the place was a cave and trees, and the cave was used as a sepulchre. Abraham and Sarah, Isaac and Rebekah, Jacob and Leah, and doubtless others of whom we have no record, were buried there.

Esau came up from the desert country of Seir, to help Jacob bury their father. The twin brothers had not seen each other in the ten years since their reconciliation and separation on the east side of the Jordan, near Succoth. After the burial of Isaac, they separated again, and there is no evidence that Esau ever rejoined Israel, to become a part of the four-hundred-years bondage in Egypt, or to inherit the promised land of Canaan afterwards.

(4) The Story of Joseph, Chapters 37-50

The remainder of the book of Genesis contains the story of Joseph and completes the great Abraham-Isaac, Jacob-Joseph saga, which occupies all the book except the first eleven chapters.

Readers for centuries have found in this epic-like narrative, not only one of the world's most engaging stories, but also God's revelation of Himself in the affairs of primitive man, and have preferred it above all other ancient stories.

The emphasis now shifts from Jacob to his eleventh and favorite son, Joseph. "Joseph, being seventeen years old, was shepherding the flock with his brothers," in the words of our historian. And Joseph brought an "ill report" of them to his father. And because of this report and because Jacob loved Joseph more than he did his other sons, they hated Joseph. And then, there was the long garment with long sleeves, draped and worn only by persons of distinction, which his father had given him.

When Joseph had a dream and told it to his brothers, signifying that he should rule over them, they hated him even more and sought to be rid of him one way or another. Some favored putting him to death; others would cast him into a dry pit and leave him to die. But Judah, the fourth brother, favored selling Joseph to a caravan of Ishmaelites. This they did. The Ishmaelites took Joseph to Egypt and sold him to Potiphar, the captain of Pharaoh's guard.

Joseph was smarter than his brothers. And because they recognized his superiority, they were jealous of him. Jacob also had recognized the superiority of his son Joseph, and doubtless had given him the long coat to symbolize, appropriately, a person who one day would achieve distinction.

The fact of Joseph's dreams also indicates a contemplative nature, which foreshadowed his pre-eminence, not merely among his brothers, but among Egyptian officials as well, with whom Joseph was to be associated as leader in the critical years of the great famine.

Thus, we have the introduction to the chief event with which the story of Joseph is concerned, namely, the migration of Israel to Egypt. In all this, we see God's purposes being worked out as announced to Abraham in chapter 15.

In Egypt, we see the Hebrews being trained to become the religious teachers of mankind in all the nations. Here, in relative peace and prosperity, they grew from a tribe of a few hundred, to a nation of two or three million. Here, too, they came in contact with a highly civilized and law-abiding nation. For in 1850 B.C., Egypt was the most enlightened nation in the world.

It was highly advanced in the arts and sciences, in architecture, agriculture, education, and in a way of life that made for peace and prosperity. Here the Hebrews learned from the Egyptians much that was of the highest value for their future. For example, this is illustrated in the education and leadership of Moses, Aaron, Joshua, and in scores of others not so well known.

In Egypt, Joseph's rise to prosperity was rapid and his career distinguished, in spite of those who would betray him. During the thirteen years of his apprenticeship, Joseph was an upright man and was loved by Potiphar his Egyptian master, and by all those who knew him.

In all this, Joseph was noted for his humility. Again and again, he gave God credit for his personal prosperity, including the interpretation of the King's dream . . . "The Lord was with Joseph, and he became a successful man."

The rulers of Egypt in the time of Joseph were of a Semitic race of kings, Hyksos or Shepherd kings they were called, and were friendly to the Hebrews who were likewise Semitic. The ruling Pharaoh therefore was happy to welcome Joseph's father and the Hebrews to Egypt. In God's providence, they would bless and prosper the Hebrews during their sojourn; and in turn the God of the Hebrews would bless and *reveal* Himself to the Egyptians, as the one true God.

Before his death, Jacob as Israel, blessed his sons and the two sons of Joseph as the heads of the Twelve Tribes of Israel, which one day would be a mighty nation. Too, Joseph forgave his brothers, recognizing that although what they had done to him was meant for "evil," God meant it for "good, to bring it about that many people should be kept alive."

Joseph's last words were to reassure his brothers and descendants that God would visit them and bring them up out of the land of Egypt "to the land which he swore to Abraham, to Isaac, and to Jacob." So great was Joseph's faith that all this would come to pass, he made them take an oath to carry his bones up from Egypt to this promised land. His final instructions were carried out, as recorded

in the last paragraph of the book of Joshua, although it was more than three hundred years later.

BIBLE CHRONOLOGY

Hebrew Chronology Showing the History of Israel from Abraham to the Close of the Old Testament

Most Old Testament dates cannot be set down with anything like mathematical accuracy. For the period before the Call of Abraham, and for many years after that call, no accurate chronology is possible in the light of our present knowledge. There have been two widely accepted schemes for dating the early history of Israel: the earlier chronology, and the later. The Chronological Table on this page follows the earlier.[7]

Abraham Leaves the Land of Ur	2150 B.C.
Abraham's Entrance Into Canaan	2100
Joseph Sold Into Egypt	1854
Jacob's Migration to Egypt	1834
Moses and the Exodus From Egypt	1444–1404
Joshua's Conquest of Canaan	1404–1380
Period of the Judges	1380–1080
The Prophet Samuel	1100–1020
Reign of King Saul	1047–1015
Reign of Saul's Son Ishbosheth	1015–1007
Reign of King David	
Judah	1014–1007
All Israel	1007– 974
Reign of King Solomon	974– 934
Divided Kingdom After Solomon's Death	
Ten Tribes of Israel	934– 721
Judah	934– 586
Return and Restoration at Jerusalem	538– 432

[7]Many scholars are of the opinion that the earlier date is almost a historical necessity to allow time for all the events from the Exodus to the early reign of Solomon. See the discussion and footnote on chronology in the introduction to the book of Exodus, pp. 87, 88.

Joseph's Tomb at the foot of Mount Ebal,
on the "parcel of ground Jacob gave his son
Joseph." © *Matson Photo Service*

Chapter 4

EXODUS

1. THE PURPOSE AND IMPORTANCE OF THE BOOK OF EXODUS

The book of Exodus, like the book of Genesis, is one of the great
fundamental books of our Bible.

The title Exodus was given to the book by the Greek translators
of the Hebrew Old Testament, the Greek word *Exodos*, Latin *Exodus*,
being the same form through Old French into English. The word
literally means *a going out,* or *departure,* and refers to the main event
which the book records — the departure of the Israelites from the
land of Egypt. The title therefore is appropriate.

The purpose of the book of Genesis, as we have seen, was to
reveal the Creator and His Creation, with particular emphasis on the
creation of Man and God's covenant with him in the promise to
Abraham and his descendants. The book of Exodus in the original
begins with the Hebrew word *And,* indicating that it is a sequel to
Genesis, although there is a gap of some 300 years between the events
of the two books.

Here in the book of Exodus we have *revealed* God in the act of
fulfilling His covenant promise to Abraham and his descendants. He
has raised up a leader, Moses, to deliver His people from slavery and
bondage. Moses under Divine guidance will be their leader in the
true way of life, and in the formation of their new nation, under God.

The book of Exodus also shares with the book of Deuteronomy
in the high value it places on the religion of Jehovah. For in no other
ancient or modern religion do we find so sublime a view of God and
His relationship to man. And nowhere else do we find such high
standards of conduct for man, as those which spring from man's relationship to God as revealed in the book of Exodus.

Because of its fundamental position in the Scriptures, the book
of Exodus, along with its revised edition in the book of Deuteronomy,
has been an inspiration to all succeeding generations. The Hebrew
poets and prophets of the Old Testament quote it and make use of its
lessons of deliverance, faith, and hope, in their songs and prophecies.
Likewise, it has also been a source of frequent quotation by the
writers and makers of the New Testament, and has been a source of
inspiration for both Jews and Christians throughout the generations.

The great underlying idea of the book of Exodus, as in the book

87

of Genesis, is that of *revelation.* In all the events connected with the lives of Abraham, Isaac, and Jacob, and their descendants, Moses and the Israelites, God is represented as in the act of *making Himself known* to His people, and as guiding their footsteps and destinies. He is constantly "speaking" to them.

To Christians of all ages, the bondage in Egypt and the deliverance, has been a symbol of personal yearning and salvation, as well as national deliverance. In the experience of Israel, men have seen and faced their own sins and weaknesses, and their need for God's forgiveness and grace.

2. The Date of the Exodus

Opinion regarding the date of the Exodus from Egypt has been sharply divided among scholars and archaeologists. One group holds to an earlier date, about 1440 B.C.; and another, to a later date, say about 1270 B.C.[1] However, more recent archaeological discoveries in Palestine have tended to confirm the earlier date. The date of the Exodus, like the date of the entrance into Canaan, has more than usual interest, because the correct interpretation of this historic event depends somewhat on chronology.

The main evidence for determining the date of Israel's Exodus from Egypt, and the subsequent Conquest of Canaan, is to be found in the Biblical record and in the evidence from somewhat recent archaeological research. The author of I Kings 6:1 states that the Exodus occurred 480 years before Solomon began to build his famous Temple, which is generally agreed to be about 967 B.C. This would place Israel's invasion of Canaan about 1407 B.C., and thus the beginning of the Exodus at about 1447 B.C.

Moreover, an earlier date seems almost a historical necessity, since only an earlier date than 1270 B.C. for the Exodus, and 1230 B.C. for the Conquest of Canaan, would give enough time for all the events of the settlement of Canaan, and the rule of the Judges during the

---

[1]One group of scholars, headed by Professor William Foxwell Albright of Johns Hopkins University, and leader of the American Schools of Oriental Research, favors the "later chronology." That is, that the Exodus probably began about 1270 B.C. See Albright's *The Archaeology of Palestine and the Bible,* pp. 108ff. (1949); G. Ernest Wright and Floyd V. Filson, *The Westminster Historical Atlas to the Bible,* Second Edition, "Excavations in Modern Palestine," Plate XVIII, pp. 110-117. (1956).

The earlier chronology is favored by Dr. John Garstang of the University of Liverpool, Director of the British School of Archaeology in Jerusalem and of the Department of Antiquities of the Palestine Government and his associates. This group prefers the earlier date of about 1440 B.C. for the Exodus. See Garstang's *Foundations of Bible History: Joshua-Judges* (1931); Wright and Filson's *Westminster Historical Atlas,* p. 114.

Excellent brief summaries by such scholars as Hugh J. Blair of the Reformed Presbyterian Church of Ireland, and F. F. Bruce of the University of Manchester, may be found in *The New Bible Commentary,* pp. 38 (Chronological Table), 224, and 237 (1954). For a more complete survey of the problems of chronology and related questions, see H. H. Rowley's *From Joseph to Joshua* (1950).

confederacy of the Twelve Tribes of Israel, before the establishment of the monarchy under Saul and David, and the early years of Solomon's reign. This point has never been sufficiently stressed.

For instance, one item which is usually overlooked is a quotation by the author of Judges 11:26 from Jephthah, one who lived near the end of the period of Judges, and referred to it as 300 years. If to these 300 years, we prefix the 40 years of the Wilderness, the years of Joshua's conquest of Canaan; then at the other end, add the years of Eli, Samuel, Saul, David, and Solomon to the building of the Temple, we shall easily have the 480 years set down by the author of I Kings 6:1. Also Acts 13:20, and Ruth 4:21-22, may have some bearing on this chronology.

3. The Contents of the Book of Exodus

The book of Exodus, as we have noted, is a sequel to the book of Genesis. It is the second part of the "five-fold volume," as many scholars prefer to translate the Greek word *Pentateuch*. The narrative begins by pointing out the very great increase in numbers of the descendants of the eleven sons of Jacob who came to Egypt after Joseph, and during the 300 years or so between the close of Genesis and the beginning of Exodus.

The author of Exodus says of them: "They multiplied and grew exceedingly strong; so that the land was filled with them."

Another way of estimating the rapid growth of the Hebrew population since they entered Egypt, is to note the complaint of the Egyptian king to his people: "Behold, the people of Israel are too many and too mighty for us. Come, let us deal shrewdly with them, lest they multiply, and, if war befall us, they join our enemies and fight against us and escape from the land" (Exodus 1:9-10).

How many Hebrews were there at the time of the Exodus? All the persons of the household of Jacob who came to Egypt were "seventy." But the writer of Genesis lists only the heads of families; and it is safe to say that the total would run into at least several hundred. Four hundred and thirty years later, at the time of the Exodus, the number of those leaving Egypt is given as "about six hundred thousand men on foot, besides women and children." A mixed multitude also went up with them (Exodus 12:37-38).

Here again only the more important males are counted, and estimates of the grand total are usually placed between 2,000,000 and 3,000,000 in all. But some scholars are of the opinion that this number is too large and altogether improbable.

The contents of the forty chapters of the book of Exodus fall naturally into three important divisions, as follows:

(1) The Status of the Israelites in Egypt: Their Oppression and Deliverance, Chapters 1 to 15:21;

(2) The Long March from the Red Sea to Mount Sinai, Chapters 15:22 to 18;

(3) Israel's Eleven Months at Mount Sinai, Chapters 19-40.

(1) THE STATUS OF THE ISRAELITES IN EGYPT:
THEIR OPPRESSION AND DELIVERANCE, Chapters 1 to 15:21

We have seen how the Israelites in Egypt fell into disfavor with the Egyptians when there was a change in the ruling dynasty from the alien Hyksos or Shepherd Kings, who were Semitic in race and akin to the Hebrews, to a native Egyptian dynasty. It is likely that this new king was the mighty Thothmes III, and the Pharaoh of the oppression preceding the Exodus, about 1501-1447 B.C. If so, the actual Exodus under Moses was probably in the early years of Thothmes' successor, Amenhotep II.

The Israelites were feared, as we have seen, chiefly because the Egyptians became alarmed at the rapidly growing numbers and strength of the Hebrews in the land. So their new masters, "who knew not Joseph," set about to "deal shrewdly" with the Hebrews and to set taskmasters over them to afflict them with heavy burdens.

But the more their taskmasters oppressed the Hebrews, the more they multiplied and the more they spread out over the land. In the words of the writer:

> The Egyptians were in dread of the people of Israel. So they made the people of Israel serve with rigor, and made their lives bitter with hard service, in mortar and brick, and in all kinds of work in the field.

Other devices for reducing the Hebrew population were tried by the Egyptians. For one thing, the midwives were ordered to kill all male Hebrew children at birth. This is why the Hebrew child Moses was hidden for three months by his mother. And when she could hide him no longer, she decided on the clever device of placing him into a little basket made of bulrushes, and of leaving him at the river's edge for the daughter of the king to find.

This "goodly child," in God's Providence, was brought up in the household of the Egyptian king, trained and educated, in all the knowledge and wisdom of the Egyptians. But God and the child's mother saw to it that his heart remained Hebrew and loyal to his people, and to the One true God. For one day this Moses would deliver the Hebrews from the bitter oppression of their Egyptian taskmasters, and lead them to freedom in a land that should be their own, "a land flowing with milk and honey."

But Moses was not yet ready for so great a task. He must first live under the stars, and let God be his teacher for another forty years, and then his opportunity would come.

How Moses left Pharoah's court is told briefly. One day he saw an Egyptian beating a Hebrew. Hot anger burned his soul and he struck down the Egyptian, and killed him, and hid him in the sand.

When he feared the thing was known, he fled in safety to the land of Midian. This was a long journey, for Midian as you can see from the map was east and south, across the peninsula of Sinai and the Gulf of Aqabah, on the edge of the great Arabian desert.

At the end of this long journey, Moses sat down by a well. Now the priest of Midian had seven daughters, and they all came to the well to water their father's flock. But the shepherds came and drove them away. But Moses opposed the ill-mannered shepherds and rescued the daughters and watered their flocks.

The grateful father, Jethro (also called Reuel), sent for Moses and entertained him. "And Moses," in the words of the writer, "was content to dwell with the man, and he gave Moses his daughter Zipporah," for a wife.

Moses remained in Midian forty years, and kept his father-in-law's flocks. The first forty years he spent in Pharaoh's court. In the Providence of God, these second forty years would be a period of special training and preparation in the wilderness, alone much of the time, and in communion with God.

Moses would also become familiar with the region in which he was to lead Israel for another forty years. We may compare this preparatory sojourn of Moses in Midian to that of John the Baptist in the wilderness round about the Jordan (Luke 1:80), and to that of Paul in Arabia (Galatians 1:17).

At long last the day of Deliverance came. In the words of the writer,

> In the course of those many days the king of Egypt died. And the people of Israel groaned under their bondage, and cried out for help, and their cry under bondage came up to God. And God heard their groaning, and God remembered his Covenant with Abraham, with Isaac, and with Jacob . . .
>
> Now Moses was keeping the flock of his father-in-law, Jethro, the priest of Midian; and he led his flock to the west side of the wilderness, and came to Horeb (Sinai), the mountain of God. And the angel of the Lord appeared to him in a flame of fire out of the midst of a bush . . . God called to him out of the bush, "Come, I will send you to Pharaoh that you may bring forth my people, the sons of Israel, out of Egypt."

The first fifteen chapters of the book of Exodus tell the complete story of how God delivered the Hebrews from Egyptian oppression, under the leadership of Moses. The writer also records their magnificent song of deliverance and thanksgiving after they had safely crossed the Red Sea by means of the miraculous parting of the waters.

It has long been thought that this magnificent hymn of praise, especially the first two stanzas (Exodus 15:2-10), was composed by Moses himself.

(2) THE LONG MARCH FROM THE RED SEA TO MOUNT SINAI,[2]
Chapters 15:22 to 18

After the day of celebration and praise to the Lord for deliverance from the Egyptians, Moses led Israel on its march from the Red Sea to Mount Sinai.

Leaving the shore of the Sea, the Israelites journeyed in a southeasterly direction, for the most part, avoiding the high plateaus on their left and the lowlands near the Sea on their right, with their vast numbers of men and women and children on foot, not to mention cattle and all that they had with them.

At length they came into the lower half of the Peninsular of Sinai, by way of the oases of Marah and Elim, to the Wilderness of Sin, by the end of their first month's journey since their departure from Egypt. At this point the supplies they brought with them had given out.

And God seeing their need, sent them quail and manna, and water, and this the people of Israel ate for forty years in the wilderness, "until they came to a habitable land . . . to the border of the land of Canaan."

The Lord's purpose in thus "raining bread from heaven" was to *reveal* Himself to the people:

> Then the Lord said to Moses, "Behold, I will rain bread from heaven for you; and the people shall go out and gather a day's portion every day, that I may prove them, whether they will walk in my law or not . . ."
> And Moses and Aaron said to the people, "At evening you shall know that it was the Lord who brought you out of the land of Egypt."

God also *revealed* Himself to the people by re-emphasizing the observance of the Sabbath which was instituted at the creation.

> On the sixth day they gathered twice as much, two omers apiece . . . Moses said to the people, "Tomorrow is a day of solemn rest, a holy Sabbath to the Lord."

From the Wilderness of Sin, Moses led the people of Israel by stages, as they could travel best, to the last stage, which took them into the Wilderness of Sinai, and there they encamped before Mount Sinai.

Now this last journey took Moses by the land of Midian and his father-in-law, Jethro, the priest of Midian. And Jethro came out to counsel with Moses concerning a system of justice and judging for all the people, and how Moses could save himself for his mighty work, by delegating part of his judicial duties to others.

According to Jethro's plans, the helpers were to be "rulers of thousands, of hundreds, of fifties, and of tens." And Moses went along

---

[2]See "The Route of the Exodus," *The Westminster Historical Atlas to the Bible,* pp. 38-39 (Revised Edition, 1956). See map, p. 127.

with the suggestions of his father-in-law, and chose able and loyal men to work under him in subordinate positions.

There was another advantage to Moses in going by way of the land of Midian, in his journey north to Canaan. He was in familiar territory. For it was in this region that Moses kept Jethro's flock for forty years, and on occasion had gone as far as Mount Horeb (Mount Sinai). And it was here, as was noted above, that while Moses led the flock one day to the west side of the wilderness, and came to Horeb, "the mountain of God," that his call came from the burning bush. In short, he had learned the roads of the wilderness, the resources, the climate, and the way of life of the people.

In addition to providing food and water, and against the hardships and murmurings of the people, Moses had other troubles. He met with opposition from the natives. The first instance of this was the Amalekites, the descendants of Esau, who originally settled as we have seen in the land of Seir in Jacob's day, and who now were spread out over much of the wilderness of the Sinai peninsula.

These wild tribes, who survived the great famine without going to Egypt, had harassed the rear of the Israelites soon after they left Egypt and entered the wilderness. And at Rephidim, as Moses approached Mount Sinai on the west side, these Amalekites engaged with Israel in battle, and were defeated.

This battle was under the leadership of a new man, who is mentioned here for the first time, Joshua, captain of the host. Soon he was to become the personal attendant of Moses.

Moses had valuable help from others, in his leadership of Israel on the great and historic march from the bondage of Egypt, toward freedom and a settled life of their own.

The first of these was his older brother Aaron. At the time of his call, Moses hesitated, because he was slow of speech. God promised him Aaron's help. Aaron acted as spokesman and agent for Moses and carried the rod, symbol of Jehovah's presence and power, in their first interviews with the elders of the people, and with Pharaoh.

Aaron was present and aided Moses at the battle with the Amalekites, and on many other strategic occasions he was Moses' first assistant. Only once did he signally disappoint Moses, and that was the making of the Golden Calf during Moses' forty days' absence on Mount Sinai. Aaron later became the first high priest, and through his sons, became the organized head of the order of priesthood.

Moses' sister Miriam, the oldest of the three, was a prophetess and leader of women in her own right. She was present as a girl when the infant Moses was placed in the basket and set in the rushes at the river's edge. She waited at a distance, to learn what would be done to the child, until the Egyptian princess and her maidens came to bathe. At the right moment, she came forth and asked the princess if she might call a nurse for the child, and then went and called the child's mother.

Again, after the people had passed safely over the Red Sea, it was Miriam who took a timbrel and led the Israelite women, with timbrels and with dances, and sang praises to the Lord, in these words:

> Sing ye to Jehovah, for he hath triumphed gloriously;
> The horse and his rider hath he thrown into the sea.

(3) Israel's Eleven Months at Mount Sinai, Chapters 19-40

The hosts of Israel, marching slowly as they did, with long halts at the various stations on their route, took two months to make the 150-mile journey from Egypt to Mount Sinai.

They spent eleven months at Sinai. During this time the people, under the leadership of Moses, began their organization as a nation, and entered into a formal Covenant with Jehovah their God.

The time had come for laws to guide the people in their religious worship and in their moral conduct toward one another. These rules, which were the basis and foundation of the Covenant, were the moral and religious laws received from God by Moses, and published and made known by him. They are briefly summarized in the Ten Commandments.

What Jesus thought of the permanence of The Law is profoundly stated in His great Sermon on the Mount:

> Think not that I have come to abolish the Law and the Prophets;
> I have come not to abolish them but to fulfill them. For truly, I
> say to you, till heaven and earth pass away, not an iota, not a
> dot, will pass from the Law until all is accomplished.

But the Ten Commandments did not come to the Israelites immediately upon their arrival at Mount Sinai; but only after much schooling, much preparation, and much "waiting before the Lord."

Only after their *agonizing reappraisal* of their sojourn in Egypt, their deliverance, their present dependence upon the Lord, and a future based upon Faith and of the Promise of things to come, did they begin to see Jehovah's *revelation* of Himself in the things that had come to pass.

Mount Sinai, the place of the giving of the Law, had special meaning and significance for the ancient Hebrews, as it has had for many travelers and pilgrims since. "When they came into the wilderness of Sinai," says the writer, "they encamped in the wilderness; and there Israel encamped before the mountain."

The wilderness in which they encamped was a small, desert-like plain, some two miles long and about one-half mile wide, lying in between two high and precipitous mountain ranges of black and yellow granite. At the end or head of this enclosed court was an enormous mountain block some 7,000 feet in height, and rising sheer from the plain like a huge altar, which many scholars take to be the mount on which the Law was given.

The Tabernacle in the Wilderness as pic
tured in the model by Dr. Conrad Schick
© *Matson Photo Service*

The whole view may be described as one of the most awe-inspiring scenes on the face of the earth. It was therefore most appropriate for the revelation of Divine Majesty to Moses, and to his people.

The giving of the Law appears in these stages:

1. Preparation for the giving of the Law, Chapter 19.
2. The Ten Commandments, Chapter 20.
3. The Book of the Covenant, Chapters 21-24.
4. The Tabernacle and the Priesthood, Chapters 25-31.
5. The Sins of the People, Aaron's Golden Calf; the Intercession of Moses; the Renewal of the Covenant, Chapters 32-34.
6. Description of the Construction of the Tabernacle and its Furniture, Chapters 35-40.

4. THE MEANING OF THE BOOK OF EXODUS

Present day Christians see in the book of Exodus the book of *redemption*.

Just as God brought the children of Israel out of bondage in Egypt, so by redemption we understand that the Redeemer delivers mankind out of the bondage of sin. Moreover, He also brings them into a special relationship with Himself, making them His people and His own purchased possession.

The Exodus therefore, beginning with the great deliverance of God's people from Egypt, and culminating in the Passover, foreshadows the still greater redemption achieved by the Saviour on Calvary.

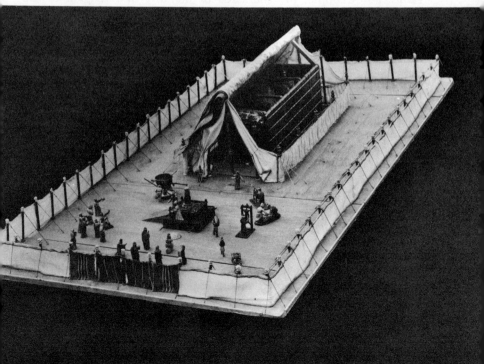

Chapter 5

LEVITICUS

1. THE BOOK

The title of the book of Leviticus was given to it by the Greek translators of the Old Testament, from the opening word in the Hebrew. Greek, *Levitikos;* Latin, *Leviticus;* English, *Leviticus.*

The title, however, is not particularly appropriate, since the Levites are hardly mentioned in the book; but Aaron and his sons are mentioned many times. Actually the book is a sort of manual of religious ceremonies drawn up for the guidance of both priests and worshipers.

The religious value of the book of Leviticus is greater than appears from a hasty examination of its contents. In these laws and directions for ritual and worship, drawn up for a people and their religious leaders more than thirty centuries ago, we get a picture of the foundations of the moral and religious life of the Hebrew people at an early stage of their development.

To the student of comparative religion the book is of great value. For example, the standards of morality and religion of the ancient Greeks, as reflected in Homer's *Iliad* and *Odyssey* of a comparable period, for example, are far below those of the Israelites of Moses' day. The same may be said of the religion of ancient India, or of ancient China, or of other ancient peoples such as the Babylonians or Egyptians, as reflected in their ancient books and landmarks.

Moreover, for their own sake, the standards set by the Hebrews are exalted. The book of Leviticus presents teachings that insist on the duty of justice and mercy, kindness to strangers and to the poor, consideration for slaves and the weak, and even for animals. Personal virtues, such as chastity and truthfulness and fidelity to trust, are pointed up in the moral code. As for religion, there is the One and only true God; and the entire system is penetrated with the idea that Israel is called to be a *holy* people, consecrated to the service of a holy God.

2. THE CONTENTS

The book of Exodus closed with the Israelites still encamped before Mount Sinai. The time of the book of Leviticus is during this same eleven months period of encampment at Sinai. The account

An orthodox Jewish scribe in Jerusalem transcribing the Torah on parchment. © *Matson Photo Service* of the construction of the Tabernacle and its furniture was given in the last part of the book of Exodus. The rules for worship in the new Tabernacle are given in the book before us, the book of Leviticus.

The contents of the book of Leviticus may be divided into four natural groups as follows:

(1) The Law of Sacrifice, or the book of directions to be followed by the worshiper and the priest at the offering of sacrifices, chapters 1-7.

(2) The Consecration of the Priesthood, or a record of the consecration of Aaron and his sons to the priestly office, chapters 8-10.

(3) The Law of Clean and Unclean, or a directory of ceremonial purity, chapters 11-16.

(4) The Law of Holiness, or the statutes concerning holiness given by Moses, chapters 17-26.

The book closes with a final chapter on Vows and Tithes, in the form of an appendix, chapter 27.

Thus, the book of Leviticus is not a book of law in the usual sense at all, but a manual for the priests, in this case Aaron and his sons, to guide them through the technicalities of the ritual, and to instruct the people in their own duties, and to exhort them to fidelity.

Chapter 6

NUMBERS

1. THE BOOK OF NUMBERS[1]

The book of Numbers gets its title from the Greek translators of the Old Testament, who chose it because it tells of the two census or enumerations of the Israelites. One was taken at Sinai in the second year of the Exodus, and recorded in chapter 1; and the other, taken at the end of their journey in the fortieth year, and recorded in chapter 26.

The title is not especially appropriate, since the story of these census numberings occupies only a small part of the book. A better title is the one given to the book by the Hebrews themselves, *Bemidhbar*, which is the fifth word of the opening verse, and means "In the Wilderness," for it exactly suits the subject matter of the book.

Our English title, *Numbers*, which has come down to us through the translation of the Greek and Latin, may have caused many readers not to read the book. They have thus missed the rich treasures of a book which is rightly the sequel of the book of Exodus.

The writer of the book of Numbers, like the author of the books of Exodus and Leviticus, is not merely recording events. For he is doing much more. He is the interpreter of the history of his people. In every event he sees the guiding hand of God, who is watching over His people and providing for their wants, keeping His Covenant with them, and preparing them by means of a long and severe discipline for serving Him, and for being His witness to the world.

2. THE CONTENTS OF THE BOOK

As the Hebrew title suggests, the book of Numbers contains the narrative of the greater part of the wilderness journey of the Israelites. The book of Exodus, as we have seen, tells how they left Egypt, and gives the story of their progress as far as Mount Sinai. But the long and round-about journey from Mount Sinai to the Plains of Moab, opposite Jericho, during a period of some thirty-nine years, is told in the book of Numbers.

The purpose of all this is that the Israelites had to be prepared for their occupation of Canaan, the Promised Land. Part of their

---

[1]A very satisfactory brief introduction of the book of Numbers is that by President A. A. MacRae. "Numbers," *The New Bible Commentary*, Part Two, pp. 162-194 (Second Edition, 1954). For further selected references, see pp. 66, 67.

schooling and discipline took place in Egypt. Another, and very different part, took place during the "forty years of wanderings in the wilderness."

The contents of the book of Numbers may be grouped into three main divisions, as follows:

(1) The Camp at Mount Sinai and Preparations for the Departure for the Land of Canaan, Chapters 1 to 10:10;

(2) The Journeyings from Mount Sinai to the Plains of Moab, Chapters 10:11 to 22:1;

(3) Israel's Encampment in the Plains of Moab, Chapters 22:2 to 36.

A. *The Camp at Mount Sinai and Preparations for the Departure for the Land of Canaan,* Chapters 1 to 10:10

The first ten chapters of the book of Numbers are a continuation of the narrative of the book of Exodus, and belong to that book.

THE FIRST CENSUS OF THE PEOPLE

While yet in camp at Mount Sinai, the first census or numbering of the people was ordered. Presumably this was to determine their strength if and when they met an enemy on the way, especially to determine the number of men able for war:

> The Lord spoke to Moses, "Every male, head by head, from twenty years old and upward, all in Israel who are able to go forth to war, you and Aaron shall number them, company by company."

Also, there was an elaborate ordering of the camps of the different tribes, and plans for the march, including the special laws for regulating their moral and religious life during the wilderness journey.

A FAMOUS BENEDICTION

An extraordinarily famous *Benediction* was introduced among the Israelites at this point. It came about in this way. Aaron, Moses' elder brother and first assistant, was high priest, and Aaron's sons served as priests under their father. Now the Lord said to Moses, "Say to Aaron and his sons, 'Thus you shall *bless* the people of Israel, you shall say to them:

> THE LORD BLESS YOU AND KEEP YOU:
> THE LORD MAKE HIS FACE TO SHINE UPON YOU,
>   AND BE GRACIOUS TO YOU:
> THE LORD LIFT UP HIS COUNTENANCE UPON YOU,
>   AND GIVE YOU PEACE.

" 'So shall they put my name upon the people of Israel, and I will bless them.' "

It was the duty of the priests to bless the people in the name of Jehovah, and this Priestly Benediction is the form of the benediction which Jehovah gave Moses to give to Aaron and his sons, just as Jesus gave His disciples the Lord's Prayer as a form of prayer for them to use. This Benediction, like the Lord's Prayer, has been in common use to this day.

Psalm 67 is evidently modeled on this Benediction. The reader may compare also the Apostle Paul's threefold Christian benediction, given in the last verse of his II Corinthians.

B. *The Journeyings From Mount Sinai to the Plains of Moab*, Chapters 10:11 to 22:1

It is important to remember that these chapters cover the main period of the wanderings, and that they give, not a complete history of the period, but a few outstanding incidents in these thirty-nine years, with the laws relating to the various occasions during the journey.

After eleven months of settled life at Mount Sinai, the Israelites once again started their slow march north; and as usual, they again complained because of hardships and misfortunes, and especially because they had no meat to eat. Also, some of them missed their cucumbers and melons, and the leeks and onions and garlic that they had in Egypt.

Once more Moses' administrative duties became very heavy. To lighten his burdens, the Lord asked Moses to go out and get seventy men of the elders of the people to assist him. The seventy were brought in, and the Lord anointed them. They ministered to the people and greatly relieved and cheered Moses.

But Moses had other troubles. His sister Miriam and brother Aaron, both older than Moses, became jealous of their younger brother because of his superior position and power as leader of Israel. As a pretext for her opposition, Miriam "spoke against Moses" because he had married a Cushite or Ethiopian woman. And she persuaded Aaron to take her part in the foolish criticism.

The Lord came down to the "Tent of Meeting" and held an interview with the three of them, and when the cloud of His Presence removed from over the tent, Miriam was found leprous and white as snow.

Aaron confessed to Moses that they had done foolishly and sinned, and pled with Moses to cry to the Lord that Miriam be healed. After she had been quarantined outside the camp for seven days, the people took up their march and went on the next stage of their journey, and encamped in the Wilderness of Paran, at Kadesh-barnea.

THE TWELVE SPIES AND THEIR REPORT

But perhaps Moses' greatest crisis came when twelve select leaders, one from each tribe, were sent north to spy out the land of Canaan.

Their expedition had a twofold purpose. First, to learn whether the inhabitants of Canaan were strong or weak. Second, to determine whether the land itself was good and worth taking.

It is one thing for a people to "go out" of one country and migrate, as the Israelites did from Egypt. It is quite a different thing for them *to take the initiative* and to invade and conquer another country, as they proposed to do in Canaan.

The reader can see in this dramatic story how God was training His people "to be on their own," so to speak, by letting them use their own intelligence in deciding their own problems, although He makes it clear that He is still their leader and protector.

The spies traversed the entire land from south to extreme north, from Kadesh-barnea where they were encamped "to Rehob, near the entrance of Hamath," a distance of about 180 miles. They had covered the fertile plains of the west and the central country down to the Jordan Valley.

After forty days the spies returned to Moses and Aaron, and to the whole congregation, with their report. Ten of them came in with the majority report, saying,

> We came to the land to which you sent us; it flows with milk and honey and this is its fruit. Yet the people who dwell in the land are strong, and the cities are fortified and very large; and besides, we saw the descendants of Anak there . . . We seemed to ourselves like grasshoppers, and so we seemed to them.

They brought with them samples of grapes and other products which they exhibited to the people. The "descendants of Anak" referred to in their report, hints at a race of giants, of which Goliath in the David story was perhaps a later descendant.

The people were in an uproar after the unfavorable report, for they feared the inhabitants of Canaan.

> But Caleb quieted the people before Moses, and said, "Let us go up at once, and occupy it; for we are well able to overcome it . . . The land which we passed through to spy it out, is an exceedingly good land. If the Lord delights in us, he will bring us into this land and give it to us, a land which flows with milk and honey. Only do not rebel against the Lord; and do not fear the people of the land, for they are bread for us; their protection is removed from them, and the Lord is with us; do not fear them."

But the people, still afraid of the giants of the north, rejected Caleb's speech, and were ready to stone him and Joshua. They even thought of choosing new leaders and of returning to Egypt.

The consequences of the people's decision were decisive. The masses of the people were guilty of open rebellion. The great works that God had done through Moses since they left Egypt were as nothing against the report of the ten unfaithful spies.

Their punishment was instantaneous. Instead of occupying the Promised Land at once, they were now sentenced to *forty years* as wanderers and shepherds in the wilderness. And not one of them would ever live to inherit the promise, except the faithful Joshua and Caleb. Moreover, the ten unfaithful spies paid the penalty with the plague and death.

All this means that they were not yet ready to occupy Canaan. They must have more training and discipline, before they would learn to trust God; and then only their offspring of a new generation would live to inherit the Great Promise. The complete story of all these years in the wilderness is not given in the book of Numbers; instead, we have only a few telling and revealing incidents and episodes to represent the whole, in chapters 14 to 21.

Kadesh-barnea seems to have been their headquarters during most of "the forty years," although their herdsmen traveled far and wide with their flocks and herds, over the dry and sparse grazing lands called the Wilderness of Paran and the Wilderness of Zin south of Palestine proper.

A glance at the Exodus map will show the reader the location of Kadesh-barnea and this wide wilderness region around about it. The *wilderness* is so-called because it consists of desert and semi-desert lands, dry and stony, ill-suited to agricultural pursuits other than the grazing of flocks and herds. The wilderness generally was *unclaimed lands,* because other tribes had found them unprofitable for the most part and had migrated elsewhere.

Thus, the territory which was to be the "home" of Israel for almost forty years extended north in the direction of Beer-sheba, to the land of the Amalekites and other Canaanite tribes; on the east to the Dead Sea and the dry lands of the Arabah and the border of Edom; on the south, as far as the Gulf of Akabah; and on the west — well, not too far, because the Philistines claimed everything within their sight on the west.

Two Rebellions

While at Kadesh-barnea, Moses' leadership was again challenged. There was another rebellion. In fact, there was a double rebellion. One against his civil authority, led by Dathan, Abiram, and Or; the other, a different sort of rebellion, led by Korah and 250 leaders of the congregation, against the ecclesiastical leadership of Moses and Aaron.

Moses and Aaron were vindicated by the Lord, and the rebels were dramatically punished. The earth opened and they were swallowed up alive! Aaron's priestly authority was confirmed (Chapter 16).

Miriam's Death

Another incident at Kadesh-barnea was the death of Miriam. She was older than her brothers Aaron and Moses. In spite of her one-time jealousy of the authority and leadership of her younger brother Moses, she had been invaluable to Moses, from birth onward, and her death now must have caused him great personal grief.

Moses Disobeys

The Water-from-the-Rock incident, also at Kadesh, is the most disappointing, because of all the events connected with the leadership of Moses, this is the only one in which he lost his patience with the incessant complaints and grumblings of the people, and disobeyed the Lord outright.

The people assembled themselves and made speeches against Moses and Aaron. Pointing to their leaders, they asked, "Why have you brought the assembly of the Lord into this wilderness, that we should die here, both we and our cattle? And why have you made us come up out of Egypt, to bring us to this evil place? It is no place for grain, or figs, or vines, or pomegranates; and there is no water to drink."

The Lord commanded him to take the rod, he and Aaron, and *tell* the rock before their eyes to yield its water. Instead of following the command of the Lord, Moses lifted up his hand and *struck* the rock twice. The water came from the rock all right, and the congregation drank, and their cattle. But the leaders had disobeyed the Lord irreparably. For the Lord said to Moses and Aaron, "Because you did not believe in me, to sanctify me in the eyes of the people of Israel, therefore you shall not bring this assembly into the land which I have given them."

At long last, the forty years of wanderings in the Wilderness of Paran were drawing to a close. Kadesh-barnea, which the tribes of Israel had long used as central headquarters as they moved back and forth over the hills seeking better pasturage, this Kadesh was about to be left behind them forever. For Moses and the people of Israel once more were ready to begin their march toward Canaan, by regular stages, but by a circuitous and zig-zag route, which would eventually bring them to the Plains of Moab, opposite ancient Jericho.

Aaron's Death

Moses, under the command of the Lord, moved south in the direction of the Red Sea, that is the Gulf of Akabah, and camped at Mount Hor. But while Moses and Aaron and the people of Israel were waiting before Mount Hor, on the border of the land of Edom, another great sadness came to Moses. His brother Aaron died. The Lord said, "Aaron shall be gathered to his people; for he shall not enter the land which I have given to the people of Israel, because you rebelled against my command at Meribah."

In Israel's religious order Aaron was high priest. He organized and trained the priesthood, including his sons, one of whom was anointed to succeed him at the time of his death. Moses would sorely miss Aaron, his only brother and chief aid.

From Mount Hor, Moses and Israel again marched north, up the valley of the Arabah to the southern shores of the Dead Sea, where they turned east up the valley of the River Zered, which separates Edom from Moab. Thence they continued east and north around the eastern border of Moab, thus avoiding the territory of both kingdoms.

As usual, there was a shortage of food and water, and the people spoke against God and against Moses. To teach them faith and humility, the Lord sent fiery serpents to bite them, and the bronze serpent on a pole to heal all who had faith to look upon it and be healed, thus foreshadowing the Crucifixion.

At the northern border of Moab, Moses rested and sought permission from Sihon, king of the Amorites, for peaceful passage through his territory. But Sihon refused permission; instead, he took his men and fought against Israel. Israel slew him and took possession of his land, from the river Arnon to the river Jabbok. Then Israel settled for the time in Heshbon, the capital, and in all the cities and villages of the Amorites.

C. Israel's Encampment in the Plains of Moab, Chapters 22-36

The Israelites had now entered upon the last stage of the journey to Canaan.

After the conquests of Sihon and the Amorites, and of Og and Bashan, the Israelites set out and encamped in the "Plains of Moab," on the east bank of the Jordan, and opposite the ancient city of Jericho. At this point three terraces form the valley of the Jordan. The camp of the tribes of Israel was located on the third and topmost terrace or tableland, and among a long grove of acacia trees some three miles or more in length. The site was called Shittim or Acacia Wood, because of the acacia trees.

But Israel's concentration on the conquest of Canaan was soon disturbed. For Balak, king of Moab, whose territory Moses had bypassed on his journey to the land of the Amorites, was afraid of the Israelites because of their recent victories over Sihon and Og, giants in the earth though they were. Since Balak had decided that he could not prevail against Israel with ordinary weapons, he resorted to magical arts, hoping in that way to outwit Moses and the Israelites.

Balak wanted the best. So he sent to Pethor on the bank of the River Euphrates for the famous magician, Balaam, to come and "curse Israel." But Balak had not reckoned that Jehovah would take a hand in this contest, and that not even the powers of darkness could stop the victorious march of Jehovah's people.

To state the matter simply and in our own way of speech, Jehovah held an interview with Balaam. In fact, several interviews. The net result was that Jehovah sold Balaam on the idea of being His witness in the supernatural contest, instead of Balak's. Balak, on his part, raised his magical fees to Balaam, hoping thereby to put an end to Balaam's hesitation, and to secure his full cooperation and use of magic in bestowing the curse on Israel.

Jehovah won the contest, of course. But the whole story, as it develops and climaxes in chapters 22, 23, and 24 in this book of Numbers, is one of the most human in the Old Testament.

Israel had other temptations. The proximity of the tribes of Moab and Midian to the encampment of Israel made it easy for them to intermingle, and to become victims of immorality and the idolatrous worship of these neighboring peoples. The chief blame for the corruption of Israel was placed with the Midianites, with whom Moses went to war to avenge his people, and to impress upon the whole congregation of Israel the seriousness of deserting Jehovah for idol worship. These stories are told in chapters 25 and 31.

The Second Census of the People

Chapter 26 tells the story of the second census or enumeration of the people since they left Egypt, or in their fortieth year. According to Numbers 1:46, the size of the male population, twenty years old and upward, at the time of the first census was 603,550. This did not include the tribe of Levi, which belonged to the priesthood and was not subject to military and other similar duties. Thirty-nine years later, at the time of the second census, there were 601,730 male adults, not counting the tribe of Levi. Mortality in the desert had been high, including deaths resulting from plagues and rebellions.

The purpose of this census was twofold: first, it was military and intended to find out the number of fighting men available for the occupation of Canaan; second, and perhaps the more important reason, was to establish a factual basis for dividing the land of Canaan, after it had been conquered, among the Twelve Tribes of Israel. "Every tribe shall be given its inheritance according to its numbers."

The complete details of the inheritance of each of the tribes, the location and name and boundaries of each, together with the method of allotment after the conquest, are given in the book of Joshua.

Joshua Chosen As Moses' Successor

The Lord made it known to Moses that his work as leader of Israel was about to end, and chose Joshua, his captain, as his successor. Then Moses, in the presence of all the congregation, anointed Joshua to lead the people in his stead and invested him with some of his own authority . . . "that all the congregation of the people of Israel may obey."

The remainder of the story of Moses is told in the fifth and last book of the Pentateuch, the book of Deuteronomy. His Farewell Address occupies most of the book.

Chapter 7

DEUTERONOMY

1. THE BOOK OF DEUTERONOMY

The book of Deuteronomy shares with the book of Exodus as the main source of the Ten Commandments and the rest of the Mosaic Law.

Indeed, the book of Deuteronomy is the later and more popular *version* of the Law, and the version which has been widely quoted during the thirty-three centuries or so since its composition.

This alone would make the book one of the great fundamental books of all time, and certainly one of the most influential ever written. It is therefore well nigh impossible to over-rate its value.[1]

Chapter 6 of the book is distinctive for its noble statement of The Great Commandment:

> THOU SHALL LOVE THE LORD THY GOD
> WITH ALL THY HEART, WITH ALL THY SOUL,
> AND WITH ALL THY MIGHT.

This is repeated over and over again by Moses, and quoted by later prophets: chapters 6:5; 10:12; 11:1, 13, 22; 13:3; 30:2, 6. It was called The Great Commandment by our Lord (Matthew 22:37) and given first place in His ministry and teaching.

Moses was the first to prophesy the coming of the Messiah, "a prophet like unto Moses":

> The Lord your God will raise up for you a prophet like me from among you, from your brethren — him you shall heed (18:15).

When Jesus was led up by the Spirit into the wilderness to be tempted by the devil, He answered the tempter with four quotations from Scripture, three of them being from the book of Deuteronomy (8:3; 6:16; 6:13). Also, as indicating the importance of the book, Professor G. T. Manley of Christ's College, Cambridge, has discovered

---

[1]One of the best short introductions to the study of the book of Deuteronomy is G. T. Manley's "Deuteronomy," *The New Bible Commentary*, Part Two, pp. 195-222 (Second Edition, 1954). See also the same author's *New Bible Handbook* (1948); Edward J. Young's *An Introduction to the Old Testament*, pp. 101-114. Of the liberal school, see G. Ernest Wright, *The Interpreter's Bible*, Vol. II, pp. 311-330; Bernhard W. Anderson, "The Rediscovery of Mosaic Torah," *Understanding the Old Testament*, Chapter 10; Gerhard von Rad, *Studies in Deuteronomy* (1953).

that the name of Moses occurs ninety-nine times in the New Testament and every reference throws light on the book of Deuteronomy.[2]

The reader, too, will not overlook the eloquence of some of the great passages in the book of Deuteronomy, unsurpassed in world literature as many think even by such classic orators as Demosthenes, Cicero, or by their modern counterparts. Take Moses' second discourse, for example, which has been called his *Great Oration,* chapters 5 to 26.

The book of Deuteronomy gets its English name from the Greek word *Deuteronomion* by the Greek translators of the Hebrew Old Testament, and means *the second law,* or *the law repeated.* That is, the second time The Law was presented, the first time being at Mount Sinai, and recorded in the book of Exodus.

But the book of Deuteronomy is much more than the repetition or copy of the Law already given at Mount Sinai.

Now, after thirty-nine years of experience in the wilderness since the old legislation was rehearsed at Mount Sinai, Israel is encamped in the Plains of Moab on the eve of the battle for the possession of Canaan. The point of view has changed. Moses now, in his Farewell Address, is reviewing and explaining laws which were previously given, and in simple terms that everyone in the congregation of Israel might understand, he is speaking directly to the people, exhorting them to gratitude, obedience, and loyalty to the Lord their God.

Thus, the point of view of the book of Deuteronomy is that of a sermon, a farewell message, by a wise and devoted leader.

2. THE DATE, OCCASION, AND PURPOSE OF THE BOOK

Many scholars are of the opinion that Moses and the Israelites began the Exodus from Egypt about 1440 B.C.[3] If so, they arrived on the Plains of Moab about 1400 B.C. From its context, we infer that the book of Deuteronomy was written shortly before Moses' death and Joshua's entrance into Canaan.[4]

The occasion also is expressly stated by the speaker and writer of the book (31:1-2). The time of his departure is at hand. His commission as leader of the great Exodus from Egypt, and as Lawgiver to the new nation, has been accomplished. His successor has been both named and installed. But before his departure, he delivered his Farewell Address to *All Israel,* implying that he knew the people were being welded into a new nation.

The purpose of the farewell message was to recount the past history of Israel as it related to the present; to rehearse before all the congregation the Law and the Covenant, and to renew their vows

---

[2]*The New Bible Commentary,* p. 197 (1954).
[3]For a discussion of the chronology of Deuteronomy and the other books of the Pentateuch, including footnote and references, see pp. 86, 87.
[4]See the discussion of authorship of the Pentateuch, including references, pp. 63, 64, 65.

to keep the same; and to issue a final and solemn warning to Israel to be obedient and faithful to the Lord their God, in the land into which they were about to enter.

3. THE CONTENTS OF THE BOOK

Two methods of analysis of the contents of the book of Deuteronomy may be used. The simplest is to regard the whole book, with minor interruptions and additions of matter not by the speaker, as the Farewell Address of Moses to the Israelites. The interruptions may provide also for the delivery of parts of the address on different days.

The other approach, the one which is used here, is to let the book divide itself naturally into *four* separate speeches or discourses, with a fifth and final division covering the installation of Joshua as Moses' successor, and the final messages of Moses to all the people, given in poetry and song. The reader will notice that the separate speeches have appropriate introductions and conclusions.

(1) *Moses' First Address,* Chapters 1-4:43

In this address Moses reviews the history of the people, especially since they left Mount Sinai.

He points out God's love and providential care of them through all those trying years, and uses that as reason and grounds for their obedience and loyalty to Him now, on the eve of their march into the Land of Promise.

(2) *Moses' Second Address,* Chapters 4:44 to 26

This is called the Great Address, both because of its great length and because it sets forth the very heart of the book. It repeats and explains, as only Moses could, the Ten Commandments and the Law and the Covenant.

It embraces the same fundamental principles and covenants as given thirty-eight years before at Mount Sinai, but adapted and motivated simply to suit the new conditions and the new day, and in language that every one of the great congregation could understand.

God was revealing Himself in new ways to His people, and more and more responsibility was being shifted to all the people, and no longer rested mainly on the priests and Levites and other leaders.

Some special passages in the Great Address:
1. The Ten Commandments, Chapter 5:1-21
2. The Great Commandment, Chapter 6:4-9
3. Holy to the Lord Are His People, Chapter 7:6-16
4. It Is a Good Land, Chapter 8
5. "And, Now, Israel, What Does the Lord Your God Require of You?" Chapters 10:12 to 11:25

(3) *Moses' Third Address,* Chapters 27-28

In this shorter discourse, Moses, assisted by the elders of the people, and the Levitical priests, *charges* the people to obey the Lord their God, and to keep His commandments and statutes:

> Keep silence and hear, O Israel: this day you have become the people of the Lord your God. You shall therefore obey the voice of the Lord your God, keeping his commandments and his statutes, which I command you this day.

Thus, at this point in his series of discourses, Moses pauses and exhorts the people on the importance of *putting into practice* the laws and high covenant agreements which he had just presented to them in the foregoing discourses.

They were about to go over into Canaan, under the leadership of Joshua. Their greatest temptation, as they came in contact with the idolatrous Canaanites, Moses well knew, would be to forsake the Lord their God and take up the worship of idols. So his final charge to the people stressed the Blessings of Obedience, and the "curses" of disobedience.

He stressed also the *abiding presence* of the Lord their God, who would go over into Canaan with them, and give them victory:

> The Lord will cause your enemies who rise up against you to be defeated before you; they shall come out against you *one* way, and flee before you *seven* ways.

In the amazing chapter Twenty-Eight, Moses presents the two contrasting pictures with great power:

In the *first*, he gives a vision of the Blessings of Obedience, the overflowing prosperity that shall come to the people of Israel in the land of Canaan — "if you obey the commands of the Lord your God, which I command you this day, being careful *to do* them" (28:8-14).

In the *second* picture, Moses sketches not only the "curses" of disobedience, but assumes the role of prophet and prophesies the evils that shall come to a disobedient nation and people. In short, in an amazing passage, he predicts the whole future history of the Hebrew Nation, its disobedience, decline and fall, including the Assyrian and Babylonian exiles . . . "And the Lord will scatter you among all peoples, from one end of the earth to the other" (28:15-68).

(4) *Moses' Fourth Address*, Chapters 29-30

In this short discourse, Moses is delivering the speech on the occasion of the *Renewal* of the Covenant, made at Mount Sinai some thirty-eight years before, and which they had quickly broken.

Now, at the end of his life, and in the true spirit of an evangelist, Moses made this sworn Covenant to all the congregation. In this act he reaffirmed that all Israel belonged to the Lord, and that he was the Lord their God.

His final warning was to offer them a choice between Life and Death:

> See, I have set before you this day
> Life and Good, Death and Evil.

Moses was a prophet indeed. Foreseeing the future and the time when Israel would disobey, and fall, and be scattered abroad from their homeland, he foresees also the way open to repentance, and return to the Lord (30:1-10):

> And when all these things come upon you, the blessing and the curse, which I have set before you, and you call them to mind among all the nations where the Lord your God has driven you, and return to the Lord your God, you and your children, and obey his voice in all that I command you this day, with all your heart and with all your soul; then the Lord your God will restore your fortunes, and have compassion upon you, and he will gather you again from all the peoples where the Lord your God has scattered you.

(5) The Last Words of Moses, Chapters 31-33

1. Chapter Thirty-One records the farewell words of Moses to the people and to Joshua, his successor. Moses exhorts Joshua to be strong and of good courage, for the Lord their God will march with the people into Canaan, and give them victory.

Moses completed the writing of the Law and gave it to the priests of Levi for safe keeping. In the future it was to be read at regular intervals, "before Israel in their hearing."

The distinction is clearly made between the Levites who were charged with the keeping of the Book of the Law, and the priests who, with the elders and heads of families, were charged with the reading and teaching of the Law.

2. Chapter Thirty-Two records Moses' Farewell Song, the theme of which is the goodness of the Lord their God in choosing the Twelve Tribes of Jacob and bringing them into the rich land they are about to possess. They are commanded to memorize the Song and to teach it to their children, as a reminder to keep the Law.

3. Before his death, Moses also composed the Song of Blessing for all the congregation (chapter 33).

Thus, as the reader will observe, the Exodus began and closed with a Song of Moses (Exodus 15:1-18). Some scholars are of the opinion that Moses also wrote Psalm 90. In this connection, the reader may compare Deuteronomy 33:27 with Psalm 90:1.

(6) The Death of Moses, Chapter 34

Chapter Thirty-Four was written, not by Moses, but by a later writer or editor. It was added to complete the story of Moses for later readers.

Many scholars today are of the opinion that the chapter was written considerably later than the death of Moses, and that the phrase, "to this day" (34:6), came long enough after the death of Moses for the writer and his generation to appreciate Moses' real greatness, as compared with the great prophets and leaders who succeeded him.

It is impossible, of course, to evaluate adequately the greatness of a great man.

However, there are many who think it just possible that Moses has had greater influence on the thinking and conduct of mankind than any other man in the history of the world and that an appraisal of Moses today would not differ substantially from the high praise given him by the writer in the famous passage with which the book of Deuteronomy closes (34:10-12).

Moses is the only person with whom Jesus ever compared Himself, not only as Lawgiver, but as prophet and revealer of the Great Truth of the Bible:

> And Jesus said to the Jews . . . "Do not think that I shall accuse you to the Father; it is Moses who accuses you, on whom you set your hope. If you believed Moses, you would believe me, for he wrote of me. But if you do not believe his writings, how will you believe my words?" (John 5:45-47).

Moses' name was a household word during Old Testament times and was on the lips of every Hebrew prophet and leader and poet for a thousand years of Hebrew history.

And as stated above, the name of Moses occurs ninety-nine times in the New Testament, all of which was written fourteen hundred years after his death.

Moses and the prophets are given the highest rating as earthly representatives of the Kingdom of God in Jesus' parable of the Rich Man and Lazarus. In the parable, the Rich Man in Hades prayed to Abraham to send a messenger to warn his brothers. Abraham replied, "They have Moses and the prophets; let them hear them" (Luke 16:29).

Remains of the excavated city walls of ancient Jericho. © *Matson Photo Service*

THE BOOKS OF CONQUEST AND SETTLEMENT OF CANAAN

Chapter 8

JOSHUA

1. JOSHUA AND THE BOOK OF JOSHUA

Thomas Carlyle, who has been called the "Prophet of Edinburgh," once said that the history of the world is but the biography of great men. Ralph Waldo Emerson said that an institution is but the lengthened shadow of one man.

Both men were right, and the Bible is full of illustrations of both. And there is no better example than Joshua and the book of Joshua. For the biography of Joshua is quite literally the history of the period.

Joshua was the son of Nun, of the tribe of Ephraim, one of the two sons of Joseph by his Egyptian wife, Asenath. Originally he had the Hebrew name Hoshea, which was changed by Moses to the more significant form of *Jehoshua,* meaning "Jehovah is salvation." It later developed into *Joshua.* The Greek form of the Hebrew name is *Jesus.* Some Christians have seen in Joshua a *type* of Jesus the Son of God, and in this book a picture of the life of victory in Him.

Some Biblical scholars feel that Hebrew history does not give Joshua his just rating. The towering greatness of Moses, and the importance of his leadership, may account for the apparent lack of recognition of Moses' successor. We read the book of Exodus down to chapter seventeen before we meet the name Joshua, but from then on he is mentioned prominently. As Moses' captain, he defeated the Amalekites. The Lord thought highly enough of Joshua's achievement to make this request of Moses,

> Write this as a memorial in a book and recite it in the ears of Joshua, that I will utterly blot out the remembrance of Amalek from under heaven.

After Joshua's defeat of Amalek, he continued to be Moses' personal attendant and colleague. He was with Moses on Mount Sinai. As prince of Ephraim, he was one of the twelve sent to spy out the land of Canaan. He showed great faith and courage when he and Caleb came back with a minority report, and stood up and defended it at the risk of being stoned to death. Like Moses, Joshua was born in Egypt and brought up under the influence of Egyptian civilization and culture, which was of great advantage to him.

The book of Joshua is important for three main reasons. In the first place, the book records the fulfillment of God's promise to Abraham and his descendants of Canaan as an inheritance. Second, the book reveals how God helped Israel to victory in a critical period of its history. Finally, the book also reveals God's own righteousness and His standards for those who follow Him. Indeed, the conquest was a holy war, led by the Lord Himself.

The question is asked, "What of the rights of the Canaanites, whose lands were invaded and possessed?" The writer states that all the tribes of the Canaanites were idolatrous and were come under God's judgment for their wickedness, "It is because of the wickedness of these nations that the Lord is driving them out before you" (Deuteronomy 9:4). Their wickedness was extreme and had placed them in the category of Sodom and Gomorrah, to be destroyed utterly. Archaeological discoveries at Gezer, Megiddo, Jericho, and other places, also tend to verify this view.

2. Authorship, Date, and Purpose of the Book[1]

So Joshua made a covenant with the people that day, and made statutes and ordinances for them at Shechem. And Joshua wrote these words in the book of the Law of God.

The Jewish tradition was that Joshua wrote the book that bears his name, although this quotation refers specifically to Joshua's Farewell Address and the covenant with the people that day. Significantly, the place was the old city of Shechem, where Abraham some seven centuries earlier set up his first altar in Canaan, in the name of the Lord.

At Mount Sinai, as recorded in the book of Exodus, Moses wrote the Ten Commandments and the rest of the Law, in what may be called the *First Edition* of our Bible.

On the Plains of Moab, as recorded in the book of Deuteronomy, almost forty years after Sinai, Moses *revised* the Commandments and the Law and explained it to all the people of Israel. This could be called the *Second Edition* of our Bible.

Joshua had received from Moses this Written Law of God. And when he crossed the Jordan he carried with him "this book of the Law" of Moses and used it as his daily guide for the next twenty-five years, during the period of conquest and settlement of Canaan.

After his Farewell Address at Shechem, Joshua wrote his own

---

[1]For the documentary theory of the authorship and composition of Joshua, see Bernhard W. Anderson, *Understanding of the Old Testament*, Chapters 3 and 4, pp. 60-121 (1957); for an archaeological analysis, see John Garstang, *The Foundation of Biblical History: Joshua-Judges* (1931); a more conservative view is contained in the excellent brief summary by Hugh J. Blair, *The New Bible Commentary*, Part Two, pp. 223-224 (1954); and Edward J. Young's *An Introduction to the Old Testament*, pp. 165-178. A more critical view is that by Wright and Filson, *The Westminster Historical Atlas to the Bible*, pp. 39-42; and R. H. Pfeiffer, *Introduction to the Old Testament*, pp. 296-301 (1948).

book and added it to the Book of Moses, which we may call the *Third Edition* of our Bible (24:26).

As in the case of Moses, it is not necessary that we assume that Joshua wrote the book as is, verbatim and unchanged, as it has come down to us. For later editors have added short introductions and interpolations for the benefit of later readers, as is evident in all these older books.

The date of the book of Joshua may be placed at about 1375 B.C., or about twenty-five years after the date of the book of Deuteronomy. Josephus, the Jewish historian of the first century A.D., states that Joshua was eighty-five years of age when he succeeded Moses, and the text gives his age at 110 at the time of his death (24:29). This would allow about twenty-five years for the conquest and settlement of Canaan.

Like the five books of Moses, the overall purpose of the book of Joshua is to reveal God to His people and His plans for their redemption. The Lord is leading Joshua and his fighting men in a victorious march throughout Canaan, and is fulfilling His promise to Abraham and his descendants. He is also charging them to loyalty and devotion to Him as their God, and warning them against idolatry and its consequences. In all this, Joshua, like Moses and Paul (many centuries later), is preaching the doctrine of the unmerited grace of God, because of His choice and love of His people, and not because of any righteousness of theirs (see Farewell Addresses, chapters 23, 24).

In the ancient Hebrew Canon, the books of Moses occupy the first division and are called THE LAW. The second division of the Canon is called THE PROPHETS and is subdivided into "Former Prophets" and "Latter Prophets." It is significant that the book of Joshua is the first to be placed in the new division called Former Prophets, indicating a new role for God's servants.

Although Moses is held the ideal prophet in both Old and New Testaments, and is specifically referred to as a prophet in Deuteronomy (chapters 18, 28, 29), the prophetic function was not so much emphasized in the books of Moses as in the historical books after Moses. Edward J. Young and others are of the opinion that the books of Joshua, Judges, I and II Samuel, and I and II Kings, are called "The Prophets," not primarily because of the prophetical contents of the books, but because the *authors* of these books occupied the office and function of prophet.[2] On the contrary, is it not due primarily to the appearance of a new type of character and leadership, and *spokesman*, culminating in the prophet Samuel, as contrasted with the emergence of civil leaders who were frequently not God's spokesmen?

[2]*An Introduction to the Old Testament,* pp. 167-169 (1958).

3. The Contents of the Book

The contents of the book of Joshua fall into these three divisions:

(a) The Conquest of Canaan, Chapters 1:12;

(b) The Division of the Land, and the Permanent Settlement of each of the Twelve Tribes of Israel, Chapters 13-22;

(c) Joshua's Farewell Addresses, Chapters 23-24.

A. *The Conquest of Canaan,* Chapters 1-12

The book of Joshua opens with the mobilization of the men of arms and with a sense of urgency for the beginning of the campaign against the Canaanites . . .

> Prepare your provisions; for within three days you are to pass over this Jordan, to go in to take possession of the land.

Joshua introduced the tactics of a holy war. The miraculous crossing of the Jordan is according to ritual, the details of which are specifically stated: the priests and the ark, the twelve stones, and the order of the march across the river. Then there are the other twelve stones and the memorial at Gilgal, which is to be headquarters, and the days of circumcision and sanctification, including the Passover. All this before the first battle, which is the battle of Jericho, and which has its own sacred ritual. On his three-mile march to Jericho, Joshua met a representative of Jehovah with a drawn sword in his hand, who called himself "the Commander of the Army of the Lord." Many scholars believe that this was the Son of God Himself.

The battle for Jericho and the other cities and strongholds proceeded according to plan, and by stages, thus:

1. The *first stage* was a frontal attack, against the cities of Jericho and Ai, which were the key to western Canaan, or Palestine. This thrust forward and westward had the strategic advantage of driving a wedge between the Canaanites of the north and those of the south.

2. The *second stage* was the campaign against the kings and cities of the south, in what might be described in modern tactical language as a "pincher movement," to defeat the left and south sector of the enemy.

The Gibeonites, being convinced of their defenselessness against "the Army of the Lord," through a strategy of their own, joined themselves as allies to the Israelites. This angered the five kings of the south, who sought revenge on Gibeon in a pitched battle before his own city. Learning of Gibeon's distress, Joshua and his men of war traveled all night from Gilgal and took the armies of the five kings by surprise . . . "The Lord threw them into a panic before Israel, who slew them with a great slaughter at Gibeon, and chased them by the way of the ascent of Beth-horon," where they were completely destroyed. Joshua spent some time "mopping up" the lesser cities and enemy territory of the south.

3. The *third stage* was the campaign in the north.

When Jabin, king of the city of Hazor, and head of all the king-doms of the north, heard how Joshua and the Israelites had defeated the five kings of the Amorites and their allies of the south, he sent messages to the kings of Madon, Shimron, Achshaph, and to the kings of the northern hill country, and to the Canaanites and the other tribes allied with them.

Like the five Amorite kings in the south, these northern kings and their allies assembled their combined strength for a strategic and decisive battle against Joshua and the Israelites, this time at the historic battle at the Waters of Merom, ten miles northwest of the Sea of Galilee. The writer describes their gathering in these words:

> And they came out, with all their troops, a great host, in number like the sand that is upon the seashore, with very many horses and chariots. And all these kings joined their forces, and came and en-camped together at the Waters of Merom, to fight with Israel.

And the Lord said to Joshua,

> Do not be afraid of them, for tomorrow at this time I will give over all of them, slain, to Israel; you shall hamstring their horses, and burn their chariots with fire.

Joshua came suddenly upon the hosts of the enemy, and slew them, and chased the remnant far into the north . . . And then, says the writer, "The land had rest from war."

Although Joshua's victories were sweeping, and the enemy cities were destroyed far and wide, still and all the conquest was far from complete. For in many instances the enemy was routed, and subdued; but not destroyed. And so the tribes of Israel, each in his own territory and inheritance, had to keep on the alert against the remnants of the enemy.

Unhappily, this was only too true of the stronger enemy groups, such as the Canaanites on the northwest plains, the Philistines on the southwest, and the Amalekites and Amorites in the east, against whom the mighty Samson and others struggled in succeeding generations, and about whom we read in the book of Judges and in I Samuel.

B. *The Division of the Land and the Permanent Settlement of Each of the Twelve Tribes of Israel,* Chapters 13-22

Chapters 13 to 22 give the story of the division of the land and the allotment to each of the Twelve Tribes. Since these chapters contain much detail and repetition, it will be helpful first to indicate in outline each tribal allotment, thus:

1. The tribes of Reuben, Gad, and the half-tribe of Manasseh already had their territory assigned to them on the east side of the Jordan, and during the lifetime of Moses. For that agreement, see the book of Numbers 32. Their final settlement is described in Joshua 13.

2. We come now to the west side of the Jordan and the first main

division of the land. The tribe of Judah, with whom Caleb was associated, was given their allotment in the south, including Jerusalem and the very desirable territory of the five kings (chapter 15), and extending all the way to Kadesh-barnea and the River of Egypt. In a later and second division of the land, the tribe of Simeon was included in Judah's territory, "because the portion of the tribe of Judah was too large for them" (chapter 19:1-9).

3. The tribes of Manasseh and Ephraim, the sons of Joseph, were allotted the large and important territory of central Palestine (chapters 16, 17). Joshua, their great leader, was of the tribe of Ephraim and chose the city of Timnath-serah in the hill country of Ephraim for his inheritance (chapter 19:49-50).

4. We come now to the second division of the land, the allotments to the smaller tribes. The tribes of Benjamin (18:11-28) and Dan (19:40-48) were assigned the small strip of territory between the two powerful inheritances of Judah, and Manasseh and Ephraim. The tribe of Dan was unable to possess its land, because the Philistines occupied it. So later they migrated to the far north, as the map will show.

5. The remaining tribes, Asher and Zebulun and Issachar and Naphtali, like Simeon and Benjamin and Dan, had their portion allotted to them in the second division of the land, and in the far north of Palestine, as a look at the map will reveal.

No land was allotted to the tribe of Levi. "No portion was given to the Levites in the land, but only cities to dwell in, with their pasture lands for their cattle and their substance" (14:4). As Levites and priests for the entire Hebrew faith, it was necessary that they should be dispersed throughout the entire nation. The location of the 48 cities and the specifications for grazing lands around them were set forth by Moses in the book of Numbers 35:1-8; see Joshua 21 for the names and tribal locations of these cities. One day someone asked Moses, who had a sense of humor, what should be the allotment of the tribe of Levi. With a twinkle in his eye, he replied, "The Lord God of Israel is their inheritance" (13:33).

All the Twelve Tribes had one thing in common. They must continue to fight the unsubdued remnants of the Canaanite tribes still living on portions of their territory. For example, the tribe of Dan, as we have seen, because of the powerful Philistines who occupied their land, moved to the far north. Also, the tribe of Manasseh complained to Joshua that the Canaanites still occupied certain fortifications and cities of their inheritance (17:11, 12; 16:10). The tribe of Judah, as we know, until the time of King David was unable to dislodge the Jebusites from the fortifications of Jerusalem. Other tribes had their particular tasks and problems.

C. *Joshua's Farewell Addresses,* Chapters 23-24

Like Moses his predecessor, Joshua at the close of his life delivered his Farewell Address to the people.

Moses' farewell was delivered in what appears to be four separate discourses, and possibly on four separate days. Joshua's was in two parts and very likely delivered at two different places. The first, which appears to have been given primarily to the leaders of the people, and possibly at Timnath-serah his home, is introduced thus:

> And it came to pass . . . that Joshua called for all Israel, for their elders and for their heads, and for their judges and for their officers, and said unto them.

In this first address, Joshua dwells chiefly upon the political and religious future of Israel, and urges them "to keep and do all that is written in the Book of the Law of Moses." And, after reminding them that it was the Lord their God who had given them victory in Canaan, and not they themselves, he was equally outspoken in his insistence that they abstain from all forms of idolatry:

> For if you turn back, and join the remnant of these nations left here among you, and make marriage with them, so that you marry their women and they yours, know assuredly that the Lord your God will not continue to drive out these nations before you; but they shall be a snare and a trap for you, a scourge on your sides, and thorns in your eyes, till you perish from off this good land which the Lord your God has given you.

In his *second address,* "Joshua gathered all the tribes of Israel to Shechem," one of the sacred places in early Hebrew history, and again reminded them of the faithfulness of God, from the days of Abraham until now, and then solemnly called upon the people to be loyal to the Lord their God.

The climax of the speech, and of the events of the day, came when Joshua shouted the great challenge, which is recorded in 24:15, as follows:

> And if you be unwilling to serve the Lord, choose this day whom you will serve, whether the gods your father served in the region beyond the River, or the gods of the Amorites in whose land you dwell; but as for me and my house, we will serve the Lord!

And the people answered,

> Far be it from us that we should forsake the Lord, to serve other gods.

So Joshua made a covenant with the people that day at Shechem. The solemn agreements were put into words, and Joshua wrote these words in the Book of the Law of God. They also became a part of the book of Joshua, which we now read.

The book closes with these words:

> And Israel served the Lord all the days of Joshua, and all the days of the elders who outlived Joshua, and had known all the work which the Lord did for Israel.

But the writer, in parting, wants the reader to know that the mummy of Joseph, which the Egyptian embalmers prepared in Egypt, and which his kinsmen had loyally brought from Egypt and kept all these years, was finally buried at Shechem, in his father Jacob's family burying place.

SELECTED READINGS ON THE CONQUEST AND SETTLEMENT OF CANAAN

Bible Readings: The Books of Joshua, Judges, and Ruth. Text: *The Revised Standard Version;* or *The New English Bible;* or *The King James Version,* preferably in modern reader's format.

Anderson, Bernhard W.: *Understanding the Old Testament,* Chapters 3 and 4, pp. 60-121.

*Blair, Hugh J.: "Joshua," *The New Bible Commentary,* pp. 223-235.

Bright, John: "Joshua," *The Interpreter's Bible,* Vol. II, pp. 541-549.

*Bruce, F. F.: "Judges," *The New Bible Commentary,* pp. 236-257.

Burney, C. E.: *The Book of Judges.*

Canon, W. W.: "The Book of Ruth," *Theology,* Vol. 16, pp. 310-319.

*Garstang, John: *The Foundations of Bible History; Joshua, Judges.*

*Rowley, H. H.: *From Joseph to Joshua.*

*Young, Edward J.: *An Introduction to the Old Testament,* pp. 165-187, and 357-361.

The pyramids of Egypt which remind us of Joseph's time. At left, top, the great pyramid of Cheops at Gizeh, near Cairo, and left, bottom, the excavated Sphinx amid the pyramids. At right, near the top of the great pyramid Cheops, showing the size of the stone blocks used in its construction.
© *Matson Photo Service*

Chapter 9

JUDGES

1. THE BOOK AND THE PERIOD OF THE JUDGES

The book of Judges gets its title from the fact that *twelve* somewhat heroic individuals served as "Judges" of Israel during the period of approximately three hundred years, immediately following the period of the book of Joshua.

Of necessity these Judges were primarily military leaders,[1] although they were the religious representatives of Jehovah, also. In the book of Joshua, we learned that the conquest of Canaan by Joshua was never a *total* conquest. Instead, strong remnants of the unconquered Canaanites of the north, the Philistines of the southwest, and the treacherous Amalekites and Amorites on the east, were left in their strongholds, ready to fight back at the first opportunity. The chief result was that the tribes of Israel had to "live with this remnant" and constantly be on the alert against them.

The writer, early in the book of Judges, tells us that Israel, not long after the death of Joshua, forsook the Lord and worshiped the foreign gods, the Baals and Ashtaroth of the Canaanites. Also, that the Lord, in His anger at their disobedience, "gave them over to plunderers."

It was at this point that the Lord "raised up Judges" who saved the people of Israel out of the power of those who plundered them (2:13-16). "But whenever the Judge died," continues the historian, "they turned back and behaved worse than their fathers, going after other gods." So the book of Judges records the exploits of a succession of Judges, one after another, whose prime duty was to rescue the people, in the name of the Lord, from their oppressors.

At best Israel was only a loosely connected confederacy of twelve independent tribes,[2] living in widely separated parts of the hill country, and out of communication with one another. The author of the

---

[1]For the role of the Judges, see Bernhard W. Anderson, *Understanding the Old Testament*, pp. 105-106 (1957).

[2]For further description of this loose type "Tribal Confederacy," see Bernhard W. Anderson, *Understanding the Old Testament*, pp. 92-121 (1957); John Bright, *The Kingdom of God*, pp. 31-32 (1953); William Foxwell Albright, *Archaeology and the Religion of Israel*, pp. 95-110 (1942).

book of Judges says of them, "Every man did what was right in his own eyes." There was no strong central government and no strong national leader like Moses or Joshua to unify the people in religion and against their enemies.

The Hebrew fathers who made up the early Hebrew Canon of Scripture placed the book of Judges as second in the new division which they called "The Former Prophets." The book of Joshua, as the reader will recall, was the first book in the new division.

In what sense were these Judges "Prophets?" And what concept of Hebrew history is the writer making use of in the book of Judges?[3]

2. Authorship, Date, and Composition of the Book

The date of the historical incidents and episodes related in the book of Judges, as we have seen, is the three hundred years or so immediately following the historical narratives contained in the book of Joshua, or about 1375 b.c. to 1075 b.c. The date of the composition of the book, however, is somewhat later, as a few internal references in the book itself will show.

In 18:31, the sentence, "So they set up Micah's graven image which he made, as long as the house of God was at Shiloh," suggests a time later than the removal of the Ark from Shiloh, which was in the early days of the prophet Samuel.

Also, in 17:6, the statement, "In those days there was no king in Israel; every man did what was right in his own eyes," implies that the writer lived at the time when there *was* a king, that is, after the beginning of the monarchy under Saul or David.

The writer's remark in 18:30 implies an even later date: "And his sons were priests to the tribe of the Danites until the day of the captivity of the land," which evidently refers to the Northern Kingdom, and probably to the first captivity and deportation of large numbers of the population by the Assyrian king, Tiglath-Pileser III, in 734 b.c.

Many scholars are of the opinion that the books of Judges, I and II Samuel, and I and II Kings, were probably written by the prophets from the eleventh to the eighth centuries b.c., chief of whom was the prophet Samuel.

The Hebrews had an ancient legend which said, "Where there is no vision, the people perish." There was little vision in the period of the Judges. The author of the book of Judges, however, while presenting a realistic picture of the low level to which leadership had fallen, yet is at pains to show that the light of true religion did not go out. With this view the author of the New Testament book of Hebrews agrees. For he names four of their leaders who were prophets

---

[3]See F. F. Bruce, "Author's Approach to History," *The New Bible Commentary*, p. 237 (1954); Edward J. Young, *An Introduction to the Old Testament*, pp. 167-169 (1958). See the author's discussion, p. 114.

as well as Judges, Gideon and Barak and Samson and Jephthah; men who were worthy to be included in his roll call of heroes, "who through *faith* conquered kingdoms, enforced justice, received promises, stopped the mouths of lions, quenched raging fire, escaped the edge of the sword, won strength out of weakness, became mighty in war, put foreign armies to flight" (Hebrews 11).

3. THE CONTENTS OF THE BOOK OF JUDGES

The book of Judges contains the story of Israel and Israel's leadership during the three hundred years or so, from the death of Joshua to the death of Samson, the last of the "Judges."

The material of the book falls naturally into three main divisions, as follows:

(1) The Meaning of the Past, Chapters 1 to 2:10a;
(2) The History of the Judges, Chapters 2:10b to 16;
(3) Two Added Stories — The Danites and the Benjaminites, Chapters 17 to 21.

A. *The Meaning of the Past*

The first one and a half chapters of the book are devoted to a brief review of the conquest of Palestine by Joshua, indicating what had been accomplished and also what remained to be done.

This review covers briefly part of the material in the book of Joshua, but from a somewhat different viewpoint. It serves as a general introduction to the main body of the book of Judges, which is contained in chapters 2:10b to 16.

B. *The History of the Judges*

At the outset, we should remind ourselves that in the book of Judges, as in all the historical books of the Old Testament, we have religious history and not secular history. That is, the record here, instead of presenting a comprehensive history of Israel's *total* life, selects those incidents and events from their religious and moral experience which illuminate the lessons of history. In short, the writer's story is told from the viewpoint of a preacher or a prophet.

1. OTHNIEL. The first of the Judges was Othniel, Caleb's younger brother. He was a native of the tribe of Judah and lived in the extreme south. He delivered Israel from the bondage of the king of Mesopotamia, Cushan-rishathaim, the invader and oppressor from the north, after Israel had paid tribute to him eight years. And there was peace in the land for "forty years."

2. EHUD. After Othniel, the next Judge was Ehud, a Benjaminite; and although he was left-handed, he was skilled with the sword. In fact, he made his own two-edged sword, which he girded on his right thigh, under his clothes.

Formerly Eglon, the king of Moab, had defeated and humiliated Judah and that part of Israel and required it to pay tribute.

When the time came, Ehud and his men were selected to go to Moab to deliver the tribute. The king of Moab was a very fat man. After his men had delivered the tribute, Ehud, as he had planned it, found himself alone with the king. As Ehud prepared to deliver "the message of God," he cunningly touched his sword and sank it completely into the protruding abdomen of the fat king, and thus opened the way for the armed men of Israel to destroy the Moabites.

Also, his reputation spread far and wide beyond the borders of Moab, so much so that he delivered Israel also from other powerful desert fighters on the east side of the Jordan, the Amalekites and Amorites, as well as the Moabites. And because of Ehud's victories, Israel enjoyed peace for eighty years, or until his death.

3. SHAMGAR. After Ehud, the next Judge was Shamgar, about whom little is recorded. Shamgar was something of an early Samson, in his giant stature and physical might.

For a long time, because of fear of the Philistines, travelers avoided the highways and crept along by-paths. Shamgar, single-handed, and with only an oxgoad, slew six hundred Philistines and cleared the highways of robbers and oppressors, and saved Israel until the days of the prophetess Deborah.

4. DEBORAH. The capable Deborah, the fourth and one of the best known of the Judges, was a Prophetess as well as a Judge.

She lived in the hill country of Ephraim, between the cities of Ramah and Bethel. Her "office" was a famous palm tree named for herself, called "The Palm of Deborah," under which she sat as the people of Israel came to her for judgment.

Deborah was diplomatic. Instead of commanding Barak her general to take his army and engage in battle with the mighty Sisera, commander of the Canaanite army, she merely "asked" Barak if the Lord had not commanded him to go!

She had a sense of humor, too, for when Barak refused to go up against Sisera in battle unless she went along with him, her reply was:

> I will surely go with you; nevertheless, the road on which you are going will not lead to *your* glory, for the Lord will sell Sisera into the hand of a woman.

Sisera and his army and chariots of iron were routed, overcome, and Sisera himself fled from his chariot on foot. He found refuge, as he thought, in the tent of Jael, the wife of Heber. But he overestimated the friendship of the Kenites, with whom the Canaanites were supposed to be at peace. Exhausted from long hours in battle, Sisera threw himself down on the floor of the tent to sleep. Jael, seeing his helplessness, killed him by driving a tent peg through his head.

This victory was the beginning of the end, the end of twenty years of oppression by the northern Canaanites and their King Jabin, one of Israel's greatest enemies. After the death of Sisera his general, Jabin continued the war, but he was finally destroyed.

Then Deborah composed a victorious song, which she and Barak sang to celebrate Israel's glorious victory (chapter 5).

Readers of all ages have regarded it as a masterpiece, and its style typical of the best in Hebrew poetry. One critic calls it, "The lyric outburst is one of the finest in any language." It should be read aloud, with due regard to its parallelism and cadence, as all Hebrew poetry is to be read.

5. GIDEON. In the days of Gideon, the Midianites and their allies, the Amalekites, were fierce, wild tribes from the edge of the desert, on the east side of the Jordan. They swarmed into the land of Israel in such numbers and with such power, for seven years, that the Israelites hid in caves and buried their grain, and feared for their lives and their future. The people cried to the Lord, because of the Midianites, and the Lord sent them a deliverer, Gideon.

Gideon was of the tribe of Manasseh, and was rated as prophet as well as Judge. While Gideon was threshing wheat in his father's wine press, to hide it from the Midianite plunderers, the Angel of Jehovah called him to deliver his people.

Gideon's father was a worshiper of Baal, and that very night Gideon threw down his father's altar to Baal and built an altar to Jehovah. Jehovah put it into the heart of Gideon's father not to resist, but to let Baal contend for himself. Yet Gideon hesitated until his call should be confirmed. Finally, in order to have Gideon depend on Jehovah for victory, and not on a large army, his fighting force was reduced to a select three hundred.

With this little band of three hundred, and faith in Jehovah as his Commander, Gideon made a night attack on the Midianite camp, in the Valley of Jezreel. The Midianites were surprised, and by means of Gideon's strategy of the torches and empty jars, they were thrown into confusion, fought each other and fled.

The men of Israel wished to make Gideon their king:

Rule over us, you and your son and grandson also; for you have delivered us out of the hand of Midian.

But Gideon would not hear them:

I will not rule over you, and my son will not rule over you; the Lord will rule over you.

More and more, however, the people felt that they should have a king to rule over them. This request was renewed from time to time, as we shall see in the book of I Samuel, and Saul became their first king.

6. TOLA. Little is known of the sixth Judge, Tola. He was a man of the tribe of Issachar, who lived in the hill country of Ephraim. He judged Israel twenty-three years, after which he died and was buried at Shamir, on Mount Ephraim.

7. JAIR. Judge Jair was a Gileadite, who dwelt on the east side of the Jordan. Our historian says of him that he judged Israel twenty-

two years, and adds: "He had thirty sons who rode on thirty asses; and they had thirty cities, called Havoth-Jair." To own an ass for riding purposes was an indication of distinction in the community. The word Havoth-Jair means tent-villages of Jair and indicates that each of the thirty sons of Jair was a prince over his own tent-village. Both Tola and Jair were "minor judges," and their duties very likely were confined to inter-tribal matters.

8. JEPHTHAH. Once more the people of Israel turned to idolatry. Of them the author says:

> And the people again did what was evil in the sight of the Lord, and served the Baals and the Ashtaroth, the gods of Syria, the gods of Sidon, the gods of Moab, the gods of the Ammonites, and the gods of the Philistines; and they forsook the Lord, and did not serve him.

Jephthah was a native of Mizpah, on the east side of the Jordan, in the territory occupied by the half-tribe of Manasseh.

Because he was an illegitimate son, Jephthah's brothers threw him out of the family. He became the leader of a band of "rough-riders," until the Ammonites made war against Israel. Then the Elders of Israel went to Jephthah with this proposal:

> Come and be our leader, that we may fight with the Ammonites . . . and be our head over the inhabitants of Gilead.

Jephthah was realistic in his reply:

> Did you not hate me, and drive me out of my father's house? Why have you come to me now when you are in trouble?
> . . . If you bring me home again to fight with the Ammonites, and the Lord gives them over to me, I will be your head.

And the Elders of Israel agreed. To secure the Lord's help and victory for his people against the treacherous Ammonites, Jephthah made a vow to the Lord, which involved the tragic sacrifice of his daughter. Although he destroyed the Ammonites, the price of victory brought him very low, for she was his only child. This development no doubt explains why he was Judge of Israel for only six years.

The next three are called "minor judges," because no important exploits are recorded about them, and because of them little is known.

9. IBZAN. Ibzan, a native of Bethlehem of the tribe of Zebulun (Joshua 19:15), judged Israel for seven years. And our author adds, "He had thirty sons; and thirty daughters he gave in marriage outside his clan, and thirty daughters he brought in from outside for his sons."

10. ELON. Elon was a Zebulunite who judged Israel for ten years and was buried at Aijalon in Zebulun.

11. ABDON. Abdon was a native of the tribe of Ephraim, who judged Israel or a portion of it for eight years. "He had forty sons and thirty grandsons, who rode on seventy asses." In the days when the Hebrews did not yet have horses or camels, as we have seen, to own an ass for riding purposes was a sign of rank and distinction.

12. SAMSON. Samson was a native of the tribe of Dan and was

born at Zorah near the Philistine border. He was known chiefly for his super-human strength and was the twelfth and last of the Judges of Israel, and perhaps the best known of all of them.

The writer of the book of Judges took five chapters to tell Samson's story, whereas he used only three to tell the remarkable story of Gideon, the next longest in the book.

An angel appeared to Samson's mother and said that the boy would be a Nazarite from birth, which meant that he should be dedicated to the Lord, and in this case to be Israel's deliverer from the Philistines, perhaps the strongest of the seven enemy tribes in possession of the land at the time Joshua invaded Canaan.

The Philistines were a strong, non-Semitic race of people who lived in southwest Palestine, along the Mediterranean coast, in five famous walled cities — Gaza, Ashkelon, and Ashdod, all on the Mediterranean coast; and Ekron, about six miles inland, and Gath among the hills of the lowlands.

The Philistines probably came from the island of Crete and belonged to the Minoan or early Greek civilization of Crete. From their name, *Philistine,* the little Hebrew nation took its name, *Palestine.*

Each Judge of Israel, it appears, was divinely appointed for a specific task. Samson's was to rid Israel of the dreaded Philistines. The reader will remember that Shamgar, one of the earlier Judges, in a one-man foray slew six hundred Philistines and cleared the highways of robbers and oppressors. But Shamgar left the task unfinished. And so Samson had the assignment of going up against the strongest of Israel's enemies.

But instead of organizing the fighting men of the tribes of Dan and Judah for the war against the Philistines, Samson went alone. All of his exploits among the Philistines seem to have been on a personal basis. At the outset, in the words of the writer, "The Spirit of the Lord began to stir him in Mahaneh-Dan, between Zorah and Eshtaol." What that means we do not know, although it suggests that special power and strength entered Samson.

In his next sentence, the author states that Samson went down to Timnah, a few miles from his home and across the Philistine border. At Timnah he saw and fell in love with one of the daughters of the Philistines. He wanted her for his wife and came home and asked his parents to arrange for the wedding, as was the custom. But his parents demurred, suggesting that he find a wife among his own kinsmen. However, Samson insisted, and they went with him to Timnah.

When they arrived, Samson soon discovered that the girl, the girl's parents and thirty of their countrymen, had "framed" him. Before the wedding feast was over, Samson knew that he had been outsmarted, lost his temper and went home to Zorah.

After a while, Samson returned with a present, thinking to patch up matters with the girl. But on arrival, he learned that the girl had married another man! Samson would have revenge. He went home and secured help and caught three hundred foxes, tied them together in pairs by the tails, with a burning torch between, and turned them loose in the ripened grain of the Philistines.

Samson again returned home; but the Philistines followed him and forced Samson's countrymen to bind him with strong cords, so that he could be delivered to his enemies. But when the Philistines came shouting for their prisoner, he burst the bands from his arms, and with a jawbone of an ass slew one thousand of them.

Samson made another sally into the territory of the Philistines. He went down to Gaza. Here Samson's daring in love almost got him into trouble again. But he became wary of a suspected trap, and walked away from the girl's house at midnight, carrying with him the locked gates his enemies had thrown around to capture him.

"After this," continues our Hebrew writer, "he loved a woman in the Valley of Sorek, whose name was Delilah." Samson's home, Zorah, was in this same valley. Delilah played the role of treachery, and lured Samson step by step to his final downfall. The complete story is told in chapter 16.

C. *Two Added Stories — The Danites and the Benjaminites,* Chapters 17 to 21

In chapters 17 to 21, the writer records two additional stories which have little or no connection with the plan of the book of Judges as a whole. In a modern book, these narratives probably would be placed in an appendix.

The first of these stories deals with the tribe of the Danites and their migration to the far north, including the story of how they robbed a certain Ephraimite, Micah.

The other narrative is the story of the unspeakable crime at Gibeah, in the tribe of Benjamin; and how the other tribes of Israel almost wiped out the tribe of Benjamin in their war of vengeance against it (chapters 19 to 21).

Chapter 10

RUTH

1. THE BOOK OF RUTH AND THE PERIOD OF THE JUDGES

Here we have an example of the Biblical short story, a masterpiece which has been called one of the world's great short stories. It is simple, natural, complete, and so true to the life according to the customs of the day, that the reader would not willingly change any part of it.

Ordinary short stories, as they appear in our magazines, we think of as *fiction*. However, here is a true story, as delightfully presented as the best of fiction.

The events recorded in the story occurred in the days of the Judges, as the author announces to the reader at the outset. And from the context of the story, we infer that the writer lived after the events of his narrative, or about the time of David or a little later.

All the translators, including the Septuagint Greek translation of the Hebrew Old Testament, the *Vulgate Version* of Saint Jerome, and the later versions in English, place the book of Ruth in between the books of Judges and I Samuel, as belonging to the same historical period.

Someone has said that the story of Ruth reads like the calm after a storm. After reading the book of Judges and its sordid stories of crime and bloodshed, of lawlessness and savage revenge, the reader once more is happy to come across such a lovely story of life as the common people no doubt really lived it.

The story of Ruth therefore supplements the book of Judges, by giving the reader a picture of domestic life such as he does not find in the other book, and thus tends to soften his judgment of the historical period of the Judges.

2. THE CONTENTS AND PURPOSE OF THE BOOK OF RUTH

In the days of the Judges, because of famine, a certain man of Bethlehem in Judea, Elimelech, went to live in the country of Moab, he and his wife Naomi, and their two sons.

While they were there, the two sons married two daughters of Moab, whose names were Ruth and Orpah. Time dealt harshly with Naomi, and her two daughters-in-law, for the three men died and left them widows.

So when Naomi learned that the famine in her own country was no more, she blessed her daughters-in-law and made ready to return to her own people at Bethlehem. Both young women wept. And Orpah kissed her mother-in-law and departed. But Ruth clung to her, because she loved her, and would not leave her. So Ruth returned with Naomi to Bethlehem.

How Ruth found a new husband in the substantial person of Boaz, Naomi's kinsman, and became the great-grandmother of David, is related in the remainder of the book. And it is for Ruth that the author has written and named his story.

At the close of his story, in verses 4:17-22, the writer puts his finger on the heart of the matter behind the story, and the reason no doubt for which the book of Ruth was written, namely, to reveal the genealogy of the Messiah.

Ages ago, Abraham had been called to found a Nation for the purpose one day of bringing a Saviour to mankind. Moses knew about God's plan and prophesied that "the Lord your God will raise up for you a Prophet like me . . . Him you shall heed." The author of the book of Ruth describes the founding of the family within the Hebrew nation from which the Saviour would come.

From here on, every true Israelite knew that the Messiah was to spring from the family or house of King David. And, too, throughout the remainder of the Old Testament, the writers again and again remind the reader of the "Branch" of David which should be the promised One.

The writer of the Gospel of Matthew follows the tradition stated here in the book of Ruth, that is, the line of Joseph (1:1-17). Luke's account, on the contrary, differs from the genealogy of Ruth and Matthew, in that it gives the line of Mary, instead of the line of Joseph (Luke 3:23-38). Evidently Matthew traces the royal line of David, and Jesus as the legal heir of David. Luke seems to be tracing the human ancestry of Jesus, showing that Jesus was "of the seed of David according to the flesh" (Romans 1:3).

THE BOOKS OF THE KINGS AND KINGDOMS

Chapter 11

I AND II SAMUEL

1. THE BOOKS OF I AND II SAMUEL

The Biblical narratives of I and II Samuel, like the stories of I and II Kings, have long been favorites with readers in every land. For here we have a stirring account of a people in their struggle and rise to greatness, and told in the classic Hebrew manner according to the best traditions of the Old Testament.[1]

In the original Hebrew text, the two books of I and II Samuel appeared as one book. Also, the historian Josephus, in his enumeration of the books of the Old Testament, listed it as one book. The famous Greek translators of the Hebrew Old Testament, in their *Septuagint Version* about 270-150 B.C., were the first to divide the book into two, which they called "Books of the Kingdoms," because the books contained the history of the first two kings of Israel — Saul and David.

The eminent Bible scholar and translator, Saint Jerome, in his Latin *Vulgate Version* (390-405 A.D.), also followed the division of the book introduced by the Greek translators, but altered the title to read, "Books of the Kings."

In 1516-1517 A.D., Daniel Bomberg printed a Hebrew Bible at Venice in which he retained the division into two books, but for the first time used the new title, first and second "Books of Samuel." Since Bomberg's time most Hebrew Bibles have followed this arrangement, as have the English versions, although some English Bibles have a sub-title, the first and second "Books of the Kings."

There is much justification for the use of the title Samuel for these books. For one thing, Samuel was the leading person during the first half of the historical period covered. And he was one of the greatest of the prophets of Israel, of any period. He presided over the change and transition of the nation from the period of judgeship to that of the kingship. And he was organizer of the kingdom. Indeed, in a later time he would have been called "a maker of kings."

---

[1]The author's account of David's reign, and Solomon's, II Samuel, Chapters 9 to 20, and I Kings, Chapters 1 to 11, have usually been regarded as examples of the finest historical writing in the ancient world. See J. R. Dummelow, *A Commentary on the Holy Bible*, p. 178b (Third Edition, 1936); Bernhard W. Anderson, *Understanding the Old Testament*, p. 124 (1957).

He was God's agent in the selection of both Saul and David for the throne. He was personal sponsor of King Saul as long as Saul remained faithful to his vows and office as king, as the "anointed" of the Lord. And when Saul was rejected by the Lord, Samuel anointed David in his stead. And long after Samuel's death, his influence over Saul and David lived on.

In the Hebrew canon, the book of Samuel, like the book of Joshua and the book of Judges, is placed in the general division of the Hebrew Scriptures called "Former Prophets."

2. The Authorship and Date of I and II Samuel

As we have seen, the fact that the book bears Samuel's name is no proof that he wrote it. He may have written part of it; that part before chapter 25 of the book of I Samuel (chapter 25 records his death). And he may have written the book of Judges. Certainly it appears that Samuel was head of the school of prophets, some of whom were writers who kept books of "Chronicles."

For example, the authors of I and II Samuel and I and II Kings did not record the authors of the sources of their historical materials; but the writers of I and II Chronicles, whose writings cover much of the same period, did give the authors as well as their sources. In I Chronicles 29:29, we read:

> Now the acts of King David, from first to last are written in the Chronicles of Samuel the seer, and in the Chronicles of Nathan the prophet, and in the Chronicles of Gad the seer.

Here we have direct testimony that Samuel and his two important successors, the prophets Nathan and Gad, each wrote Chronicles of the period. Samuel lived until near the end of Saul's reign, which included also much of David's life; and Nathan and Gad outlived David.

Thus, we may assume that Samuel, Nathan, and Gad, either as direct authors wrote the book of Samuel themselves, or at least, that they left detailed records in the form of Chronicles, from which others compiled and composed the books of I and II Samuel.

The exact date of the composition of the book is unknown. However, inasmuch as II Samuel 5:5 gives the total length of David's reign, the date of the author's composition must have come after the death of David.

Also the passage, "Ziklag has belonged to the kings of Judah to this day," reveals the period of the Divided Kingdom, and a date not earlier than that of Rehoboam, Solomon's son and successor.

Since there are no later internal references in the context, or other internal evidence to the contrary, we may assume that the work was written shortly after the death of Solomon, and during the reign of his son Rehoboam, king of Judah.

3. THE CONTENTS OF I AND II SAMUEL

The contents of I and II Samuel deal mainly with the historical stories of the three chief men of the period: The prophet Samuel, King Saul, and King David; and the organization of the Kingdom from the Twelve Tribes of Israel.[2]

The approximate overall dates of the period are from about 1100 B.C. to 974 B.C.

The contents of the book thus may be grouped according to the three leading men of the period, as follows:

A. The Prophet Samuel, I Samuel, Chapters 1-24;
B. King Saul, I Samuel, Chapters 9-31;
C. King David, II Samuel, Chapters 1-24.

A. THE PROPHET SAMUEL

Samuel was born of a pious family of Levites, Elkanah and Hannah his wife, who faithfully attended each year Jehovah's sanctuary at Shiloh, where Eli the old high priest and his two sons were in charge. They were Ephraimites of the hill country.

Hannah, who was childless, poured out her soul to God that He might give her a son, whom she vowed to dedicate to the Lord, from childhood ever afterward. Samuel was born about 1100 or 1090 B.C., and as soon as he was weaned, she took him to the tabernacle at Shiloh and placed him under the charge of the high priest Eli, to train for his sacred duties. "And the boy ministered to the Lord, in the presence of Eli the priest."

The Hebrews regarded the prophet Samuel as one of their greatest heroes and national leaders, perhaps second only to Moses.

By the close of the period of the Judges, Israel's fortunes nationally and religiously had sunk to the lowest ebb, and its future seemed hopeless. Indeed, by the end of Eli's judgeship the country was about ready to be taken over by the Philistines and the Canaanites; for even God threatened to utterly reject Israel (see I Samuel 4:10-22; Psalm 78:59-64; Jeremiah 26:6).

This was before the days of Samuel as Prophet and Judge. Chapter 7 of I Samuel describes the momentous changes[3] and reforms

---

[2]For portraits and further studies in the lives of Samuel, Saul, David, and Solomon, and the impact each made on the period, see Fleming James, *Personalities of the Old Testament,* Chapters 6, 7, and 8 (1939).

[3]There are two interpretations of the Samuel story, one of which is based upon two supposed sources: one source against the institution of a monarchy, and the other in favor of it. The liberal critics have made much of multiple sources of the book of Samuel, just as they have of the Pentateuch and other portions of the Old Testament. For a brief summary of this view of I Samuel, see Bernhard W. Anderson, *Understanding the Old Testament,* pp. 116-121; and R. H. Pfeiffer, *Introduction to the Old Testament,* pp. 341ff. On the other interpretation of the Samuel story: The best brief, conservative discussion is by Professor A. M. Renwick of the Free Church College of Edinburgh, "I and II Samuel," *The New Bible Commentary,* pp. 262-299, and specifically pp. 293-299 (Revised Edition, 1954). See also Edward J. Young, *An Introduction to the Old Testament,*

brought about by Samuel at the beginning of his leadership. First, he called for a meeting of the leaders of all the tribes of Mizpah, a mountain "watch-tower" some five miles northwest of Jerusalem.

Here the tribes dedicated themselves to the Lord their God, and, forsaking the foreign gods of Baalim and Ashtaroth, prepared to throw off the yoke of the Philistines. This they did, under the leadership of Samuel in the great battle and defeat of the Philistines at Ebenezer. This victory brought peace and independence to Israel for the next twenty years, and gave Samuel time for other reforms for which his leadership is noted.

To make his judgeship more effective, Samuel established a judicial "circuit" on which he went year after year, with headquarters at Ramah, his birthplace and home, six miles north of Jerusalem. From Ramah he went to Bethel, and from Bethel to Gilgal near Jericho, and from Gilgal to Mizpah, and doubtless to other towns not mentioned in the narrative (I Samuel 7:15-17).

At Ramah, Samuel was well established during his long life, and here he administered justice as the last and greatest of the judges of Israel, as well as prophet. And it was from Ramah, too, that he directed the founding of the monarchy and the anointing of Saul as the first king, although the kingship was the people's idea, and not Samuel's.

At Ramah also it appears that Samuel founded the first of the schools or "bands" of the prophets, which for generations afterward exercised a great influence upon the moral and religious life of the nation (I Samuel 10:5-10; 19:18-20; I Kings 2:1-7; 4:38). Other such schools seemed to have been founded at Bethel, Gilgal, Jericho, and possibly elsewhere. Out of them may have come the prophets who wrote the very historical books of the Old Testament which we are now reading, and who prepared the way for the great books of written prophecy by the prophets in the generations soon to come. And these bands of prophets may have stimulated David and the other great Psalm writers, and the authors of other great books and collections such as Job and Proverbs.

The most famous of the schools was the one at Naioth, a suburb of Samuel's home town, Ramah. It became a community of prophets who gathered about the prophet Samuel as their leader (I Samuel 19:18-20). The word Naioth is sometimes translated as a "house of learning." Saul was directed to go there as a part of his anointing, to receive "the Spirit of God." And later, David went to Naioth in hiding from Saul and his other enemies.

Although the people of Israel, under the thirty years or so of Samuel's leadership, had enjoyed relative peace and security from

pp. 188-190 (1958). For the larger problems of authorship and sources in the Old Testament as propounded by liberal scholars, see James Orr's *Problem of the Old Testament,* and Professor G. T. Manley's *New Bible Handbook,* especially Chapter 4.

the Philistines and Canaanites, yet they were dissatisfied and sent their elders to Samuel with the blunt request, "Give us a king like the other nations to rule over us."

So Samuel went to the Lord with the matter. The fault was not with Samuel; but it was with disobedient Israel, who now as on former occasions had rejected God, and followed in the footsteps of other nations, and worshiped their gods.

But notwithstanding all this, the Lord said to Samuel, "Make them a king. But warn them. It is their choice, and the consequences will be theirs, too."

So the Lord sent Saul to Samuel to be anointed as Israel's first king.

B. KING SAUL[4]

Evidently God's purpose up to this time was for Israel to be governed by a *theocracy,* that is, by direct rule of God by Himself, but under the leadership of prophets such as Moses and Joshua, and more recently, Samuel. But human nature as revealed in the people and their elders was perverse and disobedient, and so they demanded a king. This was the immediate occasion for the institution of a king. Of course, in God's plan the kingship would be established to foreshadow the Messianic kingdom.

By following their own national pride, as influenced by other nations, they had failed in God's plan. The question now was, would they do any better under an earthly *monarchy* than they had done under the theocracy? Would the purpose of the Messianic Kingdom be served under the kingship of the young man Saul?

Saul was a native of Gibeah, a town near Samuel's home at Ramah. He was of the tribe of Benjamin. As a man, Saul was a political unknown. His occupation was that of herdsman for his father Kish. His commanding physique no doubt influenced his choice, he being "taller than any of the people from his shoulders up." His giant size would likely inspire confidence and a unified following among the tribes, so necessary in saving Israel from the Philistines.

Saul began his reign with a series of brilliant victories against the Ammonites, Moab, Edom, and the Philistines, and other enemies of Israel . . . "wherever he turned he put them to the worse" (I Samuel 14:47-48). Saul, however, forgetting his dedication and Samuel's solemn words on the occasion of the anointing, allowed his successes to get the better of him. In his pride and vanity, he gave himself, and not the Lord, credit for the defeat of his enemies.

1. Saul's first great sin was on the occasion of the battle with the Philistines at Michmash. He wished to sacrifice to the Lord before the battle, and so he presumed to act as priest and to conduct the

---

[4]For the political background of the reigns of Saul and David, see Bernhard W. Anderson, *Understanding the Old Testament,* pp. 122-143 (1957).

sacrifice himself, in the absence of Samuel. Samuel appeared and rebuked the king for his disobedience, and for transgressing God's command (chapter 13).

2. Saul made another mistake when he gave the rash command to the army to abstain from eating food until he was avenged of his enemies. In consequence, he passed sentence of death upon his famous son Jonathan, who was absent fighting the enemy when the command was given. The people were quick to see how foolishly the king had acted and kept him from putting Jonathan to death (chapter 14).

3. Saul's greatest sin, however, was in his deliberate disobedience of the Lord in the battle against the Amalekites. He was commanded to destroy the enemy and all his cattle in battle. Instead, Saul spared the enemy king, and kept back all the best of the livestock for himself and his army, and then falsified his report as to what had actually taken place in battle.

Then the prophet Samuel, as spokesman for the Lord, delivered these words of impeachment to King Saul:

> Has the Lord as great delight in burnt
> offerings and sacrifices
> As in obeying the voice of the Lord?
> Behold, to obey is better than sacrifice,
> And to hearken than the fat of rams . . .
> Because you have rejected the word of the Lord,
> He has rejected you from being king.

The break between Saul and Samuel was final. For Samuel went to Ramah his home, and Saul to his house at Gibeah. And Samuel did not see Saul again until the day of his death. But Samuel grieved over Saul . . . "And the Lord repented that he had made Saul king over Israel."

Although the story of Saul continues to the end of I Samuel, from the beginning of chapter 16 on, the interest centers in David.

C. KING DAVID

Chapter 16 tells the unusual story of how David was chosen and anointed secretly to be Saul's successor and king of Israel.

David was the eighth and youngest of the sons of Jesse, a native of Bethlehem in Judah. The reader will recall the book of Ruth, and how Ruth married Boaz of Bethlehem and became the great grandmother of David. A thousand years hence, Jesus, a descendant of David, would also be born at Bethlehem.

When we first meet David, he is already noted for his skill as a shepherd boy and as a musician with the harp. Although he was not tall and handsome like his oldest brother Eleah, David "was ruddy and had beautiful eyes," the Hebrew word says "fair of eyes."

Indeed, he had a *pleasing* personality, as the story reveals, and made friends easily. He was of blond complexion, and perhaps red-headed, an oddity in the East where almost every one is dark-skinned. He certainly was not tall, for he is contrasted with his tall, oldest brother: "Do not look on his appearance or on the height of his stature . . . For the Lord sees not as man sees; man looks on the outward appearance, but the Lord looks on the heart" (16:7).

So David was anointed secretly, for Saul was revengeful and would kill David if he learned what had happened that day.

The Hebrew language symbolizes the transfer of kingship from Saul to David, thus:

> The Spirit of the Lord came mightily upon David from that day forward . . . Now the Spirit of the Lord departed from Saul, and an evil spirit from the Lord tormented him.

Actually, when Saul saw that his kingdom was gradually slipping from him, he was often seized with fits of melancholy and despair, bordering on insanity. At such times David, who was now in Saul's service, would be called in to play for the king and make him well again. Robert Browning's poem, "Saul," dramatizes this relationship between Saul and David, with a Christian interpretation.

David had another opportunity to demonstrate his service to Saul, and to show his courage and valor. The hated Philistines had invaded Israel again. They met Saul's army, some fifteen miles southwest of Jerusalem, in the valley of Elah. Instead of having the two armies fight, the giant Goliath came forward as the champion for the Philistines. He challenged the Israelites to send forth their champion, he himself bragging and taunting the people of Israel.

The practice of letting a single champion on each side settle the issue was common in ancient times. Matthew Arnold gives an interesting example of the custom in his famous poem, "Sohrab and Rustum," with its setting in old Persia.

When Saul and the people heard these words of the Philistine champion, they were dismayed and greatly afraid of Goliath, a member of the all-but-extinct Anakim race of giants, who was about nine and one-half feet tall, and who wore a coat of mail weighing 157 pounds!

David, who had come to visit his three oldest brothers on the battlefield, and to bring them food, arrived just in time to hear the insulting words of Goliath, and his challenge for the fortieth time in so many days. There was no one in all Israel to take up the challenge.

David's astonishing reply to the Philistine champion was, "Who is this uncircumcised Philistine, that he should defy the armies of the living God?"

Saul sent for David, and David convinced the king that his exploits with the bear and the lion, while he kept his father's flocks, made him equal to this fight with the Philistine, who dared insult Israel's God.

Now follows a piece of pure comedy. Saul undertakes to saddle his own giant-size armor on the short David, as protection in the fight against Goliath. The sleeves were much too long for David's short arms, and the breeches of the mail scraped the ground, and made it impossible for David to bring one foot before the other. Then, to top it all off, David girded his sword over his sagging armor; but to no purpose, for he confessed to Saul, "I cannot *go* with these!"

Then David wiggled out of his heavy war gear, quickly picked up his familiar staff and sling and five smooth stones from the brook, and put them into his shepherd's bag. And with his sling in his hand, he drew near to the Philistine.

Everyone knows the outcome of the contest, as told in chapters seventeen and eighteen of I Samuel. At once David became the hero of the nation, although he would claim no credit for himself. It was the Lord's doing, he would say. "I come to you in the name of the Lord of hosts, the God of the armies of Israel," he had said to Goliath . . . "That all the earth may know that there is a God in Israel."

The consequences of the day were far-reaching. It was not only a day of defeat for the Philistines, it also marked a turning point in the personal relations between Saul and David.

Saul's jealousy of David was aroused. As they were returning home from the slaying of the Philistines, the women came out of all the cities of Israel, "singing and dancing, to meet King Saul, with timbrels, with songs of joy, and with instruments of music." But it was their theme song which touched Saul's vanity, and made him angry, for they sang over and over again to one another,

SAUL HAS SLAIN HIS THOUSANDS,
AND DAVID HIS TEN THOUSANDS!

This song remained in the memory of Saul as long as he lived and stirred his determination to get rid of his rival to the kingship. He would say to himself,

They have ascribed to David ten thousands, and to me they have ascribed thousands; and what more can he have but the kingdom?

And so Saul eyed David from that day on, and sought to kill him on every occasion. He knew that his own popularity was decreasing, while David's was increasing, and that in the end David would have the kingdom. Indeed, he soon threw off all disguise and openly sought to slay David, by whatever means — sometimes with his own sword, at other times with the aid of spies and murderous bands, and even with an army of three thousand men.

David was hunted throughout the land, from one hill to another, from one cave to another, in the wilderness, in the Negeb. Saul was like a hunter pursuing a predatory animal. But David was too smart for his enemies.

David had many loyal friends in his struggle with Saul. For on the day on which he slew the Philistine champion, David won the abiding friendship and love of Jonathan, Saul's famous son, and from that day on the two men were as one. Jonathan was on David's side as against his father, and tried all his days to dissuade Saul from his murderous plot to kill David. And then, when he could not prevail with Saul, he entered into a covenant with David to protect him, by informing him of all Saul's secret movements.

The prophet Samuel was another faithful friend who served David when he most needed a friend. Samuel lived his last days in his beloved home at Ramah, and in Naioth, where the school of the prophets lived in a community.

To elude Saul, David would visit his old friend Samuel at Ramah, and the two of them would go in retreat among the prophets of Naioth. This was the Lord's place, and all who entered were filled with the Spirit and made to prophesy. This worked well for David until Saul's spies found out his hiding place.

David, on two different occasions, had an opportunity to slay his mortal enemy, Saul; but in each case he had mercy on Saul, leaving his punishment to the Lord. One was in the wilderness of Engedi, in the cave of the Wild-goats' Rocks (chapter 24), and the other was in the wilderness of Ziph, in Saul's tent while Saul slept (chapter 26).

For Saul, the final day of reckoning came at the decisive battle of Mount Gilboa. When he saw the mighty army of the Philistines, he was afraid and sought the advice of the Lord. When the Lord did not answer, Saul went to inquire of the Medium of Endor.

The Medium called up the spirit of Samuel, who warned Saul, "The Lord has torn the kingdom out of your hand, and given it to your neighbor, David."

On hearing these words, Saul filled with fear, fell full length upon the ground. It was with difficulty that his servants persuaded him to eat, before he left to go on his way back to the approaching battle.

The last chapter of I Samuel closes with the story of the downfall and death of Saul, the defeat and slaughter of the army of Israel, and the death of Jonathan and the other two sons of Saul.

The first chapter of II Samuel opens with David as king in his own right.

He was not present at the battle of Mount Gilboa, at which Israel suffered such an inglorious defeat. But he was at Ziklag, a desert city on the edge of the Negeb and now in the hands of the Philistines, where David had gone a year or so before to escape from Saul and his pursuing agents.

1. DAVID'S DAYS OF MOURNING. When the news of Israel's disaster, and the death of Saul and Jonathan came to David at Ziklag, he mourned their death as a personal loss and as a national calamity.

He expressed his grief in the writing of a beautiful and touching elegy, which begins with these well known words,

> Thy glory, O Israel, is slain upon thy high places!
> How are the mighty fallen! (II Samuel 1:19-27).

In his grief, David made no distinction between the loss of Saul and that of Jonathan, his faithful friend. After all, Saul in his lifetime had won many battles for Israel against her enemies. Also, Saul was the Lord's anointed. This same love of truth, and God's righteousness, had led David to spare Saul's life on two separate occasions when he could have destroyed his chief enemy. Indeed, few men have been so generous to their mortal enemies as was David to Saul.

These sentiments David thought should belong to the Hebrew race, and so he recommended that this "Lamentation over Saul and Jonathan" should be taught to the people of Judah (II Samuel 1:18). The writer of this historical narrative reveals his source for the elegy as the *Book of Jashar,* which apparently was a collection of national ballads dealing with the exploits of Hebrew heroes (see also Joshua 10:12, 13).

2. DAVID PROCLAIMED KING OF JUDAH AT HEBRON, about 1014 B.C. After seeking God's guidance, David left Ziklag and came to Hebron, where his own tribe anointed him king over the house of Judah.

Thus, the defeat and death of Saul had entirely changed David's relation to the people of Israel and their future. But Saul's followers were yet alive and had to be reckoned with, before David would be king of all Israel. These included Abner, Saul's army commander, and Saul's son Ish-bo'sheth, who continued tribal warfare for more than seven years.

3. DAVID MADE KING OVER ALL ISRAEL, AND MOVES HIS CAPITAL TO JERUSALEM, about 1007 B.C. Abner and Ish-bo'sheth quarreled, and Abner came over to David and drew up a covenant, whereby Abner agreed to bring all Israel over to David's side.

However, in the battles and intrigues that followed, first Abner, and then Prince Ish-bo'sheth, were slain, and both without the knowledge of David, and to his great dismay and sorrow. Then all the elders of the house of Saul, seeing that the last strong arm of their house had fallen, came to David at Hebron. So all the tribes of Israel in a national assembly at Hebron made David King, thus fulfilling the words of the Lord to David,

> You shall be shepherd of my people Israel,
> And you shall be prince over Israel.

But David did not yet have control of all the land, for the Jebusites had held possession of the stronghold of Jerusalem since before the days of Joshua. So David and his men went up against the Jebusites and took their stronghold, and fortified it as the City of David, although it did not yet include the city of Jerusalem.

When the Philistines, who held the Israelites vassals since the defeat of Saul in the battle of Mount Gilboa, heard that David had been anointed king, they went up to search for him. But David retreated within his fortifications. After seeking God's guidance as was his custom, he came out and defeated the Philistines in two separate engagements, and from this time henceforth became master of both the stronghold of Zion and the city of Jerusalem.

Jerusalem Becomes the Hebrew Capital

The capture of Jerusalem marked a most important event in the history of Israel. Before the capture, the nation had no real center or capital. At best the residence of a Judge or a Prophet or a King was only a temporary meeting place, such as the Palm Tree of Deborah, the home of Samuel at Ramah, or the house of Saul at Gibeah, or the military headquarters of David at Hebron.

From this time on, however, the national center was fixed at Jerusalem. All other cities grew less and less important, while the new capital increased in prestige and national importance throughout the generations.[5]

4. David's Partnership With God. David's religious heritage was unique in that God promised that his family should become an Eternal Throne, and that he should enjoy his immortality in his own lifetime. He was informed of this promise through the prophet Nathan, who came to David with these words from the Lord:

> When your days are fulfilled and you lie down with your fathers, I will raise up your son after you, who shall come forth from your body, and I will establish his kingdom . . .
> And your house and your kingdom shall be made sure for ever before me; your throne shall be established for ever.
> (II Samuel 7:12-16)

With evident humility, David made this reply to Nathan, the Lord's messenger and spokesman:

> Who am I, O Lord God, and what is my house, that thou hast brought me thus far? Thou hast spoken also of thy servant's house for a great while to come, and hast shown me future generations, O Lord God! And what more can David say to thee?

A long line of prophets repeated this promise to David and looked toward the coming of the Messiah as its fulfillment (see Psalms 89:3-4, 27-29, 34-37; 132:11-18; I Chronicles 22:8-10; Amos 9:11-12; Isaiah 9:6-7; 11:1-10; Micah 5:2-4; Jeremiah 22:2-4; 23:5-6; 33:14-18; Zechariah 3:8-9; 6:12-13; 9:9-10; 12:7-10; 13:1. See also Luke 1:30-33).

David had a deep sense of partnership with God. One of his first public acts was to take an army of men and go to Baal-judah, where the Ark of God had been in Abinadab's house for almost eighty

---

[5]For this complete story, see J. J. Simon, *Jerusalem in the Old Testament.* (E. J. Brill, 1952.)

years, and bring it to Jerusalem and place it in the Tabernacle which David made for it at Jerusalem.

David himself became the religious head of the nation, appointing and supervising the priests. He also wrote many of the early religious lyrics and Psalms for the Tabernacle worship. It is estimated by conservative scholars that David, in one form or another, was the author of almost half of the one hundred and fifty Psalms in the Old Testament collection.

David built for himself the handsome King's House; but he was not happy about it, because the Ark of God rested in a tent. He went to the prophet Nathan with his plan to build the Temple, but was never permitted to build it. However, he did amass largely the necessary materials for the building of the house, including vast quantities of silver and gold (II Samuel 7; I Chronicles 22; 28:11 to 29:9). This material was placed at the disposal of his son Solomon, who began the work in the fourth year of his reign.

5. DAVID EXTENDS HIS KINGDOM. But David still had much unfinished work to do, before Israel's enemies were all driven from the land, and his kingdom securely established at Jerusalem.

After the death of Joshua, and during the period of the Judges, the Philistines, the Amalekites, and other aggressive tribes from without had invaded Israel from every quarter, until the Israelites were almost a people without a country. At times, Saul had made considerable headway. At other times, as at Mount Gilboa, he was disastrously defeated. David was destined to drive out his enemies, north, south, east, and west. His marvelous military victories against enemy nations are briefly summarized in chapters 8 to 10, and David is shown as their overlord to whom they paid tribute.

First, he subdued the Philistines, on the west; then he turned east and defeated Moab and Edom and the Ammonites, and the trouble making Amalekites. And, finally, he began to extend his kingdom in the north as far as the Euphrates River, subduing the Syrians and their allies. In short, all the enemy nations between Egypt and the Euphrates. The writer sums up David's overwhelming military successes in this short sentence: "And the Lord gave victory to David wherever he went" (II Samuel 8:6).

6. DAVID'S PRIVATE LIFE, AND TROUBLES. Chapters 11 to 20 of II Samuel present episodes dealing mainly with the private and domestic life of King David.

The first of these is the ugly and criminal story of David and Bathsheba. Someone has said that this story proves that the writer was a great historian. For the observing reader has already noticed that David is the author's hero; and that Saul's history, for instance, is presented not so much for Saul's sake, as for an introduction to David's, the central personage of I and II Samuel. But the author's integrity and devotion to truth compels him to reveal the total story of David, the good and the bad, as other characters in his history.

David repented; and God forgave him. But the grievous consequences followed him all his life, as he lived under God's pronouncement in these words: "The sword shall never depart from thy house." This was only too true, as David lived to see. For in the chapters that follow, we read the story of how David's daughter Tamar was outraged by her brother Ammon, who in turn was murdered by their brother Absalom.

Next, we have the full-length story of Absalom's rebellion and conspiracy to overthrow his father David, David's temporary exile from his capital at Jerusalem, and the death of his son Absalom in the father-and-son struggle for the kingship. While David was in exile from the palace, his wives were violated in public by his enemies.

Finally, the rebellion of Absalom had stirred up the old feud between the followers of Saul in the north, and the followers of David in Judah. So Sheba, a Benjaminite, taking advantage of the jealousy of the men of Israel, that is, the former ten tribes of Saul, began a rebellion of his own, by blowing his horn and summoning the ten tribes to renounce their allegiance to David. However, Sheba's conspiracy against David was short-lived and soon rejected by the leaders of his own people. On the advice of a "Wise Woman," whose name is not given, Sheba was beheaded, his head thrown over the city wall to David's old commander Joab, thus ending the rebellion.

Although his great transgression, and its consequences, took some of the luster from David's glorious reign, he sincerely repented (see Psalms 32, 51) and his later life was such that he was called "the man after God's own heart." Certainly every Hebrew writer after him gave him the highest rating as the man who "did what was right in the eyes of the Lord."

Sometimes we all but forget that David's chief characteristic was his piety. With David, it was not enough to win battles *against* the enemy; battles are to be won *for* the Lord. The reader will recall that his chief criticism of the Philistine champion, Goliath, was that he had "defied the armies of the living God."

7. DAVID AS MUSICIAN AND POET. Bible readers usually think of David as a great soldier, a statesman, and prophet in the sense that he was a devout follower and champion of his God, and a wise leader. But few readers think of David as one of the world's greatest poets and musicians. If he had written nothing else but the Twenty-Third Psalm, this would have earned for him greatness as a poet and the gratitude of all mankind.

As a youth, David was noted for his skill with the harp. After the Ark was brought to Jerusalem and placed in the Tabernacle, it was David who organized and arranged the Psalms of praise, and the musical instruments of sacred song for the sanctuary (I Chronicles 6:31; 16:7, 41, 42, 43; 25:1).

It would not be too much to say that David put Psalm writing on the literary map, just as his son Solomon gave the writing of Proverbs its reputation and vogue. Young David was regarded as "the sweet Psalmist of Israel," as Shakespeare was called "the sweet bard of Avon."

David composed the "Lament over Saul and Jonathan" (II Samuel, chapter 1), the "Song of Deliverance" from all his enemies (II Samuel, chapter 22), and David's "Last Words'" (II Samuel 23:1-7).

To David also is ascribed the authorship of some seventy-three of the one hundred and fifty Psalms of the Old Testament collection.[6] These Psalms are on many subjects and themes. Two large groups of them relate to David's personal experiences with his enemies and reveal his inmost feelings and emotions.

The first of these groups of Psalms grew out of the period of persecution by King Saul and his pursuing agents, and include among others, these: Psalms 7, 11, 12, 13, 17, 18, 25, 35, 40, 52, 54, 56, 57, 59.

The second group evidently were written during the period of his son Absalom's rebellion, and include: Psalms 3, 4, 5, 6, 41, 55, 61, 62, 63, 64.

8. AN APPENDIX. Chapters 21 to 24 contain some extra matters, which in a modern book would be called an Appendix, and are placed here at the end of II Samuel in order not to interrupt the history of David's reign.

These chapters record stories of a famine; some more exploits against the Philistines; the "Song of Deliverance," which was revised and printed as Psalm 18; the "Last Words" of David; a list of thirty of David's chief heroes; and a census of the people of Israel and Judah.

SELECTED READINGS ON THE KINGS AND KINGDOMS

Bible Readings: The Books of I and II Samuel, I and II Kings, and I and II Chronicles.

Text: *The Revised Standard Version;* or *The King James Version,* preferably in the modern reader's format.

*Anderson, Bernhard W.: *Understanding the Old Testament,* pp. 122-153, and 183-356.

*Edersheim, Alfred: *The Temple — Its History and Service.*

*Ellison, H. L.: "I and II Kings," *The New Bible Commentary,* pp. 300-338.

James, Fleming: *Personalities of the Old Testament,* Chapters 6-8.

Napier, B. Davie: *From Faith to Faith,* Chapter 3.

*Renwick, A. M.: "I and II Samuel," *The New Bible Commentary,* pp. 262-299.

[6]See Introduction to the book of Psalms, pp. 211-213.

Scott, R. B. Y.: *The Relevance of the Prophets*, Chapters 3-4.

*Simon, J. J.: *Jerusalem in the Old Testament*.

Welch, Adam C.: *The Work of the Chronicler*.

*Young, Edward J.: *An Introduction to the Old Testament*, pp. 188-214, and 412-427.

For additional readings on Kings and Kingdoms, see the General Bibliography at the end of the book.

Chapter 12

I and II Kings

1. The Books of I and II Kings

The book of I and II Kings is the sequel to I and II Samuel and should be read as a continuation of the historical story of the Hebrew nation contained in the former work.

As we have seen, the narrative of I and II Samuel covers a most important period of Hebrew history — from the birth of the prophet Samuel to the close of the reign of David, or from about 1100 B.C. to about 974 B.C.

The present story of I and II Kings covers the critical period from the death of King David, 974 B.C., to the Captivity and Exile of the Northern Kingdom, in 721 B.C., and the Fall and Exile of Judah or the Southern Kingdom, in 586 B.C.

In this full length historical narrative, as presently contained in the four books of I and II Samuel and I and II Kings, we have the mighty drama of the rise and fall of the Hebrew nation. If we were to cast it in the form of a five-act tragic play, the broad outline of the plot would read something like this:

The story of the prophet Samuel, and the "stage" which he set, would be the First Act. Then, for the "rising action," the conflict between Saul and David would represent the Second Act. The growth and prosperity, or the Golden Age of the nation, during the latter half of the reign of King David and the first half of his son, Solomon's, would represent the "climax" and "crisis" of the historical action, or the Third Act. The period of the Divided Kingdom, beginning with the death of Solomon about 934 B.C., and the rapid decline of the nation, would represent the tragic elements of the "falling action," or Fourth Act. The captivity and exile of both halves of the Divided Kingdom, or the "tragic fall," take place in the Fifth Act of this historical drama.

It took many players — kings and princes and prophets, as well as the people — to play all the parts in such a drama. And it would be a dull eye that did not see that God was the Director of both the stage and the players!

History *does* repeat itself, both with respect to individuals and nations. And God speaks to all the generations through His servants

A shepherd and his flock, illustrative of David's younger life, with Bethlehem in background. © *Matson Photo Service* the prophets, who were chief actors in this play, and some of whom doubtless wrote this history which we read. God also speaks through the history itself, and the lessons it teaches, as interpreted by the prophets. So these histories are as important today as they were the day the events were enacted.

In the original Hebrew text, I and II Kings was presented as *one* book, just as I and II Samuel originally appeared as one book.

The first division into *two* books was made by the famous Greek translators of the Hebrew Old Testament. They regarded the full-length narrative of Samuel and Kings as a complete history of the kingdoms, and thus divided them into four parts which they called "Books of the Kingdoms."

Saint Jerome, the most learned scholar of his day, in his Latin *Vulgate Version* of the Old Testament (390-405 A.D.), followed the division of the book of Kings introduced by the Greek translators, but altered the title to read, "Books of the Kings," as he had done in the book of Samuel. Our English Bibles have retained both the division and the titles.

In the Hebrew canon, the book of Kings follows the book of Samuel, and is placed in the general division of Hebrew Scriptures called "Former Prophets."[1]

2. Authorship and Date of I and II Kings

The author of I and II Kings is unknown. One early Jewish tradition, that of the *Talmud,* states that the prophet Jeremiah wrote the books of Kings. No doubt the appearance of chapters 24 and 25 of II Kings in the book of Jeremiah 39-42 and 52, has led some to conclude that the same writer was author of both the books of Kings and Jeremiah.

Present day scholars, however, are not much inclined to accept Jeremiah's authorship of Kings. Josephus, the Jewish historian of the first century A.D., ascribed the authorship to "the prophets." This is the more likely view, and the one generally held today.

After the days of Samuel, the prophets banded themselves together in communities or schools and became the center of the nation's religious activity and leadership. So that, when the writer of I Chronicles states that three of these prophets wrote Chronicles, Samuel and Nathan and Gad, we may infer that I and II Kings were also written by the prophets. The custom of writing Chronicles was common among the prophets.

Although the author of I and II Kings does not name the writers of the Chronicles, he does name the Chronicles ot the different kings, as follows:

---

[1]See footnote No. 2, p. 114, and references.

"The Book of the Acts of Solomon" (I Kings 11:41);

"The Book of the Chronicles of the Kings of Israel" (I Kings 14: 19; 15:31; 16:5, 14, 27; 22:39; II Kings 1:18);

"The Book of the Chronicles of the Kings of Judah" (I Kings 14:29; 15:7, 23; 22:45; II Kings 8:23; 12:19, etc.).

The other reasons for ascribing to the prophets the authorship of Kings, as well as Samuel, are somewhat evident. In the first place, the reader has observed that these historical narratives are written from the viewpoint of the prophets, and that the interpretation of the events under review are given as the moral and religious lessons of a spokesman of Jehovah.

Everywhere these books are regarded as "prophecies," and therefore are placed in the division of the Hebrew canon of the Old Testament Scriptures called "Former Prophets."

The date of the composition of I and II Kings has been placed more or less precisely between the dates of 560 b.c. and 538 b.c.

For one thing, King Jehoiachin of Judah was deported to Babylon in the year 597 b.c., and in the thirty-seventh year of his exile and imprisonment, on March 27, 560 b.c., he was freed from prison by the Babylonian king Evil-merodach. This event is recorded in the last paragraph of II Kings.

And since no mention is made of the destruction of Babylon in 538 b.c., just twenty-two years later, it is presumed that this important event had not yet taken place when the author wrote the last paragraph of II Kings, which describes the freedom of Jehoiachin.

On the other hand, since it is likely that more than one author took part in the composition, portions of Kings could have been written much earlier than the outside dates given above. That is, the whole period covered by I and II Kings is more than four hundred years, or from about 974 b.c., the approximate date of the death of King David, to approximately 560 b.c., the last event mentioned in II Kings.

3. The Contents of I and II Kings

The books of I and II Kings take up the history of the kings and kingdoms where the books of I and II Samuel leave off and are clearly a sequel to the books of Samuel.

The contents of the books of I and II Kings fall naturally into three main divisions, as follows:

A. The Reign of King Solomon, Chapters 1 to 11 of I Kings;

B. The Divided Kingdom: The Separate Parallel Histories of Judah and Israel, until the Assyrian Captivity and Exile of Israel, Chapters 12 to 22 of I Kings, and Chapters 1 to 17 of II Kings;

C. The Divided Kingdom: The History of Judah, until the Babylonian Capture and Exile, Chapters 18 to 25 of II Kings.

A. *The Reign of King Solomon*[2]

(1) SOLOMON CHOSEN AS DAVID'S SUCCESSOR

At the outset, there was some question as to which of David's sons would be his successor. The handsome and older Absalom was already dead as a direct result of the rebellion he led against his father. Adonijah, the next oldest living son, and a handsome man like his brother Absalom, was ambitious to succeed his royal father David. He formed a plot and had the old army commander Joab, and Abiathar the priest, on his side.

But Nathan the prophet, and Zadok the priest, and David's "thirty mighty men," were not on the side of Adonijah, but with Solomon. So Nathan went to Solomon's mother Bathsheba and counseled her to go to the king's chamber, where the aged king lay on his bed, and prevail with him to keep his promise to make Solomon king after him.

And it was done as Nathan had planned. For David called in Nathan the prophet and Zadok the priest, and Solomon was anointed king, in a ceremony that took place at Gihon. Solomon rode David's mule as a sign of kingship.

(2) DAVID'S LEGACY TO HIS SON SOLOMON

The legacy that David left to his son Solomon was very great. When David came to the throne he found the tribes of Israel disorganized, over-run by powerful enemies from without, and threatened with destruction. Within a single generation of forty years he drove Israel's enemies from the land and developed the tribes of Israel into a strong nation.

He transferred the leadership of the nation from the house of Saul and the tribe of Benjamin, to Judah, and established the royal house of David.

He established Jerusalem as the Holy City and as the religious center and national capital for all Jews.

He stamped out idolatry, practically speaking, and made the worship of Jehovah universal in the land.

He made conquests of many nations, who paid tribute to Israel and its king. He extended the borders of the country to Egypt on the south, and to the River Euphrates on the north and east, including far more territory than at any other time in the nation's history.

Although an oriental monarch, with a sizable harem, David's foreign marriages were largely political, and relatively free from religious and moral corruption.

David was a poet and musician, who endeared himself to the people as the "sweet Psalmist of Israel."

David planned the Temple, which was to exalt the religious life

---

[2]For special studies on "Solomon in all his glory," see Anderson's *Understanding the Old Testament*, pp. 143-153 (1957); Fleming James, *Personalities of the Old Testament* (1939).

of the nation and the worship of Jehovah, although he was not permitted to build the Lord's house.

Although there was still rivalry of a sort between the Ten Tribes of the North, and Judah, and had been ever since the death of Saul and his son, even so David had no serious difficulty in uniting all tribes under his rule, and about the national capital at Jerusalem.

At the time of David's death, the nation was second to none in power and military prowess, and the people had a large measure of peace and freedom, as every man "sat under his own vine and fig tree."

(3) Solomon's Choices

At the beginning of his reign, Solomon made certain major choices which suggest the keynote of his forty years' rule.

(a) The first of these choices was to make a marriage alliance with Pharaoh, king of Egypt, and to bring to his court Pharaoh's daughter as his wife, thus showing that his real confidence lay in political alliances, rather than in the God of his father David.

This foreign marriage was the beginning of the collection of a harem of foreign wives, the like of which no other king or potentate ever assembled in one royal palace. The writer of Chapter Eleven of I Kings describes the disastrous effects this harem had on Solomon's religion and Solomon's reign.

(b) Solomon's second choice was religious compromise. The prophet Samuel, and Solomon's father David, had gone far toward eliminating idolatry, although the people lived near the remnants of the Canaanite tribes and the influence of their foreign gods.

Originally, the numerous so-called "high places" in the land were sanctuaries of the Canaanites, as their name implies. They were elevated platforms on which were placed the objects of heathen worship, such as the small figures and images of the mother-goddess, Asherah, or the male nature god, Baal. Samuel and David had succeeded in converting these high places largely into shrines for Jehovah worship, although many of them were still in the hands of the Canaanites and followed the worship pattern of the Canaanites.

Soon after his informal anointing at Jerusalem, by riding on David's mule to and from the anointing shelter of Gihon, Solomon set his heart on an elaborate ceremonial inauguration at the historic, semi-Canaanite sanctuary at Gibeon, five miles or so out of town northwest from Jerusalem.

Why did Solomon go to the "high place" at Gibeon for this inaugural ceremony, instead of having it at Jerusalem, in the Tabernacle of God, to which his father David had brought the Ark of God, and in which the national worship was now centered? The question has often been asked.

The prophet or the disciple of a prophet who wrote I Kings 3:3-4 gives this explanation of Solomon's religion:

> Solomon loved the Lord, walking in the statutes of David his father; *only*, he sacrificed and burnt incense at the High Places. And the king went to Gibeon to sacrifice there, for that was the great high place; Solomon used to offer a thousand burnt offerings upon that altar.

The word "only" in the writer's sentence indicates the kind of compromise, in the opinion of the prophets, with which Solomon began his administration. Later, to please his foreign wives, Solomon erected altars to their heathen gods, and even worshiped with his wives before these shrines! (I Kings 11:4-10).[3]

Was it true as it appears, that Solomon like many other Israelites, was interpreting Jehovah in Canaanite terms, and was looking upon Him as the *chief* of the gods, the God of Israel, and not as the *only* God?

(c) Solomon's third choice was Wisdom. While at Gibeon, during his inaugural rituals, Solomon had a dream. In the dream, the Lord appeared to Solomon and asked what it was the Lord could give him.

In great humility, Solomon made a speech, recalling the goodness of God to his father David, and to him, David's son, and closed with this request:

> Give thy servant therefore an understanding mind to govern thy people, that I may discern between good and evil; for who is able to govern this thy great people?

What did Solomon mean by asking Jehovah for an "understanding mind" and Wisdom to govern his people? And what was it that gave Solomon the reputation, for nearly thirty centuries, for being the wisest man who ever lived?

In the first place, Solomon had a brilliant mind. And the best educational facilities of the day were available to him, as well as the advantages and contacts of a stirring court life.

Also, Solomon was the son of a famous father. David's kingdom was the most powerful and most influential in the world of his day. His achievements introduced the Golden Age of Hebrew history, which the first twenty years of Solomon's reign brought to a dramatic climax. When Solomon came to the throne, Israel was at peace with all the world, and had large revenues for carrying out great projects.

Solomon was brought up as a child of the court. And in the atmosphere of the court, he developed a taste for luxury and grandeur. He early set his heart on building according to the grand manner. Solomon's first building project was the building of the great Temple, which his father David had planned. Although he built shrines to foreign gods and worshiped before them with his wives, Jehovah was

---

[3]Bernhard W. Anderson, *Understanding the Old Testament*, pp. 152-153.

the chief God and the God of Israel, and so the Temple would exalt Him above every other god.

Also, Solomon had the wisdom to seek the best builder of the age, Hiram, king of Tyre, and thousands of his skilled workmen, regardless of cost, to carry out his building schemes.

He spent seven years building the Temple, which was of the finest stone and cedar, and finished with rare adornments. The cedar of the interior was overlaid with gold. It was built in the midst of a series of inner and outer courts, with specially named gates and doors to each.

When completed, the Temple was the finest, most handsome, as well as the most expensive, piece of architecture in the world of Solomon's day. It was the constant wonder of all who saw it.[4]

Within the outer wall surrounding the Temple area, and near by, Solomon built his royal palace, also according to the grand manner. It required thirteen years to build.

The royal palace was a group of separate halls, connected by porches and rows of cedar pillars. There was the House of the Forest of Lebanon, so-called because it was built of the choicest cedar from Mount Lebanon; the Hall of Pillars, because of the enormous porch with pillars in front, and the canopy; the Hall of the Throne, or Hall of Judgment as it was sometimes called, where Solomon sat and pronounced judgment. It was finished in choicest cedar from floor to rafters. Next, was the King's House, where he was to dwell, and of like workmanship as the Throne. And, finally, Solomon made a house alike and to match his own living quarters, for Pharaoh's daughter whom he had taken in marriage.

This completed the handsome group of buildings within the outer court or wall, and all specially decorated and inwrought with the choicest metals, and by Hiram's master metal worker, whose name was also Hiram.

Although the Temple, and the Royal Palace group of buildings, were by far the most impressive that Solomon built, and were the ones that brought him world fame, yet his building enterprises had only begun.

Solomon built the Millo, a bastion at Jerusalem, and the great Wall of Jerusalem, against the invasion of a possible enemy. His father David built the main fort of Jerusalem, called the City of David, within which he lived and kept his men at arms while the other fortifications, and the Wall around greater Jerusalem, were under construction. Solomon completed the Wall, closing the gap around the

[4]For references on Solomon's Temple, see William Foster Albright, *Archaeology and the Religion of Israel*, 2nd ed., pp. 142-155 (1946); G. Ernest Wright, "Solomon's Temple Resurrected," *The Biblical Archaeologist*, Vol. IV, pp. 17-31 (1941); Anderson, *Understanding the Old Testament*, pp. 146-147 (1957). The Temple as an institution: Alfred Edersheim, *The Temple — Its Ministry and Service*. New Edition (1950).

fort or City of David. Portions of the city of Jerusalem were also built under Solomon.

Also, Solomon undertook to build and to fortify many of the leading cities of his kingdom. These included Hazor, Megiddo, Beth-horon, Baalath, Tamar, and many others. Moreover, all the store-cities of Solomon were fortified, as were the cities for his chariots, and the forty thousand stalls of horses for his chariots. And then he rebuilt Gezer, which Pharaoh took from the Philistines, and which he gave to Solomon as a marriage dowry to go with his daughter.

While these building projects were under way, Solomon commissioned Hiram, king of Tyre, to build him a fleet of ships. These ships were to ply their trade in two different directions. One went East by way of the Red Sea, to Ophir, and returned loaded with gold, silver, ivory, apes, and peacocks.

The other fleet went West, to Tarshish, probably in south Spain, and would bring back silver beaten into plates, and iron, tin, and lead. This is the same Tarshish to which the prophet Jonah started, on his famous detour from the Assyrian capital of Nineveh, some two hundred years later.

These are some of the main building and commercial enterprises which Solomon undertook during his reign. They are the fruits of wisdom. For only a wise king, and an "understanding" leader, can do so much for his people and country.

(4) SOLOMON'S LITERARY ACHIEVEMENTS

Much of Solomon's reputation for Wisdom is associated with his literary achievements. The writer of I Kings (4:32-34) catalogues these achievements briefly, as follows:

> He uttered three thousand Proverbs; and his Songs were a thousand and five. He spoke of trees, from the cedar that is in Lebanon to the hyssop that grows out of the wall; he spoke also of beasts, and of birds, and of reptiles, and of fish. And men came from all peoples to hear the Wisdom of Solomon, and from all the kings of the earth, who had heard of his Wisdom.

This quotation refers to three types of literary work: Proverbs, Songs, and Nature or natural history.

Unfortunately, most of Solomon's literary work has not come down to us. Present-day opinion ascribes to Solomon the writing of approximately half of the Proverbs in the book of Proverbs in the Old Testament collection.[5] Thus, most of the three thousand Proverbs mentioned in the quotation have perished with time, as have the one thousand and five Songs.

There was a tradition that Solomon wrote the book of the Song of Songs. Most Biblical scholars now, however, do not favor his authorship. On the other hand, Solomon as it appears is merely one of the

---

[5]See Young, *An Introduction to the Old Testament*, pp. 328-332 (1958); Anderson, *Understanding the Old Testament*, pp. 473ff (1957).

two chief characters of the story; and the most we can say is that the title could mean either that the Song of Songs was written *by* Solomon, or that it is *about* Solomon.

Solomon's name has been associated also with the writing of the book of Ecclesiastes. But it is unlikely that Solomon wrote it. Here again, as in the case of the book of the Song of Songs, the book appears to be *about* Solomon, and not *by* Solomon. For, on closer examination, it appears that the author does not really claim to be Solomon but places his words in Solomon's mouth. He is impersonating Solomon, as he imagines Solomon would view life in his later days of disappointment.

(5) SOLOMON'S REPUTATION FOR WISDOM

Much of Solomon's reputation for wisdom appears to have come from his conversations and oral sayings, much of which were recorded by the men of his Court.

He was a master talker, who was familiar with the wisdom of the ages, for he was highly educated for his time. His visitors and audiences were captivated with his learning. The passage quoted above (I Kings 4:32-34) closes with a reference to his talks on nature and natural history, of beasts and birds, of reptiles and fish, and how "men came from all peoples to hear the wisdom of Solomon."

It is not likely that Solomon here is speaking as a scientist, but as a moralist. The Proverbs of Solomon (see Proverbs, chapters 10 to 22:16, and chapters 25 to 29), his favorite literary form, were set down primarily for their moral value; and Solomon's reference to nature in the passage quoted would be for the purpose of pointing a moral, as was the custom among the ancients. For example, the Proverb: "Go to the ant, O sluggard; consider her ways, and be wise" (Proverbs 6:6).

Thus, Solomon was noted for his verbal wisdom — for his wise *sayings*. Our historian says that he "spoke" three thousand proverbs; and that he "spoke" of trees, and beasts, and birds, and reptiles. And that all people came to "hear" the wisdom of Solomon.

Indeed, all sorts and conditions of people — travelers, merchants, wise men, monarchs — all came to see Solomon, and to hear his wisdom, and to be dazzled with the greatest show of wisdom and magnificence on earth.

Solomon had achieved grandeur and renown as no one else had, and these traveling visitors were the patrons of his greatness, and the carriers of his reputation to distant lands. Thus, as we moderns would say, Solomon was fortunate in having good "publicity agents," who like the Queen of Sheba, told of his wisdom, and the wonders of his court, wherever they went.

And one of these publicity agents of Solomon was the prophet who wrote the book of Kings we are now reading. Listen to his words:

> Judah and Israel were as many as the sand by the sea; they ate and
> drank and were happy. Solomon ruled over all the kingdoms from
> the Euphrates to the land of the Philistines and to the border of
> Egypt; they brought tribute and served Solomon all the days of his
> life . . .
> And Judah and Israel dwelt in safety, from Dan even to Beer-Sheba,
> every man under his vine and under his fig tree, all the days of
> Solomon . . .

And he continues,

> And God gave Solomon wisdom and understanding beyond meas-
> ure, and largeness of mind like the sand of the seashore, so that
> Solomon's wisdom surpassed the wisdom of all the people of the
> East, and all the wisdom of Egypt.

Also, the priest who wrote the book of Chronicles joined in the
chorus of Solomon's praise (see II Chronicles, chapters 1 to 9).

(6) SOLOMON'S TROUBLES AND DETERIORATION

Solomon's glorious achievement reached its highest point near
the middle of his reign. Then the fatal consequences of the excesses
and evils of his rule began to appear, so that his brilliant reign ended
under a cloud.

The same prophet who wrote the books of Kings, and who had
praised so highly Solomon's wisdom and understanding and greatness
as revealed in the first twenty years of his reign, also wrote that
terrible eleventh chapter of I Kings, in which he summarizes briefly
Solomon's defection from the faith of Jehovah, in his last twenty years.

Listen to these introductory words to the chapter,

> Now King Solomon loved many foreign women: The daughter of
> Pharaoh, and Moabite, Ammonite, Edomite, Sidonian, and Hittite
> women, from the nations concerning which the Lord had said to the
> people of Israel, "You shall not enter into marriage with them,
> neither shall they with you, for surely they will turn away your
> heart after their gods." Solomon clung to these in love. He had
> seven hundred wives, princesses, and three hundred concubines;
> and his wives turned away his heart.

There were other factors also which marked the beginning of the
end of Solomon's kingdom. In his expansive conquests, Solomon's
father David had included Syria and its old capital city of Damascus,
and at the time of David's death, Syria was paying tribute to Israel.

But Solomon, while being pre-occupied with his building and
commercial enterprises, had allowed Rezon, a bandit leader of Syria,
to recapture Damascus. This was a serious blow to Solomon, since
Damascus also was on the main trade route to the North and East.

Also, Solomon, to complete payment for his enormous building
projects, had given to Hiram, king of Tyre, *twenty cities* in the district
of Galilee. Hiram had furnished Solomon with choicest cedar and
cypress and gold, with ornamental metal, and thousands of skilled
workers and artisans, for many years, for which Hiram had not been
paid.

And to make bad matters worse, when Hiram investigated the cities, they did not please him, and he said: "What kind of cities are these which you have given me, my brother?"

Moreover, Solomon had allowed the gap between the Ten Tribes of the north, and Judah, to widen greatly during his reign. Under his father David, after the death of Saul and the death of Saul's son and heir, Ish-bo'sheth, the Ten Tribes came over, voluntarily, and united with David as their king

But Solomon, by over-taxing the people, by using forced labor on a grand scale, and by spending the money and labor largely on the capital at Jerusalem and the Court, and related enterprises, had alienated the Ten Tribes of the north. So the stage was set for the division of the kingdom, upon Solomon's death.

Indeed, the stage was more than set; for action had already begun. Jeroboam, the son of Nebat, an Ephraimite by birth, under the inspiration of Ahijah the prophet, had formed a plot against Solomon, who in turn sought to kill Jeroboam. So Jeroboam fled to Egypt as a political exile, to await Solomon's death. Formerly he had been in the service of Solomon, as engineer and in charge of all the "forced labor" of the house of Joseph.

CHRONOLOGY OF THE KINGS OF THE DIVIDED KINGDOM

KINGS OF ISRAEL		KINGS OF JUDAH	
JEROBOAM I	934-913 B.C.	REHOBOAM	934-917 B.C.
NADAB	913-912	ABIJAH	917-915
BAASHA	912-889	ASA	914-874
ELAH	889-887	JEHOSHAPHAT	875-852
ZIMRI	887 (7 days)	JEHORAM	852-845
OMRI	887-875	AHAZIAH	845
AHAB	875-854	ATHALIAH	845-839
AHAZIAH	855-854	JEHOASH*	845-805
JEHORAM	854-843	AMAZIAH	805-777
JEHU	843-816	UZZIAH*	791-740
JEHOAHAZ*	820-804	JOTHAM	751-736
JOASH	804-789	AHAZ*	741-726
JEROBOAM II	789-749	HEZEKIAH	726-697
ZECHARIAH	748	MANASSEH	697-642
SHALLUM	748 (30 days)	AMON	642-640
MENAHEM	748-738	JOSIAH	639-608
PEKAHIAH	738-736	JEHOAHAZ	608
PEKAH	748-730	JEHOIAKIM	608-597
HOSHEA	730-721	JEHOIACHIN	597
		ZEDEKIAH	597-586

(Assyrian Captivity, 721 B.C.)   (Babylonian Captivity, 586 B.C.)

*Apparent discrepancies in dates of kingships are usually accounted for by overlapping reigns where an incapacitated father would be assisted by the heir apparent, his son, or parts of years counted as whole years, or in periods of anarchy when there was no lawful king.

Chapter 13

I AND II KINGS (Continued)

B. *The Divided Kingdom: The Separate Parallel Histories of Judah and Israel, Until the Captivity of Israel in 721 B.C.*

1. SOLOMON'S KINGDOM DIVIDED[1]

The deterioration which took place during the last twenty years of Solomon's reign, as we have seen, led to a division of the kingdom after his death.

Solomon's son Rehoboam was his lawful successor.[2] Upon the death of Solomon, therefore (about 934 B.C.), representatives of the Twelve Tribes assembled at the central city of Shechem to make Rehoboam king. He met with them. But a certain coldness existed between Judah and the tribes of the north, who still called themselves "Israel." During his building campaigns, Solomon had over-taxed them, and had exacted heavy tolls in "forced labor." Now they had an opportunity to seek relief from these burdens and demanded a promise of relief from Rehoboam.

In their claims, Israel had a strong leader in the person of Jeroboam, who was still an exile in Egypt. When he heard of the death of Solomon, and what his rival Rehoboam was up to, he came hurriedly from Egypt and conferred with the leaders of Israel. So, when Rehoboam announced his determination to increase the burdens of the people, and not lessen them, they revolted and returned to their own "tents," and chose Jeroboam as their leader and king (I Kings 12).

2. JEROBOAM'S REIGN AND RELIGIOUS POLICY. About 934-913 B.C.[3]
I Kings 11:26 to 14; II Chronicles 10:12 to 13.

The first thing Jeroboam did, after the people made him king of their new kingdom, "Israel," was to build and fortify Shechem in the hill country of Ephraim as his capital.

---

[1]For an analysis of the political and religious backgrounds of the Divided Kingdom, including the role of the prophets, see Anderson, *Understanding the Old Testament*, Chapters 7 and 8, pp. 183-251; Professor H. L. Ellison of the London Bible College, "The Religion of Israel under the Monarchy," "Political Alliances," and "The Great Empires During the Period of the Monarchy," *The New Bible Commentary*, pp. 333-338 (1954).

[2]See Old Testament Chronology, p. 86, and the Chronology of the Kings of the Divided Kingdom, p. 155.

[3]See James Hastings, *The Dictionary of the Bible*, Vol. I, p. 399, for a discussion of the problem of chronology in dating the reigns of Hebrew kings.

But this did not satisfy the main need of the people, which was a place to worship. In the reign of Solomon, large numbers had gone to Jerusalem to the feast days three times a year, and had worshiped in the Temple which Solomon built. So Jeroboam raised this question,

> If this people go up to offer sacrifices in the House of the Lord at Jerusalem, then the heart of this people will turn again to their Lord, to Rehoboam king of Judah, and they will kill me and return to Rehoboam king of Judah.

So Jeroboam built sanctuaries and substitute places of worship, so that the people no longer would need to go to Jerusalem to worship. He made two Golden Calves, after the manner of what he had seen in Egypt, and set one up at Bethel on the southern border of his territory, and the other at Dan in the north. Then he said to the people:

> You have gone up to Jerusalem long enough. Behold your gods, O Israel, who brought you up out of the land of Egypt.

Henceforth calf worship became the state religion of the Ten Tribes of Israel, as Jehovah worship had become identified with Judah and the family of David, although Solomon did not live up to the ideal set by his father David. In addition to the two main centers of worship, Jeroboam established numerous "high places" throughout his kingdom, many of which were the same sanctuaries used originally by the Canaanites for the worship of their false divinities.

Several evil consequences followed Jeroboam's religious policy. In the first place, although it seems that Jeroboam's plan was to worship Jehovah under the image of the calf, the average Israelite soon did not make that distinction, and adopted the golden calf as his god.

So, in defiance of the first and second of the Ten Commandments, which forbade the worship of other gods, or the adoration of the true God by means of images or idols, Jeroboam was guilty of the great sin of rooting calf worship in the hearts of the people of the Northern Kingdom. Indeed, this system of idolatry was established so firmly in the minds of the people that it was not eradicated until the Captivity and Exile of Israel, some two hundred years later.[4]

Although the masses of the people conformed, the minority, including the priests and Levites whom Jeroboam removed from office, "left their common lands and holdings and came to Judah and Jerusalem . . . to sacrifice to the Lord, the God of their fathers." In their stead, he made priests from among the people.

Jeroboam's evil example is quoted again and again by the writer, by way of explaining the idolatrous practices of the other eighteen kings of the Northern Kingdom who followed Jeroboam, and were

---

[4]Some critical scholars hold a different view, namely, that the author of I Kings, "probably the Judean historian, guilty of anti-northern propaganda," has slanted his story of Jeroboam's religious reorganization. See Bernhard W. Anderson, *Understanding the Old Testament*, p. 195, and the authors cited in his footnote.

influenced by him (see I Kings 15:26, 34; 16:19, 31; 22:52; II Kings 3:3; 10:29; 13:2, 11; 14:24; 15:9, 18, 24, 28; etc.).

3. REHOBOAM, THE FIRST KING OF JUDAH. About 934-917 B.C. I Kings 12 to 14; II Chronicles 10 to 12.

Rehoboam, Solomon's son and lawful heir to the throne after his father's death, was kept from seeking revenge on his rival Jeroboam for leading the revolt of the Ten Tribes of the north. Instead of warring with his kinsmen of Israel, he proceeded to fortify the leading cities of Judah, as well as Jerusalem his capital. Since he was not a strong personality like his father Solomon or his grandfather David, it was fortunate for Rehoboam that the whole body of priests and Levites, whom Jeroboam drove out when he erected the shrines of the golden calves at Bethel and Dan, came over to Judah. For he needed the help and strength they brought to his kingdom. So, for a brief period of three years at least, his kingdom prospered.

However, according to the writers of both Kings and Chronicles, Rehoboam soon lapsed into idolatry (I Kings 14:21-24; II Chronicles 12:1-5). For him retribution was swift and sure. For in the fifth year of his reign, Shishak, king of Egypt, came out of the South and captured the fortified cities of Judah, entered Jerusalem and took away the treasuries of the great Temple of Solomon, and the treasuries of the King's Palace, including the shields of gold and everything of value.[5] All this happened just five years after the death of Solomon.

Rehoboam, although greatly humbled by the Egyptian invasion, continued his evil ways. He came to the throne at the age of forty-one, and reigned for seventeen years at Jerusalem. Thus, Jeroboam for Israel, and Rehoboam for Judah, set an evil pattern for the kings that followed them. The historical narrative from now on therefore is heavy with warnings from the prophets of every reign and generation, with judgment and doom promised, if Israel and Judah persisted in violating the Covenant and the Commandments, especially the first two of the Ten Commandments which they were so prone to violate.

4. ABIJAH, THE SECOND KING OF JUDAH. About 917-915 B.C. I Kings 15:1-8; II Chronicles 13.

After the death of Rehoboam, his son Abijah (also, Abijam) reigned about two years. The writer of Kings finds little that is significant about the rule of Abijah for the purpose of his narrative, and so states briefly that there was war between Abijah and Jeroboam, his rival. However, the author of II Chronicles devotes a whole chapter to Abijah's war with Jeroboam, with details not given in I Kings. The kings of Judah had not yet become reconciled to the fact of the

---

[5]The famous Karnak List of Asiatic countries conquered by Egyptian kings includes Judah under Rehoboam. See Pritchard, *Ancient Near Eastern Texts*, pp. 242-243, 263-264.

revolt of the Ten Tribes. In religion, Abijah followed the evil pattern set by his father.

5. Asa, the Third King of Judah. About 914-874 b.c. I Kings 15: 9-24; II Chronicles 14 to 16.

Sometimes a worthy son is the offspring of an unworthy father. Such is the story of Asa, third king of Judah, and son of Abijah. The reader is disappointed to find such a brief account in I Kings of a rule as important as Asa's reformation, which continued over a period of about forty years. Among Asa's reforms are the following:

First, he removed the idols his father had made and drove the heathen cults out of the land.

Asa also removed his grandmother Maacah from being queen mother at the court, because she had an image made of the Canaanite goddess Ashtoreth, which she had erected in the grove. Asa cut down the large image and burned it.

Asa did not remove the "high places" during his reign, for reasons which he thought were good. As his priests conducted them, Jehovah was worshiped there, and not the false gods, although these places originally were possessed by the Canaanites. The writer justifies Asa, thus: "Nevertheless the heart of Asa was wholly true to the Lord all his days."

Solomon did not remove these high places for reasons less worthy than Asa's. However, it became a spiritual necessity to remove them later, in the reigns of Hezekiah and Josiah, as we shall see.

The writer of the book of II Chronicles devotes three whole chapters to the story of Asa's reign, as compared with the half chapter in I Kings. He stresses the ten peaceful years before the beginning of Asa's foreign wars, and includes incidents not mentioned in Kings, such as the war with Zerah the Ethiopian.

The writer of Chronicles also points out that for a long time Judah was without the true God, without a teaching priesthood, and without law. When Asa heard this message from Azariah the prophet, he was greatly encouraged, and went forward with his reforms and religious sacrifices in the presence of the people, which included also numbers who had deserted and come over from the Northern Kingdom to Judah.

6. Nadab, the Second King of Israel. About 913-912 b.c. I Kings 15:25-32.

The reader has already observed that the writer's method of composition is to present his historical story of the Divided Kingdom by means of *parallel narratives* of the kings of Israel, and the kings of Judah. So at this point, after presenting the reigns of the three kings of Judah, Rehoboam and Abijah and Asa, he returns to the kings of Israel. This method he continues, back and forth, throughout his treatment of the nineteen kings of Israel, and the twenty kings of Judah.

Nadab, son and successor of Jeroboam, ruled less than two years. Of him it could be said, like father like son, for he followed the evil pattern set by his father in the state religion of calf worship, and in other evils which characterized the reign of his notorious father Jeroboam. He began his reign over Israel the second year of King Asa's rule over Judah.

His kingship was cut short by the conspiracy of his chief rival, Baasha, of the tribe of Issachar. While Nadab and the army were engaged in battle against the Philistines at Gibbethon, Baasha plotted Nadab's death and murdered him, and then all his relatives and descendants, and took over the vacant throne. This complete destruction of the house of Jeroboam was understood to be the fulfillment of the judgment of God against the evils of Jeroboam, although Baasha himself came to the throne by means of violence.

7. BAASHA, THE THIRD KING OF ISRAEL. About 912-889 B.C. I Kings 15:33 to 16:7; II Chronicles 16.

Even though Baasha came to his throne at Tirzah by means of violence and bloodshed, he managed to remain in power almost twenty-four years. Formerly established at Shechem, the capital of Israel was removed to Tirzah by Jeroboam in the latter years of his reign, where it remained until King Omri built Samaria. In spite of the frontier fortress he built at Ramah, his kingdom was invaded by Ben-hadad of Syria, who had an alliance with King Asa of Judah.

We are told too little to have a complete picture of Baasha's reign, although the writer does give the outcome of his story. Just as Abijah the prophet interpreted the death of Nadab as judgment upon Jeroboam and the end of his royal house; so Jehu the prophet, another man of God, prophesied the doom and death of Baasha, because he continued the calf worship begun by Jeroboam and his evil influence on Israel.

8. ELAH, THE FOURTH KING OF ISRAEL. About 889-887 B.C. I Kings 16:8-14.

Elah, Baasha's son, ruled part of two years and according to the evil pattern set by his predecessors. One incident in the reign of Elah is noted by the writer, and that the last one. Zimri, one of Elah's commanding charioteers, plotted against Elah. One day while Elah was drinking himself drunk in the house of his steward at his capital Tirzah, Zimri murdered him and took the vacant throne. As soon as he had established himself, Zimri slew all the male descendants of the house of Baasha.

This tragic end was taken as the fulfillment of the prophecy spoken by Jehu. And so ended the second bloody dynasty in twenty-five years, and further weakened Israel in the hands of Syria and Israel's other enemies.

9. ZIMRI, THE FIFTH KING OF ISRAEL. About 887 B.C. (7 days). I Kings 16:15-20.

After the assassination of Elah, Zimri set himself up as king at Tirzah. However, the army proclaimed their commander-in-chief Omri king, at Gibbethon where they were encamped against the Philistines. Omri immediately marched against the capital at Tirzah and seized it. And when Zimri saw that the city was taken, he went into the citadel of the king's house and set fire to the palace and himself perished in the flames. He followed the evil pattern set by Jeroboam; his so-called reign lasted only seven days.

10. OMRI, THE SIXTH KING OF ISRAEL. About 887-875 B.C. I Kings 16:21-28.

At first the people of Israel were divided as to their new king. Half of them, including the army, wanted Omri for king; the other half supported the claims of Tibni, the son of Ginath. It was not until after the death of Tibni, five years later, that Omri became the undisputed king of all Israel.

Omri reigned six years at Tirzah, the capital since Jeroboam took up residence there. Then he bought a piece of land, called the Hill of Shemer, and fortified it, and called the name of the city *Samaria* after the name of Shemer, the owner of the hill. In the seventh year of his reign Omri moved his capital from Tirzah to Samaria.

This is important to remember, because the capital of the Northern Kingdom remained at Samaria until the defeat and captivity of Israel, some one hundred and fifty years later. Also, the people of the region were called *Samaritans*, even until New Testament times and later.

In worldly matters, Omri gained the reputation abroad for being a capable and war-like king, so much so that the Assyrian kings called his kingdom "the land of Omri." As late as 733 B.C., one of them, Tiglath-pileser, still called Israel the land of Omri.[6]

The historian of I Kings says of him: "Omri did what was evil in the sight of the Lord, and did more evil than all who went before him." This was saying a great deal. But Omri's son Ahab was to take the prize for sheer wickedness. For Ahab is universally rated as the worst of the kings, in Judah or Israel, during the long period of the Divided Kingdom.

11. AHAB, THE SEVENTH KING OF ISRAEL. About 875-854 B.C. I Kings 16:29 to 22:40.

The historian who, in a paragraph above, wrote that Ahab's father Omri had done more evil than all who went before him, wrote in this paragraph: "There was none who sold himself to do what was evil in the sight of the Lord like Ahab."

---

[6]See also James B. Pritchard, *Ancient Near Eastern Texts,* pp. 320-321, for Omri's domination of Moab as recorded on the Moabite Stone.

Politically speaking, Omri's reign was quite as important as Ahab's, perhaps more so. But since it is spiritual and not political lessons which our writer wants us to learn, he devotes twenty-six times as much space to the reign of Ahab as he does to Omri's. Ahab's reign was a period of crisis. Jehovah's religion was in jeopardy. And so the whole reign of Ahab and his queen Jezebel are given at full length.

AHAB'S QUEEN JEZEBEL

In the first place, Ahab married Jezebel, daughter of Ethbaal king of Tyre and Sidon, and the most wicked woman in the world of her day. Before he became king, her father was priest of Ashtoreth, goddess of the Phoenicians and Canaanites and wife of the god Baal.

Jezebel was a woman of masculine temperament, determined and unscrupulous. She was fanatically devoted to the worship of Baal; built temples to Baal and Ashtoreth in Samaria, and maintained 450 prophets of Baal and 400 prophets of Ashtoreth, at public expense. She slew the prophets of Jehovah and did her utmost to abolish Jehovah worship. Under the influence of Jezebel, the worship of Baal among the Ten Tribes almost supplanted that of Jehovah. The struggle between the two, as we shall see, culminated in the contest on Mount Carmel when the prophet Elijah met the priests of Baal.[7]

THE PROPHET ELIJAH

God's answer to Ahab and Jezebel was the prophet Elijah, whose mission was to defeat and discredit Baalism, and to re-establish the power and authority of Jehovah in the minds and hearts of the people. Elijah is one of the most dramatic characters in the Old Testament, and one of the greatest of all the prophets. He appeared suddenly out of nowhere, and challenged King Ahab to his face:

As the Lord the God of Israel lives,
before whom I stand,
There shall be neither dew nor rain these years,
except by my word.

We know little of Elijah's past. He is introduced simply as "Elijah the Tishbite, of Tishbe in Gilead," from the east side of the Jordan. "He wore a garment of haircloth," said Ahab's messengers, "and with a girdle of leather about his loins." This humble habit reminds us of another great prophet of later times, John the Baptist.

The dramatic story of how Elijah went into hiding for the space of three years; the contest on Mount Carmel between Elijah and the prophets of Baal and Ashtoreth, and Elijah's triumph over the prophets of Baal; how he fled from the fury of Jezebel to Mount Horeb, three hundred miles south, where he heard "the still small voice" of the

---

[7]For a description of Canaanite religion, see John Bright, *The Kingdom of God*, pp. 52-54; see also W. F. Albright, *Archaeology and the Religion of Israel*, Chapter 3.

Lord and further instructions on ridding the land of Baalism; and, finally, how he should meet his successor, Elisha, upon whose shoulders Elijah's mantle should fall — all this, and more, is related in chapters 17 to 22 of I Kings.

THE PROPHET ELISHA

Elijah departed from Horeb, and after many days' journey, found Elisha at Abel-meholah, in the upper Jordan Valley, the son of a farmer and a man of means. Elisha was plowing in his father's field, with twelve yoke of oxen before him, his yoke the twelfth.

The meeting of the old prophet and the young farmer was of the greatest importance. For Elijah had come to anoint Elisha to take his place as prophet of the Northern Kingdom. The interview was brief. Elijah passed by and "cast his mantle upon him." It was an exciting moment for Elisha, for he understood the significance of the act. He was being called to follow the older prophet.

After a farewell dinner with his family and neighbors, Elisha "arose and went after Elijah." The two men started off to anoint two new kings — Hazael to be king over Syria, and Jehu over Israel, as the Lord had directed. Their main task was to eliminate the wicked pair, Ahab and Jezebel, from the kingship and domination of the civic and religious life of Israel.

These were uneasy times, too, for Ahab and Jezebel. Everywhere around their frontiers were unfriendly neighbors, chief of whom was Ben-hadad, king of Syria. Also, Ahab and Jezebel had provoked the Lord one time too many, when they murdered Naboth, and took his fruitful vineyard for their own. For he sent his prophet Elijah to face the king with this warning of impending doom: "In the place where dogs licked up the blood of Naboth, shall dogs lick your own blood." And of Jezebel the Lord said, "The dogs shall eat Jezebel within the bounds of Jezreel." Both prophecies were carried out — Ahab's almost immediately in battle, and Jezebel's a few years later.

12. JEHOSHAPHAT, THE FOURTH KING OF JUDAH. About 876-852 B.C. I Kings 22:41-50; II Chronicles 17 to 20.

Jehoshaphat, like his famous father, King Asa, before him, was a good king. For reasons not immediately clear, the writer of Kings gives only a brief account of the important reign of Jehoshaphat, and so the reader will do well to turn to II Chronicles, chapters 17 to 20, for his complete story.

At the outset, the writer of II Chronicles summarizes briefly Jehoshaphat's religious attitude as king, thus:

> The Lord was with Jehoshaphat, because he walked in the earlier ways of his father; he did not seek the Baals, but sought the God of his father and walked in his commandments.

The most notable thing, and the most original, in Jehoshaphat's twenty-five years' reign, is that in the third year of his rule he inaugurated a system of public instruction in the Book of the Law. He sent out his own princes to teach in the cities of Judah, and with them a commission of Levites and priests. The Book of the Law, their Bible, was their main text.

Jehoshaphat also established courts of justice throughout the land, and appointed judges in all the fortified cities of Judah, city by city, and said to the judges:

> Consider what you do, for you judge not for man, but for the Lord; he is with you in giving judgment . . . Take heed what you do, for there is no perversion of justice with the Lord our God, or partiality, or taking bribes.

He also provided a court of appeals at Jerusalem (II Chronicles 19: 8-10).

He maintained a large army, fortified his main cities, and won the respect of all neighbor nations, who were envious of his peace and prosperity.

13. AHAZIAH, THE EIGHTH KING OF ISRAEL. About 855-854 B.C. I Kings 22:40 to II Kings 1.

After his father Ahab's death, Ahaziah ruled over Israel in Samaria part of two years. He was greatly influenced by his mother Jezebel, and the princes and counselors of the house of Ahab. The writer summarizes briefly this influence:

> He did what was evil in the sight of the Lord, and walked in the way of his father, and in the way of his mother, and the way of Jeroboam the son of Nebat, who made Israel to sin. He served Baal and worshiped him, and provoked the Lord, the God of Israel to anger in every way that his father had done.

The last recorded incident in the life of Ahaziah is characteristic and shows how stubbornly he, like his father Ahab and mother Jezebel, held to the belief in heathen gods. It also shows the great Elijah in his characteristic role, and last public act, as the prophet of God.

One day Ahaziah fell through a lattice in the upper chamber of his palace and was seriously injured. He was afraid for his life and sent messengers to the god Baal-zebub, the god of Ekron, one of the five cities of the Philistines, to inquire whether he would live.

This provoked the Lord, who sent his angel to Elijah and commanded him to say these words to Ahaziah's men:

> Is it because there is no God in Israel that you are going to inquire of Baal-zebub, the god of Ekron? Now therefore thus says the Lord, "You shall not come down from the bed to which you have gone, but you shall surely die."

And with these words of warning, Elijah disappeared.

Angry at Elijah's interference with his messengers, Ahaziah sent a captain with a company of fifty to arrest him. When the captain and his fifty arrived, Elijah was ready for the challenge. Instead of permitting himself to be arrested, as the king ordered, Elijah called fire down from heaven and consumed all of them.

But Ahaziah, like his father Ahab, must learn the hard way. So he sent another captain and fifty men, and these were consumed with fire; and still another company, and these were destroyed. Finally, Elijah in person went to Samaria and delivered the Lord's message to the king, before he would believe that disaster at the hand of the Lord had overtaken him.

This episode, which is the last recorded in the life of Elijah on earth, like the contest on Mount Carmel, was used to demonstrate that the Lord is God, and that the followers of Baal must recognize His supremacy.

14. JEHORAM, THE NINTH KING OF ISRAEL. About 854-843 B.C. II Kings 3 to 9.

Ahaziah left no son to succeed him, so the throne passed over to his younger brother Jehoram (also, Joram), another son of Ahab, who ruled over Israel almost twelve years.

But these were uncertain times. The house of Omri, Ahab and sons was on its last legs, so to speak. Jehu, as we were told in the story of Elijah, was secretly anointed king of Israel with the avowed purpose of wiping out this wicked dynasty, including Jehoram, which had done so much to dishonor the Lord, and to corrupt His worship throughout Israel — and now Judah, since the daughter of Ahab (Athaliah) had married Jehoram king of Judah.

It was a long story, the culminating event of which may be briefly stated as follows. Ever since the days of Ahab, a contest had been on between Israel and Syria for the territory east of the Jordan known as Ramoth-gilead. In a battle there against Hazael king of Syria, Jehoram was wounded. After the battle, he returned to the old city of Jezreel to seek a cure for his wounds.

One day his watchman came in and announced the approach of the fast-riding Jehu. Not being aware of Jehu's secret plans to assassinate him, Jehoram mounted his chariot, having his nephew Ahaziah king of Judah accompanying him in another chariot. Thus, the two men rode forth to meet Jehu. As the parties met on the road by the side of Naboth's Vineyard, where Naboth had been slain by Jezebel's agents, Jehu shot an arrow through Jehoram's heart and killed him instantly. The body was thrown from Jehoram's chariot into the field of Naboth, thus fulfilling Elijah's prophecy.

With the death of Jehoram, the evil dynasty of Omri, the fourth dynasty of Israel since the beginning of the Divided Kingdom, came to an end. But not yet in Judah.

THE PROPHET ELISHA, ONCE MORE

Elisha, after the departure of Elijah about 850 B.C., began his ministry in earnest during the rule of Jehoram (854-843 B.C.) king of Israel, and continued it through the reigns of Jehu and Jehoahaz, dying in the reign of Joash, about 800 B.C. (II Kings 3:1, 11; and 13:14-20).

Elisha's ministry, even more than Elijah's, was noted for the great number of miracles performed. This period, like the age of Moses, represents a time of crisis in the religion of Jehovah, in which miracles were performed to demonstrate, to both Israel and her neighbors, the power and supremacy of the Lord God over all other gods.

These Hebrew prophets did their utmost to save Israel from the evils of gross idolatry, and to bring the Ten Tribes of the north in line with the best traditions of Judah. And they must have had many followers among the people, although their kings and princes were wicked and largely neutralized the good influence of the prophets. However, the eventual disaster and fall of Israel, in 721 B.C., is evidence that the evil day was only postponed. But their dramatic messages still stand as enduring monuments to their immortality.

15. JEHORAM, THE FIFTH KING OF JUDAH. About 852-845 B.C. II Kings 8:16-24; II Chronicles 21.

After Jehoshaphat's death at the age of sixty, his unworthy son Jehoram succeeded him as king of Judah. For a year or two he had already been associated with his father in the government, as the oldest of seven sons. To his other six sons, Jehoshaphat gave great gifts of silver, gold, and other valuable possessions, together with fortified cities in Judah.

King Jehoram, whose name we have already noticed is the same as that of the son of Ahab and king of Israel, had for his wife a daughter of Ahab and Jezebel, who led him into all sorts of wickedness, as Jezebel had seduced Ahab. As soon as he was established on the throne, he slew all six of his brothers with the sword, and many of the princes of Judah.

As a sequel to his murders, Jehoram built in Judah a Temple to Baal, made high places in the hill country of Judah, thus leading the inhabitants of Jerusalem and Judah into unfaithfulness, and preparing for the time when his wicked queen would substitute Baal worship in Judah for the true worship of Jehovah, as had been done previously in Israel.

For this planned, national infidelity, the Lord would destroy the guilty, not Judah and the house of David. In the Providence of God, a letter was prepared by the hand of Elijah, who departed from the earth in the reign of Jehoram's father, Jehoshaphat, pronouncing doom on the king and his brood of vipers:

> Thus says the Lord, the God of David your father, "Because you have not walked in the ways of Jehosaphat your father, or in the ways of Asa King of Judah, but have walked in the ways of the kings of Israel, and have led Judah and the inhabitants of Jerusalem into unfaithfulness, as the house of Ahab led Israel into unfaith-

fulness, and also you have killed your brothers, of your father's house, who were better than yourself; behold, the Lord will bring a great plague on your people, your children, your wives, and all your possessions, and you yourself will have a severe sickness with a disease of your bowels, until your bowels come out because of the disease, day by day."

Finally, after two years of suffering from the disease predicted by the prophet, Jehoram died in great agony, thus ending the eight years of his wicked reign. He was buried without honor from his people. And the historian of II Chronicles says that "he departed with no one's regret."

16. AHAZIAH, THE SIXTH KING OF JUDAH. About 845 B.C. (One year.) II Kings 8:25-29; II Chronicles 22:1-9.

Although Ahaziah, the youngest son of Jehoram, was twenty-two years old when he began his reign, his one year's rule was not his own. For his mother Athaliah, daughter of the infamous Jezebel, was his evil genius and counselor, as were also the princes of the house of Ahab.

This young King Ahaziah of Judah, whose name the reader recognizes as the same as that of Ahaziah, son of Ahab and king of Israel, was murdered by Jehu at the time when he murdered King Jehoram of Israel on the road by Naboth's Vineyard, near Jezreel.

It is difficult for the reader to see the hand of God in these murders by Jehu, although Jehu was anointed and instructed specifically to destroy the wicked house of Ahab. And why was Ahaziah's mother, Athaliah, an evil daughter of an evil mother, Jezebel, allowed to take over the rule of Judah after his death?

17. ATHALIAH, THE SEVENTH RULER OF JUDAH. About 845-839 B.C. II Kings 11; II Chronicles 22 to 23.

Athaliah was the daughter of Jezebel, and like her mother in Israel, she was bent on establishing the most depraved system of heathen worship of the day, Baalism, in Judah. She married Jehoram king of Judah, and induced him to worship Baal during his eight years as king. And then as "Queen Mother," she did the same for her son Ahaziah's brief reign.

When she learned that her son Ahaziah was dead, and that there was no one else old enough to rule the kingdom, she murdered her own small grandchildren to remove all rivals, and usurped the throne herself! She then ruled Judah in her own right six years, making a total of fifteen years in which she controlled religion in Judah.

But hers was not a "perfect crime." For she unknowingly permitted her own daughter, Jehosheba, to outsmart her in the murder plot and to rescue the former king's infant son. And then Jehosheba and her husband, Jehoida the priest, hid the boy in the Temple during the six years of Athaliah's reign, until he could safely be proclaimed king.

So when the boy Joash was seven years old, and when Jehoida had completed plans with the priests, the heads of fathers' houses, and with the army guards at the Temple, for the removal of the hated queen, the boy was brought forth and publicly crowned king.

The queen, hearing all the people shout, came out to discover the plot which Jehoida had secretly engineered. According to the arrangement with the captains of the army guard, she was completely surrounded, so that no one could rescue her. The captains dragged her from the Temple, which she had desecrated and stripped of its sacred vessels and furnishings, to supply her temple of Baal.

It was a dramatic moment. The soldiers were determined to crush the life out of their notorious victim, then and there. But the priests were shouting over the noise of the crowd, "Do not slay her in the house of the Lord!"

So she was taken out to the horse gate of the King's Palace and there slain. And so the curtain fell on the last act of the house of Ahab, in Judah also, as it had already fallen in Israel. Many scholars feel that the book of Joel may have been written about this time, as indicating the great need the nation had to repent after this period of infidelity to the religion of Jehovah.[8]

18. JEHU, THE TENTH KING OF ISRAEL. About 843-816 B.C. II Kings 9-10.

We return now to the kings of Israel and the story of Jehu. There are two important persons of this period by the name of Jehu. One was a prophet, an older man (see II Chronicles 20:34). The other Jehu, the one we have under review here, was the younger man, the impetuous soldier, the fast-and-furious-driving Jehu. He was son of Jehoshaphat king of Judah, and the Jehu whom Elisha anointed for Elijah to be king of Israel, to destroy the house of Ahab and to eradicate Baalism.

We have already seen how Jehu shot and killed Jehoram in his chariot in the road beside Naboth's Vineyard; and how he pursued Jehoram's nephew Ahaziah, king of Judah, and fatally wounded him as he climbed the ridge to Mount Carmel; and finally, how he had Jezebel thrown from her window and killed.

This was a bloody task; but there was even more bloody work ahead of him. For after Jehoram, Ahaziah, and Jezebel, Jehu slew seventy princes of the house of Ahab, probably sons and grandsons, and piled their heads in two heaps at the gate of Jezreel! Next Ahab's great men and his familiar friends were slain, and forty-two of Ahaziah's kinsmen. And then, to climax it all, he slew all the priests of Baal, and all the prophets of Baal!

Finally, by a cunning device, he induced all the worshipers of Baal, throughout all Israel, to assemble in the house of Baal, with

---

[8]See chapter on the book of Joel.

strict orders that no servant of the Lord should be admitted or be found among them. The house of Baal was filled from one end to the other. As the worshipers of Baal went in to offer sacrifices and burnt offerings, Jehu's outside guard of eighty officers and men, entered the house and slew every one of them, allowing no one to escape.

Then the guard proceeded, under Jehu's instructions, to destroy the house of Baal, breaking up the images, the pillars of Baal, and finally burning the temple of Baal itself, thus eradicating Baal worship completely.

The Old Testament contains many illustrations of how God uses men and nations that are far from ideal to be His agents in executing His judgments on the wicked. Jehu seems to have been one of them. If we think his methods murderous and extreme, and his motives selfish, as some have thought, we must remember that Baalism and its peculiar form of idolatry was unspeakably vile and cruel, more wicked and more defiling by far than calf worship, which was also practiced in Israel.

19. JEHOASH, THE EIGHTH KING OF JUDAH. About 845-805 B.C. II Kings 12; II Chronicles 24.

The young king Jehoash, called "Joash" by the writer of II Chronicles, as we have learned, was a grandson of Athaliah, daughter of Jezebel. He "reigned forty years in Jerusalem," which probably included Athaliah's six years during which she usurped the throne of Judah.

We have seen, too, how Jehoida the priest and his wife hid young Jehoash in the Temple until he was seven years of age, until his wicked grandmother could be disposed of and Jehoash made king. This same Jehoida, a devout man and uncle of the boy, had charge of his education, and so long as he lived he caused Jehoash to be true to the worship of Jehovah. As soon as Jehoida died, however, Jehoash departed from the good influence of his uncle. He came under the evil influence of the nobles of the court, the followers of the wicked Athaliah and the tradition of idolatry which she had built up during her fifteen years of evil influence in Judah.

Thus, evil days returned to Jerusalem and Judah. Zechariah, son of Jehoida the priest, and a prophet in his own right, stood up boldly like Stephen in early New Testament times, and reprimanded them for their sins. For this, Jehoash ordered that Zechariah be stoned to death, forgetting the kindness which Jehoida, Zechariah's father, had shown him.

Within the year of Zechariah's death, the army of Syria came and plundered Judah and Jerusalem, and slew the nobles. The writer interprets the defeat of Judah by the much smaller army of Syria as their punishment "because they had forsaken the Lord, the God of their fathers."

This caused the people to turn against Jehoash. When the Syrian invaders departed, they left the king wounded. As he lay in bed, his own servants conspired against him, entered his bedroom and slew him, in revenge for the murder of Zechariah.

20. JEHOAHAZ, THE ELEVENTH KING OF ISRAEL. About 820-804 B.C. II Kings 13:1-9.

We return now to the house of Jehu and to his own son Jehoahaz, who ruled over Israel at Samaria about seventeen years. Notwithstanding all that Jehu did to destroy the house of Ahab, and its idolatrous practices, his son Jehoahaz and his nobles and followers reverted to the old order and re-established Baal and his idols, including Ashtoreth at Samaria.

For this the Lord punished them, by continually allowing them to be defeated by the kings of Syria, Hazael and his son Ben-hadad. Thus Israel was brought very low. Jehoahaz's defeats by the Syrians were so severe that he was forced to turn to the Lord for help. The "savior" which the Lord sent was probably in the persons of his two successors after his death, Jehoash and Jeroboam II.

21. JEHOASH, THE TWELFTH KING OF ISRAEL. About 804-789 B.C. II Kings 13:10 to 14:16.

Jehoash, son of Jehoahaz, should not be confused with that of Jehoash, grandson of Athaliah, and king of Judah. Although he was king of Israel about sixteen years, his record is somewhat brief. The main event is how he got revenge on Hazael king of Syria, for the several invasions of Israel in the days of his father Jehoahaz's reign. This he did by retaking from Ben-hadad, son of Hazael, the cities which he had taken from Jehoahaz. Three times Jehoash defeated him and recovered the cities of Israel.

THE ASSYRIAN EMPIRE

In our reading of Hebrew history from now on, we shall hear much of Israel's and Judah's two great enemies in the far north, the Assyrians and Babylonians respectively.

About 2150 B.C., Abraham and his family migrated from the city of Ur in Chaldea, the southern portion of the ancient Babylonian Empire. This was in the lower Mesopotamian Valley, in which the Garden of Eden was located. About the time Abraham left Chaldea, Assyria in the upper Mesopotamian Valley was founded by some colonists from Babylonia, and their capital city given the name of Asshur, after their heathen god by that name. Later the capital of Assyria was moved a little further north to Nineveh.

In time these two great powers were rivals, and lived principally by robbing each other and their neighbors, including the Hebrews in Israel and Judah. One of the Assyrian kings, Assur-nasipal II (885-860 B.C.), clashed with Omri and called Israel "the land of Omri." His successor, Shalmaneser II (860-825 B.C), fought Ahab. And he must have defeated Jehu in some contest, for he testifies that Jehu paid him tribute.

The main reason why Jehoash was able to get revenge on King Hazael by re-taking from his son Ben-hadad all the cities previously taken by Hazael was the victories of these northern Assyrians over the Syrians. For in his inscriptions, the Assyrian King Ramman-nirari (808-783 B.C.) states that he besieged Damascus and forced its ruler to bow to him and to pay tribute. Moreover, at the same time he claims to have received tribute from "the land of Omri." So it appears that Jehoash purchased the aid of the Assyrian king by sending money or presents to him.

Two other incidents are related of the reign of Jehoash. One was his war with Amaziah, king of Judah, in which Amaziah challenged him to fight. He defeated Judah in the battle of Beth-shemeth on Judah's own soil, captured King Amaziah, broke down six hundred feet of the Wall of Jerusalem, and seized all the gold and silver in the House of the Lord, the treasuries of the king's palace, together with hostages, before he returned to Samaria.

The other item is the story of Jehoash's visit to the old prophet Elisha, at the time of the prophet's last illness before his death. This story shows the good relationship that existed between prophet and king, and the influence for good the former had on the latter, in spite of the fact that the king often paid little attention to Elisha's prophecies, or to correcting the evils that existed in the land (II Kings 13: 14-19).

22. AMAZIAH, THE NINTH KING OF JUDAH. About 805-777 B.C. II Kings 14:1-22; II Chronicles 25.

Amaziah, son of Jehoash, beginning at age twenty-five, ruled twenty-nine years over Judah at Jerusalem.

As we have seen, when the army of Syria invaded and plundered Judah, they went away leaving the king wounded. As he lay in bed, his servants plotted against the king and killed him. So, when his son Amaziah found himself firmly established in power, the first thing he did was to put to death those who had slain the king his father.

Amaziah next planned an ill-starred war against Edom and received a reprimand from the prophet of God, because he undertook to go to war with "hired soldiers" from Israel. To make bad matters worse, he brought back with him the idols of the men of Edom and set them up as his gods, and worshiped them.

Flushed with this questionable victory over Edom, Amaziah next sent his messengers to Samaria to challenge King Jehoash to war. He was defeated by the army of Jehoash so disastrously, as we have seen, that his leadership became discredited in Jerusalem, and a conspiracy against him was formed there. And so the king fled to Lachish, a fortified city in Judah some twenty-five miles southwest of Jerusalem; but twelve years later he was sought out there and murdered. His body was brought back upon horses and buried with his fathers in the city of David.

23. JEROBOAM II, THE THIRTEENTH KING OF ISRAEL. About 789-749 B.C. II Kings 14:23-29.

Jeroboam II, son of Jehoash king of Israel, held the throne of Israel for about forty-one years. Although described only briefly in Kings, his reign was notable on at least three counts.

(1) For one thing, he continued the victorious wars of his father against Syria, retaking Damascus. Then he reconquered the whole of traditional Israelite territory, including Hamath and the valley of the Orantes River on the north; and restored to Israel the country from Hamath to the Dead Sea, including Transjordan, Moab and Edom.

It is noteworthy that this historical statement of how Israel had restored and extended its borders is that it came from the prophet Jonah (14:25), apparently the same Jonah whose book we have, and quoted by the writer of II Kings.

And many scholars think that the prophet Jonah helped Jeroboam II in the work of extending the borders of Israel, as against her neighboring enemies, at a time when the Assyrians of the north were inactive and unaggressive. Jonah did not like the Assyrians, for they had already caused Israel trouble, and were likely to cause even more in the future. That is why he balked at going to Nineveh, the capital city of Assyria, to preach to the Ninevites.

(2) In the second place, the material and political prosperity of Israel under Jeroboam reached its highest level since the days of David and Solomon. God had Jehu anointed king of Israel to destroy the wicked house of Ahab, and to restore His worship throughout Israel. Jehu's dynasty was given five successive kings in which to complete this work. But in many ways the dynasty of Jehu had been a disappointment.

Now prosperity to an unusual degree had come to the land in the time of Jeroboam II. Is it possible that God was giving Israel a last chance to repent, seeing whether material and political prosperity would accomplish what poverty and affliction had not?

(3) In the third place, Jeroboam II's reign was known for its notorious social and religious corruption. The true measure of this corruption is to be seen in the call of two great prophets, whose primary purpose was to counsel and to warn King Jeroboam, and his nobles and princes, and the wealthy and corrupt men and women of his reign, and principally the dwellers in the beautiful city of Samaria.

THE PROPHETS JONAH, AMOS, AND HOSEA[9]

The three prophets who figured prominently during the reign of Jeroboam II were Jonah, Amos, and Hosea. They have been called

[9]See the separate chapters on the prophets Jonah, Amos. and Hosea, pp. 272-284.

the "Latter Prophets" to distinguish them from their earlier predecessors, the "Former Prophets," such as Samuel, Elijah, Elisha, and many others, who did not reduce their prophecies to writing.

Amos delivered discourse after discourse. He counseled the king and his princes, the leaders and the wealthy, and the idolators, warning them and pronouncing their day of doom. Indeed, Israel's day of disaster did come soon; for the nation's fall came within a short thirty years after this prophecy.

The prophetic ministry of Hosea followed that of Amos and covered the last years of Jeroboam II and his successors to the final conquest of Israel by the Assyrians, in 721 B.C.

24. UZZIAH, THE TENTH KING OF JUDAH. About 791-740 B.C. II Kings 15:1-7; II Chronicles 26.

Uzziah, son of Amaziah king of Judah, began his reign as a young man and held the throne of Judah for approximately fifty-two years. However, the first twelve of these years were spent as regent for his father Amaziah, who fled from his conspirators, to Lachish, where he remained in hiding until he was discovered and murdered.

King Uzziah, who is called "Azariah" by the writer of II Kings, and "Uzziah" by the author of II Chronicles, got off to a good start as the young king. For he was singularly fortunate in being brought up under the instruction and good influence of the prophet Zechariah, "who instructed him in the fear of God."

Uzziah's reign was long and significant, and like Jeroboam II's, it deserves fuller treatment than that given by the historians. For one thing, he organized the army of Judah, bringing its total war strength in men up to the impressive total of 307,500, with 2,500 officers and "mighty men of valor" at the head of the organization. He supplied this army with improved weapons and military engines, catapults, war shields, spears, helmets, coats of mail, bows, and stones for slinging.

With this superior military strength, Uzziah went out and made war against the Philistines to the southwest, and against the Arabs and Ammonites to the east of Judah. He broke down the walls of Gath, Ashdod, and other important cities of the Philistines, and built cities of his own in their territory. So great were his victories against these traditional enemies, that his fame spread to the border of Egypt.

Uzziah's enemies to the north had their hands full for the moment. Israel was busy protecting herself against Syria; and Syria had all she could do to stave off invasion by the growing Assyrian Empire; and all three were watching the moves of one another. So Uzziah, in the south, had comparative peace for strengthening the kingdom, as Jeroboam II his neighbor and king of Israel was doing.

As an important part of his planning, Uzziah also promoted agriculture and his food supply. He built towers in the wilderness to protect his herds, and dug many water cisterns for his animals to drink, for he had large herds in many parts of the land (II Chronicles 26:10). Through his own effort and example as a farmer, he set a pattern for his people to follow and greatly encouraged the food supply of his kingdom.

Two things have been charged against the reign of Uzziah. In the first place, although he himself worshiped Jehovah, he did not take away the high places at which his people sacrificed to other gods.

The second charge is personal. Uzziah, inflated because of his prosperity in all that he had undertaken, became arrogant and entered the Temple against the opposition of eighty priests, and attempted to burn incense to the Lord, in violation of the Law of Moses, and more than six hundred years of well established practice of the Levitical priesthood. As the king struggled with the priests, he was stricken with leprosy and was hurried out of the Temple and placed in a separate house for quarantine, where he remained some fifteen years until his death. Meanwhile, his son Jotham ruled in his stead as regent.

25. ZECHARIAH, THE FOURTEENTH KING OF ISRAEL. About 748 B.C. (6 months). II Kings 15:8-12.

Zechariah, son of Jeroboam II and king of Israel, succeeded his father to the throne of Israel.

In spite of the outstanding ability and success of Jeroboam II during his long reign, the corruption of the court and the people, as revealed and denounced in the prophecies of both Amos and Hosea, was the immediate cause of the downfall of the Jehu dynasty. Indeed, extreme chaos set in, while rival and factional leaders plotted for power.

Zechariah lived just long enough to fulfill the prophecy that the fourth generation of Jehu's sons should rule after him. For Shallum, son of Jabesh, formed a plot and murdered him at Ibleam, in the sixth month of his rule. The writer of II Kings applies the old formula of faithlessness and disloyalty to Jehovah, which he so often had applied to the reigns of other evil kings, that "he did what was evil in the sight of the Lord."

26. SHALLUM, THE FIFTEENTH KING OF ISRAEL. About 748 B.C. (1 month.) II Kings 15:13-15.

The old adage that he who lives by the sword must die by the sword, was soon realized in the example of Shallum. For Shallum, who murdered Zechariah to reach the throne of Israel, was himself assassinated within a month, by Menahem when he heard that Shallum had murdered the former king. Thus, to avenge one outrage, he committed another.

27. MENAHEM, THE SIXTEENTH KING OF ISRAEL. About 748-738 B.C. II Kings 15:14-22.

At the time he left Tirzah in a rage to come to Samaria to assassinate Shallum, Menahem probably was military governor of Tirzah, an important town and former capital of Israel before Samaria was built. His reign of ten years was noted for its brutality in an age when violence and ruthlessness were the rule.

Like his immediate predecessors on the throne of Israel, Menahem was unsteady and afraid. So, when the warrior-king Tiglath-pileser III of Assyria invaded Israel, Menahem hastily agreed to buy off the invaders with the payment of one thousand talents of silver. To raise the money, he taxed some sixty thousand of the wealthiest men in Israel, mostly in Samaria, in the amount of fifty shekels or twenty-five ounces of silver, each.

Although the Assyrians had threatened invasion of the Northern Kingdom in the days of Jehu, and also in the reign of Jeroboam II, as evidenced by the prophet Jonah, the invasion here described is the first recorded of the many they were to make in the near future.

Tiglath-pileser, as recorded in the Assyrian inscriptions, claims Menahem of Samaria as one who paid tribute to him.[10] As it turned out, this invasion by the growing Assyrian Empire of the north was the beginning of the end for Israel. Israel was becoming weaker by the hour. In the words of one writer, "Never before in the history of the Northern Kingdom had there been such a tangle of murder and intrigue." And the historian's old formula, "He did what was evil in the sight of the Lord," hardly describes the religion of an age in which the people and their leaders had become so corrupt that true Jehovah worship was all but forgotten.

28. PEKAHIAH, THE SEVENTEENTH KING OF ISRAEL. About 738-736 B.C. II Kings 15:23-26.

Pekahiah, son of Menahem, managed to hold out for two years before he fell victim to intrigue. Like his earlier predecessors, Zechariah and Shallum, he was assassinated. Pekah, his captain and strong man, and fifty men of the Gileadites, plotted against Pekahiah, entered the palace at Samaria and murdered him. Then Pekah usurped the throne and ruled in his stead.

29. PEKAH, THE EIGHTEENTH KING OF ISRAEL. About 748-740 B.C. II Kings 15:27-31.

Pekah, the son of Remaliah, captain and strong man behind the preceding reigns of Menahem and Pekahiah, and possibly the reigns of Zechariah and Shallum also, is reported to have ruled over Israel at Samaria "twenty years." Actually, his reign, based on other known dates, could not have been longer than two to five years at most. He may have claimed the longer reign, inasmuch as he had been the power behind the preceding reigns. Pekah's reign, however, is im-

---

[10]James B. Pritchard, *Ancient Near Eastern Texts Relating to the Old Testament*, Second Edition, p. 283. (Princeton, 1956.)

portant because of its connection with international politics, and because it hastened Israel's downfall.

When the reign of King Jotham of Judah was drawing to a close, Pekah entered into an alliance with Rezin, king of Syria, the purpose of which was to dethrone the king of Judah, and set up in his place a king of their own choosing. As the armies of Syria and Israel marched into Judah, Jotham died suddenly and his son Ahaz came to the throne of Judah. Ahaz, contrary to the advice of Isaiah, the great prophet of Judah, undertook to purchase the aid of Tiglath-pileser III, king of Assyria. The advance of the Assyrian army south, in 734 B.C., sent terror through all Syria and Palestine, and compelled Syria and Israel to withdraw their troops from the destructive occupation of Judah, in order to protect their territories, now being invaded by Assyria from the north.

But this strategy did not prevent the invasion by the Assyrians, who had already captured the cities of Ijon, Abel-bethmaacah, Janoah, Kedesh, Hazor, Gilead, the district of Galilee, as well as all the land of northern Palestine, and carried away large numbers of the inhabitants captive to Assyria. This was part of the enemy's new military policy, to uproot conquered populations and crush national loyalties, as well as to secure needed labor for their building projects at home.

Pekah lived four years after this humiliating defeat by Assyria. Samaria alone of the important cities was left by the conquerors. Pekah himself was murdered by Hoshea, who became the last king of Israel.

30. JOTHAM, THE ELEVENTH KING OF JUDAH. About 751-736 B.C. II Kings 15:32-38; II Chronicles 27.

We return now to the kings of Judah. Jotham, whose reign was conducted largely as regent for his father Uzziah, continued in large measure the administration of his father. He kept up his father's building program. He built cities in the hill country of Judah; and, like his father, he built forts and towers on the wooded hills, for the care and protection of his herds and other agricultural interests.

Jotham conducted wars. He fought with the king of the Ammonites and defeated him. From him he collected tribute to the extent of one hundred talents of silver, and quantities of wheat and barley. Other wars are referred to but not given in the history.

Jotham "did what was right in the eyes of the Lord according to all that his father Uzziah had done," except that, unlike his father, he "did not invade the Temple of the Lord." However, Jotham, like his father, did not take away the high places at which the people sacrificed to other gods, and practiced idolatry. Indeed, some scholars are of the opinion that it is the prophet Isaiah, who as a young man just now appearing on the scene, is describing the idolatry and faithlessness in Jotham's as well as his son Ahaz's reign, in the second chapter of the book of Isaiah.

Jotham died in 734 B.C., at the age of forty-one, and his son Ahaz succeeded him to the throne of Judah.

31. AHAZ, THE TWELFTH KING OF JUDAH. About 741-726 B.C. II Kings 16; II Chronicles 28.

Ahaz ruled over Judah at Jerusalem about sixteen years, including the years in which he seems to have served as co-regent with his father Jotham, and his grandfather Uzziah. At the outset, Ahaz inherited trouble as well as a throne, as was noted in our story of Pekah's reign at Samaria. The very moment his father died, the conspiracy of Pekah, and Rezin, king of Syria, to overthrow the king of Judah, was being executed. Their separate armies were already marching toward Jerusalem as young Ahaz was crowned king.

There was panic in Jerusalem when news of the invasion reached the king and the people. The prophet Isaiah advised his fellow countrymen to be calm and to put their trust in Jehovah their God. Ahaz rejected the advice of Isaiah. Instead, as we have learned, he turned to Tiglath-pileser III king of Assyria, and undertook to purchase help with the treasures of the Temple and the king's palace (see Isaiah 7, 8, 9).

Eventually the king of Assyria appeared, forced the armies of Israel and Syria to withdraw from Judah and to return home to protect their own borders from the Assyrians. But Judah had been badly robbed by King Pekah and King Rezin, before their departure. However, they were repaid for their aggressions in the fatal defeat of their armies by Tiglath-pileser III and in his celebration of his victories at Damascus. Israel in particular suffered disastrously in what is known as the Galilee Captivity of 734 B.C.

King Ahaz received the doubtful invitation to attend Tiglath-pileser III's celebration of his victories over Israel and Syria, at Damascus, where all his vassals were gathered to do homage to the Assyrian king. For, as he was soon to learn, Ahaz's "purchased protection" was only temporary.

While at Damascus, Ahaz saw an altar and idols of Syrian gods that pleased him. He sent a model of the altar to his priest Urijah, to have an imitation made and set up in Jerusalem.

Ahaz also re-introduced Baal worship into Judah and even offered his sons as sacrifice, after the manner of the ancient Canaanites. In these and other forms of idolatry, Ahaz imitated the wicked kings of Israel, rather than following in the footsteps of his forefathers of Judah. He died about the year 726 B.C., and his son Hezekiah succeeded him.

THE PROPHETS ISAIAH AND MICAH[11]

During this time there were doubtless many prophets, as there had been in every generation for more than three hundred years since

---

[11]See the chapters on the prophets Isaiah and Micah, pp. 285-305.

the days of the prophet Samuel, who organized bands or schools of prophets. The two outstanding ones in the period we have under study were Isaiah and Micah.

Isaiah was himself of royal blood, being cousin to King Uzziah and his son and grandson, Jotham and Ahaz, respectively. As statesman as well as prophet, he counseled and advised these kings in Jerusalem as members of his own family, although on many occasions they did not listen to him or take his advice as prophet. For a picture of Ahaz's reign and its corruption, including the invasion of Judah by Pekah and Rezin, and Assyria's invasion of Syria and Israel and its consequences, see Isaiah 7, 8, 9, 10, 11, and 12. Against the background of intrigue, immorality, and idolatry, and included in the same chapters, Isaiah prophesies that God will punish all these nations, including Assyria the present punisher of the others. Finally, in the midst of it all, Isaiah again and again prophesies the coming of the Prince of Peace as the future hope of Israel (Isaiah 7:14; 9:1-7; 11: 1-16; etc.).

Micah, a native of Moresheth-gath, a village on the Philistine border near Gath, directed his preaching mainly to his own people of Judah and Jerusalem, as did his contemporary Isaiah. However, in their messages they included also the wicked and faithless of Israel and elsewhere.

32. Hoshea, the Nineteenth King of Israel. About 730-721 b.c. II Kings 17.

Hoshea, son of Elah, was the last king of Israel and the Northern Kingdom. As we have already seen, he came to the·throne by plotting against and murdering King Pekah. In this he had the secret understanding and aid of Tiglath-pileser III, king of Assyria. In return, Hoshea was to continue paying tribute to the king of Assyria.

But in 727 b.c., Tiglath-pileser died, and his successor, Shalmaneser IV as king of Assyria, made an expedition against Hoshea and forced him to continue the payment of the annual tribute. Hoshea did not like this. So he formed a secret alliance with the king of Egypt, stopped his yearly payments of tribute to the Assyrians, trusting that aid from Egypt would be forthcoming before Shalmaneser IV learned of his double-dealing.

But Hoshea miscalculated. For Shalmaneser soon learned of his treachery, again invaded all the territory of Israel, took King Hoshea captive, and for three years laid siege to Samaria the capital city. The Egyptians did not arrive to rescue Hoshea and Israel, and the city was soon reduced to the verge of starvation. Near the end of the third year, however, King Shalmaneser IV died, and his successor Sargon II claimed the honor of capturing the city, 721 b.c.

And so the curtain fell on Samaria, and the Ten Tribes of Israel passed into history and into oblivion. For Sargon II, following the

The Great High Place of Sacrifice of the Nabateans at Petra. © *Matson Photo Service* barbarous custom of holding conquered territory by deporting all the important inhabitants, like Tiglath-pileser III his predecessor, left behind only an unimportant remnant of the population. In his inscription, the Assyrian says that he deported "the whole of the inhabitants."

Where did they go? The historian says that they were carried away to Assyria, and placed in Halah, and on the Habor, the river of Gozan, and in the cities of the Medes (II Kings 17:6). From here they disappeared from history, and became the "Ten Lost Tribes of Israel." Most of them probably did what Jews ordinarily did not do in a foreign land, that is, intermarried with the natives and thus lost their identity.

Was Hoshea the cause of the Fall of Israel? In the words of one commentator, "It was not any special wickedness on the part of Hoshea that brought it on. The cup of Israel's iniquity had been filling for centuries, and Hoshea's iniquities only added the last drop which made the cup full to overflowing." The writer of that terrible chapter, chapter seventeen of II Kings, takes this view.

Chapter 14

I AND II KINGS (Continued)

C. THE DIVIDED KINGDOM: THE HISTORY OF JUDAH, UNTIL THE BABYLONIAN CAPTURE AND EXILE, IN 586 B.C.[1]

33. HEZEKIAH, THE THIRTEENTH KING OF JUDAH. About 726-697 B.C. II Kings 18, 19, 20; II Chronicles 29, 30, 31, 32.

Hezekiah, son of Ahaz, is another example of a worthy son of an unworthy and wicked father. He was twenty-five when he came to the throne; he ruled Judah twenty-nine years, plus a year or two as acting ruler during his father's illness. Hezekiah's reign is one of the most important, as well as one of the best, in the history of Judah.

To secure a complete picture of Hezekiah's reign, the student should examine the accounts of both II Kings and II Chronicles. Each historian stresses a somewhat different side of the reign. The writer of Kings is concerned mainly with the political events of the time and their consequences, especially Judah's international relations with Assyria, Babylon, and Egypt; whereas the author of Chronicles is mainly interested in Hezekiah's religious reforms, which he relates in detail. Both are important for understanding these critical years in Judah's history.

In the first year of his reign, Hezekiah began his great religious reformation. He re-opened and cleansed the Temple, and restored the worship of Jehovah under the leadership of his devoted priests and Levites. But Hezekiah's main inspiration and counsel came from his distant cousin, the great prophet Isaiah, who retained the king's complete confidence throughout his reign, although they sometimes disagreed as to policy.

The Temple had been closed by King Ahaz; now it was restored to all the people, including any of the Northern Kingdom of Israel who had not been deported by Assyria. One of Hezekiah's first religious acts was to call for a period of national repentance, followed by the observance of the Passover. The king sent letters, inviting the remnants of Ephraim, Manasseh, and of other tribes as well as the people of Judah, urging every one to come to the House of the Lord at Jerusalem.

The king's next step was to begin a crusade against idolatry. He set out to destroy the high places. This was the first real campaign to put an end to these local and community altars throughout Judah,

---

[1]For a liberal analysis of the Decline and Fall of Judah, including the role of the prophets, see Anderson, *op. cit.*, chs. 9, 10, 11.

which had co-existed with the Temple of Jerusalem as places of worship since the time of Solomon. But the undertaking was a difficult one and was not completed until the reign of King Josiah, some ninety years later (II Kings 23:13-20).

One of Hezekiah's main problems was how to keep out of trouble with the great rival powers of his day — Assyria, Egypt and Babylon.

In the sixth year of his reign, 721 B.C., Sargon II took Samaria and completed his conquest of the Ten Tribes of Israel, which his predecessors, Tiglath-pileser and Shalmaneser, began. It was now only a question of time before the successful Assyrians would extend their invasions further south and include Judah. Hezekiah was afraid of the strong power of the north.

In the fourteenth year of Hezekiah's reign, about 713 B.C., Sennacherib as commander of his father Sargon's armies, invaded Judah and took many of the fortified cities of Hezekiah's kingdom. And then from his military headquarters at Lachish, in Judah, Sennacherib threatened to take Jerusalem. Being unable to withstand the invader, Hezekiah, to save his capital, bowed to the enemy by handing over to him large quantities of silver and gold.

But this did not satisfy the invader's thirst for conquest. So Sennacherib sent Rabshakeh his commander with a large army to Jerusalem, with insulting demands upon Hezekiah, which also insulted and dishonored Jehovah the God of Israel. Hezekiah conferred with Isaiah and asked God for His protection. Isaiah assured the king most solemnly that the Lord would not permit the arrogant Assyrian to take the city. So Jerusalem was saved, for the present at least, and the capital city spared the might of the Assyrian armies, although Sennacherib conducted wars against the Philistines and Egyptians on more than one occasion, and crossed and re-crossed the territory of Judah. However, Sargon II was murdered in 705 B.C. and his ambitious son Sennacherib became king in his own right.

Sennacherib was determined to crush the subject states in the south, including Judah, because they formed alliances against him and refused to pay him tribute. In 701 B.C., after he put his own house in order, he marched south once more to put down growing rebellion and conspiracy. Coming down the Mediterranean coast from the north, he overran Phoenicia, Philistia, robbing their chief cities. Then he turned east and captured Lachish, in Judah, and according to his own count, took forty-six fortified cities of Judah, and carried away more than 200,000 captives, and seized multitudes of horses, mules, asses, camels, and sheep.[2]

He next sought out the Egyptian army, just now stationed at Eltekeh, in Dan near the Philistine border.

Sennacherib's final plan included the capture and destruction of

---

[2]See James B. Pritchard, *Ancient Near Eastern Texts Relating to the Old Testament,* Second Ed.. pp. 287-288. (Princeton, 1956.)

Jerusalem. But he miscalculated. The Lord was not on his side. According to our historian, when he proceeded in the direction of Jerusalem, an insurmountable barrier stood in his path:

> And that night the angel of the Lord went forth, and slew a hundred and eighty-five thousand in the camp of the Assyrians; and when men arose early in the morning, behold, these were all dead bodies. Then Sennacherib king of Assyria departed, and went home, and dwelt at Nineveh.

And he returned no more to molest the Hebrews. Some years later he was murdered by two of his sons.

Hezekiah's latter days appear to have been spent in search of peace and security for his people. When told by Isaiah, who was prophesying the future, that the day would come when Babylon would carry them into exile, he replied simply,

> Why not, if there will be peace
> and security in my days?

This he said, thinking doubtless that his descendants could avert the prophesied disaster, as he had done, by their loyalty to Jehovah.

34. MANASSEH, THE FOURTEENTH KING OF JUDAH. About 697-642 B.C. II Kings 21:1-18; II Chronicles 33:1-20.

Hezekiah died about the year 697 B.C., and his son Manasseh ruled Judah at Jerusalem for the long period of fifty-five years, beginning at age twelve.

Manasseh is conceded to be the most wicked king Judah ever had, just as Ahab was the worst king of Israel. Both the historians of II Kings and of II Chronicles emphasize the evils of Manasseh's reign.

He reversed entirely his father's religious policy, and re-introduced all the forms of idolatry practiced by his wicked predecessors of both Israel and Judah, except possibly calf worship. At least on one occasion he sacrificed his own son on the altar of his heathen god!

As did Ahab's wicked queen Jezebel, he put to death large numbers of those who worshiped Jehovah, primarily because they opposed his religious practices:

> Moreover, Manasseh shed very much innocent blood, till he had filled Jerusalem from one end to another.

Some scholars are of the opinion that the prophet Isaiah was likely one of those put to death by Manasseh. The prophet Micah, in 7:1-6, seems to be describing Manasseh's reign.

The extreme length of Manasseh's reign indicates that the masses of the people went along with his injustice and wickedness, and that there was no effective opposition. The extreme corruption of the age had created a situation that could not, humanly speaking, be reversed, and from which there could be no return, as the reader saw in the closing days of Israel:

> Because Manasseh king of Judah has committed these abominations, and has done things more wicked than all that the Amorites did, who were before him, and has made Judah also to sin with his idols;

therefore thus says the Lord, the God of Israel, "Behold, I am bringing upon Jerusalem and Judah such evil that the ears of every one who hears of it will tingle. And I will stretch over Jerusalem the measuring line of Samaria, and the plummet of the house of Ahab; and I will wipe Jerusalem as one wipes a dish, wiping it and turning it upside down. And I will cast off the remnant of my heritage, and give them into the hand of their enemies."

(21:11-14)

35. AMON, THE FIFTEENTH KING OF JUDAH. About 642-640 B.C. II Kings 21:19-26; II Chronicles 33:21-25.

Amon, son of Manasseh, was twenty-two years old when he succeeded his father as king, and he ruled over Judah about two years.

Both of our historians dispose of the reign of Amon with a single paragraph each, implying that little of note took place during his two years as king. For here we have another illustration of, like father, like son. Amon imitated the wickedness of his father and prolonged the evils which his father instituted over Judah, for two more years.

Amon's servants plotted against him and killed the king in his palace. But the people, not approving this sort of violence, slew all those who had conspired against the king, and then placed his eight-year-old son on the throne in his place.

36. JOSIAH, THE SIXTEENTH KING OF JUDAH. About 639-608 B.C. II Kings 22 to 23:30; II Chronicles 34 and 35.

The most important thing connected with Amon's story is that he was father of Josiah, who became the best king Judah ever had during the three hundred and fifty years of the Divided Kingdom.

Josiah began his reign at the age of eight, with the assistance of his teacher and counselor, Hilkiah the high priest. He ruled Judah for thirty-one years. From his boyhood, Josiah seems to have been under the direct educational and religious influence of Hilkiah. One of our historians says:

In the eighth year of his reign, while he was yet a boy, he began to seek the God of David his father.

He was then about the age of fifteen. At age twenty Josiah began his reforms. And this reformation was more thoroughgoing and complete than any undertaken before in Judah, including the reforms of such good kings as Asa, Uzziah, and Hezekiah.

Josiah's reforms included the repairing and rebuilding of the Temple, and the removing and destroying of all altars, idols, and every emblem of idolatry and ungodly worship from the Lord's House.

After cleansing the Temple, he next went to the city of Jerusalem, and to all the cities and provincial centers of worship, destroying every "high place," every altar, every idol, every monument or pole dedicated to Baal and Asherah, and every property of incense and sacrifice to strange gods — all these were taken away and destroyed, as an abomination in the eyes of the Lord.

One day, when Josiah was twenty-six years of age, Hilkiah, his high priest, found a Book in the Temple. It was the Law of Moses. The book seems to have been a copy of Deuteronomy and not the whole Pentateuch, since Josiah read it to the people at one hearing. Although Josiah's reforms began about six years earlier, when he was twenty, the finding of this Book influenced him profoundly and became the main inspiration of a renewed crusade against idolatry.

After his public reading of the Book, Josiah led the Elders and the people to a solemn renewal of the Covenant as revealed in the Word of the Lord by Moses. And then the king, to solemnize their renewed vows, kept the Feast of the Passover with all the people. So many were those who attended, and so sincere and devout was their purpose, that no Passover since the days of the prophet Samuel was like it.

In 608 B.C., in the thirty-first year of his reign, Josiah became involved in international politics, as between Egypt and Assyria, and met his death quite suddenly. Under his leadership, Judah had enjoyed peace for many years. But now he became afraid that he was about to lose his independence.

Many things had happened recently on the international scene. In the year 626 B.C., in the thirteenth year of Josiah's reign, hordes of barbarians from the far north (now part of Russia), Scythians they were called, swarmed like locusts, and overran and terrorized the nations of southwest Asia.

For one thing, they dealt a terrific blow to the Assyrian Empire, from which it never really recovered.

On one of their expeditions the Scythians came south, along the coast of the Mediterranean in the direction of Egypt. But they were met and bought off by Pharaoh, at Ashdod in Philistia; otherwise they may have invaded and destroyed Judah also, as a part of their southern exploits. The prophet Zephaniah refers to the presence of the Scythians as the scourge of the Lord (Zephaniah 2).

The Assyrians, thus weakened by the Scythians, continued on the decline until 612 B.C., when Nabopolassar, king of Babylon, and his ally Cyaxeres king of the Medes, attacked Nineveh, the great capital city of Assyria, and destroyed it.

In 608 B.C., Necho, Pharaoh of Egypt, taking advantage of Assyria's defeat by the Babylonians, decided to march north and "get in on the grab" of the fallen Assyrian Empire; in particular that part of it south and west of the Euphrates river.

King Josiah of Judah saw in all this danger to his newly acquired freedom. So, taking his own advice, and not that of Jeremiah who steadfastly opposed him, Josiah foolishly decided to resist Necho's passage through his territory on the way north, although Necho expressly informed him that he had more important business on hand than to fight Judah (II Chronicles 35:22).

Josiah's forces and the army of Necho met in battle at the strategic and historic battlefield of Megiddo, on the plains of Jezreel. Josiah was disguised and fought from his chariot as a soldier. An arrow from the enemy struck and mortally wounded him. He was transferred to another chariot, and hurried to Jerusalem some sixty miles distant, but when he arrived he was dead.

The people were stunned by the sudden loss of their king. And from this loss Judah never rallied, for there was no one to take his place. Chief of those who mourned for Josiah was the great prophet Jeremiah.

THE SWIFT DECLINE AND FALL OF JUDAH

There are two somewhat different views regarding the thoroughness of Josiah's reforms.[3]

One view is that the reforms were substantial and far-reaching, and that if Josiah had had a long reign of a half century or so, such as that of his wicked grandfather Manasseh, Judah could have been saved. Indeed, the historian of II Kings and the writer of II Chronicles, both make a strong case for Josiah and his devoted collaborators.

On the other hand, there are those who interpret the events to mean that, however well-meaning Josiah and his fellow-reformers had been, the reformation itself was never more than superficial. They hold to the view that the total collapse of the nation immediately after Josiah's death is evidence of deep-seated, internal corruption. God had already pronounced judgment against Judah by the close of Manasseh's reign (II Kings 21:11-15).

Moreover, the great prophet Jeremiah, who took a most active part in civic and religious affairs of his day, as Isaiah had done a hundred years earlier, virtually ignored Josiah's reformation, in these words:

> The Lord said to me in the days of King Josiah: "Have you seen what she did, that faithless one, Israel, how she went up on every high hill and under every green tree, and there played the harlot? And I thought, 'After she has done all this she will return to me'; but she did not return, and her false sister Judah saw it . . . Yet her false sister Judah did not fear, but she too went and played the harlot . . . Judah did not return to me with her whole heart, but in pretence," says the Lord (Jeremiah 3:6-10).

And again,

> Run to and fro through the streets of Jerusalem,
>   look and take note!
> Search her squares to see if you can find a man,
>   one who does justice and seeks truth;
>   that I may pardon her . . .
> They have made their faces harder than rock;
>   they have refused to repent (Jeremiah 5).

---

[3]See John Bright, *The Kingdom of God*, pp. 102-109 (1953); Anderson, *Understanding the Old Testament*, pp. 305-309 (1957); H. L. Ellison, *The New Bible Commentary*, p. 332 (1953).

37. Jehoahaz, the Seventeenth King of Judah. About 608 b.c. (3 months). II Kings 23:30-34; II Chronicles 36:1-4.

After Josiah's death, the people made his third son, Jehoahaz, king of Judah in his stead. Presumably the oldest son of Josiah was dead. And it appears that the people passed over the second son and chose the third, as most likely to continue his father's policies. His real name was *Shallum;* Jehoahaz was adopted as his throne name.

Within three months, however, Jehoahaz was deposed by Pharaoh Necho and carried in chains to Riblah, in Hamath, where the Egyptian army was engaged in war with the Babylonians, the recent conquerors of Assyria. Afterward, he was taken to Egypt, where he died.

38. Jehoiakim, the Eighteenth King of Judah. About 608-597 b.c. II Kings 23 to 24:6; II Chronicles 36:5-8.

When Pharaoh Necho deposed Jehoahaz, he made Jehoiakim, Josiah's second son and Jehoahaz's elder brother, king in his place. His real name was *Eliakim;* Necho changed it to the throne name of Jehoiakim. He began his rule over Judah about 608 b.c., at the age of twenty-five, and continued about eleven years.

In 605 b.c., however, in the famous battle at Carchemish on the west bank of the Euphrates, Nebuchadnezzar utterly defeated Pharaoh Necho and drove his army back to his own land. Thus, Jehoiakim, who had been a vassal of Pharaoh Necho since he was placed on the throne of Judah in 608 b.c., suddenly found it necessary to change his allegiance and pay tribute to Nebuchadnezzar.

A few years later Jehoiakim was foolhardy enough to rebel against Nebuchadnezzar. Finally, losing his patience with the Jewish king, Nebuchadnezzar and his army entered Jerusalem and bound Jehoiakim, with the intention of bringing him in chains to Babylon. But for some reason the sentence was not carried out. He died or was murdered, and his body was dragged outside the city gates, as the prophet Jeremiah had predicted, and given the burial of an ass. That is, given no burial at all, but left for the vultures.

Jehoiakim was one of Judah's worst kings. He thoroughly hated the prophet Jeremiah, and again and again sought to have him put to death. For the prophet's opinion of him, see Jeremiah 22:13-15, 17-19; 26:20-23; 36:21-26.

The First Stage of the Captivity of Judah, 605 b.c.

The defeat of Jehoiakim and Jerusalem by Nebuchadnezzar's army in 605 b.c., marked the beginning of the end of Judah, and may be called the *First Stage* of the final conquest and captivity of the Southern Kingdom. For at this time the first installment of the population of Judah was carried away as captives to Babylon. Included in the number was a youth, Daniel by name, who was to become famous in the court of the king in Babylon. (For his story, see the book of Daniel.)

39. JEHOIACHIN, THE NINETEENTH KING OF JUDAH. About 597 B.C. (3 months, 10 days.) II Kings 24:6-17; II Chronicles 36:8-10.

Jehoiachin, son and legal successor of Jehoiakim, was king of Judah only three months and ten days. Jehoiachin was his throne name; his real name was *Jaconiah*, often shortened to *Coniah*. Jeremiah refers to him by these names.

THE SECOND STAGE OF THE CAPTIVITY OF JUDAH, 597 B.C.

Not long after Jehoiachin came to the throne of Judah, Nebuchadnezzar made another campaign of conquests into the south, deploying his army in several directions. He subjugated Tyre and other neighbors of Judah, and laid siege to Jerusalem, which was the main objective of this campaign. During the siege, King Nebuchadnezzar in person came to Jerusalem.

Jehoiachin, seeing that he could not hold out against so valiant an enemy, gave himself up to the king of Babylon, his mother, his wives, servants, princes, and palace officials. All these, including the king, were carried into captivity from Jerusalem to Babylon. Says our historian of II Kings,

> He carried away all Jerusalem, and all the princes, and all the mighty men of valor, ten thousand captives, and all the craftsmen and smiths; none remained, except the poorest sort of people of the land.

The most famous of the captives was the prophet Ezekiel, just eight years after the deportation of Daniel, who was carried away with the captives of 605 B.C. Daniel was placed in the city of Babylon; Ezekiel was located in the country, on the river Chebar, a great canal southeast of Babylon.

Nebuchadnezzar's method of deporting conquered peoples followed a well-established policy which both Assyria and Babylon carried out, namely, that of transporting large numbers of the most important inhabitants, including trained and skilled workers of all sorts, to other parts of the empire.

The policy had two unquestioned values for the conqueror. It supplied the conquering king with much needed labor. Also, captives transferred to a distant land break their ties with the homeland, and adjust themselves more quickly to new ways of life.

Nebuchadnezzar was a great builder. He seems never to have tired of building and beautifying the great city of Babylon. He built the great wall of Babylon; he erected a magnificent Palace for himself; he repaired the great Temple of Marduk, the patron god of Babylon; and, for his wife, he built the famous Hanging Gardens, one of the Seven Wonders of the ancient world, not to mention the famous sanctuaries and reservoirs which he built away from Babylon. All these enterprises required much labor and money, both of which he looted from conquered peoples and lands.

King Jehoiachin remained in prison in Babylon from his capture in 597 B.C. to 562 B.C., when Nebuchadnezzar died and his son, Evil-merodok, released Jehoiachin from prison and permitted him to eat at the king's table the rest of his days. It is somewhat likely that Daniel, who was a friend and favorite at the court, had a hand in having the old king removed from prison.

40. ZEDEKIAH, THE TWENTIETH KING OF JUDAH. About 597-586 B.C. II Kings 24:17 to 25; II Chronicles 36.

Zedekiah was the last of the kings of Judah. His real name was *Mattaniah*, an uncle of Jehoiachin and a brother of Jehoiakim. As his vassal king, Nebuchadnezzar gave him the throne name *Zedekiah*. He was twenty-one when he became king, and ruled eleven years, until he rebelled against King Nebuchadnezzar.

Zedekiah was a weak king and subject to all the evils and vices of the age. His princes and advisers unduly influenced him, frequently swaying him from his own best interests and those of the nation, and against the advice of Jeremiah, the leading prophet of the period. Zedekiah was bound by oath to Nebuchadnezzar; but pressure from Egypt, Edom, Moab, Tyre, and other countries, aided by the princes of his own Court, led him away from his allegiance to Babylon, to join an alliance against Babylon by these states.

Jeremiah advised the king to remain faithful to his oath to the king of Babylon, as the best prospect for Jerusalem and peace. For this Jeremiah was accused of disloyalty to Judah, and put in stocks or in prison. However, unlike Jehoiakim, when the princes of the court had Jeremiah put in prison on the charge of deserting to the enemy, Zedekiah delivered him (Jeremiah 37:11-21). On another occasion, when Jeremiah was cast into a foul cistern, he was rescued by the king's help (Jeremiah 38:6-13).

THE THIRD AND FINAL STAGE OF THE CAPTIVITY OF JUDAH, 586 B.C.

When word finally reached Nebuchadnezzar that Zedekiah had broken his solemn oath of loyalty and joined an alliance with Egypt and others against Babylon, he marched south with his armies with the firm intention of destroying Judah and Jerusalem, once and for all. He laid siege to Jerusalem in 588 B.C., and for a year and a half the city was surrounded, and the people within were brought to the verge of starvation.

There was a brief relief period, when the Babylonians temporarily retired from their siege to fight off an Egyptian force, which had advanced to the relief of Jerusalem. But the relief was only temporary, and the siege was resumed.

On July 9, 586 B.C., a breach was made in the city wall. When Zedekiah saw that the city was about to be taken, he and all his men of war fled the city by night, on the old highway in the direction of Jericho. The Babylonians pursued and overtook them in the plains of Jericho and brought them to the king of Babylon, who was stationed at Riblah in Hamath, where he passed sentence upon them.

They slew Zedekiah's sons, put out the eyes of Zedekiah, bound him in fetters, and imprisoned him in Babylon to the day of his death. The next month, August 586 B.C., Nebuchadnezzar and his captain of the guard, Nebuzaradan, returned and completely destroyed Jerusalem. They burned the magnificent Temple which Solomon had built, and the palatial house of the king, and all the "great houses."

Then the captain took his army and broke down the walls around Jerusalem, and the Millo, the famous bastion at Jerusalem, built by David and repaired by Solomon as a precaution against siege or invasion and every other fortification.

The inhabitants were taken captive, including persons of all ranks and worth, and skills, except a remnant of the poorer sort "to be vinedressers and plowmen." Archaeologists have confirmed the virtual depopulation of all Judea, including all those who fell by the sword.[4]

Finally, the conquering Babylonians took anything and everything of value left in the Temple, gold, and silver, and bronze, and the Temple vessels and utensils of every sort. Jeremiah (in chapter 52: 17-23) gives a complete list, longer than the list in II Kings. The city was looted and all the precious things that could be transported taken.

THE FOURTH STAGE: THE CAPTIVITY OF THE REMNANT, 581 B.C.

After the destruction of Jerusalem, Nebuchadnezzar appointed Gedaliah, son of Abikam and a person of quality, to serve as vassal governor over the remnant which he left in Judah.

In the five years that followed, many mishaps had befallen the land. The climax came when Ishmael, who was leader of the band opposing the governor, and who was instigated by the king of the Ammonites, treacherously assassinated Gedaliah in his official residence.

When the inhabitants of Jerusalem were being taken to Babylon, Nebuchadnezzar gave the prophet Jeremiah the choice of going to Babylon with the Jewish exiles, or of remaining in Judah with the remnant. Jeremiah chose to remain. In the midst of the feuding that followed the death of Gedaliah, the leaders of the remnant came to Jeremiah to inquire what they should do. Jeremiah replied that it was the Lord's wish that they remain in the land. But, being afraid of reprisals by Nebuchadnezzar because of the death of his governor, they fled tó Egypt, compelling Jeremiah against his will to go along.

So, in 581 B.C., Nebuchadnezzar's captain came back and dealt severely with Judah, taking with him the last remaining remnant of the people.

---

[4]See James B. Pritchard, *Ancient Near Eastern Texts*, pp. 321-322, for the Lachish Letters describing the Babylonian invasion. See also Jeremiah's Elegy, *Lamentations*.

ISRAEL AND JUDAH
THE DIVIDED MONARCHY
(C. 850 B.C.)

Chapter 15

I and II Chronicles

1. The Character and Purpose of I and II Chronicles

In the original Hebrew, I and II Chronicles not only formed a single book but probably was one continuous work with the books of Ezra and Nehemiah.

One main characteristic of Chronicles is that it is not a continuation of the history of the Hebrew nation, but is a *duplication* and a *supplement* to parts of I and II Samuel and I and II Kings.

Another characteristic of Chronicles is that it deals almost exclusively with the fortunes of Judah or the Southern Kingdom, and with Israel or the Northern Kingdom not at all, except where it touches the fortunes of Judah.

Thus, the title Chronicles is significant. For a chronicle differs from a history. The meaning of the original title Chronicles suggests "supplement" or "things passed over," by the preceding works of I and II Samuel and I and II Kings.

Also, the purpose of the writer of Chronicles seems to have been different from that of the writers of Samuel and Kings. One commentator, Professor H. L. Ellison of the London Bible College, sees a very clear principle both in the writer's *additions* to the books of Samuel and Kings and in his *omissions*.[1] And with this opinion most careful readers will agree.

For instance, the chronicler's additions concern mainly the Temple and its services and such incidents as stressed the religious aspects of the nation, in contrast with the civil. His omissions show that he is primarily interested in what Ellison calls "two divine institutions": The Temple worship and ritual, and the Davidic line of kings.

This viewpoint leads the writer of I and II Chronicles to omit Saul, except incidental reference to his death, and to omit David's troubles, including the Bathsheba episode, Absalom's rebellion, Adonijah's attempted usurpation of the throne, and other sins related to the house of David. And the same may be said for his treatment of the reigns of Solomon and the subsequent kings of Judah during the period of the Divided Kingdom.

That is to say, the writer omits most of the sins and weaknesses of David and Solomon, and sometimes those of the later kings of Judah. And a notable *addition* the writer of Chronicles makes to the

---

[1] *The New Bible Commentary*, Second Ed., pp. 339-340 (1954).

story of Kings, for example, is the stress he places on the Temple worship and ritual during Josiah's reign, and the relative lack of attention he gives to King Josiah's reforms.

It has been said, and correctly, that the writers of Samuel and Kings were primarily interested in working out the double theme of God's revelation of Himself, and His dealings with His people, in what has often been called the "prophetic viewpoint," for the prophets were supposed to have written these books.

On the other hand, the writer of Chronicles is chiefly concerned with the nation as a religious community, and its Temple organization, rituals and ceremonials, and thus the books were written from the Levitical or priestly point of view.

For these reasons, I and II Chronicles should be read in conjunction with the books of I and II Samuel and I and II Kings, and as supplementing these books; otherwise, Chronicles would give an unbalanced view of the history of the Hebrew nation. Indeed, it seems quite likely that its author presupposed a knowledge of Samuel and Kings on the part of his readers.

2. Authorship and Date of I and II Chronicles

The author of Chronicles is unknown. But from what has been said above, and from the prominence given in the book to the Levitical order, it has been presumed that the writer himself was a Levite, as contrasted with the authors of I and II Samuel and I and II Kings, who were supposed to have been prophets.[2]

A Jewish tradition ascribes the authorship of Chronicles to Ezra, at least as the tradition has been interpreted. But perhaps the genealogies were attributed to him, and not the whole book (I Chronicles 1 to 9). This is the same Ezra whose name furnishes the title for the next historical book, and who came from Babylon to Jerusalem with a second body of exiles, in 457 B.C.

Of late, however, scholars have concluded that Chronicles and Ezra and Nehemiah were originally one book. And although he could have written all three books, it is much more likely that Ezra contributed such material as the genealogies (I Chronicles 1-9), and was the compiler of much of the material which a later writer used in his composition of the Chronicles-Ezra-Nehemiah book.

The date of the writing of Chronicles, and its sequels, Ezra and Nehemiah, is much later than the dates of Samuel and Kings. In I Chronicles 3:19-24, the writer lists the descendants of Zerubbabel to the sixth generation,[3] which suggests a date not earlier than about 400-340 B.C. Moreover, the writer of the book of Nehemiah (12:10-22)

---

[2]Although the writer of I and II Kings does not name the sources he used, the author of I and II Chronicles does. See I Chronicles 29:29; II Chronicles 9:29; 12:15; 13:22; 26:22; 33:19.

supports this late date by his reference to Jaddua, who was high priest in the time of the Persian King Darius Codomannus (335-330 B.C.) and of Alexander the Great (336-323 B.C.).

It would seem from this internal evidence that the date of the composition of the Chronicles-Ezra-Nehemiah trilogy was thus not much before 300 B.C. Consequently the author of I and II Chronicles was removed from the events he records by a much longer period of time than were the authors of I and II Samuel and I and II Kings, and therefore he cannot be considered so good an authority.

3. The Contents of I and II Chronicles

The contents of I and II Chronicles fall historically into three main divisions, as follows:

(1) Hebrew Genealogies, I Chronicles, Chapters 1-9;
(2) The History of David and Solomon, I Chronicles 10-29 to II Chronicles 9;
(3) The Divided Kingdom: The History of Judah, II Chronicles 10-36.

(1) *Hebrew Genealogies*

The writer, without heading or introduction, begins at once with a series of genealogies. These are taken, with a few unimportant variations, directly from chapters 5, 10, 11, 16, 21, 25, 36, of the book of Genesis.

One group refers to *peoples*, another to *locations*, and a third and much larger group refers to *families*, which are genealogies in the strict sense.

This last group became extremely important after the exile when descent from Aaron was faithfully required as a condition for the priesthood, and when strong efforts were made to prevent inter-marriage with foreigners and to maintain the purity of the Jewish race.

(2) *The History of David and Solomon*

Briefly: The death of Saul; David made king, first of Judah, and then of all Israel; David's wars, victories, and triumphs; the Ark of the Lord brought to Jerusalem; a Psalm of thanksgiving; David's further victories against the Philistines; his purpose to build a House of the Lord, its plans and specifications; David's farewell, and death.

Solomon anointed king; Solomon, not David, builds the great Temple, the House of the Lord; the dedication of the new Temple; Solomon consolidates his kingdom and extends its borders until "he ruled over all the kings from the Euphrates to the land of the Philistines, and to the border of Egypt"; the visit of the Queen of Sheba; the declaration of Solomon's riches and wisdom.

---

[3]Scholars differ as to the correct reading of I Chronicles 3:19-24. See Edward J. Young, *An Introduction to the Old Testament*, pp. 414-415. According to this view only two generations after Zerubbabel are stated, and thus there would be no obstacle to Ezra's authorship.

And then the writer closes his history abruptly and refers the reader to other sources for "the rest of the acts of Solomon." No mention is made of Solomon's great defection in the second half of his reign, such as that recorded in the eleventh chapter of I Kings.

(3) The Divided Kingdom: The History of Judah

Chronicles, unlike Kings, omits entirely the history of Israel or the Northern Kingdom. The list of the twenty kings of Judah during the period of the Divided Kingdom, their references in II Chronicles, and their approximate dates are given in the chart below. The references in II Chronicles to the kings of Judah are also consolidated with the references in I and II Kings to these same kings, as the reader has observed, so that both may be read together.

THE DIVIDED KINGDOM: THE KINGS OF JUDAH

Rehoboam	Chapters 10-12	934-917 B.C.
Abijah	Chapter 13	917-915
Asa	Chapters 14-16	914-874
Jehoshaphat	Chapters 17-20	876-852
Jehoram	Chapter 21	852-845
Ahaziah	Chapter 22:1-10	845
Athaliah	Chapters 22:11 to 23	845-839
Joash	Chapter 24	845-805
Amaziah	Chapter 25	805-777
Uzziah	Chapter 26	791-740
Jotham	Chapter 27	751-736
Ahaz	Chapter 28	741-726
Hezekiah	Chapters 29-32	726-697
Manasseh	Chapter 33:1-20	697-642
Amon	Chapter 33:21-25	642-640
Josiah	Chapters 34-35	639-608
Jehoahaz	Chapter 36:1-3	608 (3 months)
Jehoiakim	Chapter 36:4-8	608-597
Jehoiachin	Chapter 36:9-10	597 (3 months, 10 days)
Zedekiah	Chapter 36:11-21	597-586

Judah was captured and carried into exile by Nebuchadnezzar king of Babylon in four separate stages: 605, 597, 586, and 581 B.C. The main captivity and destruction of Jerusalem was in 586 B.C.

These dates are approximately correct. The dates of reigns frequently overlap, because the son was often co-regent with the father. Also, fragments of years in Hebrew chronology are often counted as entire years.[4]

---

[4]Selected References: Adam C. Welch, *The Work of the Chronicler — Its Purpose and Its Date* (1939); Edward J. Young, *An Introduction to the Old Testament*, pp. 412-427 (1958). A more liberal view is that of Bernhard W. Anderson, "A Kingdom of Priests," *Understanding the Old Testament*, pp. 430-463 (1957).

BOOKS OF THE RETURN AND RESTORATION

Chapter 16

EZRA

1. THE CHARACTER AND PURPOSE OF THE BOOK OF EZRA

We come now to the last of the historical books of the Old Testament: Ezra, Esther, and Nehemiah.

Unlike the books of Samuel, Kings, and Chronicles, which tell the historical and dramatic story of the rise and fall and exile of the Jewish nation, these last books tell of the Return and Restoration at Jerusalem *after* the half century and more of Exile in Assyria, Babylonia, and Persia, but principally in Babylonia.

Two of them, Ezra and Nehemiah, are especially important, because they give us nearly all the direct information we have of the Return and Restoration: who came and when, and what they did after their return.

In the original Hebrew Scriptures, the book of Ezra and the book of Nehemiah were one book. They were retained as one book in the *Septuagint Version* by the Greek translators of the original Hebrew Scriptures, and were not divided into two separate books until Jerome's *Vulgate Version* of 390-405 A.D.

Because the opening verses of Ezra repeat the concluding verses of II Chronicles, and because of the similarity of style and content, as well as viewpoint and purpose, the general opinion among scholars now is that the three works form one consecutive history, of which I and II Chronicles is the first half.[1]

The modern reader, however, is interested in the book because it reveals God's purpose and plan for His people. Indeed, the first sentence introduces the reader to that purpose: The Hebrews have been in exile for "seventy years," and now they are about to be released. God has raised up a new king, Cyrus king of Persia, "that the word of the Lord by the mouth of Jeremiah might be accomplished."[2]

The prophet Jeremiah had warned that Judah would be punished for her disobedience and wickedness, by the Babylonians, and that Babylon in turn, because of her cruelty and wickedness, would then be destroyed:

---

[1]See Adam C. Welch, *Post-Exilic Judaism*, p. 242ff (1935); also *The Work of the Chronicler,* same author (1939).
[2]For Cyrus' testimony, see the translation of the famous Cyrus Cylinder, James B. Pritchard, *Ancient Near Eastern Texts*, p. 316.

This whole land shall become a ruin and a waste, and these nations shall serve the king of Babylon seventy years. Then after seventy years are completed, I will punish the king of Babylon and that nation, the land of the Chaldeans, for their iniquity, says the Lord, making the land an everlasting waste. (Jeremiah 25:11-12)

Isaiah, more than a hundred years before the event, prophesied the capture and exile of Judah by Babylon, and the subsequent destruction of that cruel and wicked nation:

> And Babylon, the glory of kingdoms,
> the splendor and pride of the
> Chaldeans,
> Will be like Sodom and Gomorrah
> when God overthrew them.
> It will never be inhabited
> or dwelt in for all generations. (Isaiah 13:19-20)

And of Cyrus, not as yet born, Isaiah said:

> Thus says the Lord . . . concerning Cyrus, "He is my shepherd, and he shall fulfill all my purpose." (Isaiah 44:28)

Thus, the book of Ezra is the story of the fulfillment of the promise to all Israel. Further, it shows in clear and unmistakable terms how God presides over the destinies of men and nations.

The Seventy Years, which Jeremiah prophesied, extends from the first stage of Judah's captivity, in 605 B.C., to Cyrus' proclamation granting all Jews their freedom to return to Jerusalem, in 538 B.C.

Two other books, the prophecies of Haggai and Zechariah, should be read as a part of the study of the book of Ezra and the fortunes of those who first returned to Jerusalem. They both deal with the early part of the period, and especially with the re-building of the Temple under the first provincial governor, Zerubbabel.

2. AUTHORSHIP AND DATE OF THE BOOK OF EZRA

The author of the book of Ezra is unknown. A Jewish tradition ascribes the authorship of Ezra, as well as Chronicles, to the priest and scribe Ezra, at least as the tradition has been interpreted. Ezra was not only scribe, but a scholar and teacher of the Law of Moses as well. He came from exile in Babylon to Jerusalem with the second company or contingent of those who returned in 457 B.C.

More recently, however, the prevailing view among scholars is that an unknown historian or chronicler compiled and composed Ezra as a part of his Chronicles-Ezra-Nehemiah history, gathering his materials from many sources, reference to which is made in the books themselves.

Parts of Ezra are written in Aramaic, a language used by Israel's neighbors to the east and northeast, and which became the diplomatic language of the Near East. The book is composed largely of copies of public records and official documents, and these together with the connecting history, are in Aramaic. In Aramaic, too, were copies of letters sent to the Persian kings by officials of the Jewish province, and the royal replies and decrees giving instructions and commands to these officials.

The remainder of the book was written in Hebrew, including the domestic history of Judah as taken from a variety of historical documents, and the connecting history composed by the writer himself.

A feature of the book is the quoted matter by the historian from the personal memoirs of Ezra, which is copied with the first personal pronoun "I" and "we," just as the writer evidently found it in the original. The rest of the book generally is in the third person.

The date of the composition of Ezra, based on internal evidence, would of necessity be later than the arrival at Jerusalem of the second company of exiles under the priest and scribe Ezra, in 457 B.C. Moreover, based on the assumption that all three works of Chronicles and Ezra and Nehemiah are one connected history, the date would be later. That is, as late as Darius Codomannus (335-330 B.C.), as referred to in the book of Chronicles, and Alexander the Great (336-323 B.C.) as referred to by the Jewish historian Josephus.[3] The main events as related in the histories of Ezra and Nehemiah, however, bring the story of the Jews down to about 432 B.C.

3. THE CONTENTS OF THE BOOK

The contents of the book of Ezra fall naturally into these two main divisions:

(1) The First Return to Jerusalem, under the Leadership of Zerubbabel, 538 B.C., Chapters 1-6;

(2) The Second Return to Jerusalem, under the Leadership of Ezra, 457 B.C., Chapters 7-10.

(1) *The First Return to Jerusalem*

1. The first six chapters tell the story of the historic return to Jerusalem by the Jews from their exile in Babylon, under the leadership of Zerubbabel, the first governor appointed by Cyrus king of Persia, and Zerubbabel's chief aid Joshua the priest, in 538 B.C.

Two items stand out in the narrative: the restoration of Divine service, and the building of the second Temple, the main purpose for which they returned.

2. Another feature of the book is the author's particular interest in genealogy: the persons who came with Zerubbabel, their quality and standing among the Jews, as well as their respective numbers. He mentions the heads of fathers' houses, the priests and Levites, and other important persons, with the precise numbers in each group.

Certain items attract the reader's interest. For example, there were only 341 Levites returned, whereas of the priests there were as many

[3]For the argument in favor of an earlier date, and Ezra authorship, see Edward J. Young, *An Introduction to the Old Testament*, pp. 401-406 (1958); R. Dick Wilson, "Ezra-Nehemiah," *International Standard Bible Encyclopedia;* and Adam C. Welch, *op. cit.*, p. 242 (1939).

as 4,289. Here is evidence of a reluctance on the part of the Levites to return to Jerusalem from their positions of prominence in Babylon.

The writer enumerates a total of 42,360 Jewish citizens who came, besides 7,337 servants, and 200 singers. These last were secular entertainers and not the Levitical singers who performed at religious services in the sanctuary. The grand total is approximately 50,000 of those in the first body to return, which seems small as compared with the total in exile.[4]

3. The writer also enumerates the livestock the farmers and others brought along with them, with which to start their new life in Judah. These include 736 horses, 245 mules, 435 camels, and 6,720 asses.

4. Cyrus further demonstrated his generosity by permitting the Jews to take back with them large quantities of gold and silver vessels, which Nebuchadnezzar had taken from the Temple and from the people of Jerusalem at the time of that city's total destruction. One author estimates as many as 5,400 gold and silver vessels.

(2) The Second Return to Jerusalem

1. The last four chapters of the book of Ezra tell the story of the return to Jerusalem and Judah of the priest and scribe Ezra, and the second body of exiles who came with him, 457 B.C.

2. The primary purpose of Zerubbabel's mission,[5] as we have seen, was to build the new Temple. Ezra's chief mission, on the other hand, was to investigate the religious laxity of the people of Jerusalem, news of which had reached Babylon, and to introduce reforms.

Ezra was to teach the people, so that every one would know the Law of Moses. In addition, the Persian king, who although a non-Jew was a follower of Jehovah, expressly gave his authority to Ezra to enforce the observance of the Law, and by means of penalties, if need be. And so the writer makes a point of the fact that Ezra brought with him his Bible, which was the "Law of Moses," his purpose being "to study the Law of the Lord . . . and to teach his statutes and ordinances in Israel."

3. Those mentioned who came with Ezra were 1,496 males. But since so often in Hebrew enumerations, women and children are not included, there is no reason for believing that no women and children were present in Ezra's company. These inhabitants were making a

---

[4]For the reasons why many of the Jews did not return to Jerusalem after Cyrus' edict, see the famous Jewish historian Flavius Josephus, *Antiquities of the Jews*, Book XI, 1, 3. They were reluctant to leave their businesses and possessions. Indeed, some scholars are of the opinion that the number may have been even less than 50,000. See William Foxwell Albright, *The Biblical Period* (a reprint from the larger work, *The Jews: Their History, Culture and Religion*, edited by Louis Finkelstein, 1949), p. 53 (1950), for a discussion of the matter.

[5]For a discussion of the religious motives of Ezra and Nehemiah in returning to Jerusalem, see H. H. Rowley, *The Rediscovery of the Old Testament*, pp. 161-186 (1946).

permanent migration from Babylon to Judah, some 900 miles, and it is not likely that they would have left their families back in Babylonia.

4. Ezra had another purpose in coming to Jerusalem. Artaxerxes, now king of Persia, and his counselors had generously donated large sums of silver and gold for the Lord's work in the province of Israel. To this was added a generous freewill offering by the Jewish people and priests of Babylonia. Included in the king's gifts were also large quantities of wheat, oil and wine. It was a part of Ezra's mission to convey all these gifts to the colony at Jerusalem.

5. When he arrived in Judah after four months of travel, one thing embarrassed Ezra above everything else. He found his fellow countrymen in large numbers were marrying non-Jewish or "foreign women," and the worst offenders were the officials and chief men of the colony!

Ezra undertook to enforce extreme but successful measures to stop Jewish marriages with foreign women, by making a covenant in which the Jews pledged themselves to give up their non-Jewish wives and families.

In the book of Nehemiah, we learn more of the work of Ezra, and how he and his assistants read, and interpreted publicly the Bible to all the people.

The reader has noticed the gap of 59 years between the two parts of Ezra. The first half extends from 538 B.C. to 516 B.C., the building of the Temple; and the second from 457 to 444 B.C., the beginning of Nehemiah.

Suggestions for Additional Reading[6]

The student has now finished reading the seventeen historical books of the Old Testament and has secured a foundation for the reading and study of the other books of the Old Testament. Also, in the course of these readings, if he has been resourceful, he has read a number of books and parts of books on these Biblical texts. One lesson the student should learn early, and that is the importance of *evaluating* the materials he reads. While the references have emphasized the conservative and constructive viewpoint, they include also many writers of a more liberal view.

Bible Readings: The Books of Ezra, Esther, Nehemiah, and the Prophets Haggai and Zechariah. Text: *The Revised Standard Version;* or *The King James Version,* preferably in modern readers' format.

*Anderson, Bernhard W.: "A Kingdom of Priests," *Understanding the Old Testament,* Chapter 14, pp. 430-463.

*James, Fleming: *Personalities of the Old Testament,* Chapter 25.

MacDonald, A.: "Esther," *The New Bible Commentary,* pp. 380-386.

Rowley, H. H.: *The Rediscovery of the Old Testament,* Chapter 7.

[6]For other references, see the reading list on pages 60, 194, 198. See also the General Bibliography at the end of the book, which includes publishers, dates, and brief comments.

Welch, Adam C.: *Post-Exilic Judaism.*

*Welch, Adam C.: *The Work of the Chronicler.*

*Wright, J. Stafford: "Ezra and Nehemiah," *The New Bible Commentary,* pp. 365-379.

*Young, Edward J.: *An Introduction to the Old Testament,* pp. 374-379, and 400-411.

Ruins, possibly of the palace of Ahasuerus (Xerxes) at Susa, ancient Shusha, very likely the place of Esther's banquet. (Modern building is arachaeological headquarters). *Photo courtesy Dr. S. H. Horn, Andrews University.*

Chapter 17

ESTHER

1. THE BOOK OF ESTHER AND ITS BACKGROUND

The book of Esther is in the form of a short story, like the short stories of Ruth and Jonah.

The setting of the story is laid in the palace at Shushan, or Susa, one of the three capitals of the Persian Empire. The date of the opening of the story is 483 B.C., and the close 470 B.C., the date to which the book of Esther brings us.

The Ahasuerus of the story is King Xerxes of Persia (485-465 B.C.), the same Xerxes the Great whose vast army and navy fought the Greeks at the famous battles of Thermopalyae and Salamis, 480 B.C. The feast and assembly of all the leading men of the empire at Susa, described in the opening chapter of the book, was held in the third year of his reign (483 B.C.) to plan the expedition against Greece.

It appears that the king deposed Queen Vashti about 482, before he left, and married the Jewess, Esther, about 478 B.C., after the return from his disastrous war against the Greeks.

The story of Esther gives a vivid picture of the Jews in exile, and their treatment by their non-Jewish enemies in Persia and in the provinces of the Persian Empire.

One of the themes of the story is the intense loyalty and patriotism of the Jews for their fellow countrymen, in a foreign land, in this instance, in Persia. Thus, many scholars have regarded the book as a historical romance, written to glorify the Jews at a time when they were hated and threatened with wholesale massacre, and even extinction.

A deeper purpose of this historical narrative, however, seems to be the deliverance of Israel from annihilation, in the latter days of their Babylonian and Persian exile, by the overruling power of providence.

And yet this may seem strange to the reader in view of the fact that, in the original Hebrew of the book, not a single reference is made to the God of Israel; and neither prayer nor supplication is made to their God, in the time of their terrible ordeal. Could it be that the book was written at a time when it was extremely dangerous to make any open profession of the worship of Jehovah (see Daniel 6:7-17)?

Despite the fact that the author carefully refrains from saying the Jews cried to their God, the whole story implies a belief that Esther was an instrument in God's hand to bring about the deliverance of her people. For in Mordecai's message to Queen Esther, are these words:

> And who knows whether you have not come
> to the kingdom for such a time as this?

2. AUTHORSHIP AND DATE OF THE BOOK

The author of the book of Esther is unknown. Whoever he was, the writer was familiar with Persian customs and Persian words, and the layout of the King's palace and the court.[1]

In the course of his narrative, he refers to Persian state records at least three times (Esther 2:23; 6:1; 10:2), as well as to documents written by Mordecai, upon which some of the facts of the story probably are based.

Also, he was familiar with the dates of such events as the gathering of the Persian leaders at Susa the capital. And at the end of his story, he refers the reader for further information to one of his main sources, the *Chronicles of the Kings of Media and Persia*.

Chronologically, the events of the book of Esther come between the books of Ezra and Nehemiah. That is, Ezra covers the historical period 538-516 B.C., and 457-444 B.C.; Nehemiah, 444-432 B.C., or possibly a little later than 432 B.C.

The events related in the book of Esther come, as we have seen, during the reign of the Persian king Xerxes, 485-465 B.C., who is the Ahasuerus of the story.

The date of the writing of Esther, however, is later than the date of the events related in the story. For instance, Xerxes the king is described in language which implies that his reign was past (10:2). But scholars are of the opinion that the date of writing is not too much later than the date of the events described.

For example, the author's familiarity with the palace, which was destroyed by fire within some thirty years after Xerxes' death, suggests that he was close to his material. Moreover, the style of Esther clearly resembles that of Chronicles, Ezra, and Nehemiah. Also, Josephus the Jewish historian assigns the date to the reign of Artaxerxes (464-424 B.C.).

3. THE PLOT OF THE STORY OF ESTHER

The book of Esther is valuable because, like the books of Daniel and Ezekiel, Ezra and Nehemiah, it gives us a picture of the Jews

---

[1]There has been a great diversity of opinion among scholars on both the authorship and date of Esther, as well as its character and purpose in the Scriptures. Josephus says that Mordecai wrote the book (*Antiquities of the Jews*, 11:6:1); many modern scholars regard the book as a historical romance by an unknown author. Selected references: Edward J. Young, *op. cit.*, pp. 374-379; Anderson, *op. cit.*, pp. 504-508; A. Macdonald of Glasgow, *The New Bible Commentary*, Part Two, pp. 380-386. See also Bernhard W. Anderson's article in *The Interpreter's Bible*, Vol. III, pp. 825-828.

in exile. The picture is made more valuable because it gives us the views of those in authority, of non-Jews as well as Jews.

One of the biggest problems of Jews in exile was survival, survival as individuals and as a race. Although many Jews had returned to Jerusalem and Judah under Zerubbabel in 538 B.C., yet the vast majority were still scattered widely over the provinces of the Persian Empire, as the story reveals.

The story of Esther dramatizes thé conflict and struggle between Jews in exile and their non-Jewish enemies. In this instance the contest is at the Persian court itself, Susa, one of the three capitals of the Persian Empire.

The principal characters in the story are these: King Xerxes; his royal favorite, Haman, whom he has lately promoted above all other princes; the Jew, Mordecai; and Esther, Mordecai's beautiful and lovely cousin, an orphan, whom he has adopted as his own daughter.

When Haman was promoted to the second place in the kingdom, the king commanded that every one in the household should "bow down" and do obeisance to Haman. Now Mordecai, with the pride of his race and his loyalty to God, refused to bow to Haman, who in turn became very angry and sought revenge on Mordecai and all the Jews.

Craftily, Haman went before the king and bribed him with an offer to pay the enormous sum of 10,000 talents of silver into the king's treasuries, if it please the king to go along with his scheme to destroy the Jews. This short speech to the king shows his cunning and treachery:

> There is a certain people scattered abroad and dispersed among the peoples in all the provinces of your kingdom; their laws are different from those of every other people, and they do not keep the king's laws, so that it is not for the king's profit to tolerate them. If it please the king, let it be decreed that they be destroyed, and I will pay ten thousand talents of silver into the hands of those who have charge of the king's business, that they may put it into the king's treasuries.

The king gave Haman his permission, and his signet ring to make valid the edict, called in the king's secretaries to write the official document, and forwarded it by swift horsemen to the satraps and governors of all the 127 provinces of the vast Persian Empire.

Moreover, letters were sent by couriers to all the king's provinces, to destroy, to slay, and to annihilate all Jews, young and old, women and children, in one day, and to seize their goods and their possessions. A copy of the document was to be issued as a decree in every province by proclamation to all the peoples to be ready for that day.

Haman and his non-Jewish friends, eager to begin executing their plan to destroy the Jews, went out and built a gallows fifty cubits high (75 feet), and would go in the morning to request the king to have Mordecai hanged upon it.

Meanwhile, Mordecai rent his clothes and put on sackcloth and ashes, and went out into the midst of the city, wailing with a loud and bitter cry. And in every province, wherever the king's decree came, there was great mourning among the Jews, with fasting and lamenting.

But Mordecai was not one to waste many hours in wailing. He sent a message to Esther, who had long since won the royal favor and had become the king's queen. He pled with Esther to go to the king, to make supplication to him, and to entreat him to save her people.

Esther's reply:

> Go, gather all the Jews to be found in Susa, and hold a fast on my behalf, and neither eat nor drink for three days, night or day. I and my maids will also fast as you do. Then I will go to the king, though it is against the law; and if I perish, I perish.

Then on the third day, Queen Esther put on her royal robes and stood in the court of the King's palace. And when the king saw her, she found favor in his sight, for he held out the golden scepter, which meant that she was welcome, and that her request would be granted . . .

> If it please the king, let the king and Haman come this day to a dinner that I have prepared for the king.

But at the dinner, Queen Esther postponed her petition to the king until tomorrow, when she invited her royal guests back for another dinner.

On that night the king was unhappy and could not sleep. And so he gave orders to bring the "Book of Memorable Deeds, the Chronicles," to be read to him. In the book it was recorded how Mordecai had saved the king from two of his unfaithful servants, and that Mordecai had gone unrewarded for his good deed.

Events in the court now came to a swift climax. Haman, who had just entered the court of the King's palace, with plans to have Mordecai hanged upon the gallows he had prepared for him, was now commanded by the king, much against Haman's wish, to honor Mordecai publicly, in royal parade as the king's new favorite.

At Queen Esther's second banquet for the king and Haman, the moment had come for her to present her petition to the king:

> If I have found favor in thy sight, O King, and if it please the king, let my life be given me at my petition, and my people at my request. For we are sold, I and my people, to be destroyed, to be slain, and to be annihilated.

And the king said,

> Who is he, and where is he, that would presume to do this?

Esther replied quickly,

> A foe and enemy! This wicked Haman!

And then the king rose from the feast in wrath, and went into the Palace Garden. When he returned, he found Haman falling upon the couch where Esther was, to dishonor her. In a burst of anger, he said,

Will he even assault the queen in my presence, in my own house?

And then he commanded that Haman be hanged upon the gallows which Haman had prepared for Mordecai.

On that same day King Ahasuerus gave to Queen Esther the house of Haman, the enemy of the Jews. And the king took off his signet ring, which he had taken from Haman, and gave it to Mordecai. And Esther set Mordecai over the house of Haman, which made him prime minister and second only to the king.

The king issued a new edict to take the place of the old one, and overruled the evil design of Haman and the wicked plot he had devised against the Jews.

In this, the Jews were permitted to defend themselves, and to get revenge on their enemies throughout the 127 provinces of Ahasuerus' kingdom.

Thus, Esther saved her people, the Jewish race, from destruction and annihilation.

To show their gratitude, the Jews instituted a memorial, the Feast of Purim, the fourteenth and fifteenth days of the month of Adar (March), because on these days the Jews were saved from their enemies, and the days of sorrow were changed into days of gladness.

Esther and Nehemiah

Esther's marriage to King Xerxes must have given Jews great prestige and influence at the Persian court. For instance, when Xerxes died in 465 B.C., his son Artaxerxes, and Esther's step-son, succeeded him, 465-425 B.C. This Artaxerxes was the king at Susa for whom Nehemiah was cupbearer in 444 B.C., when he was given permission to come to Jerusalem to re-build the Wall of Jerusalem.

Who knows but that Esther's influence at the Persian Court greatly aided Nehemiah in his mission to Jerusalem? And thirteen years earlier, in 457 B.C., may she not have had a hand in fitting out Ezra's expedition from Babylon to Jerusalem?

Chapter 18

NEHEMIAH

1. THE CHARACTER AND PURPOSE OF THE BOOK OF NEHEMIAH

The book of Nehemiah is a sequel to the book of Ezra, just as Ezra is a sequel of I and II Chronicles. All three works were probably written by the same author, and form one consecutive chronicle history, of which I and II Chronicles are the first half.[1]

The purpose of the book is to record the story and heroic fortunes of Nehemiah and the third body of exiles to return from captivity to Jerusalem, 444 B.C., thirteen years after the arrival of Ezra and his second company of exiles.

Nehemiah, who was cupbearer to Artaxerxes king of Persia, was appointed by the king as the new governor of Judah. He and his exiles came from Susa, the Persian capital; whereas Zerubbabel and Ezra and their returning exiles came from Babylonia. Ezra the priest and scribe, with his Bible the Book of the Law, was engaged in teaching religion when Nehemiah arrived at Jerusalem.

Nehemiah's main mission was to re-build the Wall of Jerusalem, and to restore Jerusalem as a fortified city. He came with authority from the king of Persia to build the fortifications at government expense, and to withstand the hostility and intrigues of their powerful neighbors who formerly had caused the building of the wall to be postponed.

In the original Hebrew Scriptures, the book of Nehemiah and the book of Ezra were one book. They were retained as one book in the *Septuagint Version* by the Greek translators of the original Hebrew Scriptures, and were not divided into two separate books until Jerome's Latin *Vulgate Version*, 390-405 A.D.

2. AUTHORSHIP AND DATE OF THE BOOK

The author of the book of Nehemiah is unknown. A Jewish tradition assigns the authorship of the Chronicles-Ezra-Nehemiah trilogy to the priest and scribe Ezra, who was a noted writer and student of the Law of Moses, and the most outstanding teacher and preacher of the province of his time. Some think that Nehemiah himself wrote the book of Nehemiah.

Many present day scholars are of the opinion that an unknown priestly chronicler, later than either Ezra or Nehemiah and probably

[1]See footnote, Introduction to the book of Ezra, p. 195.

as late as 330 or 320 B.C., compiled and wrote these books from materials which he selected from many different sources.[2] The obvious similarity of the books in substance and purpose, and style, and viewpoint, suggests a single author.

The writer quotes from the memoirs of Nehemiah, just as he quoted from the letters of Ezra; likewise, he copies letters and decrees, genealogies and registers and other documents, as well as incidents about Nehemiah. Part of this material is in the first person, and part in the third person, presumably as he found it in the source from which he gathered the material. Also, some of the writing is in Aramaic, and some in Hebrew, just as we found it in the composition of Ezra.

All these are marks of a compiler or chronicler, in contrast with the method of a writer of an original composition, say for example, the book of Job or the book of Ecclesiastes.

3. The Contents of the Book

The book of Nehemiah contains the narrative of the return of Nehemiah in 444 B.C. to Jerusalem as governor of the province, the rebuilding of the city walls, and the restoring of obedience to the Law of Moses among the Jews.

After governing the province of Judah for twelve years, Nehemiah in 432 B.C. returned to Susa, the capital of Persia, to talk with Artaxerxes about the problems of the province, and to secure a further leave of absence for his work at Jerusalem. He returned within a few months.

The same method of composition is used in Nehemiah as was used in Ezra, that is, the chronicler confines his history to an account of a few critical incidents and events, instead of presenting a complete and comprehensive narrative of the whole or total history of the period, which indeed is the general method used in the narratives of Chronicles and Ezra.

A Brief Analysis of the Book

1. Distressing news of his fellow countrymen in Jerusalem came to Nehemiah while in exile as cupbearer to King Artaxerxes in the Persian capital at Susa; his prayer and resolve to re-build Jerusalem, with the permission of the king. Chapters 1 and 2.

2. The re-building of the Wall of Jerusalem, and a list of the leaders who helped, in the face of great opposition by the Samaritans and other powerful enemies of the Jews. Chapters 3, 4, 6.

3. Nehemiah's measures to alleviate poverty among his people. Chapter 5.

4. A list of exiles who returned from Babylon with Zerubbabel. Chapter 7.

5. The public reading of the Law of Moses by Ezra and his

---

[2]See footnote, Introduction to the book of Ezra, p. 195.

helpers, the renewal of the covenant by the people and their leaders, and a list of those who participated. Chapters 8 to 10.

6. Measures to supplement the population of Jerusalem, the dedication of the Wall of Jerusalem, and the correction of certain abuses, such as breaking the Sabbath and intermarriage with "foreign women." Chapters 11 to 13.

A view of Bethlehem from the southwest.
© *Matson Photo Service.*

PART THREE

THE BOOK OF PSALMS

Chapter 1

PSALMS

1. THE BOOK OF PSALMS

The book of Psalms has often been called the best loved book in the Old Testament.

The reason for this popularity is pointed out by Leslie S. M'Caw, in these words: "The continued freshness and enduring quality of the Psalms is primarily due to their spiritual intensity."[1] Each Psalm is remarkably personal and comes directly from the heart of the Hebrew who produced it; and yet the feeling of Divine worship is so universal that these Psalms speak the language of devotion for every heart.[2] Because of this, the Psalter not only was the hymnbook of the Hebrews but became the hymnbook for the Universal Church as well.

"From earliest times," says Professor John Paterson, "the Christian church has treasured the Psalter: of 287 quotations from the Old Testament appearing in the New, 116 are taken from the Psalter."[3] Even a casual examination of our present day church hymnals and prayerbooks will reveal how great has been the influence of the book of Psalms.

The inspiration and authority of the Psalms was stressed by our Lord, in His final appearance to His disciples after the Resurrection, in these memorable words:

> These are my words which I spoke to you, while I was still with you, that everything written about me in the Law of Moses and in the Prophets and the Psalms must be fulfilled. (Luke 24:44)

The book of Psalms is a collection of one hundred and fifty Psalms under the Hebrew name *Tehillim*, which means "Songs of Praise." As it comes down to us, the collection represents the hymns of perhaps a thousand years. In fact, our book of Psalms is a collection of collections. As one writer put it, the book of Psalms was not made. It grew.

The editors who compiled and arranged the Psalms, about the second century B.C., were conscious of the long history back of them when they divided the whole into five books, with a doxology to close each book. Some present day versions of the Bible retain this five-fold division, including the *Revised Standard Version* of 1952. They are: Book One, Psalms 1-41; Book Two, Psalms 42-72; Book Three, Psalms 73-89; Book Four, Psalms 90-106; Book Five, Psalms 107-150.

---

[1]*The New Bible Commentary*, Rev. Ed., 1954, p. 412.
[2]See Arnold B. Rhodes, *The Book of Psalms*, pp. 7-8 (1960); Anderson, *Understanding the Old Testament*, pp. 444-445 (1957).
[3]*The Praises of Israel*, p. 7 (1950).

A "modern David," a shepherd boy with sling. © *Matson Photo Service*

However, there is reason to believe that the editors were following an ancient tradition when they chose and divided the hymns into five books, which is thought to be in imitation of the five books of Moses, or the Pentateuch.

Also, if we go back beyond this tradition, we find on closer examination that smaller collections of hymns existed in earlier times, and that these formed the basis of later collections. For example, if the reader will turn to Psalm 72:20, which is a footnote that closes the Second Book, he will read: "The prayers of David, the son of Jesse, are ended." This indicates that the writer of the note regarded these Psalms as in some sense "belonging to David," and that he knew of no others by David.

Moreover, certain Psalms occur more than once in slightly differing forms, indicating that Psalms in earlier collections appeared also in later collections or books, and that the final editors did not eliminate these duplications. For example, compare Psalm 14 with 53; Psalm 40:13-17 with 70; and Psalm 108 with 57:7-11 and 60:5-12.

There are a number of ancient Psalms, reference to which is made in the earlier books of the Old Testament, and which do not appear in our present collection of 150. One of the most famous is the song Moses wrote and the people of Israel sang to celebrate their victory over the Egyptians, when they had crossed the Red Sea (Exodus 15).

Two other songs of Moses, the Farewell Song and the Song of Blessing in which he blessed all the congregation of Israel, are recorded in Deuteronomy 32 and 33. And one of the best of the early songs is the Song of Deborah, in the form of a ballad, which celebrates a famous victory over Sisera and Jabin, the king of Canaan.

The first and second Psalms may be taken as a fitting introduction to the collection as a whole. Psalm 1 divides all people according to their covenant relationship to God — the *godly* and the *ungodly*. Those who have had a *personal* encounter with God, and those who have not; those whose "delight is in the Law of the Lord," and those who take no such delight. Psalm 2, on the other hand, represents *the whole world* set over against the Lord and in deliberate opposition to His rule. The point in the Psalm is its application to the Messianic King, who one day will be Lord of all. Thus, the psalmist, like a wise counselor and prophet, in his preface points to the scope and purpose of the book of Psalms.

2. Authorship and Dates of the Psalms[4]

David was far and away the most famous musician of his age, which was the Golden Age of Israel. He was a noted musician and a poet of the first rank.

In the background of David's religious songs was a man after

---

[4]For a summary of the diversity of opinion on the authorship of the Psalms, see Young, *An Introduction to the Old Testament*, pp. 313-322 (1958).

God's own heart, in spite of his human weaknesses. He had many remarkable religious experiences. He was traditionally and intimately connected with, and a chief promoter of, organized worship. Indeed, he as king was head of Jehovah worship in his day, and unlike his son Solomon, he never permitted the worship of his God to become corrupted, or Jehovah to have a rival in his kingdom.

All the Hebrew prophets after David remembered him for his brave and heroic loyalty to Jehovah and said so in their histories and prophecies.

The writer of II Samuel described David as "the sweet Psalmist of Israel." Indeed, he was. And with this great reputation during his lifetime, it was easy for those coming after him to build up a tradition, and to ascribe to him the authorship of the book of Psalms. In fact, the earlier books were called the "Psalms of David."

Since the subject matter of the Psalms covers so many centuries, especially after the time of David, he could not historically speaking have written all of them, or perhaps even most of them. That he did write many of them, however, is certain.

For example, Psalm 18 was most surely written by David. It appears in II Samuel 22, and also in our collection of One-Hundred-and-Fifty. In both instances a head-note is prefixed, stating that the Psalm was written by David to celebrate his deliverance from the hand of all his enemies, and in particular from Saul.

This Psalm is noted for its fervent praise and adoration, and absolute trust, and may well be taken as representative of David's subject matter and mode of composition. The wholehearted declaration of his love and gratitude, as well as the style of his lyrics, undoubtedly influenced many other psalmists who came after him. And also the prophets, whose ecstatic rhapsodies frequently show this type of poetic style.

Thus, using Psalm 18 as a general pattern, many have assigned to David most of the songs of Book One, Psalms 1-41, omitting possibly Psalms 1 and 2, which are of the nature of a general introduction to the collection. This would suggest that the Psalms of David may be taken as a *nucleus* or foundation for later collections.

Also ascribed to David are Psalms 51-71 of Book Two; that is, the Psalms with the label "A Psalm of David," the same label we found attached to the Psalms of David in Book One.

In addition to the Psalms listed in Books One and Two, Psalms 101 and 103 of Book Four are also ascribed to David. And in Book Five, the following are listed as belonging in some sense to David: Psalms 108, 109, 110, 138, 139, 140, 141, 142, 143, 144, and 145.

It has been suggested by some scholars that the head-notes or titles containing the phrase "*of* David" is no certain indication of Davidic authorship, since the same preposition in Hebrew is translated in English as "of," "to," and "for." That is to say, a Psalm "of"

David may be one he himself wrote, or that was dedicated "to" David, or even written "for" David. However, long-established Hebrew tradition favors David's authorship of Psalms under this title, and that have been handed down to the compilers of our present one-hundred-and-fifty collection still under David's name.

Thus, at least seventy-three of our one-hundred-and-fifty collection are labeled in the head-notes or titles as "A Psalm of David."

Other individuals or groups are credited with the authorship of part of the Psalms. Twelve songs, Psalms 50, 73-83, are ascribed to Asaph, or the family of Asaph. Asaph's family, with Asaph himself as head, was one of three families of musicians permanently charged by David with furnishing music and songs for the worship service. Asaph himself was given the permanent office of sounding cymbals during the service. He was a Levite, and like other chief singers, was called a *seer*.

To the "Sons of Korah" are ascribed eleven Psalms: Psalms 42 (which originally included Psalm 43), 44-49, 84, 85, 87, and 88. Korah was a historical character, one of four leaders who rebelled against Moses and Aaron (see Numbers 16). The Sons of Korah were his descendants, and were organized by David as singers of sacred songs in the Tabernacle.

Two Psalms are ascribed to Solomon, Psalms 72 and 127; and one to Moses, Psalm 90. More about these later. Psalm 88 is attributed to Heman, and is the saddest and most despairing of all the Psalms. Psalm 89 is assigned to Ethan, another Levite who was appointed a singer in the time of David.

Fifty of the Psalms are anonymous. It is likely that some of these were written by the authors immediately preceding them, the author's name not being repeated.

It is generally agreed that David lived in the creative age of Hebrew song and poetry, and that he himself was a great and original poet, by any standards. And it is not surprising to discover that his thought and style greatly influenced other psalmists.

Indeed, a close examination of the later Psalms in our collection will reveal that they were written in an age when authors somewhat generally imitated and copied the earlier and greater Psalms. Psalms 140-144, for example, are made up mainly of ideas, quotations, and adaptations from earlier Psalms.

3. THE BOOK OF PSALMS AND ITS ENGLISH TRANSLATORS

The excellence of the book of Psalms as it comes down to us is due in no small part to the excellence of its translation into English.

It can be truthfully said that God loved poets, because He employed so many of them, both as original writers and as translators of His Book. The book of Psalms was written, and translated, by poets.

For a thousand years English-speaking peoples have been translating their Bible into good English. In Anglo-Saxon times — that is, before 1200 A.D. — portions of the Scriptures, especially the Psalms and the Ten Commandments and parts of the gospels, were translated into Old English. As early as 1382-1388, John Wycliffe and his associate, John Purvey, translated important portions of the Bible into the English of their day, and helped "to mold the language" as well as to exert a great influence on the life of the English people.

However, the standard of excellence for English translation of our Bible was set by the joint work of two great English scholars and poetic translators, William Tyndale and Miles Coverdale. Although much of their work was done in the 1520's, their translations were not published until 1530, 1531, 1534, and the complete Bible in 1535. The translation of the book of Psalms was done by Coverdale. All subsequent English translations of the Bible, including the *King James Version,* are greatly indebted to the work of these two men.[5]

4. READING HEBREW POETRY[6]

The construction or pattern of Hebrew poetry is different from that of English poetry.

English poetry depends for its musical effects on *rhyme* and regular rhythms or *meters.*

Hebrew poetry depends upon *rhythm of thought* and *balance* of sentence members. These members appear in the form of a *parallelism.*

The simplest and most common form of this parallelism in Hebrew poetry is when two thought sentences match each other in a couplet, for example, in Psalm 19:

> The heavens declare the glory of God;
> And the firmament showeth his handy work.

In Psalm 24:

> The earth is the Lord's and the fullness thereof,
> The world and those who dwell therein.

And in Psalm 46:

> The Lord of hosts is with us;
> The God of Jacob is our refuge.

In these couplets, the second line repeats the sense of the first, and adds emphasis as well as rhythm to the thought. This is called *synonymous* or equal parallelism.

Frequently, however, the second line contains the *opposite* thought of the first, in what may be called antithesis or contrast, for example, in Psalm 1:

> The Lord knows the way of the righteous,
> But the way of the wicked shall perish.

---

[5]For more on English translators, see "The Greater English Versions of Our Bible," p. 38ff.
[6]See F. F. Bruce, "The Poetry of the Old Testament," *The New Bible Commentary,* pp. 39-41 (1954); Arnold B. Rhodes, *The Book of Psalms,* pp. 12-14 (1960).

Sometimes a parallelism in thought has three members, or triplets, for example, in Psalm 24:

> And who shall stand in his holy place?
> He who has clean hands and a pure heart,
> Who does not lift up his soul to what is false,
> And who does not swear deceitfully.

Occasionally a parallelism may have even four members, or quatrains, for example, in Psalm 19:

> The Law of the Lord is perfect,
>   reviving the soul;
> The testimony of the Lord is sure,
>   making wise the simple;
> The precepts of the Lord are right,
>   rejoicing the heart;
> The commandment of the Lord is pure,
>   enlightening the eyes.

A close examination of the composition of the Psalms will show a great variety of forms, and reveal how the writers of these sacred lyrics avoided the sameness and monotony of didactic verses, such as the reader finds in the Proverbs and other more formal verse.

For example, in the triplet above, notice how the rhetorical question introducing the three members aids in variety. Also, notice the variety and pleasing effect secured in the quatrain above, by the use of *cadence* or concluding strain, in the end of each of the four parallel members, "reviving the soul," "making wise the simple," etc. These and many other instances show how the order and symmetry of life may exist along with the surprise of endless variety.

A few of the Psalms were used in *antiphonal* singing and chanting. Psalm 24, for example, appears to have been used on the occasion when David brought the Ark of the Lord from the house of Obededom to Jerusalem, to the tent prepared for it on Mount Zion. This Psalm is a processional for the occasion. It may be dramatized by dividing a group of singers or readers into two or more units, and by reading or singing the Psalm antiphonally.

Psalm 68 is a magnificent processional hymn and appears to have been written for the same occasion as that of Psalm 24, that is, for the ceremony of bringing the Ark to Jerusalem, and upon the hill called Mount Zion. Verses 1-3 describe the beginning, verses 4-10 the procession, verses 11-18 the approach to the city, and verses 19-35 the arrival. Two sub-hymns complete the Psalm: verses 28-31 contain the Hymn of Israel, and verses 32-35 the hymn of all the kingdoms of the earth.

Psalm 118 appears to be another processional hymn, to be chanted antiphonally. Verses 1-18 should be read or sung in half-verses, and the remainder of the Psalm in whole verses, for each unit or group.

Certain groups of Psalms, such as the liturgical Psalms 95-100, were sung antiphonally. These are songs of praise. Notice that the

The mosque marking the Tomb of David on Mount Zion. © *Matson Photo Service* parallel themes alternate from verse to verse, as between groups of singers.

Two other groups of Psalms which may be read or sung antiphonally are the Hallel Psalms 113-118, and the Hallelujah Psalms 146-150.

An understanding of these and other characteristics of Hebrew poetry will help the student to understand better the text of Scripture, and the essential meaning and beauty of the Psalms.[7]

Suggestions for Additional Reading

Bible Readings: The Book of Psalms. Text: *The Revised Standard Version;* or *The King James Version,* preferably in modern readers' format.

*Alexander, J. A.: *The Psalms.*

*Bruce, F. F.: "The Poetry of the Old Testament," *The New Bible Commentary,* pp. 39-41.

James, Fleming: *Thirty Psalmists.*

Leslie, E. A.: *The Psalms.*

*Leupold, H. C.: *The Psalms.*

*M'Caw, Leslie S.: "The Psalms," *The New Bible Commentary,* pp. 412-514.

Oesterley, W. O. E.: *The Psalms.*

*Paterson, John: *The Praises of Israel.*

*Rhodes, Arnold B.: *The Book of Psalms.*

Robinson, T. H.: *The Poetry of the Old Testament.*

Terrien, Samuel: *The Psalms and Their Meaning for Today.*

Welch, Adam C.: *The Psalter, in Life, Worship, and History.*

*Young, Edward J.: "The Psalms," *An Introduction to the Old Testament,* Chapter 19, pp. 307-327.

---

[7]T. H. Robinson, *The Poetry of the Old Testament,* p. 46 (1947).

Chapter 2

PSALMS (Continued)

5. THE CONTENTS OF THE BOOK OF PSALMS

The contents of the one-hundred-and-fifty Psalms of the book of Psalms may be classified for the purpose of reading and study according to the following subjects or themes:

(1) Songs of Praise

The key to the contents of the book of Psalms is to be found in its Hebrew title *Tehillim,* meaning "Songs of Praise." For it is preeminently a book of praise and thanksgiving.[1]

It contains grateful praises to the Lord for His help on all occasions: For the harvest; for victory in battle; for faith and trust; for God's mercy and lovingkindness; for assurance in time of national disaster; for recovery from severe illness; for security from a treacherous, personal enemy; for forgiveness of sins; for deliverance from death; for God's Word; for the sun, moon, and stars as the handiwork of God.

There are praises for God's House; for God's love; for the Sabbath of Creation, and the Eternal Sabbath; for the dedication of the king's palace; for the defeat of a foreign foe; for the promised Messiah; for deliverance from the Philistines; for the glories of Creation and the perfection of God's Laws; for the return from captivity; for the majesty and glory of God's eternal reign; for God's peace; for God's wonderful works, etc., etc.

More than a third of the total collection have praise and thanksgiving as their central theme, and many more have praise as a secondary motive. This list includes the main ones: Psalms 8, 9, 18, 19, 21, 30, 32, 33, 36, 40, 47, 48, 65-68, 75, 76, 84, 92, 93, 95-100, 103-106, 107, 113-118, 136, 138, 139, 144, 145, 146-150.

Of the Psalms of praise, here are seven that have won special favor with readers generally: Psalms 8, 19, 68, 84, 96, 100, and 107.

(2) The Cry of the Righteous in the Presence of Trouble

Another common theme in the Psalms is that of the cry for help in time of trouble. As in the other group, the occasion for these Psalms varies as widely as the needs of human beings. Here are the main

---

[1] See Anderson, *Understanding the Old Testament,* pp. 444-445; Arnold B. Rhodes, *The Book of Psalms,* pp. 21-22; John Paterson, *The Praises of Israel.*

Psalms which feature this theme: Psalms 3, 4, 6, 7, 13, 17, 22, 25, 26, 31, 35, 38, 39, 57, 74, 77, 79, 83, 86, 88, 94, 102, 109, 120, 130, 140, 141-143. Many of the Psalms in this group appear to have been written by David. Although he led a many-sided life, and was one of the most successful of men, David's personal life was never far from trouble.[2]

Eight of the Psalms should be read with this background of David's story in view:[3] Psalms 7, 34, 35, 52, 54, 56, 57, and 142.

(3) *Trust and Steadfastness in the Lord*

Still another frequent theme in the Psalms is that of quiet, confident trust in the Lord. In this group are some of the best loved Psalms in the entire collection. Any list should include the following: Psalms 3, 4, 5, 11, 16, 20, 23, 27, 28, 46, 56, 62, 63, 91, 108, 121-123, 125, 131.

The special favorites with readers in this group include Psalms 16, 23, 27, 46, 121, 122, 125. Psalm 23 is the best loved Psalm in the collection. If David had written nothing else, this Psalm would have entitled him to everlasting fame.

(4) *The Greatness and Majesty of Jehovah*

Faithful Hebrews held in awe the greatness and majesty of their God, and their devoted psalmists delighted in portraying Him in all His exalted glory.

The following list contains the main Psalms in the group, although some of them overlap the Psalms in the first group: Psalms 8, 19, 24, 29, 33, 46, 47, 68, 90, 93, 96, 97, 103, 104. Some special favorites in this group are Psalms 8, 19, 24, 46, 90, 96.

Psalm 90 is ascribed to Moses, who lived some four hundred years before David. It is one of the most comprehensive and mature, as well as one of the most beautiful, in the collection. It is easily one of the greatest of the great.

(5) *National and Historical Psalms*

The ancient Hebrews were intensely patriotic. Too, they were jealous of the fact that they were "chosen" of the Lord, and their psalmists, like their prophets, frequently reminded the people of how the Lord had led them to victory on many historic occasions.

Also, both psalmists and prophets reminded them of how often they were willful and disobedient, and how the Lord had to punish them, even at the hands of their most hated enemies. These feelings and attitudes are reflected in many of the Psalms, including Psalms 74, 78, 79, 80, 81, 83, 89, 94, 105, 106, 107, 114, 132, 135, 136, 137. Some of the favorites in this group are Psalms 105, 107, 132, 135.

(6) *The Prosperity of the Wicked*

From the days of Job on, ancient Hebrews wrestled with the problem of the prosperity of the wicked. It perplexed them to know

---

[2]For David's story, see p. 135ff.
[3]For a list of Psalms with a strong Davidic autobiographical interest, see Edward J. Young, *An Introduction to the Old Testament*, p. 314.

that Jehovah permitted the wicked and unfaithful, as well as the righteous, to prosper in this life.

Some of the psalmists gave good and final answers to their fellow countrymen who were disturbed with this problem. The most devastating answer is that the wicked do not prosper — in the long run.

It is interesting to see how these answers are developed in Psalms 10, 12, 14, 37, 53 (same as 14), 73, 94. The question of the prosperity of the wicked is well answered in Psalms 37, 73, 94.

(7) Psalms of Wisdom

In the next chapter of this book, we deal with what has been called Wisdom Literature, that is, books written by a class of writers known as the Wise Men of Israel. Scholars have long noted that several of the Psalms also belong to this classification.

The writer of the preface to the book of Proverbs states that the purpose of proverbs is "instruction." And so does the author of the book of Ecclesiastes, in his last chapter, claim that instruction is his chief purpose. This is the viewpoint from which the Psalms in this group are presented. The Psalms in this group are 1, 19:7-14, 37, 49, 73, 78, 90, 111, 112, 119, 127, 128.

(8) Psalms of Deep Penitence

In a few of the Psalms the psalmists cry out in anguish and deep penitence. These include Psalms 6, 32, 38, 51, 102, 130. Nearly all of them appear to refer to David's personal experiences.

(9) Psalms on the Hebrew Bible

The early Hebrew Bible was called the Law. It was the Law as recorded by Moses in the book of Exodus. It was enlarged by the books of Leviticus and Numbers, and especially by the revised and enlarged edition contained in the book of Deuteronomy.

This Law or Bible was the basis of instruction of all Hebrew children, and the religious guide of all Israel for centuries. Three of the Psalms in particular, Psalms 1 and 19 and 119, are on this Hebrew Bible. Psalm 119 is a continuation and an enlargement of the ideas in Psalms 1 and 19. It is a long, ingenious, and passionate meditation upon the glories of God's Word. It is the longest chapter in the Bible.

(10) Psalms Relating to the Exile and the Return

Psalm 137 is a lament of an exile "by the waters of Babylon," probably written not long after he was deported from his homeland. Psalm 126 appears to have been written shortly after the proclamation of Cyrus, king of Persia, permitting the Jews to return to Jerusalem. The event was unexpected and too good to be true. "We were like those who dream," wrote the psalmist.

A much longer, and a beautifully written Psalm, is 107, which describes how the dispersed Jews from the four corners of the earth were gathered together "to their desired haven," Jerusalem. The psalmist is full of praise to the Lord for His goodness in thus bringing His people home again. Other later Psalms contain references to the period of Captivity and Exile, and indicate that they were written much later than the time of David. Most of the Psalms of Book Five, Psalms 107-150, appear to belong to this later period.

(11) *Psalms Which Foretell the Coming of the Messiah*[4]

Some of the most significant Psalms in the collection are those which foretell the coming of the Christ, the Saviour and Hope of the world. These Psalms assumed greater significance when it was discovered that they were quoted and interpreted specifically by persons and writers of the New Testament, as referring to Christ's coming and mission. Of these there are at least fourteen Psalms, and no less than twice that many specific references quoted and interpreted in the New Testament, as follows:

Psalm 2:6-9 is the first to speak of the Messianic Age: "You are my son, today I have begotten you." Quoted by Paul in his sermon at Antioch of Pisidia, Acts 13:3.

Psalm 8:6 presents man, through the Messiah, as the Lord of Creation: "Thou hast given him dominion over the works of thy hands; thou hast put all things under his feet." Quoted by the author of Hebrews 2:6-10; also quoted by Paul in I Corinthians 15:27.

Psalm 16:8-11 refers to the Resurrection of Christ. Quoted by Peter to prove that the Resurrection was in accordance with prophecy, Acts 2:25-31.

Psalm 22:1 contains the words quoted by our Lord on the cross in the hour of His great suffering, Matthew 27:46. Psalm 22:8 contains the very words used by the priests in mocking our Lord as He hung on the cross, Matthew 27:43. Psalm 22:16, "They have pierced my hands and feet," which is the language Thomas used when he required of the other disciples evidence of the Resurrection, John 20:25. Psalm 22:18, "They divide my garments among them, and for my raiment they cast lots," quoted by John 19:23-24.

This remarkable Psalm, Psalm 22, for its realistic picture of incidents and details foretold of the Crucifixion, should be compared with the famous fifty-third chapter of the book of Isaiah.

Psalm 40:6-8 refers to the willingness of the Son to obey the Father in the sacrificial death, Hebrews 10:5-10.

Psalm 41:9 is quoted by Jesus after He had washed His disciples' feet on the night of the Last Supper, and referred to Judas as the traitor, John 13:18.

Psalm 45:6-7 is quoted by the author of the book of Hebrews 1:8-9, and refers to the Messiah as the ideal King.

Psalm 69:4 is quoted by Jesus at the Last Supper, against His

[4]See Henry H. Halley, "Messianic Passage," *Halley's Bible Handbook*, p. 233 (22nd ed., 1961).

enemies, "They hated me without cause," John 15:25. Psalm 69:9 was remembered by His disciples at the time Jesus drove the money-changers out of the Temple: "Zeal for thy house will consume me," John 2:17. Also quoted by Paul, Romans 15:3. Psalm 69:21 relates to the cross and the vinegar they gave Him to drink, Matthew 27:34. Psalm 69:25 was quoted by Peter concerning Judas' death and burial, Acts 1:20.

Psalm 72 presents the eternal reign of the righteous King, and is recalled in Luke 2:14; Ephesians 1:21; Hebrews 11:16.

Psalm 89 repeats God's covenant with David and David's house, and the promise of the everlasting throne, Hebrews 1:5-13; Colossians 1:16.

Psalm 91:11-12 is quoted by Satan at the time of the Temptation in the Wilderness, except that the Tempter in his craftiness *misquotes* Scripture for his own purpose, when he omitted the significant phrase, "to guard you in all your ways," in verse 11, Matthew 4:6.

Psalm 109:8 is quoted by Peter concerning Jesus' betrayer, Judas, Acts 1:20.

Psalm 110:1 was quoted by Jesus to the Pharisees as evidence of His Sonship, and the writer added, "Nor from that day did any one dare to ask Him any more questions." Jesus thus verified the prophecy of the Psalms. The passage is recorded by Matthew 22:43-45; Mark 12:36; Luke 20:42; Acts 2:34; Hebrews 1:13. Psalm 110:4 was quoted by the author of the book of Hebrews 5:6; 7:17.

Psalm 118:22 is quoted in Matthew 21:42; Acts 4:11; Ephesians 2:20; I Peter 2:7: "The stone which the builders rejected has become the chief corner stone. This is the Lord's doing; it is marvelous in our eyes." Psalm 118:26 contains the shouts of the crowds as Jesus made His triumphant entry into Jerusalem the week before His Crucifixion: "Blessed be he who comes in the name of the Lord!" (Matthew 21:9).

Psalm 132:17 is quoted by Zechariah, the father of John the Baptist: "Blessed be the Lord God of Israel . . . for he has . . . raised up a horn of salvation for us in the house of his servant David," meaning that the Messiah would be the Eternal Inheritor of David's throne.

(12) The Hallel Psalms

There are a few special groups of Psalms which deserve notice in our classification of the contents of the book of Psalms. The Hallel Psalms, Psalms 113-118, have always been associated in the Jewish Church with the three great pilgrim festivals of the Jewish year, the Passover, Pentecost, and the Feast of the Tabernacles. The Passover hymns were sung also in Jewish families on the night of the Passover.

One fact which attaches special interest to Psalms 113-118 in this group is that they were probably sung by our Lord and His disciples after the Last Supper.

(13) *Songs of Ascents*

Another special group of Psalms is the Songs of Ascents, each one having the title, "A Song of Ascents." They are the fifteen Psalms 120-134.[5] These Psalms are usually interpreted as "Songs of Pilgrimages," meaning literally "goings-up." They were often sung by pilgrims on their annual journeys to keep the various feasts at Jerusalem. Indeed, some of the Psalms indicate progress of the pilgrims. Psalm 121 suggests that it was sung by pilgrims as they first sighted Jerusalem or the mountains surrounding the famous city. Psalm 122 pictures pilgrims at the end of their journey and standing within the gates of Jerusalem. Psalms 123, 124, 125, were sung within the Lord's house, the Temple.

(14) *The Hallelujah Psalms*

The final group is called "The Great Hallel," or Hallelujah Songs. They are Psalms 146-150.

These Psalms are praise-hymns in an extraordinary sense. In the earlier groups of hymns other motives and elements besides praise were present. But in the Hallelujah Psalms there is singleness of purpose, and that purpose is the adoration of Jehovah.

Each of the five Psalms opens with a prologue of *Hallelujah,* and closes with an epilogue *Hallelujah,* which translated into English means "Praise the Lord." Indeed, as someone has observed, these last Psalms form an elaborate and comprehensive doxology to the whole collection, just as each division of the book has its individual doxology (see last stanza of Psalms 41, 72, 89, 106).

---

[5]See Anderson, *op. cit.*, p. 445, including footnote.

Dr. Conrad Schick's famous model of Solomon's Temple. © *Matson Photo Service*

PART FOUR

BOOKS BY THE WISE MEN OF ISRAEL

A partial reconstruction of Solomon's Stables
at Megiddo, showing clearly at right the
posts to which the horses were tied. *Courtesy Oriental Institute of the University of Chicago*

Chapter 1

INTRODUCTION

1. THE PRESENCE OF WISE MEN AS A CLASS OR PROFESSION

The whole Bible was produced by wise men, and it is pre-eminently a Book of wisdom.

What this section refers to, however, is the presence of a class or profession of Wise Men, such as were to be found in every generation and in every land of the ancient East.[1] The prophet Jeremiah, for example, indicates that in his time the Wise Men were as authoritative as the priests and the prophets, as voices of God's revelation:

> Then they said, "Come, let us make plots against Jeremiah, for the Law shall not perish from the *priest*, nor counsel from the *wise*, nor the word from the *prophet*." (Jeremiah 18:18)

In Genesis 41:8, an early reference is made to Pharaoh's wise men, who with the magicians, were called in to interpret the king's dream. In Job 15, Eliphaz (probably a non-Israelite) in his answer to Job, regarded himself as one of the wise men who had consulted other wise men regarding Job's problem. Obadiah, verse 8, refers to Edom's wise men. The author of the book of Daniel 2:48, relates how Daniel was made ruler not only of the whole province of Babylon, but also was made "chief prefect over all the wise men of Babylon."

The Wise Men who came from the "East" and worshiped the Child Jesus belonged to the religious caste known as Magi, and found among the Persians, Babylonians, Arabians, and other Eastern nations. From the days of the Captivity, the Jews and their synagogues in exile exercised an influence that was particularly strong in Babylonia and Persia, as is evidenced by the stories of Daniel and Esther.

It is more than likely, therefore, that these Wise Men came from Babylonia or Persia, or perhaps Northern Arabia, where many of them no doubt worshiped the God of Israel, and like the Jews, looked forward to the coming of the prophesied Messiah.

The wise of counsel are met with throughout Israel's national history. In II Samuel 14, the story is told of the wise woman of Tekoa; and in II Samuel 20:16, the work of the wise woman of Abel of Beth-

---

[1]See W. O. E. Oesterley, *The Wisdom of Egypt and the Old Testament;* John Paterson, *The Book That Is Alive,* pp. 41-44.

maacah, who took the part of David in crushing Sheba's rebellion. At the top of the list, however, were the four wise men, Ethan and Heman and Calcol and Darda, with whom the wisdom of Solomon is compared, I Kings 4:31.

However, the Jews universally regarded Solomon as their wisest man, and justly so. As a young man he loved the Lord, and prayed for an understanding mind and heart, to know good from evil, and to govern his people justly.

God gave him wisdom such as no other man had ever received, and with it deep humility.

> And God gave Solomon wisdom and understanding beyond measure, and largeness of mind like the sand on the seashore, so that Solomon's wisdom surpassed the wisdom of all the people of the East, and all the wisdom of Egypt. For he was wiser than all other men, wiser than Ethan the Ezrahite, and Heman, Calcol, and Darda, the sons of Mahol; and his fame was in all the nations round about.

2. The Books by the Wise Men

The Wise Men had habits of thought and a literature somewhat peculiar to themselves. The Proverbs, for example, deal with *practical life*, something new in Hebrew literature, and rather different from the books of the Prophets and their denunciation of sin, and the songs of praise and worship in the book of Psalms.

However, the Wise Men reached the same conclusions as the prophets and the psalmists, although they say next to nothing about Israel as a chosen people. Moreover, there is no single hint of the Messianic Hope; and only one reference to Temple worship. There is little said even of a personal God.

But, as Professor Richard G. Moulton has said, "It would be a great mistake to describe their works as secular. The whole is pervaded by a spirit of devoutness" (*Modern Reader's Bible*, p. 1451). If there is little mention of God in some of these works, it is plainly because the idea of God is so entirely taken for granted.

The book of Job differs in one important particular from the other books of Wisdom, in that it comes face to face with God, and like John Milton's *Paradise Lost*, undertakes "to justify the ways of God to man." And it does so by a non-Jewish and wholly unorthodox approach. The book deals with the mystery of evil, and the problem of human suffering in the world, and is the author's answer to that problem. In the book we meet with a group of wise men, all of them apparently non-Jews, except perhaps the author, the wisest of them all.

The book of Ecclesiastes is unique in that it is the most pessimistic book in the Bible, although no one would wish to be without it. It was written by one wise man about another wise man, Solomon, whom he impersonates. The author makes Solomon his speaker, after the manner of a dramatic monologue. After the manner of the dramatic monologue, too, the author selects one particular viewpoint in Solomon's life for his study, Solomon's old age.

If the book of Ecclesiastes impersonates Solomon in his old age, the Song of Songs presents an idyllic love story of Solomon's earlier life and kingdom. Again Solomon is a character in the book and not its author. The authorship is assigned to one of the wise men. There were many other books by the Wise Men that were not thought to be worthy of a place in the Old Testament canon. (See the Apocrypha.)

SUGGESTIONS FOR ADDITIONAL READING ON WISDOM LITERATURE

Bible Readings: The Books of Proverbs, Job, Ecclesiastes, Song of Songs. Text: *The Revised Standard Version;* or *The King James Version,* preferably in modern reader's format.

*Anderson, Bernhard W.: "The Beginning of Wisdom," *Understanding the Old Testament,* Chapter 15, pp. 464-500.

*Bruce, F. F. and Francis Davidson: "The Wisdom Literature of the Old Testament," *The New Bible Commentary,* pp. 42-44.

Irwin, William: "Wisdom Literature," *The Interpreter's Bible,* Vol. I, pp. 212-219.

*Oesterley, W. O. E.: *The Wisdom of Egypt and the Old Testament.*

*Paterson, John: *The Book That Is Alive,* Chapters 3-9.

Rankin, O. S.: *Israel's Wisdom Literature; Its Bearing on Theology and the History of Religion.*

Ranston, Harvey: *The Old Testament Wisdom Books and Their Teaching.*

Rylaarsdam, J. Coert: *Revelation in Jewish Wisdom Literature.*

Terrien, Samuel L.: "Job," *The Interpreter's Bible,* Vol. III.

Chapter 2

PROVERBS

1. THE CHARACTER AND PURPOSE OF THE BOOK OF PROVERBS

The book of Proverbs, like the book of Psalms, is a collection of collections. That is to say, the Proverbs as we have them came from many sources, although Solomon is represented as the chief contributor.

The book is made up of five main divisions or collections. They are:

(1) Introduction: In Praise of Wisdom, Chapters 1-9;

(2) The Proverbs of Solomon, Chapters 10 to 22:16;

(3) Proverbs by the Wise Men, Chapters 22:17 to 24;

(4) Proverbs of Solomon Copied Out by the Men of Hezekiah King of Judah, Chapters 25 to 29;

(5) The Proverbs of Agur, and King Lemuel, Chapters 30 and 31.

The Proverbs of the last division appear to be an appendix to the book as a whole.

The Hebrew word *mashal*, from which our English word *Proverb* comes, has a much fuller meaning than the English word as we use it. Our word proverb signifies a pithy, pointed saying. A maxim, with practical implications, such as, "He profits most who serves best."

The Hebrew proverb, on the contrary, seeks to instruct in what is good and upright in the whole of one's daily life, and to present the theme that there is no true wisdom apart from the faith in the One God.[1]

2. AUTHORSHIP AND DATE

It is impossible with our present information to determine the authorship of all the Proverbs in this collection.

The Jews regarded Solomon as the founder of Proverbs, just as they regarded Moses as the giver of their Law, and David as the author of the Psalms.

We know, however, that David did not write all the Psalms; and we have every reason to believe that Solomon did not write all the Proverbs.

---

[1]For an analysis and interpretation of the book of Proverbs, see Bernhard W. Anderson, "An Anthology of Proverbs," *Understanding the Old Testament*, pp. 473-477 (1957); W. A. Rees Jones and Andrew F. Walls, "The Proverbs," *The New Bible Commentary*, pp. 515-537 (2nd ed., 1954).

For instance, at different points of the book, rubrics or section headings occur giving the group or individual authorship. The rubric at the heading of chapter 10 assigns this section to Solomon, and at chapter 22:17 and 24:23 the Proverbs are ascribed to "The Wise."

At chapter 25:1, the rubric reads: "These also are Proverbs of Solomon which the men of Hezekiah (scholars) king of Judah copied." And at chapter 30:1: "The words of Agur son of Jakeh of Massa"; and at 31:1: "The words of Lemuel, king of Massa, which his mother taught him."

So it appears that the general heading of chapter 1, "The Proverbs of Solomon, son of David, king of Israel," does not mean to imply that Solomon was the author of all the Proverbs of the book, but that it is likely a label placed there by an editor or publisher.[2]

Who was the author of the important introductory section, chapters 1 to 9, in Praise of Wisdom? Some wise man, or group of wise men, prepared the section, including the long title giving the purpose of the book.

In our day, we would call him a teacher or director of religious education, whose purpose was to provide instruction not merely in Proverbs but through them instruction in the Law and other portions of the Old Testament. This purpose was intended first for the instruction of the youth, and then for all the people.

Solomon was noted for his verbal wisdom, his wise *sayings*. He conversed with many individuals and with many peoples. The historian of I Kings 4:32 states that Solomon "uttered" three thousand Proverbs. The Proverbs in chapters 10 to 22:16, may well represent his manner and temperament, which was ethical and practical.

The fourth section, chapters 25 to 29, which King Hezekiah's scribes or wise men copied, may well have been a second gleaning of proverbs from the Solomon collection of 3,000, of which the historian wrote.

The date of the Proverbs is also impossible to determine, with the information we now have.

We know that proverbial literature is very ancient and that it is to be found in all lands. In I Samuel 24:13, David quotes an ancient proverb to Saul, when Saul's life was in David's hands: "As the proverb of the ancients says, 'Out of the wicked comes forth wickedness'; but my hand shall not be against you."

In his many wise utterances, Solomon made proverbs popular, and not only headed up the wise men of his generation, but he gave proverbial literature a vogue and prosperity it had not known before.

So, after Solomon's death, about 934 B.C., there came into greater prominence in Israel the class or society known as the Wise Men.

---

[2]See John Paterson, "Schools, Scribes and Sages," *The Book That Is Alive*, pp. 61-81 (1954), for the role of the Wise Men.

They shared with the priests and prophets not only as the chief agents of God's revelation, but they also shared with them the responsibility of public instruction. And their teachings were highly esteemed. Moreover, they collected and composed proverbs until eventually there were many collections.

These Proverbs became a part of Hebrew tradition and were quoted widely by priests, prophets, and rulers and others of succeeding generations. They also became an important part of the instruction of Hebrew youth.

Jesus was familiar with these Proverbs and quoted many of them in His discourses. The method of instruction suggested in chapter 1:6, by proverbs, figures or parables, and epigrams, is substantially the method Jesus used in His parables and other figures.

3. The Contents of the Book of Proverbs

(1) *The Title and Introduction*

The book of Proverbs has the longest title of any book in the Old Testament, covering the first six verses of the opening chapter. From his title, which is also the writer's introduction to his book, we learn both the purpose of Proverbs, and something about the writer himself.

He is a teacher, one of the Wise Men of Israel, who is introducing these Proverbs as a book of instruction. His aims are high: that all men may know wisdom and receive instruction, in wise dealing, and in justice and righteousness; that youth and the inexperienced may receive knowledge, and learn discretion and prudence; and that the wise may increase his understanding and wisdom.

These are the ideals of the Good Life, as set forth by the Wise Men.

(2) *The Praise of Wisdom,* Chapters 1-9

The chapters of this section are made up mainly of short poems on a variety of topics or themes. The wise man, who is writing these Proverbs, plays the role of the teacher and addresses the learner as "My son."

Verse 7, chapter 1, is an appropriate motto for the book as a whole as well as for this section: "The fear of the Lord is the beginning of knowledge; fools despise wisdom and instruction."

Chapter 1:7-19, in the form of a sonnet, is a warning against companionship with robbers; verses 20-33 is an ode in praise of wisdom. The writer lets the Voice of Wisdom be his speaker.

Chapter 2 is on the blessings of wisdom, or the art of living the Good Life.

Chapter 3 is a grand chapter on the major theme of the book: *Happy is the man who finds wisdom, and the man who gets understanding, for by wisdom the Lord founded the earth, and by understanding he established the heavens.*

In chapter 4, the teacher turns autobiographical, and repeats the instruction he received from his father. The main poem of the chapter is on the two paths or ways of life: the path of the *upright,* and the way of the *wicked.*

Chapter 5 contains three related poems, mainly on the theme of the disastrous consequences of adultery.

In chapter 6, we have a group of poems on four somewhat unrelated themes: verses 1-6 contain a warning against making one's self responsible for another's payment of debt; verses 6-11, against idleness; verses 12-15, against lying; and verses 16-19, seven evils the Lord hates. This last is a "numerical proverb." (See chapter 30 in Proverbs for other numerical proverbs.)

Verses 20-35 resume the theme of chapter 5 and are on the evil consequences of adultery. Likewise, chapter 7 is a continuation of the latter part of chapter 6, and is on the same theme.

This introductory section of Proverbs closes with two special chapters in praise of wisdom, the main theme of the section. Chapter 8 contains two odes. In the first the writer speaks with the voice of wisdom again, verses 1-21; in the second Wisdom relates her part in the work of Creation, verses 22-31.

Chapter 9, in two separate sonnets, presents in contrast two rival hostesses: Mrs. Wisdom and Mrs. Folly. Their invitations, and the consequences of accepting either, present a somewhat novel approach to the writer's study of the rival claims of Folly and Wisdom.

(3) *The Proverbs of Solomon,* Chapters 10 to 22:16

This section is generally regarded as the Proverbs of Solomon. It is definitely the largest collection in the book.

Whether the collection was made by Solomon himself, by some scholar or scribe of his court, or by a later collector, we have no way of determining. But the historian's statement in I Kings 4:32 suggests that collections may have been made in Solomon's lifetime. However, the rubric at the head of chapter 25 suggests that later collections were made, and that Hezekiah's scholars made them. Hezekiah's reign was more than 200 years after Solomon's time.

One thing we notice about the Proverbs of Solomon is that most of them consist of two lines, or are in couplets. Also, the two lines are parallel to each other, and nearly always the parallelism is one of contrasting ideas, as:

> A wise son makes a glad father,
> But a foolish son is a sorrow to his mother.

Another thing the reader notices is that the Proverbs of Solomon are without any order or principle of arrangement. Proverbs on rather different subjects are often placed side by side without any apparent reason.

In chapters 10 to 15, the contrasted theme of the Upright and the Wicked, their ways, rewards and punishments, appears more or less prominent. This heading therefore may serve as a rough classification for readers who wish to group the Proverbs.

Likewise, in chapters 16 to 22:16, the prevailing theme appears to be the general one of man's life and his conduct, in a world created and governed by the Lord.

The student will be impressed, too, with the high standard of morality and religion which the Proverbs of this section uphold. Also, the reader will do well to remember that the Proverbs were written many centuries before the days of the Gospel and the New Testament.

Again, the reader has noticed how practical in nature are these Proverbs, and how modern many of them appear — as if they had been uttered in the twentieth century A.D., instead of in the tenth century B.C., as some of them were.

(4) *Sayings by the Wise*, Chapters 22:17 to 24

This section of the book of Proverbs consists of two other small collections or fragments of collections, both labeled "Sayings of the Wise."

The first of these, in chapters 22:17 to 24:22, is announced by the writer (22:17-21) as "Thirty Sayings of Admonition and Knowledge." Then follows his list of thirty precepts and warnings.

We cannot help noticing that these proverbs are much unlike those of Solomon in the preceding section, in both attitude and style. The sage here is more personal and didactic, showing a good opinion of himself and of his wisdom.

Also, his proverbs are composed, not in sonnets or odes of some length like those of our first section, or in couplets like Solomon's, but in *strophes* or short choral-like stanzas.

Some scholars have held that these proverbs are rather similar in many respects to the proverbs in an Egyptian collection, under the title "Wisdom of Amen-em-ope."[3] Too, since the Egyptian manuscript has thirty chapters, his work may have influenced our writer, who has thirty sayings of the wise.

The other of the small collections of this section, in chapter 24: 23-34, has the rubric heading "These also are sayings of the wise." Verses 23-26 deal with legal procedures. Verse 27 reads like modern advice on pre-fabricating of building materials before the house is ready to be built. Our author closes his work with a homily on the sluggard, who are the lazy and idle of all ages.

(5) *The Second Book of Proverbs of Solomon*, Chapters 25-29

The rubric heading for this section of the book of Proverbs reads, "These also are Proverbs of Solomon which the men of Hezekiah king of Judah copied." What this means is that the scholars or literary men

---

[3]See John Paterson, *The Book That Is Alive*, p. 52.

at King Hezekiah's court, more than 200 years after the death of Solomon, transcribed these proverbs from some other collection or collections.

The word "also" suggests that a previous collection of proverbs of Solomon was known to exist, and that the present one is an additional collection. Moreover, several of the proverbs here are more or less identical copies of the proverbs in chapters 10 to 22:16, which further suggests that by this time copies of Solomon's proverbs had been made and were in circulation.

The proverbs of Solomon's second book differ in certain particulars from those of the first book. For example, the proverbs in chapters 25-27 in general deal with miscellaneous *comparisons,* instead of *contrasts,* in presenting moral lessons. However, in chapters 27-29, the method of contrast or antithesis is again resumed for most of the remainder of the section.

Although most of the proverbs in this section consist of two lines in parallel couplets, as was universally true in chapters 10 to 22:16, several appear in three or four lines.

(6) *The Sayings of Agur, and King Lemuel,* Chapters 30-31

Of Agur we know nothing except what his proverbs themselves reveal. It has been suggested that he may have been a non-Israelite, like Job and Balaam, who had knowledge of the true God. An Ishmaelite perhaps, from the borders of the Arabian desert.

His proverbs, in chapter 30, are certainly unlike any we have previously met in this book. At the outset he professes great humility and lack of wisdom to fathom the mysteries of nature, or to know the Holy One. Yet he professes faith; "every word of God proves true," he says.

Agur is one of the wise men, full of experience and wisdom. He delights to compose his general observations in the form of "numerical proverbs," for which his short book is noted.

The other wise man in this group, King Lemuel, like Agur son of Jakeh, may have been an Ishmaelite. One scholar asks the question, "Is it possible that Lemuel was an Ishmaelite whose mother came from Israel?"

At any rate, he records the wise sayings his mother taught him on the duties of a king and on how to avoid the evils of his day. And was his mother also the inspiration for the fine poem on the virtues of a good woman, at the close of his book?

A glance back over the book of Proverbs shows what diversity of material it contains. In the words of one scholar, "The book of Proverbs represents a complex tradition, extending throughout almost the whole of the Old Testament period."[4] Too, over the centuries Israel had many vital contacts with Egypt and Babylonia and Arabia,

---

[4]See Anderson, *Understanding the Old Testament,* pp. 475-476.

not to mention her other neighbors. Indeed, this anthology represents the ancient wisdom of the East as well as that of Israel.

But it was Israel, to which was added also the prophetic and priestly tradition, that developed the faith that "the fear of the Lord is the beginning of wisdom." The sages of Israel, in their spiritual maturity, emphasized the concept: *Wisdom comes from God and is a part of the Divine plan for the whole creation.*

Special References on the Book of Proverbs

*Anderson, Bernhard W.: "An Anthology of Proverbs," *Understanding the Old Testament,* pp. 473-477.

*Jones, W. A. Rees and Andrew F. Walls: "The Proverbs," *The New Bible Commentary,* pp. 515-537.

Moulton, Richard G.: "The Proverbs," *The Modern Reader's Bible,* pp. 901-954, and 1452-1458.

Oesterley, W. O. E.: *The Book of Proverbs.*

*Paterson, John: "Wise Men and Fools," and "Schools, Scribes, and Sages," *The Book That Is Alive,* pp. 41-81.

*Young, Edward J.: *An Introduction to the Old Testament,* pp. 328-335.

Chapter 3

JOB

1. THE DRAMA OF JOB

The book of Job deals with a question as old as man; a question which has both fascinated and puzzled every generation. It is the mystery of evil, and the problem of human suffering.

Of the book of Job, Thomas Carlyle wrote:

> I call it, apart from all theories about it, one of the grandest things ever written with pen. One feels, indeed, as if it were not Hebrew: such a noble universality, different from noble patriotism or noble sectarianism, reigns in it. A noble book: all men's book! It is our first, oldest statement of the never-ending problem — man's destiny and God's way with him here on this earth . . . There is nothing written, I think, in the Bible or out of it, of equal literary merit.[1]

The book, which is in the form of a poetic drama, consists of three parts: A Prologue; the Body or main action of the play; and an Epilogue. The Prologue and the Epilogue are in prose; the main action is in verse.

Why do the *righteous* suffer? And why are the *unrighteous* allowed to continue in their wrongdoing, and permitted to prosper, whereas the innocent must often pay the penalty for the misdeeds of the wicked?

The writer presents three answers to the problem: (1) the traditional Jewish answer, as given by Job's three friends Eliphaz, Bildad, and Zophar; (2) the answer by the young man Elihu; (3) and the answer of the Almighty.

If the reader will read the entire book at one sitting, and imaginatively and freshly as if for the first time, he will agree with Martin Luther, who said that Job is "magnificent and sublime as no other book of Scripture."

2. THE SETTING AND CHARACTERS OF THE BOOK OF JOB

There was a man in the land of Uz, whose name was Job.

Who was this man Job, and where was the land of Uz?

In general, these questions are answered in the Prologue, the first two chapters of the book.

Abraham's brother Nahor's first-born son was named Uz (Genesis 22:21). According to the Jewish historian Josephus, Uz was the founder of the old city of Damascus. And from the evidence generally, it appears that the descendants of Uz occupied a portion of the

---

[1] "The Hero As Prophet," from *Lectures on Heroes.*

A pastoral scene on the Plain of Sharon.
Job's flocks must have grazed much like this.
© *Matson Photo Service*

Syrian and Arabian deserts east of Palestine, and between the latitudes of Damascus and Edom.

The home of Job, according to early tradition, appears to have been in the somewhat fertile district east of Damascus and a large lake, famous later as the Sea of Galilee. This region was once thickly populated, as is indicated now by the ruins of some three hundred ancient cities.

The writer, in Job 1:3, states that "this man was the greatest of all the people of the East," a term which applied to the tribes dwelling beyond the eastern borders of Palestine, in Syria and Arabia, and which later included also Chaldea, Media, and Persia.

The part of the East where Job lived is further indicated by two bands of robbers to which he was exposed, the Sabeans and the Chaldeans. The Chaldeans we know, for they occupied the southern portion of Babylonia. And according to an Assyrian inscription, in the eighth century B.C., the Sabeans were living in northwest Arabia, in the general latitude of Damascus. This would place the Sabeans of the Job story in the general geographical area of the Chaldeans, the other robbers of the story.

The time or historical background of the story of Job is indicated by the ancient customs and patriarchal atmosphere. Job is a great prince, whose ten sons and daughters are married and set up in their separate tents and houses in the prince's realm. Like a true patriarch, Job reckons his wealth by the number of cattle of each kind he possesses. Also, he is his own priest.

In the Prologue, the author makes it clear that Job is a non-Israelite, but nevertheless a pious and faithful worshiper of the invisible God, the same God worshiped by the Hebrews of the Old Testament, and that spiritually he belongs to the same "people from the East" from whom Abraham himself went forth, the first missionary to Canaan. In short, the patriarch Job worshiped Israel's God, outside the ranks of Israel.

The setting of the drama of Job has two different scenes. The first is the scene of the Council of Heaven, in which Satan is given permission to test Job's piety and integrity — presented in two stages, as Job's first and second trials.

The second scene is that of Job, after all his misfortunes have come upon him. The scene is an unforgettable one. We see coming in the distance Job's three friends, who have made an appointment together to "comfort" Job. Job is sitting on a mound, in ashes, outside his village. For in addition to all the other evils that have befallen him, Job is now afflicted with a terrible form of leprosy.

A considerable interval has elapsed before his friends' arrival. Job has suffered until he is only a shadow of his former self. At first his friends do not recognize him. Then they raised their voices, and wept, sprinkling dust upon their heads, as was the custom of those in great grief.

> . . . And they sat with him on the ground seven days and seven nights, and no one spoke a word to him, for they saw that his suffering was very great.

These three friends·were princes and persons of importance, like Job himself. Eliphaz was a Temanite. Esau had a son named Teman, and thus Eliphaz was probably a descendant of Esau. As a leader of the three, he was a stately, dignified prince, more considerate, and with more finesse in his criticism of his friend Job.

Bildad was a Shuhite. Abraham had a son by the name of Shuah, and it appears that the Arab tribe of Shuhites were descended from him. Bildad is a narrow traditionalist, who finds the wisdom of the past quite good enough for him. Zophar was a Naamathite, a native of Naamah in northern Arabia. Oldest of the group, Zophar is a dogmatist who assumes a holier-than-thou attitude toward his friend Job.

Elihu was a Buzite, that is, he belonged to the Arabian tribe of Buz. He was a young man, an outsider and perhaps a foreigner, who sat on the sidelines while Job and his friends argued at length on the cause of Job's suffering. When finally the friends refused to answer Job further, the young man came forth with *his* answer.

The Almighty appears as a Voice out of the Whirlwind, and gives the third and final answer to the mystery of Job's suffering.

3. AUTHORSHIP AND DATE

The author of the book of Job is unknown. Various suggestions have been made as to the authorship, including such names as Moses, Solomon, Isaiah, Jeremiah or his friend Baruch, or one of the other prophets in the age of the captivity of Judah (586 B.C.). But the evidence is not available to prove or disprove any one of them.

However, distinction must be made between the date of the materials of the book, and the date of its author and composition. We know that the patriarch Job and his friends belong to the ancient world, the age of the patriarchs. Also, the author of the book of Ezekiel refers to the historical person Job, along with two other personages of great piety, Noah and Daniel, indicating that Job belonged to the past (Ezekiel 14:14).

The date of composition, on the contrary, very likely was much later, as late possibly as the great upheaval produced by the captivity of Judah, in which the prophets saw the hand of God disciplining individuals and nations toward nobler ends and destinies.[2]

One thing is certain, the book is highly reflective, shows a knowl-

---

[2]For the date of Job, see Samuel L. Terrien, "The Book of Job," *The Interpreter's Bible,* Vol. III, pp. 888-890, who favors a date between 580 and 540 B.C. Some scholars prefer a later date, say fifth or fourth century B.C. A date around the time of the captivity of Judah, 597 to 586 B.C. or a little later, seems highly plausible.

edge of distant lands, travel, and the experience and influence of out-side people and events, such as would be true only of a later age. Also, the poetic interpretation of events and Divine disciplines is that of one of the great prophets, like Isaiah or Jeremiah, one of the wisest of the wise.

If the author was a prophet, and a Hebrew as is likely, he writes his book from a non-Jewish and wholly unorthodox viewpoint. For example, all his characters are non-Israelites, and his *philosophy of suffering* advances far beyond the traditional Jewish view, namely, that suffering is caused by some specific sin.[3]

4. THE MAIN ACTION OF THE DRAMA OF JOB

Chapter 3 introduces the main action or argument of the drama of Job. It is conducted by means of a series of speeches by Job and his three friends, somewhat after the manner of our modern panel questions and discussions, in open forum.

As the curtain rises, Job and his friends are sitting in silence on the ash mound outside the village. Words of consolation fail them as they sit beside him for seven days and seven nights, uttering never a word.

At length, Job breaks silence and gives vent to his suffering and anguish. Probably a considerable interval has elapsed before the arrival of his friends.

(1) *Three Rounds of Speeches: The First Answer to the Problem of Suffering*

Chapters 3 to 31 present three rounds of speeches between Job and his friends, in which Job answers the arguments and criticisms of each, and at the same time defends his own integrity.

THE FIRST ROUND, chapters 3-14. In his opening speech, Job curses the day of his birth and contrasts the quiet sleep of death with the troubles of this life, which Shakespeare called "the slings and arrows of outrageous fortune."

Eliphaz (chapter 4), after complimenting Job for a life of good deeds, begins the argument with a general statement on the sinfulness of man, and diplomatically hints at Job's secret sin as the only explana-tion of his misfortunes and suffering. He advises Job:

> As for me, I would seek God,
>   and to God would I commit my cause;
> Who does great things and unsearchable,
>   marvelous things without number.

---

[3]The date of the composition of the book of Job, however, is not the important thing. As one scholar expressed it, "There are few poems in all literature whose date and historical background are of less importance than they are in the book of Job." For an introduction to the interpretation and message of Job, see E. S. P. Heavenor, "Job," *The New Bible Commentary*, pp. 387-411 (1954); Richard G. Moulton, "The Book of Job," *The Modern Reader's Bible*, pp. 1480-1495; John Paterson, *The Book That Is Alive*, Chapters 6 and 7.

Job replies to Eliphaz, declaring his innocence.

Bildad, the second speaker, using the same line as his predecessor, insists that God is just and that sinful man cannot compare his
righteousness with the righteousness of God, but instead must confess
his sins and make supplication to the Almighty for forgiveness and
restoration to his former prosperity. He rebukes Job for not remembering the wisdom of the past: how everyone perishes who sins and
forgets God. Job's children, who have been destroyed, must have
sinned; the same is in store for Job, unless he repents.

Job, as before, insists on his innocence. Although he is conscious
that he has not sinned, Job for the first time introduces and develops
at length the principle of the impossibility of mortal man's appearing
just before God, and that it is hopeless for him to attempt to clear
himself.

> Though I am innocent,
> I cannot answer him;
> I must appeal for mercy
> to my accuser.

Zophar, the last speaker in this round, accuses Job of iniquity
and denounces him for accusing the Almighty and for attempting to
"find out the deep things of God."

He appears even more dogmatic than the two friends who preceded him. Job has sinned; there is no further argument, no other
answer. And he concludes: "Know then that God exacts of you less
than your guilt deserves!"

In the SECOND and THIRD rounds of speeches, chapters 15 to 21,
and 22 to 31, respectively, there are ever widening arguments and
answers between Job and his three friends, but with the same orthodox conclusion, namely, that Job's claims to innocence and integrity
cannot be defended.

And thus the drama concludes its FIRST ANSWER to the problem of
suffering: *That suffering is judgment upon sin.*

(2) The Answer of Elihu: The Second Answer to the Problem of Suffering

The old man Zophar, for reasons of his own, declined his third
speech. Job remained silent. At this point a young man by the name
of Elihu, who had been impatiently listening from the sidelines to all
the arguments of his elders, enters and speaks.

He is angry, he says, at the failure of the three friends to answer
Job properly and correctly. Too, he is angry with Job because Job
justifies himself rather than God. Job was righteous in his own eyes
and it is this spiritual pride of self-righteousness which Elihu proposes
to answer. He has his answer, too, to the problem of suffering.

Elihu chides Job for his presumptuousness — for claiming to be
without transgression, for asserting that the Almighty had been unfair
to him, and for contending against God as if he were mortal man and

could be held accountable as one person holds another amenable for his misdeeds.

Elihu paraphrases Job's complaints in these words:

> Behold, he finds occasions against me,
> he counts me as his enemy;
> He puts my feet in the stocks,
> and watches all my paths.

In all this, in the opinion of Elihu, Job is wrong. God is not an unjust God, who seeks to trip and to punish His creatures.

Instead, God speaks and makes His will known in many ways not observed by man. He may speak through a dream or vision in the night. He may speak through the voice of the storm, bringing punishment to some and bounty to others. Or, He may speak through suffering and misfortune, or the discipline of illness (Job 33:19-33). This last is apropos to Job's present situation.

Thus, God is a Teacher, who remembers that His children are created in His own Image, and His revelations in whatever manner, have purpose, and that is to bring His children closer to Himself.

The speaker closes the passage with these words:

> . . . Where is God my Maker,
> Who gives songs in the night,
> Who teaches us more than the beasts
> of the earth,
> And makes us wiser than the birds
> of the air? (35:10-11)

And,

> Behold, God is exalted in his power;
> Who is a teacher like Him? (36:22)

Two ideas stand out in the speeches of Elihu: (1) He maintains the wisdom and impartial justice of God's government of the universe; (2) he holds that God's purpose is to discipline and to improve men, even by their affliction, reproving and correcting the wicked, and purifying and making better, even the good.

And thus, Elihu's answer to Job and the three friends is the book's SECOND ANSWER to the problem of suffering: *That, in God's Providence, Suffering and Misfortune Are Intended to Teach, to Discipline, and to Improve Men and Nations, and to Bring Them Ever Nearer to the Mind and Will of the Creator.*

(3) *The Answer of the Almighty: The Third and Final Answer to the Problem of Suffering*

Chapters 38 to 41 present the speeches of the Almighty and complete the dramatic action of the book proper.

What is the author's purpose in having the Almighty appear in person, as one of the dramatic persons, at this stage of the dramatic action?

The most obvious motive is to make Divine Intervention the climax and finale of the whole piece. The poet has undertaken to dramatize the ways of God to man, which stresses His government of the whole universe, the earth and its creatures, and especially the affairs of men in the earth. The problem is to relate Job and His present misfortunes to this government.

Moreover, Job has questioned the ways of the Almighty and has demanded a personal interview. This interview he gets in the last act of the play.

And it is a surprise to some that the author has the Almighty by-pass the lengthy arguments of Elihu and makes no reference to his answer to Job and his friends. It is even more of a surprise when the Lord is silent on the important question of the cause of Job's suffering.

The reader feels that Job has been given a good, tentative answer at least, in the reply of Elihu. And some readers feel that Elihu's role is that of a messenger or forerunner of the Lord, to prepare Job in some sense for what is yet to come — that is, for the final revelation and answer to Job's tragedy, and the tragedy of mankind.

At any rate, what the Divine Intervention in this drama does is to lift the discussion and vision into a wider sphere. Job and his friends have become self-centered, so to speak, upon the problem of suffering and evil, and have made no progress because of the infinity of the mystery and their severe limitations as mortal men.

What is this wider sphere, into which the Almighty as a dramatic person has lifted the discussion and theme of the play?

In the first place, the author, like many other dramatists since his time, uses the storm as the background of his dramatic action. As the Almighty appears, the storm has reached whirlwind intensity. The Almighty speaks out of the whirlwind.

Job is shown the marvels of Creation, which reveal infinite wisdom, power, and loving care that only the Creator could bestow on the details of His marvelous universe.

This vision of God, as seen in the wonders of earth and heaven, produced in Job a feeling of *total humility*. He realized how little and insignificant his troubles were, as compared with the vastness and harmony of the whole. He was made ready and willing to confess his own weakness and ignorance, and presumption, in daring to contend with such a kindly World-builder and Creator.

Thus, although God does not explain to Job the cause of his suffering, he becomes so sure of God's wisdom and competence that he knows his affliction somehow is in harmony with God's righteousness. *Job has learned to trust where he cannot understand.* This is the supreme lesson of the book.

This is the author's THIRD ANSWER to the problem of suffering: *That Suffering, in God's Providence, Is a Price Human Beings Pay for Some Higher Good.*

Indeed, this Way of Life seems to be the Law of the Universe.

The classic statement of it is that of John 3:16. *God so loved the world that He gave his only Son. And the Son so loved the world that He gave Himself.*

Here we have the supreme sacrifice and suffering, if we may so phrase it, for a Supreme Good.

In his Epilogue, chapter 42:7-17, the author presents the dramatic conclusion to the story of Job — that is, that which follows Job's confession and acceptance by the Lord.

Three friends of Job are called in and reprimanded by the Lord, because they have not spoken the truth concerning their Lord, as has Job. Job's honest questioning of the motives of the Almighty and His government of the world, because it gave evidence of equality in some sense between the Creator and His creature, honored the Almighty. On the other hand, the concept of the Almighty by the three friends was unworthy and therefore they discredited their Maker.

The story closes with a happy ending. As penitence, the three friends were required to go to Job and offer up for themselves a burnt offering of seven bulls and seven rams, a perfect sacrifice according to their custom. Job prayed for them, and the Lord accepted Job's prayer in their behalf.

Job's trials were ended and he was restored to prosperity in twofold measure. Job's petition for his friends was evidence that he had completely learned his lesson. Seven sons and three daughters were given to him, and twice as many cattle of each kind as he had possessed before. Then Job gave a feast, to which all his brothers and sisters, and friends, came.

And the Lord blessed the latter days of Job more than his beginning.

SELECTED REFERENCES FOR THE BOOK OF JOB

Anderson, Bernhard W.: "The Book of Job," *Understanding the Old Testament,* pp. 484-497.

*Heavenor, E. S. P.: "Job," *The New Bible Commentary,* pp. 387-411.

Moulton, Richard G.: "The Book of Job," *The Modern Reader's Bible,* pp. 1480-1495.

*Paterson, John: "The Ways of God with Men," and "The Book of Job," *The Book That Is Alive,* Chapters 6 and 7, pp. 82-128.

*Strahan, James: *The Book of Job.* Second Edition.

Terrien, Samuel: "The Book of Job," *The Interpreter's Bible,* Vol. III.

Terrien, Samuel: *Job, Poet of Existence.*

*Young, Edward J.: *An Introduction to the Old Testament,* pp. 336-349.

Chapter 4

ECCLESIASTES

1. AUTHORSHIP AND DATE OF THE BOOK

The authorship of books of the Bible ordinarily is not thought to be a matter of the first importance. In fact, the names of many of the authors have long since been lost.

However, in the case of the book of Ecclesiastes, where a mistaken view of authorship has led many a reader astray, authorship may be essential to the reader's understanding and interpretation of a great classic in Biblical literature.

The traditional view is that the book was written by King Solomon. This is extremely unlikely. Indeed, the author really does not claim to be Solomon. What he does is to place his words in Solomon's mouth. A closer examination of the introductory headnote will show this. King Solomon then is referred to not as the author, but the *hero* of the book. That is to say, the composition is *about* Solomon and not *by* him.

Moreover, because of the ideas of the book, the vocabulary, idioms, style, and other details of language which tend to fix the date of a book, present day scholars hold the view that it was written centuries after the reign of Solomon (which was about 974-934 B.C.). In addition, they say that a proud monarch like Solomon, even in the closing days of his reign, would hardly admit failure of the type which the book reflects.

If not Solomon, who then is the author?

The title of the book in the original Hebrew was *Qoheleth*, which was the chosen name of the author, or what we would call his "pen" name. The Greek translators of the original Hebrew called him *Ekklesiastes*, and Jerome in his Latin *Vulgate Version*, Ecclesiastes. In English it means "The Preacher."

The "pen" name *Qoheleth* which he chose for himself appears to be connected with another Hebrew word, *qahal*, the public assembly, suggesting that the role the Preacher had set for himself was that of a speaker of wisdom to those in the outer court, or perhaps to audiences-at-large such as the readers of every generation.

He classifies himself as one of the Wise Men, in these words:

Besides being wise, the Preacher also
taught the people knowledge . . .

Many readers, because of the gloomy and pessimistic nature of the book, still make the mistake of branding Ecclesiastes as a skeptic, or an apostle of futility and despair. The melancholy refrain, "Vanity of vanities, all is vanity," he puts not in his own but in the mouth of Solomon, the reader will do well to remember.

In short, the role of Ecclesiastes, the author, evidently is to offer counsel, based on his own experience, regarding the things that make for wise conduct in this life, remembering that the Divine Creator governs the world in accordance with a plan, although that plan may be hidden from us.[1]

2. THE COMPOSITION OF THE BOOK OF ECCLESIASTES

The style or method of composition of the book of Ecclesiastes throws light on its meaning.

As we have seen, Ecclesiastes lets King Solomon be the speaker in his composition. From the viewpoint of this imaginary mouthpiece, the author develops his discourse on the vanity and unreality of a philosophy which limits life to the short, incomplete, and often unsatisfactory days of man's present existence here on the earth. The Solomon through whom the author speaks, is not the wise and prosperous king we meet in the early years, but the Solomon of old age, at the end of his days, when life for him was full of disappointment and futility, perhaps mainly because of the evil influences surrounding the Court in the later years, including his own defection.

The practice of using famous names as subjects of their compositions was common among the writers of so-called apocryphal books. Some of these are the *Assumption of Moses, Testament of the Twelve Patriarchs,* the *Psalms of Solomon,* the *Wisdom of Solomon, Ascension of Isaiah, Baruch,* and other names such as Enoch, Noah, and other Old Testament characters. Thus Ecclesiastes was following a familiar tradition.

The practice was familiar also in other lands, as for example with Plato, among Greek authors. Socrates wrote no books; yet he appears as the *hero* in the superb Dialogues of Plato. Plato's ideas were put into the mouth of Socrates, along with the ideas of Socrates, his famous teacher.

Among modern authors, the English poet Robert Browning made use of the method of impersonation to great advantage in such dramatic monologues as *Andrea del Sarto, Fra Lippo Lippi,* and many others.

---

[1]For two somewhat different interpretations of the book of Ecclesiastes, see Bernhard W. Anderson, who says the sage "looks upon the world with a pessimistic eye," in *Understanding the Old Testament,* pp. 477-484 (1957); and Edward J. Young, who says that "the author is not a pessimist," *An Introduction to the Old Testament,* pp. 370-371 (1958).

The reader has observed that the *dramatic monologue* is precisely what we have here in the book of Ecclesiastes. Browning selected a particular moment or period in the life of his Italian painters, Andrea del Sarto and Fra Lippo Lippi, and dramatized that moment, using the painter as his sole speaker.

So also, Ecclesiastes selects Solomon's old age and defection for his moment of dramatization, and uses Solomon as his solo speaker. However, as the reader has observed, as the author advances with his discourse, Solomon gradually fades from the writer's mind, and he proceeds to give us, not what Solomon thought and felt, but what he the author wished to say to the reader.

The reader should not be unduly disturbed because he does not find in the book of Ecclesiastes an orderly and systematically written composition.

The book has unity and a plan;[2] but the plan is like that of a conversation or an informal essay. It does not proceed in a straight line. After all, his is a book of experience, containing maxims for the cultivation of wisdom.

3. THE MEANING AND PURPOSE OF THE BOOK

The prudent reader will distinguish, if he can, between the views of Solomon, as he is impersonated, and those of the author. In short, what were the real views of the writer, who labels himself "The Preacher," meaning by that one who exhorts others to wise conduct?

Finding the answer to this question, and the author's purpose in writing the book, is one of the intriguing features of a work that has fascinated readers for many generations. And no two people ever come up with quite the same answer.

Rider Haggard, an English novelist, in this passage expresses the keynote of the book:

> There is one immortal work that moves me still more; a work that utters all the world's yearning anguish and disillusionment in one sorrow-laden and bitter cry, and whose stately music thrills like the voice of pines heard in the darkness of a midnight gale; and that is the book of Ecclesiastes.

In what sense does the book of Ecclesiastes "utter all the world's yearning anguish and disillusionment in one sorrow-laden and bitter cry"?

Is it not precisely because human beings are in search of an answer to the mystery of life? Where did we come from? What are we doing here? And where do we go from here? And all the related questions, such as, Why do the good people of the earth suffer? And why do the wicked often prosper and go unpunished?

---

[2]For a different view of the composition of Ecclesiastes, see Anderson, *Understanding the Old Testament*, p. 479. Young thinks the book has "unity of composition," and gives reasons, *Introduction to the Old Testament*, pp. 369-370.

Jesus said to a group of Pharisees, "You *search* the Scriptures, because in them you think you have eternal life."

Billy Graham said of the people of a great city:

> Fifty-eight per cent of the people of New York attend no church. Yet deep within their hearts are the same *yearnings*, the same longings and the same hunger for fellowship with God that exist in the hearts of people everywhere.

The book of Ecclesiastes is a book of yearnings; and the reader must remember that it was written before Jesus and the New Testament, when the answers were still vague. It was written in the darkness before the dawn, so to speak.

It has been said that if a reader is in doubt about the meaning and purpose of an editorial, he should read the last paragraph. For it is there that the editor reveals what he wishes to say to the reader.

The same is true of the book of Ecclesiastes. At the close of his book, the writer says:

> Besides being wise, the Preacher also taught the people knowledge, weighing and studying and arranging proverbs with great care. The Preacher sought to find pleasing words, and uprightly he wrote words of truth. The sayings of the Wise are like goads, and like nails firmly fixed are the collected sayings which are given by One Shepherd. My son, beware of anything beyond these.

The "One Shepherd" of course is God, and Ecclesiastes claims that his message on wise conduct, his "words of truth," are inspired, and given by the One Shepherd. They are like "goads" to prod the unwise onto the way of wisdom.

But Ecclesiastes traveled over many a thorny path in his mental journey to reach this destination, this conclusion based on his experience and observation, as we shall see in our analysis of the book.

There are those who think that the book of Ecclesiastes bears distinct traces of Greek ideas and culture established throughout the civilized world by Alexander the Great (336-323 B.C.). One form of the Greek influence appeared as the doctrine of Epicureanism, after the Greek philosopher Epicurus (342-270 B.C.), who advocated the sensualist view of life, with emphasis on the present pleasures of eating and drinking.

The reader has observed how much emphasis Ecclesiastes places upon enjoyment of simple, physical pleasures, for example, this passage among many others:

> What I have seen to be good and to be fitting is to eat and drink and find enjoyment in all the toil with which one toils under the sun the few days of his life which God has given him, for this is his lot . . .
> For who knows what is good for man while he lives the few days of his vain life, which he passes like a shadow?

Is this passage a paraphrase of Solomon, who himself made much of feasting and the physical pleasures of this life? And is the writer setting up this philosophy of life, in order to oppose it?

Professor Richard G. Moulton thinks he is not. There is, he says, throughout no note of abandonment to reveling. "I say boldly that there is nothing unwholesome in Ecclesiastes," he continues. "The tradition of Hebrew and Christian religion has in actual fact laid too much stress on the sterner side of things; it is good that at least one of the sacred canon should be found to remind us that one duty of life is happiness, and that nothing in religion can be higher than praise."[3]

But Ecclesiastes is not a book of happiness. For the writer pours forth one long drawn out and bitter cry of pain and disillusionment, because there was no escape from present misery, either in this life or in the one to come. The most he can offer is resignation, and a struggling hope that somehow God, who is a God of order, will end things well for man who lives his appointed life.

Finally, is it not true that the book's aim is to *state* rather than to *solve* the difficulties of life?

4. THE CONTENTS OF THE BOOK

The author's message is confined largely, if not entirely, to the things of this world. If it appears worldly, as it surely does, it is because Ecclesiastes is addressing the public of his day, in the midst of a selfish and corrupt society, perhaps about the fourth or third century B.C., whose understanding was bounded largely by the horizons of this world. He meets them on their own ground, and writes the most realistic, most down-to-earth book in the Old Testament.

Although the book of Ecclesiastes has little or no connected sequence running through it, a brief analysis will show these main topics or themes:

(1) *The Prologue: All Is Vanity*, Chapter 1:1-11

The writer, impersonating Solomon, takes a wholly negative view of life. All is vanity. Man and nature move in a circle, with endless repetition and monotony, both incomprehensible. "All things are full of weariness, man cannot utter it."

(2) *Solomon's Search for Wisdom*, Chapter 1:12-18

Solomon, who was reputed to be the wisest man of antiquity, "applied his mind to seek and to search out by *wisdom* all that is done under heaven." But in a lifetime he found no profit, no enduring satisfactions from wisdom, "for he who increases knowledge increases sorrow."

(3) *Solomon's Pursuit of Pleasure*, Chapter 2

After proving that the search for wisdom and knowledge brought only sorrow and disappointment, our hero next turns to the pursuit of *pleasure*. "I said to myself, 'Come now, I will make a test of pleasure; enjoy yourself.'"

[3]*The Modern Reader's Bible*, p. 1451.

Solomon then recounts all those things he pursued to his heart's content, including wine, folly, building great works, houses, planting vineyards, making gardens and parks, and pools, and gathering about him singers and concubines. Thus, he became great and surpassed all who were before him in Jerusalem.

> Then I considered all that my hands had done and the toil I had spent in doing it, and behold, all was vanity and a striving after wind, and there was nothing to be gained under the sun . . .
> So I turned about and gave my heart up to despair over all the toil of my labors under the sun.

And this is how he came to the conclusion,

> There is nothing better for a man than that he should eat and drink, and find enjoyment in his toil.

(4) *The Orderliness of Creation,* Chapter 3

The writer, baffled and defeated in his search for happiness, and in his inability to explain the mystery of existence, indulges himself for the moment in the luxury of contemplating the orderliness of the universe about him.

God is a God of order, the writer concludes, in one of the famous passages in the Old Testament:

> For everything there is a season, and a time for every matter under heaven . . . He has made everything beautiful in its time.

But there is no understanding God, and his ways:

> He has put eternity in man's mind, yet so that he cannot find out what God has done.

All this the writer, in verses 16-22, contrasts with the wickedness of the world, and the beastly outlook and fate of man.

(5) *The Injustices and Hopelessness of Life,* Chapters 4-5

The world is full of trouble. The weak are oppressed by the strong, and suffering and misery are on every hand.

> Again I saw the oppressions that are practiced under the sun. And behold, the tears of the oppressed, and they had no one to comfort them!

The most the wise man can offer by way of consolation is his counsel to wise conduct, and his many proverbs of experience. He concludes again, as in a former discourse, that the most fitting thing for man is to eat and drink and find enjoyment in his labor the few days of his life which God has given him.

(6) *Life Is an Enigma,* Chapter 6

One of the puzzles of life is that God gives to a man wealth, so that he lacks nothing, and yet he does not give to man the power to *enjoy* his riches.

And another puzzle is that all the toil of man is for his *"mouth,"* yet his appetite is not *satisfied.*

And so the wise man, the writer, asks this fundamental question:

For who knows what is good for man while he lives the few days
of his life, which he passes like a shadow?

(7) *Practical Proverbs,* Chapter 7

Experience is the best teacher. Since riches and the other circumstances of life will not secure happiness, either in the present or future, the wise man offers practical proverbs, things useful to remember in life.

One thing man can do, and that is to guide himself in the conduct of life by bearing in mind these truths based on experience.

(8) *"The Whole.World Is in His Hands,"* Chapters 9 and 10

Man's destiny is in the hands of God. In 8:12, he says,

Though a sinner does evil a hundred times and prolongs his life,
yet I know that it will be well with those who fear God . . . but
it will not be well with the wicked.

And again, in 9:1,

But all this I laid to heart, examining it all, how the righteous
and the wise and their deeds are in the hand of God; whether it is
love or hate man does not know. Everything before them is vanity,
since one fate comes to all, to the righteous and the wicked, to the
good and the evil . . . As is the good man, so is the sinner.

What began as positive faith, ends in apparent paradox. This passage illustrates one difficulty readers have in understanding Ecclesiastes. The paradox. Ecclesiastes himself complains of the apparent contradiction, in these words:

This is an evil in all that is done under the sun, that one fate
comes to all.

But the remedy is the one he so often counsels, *carpe diem:*

Go, eat your bread with enjoyment, and drink your wine with a
merry heart.

(9) *More Practical Proverbs Bearing on Life's Puzzles,* Chapter 10

A short chapter on the excellence of wisdom, as stated in a variety of original proverbs.

Although wisdom often is at a disadvantage in competition with folly, yet time and judgment are on the side of the wise, who can well afford to wait and bide their time.

(10) *Remember Thy Creator in Youth,* Chapter 11 and 12:8

Chapter Twelve, in the *King James Version* of Ecclesiastes, begins with these words:

Remember now thy Creator in the days of thy youth.

William Hazlitt, the English essayist, began one of the most important of his essays with the words: "No young man thinks he shall ever die."

The writer, in one of the famous passages in the Old Testament, gives this symbolic and poetic description of creeping old age, and its infirmities, as a contrasting picture with youth and its disregard for the counsel of the wise. And it is one of several beautiful passages which add weight and substance, and value, to the book of Ecclesiastes.

(11) The Epilogue: Fear God and Keep His Commandments, Chapter 12:9-14

In these closing verses, the writer states his method and purpose in writing the book, and sums up the conclusions of his teaching.

The Preacher as one of the Wise Men has taught the people knowledge, and to order their lives according to wise conduct, although they may know little about the Creator and His future plans. These utterances of his have been inspired by the One Shepherd, God Himself. He warns them to beware of books not so inspired.

The heart of the matter is in his parting counsel: to fear God and keep His commandments, for this is the whole duty of man.

Some readers have found it difficult to see how a *positive duty* for man could be logically deduced from the pessimistic premise running throughout the book, that all things "under the sun" are vanity.

This is another one of Ecclesiastes' paradoxes or apparent contradictions.

In the view of Ecclesiastes, unquestionably his was a world of *vanity*. He uses the word thirty-seven times in his book; but he also uses the word *God* forty times. The theme question was, What is it that is good for man to do, in a world where all is vanity? What is the answer for those with a minimum of faith? Ecclesiastes answers: Eat, drink, labor, and enjoy the simple things of life as God has provided them; and above all, Fear God, and keep His Commandments. "Yet I know that it will be well with those who fear God." (See the Apostle Paul's answer, Romans 8:18-25.)

SPECIAL REFERENCES ON THE BOOK OF ECCLESIASTES

*Anderson, Bernhard W.: "The Skepticism of Ecclesiastes," *Understanding the Old Testament*, pp. 477-484.

Gordis, Robert: *The Wisdom of Ecclesiastes.*

*Moulton, Richard G.: "Ecclesiastes and the Wisdom of Solomon," *The Modern Reader's Bible*, 1469-1475.

*Paterson, John: *The Book That Is Alive*, Chapter 8, pp. 129-150.

Ranston, Harry: *Ecclesiastes and the Early Greek Wisdom Literature.*

See also chapters on Ecclesiastes in the books listed on page 229.

Chapter 5

THE SONG OF SONGS

1. THE TYPE AND CHARACTER OF THE SONG OF SONGS

The book of The Song of Songs is a beautiful love story of an Oriental bridegroom and his bride. Its title, which means the most beautiful of songs, is well chosen. It is the only book of the Bible which has love for its sole theme.

The two main characters are King Solomon and the country maiden of Shulam (Shunem), who becomes his bride.

Here again Solomon is the hero of the book (as we found in the book of Ecclesiastes) and not its author. That is, the composition is *about* Solomon, and not *by* him.[1]

The story is presented by means of a series of seven scenes or lyric idyls, each connected with and related to the whole. Each closes with a *refrain*, presumably by the author.

The story progresses by means of dramatic dialogue from scene to scene, in which the king and his bride are assisted by a Chorus of palace ladies called the "Daughters of Jerusalem," which echoes from the background, after the manner of the chorus in an ancient Greek play. The bride's brothers, and a court crier, are also in the background.

Originally an idyl dealt with shepherd and pastoral life, in a rustic setting, and treated themes of love and domestic relations. Frequently the shepherd or shepherdess was related in some way to the court and court life, as in The Song of Songs. Theocratus, a Greek poet of the third century B.C., was supposed to have originated the literary type of the idyl.

The idyllic character of The Song of Songs reminds us at once of Alfred Tennyson's *Idylls of the King*, in which King Arthur and his knights and ladies of the Round Table present situations not unlike some of those in our Hebrew poem.

In the Old Testament, we have other narrative and romantic idyls such as the Wooing of Rebekah, Samson and Delilah, and the story of Ruth, the latter being an excellent type of the narrative idyl.

The poet of The Song of Songs has composed a masterpiece, in the lyric mood of spring and love. He takes the reader out into the

---

[1]Richard G. Moulton, *The Modern Reader's Bible*, pp. 886-897, and 1442-1450, has the best analysis and interpretation of The Song of Songs.

open air, to the hills and mountains of Lebanon, the gardens and orchards as well as the wilderness, as if to contrast with the Court the pleasures of nature. The poem, too, is noted for its rich, oriental imagery and symbolism. In the words of one reader, "It would be a dull eye that missed the beauty of the poem."

2. AUTHORSHIP AND DATE

The author of The Song of Songs is unknown. Among the ancients, authorship was not particularly important, and so most of the manuscripts or books of the Old Testament have come down to us without any author's name attached. The question they asked was not *who* wrote it, but *what* does it say?

Jewish tradition associated Solomon's name with the composition of The Song of Songs, just as it ascribed the writing of the books of Proverbs and Ecclesiastes to Solomon. For Solomon acquired an enormous reputation for being wise and learned, and competent in almost all departments of life.

Solomon's literary capabilities, however, seem to have been in the area of wisdom literature, that is, in wise sayings, and in collecting and composing proverbs, which became the flower of his conversation, not only with the men of his own court, but with the kings and princes of other lands who visited him.

It is not likely that lyrical songs of such excellence as the ones in The Song of Songs were composed by the same author to whom is ascribed at least one-half of the wise maxims and proverbs of the book of Proverbs. It would be like saying that Francis Bacon wrote the plays of William Shakespeare.

The date of the composition of The Song of Songs is still uncertain, although opinion favors a later date, much later than that of Solomon's reign (974-934 B.C.), and not earlier than the fourth century B.C. Some think the date of the book is as late as the Greek period, which began with the conquests of Alexander the Great (336-323 B.C.).

3. THE MEANING AND PURPOSE OF THE BOOK[2]

Along with the discussion of authorship, has grown up also a difference of opinion regarding the meaning and purpose of the book. If we take The Song of Songs at its face value, we must interpret it as a beautiful romantic story of a bride and bridegroom in the days of their courtship and marriage.

Would this in itself make it unworthy of a place in the Bible canon? Did not God, whose great love for His creatures is the main theme of His Book, also ordain the mutual attraction and love of the sexes? And next to His own love, is not this love His basic plan for perpetuating and blessing the human family?

[2]For a summary of the different interpretations of The Song of Songs, see Young, *An Introduction to the Old Testament*, pp. 350-356.

The Apostle Paul, writing in Ephesians 5:28-33, points out this relationship between human and Divine love, and concludes: "This is a great mystery, and I take it to mean Christ and the Church."

What Paul seems to be saying is that all true love is a *mystery* which foreshadows the love of Christ, and somehow lifts the Christian upward toward the union of the soul with Christ. Thus, as someone has well said, the earthly love becomes a stepping stone to the heavenly.

Devout Jews, however, almost from the time of its first appearance regarded The Song of Songs as an allegory portraying the relations of Jehovah and Israel. It was read at the Passover as referring to the Exodus from Egypt, where God espoused Israel as His Bride.

The early Christian Church followed the same general line, regarding The Song of Songs as a pre-nuptial song of Christ and His Church. In the New Testament the Church generally is referred to as the "bride" of Christ, although no quotation is taken from, or reference made to The Song of Songs (see Matthew 9:15; 25:1; John 3:29; II Corinthians 11:2; Ephesians 5:23; Revelation 19:7; 21:2; 22:17).

The book of The Song of Songs appears to have been written by another one of the Wise Men, and from a somewhat unorthodox Jewish point of view, as was the case in such books as Job, Proverbs, in Ecclesiastes, and in some of the so-called apocryphal books. For this reason it is grouped with the other books by the Wise Men.

4. THE CONTENTS OF THE BOOK

THE PLOT: [3] King Solomon with a courtly retinue, visiting his royal vineyards upon Mount Lebanon on the northwest boundary of Palestine, suddenly by surprise comes upon the fair maiden of Shulam. Startled, she runs away from the royal company, but not before her rustic charms have won the favor of the king. So, at a later date, Solomon returns and visits her in the disguise of a shepherd, and so woos and wins her love. Now he returns to visit the Shulammite in royal state, and calls upon her to leave Lebanon and become his queen. They are approaching the Royal Palace at Jerusalem on their Wedding Day when the poem opens.

CHARACTERS

King Solomon
Shulammite Maid, the Bride
Her Brothers
Chorus of Court Ladies, Daughters of Jerusalem
Scene 1. *The Wedding Day* (Chapters 1 to 2:7)

Outside. The bridal procession approaches the Palace: Solomon leads the bride, the court ladies following. The bride is speaking; verse 4 refers to the ancient ceremony of lifting the bride across the threshold.

---

[3]See Richard G. Moulton, *op. cit.*, p. 1445.

Inside. Verse 5: the party on the inside, the bride is explaining gracefully to the court ladies how she came by her swarthy complexion. In verse 7, the king approaches her side and the two lovers exchange reminiscences of their courtship, as lovers like to do.

Between verses 8 and 9, the wedding ceremonies, including the formal dinner in the banqueting house, have taken place. Verse 9 marks the procession from the banqueting house to the bridal chamber, and the close of the wedding day ends the events of scene 1. The poet, somewhat in the role of minstrel, closes the scene with a fitting refrain, warning the maids not to interrupt the lovers.

Scene 2. *The Bride's Reminiscences of the Courtship*
(Chapters 2:8 to 3:5)

The bride delights to remember how in the springtime her lover (Solomon disguised as a shepherd) came to her mountain home to woo her. (In point of time, this scene takes us back to events earlier than the events of the Wedding Day, in scene 1.)

In verses 2:10-13, the bride in her reminiscences quotes the king's Love Song, which is the most beautiful and most famous in the book.

Verse 2:15 interrupts the wooing, by the loud alarms of the brothers who chase away the foxes from the vineyards. But the incident of the foxes is reminiscencing, too, and so she closes it with the sweet refrain, "My beloved is mine, and I am his," etc.

Verses 3:1-4 record a happy dream, a dream of how she lost her lover, and how she found him! The poet then closes scene 2 as he closed scene 1, with the refrain, "I adjure you, O Daughters of Jerusalem. . . ."

Scene 3. *The Day of the Betrothal* (Chapters 3:6 to 5:1)

"What is that coming up from the wilderness . . .?"

Here we have a true Oriental scene. Solomon, in all his glory, is coming in state across the wilderness to the mountain home of his bride in Lebanon, in the royal litter, prepared to bring her to his palace at Jerusalem. With great skill and magnificence, Solomon has built for himself this royal palanquin for his bride, framed of cedar, adorned with pillars of silver, and cushioned with rich gold and purple. It is drawn by two royal camels. In the retinue are sixty mighty men, renowned in battle, the king's special guards, girt with swords of gleaming steel.

This scene is a sequel to scene 2, in which Solomon in disguise as a shepherd, wooed and won the mountain maid; both scenes go back in point of time to a date earlier than the Wedding Day, described in scene 1.

Once in the presence of the Shulammite maid, Solomon pours forth his love in rapturous praise of his beloved (4:1-6).

Then the king proposes marriage (4:7-15) and is accepted by her (4:16). The king expresses his happiness (5:1).

The poet, again in the role of minstrel, blesses the betrothed lovers and closes scene 3 (5:1-b).

Scene 4. *The Bride's Troubled Dream* (5:2 to 6:3)

The bride dreamed that her lover came in the night and knocked at her door. While she hesitated, before opening the door, she had lost him. She wanders forth into the night to find him and is buffeted rudely by the watchman when she inquires of her lover (5:2-7).

Next, she finds herself (in the dream) in conversation with the Daughters of Jerusalem (5:8 to 6:1). And then, as dreams have a way of doing, this one fades out, and she remembered that her lover had "gone down to the garden." This calls for a happy refrain, with which the poet closes the scene, "I am my beloved's, and my beloved is mine."

Scene 5. *The King's Soliloquy on the Beauty of His Bride* (Chapters 6:4 to 7:10)

The king is the sole speaker in this scene. The time here goes back to the time of scene 1, the Wedding Day, and is part of the conversation which took place in the royal palace between the bride and the bridegroom, in their procession from the banqueting house to the bridal chamber. Another moment of reminiscences.

The scene opens, verses 4-9, with the king's passionate praise of the charms of his bride.

After the reminiscences, verses 7:1-9 take up again the king's rapturous praise of his beloved bride.

And again the poet closes the scene with his happy refrain:

> I am my beloved's,
> And his desire is for me.

Scene 6. *The Bride's Wish to Visit Her Home on Mount Lebanon* (Chapters 7:11 to 8:4)

The bride is the sole speaker in this scene, as the king was in the preceding scene. She is addressing her husband the king.

Happy as has been the honeymoon at the king's palace, the bride, like all brides, longs now to visit her former home on Mount Lebanon . . .

> I would lead thee, and bring thee
> Into my mother's house.

This scene follows in sequence the events of scene 1 and scene 5, and may be said to mark the end of the first honeymoon. However, in her plea that they may visit together, she promises to renew her love there.

The poet closes the scene with the happy refrain he used at the close of both scene 1 and scene 2, "I adjure you, O Daughters of Jerusalem," etc.

Scene 7. *The Renewal of Love in the Vineyard of Lebanon*
(Chapter 8:5-14)

This scene carries out the purpose wished for in scene 6. That is, that the lovers may go together to the bride's home on Mount Lebanon.

The poet, in the role of chorus, announces the arrival of the royal pair from their wilderness journey, thus:

> Who is this that cometh up from the wilderness,
> Leaning upon her beloved?

Unattended, the lovers reach the familiar scene where the bride was born, the spot where the king found her asleep under the apple tree, and how he startled her by surprise.

In the midst of this scene, the bride in a burst of pride and devotion to her husband, gives one of the finest descriptions of love ever written, verses 6-7.

And so the scene continues, in reminiscent mood as well as their present happiness, until the king's royal escort comes to conduct the lovers from Lebanon back to the king's palace (verse 13).

This is signal to the lovers for one final embrace, before they leave the country.

The play closes with a human touch, the bride having the last word, and urging her husband to hurry, "Make haste, my beloved," etc.

ADDITIONAL REFERENCES FOR THE SONG OF SONGS

*Moulton, Richard G.: "The Song of Songs," *The Modern Reader's Bible,* pp. 886-897, and 1442-1450.

Waterway, Leroy: *The Song of Songs.*

*Young, Edward J.: "The Song of Solomon," *An Introduction to the Old Testament,* pp. 350-356.

Solomon's Pools, the finest of the three pools, south of Jerusalem. © *Matson Photo Service*

PART FIVE

BOOKS BY THE PROPHETS

In many and various ways God spoke of old to our fathers by the prophets. — Hebrews 1:1

Chapter 1

INTRODUCTION

1. THE PROPHETS AS GOD'S SPECIAL AGENTS

The seventeen historical books of the Old Testament, from Genesis to Esther, tell the story of the rise and fall of the Hebrew nation.

The most important individuals in that long history, and the most influential, were the prophets. If God chose Israel for the supreme purpose of being His *teacher* of mankind until the arrival of the Messiah, He called the Prophets to *reveal* Himself and His plan for the redemption of the human family.

From early times God promised to raise up prophets from among the people, to qualify them by endowing them with His Spirit, as His spokesmen.[1] According to early Hebrew tradition, the prophets were divided into two groups: Former Prophets and Latter Prophets. The Former Prophets gave their messages orally, and thus may be called *speaking prophets*. For reasons we do not know, their messages were not reduced to writing. But their activities are described in the historical books.

2. THE SPEAKING PROPHETS

Although the word *prophet* occurs many times in the Old Testament before the time of the prophet Samuel, the prophetic office appears to have assumed much more prominence from his time on.

After organizing the national life of Israel at the close of the period of Judges, Samuel appears to have founded an order or society of prophets, with schools for the training of younger prophets. He had units of these schools at Naioth in the suburbs of his native city Ramah, at Bethel, Jericho, and at Gilgal (II Kings 2:3-5; 4:38).

Samuel's schools of prophecy for generations afterwards led the religious life of Israel, and exercised a profound influence upon the life of the nation. Samuel anointed both King Saul and King David, and was counselor to both, and greatly influenced their reigns after his death. Samuel, too, may have had a hand in the writing of some of the historical books of the Old Testament. And for him, two of the great historical books are named.

Although Samuel was the earliest of the great Hebrew prophets after Moses, other prominent names follow his. Nathan, who reproved

---

[1]See Deuteronomy 18:9-22.

n the hill country of Ephraim, birthplace
f Samuel. © *Matson Photo Service.*

David for his great sin, causing him to repent and return to the Lord, was a distinguished prophet during the reigns of both David and his son Solomon.

Another is Elijah, one of the greatest of the speaking prophets, who under divine guidance successfully defeated Baal worship at Mount Carmel, and for the second "miracle period" in redemptive history (Moses' was the first) turned the tide of heathen worship in favor of the worship of Jehovah.

And finally, there was Elisha, the farmer who left his plow in the field, to accept the call of prophet. Elisha, upon whose shoulders fell the mantle of Elijah, not only became God's anointed and Elijah's successor as prophet, but by many miracles and simple deeds of kindness, and in a manner similar to that of Jesus nearly nine hundred years later, further demonstrated the victorious power of Jehovah in the struggle against Baal worship.

The oral or speaking prophets served Israel for more than three hundred years, or until about 800 B.C., when the writing or literary prophets appeared on the scene.

3. THE WRITING PROPHETS[2]

The age of the writing prophets, sometimes called "Latter Prophets" to distinguish them from the "Former Prophets," was roughly from 800 B.C. to 400 B.C.

The writing prophets wrote the seventeen books of prophecy, Isaiah to Malachi, which are listed in the last division of the Old Testament. In general each book bears the name of its author, except the book of Jonah, which likely was written by a later writer. Two books are ascribed to Jeremiah.

Thomas Carlyle once said that whenever there was a crisis in history, an emergency or moment of great need, God always provided a leader. This is what God did when He called Moses, and Samuel, and David, and Elijah, and many others we could name.

Certainly the events that rapidly developed after the death of Solomon, about 934 B.C., brought about such a crisis in the Hebrew nation. Solomon's biographer and historian, in I Kings 11, explains the evil influences surrounding the court, and the deterioration that took place during the last days of Solomon's reign.

The nation, during the early reign of Solomon, had reached its climax, and now was on its way toward rapid decline. (For that story and analysis, the reader is referred to the chapters on Kings.)

It was the age of the Divided Kingdom and of idolatry. All nineteen of the kings of Israel were evil in many ways. And only eight of

---

[2]A good, brief introduction to the prophetic writers of the Old Testament and their books is that of Professor W. J. Cameron of the Free Church College of Edinburgh, in "The Prophetical Literature of the Old Testament," *The New Bible Commentary*, pp. 45-51 (2nd ed., 1954). See also John Paterson, *The Goodly Fellowship of the Prophets* (1948).

the twenty kings of Judah could be rated "good" in any important sense of the word.

And to meet the continuing crisis, God "raised up" a whole galaxy of mighty prophets as His spokesmen and leaders in the generations that followed.

And when we realize that the Priests, who were the regularly appointed teachers of the nation, were often as corrupt and ungodly as their kings, we indeed wonder at the work accomplished by the prophets.

4. Who Is a Prophet?[3]

(1) In the first place, it seems almost impossible to eliminate from the popular mind the idea that *prophecy* means *prediction*, which it is not.

The erroneous notion rests upon a false etymology of the word. For *pro* in prophecy is not the *pro* which means *beforehand*, as in *prospectus;* but the other *pro* which means *in place of*, as in *pronoun*. The other part of the word prophet, the Greek word *phanai*, means *to speak*. A prophet then is one who speaks *in place of another* — that is, in place of or for God.

(2) In the second place, a prophet is primarily a *statesman*.

Israel began as a theocracy. The government of God was exercised through such leaders as Moses and Joshua. But when in a later period the people insisted upon earthly kings, then God gave them their wish, for it was God's plan to continue the theocracy through His appointed kings. The prophets were sent to reveal God's message, particularly in days of apostasy. Thus, one of their main functions was to counsel with kings and princes of their time, revealing and interpreting the will of God for the nation.

(3) But the prophet was also a *preacher* to the whole people. Jonah's message was to both the rulers and the people of Nineveh. So also was Amos' to the Northern Kingdom, especially the wealthy of Samaria, along with their wicked rulers.

The true prophet was an interpreter of the times and God's will for His people, in particular His true worship as opposed to idolatry. The highest duty of his prophetic profession was to work mightily to make God's will prevail, in the individual and in the national life.

(4) However, the prophet did *predict* things to come; but this was incidental to his larger ministry.

(5) The prophet was conscious that his message came directly from God. He prefaced his message with, "Thus says the Lord," or "The word of the Lord that came to the prophet" So and So. The prophet was "called" and specially commissioned to perform his duties

[3]For a discussion of this topic, see W. J. Cameron, *op. cit.*, p. 45; Edward J. Young, *My Servants the Prophets*, pp. 56-75; Bernhard W. Anderson, *Understanding the Old Testament*, pp. 183-185 (1957).

as a "Man of God." Thus, the prophet was the servant of servants of his Lord.

5. Grouping the Books by the Prophets

The method used in arranging the books by the prophets in our Bible seems to have been to list first the longer books, and then the shorter ones, although among the shorter books there seems to be some effort to arrange them chronologically.

To simplify the reader's approach, in this volume the prophets and their books have been *grouped* and *arranged* in their approximate chronological order.

Although there is still some difference of opinion regarding the historical order of many of the prophets, the chronology here given, based on internal and external evidence, is believed to be approximately correct and trustworthy. The dates given are the approximate dates of each prophet's *active years,* and not necessarily the dates of his whole biography.

Chronology of the Prophets

1. *Prophets of the First Period: the Decline and Fall of the Northern Kingdom, 934-721* B.C. (Period of the Assyrian Empire, 885 to 612 B.C.)

Joel	845-791 B.C.
Jonah	789-749
Amos	775-750
Hosea	760-720
Isaiah	755-695
Micah	751-697

2. *Prophets of the Second Period: the Decline and Fall of Judah, 934-586* B.C. (The Fall of the Assyrian Empire, and Babylonian Supremacy, 612 to 538 B.C.)

Zephaniah	639-608
Nahum	621-612
Jeremiah	626-582
Habakkuk	608-597

3. *Prophets of the Third Period: the Period of Babylonian Captivity and Exile, 605 to 538* B.C.

Ezekiel	597-570	
Daniel	605-534	
Jeremiah	586	(Lamentations)
Obadiah	586-582	

4. *Prophets of the Fourth Period: the Period of the Return and Restoration, 538 to 432* B.C.

Haggai	538-516	(520)
Zechariah	538-516	(520-518)
Malachi	450-430	

Chronology of the Prophets and the Kings
of the Divided Kingdom

Israel			Judah		
Jeroboam I	934-913	(Iddo, Ahijah)	Rehoboam	934-917	
Nadab	913-912		Abijah	917-915	
Baasha	912-889	(Jehu, Ahijah)	Asa	914-874	
Elah	889-887		Jehoshaphat	876-852	(Jehu, Micaiah
Zimri	887	(7 days)			Eliezer)
Omri	887-875		Jehoram	852-845	
Ahab	875-854	(Micaiah,	Ahaziah	845	(Joel)
		Elijah, Elisha)			
Ahaziah	855-854	(Elijah, Elisha)	Athaliah	845-839	(Joel)
Jehoram	854-843	(Elijah, Elisha)	Jehoash	845-805	(Joel)
Jehu	843-816	(Elisha)	Amaziah	805-777	
Jehoahaz	820-804	(Elisha)	Uzziah	791-740	(Isaiah)
Joash	804-789	(Elisha)	Jotham	751-736	(Isaiah, Micah)
Jeroboam II	789-749	(Jonah, Amos,	Ahaz	741-726	(Isaiah, Micah)
		Hosea)	Hezekiah	726-697	(Isaiah, Micah)
Zechariah	748	(Amos, Hosea)	Manasseh	697-642	(Isaiah, Micah)
Shallum	748	(Hosea)	Amon	642-640	
		(30 days)	Josiah	639-608	(Zephaniah,
Menahem	748-738	(Hosea)			Nahum, Jeremi-
Pekahiah	738-736	(Hosea)			ah, Habakkuk)
Pekah	748-730	(Hosea)	Jehoahaz	608	(Jeremiah,
Hoshea	730-721	(Hosea)			Habakkuk)
(Assyrian Captivity, 721 B.C.)			Jehoiakim	608-597	(Jeremiah, Ha-
					bakkuk, Daniel)
			Jehoiachin	597	(Jeremiah,
					Daniel, Ezekiel)
			Zedekiah	597-586	(Jeremiah,
					Daniel, Ezekiel,
					Obadiah)

(Babylonian Captivity, 586 B.C.)

Suggestions for Additional Introductory Reading
on the Books of Prophecy[4]

*Anderson, Bernhard W.: *Understanding the Old Testament*, Chapters 7, 8, 9, pp. 183-387; and Chapter 11, pp. 325-356.

Calkins, Raymond: *The Modern Message of the Minor Prophets.*

*Cameron, W. J.: "The Prophetical Literature of the Old Testament," *The New Bible Commentary*, pp. 45-51.

*Paterson, John: *The Goodly Fellowship of the Prophets.*

Rowley, H. H.: *The Relevance of Apocalyptic.*

---

[4]See also Books by the Prophets in the General Bibliography in the back of the book, and the individual reading lists after each prophet in the chapters that follow.

Scott, R. B. Y.: *The Relevance of the Prophets.*

*Smith, George Adam: *The Book of the Twelve Prophets.*

Smith, J. M. Powis: *The Prophets and Their Times.* Second Ed. by W. A. Irwin.

Wright, G. Ernest: *God Who Acts.*

*Young, Edward J.: *An Introduction to the Old Testament,* pp. 215-304.

*Young, Edward J.: *My Servants the Prophets.*

I. BOOKS BY THE PROPHETS OF THE FIRST PERIOD: THE DECLINE AND FALL OF THE NORTHERN KINGDOM, 934-721 B.C.

Chapter 2

JOEL

1. AUTHORSHIP, DATE, AND BACKGROUND OF THE BOOK

The book of Joel is one of the great, short masterpieces of the Old Testament. It was carefully planned and built up with dramatic effect, as a single, complete, and unified composition.

There is no evidence that it was delivered orally as a prophetic discourse, on some previous occasion and then reduced to writing, as the prophet Amos and many other prophets composed their works.

What we know of the life and work of Joel must come from the book itself. From it we learn that he was the son of Pethuel (1:1), that he lived in Jerusalem, and had a great love for it and Judah. From the many references, too, we learn of his intimate knowledge of the city, its history and Temple worship (1:9, 13, 14; 2:1, 15, 17; 3:1, 2, 6, 17, 20, 21). From 1:13, 14; 2:17, we infer that he was not a priest, although he shows intimate knowledge of the priestly properties and ritual, including its meat, cereal, and drink offerings, all of which just now are in short supply because of the unprecedented plague, and the resulting famine.

Joel makes almost no reference to contemporary people and events, such as are common in the writings of other prophets. For example, he says nothing about the king of his own beloved Judah, or of the Northern Kingdom or its king, of Assyria, or of Babylon. What he says about nearby enemy nations, such as the Phoenicians of Tyre and Sidon, of the Philistines, or Egypt, or Moab, are general references and do not appear to be called forth by any recent or present day events.

The date of the book of Joel is unknown. Recent opinion, however, is swinging back to the earlier and traditional view, namely, that the book is one of the oldest, if not the oldest of written prophecy. From internal evidence, the book appears to belong to the pre-Jonah era, and the prophet Jonah is placed definitely in the reign of Jeroboam II (789-749 B.C.).[1]

---

[1]For representative scholars in favor of the earlier date, see J. T. Carson, *The New Bible Commentary*, pp. 690-691 (1954); Kirkpatrick, *The Doctrine of the Prophets*, pp. 63-65; Young, *An Introduction to the Old Testament*, pp. 270-273. For a late date, see Anderson, *Understanding the Old Testament*, pp. 449-450 (1957); Oesterley and Robinson, *An Introduction to the Books of the Old Testament*, "Joel."

A swarm of locusts devouring herbage, as in the plague of locusts (Exod. 10, etc.) and the book of Joel. © *Matson Photo Service*

If the prophet Joel in his book makes no reference to the kingdom of Assyria, or Babylon, it is urged, it would be because these northern empires had not begun their aggressive movements against Judah or Samaria as early as 845-791 B.C., the general dates which we have assigned to Joel and his prophecy.

Moreover, if Joel wrote during the minority of King Joash, shortly after 839 B.C. as many feel that he did, failure to mention the young eight-year-old king, whose public and private life was largely in the hands of Jehoida the priest, would also be understandable.

The "sins of the people," which is the burden of Joel's book, and because of which God has sent the plague in judgment upon them, is likewise understandable. Although Joel lived and prophesied at a time when the people of Judah had not fallen so low in wickedness as in later times, their sins were great, in that many of them had followed the evil leadership of Athaliah, the wicked daughter of the iniquitous Ahab and Jezebel.[2]

So, with reason enough, the prophet Joel could proclaim a national fast and day of repentance, as a condition of God's forgiveness and restoration to their former prosperity.

Furthermore, Joel's book has the simple, direct approach of the earlier writers, such as we find also in Hosea. Also, it sets forth primitive ideas such as the spirit of retaliation and revenge on Judah's enemies. For example, on the topic of war and peace, Joel's ideas are just the opposite of those of Isaiah and Micah, when he challenges his enemies:

> Beat your plowshares into swords,
> And your pruning hooks into spears.

Is it not likely that the younger prophets Isaiah and Micah, being impressed with the novelty of Joel's "plowshares-pruning-hooks" phrase, borrowed it, but recast it as a weapon of peace instead of an instrument of war, in line with their later and more enlightened understanding of the revelation of the will of God?

For a long while, it was thought that possibly the prophet Joel borrowed ideas and even phrases from the prophet Amos, in such passages as these: Amos 1:2, and Joel 3:16; Amos 4:6, and Joel 2:12; Amos 9:13, and Joel 3:18. And some have thought that Joel borrowed from the prophets Isaiah and Micah, and also from Obadiah.

Now, however, many are of the opinion that the opposite may be true, namely, that Amos began to prophesy where Joel left off, and that the borrowing was done by the younger from the earlier and older prophet, Joel.[3]

These circumstances may well be the background of Joel's prophecy and his reason for calling a day of national repentance and

---

[2]For her reign and evil influence, see p. 162ff.
[3]J. T. Carson, *op. cit.*, p. 690. See also Kirkpatrick, *op. cit.*, pp. 63-65.

solemn fast, and a return to the Lord under the young king Joash, who with the strong aid of Jehoida the priest, was to bring about many reforms.

2. The Composition and Purpose of the Book

Joel selected for the occasion of his composition what the modern reader would call *current events,* the most important current event of a lifetime. On this occasion it was an unprecedented plague of locusts and the drought that followed it, which was so dire and distressing as to leave the people in misery and great want.

The plague is to be a symbol of the *spiritual need* of his people, and the coming Day of the Lord. So Joel will dramatize it mightily, to bring home his lesson and to make impressive the theme of the book.

And so at the outset, as with a loud trumpet, he calls the nation to attention:

> Hear this, you aged men,
> Give ear, all you inhabitants of the land!
>
> Has such a thing happened in your days,
> Or in the days of your fathers?
>
> Tell your children of it,
> And let your children tell their children,
> And their children another generation.

Then, with poetic realism, he describes the devastating march of the army of locusts (oriental grasshoppers) as they go through the land. They came like a cloud in vast swarms, darkening the sun, and making a sound like the approach of a storm, or the rushing of a mighty wind. They light upon the earth, devour every green thing, climb bush and tree, and even penetrate houses. Nothing can break their ranks or turn them back, until they have run their course, or are pushed by a violent wind into the sea, or driven into the desert.

The book has many overtones. As a truly inspired prophet, Joel becomes spokesman for and quotes the Lord at length, and covers the whole range of prophecy, hinting at Israel's exile and restoration and the subsequent punishment of her enemies (chapter 3).

The climax comes in the great passage in which Joel prophesies the coming of the Holy Spirit, which the Apostle Peter quotes as being fulfilled on the Day of Pentecost (Joel 2:28-32; Acts 2:16-21).

3. Joel Sets a Pattern for Other Prophets

At this point, the student's attention is called to the fact that we have here in Joel an early book which sets a pattern for other prophets and prophecies. This pattern appears in a form which may be called a *prophetic cycle,* thus: (1) The presence of trouble and suffering as a judgment upon sin; (2) repentance and restoration called for, against the coming Day of the Lord; (3) God, who is "gracious and merciful," promises forgiveness, and a return of their prosperity and freedom from enemies; (4) and finally, the prediction of Israel's glorious future.

If Joel was the first to write a book of prophecy, which seems likely from internal evidence and the context, and the first thus to introduce a whole chain of great prophetic books, it is of primary interest to the student to examine that pattern and its implications more closely.

For, although at the outset the symbolic plague, and the warning of judgment to come was restricted to Judah and Jerusalem and their immediate neighbors, before the writer closes his book, he widens its scope and heralds Jehovah as the judge of all mankind. He will grant temporal and spiritual blessings to His faithful, without distinction, and will punish all evildoers. To accomplish this, God will pour out His Spirit upon all flesh.

To what extent did the other great prophets duplicate, each in his own way, the ideas and methods revealed in the book of Joel?

4. THE CONTENTS OF THE BOOK

Here is a brief topical analysis of the contents of the book of Joel:

(1) The prophet describes the plague of locusts, and the famine that followed, and interprets the event as God's judgment upon the people for their sins. Also, the plague is interpreted by Joel, not as the Day of the Lord, but as the herald and omen of that Day (1:2-11).

(2) Blow the trumpet in Zion! Joel represents himself as appearing before the people, as a trumpeter, to call a day of national repentance and solemn fast in the House of the Lord. Because of their great distress, the people are brought to their knees. In deep humiliation and repentance, they come to the sanctuary and confess their sins.

Then the Lord heard them and had pity on His people. Joel prophesies the return of God's favor, and an era of prosperity, in which the land once more should be fruitful (2:12-27).

(3) But the perfect fulfillment of this promise is in the prophet's vision of the Future. As one writer put it, "Joel felt that Israel needed more than a penitence born in the midst of austerity and famine. She also needed to be transformed, sanctified and made conformable to the mind and will of God. This could come about only if God would send down His Spirit into the hearts of His people."

So the prophet Joel predicted just that. That is, in a special section of his book, chapter 2:28-32, he prophesied that there would be an outpouring of the Holy Spirit of God before there would be any act of final judgment on the world.

(4) From here, Joel goes on to prophesy the final destruction of all the enemies of God, and the deliverance of all God's people (chapter 3).

(5) The final word on Joel's message is to be found in the Apostle Peter's quotation and interpretation of Joel's prophecy as a prophecy of the Age of the Gospel (Acts 2:14-21).

It was the day of Pentecost. In his famous sermon on that day, Peter quoted Joel's passage and applied it to the day of the Gospel, which Peter himself at that moment was inaugurating in Jerusalem.

Joel's message also predicted the presence and work of the Holy Spirit in the Gospel Age, which should continue until the end of time and the Final Judgment.

Selected Readings on the Prophets of the First Period

Bible Readings: The Books of Joel, Jonah, Amos, Hosea, Isaiah, and Micah. Text: *The Revised Standard Version;* or *The King James Version,* preferably in modern reader's format.

Joel

*Carson, J. T.: "Joel," *The New Bible Commentary,* pp. 690-697.

*Myers, Jacob M.: *The Books of Hosea, Joel, Amos, Obadiah, Jonah.*

*Young, Edward J.: *An Introduction to the Old Testament,* pp. 270-273.

Note: See also chapters on the book of Joel by Raymond Calkins, George Adam Smith, and others listed on page 324 and the General Bibliography at the end of the book.

Chapter 3

JONAH

1. THE BOOK OF JONAH AS A HISTORICAL SHORT STORY[1]

The book of Jonah tells the story of the main episode in the life of the prophet Jonah, who lived and worked during the reign of Jeroboam II (789-749 B.C.). Jonah is the hero, and for him the story is named.

In a one-sentence summary, the writer of II Kings (14:25) quotes Jonah on Jeroboam's success in recapturing the lost territory of Israel, and at the same time gives a bit of information about Jonah himself. He was the son of Amittai and a native citizen of Gath-hepher, in Galilee, a town a few miles north of Nazareth, the home of Jesus.

Many think that Jonah helped Jeroboam to recapture some of Israel's lost border territory, as the prophet Elisha helped the kings of Israel in his day. As we have noted, one of the functions of the prophet was to counsel with the king and to assist him in the role of statesman, as well as prophet. Jonah was a patriot.

The book, like the book of Ruth and the book of Esther, is in the form of a short story.

As a historical narrative, it is unsurpassed in what it reveals of the character of Jonah, and of the Lord, who was directing Jonah's destiny, and revealing His own purposes with men and nations.

2. JONAH'S STORY

Jonah, an Israelite of the Northern Kingdom in the reign of Jeroboam II, was commanded by the Lord to go to Nineveh, the capital of the Assyrian Empire and the greatest city on the earth in his day, and "cry against it." That is to say, preach repentance to the vast city and warn the people of their approaching doom.

But Jonah was unwilling to go, because the Assyrians had been engaged in destroying his native land. Accordingly, instead of going to Nineveh, he started in the opposite direction, and took ship at the old seaport city of Joppa to flee to Tarshish (Tartessus, in Spain) from the presence of the Lord.

A great storm arose. The ship was in danger. The sailors cast

---

[1]For two rather different analyses and interpretations of the book of Jonah, one "liberal" and one conservative, see Jacob M. Myers and D. W. B. Robinson listed at the end of this chapter.

lots to determine on whose account the storm had been sent. The lot fell upon Jonah. So Jonah was thrown overboard and the sea became calm.

After three days and nights in the belly of a great fish, during which Jonah prayed for deliverance, he was cast upon dry land.

Commanded a second time to go to Nineveh, Jonah obeyed and delivered his message. The prophet, turned evangelist, preached with such power for forty days that the people of the great city believed God. They proclaimed a fast and put on sackcloth, from the greatest to the least of them. Even the king of Nineveh, on hearing the tidings, rose from his throne, removed his robe, and covered himself with sackcloth, and sat in ashes.

And then by royal proclamation, the people and the princes were commanded to engage in a solemn fast, and to "cry mightily" to the Lord, in the hope that the Lord might repent and turn from His purpose to destroy the wicked city.

Had Jonah actually preached better than he had intended? And would the Ninevites actually repent, and the Lord spare the city?

Jonah went outside the walls of the city and built a booth to sit in, "till he should see what would become of the city."

Jonah had a feeling that the Lord would spare Nineveh, and he again feared for the safety of Israel. For he says, "I knew that thou art a gracious God and merciful, slow to anger, and abounding in steadfast love, and repentest of evil."

Then the Lord performed another miracle. He caused a gourd vine to spring up overnight, to furnish shade for the doorway of the prophet's booth. Jonah was glad because of the plant, and loved it. But when dawn came the next day, a worm had cut the vine and it withered.

Jonah pitied the gourd, and was most unhappy, and wished to die.

And the Lord said to Jonah, "You pity the plant, for which you did not labor . . . And should not I pity Nineveh, that great city, in which there are more than a hundred and twenty thousand persons who do not know their right hand from their left, and also much cattle?"

3. The Message of the Book of Jonah

The reader should regard Jonah as the hero of the book, and not as its author.

The book was written by an unknown writer, presumably many years after the time of the events of the story. Jonah's ministry to the Ninevites took place when the Assyrian Empire was at the height of its prosperity and glory. The story is told, on the contrary, as if Nineveh were a thing of the past, and the ruler referred to as "king of Nineveh," a title which no contemporary writer would ever think of using to describe the king of Assyria. Moreover, the book of Jonah nowhere claims to have been written by the prophet himself.

But as the reader is well aware, the matter of authorship in no way detracts from the validity of the book, or its message.

(1) In the first place, the book of Jonah teaches the lesson — which few Jews before Jonah had learned, but which many after him were to learn — namely, that the children of Abraham were not the only inheritors of Divine grace and mercy.

The Chosen People were "chosen," not as the sole wards of the Heavenly Father, but specifically as the *religious teachers* of all nations, and as the agents through whom God would reveal Himself and His plan of salvation to all people. . . . "And in thee shall all the families of the earth be blessed," was the promise made to Abraham.

The Ninevites, Jonah was to learn, were included in this promise made to Abraham, provided the Ninevites repented and returned to the Lord.

Thus, God was making it clear in these early prophecies that He is the God of universal salvation. In the first book of prophecy, in the book of Joel, God moved the prophet to say, "I will pour out my Spirit on *all* flesh."

(2) By the example of the withering gourd, the Lord taught Jonah the important lesson of Divine compassion.

The great, Divine heart of God was touched by the thought of one hundred and twenty thousand innocent children, in this enormous city, and no one to pity them:

> And should not I pity Nineveh, that great city, in which there are more than a hundred and twenty thousand persons who do not know their right hand from their left, and also much cattle?

(3) While on earth, our Lord was greatly interested in the prophet Jonah and his story, and through Him the book of Jonah has had a message, and an immortality, far beyond that of most books.

The Scribes and Pharisees of Jesus' day were in the habit of asking trick questions, intended to trip Jesus in the midst of His discourses.

On one such occasion they asked Him to give them a "sign," meaning some miracle or unusual demonstration of His Divine power.

His reply always to this question was, "This generation is an evil generation; it seeks a sign, but no sign shall be given to it except *the sign of Jonah.*"

The quotations recorded in the Gospels of Matthew, Luke, and John indicate clearly that the "sign of Jonah" meant two things.

The first sign of Jonah was his preaching, and the repentance of the Ninevites that followed:

> For as Jonah became a sign to the men of Nineveh, so will the Son of Man be to this generation (Luke 11:30).

The Yunis Mound, the traditional Tomb of Jonah in Nineveh, in Iraq, ancient Babylonia. © *Matson Photo Service*

The second sign of Jonah was our Lord's Resurrection:

> For as Jonah was three days and three nights in the belly of the whale, so will the Son of Man be three days and three nights in the heart of the earth (Matthew 12:40).

What a tribute to the prophet Jonah, to be compared with Jesus in these two particulars!

SPECIAL REFERENCES

JONAH

*Anderson, Bernhard W.: *Understanding the Old Testament,* pp. 503-504.

Calkins, Raymond: *The Modern Message of the Minor Prophets.*

*Myers, Jacob M.: *The Books of Hosea, Joel, Amos, Obadiah, Jonah.*

*Paterson, John: *The Goodly Fellowship of the Prophets,* pp. 271-283.

*Robinson, D. W. B.: "Jonah," *The New Bible Commentary,* pp. 714-719.

Smith, George Adam: *The Book of the Twelve Prophets.*

*Young, Edward J.: "Jonah," *An Introduction to the Old Testament,* pp. 277-282.

Chapter 4

AMOS

1. THE BOOK AND ITS BACKGROUND

Unlike some of the other books of prophecy, the book of Amos tells us a great deal about the prophet Amos himself, and the times and the people to whom his daring message was delivered.

Among the writing prophets, he was the first of a new school. For like Elijah and John the Baptist, Amos was outspoken and hard-hitting in denouncing the evil-doers of his day.

Amos was a native of Judah or the Southern Kingdom, in the reign of King Uzziah (791-740 B.C.). He was sent on a mission to the Northern Kingdom during the latter part of the reign of King Jeroboam II (789-749 B.C.).

Before Jeroboam II came to his throne, "The Lord saw that the affliction of Israel was very bitter, for there was none left, bond or free, and there was none to help Israel . . . so he saved them by the hand of Jeroboam" (II Kings 14:25-27).

This "affliction" of the Northern Kingdom, or "Israel" as it had been called since the days of King Saul when the Ten Tribes of the north separated themselves from Judah, had been brought about by the conquests of Assyria, as we discovered in our study of the book of Jonah, and was the reason why the prophet Jonah was unwilling to preach to the Ninevites.

But in the Providence of God, Jonah finally did preach to the Ninevites, their city was saved from destruction; and it seems that the Assyrians, at least temporarily, refrained from further aggressive wars of conquest against Israel and Judah, along with other western Asiatic nations.

Thus Jeroboam, as the result of "the mighty works of Jonah," was able to recover the lost border territory of Israel, and to achieve a prosperity in the latter half of his reign such as his kingdom had not known before. His capital, Samaria, became a meeting place for merchants from the various parts of the eastern world, and especially for caravans traveling between Mesopotamia and Egypt.

But as a result of this prosperity, the social, moral, and religious conditions in the land became unspeakably bad. The center of this profligate living was in the capital city of Samaria, which at the time was probably the most beautiful city in all Palestine. The strong oppressed the weak; and the rich became more wealthy by exploiting the poor.

Religion had fallen upon evil days. When Amos arrived at his mission, what he saw shocked him. There was calf worship, with the young bull to represent the deity, as the national religion of Israel, to say nothing of lingering Baalism that had never been destroyed. False shrines filled the land; and Jehovah worship, such as it was, too often was no more than a form and a hollow mockery.

It was to such a people, and at such a time, that the prophet Amos came with a bold message.[1] Amos spared no one, in Samaria and Bethel, the two famous centers where he visited and preached; King Jeroboam, his princes and wealthy noblemen, the society women, corrupt priests and false prophets — all were singled out for accusation and impending judgment.

2. THE PROPHET AMOS AND HIS CALL

Amos was a native of the village of Tekoa, Judah, in the hill country about eleven miles south of Jerusalem — and a good, long country walk from the old city of Bethlehem.

Amos makes no mention of his parents, or his personal family. He introduces himself simply, "I am a herdsman, and a dresser of sycomore trees."

On the broad hills he pastured his flocks of sheep, and cared for his sycomore figs, which required some "dressing" to assist them in the ripening process. How did this shepherd and native horticulturist become a prophet? He tells us:

And the Lord took me from following the flock, and the Lord said to me, "Go, prophesy to my people Israel" (7:15).

So Amos turned his flocks over to the care of others, left his native tribe of Judah, and journeyed to Bethel and Samaria to deliver the message of the Lord. Although he appears to have gone directly to Samaria the capital for his first appearances, part of Amos' preaching was at Bethel, the religious center of the Northern Kingdom.

Amos, in the opening sentence of his book, states that the time of his mission was "two years before the earthquake." This is the great earthquake which so many people remembered so long. The prophet Zechariah refers to it two hundred years later (Zechariah 14:5).

The Jewish historian Josephus states that the earthquake is associated with the leprosy of King Uzziah, which took place about 751 or 749 B.C. If we may depend on these dates, Amos' prophecy should be dated approximately 753 to 751 B.C.

At any rate, Amos' mission was urgent; for, as the reader knows,

[1] A highly satisfactory short introduction to the book of Amos is that of Dr. O. Bussey of Glasgow, in "Amos," *The New Bible Commentary*, pp. 698-709 (2nd ed., 1954). See also the excellent interpretation of Bernhard W. Anderson, "The Herdsman from Tekoa," *Understanding the Old Testament*, pp. 228-237 (1957).

in less than twenty years the Assyrian king, Tiglath-pileser III, in the Galilee and Transjordan Captivity of 734 B.C., carried away large numbers of the inhabitants of Israel; and that his successor, Sargon II, completed Israel's conquest in 721 B.C.

Amos was one of a distinguished group of contemporary prophets. Some think that Amos and Jonah may have been co-workers. However, Jonah's work as prophet seems to have been in the first half of the reign of Jeroboam II, before the greater prosperity of the reign was achieved; whereas Amos' came in the latter half, perhaps near the end.

Other contemporaries, but younger than Amos, were the prophets Hosea, Isaiah and Micah.

3. THE CONTENTS OF THE BOOK OF AMOS

The book of Amos presents a special problem for the reader. Unlike the books of Joel and Jonah, which were well organized, unified compositions, the book of Amos is an informal composition, evidently written from his rather full speech notes after his return from Samaria and Bethel to Tekoa, in Judah.

There is little or no attempt to separate each of the several addresses, or to indicate precisely where one ends and another begins. However, the reader may conveniently group the nine chapters of the book into three main divisions, with a special prophecy contained in the last five verses as a conclusion of the whole, thus:

(1) God's Impeachment of the Nations, Judah and Israel Included, Chapters 1 and 2;

(2) The Prophecies of the Three Main Discourses, Chapters 3 to 6;

(3) The Prophecy of the Five Visions, Chapters 7, 8, 9:1-10;

(4) The Prophecy of the Future Glory of Israel, Chapter 9:11-15.

(1) *God's Impeachment of the Nations*

The first two chapters include material which probably was not a part of the discourses delivered at Samaria and Bethel, but which the prophet wished to include as an introduction to his main prophecy. In these chapters, Amos denounces the crimes of the surrounding nations to one another, and pronounces God's judgment upon them — Syria, Philistia, Edom, Ammon, Moab, and finally Judah and Israel.

(2) *Prophecies of the Three Main Discourses*

Amos' mission was to the Northern Kingdom, and so the three main discourses or addresses are directed at Israel, and are the heart of the book.

1. *The First Discourse*, Chapter 3.

In the first discourse Amos appears to be speaking to the nation from the capital city of Samaria, and addresses them, "O people of Israel!" And at the outset, he justifies his claim to be heard as a spokesman for God. Things do not just happen, he is saying to them. I am here because "the Lord has spoken."

The substance of the first message, already announced in chapter 2:6-16, is the apostasy and wickedness of Israel, and her certain doom. The nation, he warns, is on the brink of disaster.

Then he pronounces God's judgment: "On the day I punish Israel for her transgressions," evidently meaning Samaria, "I will punish the altars of Bethel." The special judgment is upon the wealthy, whose palatial houses were built by their oppression of the poor:

> I will smite the winter house with
>   the summer house;
> And the houses of ivory shall perish,
> And the great houses shall come to an end.

2. *The Second Discourse*, Chapter 4.

"Hear this word, you cows of Bashan!" With these outspoken and uncomplimentary words, Amos addressed the society women of Samaria at the beginning of his second discourse. Bashan was the territory east of the upper Jordan Valley and noted for its rich pastures and large, fat cattle.

Next, Amos denounces the worshipers at Samaria, Bethel, and Gilgal for their idolatry, and their meaningless rituals and sacrifices.

To close his address, Amos tells his audience of five historic disasters in the natural world which had come upon Israel, and which should have reminded the people of their great need for repentance. "Yet, you did not return to me," says the Lord.

3. *The Third Discourse*, Chapters 5-6.

The third address begins with a lamentation, in the form of a poetic dirge, over the fall of Israel. For the destruction of the nation is imminent; and so sure of it is the prophet that he laments it as an accomplished fact.

Longer than the other two discourses — or, is it two discourses in one? — it presents a message of many moods. In one sentence he is denouncing the people for their impiety and wickedness; in the next he is making a hopeless plea for them to "seek the Lord and live."

The discourse closes with another pronouncement of woes upon the rich and upper classes, whose luxury and debauchery have resulted from the oppressions of the poor.

(3) *The Prophecy of Five Visions*

These five visions are symbols of the coming destruction of Israel. They were delivered at Bethel, the religious center of Israel and the king's sanctuary, and not at Samaria the capital, where apparently the other discourses were given.

At Bethel, Amos came in contact with Amaziah, the priest of Bethel, who sought to silence the prophet. Amaziah's first move was

to send word to King Jeroboam II at Samaria of the effect of Amos'
messages: "The land is not able to bear all his words."

To move the king, he quoted from a discourse of Amos:

> Jeroboam shall die by the sword,
> And Israel must go into exile
> away from his land.

Jeroboam apparently paid little or no attention to his priest at Bethel,
or to Amos.

Then Amaziah, interrupting the prophet in the midst of his "Third
Vision," challenged Amos to leave Bethel and go home:

> O seer, go, flee away to the land of Judah,
> And eat bread there, and prophesy there;
> But never again prophesy at Bethel.

(4) The Prophecy of the Future Glory of David's Kingdom

Did Amos' preaching do any good in Israel, seeing that the
Captivity of 734 B.C. and 721 B.C. completely destroyed the Northern
Kingdom as a nation, and that shortly after Amos' mission?

Undoubtedly he greatly encouraged the small minority of loyal
followers of Jehovah, the faithful "remnant," and added to their number as a result of his prophesying. This was important.

The last five verses of the book, moreover, describe the future
glory of David's kingdom, when the remnant shall come out of exile
and be restored to prosperity in a kingdom which shall no longer be
divided.

SPECIAL REFERENCES

AMOS

*Anderson, Bernhard W.: "The Herdsman from Tekoa," Understand-
    ing the Old Testament, pp. 228-237.

*Bussey, O.: "Amos," The New Bible Commentary, pp. 698-709.

Myers, Jacob M.: The Books of Hosea, Joel, Amos, Obadiah, and
    Jonah.

*Paterson, John: The Goodly Fellowship of the Prophets, pp. 11-37.

Snaith, Norman H.: Amos, Hosea, and Micah.

Chapter 5

HOSEA

1. HOSEA AND HIS FAMILY TRAGEDY

Hosea was a younger contemporary of Amos. It appears that his prophetic career began about where that of Amos left off, that is, about the closing years of the reign of Jeroboam II (789-749 B.C.), and ended sometime during the reign of King Hezekiah of Judah (726-697 B.C.), the last mentioned king in the opening sentence of his book.

Like Amos', his message was primarily to Samaria and the Northern Kingdom, although Hosea, unlike Amos, was himself a native of the Ten Tribes of the north.[1] Hosea's career was a long one, as indicated by the list of kings at the head of his book under whose reigns he lived and prophesied. It is likely that he witnessed the final fall of Israel, in 721 B.C., and that he may have been a victim himself, although he probably lived further on into the reign of Hezekiah of Judah.

One striking thing about the book of Hosea is that, like the book of Joel and the older Hebrew prophecies, it is based upon a realistic event. In this case, it is the personal tragedy of Hosea and his family, and to that extent the book is autobiographical. His wife, Gomer, became unfaithful to her husband and her own children, and strayed off after other lovers. Hosea's patient love followed her, and eventually he won her back, although she had to be redeemed from the depths of sin and slavery, at the price of a slave.

This personal, family episode, like the plague in the book of Joel, becomes a symbol in the book of God's patient love, and forgiveness of His people, at whatever sacrifice His love and Providence wills.

2. THE STYLE AND METHOD OF COMPOSITION

The style of the book, like that of the book of Amos, is fragmentary and lacking in apparent logical organization, such as the modern reader delights to find in his reading of an ancient and famous book such as this one.

Indeed, the reader will look in vain for introductory statements,

---

[1]See Bernhard W. Anderson's splendid analysis of the historical backgrounds of the books of Amos and Hosea, and his interpretation of Hosea, in *Understanding the Old Testament*, pp. 237-251 (1957). See also the selected reading list at the end of the chapter.

Ruins of Tekoah, the birthplace of the prophet Amos. © *Matson Photo Service* transitions, and other devices of prose writing for indicating logical discourses. What he will find, instead, is the Hebrew method of movement by *waves,* repetition, bold statement, rhapsody, and a style otherwise essentially poetic.

In the book of Hosea we have fragments of teaching, rather than complete discourses, and a style marked by rapid change of thought and feeling. However, in spite of the uncertainty of meaning in particular passages, the theme and meaning of the book is remarkably clear.

For the central and dominant idea of Hosea's book is the passionate love of Jehovah for His fallen people.

The prophet's method of persuasion, unlike that of Amos and the wilderness school of bold *denunciation,* was that of wooing the fallen by means of God's love and *entreaty.*

3. THE CONTENTS OF THE BOOK

Here is a brief outline analysis of the contents of Hosea, according to its two main divisions, as follows:

THE ANALYSIS

The first section includes chapters 1-3, and presents the different stages of the domestic tragedy of Hosea's life and its symbolic interpretation.

The second section, chapters 4-14, embodies Hosea's prophecies, or summaries of prophecies, dealing with Israel's moral, religious, and political sins, and the impending consequences of those sins. Or more briefly, the section may be called divine yearning for a lost people, now on the brink of destruction.

(1) Hosea, like Joel, dramatizes his message by using three preliminary chapters in which to present the frank story of his personal history: how he chose his wife, her character, three children and their symbolic names, how she ran away with her paramours, and how he bought her back with the purchase price of a slave.

All this is done at the expressed command of the Lord, to illustrate with true-to-life allegory the harlotry of Israel by forsaking the Lord, and especially to pin-point God's love for His estranged people Israel.

(2) The second division, which contains the prophet's main discourses and message, may be viewed as so many stages of the theme of the book. This material appears to the reader, not so much as a series of discourses, but more as a summary of Hosea's prophetic teaching, and possibly prepared by him toward the close of his ministry. Here are the high points:

(a) The Lord has a "controversy," that is, a lawsuit and a bill of particulars against Israel, which includes also the sins of both priests and prophets, who, like the people, are not faithful to their trust and the cause of Jehovah (chapter 4).

(b) Then for the length of two chapters the prophet rebukes priest, king, and the people for their great apostasy, and chides them for the shallowness of their repentance, and their love, which is "like a morning cloud" for instability (chapters 5 and 6).

(c) Hosea chides Israel also for its shilly-shally politics. The opposing political parties are guilty of "calling to Egypt, going to Assyria," turning from one power to the other, only eventually to make enemies of both. Thus Hosea, like Isaiah, counseled the avoidance of entangling alliances with any foreign nation, and urged Israel's dependence on the Lord for its security.

Too, Hosea denounced their idolatry, especially calf worship as represented by the golden calf at their national shrines (chapters 7-8).

(d) Hosea was despondent because Israel "has played the harlot, by forsaking her God," and because the long-merited retribution was imminent. The enemy was at hand.

Israel's iniquity is so great, and she is so wicked and so obstinate, Hosea wonders how she can be saved. This undertone of sadness and hopelessness runs especially through chapters 7 to 10, and reveals the gentle prophet's love and yearning for his erring people, as he loved and yearned for the return of his beloved Gomer (chapters 7-10).

(e) Hosea's tender compassion for his people is exceeded only by Divine compassion and yearning for Israel, to return to the Lord and live.

In verse after verse, in the last four chapters of the book, the prophet Hosea becomes special pleader for the Lord, and reveals the Divine love and yearning.

Throughout his book, Hosea has used the name *Ephraim* as synonymous with Israel or the Northern Kingdom.

In the days of Joshua, Ephraim was the largest of the northern tribes, and was a symbol of power and strength. The reader will recall that Ephraim was the favorite son of Joseph, after whom the tribe was named. But during the period of the Divided Kingdom, Ephraim became a symbol also of idolatry and wickedness, as seen in Hosea's words,

Ephraim is joined to his idols,
Let him alone.

Despite this reputation, Ephraim here is referred to with endearment.

SPECIAL READINGS — HOSEA

*Anderson, Bernhard W.: "The Prophecy of Hosea," *Understanding the Old Testament*, pp. 237-251.

*Hadjiantoniou, G. A. and L. E. H. Stephens-Hodge: "Hosea," *The New Bible Commentary*, pp. 682-689.

Myers, Jacob M.: Chapter on "Hosea" in *The Books of Hosea, Joel, Amos, Obadiah, Jonah.*

*Robinson, H. Wheeler: *Two Hebrew Prophets; Studies in Hosea and Ezekiel.*

Snaith, Norman H.: *Amos, Hosea, and Micah.*

Chapter 6

ISAIAH

1. ISAIAH AND THE BOOK OF ISAIAH

Isaiah is easily one of the great characters in world history. Of the two major ideas developed in the Old Testament, the Law and the Prophets, Isaiah stands forth pre-eminently among Prophets, as Moses for the Law. For almost a half century, Isaiah was not only Jehovah's leading spokesman but he was also Jerusalem's chief citizen.

The late Professor Richard G. Moulton of the University of Chicago, after a lifetime study of the great literatures of the world, made this comment on the book of Isaiah:

> It may be safely asserted that nowhere else in the literature of the world have so many colossally great ideas been brought together within the limits of a single work . . . Quite apart from any question of theology, it may be said that no more precious legacy of thought has come down to us from antiquity than this Hebrew conception of a Golden Age to Come.[1]

Indeed, it is difficult to overestimate the moral and religious influence of Isaiah's statement of an "Ideal Future," the fulfillment of which is the Gospel of the New Testament. To appreciate his contribution, we need only to remind ourselves that the classic thought of Greece and Rome, the two other great contributors to our present day civilization, was that their Golden Age was essentially in their *past*, and that the passing of time with them had only one direction, that of a *decline*.

There were other prophets who hinted at or predicted in one way or another the coming of the Christ. But it was Isaiah who, according to the Apostle John, "SAW the glory of Christ, and spoke of him" (John 12:41). Indeed, Isaiah was THE Messianic prophet.

This "glory" or Vision Isaiah steadfastly kept before his people. He saw that Israel was the Messianic Nation to the world, and that through it one day a great and wonderful blessing would come from "the Holy One of Israel" to all the nations. This blessing would be the coming of the expected Messiah.

Of his many statements of this Vision, the clearest is that given in the fifty-third chapter of his book. In this chapter, one of the

---

[1] *The Modern Reader's Bible*, p. 1395. (Macmillan, 1895.)

A page from the book of Isaiah, 47:2-48:6, from the Dead Sea Scrolls. *Courtesy American Schools of Oriental Research* most beloved chapters in the Bible, Isaiah presents a biographical sketch of the Saviour from boyhood to the Cross. The passage begins at 52:13. The details are so vivid that the reader can almost see Isaiah standing at the foot of the Cross, delivering as it were his funeral message. It is even given in the *past tense*, as an accomplished fact. And what has amazed millions is that it came to pass in almost exact detail, although it was written more than seven centuries before Calvary!

Not many details of Isaiah's personal life are known, although he reveals much of his character and personality in the sixty-six chapters of his long and wonderful book. He was son of Amoz (not *Amos* the prophet), who according to a Jewish tradition was a brother of King Amaziah. Thus Isaiah would be cousin to King Uzziah, and to his successors Jotham and Ahaz and Hezekiah, the other kings mentioned at the head of his book, during whose reigns Isaiah lived and delivered his messages.

By about the year 734 B.C., Isaiah was already married. He called his wife "the prophetess" (8:3), and his two sons Shear-jashub (7:3) and Maher-shalal-hash-baz (8:3), both of whom were symbolic and a forewarning of evils to come. Isaiah states that his call to the office of prophet came in the year King Uzziah died, or about 740 B.C. He was in the Temple and may have been engaged in some religious ceremonial as priest when the call came.

Isaiah's ministry was a long and an eventful one. As statesman and prophet, he never grew weary of ministering to his people, or of counseling with and advising their leaders, in crisis after crisis, often assuming a major responsibility for their security and destiny. There is a Jewish tradition that he lived on into the reign of the wicked Manasseh (697-642 B.C.), and having resisted Manasseh's idolatrous decrees, was seized and put to a horrible death, as late as the eighteenth year of that reign. It is reasonably sure that he spent his entire life in Jerusalem, in close connection with the kings and the Court and the national life of the people.

Isaiah wrote other books, which have not come down to us. These include a *Life of King Uzziah* (see II Chronicles 26:22), and the *Book of the Kings of Judah and Israel* (II Chronicles 32:32). He was thus a historian, as well as a statesman and prophet of the highest rank. His reputation, however, rests entirely with his great work, the book of Isaiah, which is the written record of God's revelation to Isaiah in relation to both his time and all time. Much of the book is in poetry, including the great passages, which are unsurpassed by anything of the other great poets, such as Homer or Milton or Shakespeare.

2. THE BACKGROUND OF ISAIAH'S PROPHECIES

Geographically and historically, Isaiah's fellow countrymen occupied the territory situated as a sort of land-bridge between two great empires. These powers were Egypt on the south, and Assyria on the north. They were natural rivals for the domination of Palestine and the other small states, such as Syria, Phoenicia, Philistia, and Edom, between them. At the time of his call, about 740 B.C., Isaiah found himself in the midst of a rapidly developing crisis for Judah, as well as for Israel of the Northern Kingdom.

(1) The Assyrian Empire

The more powerful of the two contesting parties was Assyria. Assur-Nasipal II (885-860 B.C.), a cruel and warlike Assyrian king, was probably the first to match swords with Israel in the reign of Omri (887-875). Shalma-neser II (860-825) came in contact with Israel during the reign of King Ahab (875-854 B.C.). Tiglath-pileser III (747-727 B.C.) is the king whose aid King Ahaz "purchased" against the invasion of his neighbors, Rezin king of Syria, and Pekah king of Israel, and contrary to the advice of Isaiah. Tiglath-pileser is also the king who defeated Israel in the Galilee Captivity of 734 B.C. His successor, Shalmaneser IV (727-722 B.C.), laid siege to the city of Samaria, but died before the conquest was completed. His son Sargon II (722-705) took over and completed the siege and captivity of Samaria and all the Northern Kingdom, in 721 B.C. The fall of Israel took place about the twentieth year of Isaiah's ministry in Jerusalem, and greatly influenced that ministry.

(2) The Judean Kings and the Jerusalem Parties

Isaiah's prophetic ministry was carried on during the reigns of four Judean kings: Uzziah, Jotham, Ahaz, Hezekiah, and possibly the early part of Manasseh's; and according to a Jewish tradition he was their royal kinsman. He was born during the reign of King Uzziah, and received his call in the last year of that reign. Uzziah was rated by the historians as a good king, who greatly strengthened the military defenses of the land, and increased the food supply by improved agriculture. He showed the spirit of true piety and encouraged the worship of Jehovah, although idolatry was so strongly entrenched that he was unable to destroy the "High Places" of worship in his kingdom. Since Uzziah's name heads the list, it is likely that Isaiah was serving in some religious capacity in the Temple during part of his reign. (See also p. 173ff.)

After Uzziah, his son Jotham came to the throne of Judah in his own right, following a regency which he served during his father's illness. In most respects he continued the policies and programs of his father. Like his father, he continued true Jehovah worship in the Temple; but like his father, too, he was unable to remove the "High Places" in the country, or to successfully oppose the strong drift toward impiety and immorality. This rapid deterioration of the national character in the last days of Jotham was of the greatest concern to Isaiah.

Jotham died about 736 B.C. and his evil son Ahaz succeeded him. For the story of the conspiracy of Pekah king of Israel, and Rezin king of Syria, to overthrow the king of Judah, and Ahaz's alliance with Tiglath-pileser III king of Assyria to checkmate the conspiracy against him, contrary to the advice of Isaiah, see pp. 175, 176; and Isaiah 7, 8, 9. What disturbed Isaiah most was the absolute abandon with which Ahaz gave himself over to the overthrow of the established worship of the two preceding kingships. In fact, he destroyed the Temple worship, stripped the Temple and the King's Palace of its precious furniture to purchase favor with the Assyrians, and finally closed the doors of the house of God itself. He re-introduced Baal worship, and even offered his sons upon the altar of foreign gods.

Hezekiah, unlike his father Ahaz, undertook to revive the worship of the sanctuary by re-opening and cleansing the Temple, and restoring the worship of Jehovah under the leadership of his devoted priests and Levites. He did his best to abolish idolatry in all its forms, and to deliver his people from foreign domination. In these reforms Hezekiah received much encouragement and support from the prophet Isaiah, whom the king regarded with very great favor.

In Jerusalem, in Isaiah's day, there were two political parties: those who favored an alliance with Egypt for protection and security *against* Assyria, and those who favored an alliance *with* Assyria. Isaiah was against both, and strongly counseled and advised faith and trust in the Lord their God as the only real security.

This conflict of opinion reached great intensity during the invasion of Judah by the Assyrian king Sennacherib and the threatened destruction of Jerusalem itself, in the period 705-701 B.C. King Hezekiah was under great pressure to side with the party who would join Egypt and the other small neighboring states in the south, in an alliance against Sennacherib. Isaiah advised against the alliance, and counseled the king to depend on the Lord for victory. Isaiah and Hezekiah won, and Jerusalem was saved from destruction for another hundred years. This deliverance of Jerusalem from the Assyrians is one of the great achievements of Isaiah's life. (See p. 177ff.)

3. Authorship

Most present day scholars are of the opinion that the book of Isaiah in its entirety was written by one author, and that he is the same Isaiah to whom tradition and common acceptance have ascribed the authorship of the book from the beginning. The present writer takes this historic view, and is of the opinion that to take the view of multiple authorship is to lead readers astray, and to make it impossible for them to have a correct understanding of this great book.

Although the matter of authorship of the book, admittedly, is not a question of "faith and practice," there are still those who hold to the theory that the first thirty-nine chapters were written by *one*

Isaiah, and that the last twenty-seven chapters were by a "second" Isaiah.[2]

Here are a few of the main reasons in favor of a single authorship:

(1) Isaiah is quoted in the New Testament more than any other prophet. In fact, he is quoted nearly as often as all the other prophets taken together, and the reference is always "Isaiah the Prophet," irrespective of the part of the book from which the quoted passage is taken. This is significant, since the quotations are taken about equally from both sections of the book.

(2) It is significant, too, that for nearly nineteen hundred years no one ever questioned or doubted that Isaiah was the sole author of the book that bears his name. It is only in the last two generations or so that the question has been raised.

(3) If there ever existed a "second Isaiah," as some venture to call him, how did he appear and write so great a manuscript as that contained in the last twenty-seven chapters of the book, without leaving any name, or any historical reference, or any association in the mind of any contemporary? Did this, we ask, ever happen before to any other so important a document in the history of writing?

(4) Any one who reads and re-reads the book of Isaiah, in its entirety, is impressed with the similarity of style throughout. The vocabulary, the characteristic phraseology, the peculiar ideas and compositional ways of expressing them, even in English translation, betray a unity of purpose and method which strongly suggests a single authorship.

Take one expression, for example. The epithet for the Deity, "the Holy One of Israel," is peculiarly Isaiah's, and is hardly found elsewhere in the Bible. The expression occurs *fourteen* times in chapters 1-39, and *sixteen* times in chapters 40-66, with the significant implication in this case that one author made use of it in both sections of the book.

(5) Additional weight has been given to the case for a single authorship in the recent discovery of the Dead Sea Scrolls in 1947. One of the scrolls is that of the book of Isaiah, which is more than a thousand years older than any other known manuscript of any Hebrew Old Testament book.

In this scroll there is no break in the manuscript of Isaiah between

---

[2]For a brief, but excellent summary for and against the unity of Isaiah, see W. Fitch, "Isaiah," *The New Bible Commentary*, pp. 558-562 (1954). For a more comprehensive summary of the history of the literary criticism of Isaiah, but favoring unity, see Edward J. Young, *An Introduction to the Old Testament*, pp. 215-242 (1958). For one of the best defenses of unity of authorship, see O. A. Allis, *Unity of Isaiah*. The theory of multiple-Isaiahs was popularized in 1889 by George Adam Smith in his lectures on Isaiah, *The Book of Isaiah*, Rev. ed., 1927. For a recent exposition of the theory of multiple-Isaiahs, see Bernhard W. Anderson, *Understanding the Old Testament*, pp. 256-287, and 395-429 (1957). See also R. B. Y. Scott's article in *The Interpreter's Bible*, Vol. V, pp. 151-164.

the end of chapter 39 and the beginning of chapter 40. In fact, chapter 40 begins on the last line of the page, thus indicating that the copyist found no break in the manuscript, or change of author at this point.

4. THE PLAN AND COMPOSITION OF THE BOOK OF ISAIAH

The book of Isaiah, like most of the other books of Prophecy, presents some special problems for the reader. The reading and understanding of the book will be facilitated somewhat if one will keep in mind certain facts regarding its plan and composition.

(1) The first thing to keep in mind is that Isaiah lived a long and active life of some forty or fifty years as Jerusalem's leading minister and prophet; and that the book is the *written record* of that long lifetime during the reigns of at least four kings of Judah.

(2) Another thing to remember is that the composition of the book has a wonderful plan, although the newcomer to its pages may not recognize it at first sight.

According to this plan, the book is divided into two halves. The first section, chapters 1-39, contains messages which deal primarily with the corrupt social and religious conditions of Jerusalem and Judah in Isaiah's day, including the crimes of surrounding nations as they relate to God's purposes and his people.

The second half of the book, chapters 40-66, deals primarily with the Future of Israel, Redeemed, and the Golden Age of Mankind during the Christian Era to come. The messages and prophecies of the second half of the book are an outgrowth and a fulfillment of those of the first half. A short lapse of time may have taken place between the writing of the first and second halves of the book.

(3) Still another thing to observe is how the author changes his pattern. That is, within the halves of the grand plan of composition as stated above, the reader will meet with much variation and shifting of point of view by the author. For example, the first chapter of the book contains a terrible *arraignment* of Judah, because of religious rebellion and the corrupt internal condition of the nation. Then, in chapter 2, the author shifts suddenly to a prophecy of the Future and the glory of the Messianic Age.

This method of shifting, from *the evils of the present* to the *rewards of the faithful Remnant after the Redemption*, the reader may expect throughout the book, sometimes in smaller units, and at other times in passages of two or three chapters length.

(4) Still another thing to observe is that, although in the main the prophecies are arranged in chronological order, there are certain chapters and passages which are not so arranged.

For example, Isaiah tells the story of his call to be prophet in chapter 6, which was in 740 B.C.; whereas the preceding five chapters for the most part deal with the early part of King Ahaz's reign, about 736 B.C. Thus, chapter 6 is out of chronological order. So also, chapters 28, 38, 39, are out of chronological order, not to mention shorter passages here and there throughout the book.

(5) The book of Isaiah, like Hebrew style generally, is highly condensed; the writer says much in small space. Too, the sudden shifts from one subject to another, referred to in the paragraph above, and often without introduction or transition or other indications of logical discourse, make a highly condensed style even more difficult for the reader to follow.

(6) In the book of Isaiah we have poetry of great beauty and power. Unlike the poetry of such books as Amos or Zephaniah, where the contents are reduced to extreme brevity and fragmentariness, the poetic stanzas of Isaiah have length and fullness and climax. For example, take the stanza on the Lord's Universal Reign (2:2-4), or the one on the Coming of the Prince of Peace (9:2-7), or the oracle concerning the Fate of Babylon (13:17-22), or any one of many others. Here is poetry in the grand manner. The reader must look for prose too; for, although Isaiah's style is mainly poetic, he mixes poetic and prose passages, and like Shakespeare, he no doubt is suiting the style to the occasion (see *Revised Standard Version*).[3]

5. The Contents of the Book of Isaiah

As previously noted, the contents of the book of Isaiah fall naturally into two grand divisions. Chapters 1-39 belong to the first part of the book, and chapters 40-66 to the second part.

A. *Prophecies Which Deal Primarily With Contemporary Events in Judah and the Surrounding Nations*, Chapters 1-39

1. The Rebellion of Israel. Chapter 1 contains a terrible arraignment of Jerusalem and Judah for their disloyalty and unspeakable corruption. The term "Israel" here includes All Israel, the Northern Kingdom as well as Judah. The chapter serves as a general introduction to the book, and reveals at the outset Isaiah's characteristic teaching and approach to the major problems of the age.

2. Jehovah's Universal Reign. Chapter 2:1-4, suddenly and without transition or introduction, presents the first of many famous passages on the Coming of the Lord, and his Universal Reign. It closes with the famous passage on disarmament and universal peace.

3. The Day of the Lord. The social and political corruption in the evil reign of King Ahaz provokes Isaiah to preach of the Day of the Lord or day of judgment. Chapters 2:5 to 5 deal with the early part of that reign, about 736 or 734 B.C. Chapter 5 is an allegory of Judah, God's unfaithful "vineyard," and his judgment upon it. Verses 2-6 of chapter 4 contain the second of the passages on the future, when "the Branch of the Lord shall be beautiful and glorious."

4. Called to Be the King's Servant. The famous chapter 6 contains Isaiah's vision of God, "I saw the Lord sitting upon a throne,"

---

[3]For more on the style of Hebrew poetry, see p. 215ff, and footnotes.

and his call and commission to become a prophet. It was the greatest moment in Isaiah's life, one which he remembered joyfully all his days. It should be compared with the visions of Moses (Exodus 3-4), Jeremiah (Jeremiah 1:4-19), and Ezekiel (Ezekiel 1, 2, 3:1-15).

5. THE UNHOLY ALLIANCE OF SYRIA AND ISRAEL AGAINST JUDAH. Chapters 7 and 8 deal with the alliance of King Rezin of Syria, and King Pekah of Israel, and their invasion of Judah. They were subsequently defeated and punished by the Assyrian armies, as Isaiah had predicted.

6. THE SIGN IMMANUEL. While Isaiah the prophet is meditating upon the captivity and exile of Israel, and upon the evil days in his own Judah, and how the Lord would use Assyria to punish his rebellious people, he suddenly shifts his viewpoint again. In chapter 9:2-7, he gives us another picture of the future and the coming of the Prince of Peace (see 7:14).

7. THE ASSYRIAN INVASION AS DIVINE JUDGMENT UPON ISRAEL, AND ITS SEQUEL. Chapters 10 and 11 complete the period from about 734 to about 720 B.C.: the two invasions of Israel, and her final captivity in the campaigns of 734 and 721 B.C.

8. THE FUTURE HOPE OF ISRAEL. And then, closing this section of his prophecy, in chapters 11 and 12, Isaiah turns again to the future hope of Israel in the reign of this Ideal Ruler, this Prince of Peace, who "shall come forth a shoot from the stump of Jesse," that is, the line of David. Chapter 12 is a Song of Thanksgiving for this message of Hope, which will be sung by the Redeemed of the Lord, "in the hymn-book of heaven."

It will be useful at this point for the student to review the passages which predict the coming of Christ and His eternal reign: 2:2-4; 4:2-6; 7:14; 9:1-7; chapters 11 and 12.

9. PROPHECIES DIRECTED AGAINST ENEMY NATIONS. Chapters 13 to 23 contain prophecies directed against foreign and hostile nations — Babylon, Assyria, Philistia, Moab, Damascus (Syria), Ethiopia, Egypt, Edom, Arabia, and Tyre — and indicate the wide range of Isaiah's interests. They may be called prophecies of doom. The reader has noticed that each of these prophecies has its own introduction.

Chapters 13, 14:1-23, deal with the fall of Babylon. In Isaiah's time, as we have seen, the Assyrian Empire ruled the world, and that Babylon was subject to Assyria. It was not until 612 B.C., a hundred years after the prophecy, that the Babylonians defeated the Assyrians, and the Babylonians rose to power. In time the Babylonians themselves became indifferent rulers, and so the Medes and Persians, under their King Cyrus, defeated the Babylonians, in 538 B.C.

Thus, Isaiah in this prophecy, with his eyes turned toward the future, predicted the fall of Babylon nearly two hundred years before the event. In later chapters (44, 45), Isaiah mentions Cyrus by name.

10. WHEN EGYPT AND ASSYRIA TURN TO THE LORD. In chapter 19: 16-25, Isaiah makes another of his famous shifts in viewpoint. While he is prophesying the present humiliation of Egypt, he suddenly lifts his eyes toward the future, and describes a redeemed Egypt and Assyria, when "the Lord will make himself known to the Egyptians."

Here is a great passage which Bible readers have too often overlooked. It presents an enlightened version of the missionary influence of the religion of Judah on its would-be conquerors, the Egyptians and Assyrians, and on all the others with whom it came in contact. Isaiah closes his picture of the future regarding these nations with these significant words:

> In that Day there will be a highway from Egypt to Assyria, and the Assyrian will come into Egypt, and the Egyptian into Assyria, and the Egyptians will worship with the Assyrians.

> In that Day Israel will be the third with Egypt and Assyria, a blessing in the midst of the earth, whom the Lord of hosts has blessed.

11. ISAIAH DRAMATIZES JUDAH'S DANGERS. Chapter 20 presents something unique in prophecy. Against Isaiah's advice and counsel, a strong party in Hezekiah's reign urged an alliance with Egypt as protection from the mighty Assyrian army (about 711 B.C.). Isaiah was stoutly opposed to it, on the grounds that Egypt was militarily weak and not dependable, but especially because the Lord had promised to be Israel's defense.

To dramatize his opposition, Isaiah stripped and walked barefoot through the streets of Jerusalem, in the garb of a slave being led by his Assyrian conqueror. This demonstration he repeated again and again for the space of three years, "as a sign and portent against Egypt and Ethiopia."

12. ISAIAH'S APOCALYPSE. Chapters 24-27 present Isaiah's vision of the end of time, and the final judgment of all the peoples of the earth. It is an awe-inspiring picture, such as only a great poet could imagine.

The reader will recall at this point that the book of Isaiah is described as the "vision of Isaiah," in its opening sentence. In the last section, chapters 15 to 23, the prophet in the words of the Lord, has pronounced judgment and doom upon the wicked nations, including Judah.

In the present chapters, the reader meets with prophecies dealing with the outcome of that wickedness, namely, the end of time and the final judgment. As usual, these passages present two phases of the story: punishment of the wicked, and those who forgot God; and the future reward of the redeemed remnant.

Chapter 24 contains a picture of world convulsions as the earth reels and approaches its final destiny, in the Providence of God. Jesus, as recorded in Matthew 24, seems to be referring to the same end of time which Isaiah "saw."

13. THE RESURRECTION AND ETERNAL LIFE. Chapter 25:1-5 contains

a hymn of praise and thanksgiving to the Lord, by the redeemed. In the second half of the chapter, verses 6-12, Isaiah makes the greatest of all his prophecies, namely, the Lord's promise of eternal life, by the abolition of death, through the Resurrection.

> He will swallow up death for ever, and the Lord God will wipe away tears from all faces . . .

This is the clearest reference to the Resurrection of Jesus, and the promise of eternal salvation, to be found anywhere in the Old Testament. Chapter 26 continues the Song of Triumph of the preceding chapter, and closes with a widened concept of the Resurrection for all of God's people, to be found elsewhere only in the New Testament:

> Thy dead shall live, their bodies shall rise. O dwellers in the dust, awake and sing for joy!

14. PRECEPT UPON PRECEPT, LINE UPON LINE. In chapters 28-33, we have prophecies dealing primarily with warning to Jerusalem and Judah, in relation to Egypt and Assyria. Chapter 28, in denunciation of both Samaria and Jerusalem, appears to have been written just prior to the fall of Samaria, in 721 B.C. Chapters 29-33 deal mainly with events on the eve of Sennacherib's grand invasion of the south, Judah in particular, in 701 B.C. Isaiah is enraged over the controversy of the two parties in Jerusalem, especially against the defeatists who would seek help from Egypt in their struggle with Sennacherib's armies. There are about six separate addresses, each beginning with the word "Woe."

After his visions and prophecies concerning the "glorious future," in chapters 24-27, Isaiah returns again to the practical consideration of the immediate present. It was a terrifying present. Sennacherib's army was pillaging and ravaging the land. He had taken fortified city after fortified city, 46 of them, and more than 200,000 of their inhabitants, he boasted in his official inscription.[4]

Jerusalem was in a panic. King Hezekiah, after negotiations had failed, finally agreed to pay the Assyrian a large sum of silver and gold. But Sennacherib had treacherously broken his agreement and was getting ready to march upon Jerusalem. But Isaiah's faith was steadfast as he communed with God. Thus, he spent the hours, calmly reassuring the people that the strong arm of the Lord was encircling their city, and defending them from an enemy whose army presently would be routed and destroyed. Chapter 29 describes the impending siege of Jerusalem; the city is called "Ariel," which under David was called "The Lion of God."

Chapter 30 tells the story how Hezekiah, contrary to Isaiah's advice, sent caravans of asses and camels through the "bad lands" of the southern desert, laden with riches for Egypt and Egypt's help in Judah's war against Assyria. Chapters 31-33 contain a continuation

---

[4]James B. Pritchard, *Ancient Near Eastern Texts Relating to the Old Testament,* Second Ed., pp. 287-288. (Princeton, 1956.)

of the case of Jerusalem versus Assyria, with repeated warnings against trusting in Egypt, and with pleas for his people to return to the Holy One of Israel for present help.

15. WHEN THE GRACE OF GOD COMES TO ISRAEL. In chapters 30: 18-26, 32:1-8, and much of chapter 33, Isaiah once again shifts his viewpoint suddenly from the *present* to the *future*, from earth to heaven, and gives a prophetic picture of Israel, after her period of tribulation and gracious redemption, under the reign of the King of Kings:

> There the Lord in majesty will be for us
> a place of broad rivers and streams,
> Where no galley with oars can go,
> nor stately ships can pass.

16. SENTENCE UPON THE NATIONS. The prophet sees God's wrath upon the nations for their continued wickedness and disobedience as an accomplished fact, and so in chapter 34 he pictures them as already fallen. He therefore proclaims their sentence and doom.

17. ZION'S GLORIOUS FUTURE. Chapter 35 is another one of the great chapters of the book of Isaiah. It is another version of the redeemed remnant of Israel, and recites the blessings in store for God's faithful. The last three verses is a song of everlasting triumph.

AN APPENDIX

10. HISTORICAL SUMMARY. Chapters 36-39 are in prose and are *extras*. In a modern book they probably would be called an *appendix* and printed in the back of the book for reference.

These historical narratives are practically a verbatim transcript of II Kings 18:13 to 20:19, except for King Hezekiah's song of thanksgiving in Isaiah 38:9-20.

These extra chapters cover the invasion of Judah by Sennacherib, Hezekiah's prayer and Isaiah's message to the king, and Sennacherib's overthrow as Isaiah had predicted. Included also is Isaiah's opposition to an alliance with Babylon, at the time when King Merodach-baladan sent envoys to Jerusalem for that purpose.

Thus, these chapters give the outcome of the historical struggle between two great leaders: Sennacherib, king and army commander of the Assyrian Empire, and Isaiah, God's prophet and spokesman to Jerusalem and Judah. God was on Isaiah's side and made for the balance of power. Isaiah had prayed unceasingly that Jerusalem and its people might be spared. His prayer was granted, and the fall and captivity of the nation was postponed for another hundred years. It was a grand achievement and a personal triumph for Isaiah.

B. *Prophecies Which Deal Primarily With the Future of Israel,*
and the Golden Age of All Mankind, Chapters 40-66

At this point, the book of Isaiah, like a great drama, has reached a certain crisis. During his lifetime, Isaiah's real protagonist was

Satan, under the guise of the Assyrian Empire and its cruel and merciless kings.

The Assyrians had destroyed most of the Northern Kingdom of Israel in 734 B.C., and then took Samaria and the rest of it in 721 B.C. They invaded Judah in 720 B.C., again in 713, and finally by 701 B.C. had taken all the fortified and unfortified cities of Judah except Jerusalem itself.

Isaiah knew that Jerusalem would not fall into the hands of the Assyrians. God had so promised, and this promise Isaiah had steadfastly believed and proclaimed to his people. Now, with the destruction of Sennacherib's army, the city had been saved.

But the prophet also knew that his willful and disobedient people, like their kinsmen of the Northern Kingdom in the days of the prophets Amos and Hosea, would not repent and return to the Lord. So he had prophesied, in chapter 39:6-7, that his beloved Jerusalem would later be defeated and carried into captivity by Babylon.

And so in chapter 40, the beginning of the second half of his book, Isaiah assumes that the Babylonian Captivity is an accomplished fact, and his duty now as God's spokesman is to "comfort" his people. This he does in the grand visions of the future, which occupy most of his attention in the remainder of the book.

This second part of the book of Isaiah divides itself naturally into three sections of about equal length, as follows:[5] (1) The Proclamation of Deliverance, chapters 40-48; (2) the Servant of the Lord, chapters 49-57; and (3) the Future Glory of Zion and the Coming of the Golden Age of Humanity, chapters 58-66.

(1) *The Proclamation of Deliverance*

1. COMFORT YE, COMFORT YE MY PEOPLE. Chapter 40 is one of the grandest in the book. In the words of W. Fitch of Glasgow, who is speaking also of other chapters that follow:

> Nothing in all the sacred writings of the Jewish people can surpass these passages for sublimity of thought, felicity of expression and majestic depth of spiritual understanding. Here is unconquerable hope and unquenchable joy. The thrilling tidings that he is called upon to bear transport the prophet and give to him words winged with divine and holy inspiration.

Thus, the "comfort" Isaiah brings is that one day God will restore the exiles to their own land and will bless them beyond measure. The purpose of this prophecy is to herald the coming of the Saviour, reference to whom is made in verses 3-5 of chapter 40, and quoted in all four gospels as being fulfilled seven hundred years later (Matthew 3:3; Mark 1:2-3; Luke 3:4-6; John 1:23). The role of John the Baptist, though not named, is announced.

2. CYRUS AS GOD'S AGENT. Chapter 41 follows closely upon the

---

[5]See J. R. Dummelow (Editor), *A Commentary on the Holy Bible*, pp. 439-449. (Macmillan, 1936.)

revelation given in chapter 40, showing God as sovereign Lord of history, and introduces King Cyrus of Persia, who is to become God's agent in restoring Israel. Cyrus is referred to without name as "one from the East" (verses 1-2, and 25-27), but is named by the prophet later (44:28, and 45:1).

Some Bible scholars are bothered that Isaiah made these prophecies and died 150 years before the days of Cyrus, and that his visions describe so accurately Cyrus' rapid conquest of the world, including Babylon. These same scholars appear less disturbed over Isaiah's many prophecies of the coming of the Christ, which were also made seven centuries before His Advent.

(2) *The Servant of the Lord*

3. ISRAEL AS THE SERVANT OF THE LORD. In chapter 42 Isaiah introduces a new stage in his vision of the Messiah. Here we have from Jehovah's chief spokesman the beginning of a series of passages that *reveal* the Divine plan of salvation, and His Servant or minister by whom the divine will is to be carried out (42:1-9; 49:1-12; 50:49; 52:13-15; 53:1-12).

In the passage 42:1-9, Jehovah has called His servant, put His Spirit upon him, and filled him with a sense of mission. He is to establish justice in the earth, and to be a light to the nations, and to glorify the name of the Lord throughout the world. In this passage Jehovah is the speaker.

Who is this Servant of the Lord? Since the days of the promise to Abraham, Israel has had an important part in the divine plan of salvation; and a sense of being chosen has rested upon the leaders and people of Israel. Here perhaps Isaiah is thinking of "Ideal Israel," and the faithful remnant of every generation, and now being led by the true prophets of Jehovah.

> I have given you as a covenant to the people,
> a light to the nations . . .

> Behold the former things have come to pass,
> and new things I now declare;
> Before they spring forth
> I tell you of them. (Isaiah 42; see also 49.)

4. THE MESSIAH AS THE SERVANT OF THE LORD. Readers of the New Testament universally point to John the Baptist as the forerunner of the Christ. Here we have also in the writers of the books of prophecy, and the Psalms,[6] the earlier forerunners. Indeed, however real was Israel in the mind of Isaiah when he wrote these wonderful passages, there is no doubt that the main emphasis is upon the Messiah, the Son of God, who is Servant of the Lord.

However, it is not until chapter 49:1-12 that the Divine Son, not Jehovah as in chapter 42, in another dramatic monologue comes

---

[6]For "Psalms Which Foretell the Coming of the Messiah," see pp. 221, 222.

forth as the Speaker to reveal His place in the plan of salvation. He is conscious that His mission is very difficult, and will entail much suffering, and sees apparent failure in that He is rejected by His own people. But only through suffering will Israel be redeemed, and that in the end not only Israel but all the earth will be brought to Him.

In all these passages, it is most important for the reader to remember that Isaiah, as spokesman for God and His interpretative prophet, here is running ahead of history and is *revealing things to come.*

Chapter 50:4-9 continues the monologue by the Son of God as Servant, whose sense of mission has deepened, as well as His ability to endure personal pain and rebuffs. However, it is not until the last three verses of chapter 52, and the whole of chapter 53, that the prophet Isaiah reveals in complete outline the Messianic Person and the Messianic Mission, "a Man of Sorrows and acquainted with grief."

5. MORE ON THE MISSION OF CYRUS. Chapter 45 continues the theme of the commission to Cyrus and interprets the meaning of Cyrus' conquest of Babylon. Cyrus is the God-appointed "shepherd" or instrument of the Restoration of Israel, just as Assyria was Jehovah's agent in Israel's chastisement. Isaiah represents Jehovah as making a speech to Cyrus, and in typical Isaiahan rhapsody.

Chapters 46, 47, 48, are on Babylon, warning against its idolatry, and with a plea to trust in Jehovah. Babylon's fall is predicted. Chapter 44:9-20 is on the impotence of idols and the folly of idolatry, and is one of the most realistic passages in the book of Isaiah.

6. ZION ONCE MORE. In chapters 54-56, Isaiah again returns to Israel and her promised restoration. These passages follow naturally the preceding messages of the vision of the "Suffering Servant," and offer *comfort* to the faithful exiles. In chapter 55, Isaiah enlarges his invitation to include all mankind, which is the invitation of the Lord's Servant:

> Ho, every one who thirsts,
> Come to the waters!

These are the blessings which Jehovah has covenanted from the beginning to all His faithful ones.

Thus, the several passages in chapters 49-57 have stressed, in Isaiah's inimitable poetic style, redemption through suffering and sacrifice of the Son and Servant of Jehovah. Here is revealed Jehovah's gracious providence and mercy, and everlasting love, and longing not only for Israel's salvation, but for the salvation of the whole earth.

(3) *The Future Glory of Zion and the Golden Age of Humanity*

7. THE TRIUMPH OF THE KINGDOM AND THE UNIVERSAL DOMINION OF JEHOVAH. We come now to the third and last section of the second half of the book of Isaiah. The prophecies in these passages are what we should expect, that is, they are the outcome and culmination of

the book as a whole. Briefly, here is what the prophet is saying in these last chapters, 58-66:

Although Zion's redemption and restoration have been long delayed, because of the disobedience and wickedness of the people and their leaders, here is prophesied the triumph of the Kingdom and the Sovereignty of Jehovah, in which there is to be a glorious future for the Hebrew race, and the Golden Age for the whole human family.

From the beginning of his book, we have seen how Isaiah warned his people, and pled with them to put their trust in the Lord and return to Him, as their only hope of salvation and sure defense against the common enemy. And, alternately, we have seen how he held before them the reward of a glorious future for those who were faithful. But we have also seen how in the main that Judah, like Ephraim and the Northern Kingdom, rejected God and His promises and would eventually, like Ephraim, be punished and disciplined by exile in a foreign land. But hope for their future was always held before his people.

8. "CRY ALOUD, SPARE NOT." Isaiah is charged by Jehovah, thus:

> Lift up your voice like a trumpet;
> Declare to my people their transgression.

In chapter 58 the prophet deals with true and false worship of Jehovah. Judah was guilty of mere outward service, of fasting and sacrificing without repentance and reform. Isaiah, like Amos, preached that what Jehovah requires is mercy and social justice, rather than empty and vain sacrifice. Chapter 59 is a continuation of the theme of Judah's ungodliness, and how it had delayed the fulfillment of the divine purpose.

9. THE LIGHT OF THE WORLD. In chapter 60 the prophet shifts his viewpoint again, and in another beautiful passage gives a vision of the Light of the World, which one day will come to Jerusalem and Zion. And the restored city will be the center of the world's Light.

Chapter 61 continues the prophecy of the future glory of Zion. Here we have another dramatic monologue in which the speaker is the Son, the Servant of the Lord. Jesus quoted this passage at the very beginning of His ministry as referring to Himself (Luke 4:16-19). The Servant of Jehovah continues His message in chapter 62, and with a sense of urgency.

10. THE SERVANT AS THE DIVINE DELIVERER. In chapter 63 the prophet pictures the Servant as the Divine Deliverer, coming out of Edom "in crimsoned garments," from the battle with the enemies of righteousness and truth. Edom, the traditional enemy of Israel, is here chosen as the great type of the enemies of Jehovah. It is probably significant that the Herods of the New Testament all came from Edom.

In this chapter, and in chapter 64, the prophet Isaiah fully understands the "battle" of the Servant of the Lord, and associates himself on His side, and bursts forth with praise (63:7-9), as he does later with prayer for mercy and help (chapter 64), and for the accomplishment of the holy work of Zion's Redeemer. The symbol of the Messiah as warrior is used also by the writer of the book of Revelation (19:11-16).

11. A NEW HEAVEN AND A NEW EARTH. Chapter 65 presents Jehovah as ready and waiting to receive His own, before ever they come seeking His face, which alas, is often only in time of trouble. In the judgment to come, the faithful will be rewarded; but those who forsake the Lord will be utterly cast off.

The chapter closes, however, with a picture of the glorious future and the coming of the Golden Age for all humanity. This picture of a new heaven and a new earth is continued in the 66th and final chapter of the book, in what may be called the epilogue or conclusion of the whole.

SPECIAL READINGS ON THE BOOK OF ISAIAH

*Allis, O. A.: *The Unity of Isaiah.*

Anderson, Bernhard W.: "The Book of Isaiah," and "The Second Isaiah," *Understanding the Old Testament,* pp. 256-287, and pp. 395-429.

*Calvin, John: *The Prophet Isaiah,* 4 Vols.

*Fitch, W.: "Isaiah," *The New Bible Commentary,* pp. 556-607.

Moulton, Richard G.: "Isaiah," *The Modern Reader's Bible,* pp. 1388-1398.

North, C. R.: *The Suffering Servant in Deutero-Isaiah.*

Paterson, John: "Isaiah: Prophet of Faith," *The Goodly Fellowship of the Prophets,* pp. 59-82.

Robinson, H. W.: *The Cross in the Old Testament.* (Westminster Press, 1955.)

Rowley, H. H.: *The Servant of the Lord and Other Essays on the Old Testament.* (Lutterworth Press, 1952.)

Scott, R. B. Y.: "Isaiah," *The Interpreter's Bible,* Vol. V, pp. 151-164.

Smith, George Adam: *The Book of Isaiah,* Revised Edition.

Wright, G. Ernest: *The Book of Isaiah.*

*Young, Edward J.: "Isaiah," *An Introduction to the Old Testament,* pp. 215-242.

*Young, Edward J.: *Studies in Isaiah.*

Chapter 7

MICAH

1. MICAH, THE DATE AND BACKGROUND OF HIS BOOK

We come now to the last of the prophets of the First Period, the prophet Micah, who was a native of Moresheth-gath, a Judean village on the Philistine border near Gath, about thirty miles southwest of Jerusalem.

According to the opening words of his book, the prophecies of Micah came in the reigns of Jotham (751-736 B.C.), Ahaz (741-726 B.C.), and Hezekiah (726-697 B.C.), kings of Judah. And some think that Micah, like Isaiah, lived on into the reign of the wicked Manasseh (697-642 B.C.). The picture of conditions described in chapters 6-7 of the book of Micah seems to bear that out.

Micah was a younger contemporary of Isaiah, and both were younger contemporaries of the prophets Amos and Hosea. Isaiah was an aristocrat, a member of the ruling class, a great cosmopolitan preacher of righteousness, a social reformer, and a major prophet and spokesman of Jehovah. He was a native of Jerusalem.

Micah, on the contrary, and like Amos, was from the country or village. Some think that Micah may have moved to Jerusalem, and in some sense may have become a colleague of Isaiah. Certainly, his book reveals intimate knowledge of the social evils and corruption in the great city.

Micah's viewpoint, however, is that of the oppressed; and he writes with first hand acquaintance and sympathy with the miseries of the poor, and is on their side. He is acutely sympathetic toward those who have been deceived by their rulers, and have been robbed by the wealthy land-grabbers and merchants of the city. He may himself have been a farmer, and may have been foreclosed and dispossessed of his land by some greedy landowner. He says,

> They covet fields, and seize them;
> and houses, and take them away;
> They oppress a man and his house,
> a man and his inheritance.

In our study of the prophets Amos and Hosea, we saw how the growth in trade and economic prosperity, during the latter part of the reign of Jeroboam II, brought with it also the extreme oppression of the poor. It was against this moral evil, as well as against other

301

forms of social and political corruption, that Amos and Hosea preached.

In Isaiah and Micah's day in Judah, which was only a few years later, the same social and political evils existed in Jerusalem and Judah, and formed the background of their social and religious messages.

Also, Micah's village of Moresheth-gath was near the great coastal highway which connected Asia and Africa, and ran between his native village and the Mediterranean Sea. Over this road for many centuries had passed the armies of conquerors, caravans of trade, and the pilgrims of many lands. Thus, Micah was brought up on a natural land-bridge, so to speak, between Egypt and the south, and Assyria and Babylonia on the north, on what might be called the highway of the ancient world.

Indeed, Micah in his lifetime, like the prophet Isaiah, labored under constant threat of the Assyrian Empire. In 721 B.C., after his final defeat of Samaria, Sargon II king of Assyria, proceeded with his army southward over the famous highway to overwhelm the forces of Egypt at Raphia, in 720 B.C., including certain Philistine cities. At this time parts of Judah were also invaded. Again, in 713, Sargon came south to punish another rebellion of his subject states. As was evident from the outset, the combined strength of Philistia, Edom, Moab, and Egypt, was no match for the Assyrian army, and they were soundly beaten in the battles of Ashdod and Gath, not far from Micah's home village.

Still later, in 701 B.C., when Sargon's son Sennacherib, now king of Assyria in his own right since the death of his father in 705 B.C., came south once more to re-conquer and to punish his rebelling states. This story we followed in some detail in our study of the book of Isaiah. Micah's home at Moresheth-gath lay in the path of these battles of Sargon and his son Sennacherib, and it must have been overrun more than once, and plundered by foreign armies during his time.

2. The Composition of the Book of Micah

(1) The reader's attention is called to the fact that Micah's messages of a lifetime are condensed into the brief space of seven short chapters. This indicates that the book as we have it, is an abridgement of the prophet's teachings, and not a book of complete discourses as we would find in a modern book of sermons.

(2) In addition to brevity, the book contains abrupt changes from one topic or theme to another, from one occasion to another, and even from one period of time to another, without transition or notice to the reader. Some of these features of style are pointed out in our analysis of the contents of the book.

(3) Micah's method of composition, in one important particular, was similar to that of Isaiah's. Like his famous contemporary, Micah

presents messages dealing with present day events, and messages concerning the future of Israel and that of the whole human family. This method is the occasion for his abrupt shifts in style, as we find in many of the prophets.

(4) Portions of the book of Micah appear to have been written in different periods of the prophet's life. Chapter 1 refers to the social and religious corruption of Samaria as well as that of Jerusalem, and thus was written before the fall of the Northern Kingdom in 721 B.C. Chapter 3 was written during the reign of Hezekiah; for Jeremiah, quoting Micah 3:12 a hundred years later, affirms the historical reference to Hezekiah (Jeremiah 26:17-19). Chapters 6-7 appear to have been written after the death of Hezekiah, and likely some time during the earlier part of the reign of Manasseh (697-642 B.C.).

3. The Contents of the Book of Micah

(1) Chapter 1 in the book of Micah, like chapter 1 in the book of Isaiah, is a general chapter containing the Lord's indictment and coming judgment of His people for their wickedness. Both capitals of the Divided Kingdom, Samaria and Jerusalem, are included in the judgment, because they are the centers of moral and religious corruption.

(2) Chapters 2 and 3 should be read together, for they continue the case of Jehovah against His people, but with a bill of particulars against each class of the guilty: the wealthy landlords, the unjust rulers, the false and unworthy priests and prophets.

The reader of the book of Micah must be prepared for abrupt changes, without notice. Verses 12-13 of chapter 2 present such a change. Micah has just left off denouncing the rich for their unlawful and merciless treatment of the poor; for seizing their fields, houses, and even their clothes; and for ejecting women and young children from their homes. Here, like Isaiah, Micah pauses to give a picture and ·prophecy of Israel's future when the faithful remnant shall be restored.

In the close of chapter 3, Micah climaxes his indictment of the rulers and religious leaders by pronouncing the doom of Jerusalem itself, just as earlier he had pronounced the doom of Samaria, in these words which the prophet Jeremiah quoted a hundred years later:

> Therefore because of you
> Zion shall be plowed as a field;
> Jerusalem shall become a heap of ruins,
>   and the mountain of the house
>   a wooded height.

(3) In chapter 4, Micah suddenly shifts his viewpoint from Jerusalem and her present evil days, to her glorious future in the day of her re-generation.

Indeed, the book of Micah, like the book of Isaiah, is a book of contrasts. Here we have, in verses 1-4, Micah's vision of the future of his people. He believes that God in the beginning chose Israel to teach His true religion to all the nations, and that in this accomplishment lay her greatness. Zion is to be the religious center of the whole earth:

> FOR OUT OF ZION SHALL GO FORTH THE LAW,
> AND THE WORD OF THE LORD FROM JERUSALEM.

And the peoples of the earth shall come up to the mountain of the Lord, and learn of His ways. Then wars shall cease, and there will be a reign of universal peace.

Verse 3 of chapter 4 contains the famous swords-plowshares-pruning hooks passage, the most famous in the seventeen books of prophecy, because it expresses beautifully mankind's longing for peace in language that everyone can understand.

The longer passage in Micah 4:1-4, is recorded in Isaiah 2:2-4 in virtually the same language. The question is, who borrowed from whom? Also, the prophet Joel, in 3:10, makes use of the famous swords-plowshares-pruning hooks theme, but with reverse meaning. (See introduction to Joel.)

However, before chapter 4 is finished, Micah brings the reader back to earth, back to his prophecy of the evil days and the doom of Jerusalem, the same as given in 3:12. For, in verse 4:10, he prophesies a hundred years before the event that the people of Jerusalem shall be carried away captive to Babylon. This is God's plan to punish and to discipline His wicked and disobedient people.

This prophecy of Micah's presents a strange situation to the reader. For at the moment Micah was prophesying Jerusalem's captivity and exile to Babylon, the Assyrian army, now master of the world and not Babylon, was actually invading large portions of Judah, and threatening the capture and destruction of Jerusalem itself, as we learned from our study of Isaiah.

(4) Chapter 5 contains Micah's vision of the coming Messiah, whose birth is to be at Bethlehem. He is to come as a Deliverer and as a true Shepherd of God's people.

In Micah's immediate view, this Ruler is to deliver Israel from the Assyrians. But since "He shall be great to the ends of the earth," he is at one and the same time Micah's prophecy of the Messiah.

(5) In the last two chapters of his book, Micah returns once more to the theme which he presented in chapters 2 and 3, namely, the indictment of his people for their evil ways.

Their wickedness and confusion had grown progressively worse in the latter years. The criminal and bestial elements in the city and nation, somewhat held in check by Isaiah's and Hezekiah's good influence, broke loose once more after the death of Hezekiah, in 697 B.C. These same criminal elements certainly found a sympathetic leader in the new king, Manasseh, the most wicked of the twenty kings of Judah of the 350 years of the Divided Kingdom.

Micah's messages in these last two chapters, 6 and 7, appear to have been given in the earlier years of Manasseh's evil reign, when the social and religious conditions were about as corrupt as they could well become. Micah represents the Lord as having a *controversy* with Israel, in which he invites the people to reason with Him on the subject of their conduct.

Micah anticipates the outcome of the controversy, and gives his famous answer to the question, What does the Lord require of his people? It is given in chapter 6:6-8 and, like the other famous passage in chapter 4:1-4, well merits a place in your collection of *famous memory passages*.

These are high standards of moral and religious performance for any age, and indicate that Micah was one of the most modern of the great prophets, although his messages were given some twenty-seven centuries ago.

In the concluding stanza of his book, Micah closes the "controversy" with his people by giving a brief character portrait of the God he knew. He is a God of compassion and mercy, a God of love to all of His people, now and from the days of old. "He will again have compassion upon us."

SELECTED REFERENCES ON THE BOOK OF MICAH

Anderson, Bernhard W.: "Anonymous Prophecies," *Understanding the Old Testament*, pp. 296-297.

Bright, John: *The Kingdom of God*, pp. 79-80.

*Fraser, A. and L. E. H. Stephens-Hodge: "Micah," *The New Bible Commentary*, pp. 282-286.

Gailey, James H.: *The Books of Micah, Nahum, Habakkuk, Zephaniah, Haggai, Zechariah, Malachi*.

*Paterson, John: "Micah: Prophet of Democracy," *The Goodly Fellowship of the Prophets*, pp. 83-96.

*Smith, George Adam: *The Book of the Twelve Prophets*.

*Snaith, Norman H.: *Amos, Hosea, and Micah*.

*Young, Edward J.: "Micah," *An Introduction to the Old Testament*, pp. 282-286.

(See also chapters on Micah in other books on the prophets.)

II. BOOKS BY THE PROPHETS OF THE SECOND PERIOD: THE DECLINE AND FALL OF JUDAH, 697-586 B.C. (The Period of the Fall of Assyria, and the Rise of the Babylonian Empire, 612 to 538 B.C.)

Chapter 8

ZEPHANIAH

1. THE PROPHETS OF THE SECOND PERIOD, 639 TO 582 B.C.

The First Period of the prophets closed with the ministries of Isaiah and Micah. It is generally supposed that they completed their prophetic careers early in the long and evil reign of Manasseh, who may very well have been the direct cause of the death of one or both of them. After their death, there was prophetic silence in Jerusalem and Judah for more than fifty years.

The wicked Manasseh was on the throne from 697 until about 642 B.C., and his son Amon, who followed in his father's evil footsteps, reigned for another two years, or down to about 640 B.C. All the evils of Baalism and idolatry and imported heathen institutions, which both Israel and Judah had known in the past, were revived and allowed full sway in the nation during these years.

Young Zephaniah was the first to break the long silence;[1] but his young contemporary, Jeremiah, was soon to follow him.

These young prophets came directly from the Lord, with a message of utmost urgency, a prophecy of judgment and doom upon the wicked nation. Like all true prophets, however, they aimed to arouse the moral and religious conscience of their contemporaries, and thus they hoped to render unnecessary the fulfillment of their grim predictions of Captivity and Exile.

Both Zephaniah and Jeremiah lived with the constant reminder that God's judgment had already been visited upon their kinsmen of the Northern Kingdom, who were now in Exile, and that this judgment could be repeated for Judah.

Although the prophets Nahum and Habakkuk are not so well known as some of the others, their messages were important historically, and for succeeding generations.

---

[1]For the background of the analysis of the book of Zephaniah, see J. T. Carson, "Zephaniah," *The New Bible Commentary*, pp. 736-742 (2nd ed., 1954). See also Anderson, *Understanding the Old Testament*, pp. 298-300 (1957).

2. ZEPHANIAH AND THE OCCASION AND DATE OF HIS BOOK

The young prophet Zephaniah was a person of quality. He was a member of the royal family, and a poet. He was a great-great grandson of King Hezekiah, and a distant cousin of the present king Josiah, and a relative also of the prophet Isaiah.

According to his opening sentence, the prophecies of Zephaniah were given "in the days of Josiah." Josiah came to the throne of Judah about 639 B.C., when he was eight years of age, and ruled over Judah until his sudden death in battle, in 608 B.C. He was the best king Judah ever had. It is likely that the prophet Zephaniah, who was not many years older than his cousin Josiah, was living in Jerusalem at the time, and had an important influence on the religious education and reforms of the young king.

It is generally agreed that the immediate occasion for the prophecies of Zephaniah was the Scythian invasion of western Judah and the Philistine cities along the coast of the Mediterranean. The Scythians were wild, fierce tribes from the far north, from the region in modern times occupied by the Russians. They broke through the Caucasus and invaded Media and Assyria as early as 632 B.C., robbing, looting, and leaving destruction in their path. They ravaged Syria; and were about to invade Egypt, when Pharaoh Psammitichus I bought them off with rich gifts, thus saving Judah and her neighbors from sudden and complete destruction.

Evidently, Zephaniah saw in the presence of these fierce barbarians and professional robbers God's terrible scourge of the nations, including Judah, for their wickedness.

> I will cut off mankind from the face of the earth,
>   says the Lord.
> I will stretch out my hand against Judah,
>   and against all the inhabitants of Jerusalem . . .

The threat of the Scythians is evidently referred to in chapter 2 of the book of Zephaniah, and from this occasion Zephaniah's prophecies may be somewhat accurately dated, as between about 630 and 624 B.C., the period of the Scythian invasion of the nations of Western Asia.

Thus, since the reforms of King Josiah did not really begin until 621 B.C., when the copy of the Book of the Law was found in the Temple by Hilkiah the priest, it appears that the work of Zephaniah preceded, rather than followed, Josiah's religious reformation.

Many scholars are of the opinion that the earlier prophecies of Zephaniah helped to prepare the way for Josiah and his collaborators. In fact, there is little doubt that both of the young prophets Zephaniah and Jeremiah were prime movers in this reformation.[2]

---

[2]Anderson, *Understanding the Old Testament*, pp. 298-300; J. T. Carson, *The New Bible Commentary*, pp. 736-742.

3. The Contents of the Book of Zephaniah

The prophet Zephaniah has concentrated the messages of a lifetime in the extremely brief space of three short chapters. The reader therefore must be prepared for even more brevity here in the book of Zephaniah than he found in the brief and sketchy discourses in the book of Micah.

Here is a brief analysis of the main contents of the book:

(1) The Lord has placed upon the prophet Zephaniah the burden of declaring His judgment and doom upon guilty Jerusalem and Judah.

Chapter 1 contains more than an arraignment or indictment of the nation, such as we find in chapter 1 in the books of Isaiah and Micah; it is a warning that time is up, and that doom is imminent.

> For the day of the Lord is at hand . . .
> The great day of the Lord is near.

(2) The second half of chapter 1, and verses 1-3 of chapter 2, lay bare the crimes of a people on the brink of disaster, and reveal the cause of impending doom. Even so, Zephaniah is reluctant to believe what he knows to be true, and in verses 2:1-3 toys with the idea that judgment may yet be avoided.

(3) The reader of the book of Zephaniah must be prepared for abrupt changes in the author's viewpoint. For here the judgment which the prophet has declared against Judah, is also extended against Judah's neighbors and foes — against Philistia, Moab and Ammon, Egypt (here called "Ethiopians" because at the time the Ethiopians ruled the Egyptians), and finally against the greatest of them all, Assyria (chapter 2:4-15).

Verses 5-7 refer to the Scythian invasion. Zephaniah evidently felt that these Scythian barbarians were being used by the Lord as the instrument of His judgment.

(4) In chapter 3, verses 1-8, Zephaniah again shifts his viewpoint, from Judah's foreign foes, back to the indictment and impending judgment against his own people, especially their corrupt rulers.

(5) In verses 3:9-13, Zephaniah presents his vision of the future, in which he sees his people using a *new speech*. It is to be a pure language, the speech of the redeemed.

Too often Judah and the peoples of the earth have called upon the name of heathen gods, and have used the language of idolatry (see Isaiah 6:5; Hosea 2:16-17). In the day of redemption, they will no longer profane the holy name of the Lord with unholy speech.

(6) Zephaniah closes his book with a Messianic hymn, verses 14-20.

In his book, the prophet has spoken of the faithful remnant of Israel, and how it is to be restored (2:3, 7; 3:1-13). The Messianic hymn is a song of rejoicing by Zion and all the redeemed of the earth, in praise of the Lord, who has taken away the judgment against them.

Thus, we have in the book of Zephaniah a complete cycle of Divine prophecy: (1) The judgment against a wicked and disobedient people; (2) their purification and redemption in exile; and (3) the restoration of the faithful remnant, and their glorious future. This is substantially the overall theme of the book of Isaiah, although Isaiah emphasized the Messianic theme and Israel's future; whereas Zephaniah stressed the imminent judgment upon the people for their sins, and his hope for their return to the Lord.

As scholars have pointed out, Zephaniah seems to have been influenced by the ideas of Isaiah, and even by Isaiah's poetic, imaginative style.

Selected Readings on the Prophets of the Second Period

Bible Readings: The Books of Zephaniah, Nahum, Jeremiah, Habakkuk. Text: *The Revised Standard Version;* or *The King James Version,* preferably in modern reader's format.

Zephaniah

Anderson, Bernard W.: "The Prophet Zephaniah," *Understanding the Old Testament,* pp. 298-300.

*Carson, J. T.: "Zephaniah," *The New Bible Commentary,* pp. 736-742.

Gailey, James H.: *The Books of Micah, Nahum, Habakkuk, Zephaniah, Haggai, Zechariah, Malachi.*

*Paterson, John: "Zephaniah: Prophet of Puritanism," *The Goodly Fellowship of the Prophets,* pp. 97-108.

*Pilcher, C. V.: *Three Hebrew Prophets and the Passing of Empires.*

*Smith, George Adam: *The Book of the Twelve Prophets.*

Chapter 9

NAHUM

1. NAHUM AND THE DATE AND OCCASION OF HIS BOOK

The book of Nahum should be read as a sequel to the book of Jonah, although the prophet Jonah appeared about 150 years before the prophet Nahum. Both have to do with the great city Nineveh, the famous capital of the Assyrian Empire.

Jonah was sent to Nineveh, about 785 B.C., on a Divine mission of mercy and repentance. He preached to the Ninevites in the heyday of their prosperity and power. They repented at his preaching, and restrained themselves, for a time at least, from their wars of conquest and cruelty to other nations.

The book of Nahum, on the contrary, was written in the period of decline and approaching fall of Nineveh and the Assyrian Empire. The prophets Isaiah, Micah, Zephaniah, all had prophesied the fall of Assyria. Nahum came with a prophecy of retribution and doom. His message, shortly before the capital's fall, came like a funeral dirge, as if Nineveh's destruction was already an accomplished fact.

Little is known about Nahum the author.[1] According to the opening statement of the book, his birthplace was Elkosh. But efforts to locate such a place have been unsuccessful. However, there is one bit of interesting etymology: The author's name is contained in the latter half of the word *Capernaum,* which is the Greek spelling for *Nahum,* and means "village of Nahum." Could it be that Nahum was a resident or founder of Capernaum, which Jesus used as headquarters for most of His ministry?

It is easier to determine the approximate date of the book. Nineveh was captured and destroyed by the Babylonians in 612 B.C. In chapter 3:8-10, Nahum describes the destruction of the Egyptian city of Thebes, which took place in 663 B.C. The book of Nahum therefore was written between these two dates. However, the contents of the book, and the vividness with which its story is told, suggest to many scholars that it was composed shortly before the fall of the city of Nineveh — say, between 621 B.C., the beginning of Josiah's reformation, and 612 B.C., the date of Nineveh's fall.

---

[1]Kirkpatrick, *The Doctrine of the Prophets,* p. 237ff, places him as a contemporary of Zephaniah.

This would make the prophet Nahum a contemporary of the prophets Zephaniah, Jeremiah, and Habakkuk.

2. The Contents of the Book of Nahum

Unlike the books of Isaiah, Micah, and Zephaniah, whose prophecies were devoted largely to Jerusalem and Judah, Nahum's message was directed entirely to a foreign foe, Nineveh, Judah's arch-enemy for generations.

One commentator gives this two-sentence sketch of Nineveh:

> At the time of Nahum's prophecy Nineveh was the queen city of the earth, mighty and brutal beyond imagination, head of a warrior state built on the loot of nations. Limitless wealth from the ends of the earth poured into its coffers.[2]

This same enemy destroyed Israel in the two campaigns of 734 and 721 B.C., and carried away its inhabitants into captivity. Moreover, in the lifetime of Isaiah, in the campaigns of 719, 713, and 701 B.C., the Assyrians captured 46 fortified and many other unfortified cities of Judah, and carried away more than 200,000 inhabitants. Divine intervention only saved the destruction of Jerusalem itself.

Here is a brief analysis of the book:

(1) The prophet Nahum has a vision of what is about to come to pass. This prophecy is the *burden of Nineveh*. The day of retribution and doom of the wicked city of Nineveh is at hand. The Lord will destroy it utterly, so that it will never again rise to be the terror to the nations.

For Judah, this means deliverance from a tyrant and conqueror of long standing. For all Israel, it is good tidings and joyful peace. For at long last her chief enemy is about to be laid low (chapter 1).

(2) Chapter 2 gives a poetic picture of the siege, the capture, and looting a city rich in treasure.

(a) Nineveh is called upon to face its enemy and invader, the Babylonians and their allies, the Medes. The siege begins, which historically lasted part of two years (verses 1-5).

(b) According to historical records, after the two years siege, a sudden overflow of the river through the city washed away part of the city walls. This opened the gates and the way for the destroying army.

The city was soon sacked and its inhabitants taken. The queen and her women were carried off, and the inhabitants slaughtered (verses 6-10).

(c) The king and the royal brood were sought out and slain with the sword. Then Nahum adds a footnote, which is a prophecy giving the Lord's judgment against Nineveh, a judgment which cannot be escaped (verses 11-13).

(3) Chapter 3 contains a victory song. Some have called it

---

[2]Henry H. Halley, *Halley's Bible Handbook*, p. 339 (22nd Revised Ed., 1961).

Nineveh's Death-Song. It is a special kind of victory song, in that it is not by the Babylonians and Medes, the military victors. It is by the prophet and God's people, who have been persecuted so long by the ruthless, now fallen enemy.

(a) Here we have a picture of the attack, beginning with the fierce cry, "Woe to the bloody city!" and describing the whirling and dashing cavalry and chariots. This passage reveals Nahum's superlative descriptive power, in one of the most vivid battle scenes in Hebrew literature (verses 1-3).

(b) The pay-off for Nineveh's wickedness is her present doom. By her clever seductiveness, Nineveh has played the part of a harlot and has betrayed nations. Like another great city, Thebes, a city "that sat by the Nile," Nineveh will be sacked and destroyed. Jehovah now assumes responsibility for the execution of judgment and impending doom against her.

There is no escape for Nineveh. The enemy's powerful invading armies are like locusts for numbers. Nineveh's men of war are numerous as grasshoppers, too; but just now they are terrorized and are ready to fly away at the first opportunity, and offer no loyalty or protection to the city.

Woe to the city of Nineveh! It is like a flock "scattered upon the mountains," with no shepherd (prophet) to lead it back to the fold (verses 4-18).

(c) *The Clapping of Hands.*[3] In chapter 1, Nahum called upon Judah to proclaim peace and to rejoice because of its deliverance from the ancient enemy.

Here in the book of Nahum 3:19, the prophet calls upon all the nations that have been oppressed and have suffered from the evil influence of the common enemy, to rise up and clap their hands at the good news!

The destruction took place substantially as predicted by Nahum, and shortly after his prophecy. Historians have related that the great city's destruction was so complete that even its site was lost to succeeding generations.

Selected References
Nahum

Calkins, Raymond: *The Modern Message of the Minor Prophets.*

*Fraser, A.: "Nahum," *The New Bible Commentary,* pp. 727-731.

Gailey, James H.: *The Books of Micah, Nahum, Habakkuk, Zephaniah, Haggai, Zechariah, Malachi.*

*Paterson, John: "Nahum; Prophet of Vengeance," *The Goodly Fellowship of the Prophets,* 109-125.

*Smith, George Adam: *The Book of the Twelve Prophets.*

---

[3]See James B. Pritchard, *Ancient Near Eastern Texts Relating to the Old Testament,* 2nd ed. (1956), pp. 303-305.

Chapter 10

JEREMIAH

1. JEREMIAH'S LIFE AND DEDICATION AS A PROPHET

Jeremiah, like Isaiah, stands at the head of a long line of great prophets, and perhaps second only to Isaiah.

Like Isaiah, too, he was great not only as preacher and statesman, which were his primary functions; but he was of the first rank also as an imaginative and creative poet. Both prophets composed divine poems of great power and beauty, in their present literary forms, and give every evidence of having been written for a wider audience than that to which the prophets' oral discourses were given.

But Jeremiah, unlike Isaiah, who used the arts of diplomacy and eloquence and *persuasion,* belonged to the school of Elijah, John the Baptist, and Amos, prophets who were outspoken and hard-hitting in their *denunciation* of the evildoers of their day. So powerful were Jeremiah's messages of doom, that they won for their author the distinction of being called *Jeremiads,* after the force and personality of the man himself.

One thing that has endeared Jeremiah to his readers is his utter frankness in revealing the details of his life-story. No other prophet has so taken the reader into his confidence, into his public and private life, and told him so much.

We learn how his prophecies were delivered, how they were written and re-written, what happened to them, and to the prophet himself in consequence. We learn when and why he was put into stocks, or thrown into prison, or into a pit, and the many times he narrowly escaped death. In fact, after the death of the good king Josiah, Jeremiah found himself constantly in open conflict with Josiah's evil successors, Jehoiakim and Zedekiah, and their court officials.

But he never quit or gave up. If he were in prison, as he often was, or otherwise not permitted to deliver his bold and outspoken messages in person, he would send his faithful secretary and associate, Baruch, to deliver them for him. Their favorite *pulpit* was the court of the Temple, where the people came in numbers on feast days.

In his introductory chapter, Jeremiah tells us of his call and dedication to be a prophet, which reminds us of the call of two other

313

famous leaders and prophets, Moses (Exodus 3, 4) and Ezekiel (Ezekiel 1, 2, 3). He was a young man scarcely more than twenty years of age, in the thirteenth year of King Josiah's reign (626 B.C.). In the vision, the Lord had told him of the Divine plan for the prophet's life, even before birth, thus:

> Before I formed you in the womb I knew you, and before you were born I consecrated you; I appointed you a prophet to the nations.

Besides, Jeremiah's father Hilkiah was a priest in the village of Anathoth, the prophet's birthplace, a few miles northeast of Jerusalem. According to family traditions, Jeremiah himself would be expected to become a priest.

Jeremiah was a bachelor. The Lord had revealed to him that he should not have a family, in a land that was doomed:

> You shall not take a wife, nor shall you have sons or daughters in this place.

This seemed satisfactory to Jeremiah, who was wholeheartedly wedded to Jehovah and needed no other spouse. Although at times he complained that the Lord had forsaken him, the Two formed a most intimate partnership over the long years that followed. Indeed, the Lord revealed to him that he would meet with violent opposition from kings, priests, and people, but that they would not prevail against him.

2. JEREMIAH AND INTERNATIONAL POLITICS[1]

Jeremiah lived about a hundred years after the prophet Isaiah. As Jehovah's chief emissary, Isaiah had saved Jerusalem from Sennacherib and the Assyrian army, and had predicted its sure downfall. Now Assyria, like Judah, was in the period of its rapid decline. Other prophets had "seen" its early fall and destruction; and before one-third of his ministry was accomplished, Jeremiah was to see Nineveh destroyed and its empire taken over by the Babylonians, in 612 B.C.

Meanwhile, as the young Jeremiah came upon the scene, the three great powers — Assyria, Babylon, and Egypt — were engaged in a three-cornered contest for world supremacy.

For three hundred years, Assyria from her capital at Nineveh in the upper Mesopotamian Valley, had ruled the world.

Babylon, in the lower Mesopotamian Valley, during the same period had been under the influence and domination of Assyria. But just now, as Assyria was growing weak, Babylon was becoming strong and powerful.

Nineveh was finally destroyed by the Babylonians and Medes, in 612 B.C., as Isaiah had prophesied, and as the prophet Nahum had so vividly portrayed in his message and book shortly before the event. Egypt, which at best had been only a second-rate power for centuries,

---

[1]See John Bright, *The Kingdom of God*, pp. 105-127 (1953).

was now ambitious under her Pharaoh Necho to contest with Babylon for the empire of the fallen Assyria.

The controversy between Egypt and Babylon was settled in the famous battle at Carchemish, in 605 B.C., in which Necho and his Egyptians were decisively defeated and sent back to Egypt, never to return to contest with Babylon again. So, until her final defeat and exile in 586 B.C., Judah was under the domination of Babylon. The details of this contest will be brought out in our analysis of the contents of the book of Jeremiah.

3. JEREMIAH'S MESSAGE AND ROLE AS PROPHET[2]

As we have seen, after the decisive defeat of Egypt by Babylon, in 605 B.C., the contest now was between Judah and Babylon — or more accurately, between the prophet Jeremiah and Babylon's King Nebuchadrezzar, the real genius of the Babylonian Empire during his long reign from 605 to 562 B.C., and who finally captured Jerusalem. The question now therefore was, What would be Jeremiah's role in this contest?

Long before Jeremiah began his ministry, substantially all Judah, except the city of Jerusalem, had been lost to the Assyrians and their armies. Judah had been invaded and its cities taken, together with large portions of its inhabitants. Jerusalem alone had been spared.

The prophets had all given up Jerusalem and Judah for lost — lost spiritually, as well as geographically and militarily. Jeremiah at the outset agreed with the other prophets. So there seemed little left for him to do except to reveal God's plan for all Israel, in defeat and in exile. But, like all true prophets, he held out hope that at last Israel might repent, and Jerusalem might be saved.

His book, therefore, contains the prophecies to a nation on the brink of disaster, with the period of grace fast running out. A brief summary of Jeremiah's message and role as God's chief minister may be stated, thus:

(1) Jeremiah warned Jerusalem that it would be destroyed presently by Babylon, the recent conqueror of Assyria and the new power of the north.

(2) Even so, if Judah would now repent and return to the Lord, God in His mercy would yet save it from destruction at the hands of Babylon.

(3) Long before his book closed, however, Jeremiah had reached the conclusion that there appeared no reasonable hope of Judah's repentance. So, at the risk of being misunderstood by his own people,

---

[2]For an excellent study of Jeremiah, see Anderson, "The Prophet Jeremiah," *Understanding the Old Testament*, pp. 300-358 (1957). For a good brief summary of critical opinion and analysis of the book of Jeremiah, see E. J. Young, *An Introduction to the Old Testament*, pp. 243-255 (1958).

he recommended that they surrender to Babylon, as the best way of being spared a greater calamity.

(4) Jeremiah, like his predecessors, accompanied the idea of Judah's captivity and exile with its companion idea, namely, that Judah would eventually be redeemed and restored through the faithful remnant, and that its influence in the future would cover the earth.

(5) And conversely, that Babylon, God's instrument in punishing Judah for its sin and willful disobedience, would itself be destroyed never to rise again, the same as the prophecy against Nineveh and the Assyrian Empire.

(6) The destruction of the Temple and the physical overthrow of Judah's present religion, has become a practical necessity, as a forerunner of the "New Covenant," which is to be *written in the hearts of men*. This interpretation is Jeremiah's major contribution to the understanding of the religion of Jehovah.[3] Thus, Jeremiah is to be recognized as the central point in the religious history of his people.

(7) Finally, is it not Jeremiah who gives us our best concept of prophecy itself? According to the prophet, the Divine purpose is to reveal God Himself; to help us to understand His will and character, His ordering of events, of peoples and nations, as well as the inner life of individuals. This concept Jeremiah expressed, in what the late Professor Richard G. Moulton called the most sublime of his many sublime sayings, thus:[4]

> Thus says the Lord: "Let not the wise man glory in his wisdom, let not the mighty man glory in his might, let not the rich man glory in his riches; but let him who glories, glory in this, that he understands and knows Me, that I am the Lord who practice kindness, justice, and righteousness in the earth; for in these things I delight" (9:23-24).

4. The Contents of the Book of Jeremiah

The book of Jeremiah, like most of the other books of prophecy, presents certain difficulties for the modern reader. A brief look at the writer's plan and organization of his materials will help us better to understand and appreciate the book.

The Plan of the Book

In chapter 36, Jeremiah tells us how, after twenty years of prophesying, he came to write his book. Jeremiah had been most outspoken in condemning the wickedness of Jerusalem, and in predicting the destruction of the city by the Babylonians. So, because of his frankness and boldness, he was officially debarred from public appearances, under threat of severe punishment or death. The immediate occasion for the writing of the first edition of his book, therefore, as the author

---

[3]See John Bright, *The Kingdom of God*, pp. 116-126.
[4]*Modern Reader's Bible*, p. 1402.

tells us, was that Jeremiah's message in the absence of the prophet himself, might be read publicly by Baruch, his secretary and associate. On certain feast days, Baruch with a copy of Jeremiah's scroll in his hand, took his place in the court of the Temple, where large numbers came from Jerusalem and the cities of Judah outside of Jerusalem. The boldness of the message both impressed and confused the crowds. Micaiah, a young man and grandson of Shaphan the court scribe, standing in the Temple court, heard Baruch read the words of Jeremiah's scroll. He immediately went down to the King's House and reported the matter to the princes. The complete story of how the scroll reached King Jehoiakim, was read and burned page by page, and how Jeremiah dictated and Baruch copied a second and much larger edition of the book, all is told in chapter 36. The book of Jeremiah as we have it is a third and still larger edition, containing the prophecies after Jeremiah's encounters with the king, that is, after 605 B.C. The following chronology will further indicate the plan of the book.

The Chronology of the Book

From this brief story of how Jeremiah's book came to be written, we should expect his materials to be arranged in chronological order. But such is not the case. Some of the messages are given according to time order; others according to similarity of subject matter.

Since the messages come at a most critical period in Judah's history, and are inter-related to the kings of the time and their fortunes, as well as the fortunes and destiny of the nation, we may profitably group the chapters by kings and their reigns. Jeremiah gives date lines for many of the chapters and divisions of his work; for some he does not. There is enough of the material dated, however, to guide the reader from one section or reign to another; and from these, and the context, we can infer most of the others.

The date lines for King Josiah's reign (639-608 B.C.) are chapters 1:2; 3:6. For Jehoahaz's reign (608 B.C., 3 months): none. For Jehoiakim's reign (608-597 B.C.): chapters 22:18; 25:1; 26:1; 35:1; 36:1; 45:2. For Jehoiachin's reign (597 B.C., 3 months): none. For Zedekiah's reign (597-586 B.C.): chapters 21:1; 24:1, 8; 27:1, 12; 28:1; 29:3; 32:1; 34:2; 37:1; 38:5; 39:1; 49:34; 51:59.

From these date lines, and from the context of the passages themselves, we can construct a chart giving the approximate dates of the chapters and sections, as follows:[5]

1. Josiah's reign (639-608 B.C.):
    In the thirteenth year, 626 B.C., chapter 1.
    In the years immediately following 626 B.C., chapters 2 to 6;
    and nearly all the material in chapters 7 to 20 (except chapter

---

[5]For the main outlines of this chart, see John D. Davis, Editor, *The Westminster Dictionary of the Bible*, pp. 291-292 (Fifth Ed., 1944). See also G. T. Manley, *The New Bible Handbook*.

13) are usually assigned to the reign of Josiah. Chapter 11 may be dated about 621 B.C., when the Book of the Law was found by Josiah's high priest.

2. In Jehoahaz's reign (608 B.C., 3 months): none. However, reference is made to his being carried captive to Egypt, where he was held prisoner until his death, chapter 22:10-12.

3. In Jehoiakim's reign (608-597 B.C.):
   In the beginning of his reign, 608 B.C., chapter 26, and part or all of chapter 22.
   In the fourth year, 605 B.C., chapters 25, 36, 45, 46 (verses 1-12 seem to belong here, but 13-28 are more intimate in nature, and may have been composed in Egypt after 586 B.C.), 47, 48, 49.

4. In Jehoiachin's reign (597 B.C., 3 months): probably chapter 22:24-30; and part or all of chapter 13 (with which compare II Kings 24:12). The reference to "queen mother," Jehoiachin's mother Nehushta, suggests the date of these passages.

5. In Zedekiah's reign (597-586 B.C.):
   In the beginning of his reign, 597 B.C., chapters 23, 24, 27, 28, 29, and 49:34-39.
   In the fourth year, 593 B.C., chapters 50 to 51:59-64 (see 51:49).
   Between 597 B.C. and 588 B.C., the date of the beginning of Nebuchadnezzar's siege of Jerusalem, chapters 30-31.
   In the ninth year, 588 B.C., the beginning of the siege, chapters 21, 34. While Jeremiah was out of prison, and yet free.
   During the interruption of the siege. Nebuchadnezzar withdrew from Jerusalem to fight back the approaching Egyptian army from the south. Chapter 37.
   In the tenth year, 587 B.C., after resumption of the siege, and while Jeremiah was in prison, chapters 32 and 33.
   In the eleventh year, 586 B.C., the fall and destruction of Jerusalem by Nebuchadnezzar, chapters 38, 39. Chapter 52 contains a brief historical summary or appendix to the story of the fall and destruction of the city.

6. In Jerusalem and Judah after the fall of the city, chapters 40 to 43:7.

7. In Egypt, where Jeremiah was forced against his will to go with the remnant. Baruch went with him. Chapters 43:8 to 44.

THE PROPHECIES OF JEREMIAH

A Brief Analysis

1. JEREMIAH'S CALL AND COMMISSION. Chapter 1 contains Jeremiah's call and commission to the people of Jerusalem and Judah:

> I have set you this day over the nations and kingdoms,
>> to pluck up and to break down,
>> to destroy and to overthrow,
>> to build and to plant.

At the same time Jeremiah is warned that the kings of Judah, its princes, priests, and people of the land, will oppose his drastic message of doom:

> They will fight against you; but they shall not avail against you, for I am with you, says the Lord, to deliver you . . .
> And I will utter my judgments against them, for all their wickedness in forsaking me.

2. The Great Apostasy. Chapters 2 to 6 contain a recital of the story of the great apostasy of Israel, and the prediction of the approaching judgment. *Israel* here refers to all the Jews and not merely the people of Jerusalem and Judah. In fact, Judah is condemned as worse than the Northern Kingdom, seeing that it had greater opportunities to be loyal to the true God.

Jeremiah's first duty, as was the duty of all true prophets, was to warn the people of their wickedness and disobedience. But appearing as he did in their last days, Jeremiah also had the solemn duty of shocking the people into seeing that disaster was at hand. Time for them was up.

So, in the close of this group of chapters, Jeremiah warns of the approaching invasion by fierce enemies from the north. Like the prophet Zephaniah, Jeremiah here appears to refer to the threatened invasion by the Scythians from the far north (Russia), especially in chapter 6. In other references, he has in mind the coming invasion of the Babylonians.

3. The Temple Has Become a Stumbling Block. In chapters 7-10, Jeremiah takes his bold message to the people. For the Lord has commanded him to take his stand in the court of the Temple, "and proclaim there this word":

> Behold, you trust in deceptive words to no avail. Will you steal, murder, commit adultery, swear falsely, burn incense to Baal, and go after other gods that you have not known, and then come and stand before me in the House, which is called by my name, and say, "We are delivered!"—only to go on doing all these abominations?

Indeed, here begins a series of daring discourses and prophecies which were to stand the rulers and religious leaders of Jerusalem on their heads, and which were to cause the prophet again and again to be put into stocks or thrown into prison.

It is of the greatest importance that we understand Jeremiah's prophetic interpretations in these passages. What he is saying is that the Temple, important as it had been in the worship of Jehovah in the past, *has now become a stumbling block to true religion.* It is because the people have substituted the Temple for God Himself, and have offered animal sacrifice, instead of obedience and a pure heart.

Even the oldest of the prophets had said, "Obedience is more than sacrifice."

> I hate, I depise your feasts,
> and I take no delight in your
> solemn assemblies, says the Lord (Amos 5:21).

Jeremiah, therefore, in recognizing the need for thoroughgoing regeneration as well as reform in Israel, proclaimed Jehovah's purpose to destroy the Temple as completely as He had destroyed the sanctuary at Shiloh, because of its idolatry in the days of Eli. And as true religion had continued without Shiloh, so it could continue without Jerusalem and its Temple.

This prophecy reminds us how Jesus, more than six hundred years later, predicted the destruction of the second Temple of Jerusalem, the Temple of His day, and for the same reason that the Temple in Jeremiah's time had to be destroyed.

Thus, Jeremiah was one of the few who believed that the reforms of Josiah, although praised for whatever good they promised, touched only the surface and would not cure Israel's evils and manifest corruption.[6]

It is easy for the modern reader to see what a tidal-wave of opposition such bold prophecies would bring upon the head of Jeremiah. First the false priests and prophets, and then other officials, sought to silence him.

4. THE BROKEN COVENANT. Chapter 11 deals with the episode of finding the Book of the Law in the Temple by King Josiah's high priest. The finding of the Book is the occasion for Jeremiah again to call attention to how the people had broken the "Covenant of the Law of Moses," and possibly to infer that *the reforms of Josiah* were not enough!

5. THE YOUNG MEN OF ANATHOTH. In one of his many personal references to himself, Jeremiah in this same chapter complains of a secret plot to murder him by the young men of Anathoth, his native village near Jerusalem. Jeremiah had preached against their wickedness, and like the people in downtown Jerusalem, they formed a plot to silence him. They warned,

> Do not prophesy in the name of the Lord, or you will die by our hand.

But the Lord stood by Jeremiah:

> Concerning the men of Anathoth, who seek your life . . . Behold, I will punish them; the young men shall die by the sword . . . And none of them shall be left.

6. WHY DO THE WICKED PROSPER? In chapter 12, Jeremiah asks an old question which was often in the mind of Jews, "Why do the wicked prosper?" And, as in the present instance, why are the *treacherous* permitted to plot against God's servants? The chapter gives Jeremiah's complaint and God's answer, which contains no direct solution. The prophet must gird himself for an even greater struggle than he has yet faced, and an even greater tax on his faith and courage. In the end Judah will see exile, and so also "the evil neighbors."

7. THE LINEN GIRDLE. In chapter 13, the prophet preaches in symbols. The girdle represents the people of Judah. Jehovah chose them for His service and glory, but they turned away and served other gods. The other symbol was the jar filled with wine. This imagery bears

---

[6]See the discussion, and footnotes, p. 183ff.

the warning that just as strong drink confuses, so will Jehovah's judgment be. But these appeals are all lost on Judah. The chapter contains one of the most famous of all quotations:

> Can the Ethiopian change his skin
> or the leopard his spots?

8. WOES, AND MORE WOES. Chapters 14 to 17 deal with prolonged drought, pestilence, and exile for Judah. In these prophecies, we see Jeremiah caught between two desires: human compassion for his suffering countrymen and his yearning for their salvation, before the day of grace runs out; and his Divine mission to proclaim the grim message of approaching destruction and exile for the city and the nation.

But the ways of the Lord are inscrutable; and His judgments must be carried out. Jeremiah is told that even if Moses and the prophet Samuel, two great pleaders in the past history of Israel — even if they were to come back and plead for Jerusalem and Judah, the Lord would not be moved!

The wicked reign of Manasseh of the preceding generation is blamed for the evils of the present (15:4).

The prophet Jeremiah himself is forbidden to marry, because of the approaching destruction and slaughter of the inhabitants of Judah. In short, the end of the nation is near. Thus, the "barren prophet" becomes a symbol of the unfruitful age and the pestilence that has befallen it.

9. THE SYMBOLS OF THE POTTER AND HIS CLAY. Here we have two prophecies, illustrated by the art of the potter, and the consequences to Jeremiah personally. In chapter 18, the prophet gives a parable of the potter and his clay, in which he illustrates the power of God to alter and re-shape the destinies of a people. In chapter 19, however, the parable of the *broken flask* teaches that the time may come when alteration must take the form of breaking, "as one breaks the potter's vessel."

The scene shifts from the potter's house, and Topheth, to the Temple court, where Jeremiah is boldly denouncing the city and predicting its destruction. Jeremiah's enemies, who recently had dared plot his death openly (18:18), were now ready to lay hands upon him (chapter 20). So, while he was addressing the Temple court audience, Pashhur, the priest and chief officer of the Temple, and one who heard him, seized Jeremiah, beat him, and put him in the stocks. Pashhur became afraid of what he had done and released Jeremiah from the stocks on the following day. For his pains, Jeremiah rebuked him, and predicted that Pashhur and his household would be taken to Babylon in captivity, die there, and be buried there.

10. THE VISION OF THE END OF JERUSALEM. In chapter 22, Jeremiah states that he was commanded to go down to the King's house and deliver the startling message that unless the king (Jehoiakim in

608 B.C.) obeyed the stern message of the prophet, his house and all Jerusalem were doomed for destruction.

In this prophecy we learn of the recent death of King Josiah — "Weep not for him who is dead" (22:10). We learn also that his third son, Jehoahaz (called "Shallum"), whom the people of Judah put on the throne, after a brief reign of three months, was carried away captive to Egypt by Pharaoh Necho, who in turn placed Jehoahaz's elder brother Jehoiakim on the throne of Judah in his place.[7]

Jehoiakim treated with scorn Jeremiah's words of doom, and his prophecy that the king would die an unheroic death and have the funeral and burial of an ass; that is, no funeral at all, but be "dragged and cast forth beyond the gates of Jerusalem."

11. "THIS MAN DESERVES THE SENTENCE OF DEATH." In chapter 26, Jeremiah relates the story of his clash with the popular priests and prophets and their followers. He was commanded to go again and stand in the Temple court, and declare this message:

> If they will not heed the words of my servants the prophets whom
> I send to you urgently . . . then I will make this house like Shiloh,
> and I will make this city a curse for all the nations of the earth.

The priests and prophets were present and heard the words of Jeremiah. When he finished speaking, they laid hands on him, saying, "You shall die!"

When the princes, who happened to be at the king's house, heard the uproar, they came quickly. Not being prejudiced against Jeremiah, they were able to give a fair decision. It is interesting to note that the crowd, who a moment before were on the side of Jeremiah's enemies, now came to the side of the princes in the declaration, "This man does *not* deserve the sentence of death."

Also, a certain elder arose and spoke in Jeremiah's behalf, giving a similar incident in the life of the prophet Micah, and declaring how King Hezekiah refused to put Micah to death on a similar charge (see Micah 3:12). Jeremiah's life was saved.

12. THE BEGINNING OF THE END. The year 605 B.C. was momentous for more reasons than one. For in that year Nebuchadnezzar, one of the mightiest monarchs of all time, became king of the Babylonian Empire. In that same year he broke the power of Egypt, in the famous battle of Carchemish, and invaded Judah and carried away to Babylon the first installment of Jewish captives,[8] including a young man by the name of Daniel. This has been called the first stage of the captivity of Judah, the beginning of the fulfillment of Jeremiah's prophecies concerning Jerusalem and Judah (see chapters 25, 45).

13. "THE GRAPES OF WRATH." The day of grace *has* run out. In chapter 25, Jeremiah is called upon to deliver the bitterest of all his many decrees of doom. "Thus the Lord, the God of Israel, said to me":

---

[7]For this historical background, see p. 186ff.
[8]For the four stages of the captivity of Judah, see p. 186ff.

Take from my hand this cup of wine of wrath, and make all the nations to whom I send you drink it.

The bitter cup is that these nations shall be deported from their homeland and be made to serve the king of Babylon for *seventy years.* Then this cruel king and his warriors shall be punished "for their iniquity."

14. THE WORD OF THE LORD CONCERNING NON-JEWISH NATIONS. In chapters 46 to 51, Jeremiah delivers a series of prophecies concerning Jehovah's judgment upon non-Jewish nations — Egypt, Philistia, Moab, Ammon, Edom, Syria (Damascus), and Babylon, the most notorious of all.

15. JUDAH'S BACK IS BROKEN. In chapters 13; 22:24-30; 23; 24; 27-29; 49:34-39, Jeremiah tells the story of events centering in the year 597 B.C., which includes the death of King Jehoiakim, the three months' reign of his son and successor Jehoiachin, and his deportation along with his family to Babylonia. This is known as *the second stage* of the captivity of Judah, in which were included large numbers of skilled artisans, mechanics, and other citizens of quality, as captives to Babylon. A young priest, later to become a famous prophet by the name of Ezekiel, was also included in the 597 deportation.

16. THE GOOD AND BAD FIGS. In chapter 24, we have a parable of two baskets of figs. The good figs are the good exiles from Judah in the 597 removal to Babylon, and who later are to return to the homeland. The *bad figs* include the new King Zedekiah, who came to the kingship of Judah after Jehoiachin's removal, and his princes, and the remnant of Jerusalem who remained in the land. Is there a meaning of "depth" in this parable?

17. JEREMIAH'S LETTER TO THE EXILES. Chapter 29 reproduces a letter of consolation and wisdom, which Jeremiah wrote to the exiles in Babylonia. What is the far-reaching significance of what he says in verses 4-7?

18. THE LITTLE BOOK OF COMFORT. The general character of Jeremiah's prophecies thus far have been gloomy. In chapters 30 to 33, however, Jeremiah like Isaiah, shows that he can prophesy a cheerful future. These chapters deal with the restoration after the seventy years of exile mentioned earlier, and picture an era of peace and prosperity for both Israel and Judah. The prophet is instructed to write this in a book.

19. THE NEW COVENANT. In the "Little Book" there is given a new interpretation of religion. Jehovah is making a *new covenant* with the house of Israel and the house of Judah (see 31:31-34).

I will put my Law *within them,* and I will write it upon their hearts.

The religion of the new covenant is to be *spiritual* and *personal* in character, not *external* and *national,* as it had largely been hitherto. This is clearly a forerunner of the spiritual message of our Lord as revealed in the New Testament.

20. THE PROMISE OF THE MESSIAH. By way of continuing his gospel of hope, in chapters 23:5-8, and 33:14-26, Jeremiah prophesies the coming of the Lord, a "righteous Branch" from the house of David. This again is in the tradition of Isaiah, who in passage after passage stresses the coming of the Saviour of mankind.

21. NEBUCHADREZZAR LAYS SIEGE TO JERUSALEM. In chapters 32, 34, 37, 38, Jeremiah's prophecies of doom reach their climax in the appearance of the army of Nebuchadrezzar before the walls of Jerusalem. The Babylonians laid siege to Jerusalem in 588 B.C., and for a year and a half the city was surrounded, and the people within were brought to the verge of starvation.

Except for a brief relief period, when Nebuchadrezzar temporarily retired from the siege to fight off an Egyptian force which had advanced to the relief of Jerusalem, the siege was complete. On July 9, 586 B.C., a breach was made in the city wall, and the end came soon. During the siege Jeremiah spent most of the time in prison.

22. THE FALL OF JERUSALEM. In chapters 39 to 43:7, Jeremiah tells the story of the fall of the city and the occupation of the land by the Babylonians thereafter, as well as that of his own fate and that of his friend and associate, Baruch. For the complete narrative of King Zedekiah, and the events preceding and following the fall of Jerusalem, including Jeremiah's part in these events, see pages 187, 188; and also II Kings 24:17 to 25, and II Chronicles 36.

23. JEREMIAH IN EGYPT. Jeremiah was carried to Egypt against his will, by the rebels who murdered Gedaliah whom Nebuchadrezzar appointed to serve as vassal governor over the remnant which he left in Judah. Previously the king of Babylon had given Jeremiah his choice of going captive to Babylon or of remaining with the remnant in Judah. He chose to remain in Judah.

In Egypt Jeremiah continued to preach, to all the faithless Jews dwelling in Egypt, and to the godless of every land. These prophecies are related in chapters 43, 44, and 46 to 51.

24. HISTORICAL SUMMARY, AN APPENDIX. Chapter 52 contains a historical summary of the reign and last days of King Zedekiah, the burning and total destruction of the Temple, the King's House, and all the houses of Jerusalem, including the deportation of the inhabitants. This chapter may be compared with chapter 39, which is substantially the same, and II Kings 24:18 to 25:30, which may be the original source for both passages in the book of Jeremiah.

SELECTED REFERENCES

JEREMIAH

*Anderson, Bernhard W.: "The Prophet Jeremiah," *Understanding the Old Testament,* pp. 300-358.

*Bright, John: *The Kingdom of God,* pp. 105-127.

*Cawley, F.: "Jeremiah," *The New Bible Commentary,* pp. 608-639.

The birthplace of Jeremiah, the little village of Anathoth, northeast of Jerusalem.
© *Matson Photo Service*

Hopper, Stanley R.: "Jeremiah," *The Interpreter's Bible*, Vol. V.

*Hyatt, J. Philip: *Jeremiah, Prophet of Courage and Hope.*

Kuist, Howard T.: *The Books of Jeremiah and Lamentations.*

*Manley, G. T.: "Jeremiah," *The New Bible Handbook.*

Moulton, Richard G.: "Jeremiah," *The Modern Reader's Bible*, pp. 1398-1402.

Paterson, John: "Jeremiah — Prophet of Personal Religion," *The Goodly Fellowship of the Prophets*, pp. 139-159.

Skinner, John: *Prophecy and Religion — Studies in the Life of Jeremiah.*

*Young, Edward J.: "Jeremiah," *An Introduction to the Old Testament*, pp. 243-255.

Chapter 11

HABAKKUK

1. HABAKKUK AND THE DATE AND BACKGROUND OF HIS BOOK

The prophet Habakkuk is the fourth and last in the group of prophets we have called the Second Period. One writer praises him in these strong words, "All that we know of the person of Habakkuk is that he was a great prophet who has left us one of the noblest and most penetrating words in the history of religion" (2:4-b).[1] Indeed, if Habakkuk gave us the word *faith*, this praise is none too strong.

Although Habakkuk gives us little or no direct biographical information about himself, yet we learn much about him from his ideas, his attitude toward the great issues and events of the day, and from the style of his composition.

He is a poet as well as a prophet. And although his work is brief, his interpretation of religion shows him to be progressive, thoughtful, and wise, like the author of the book of Job, or of the Ninetieth Psalm. Surely, such an excellent poet, like the poet Joel, wrote other works which have not come down to us.

The situation in the book of Habakkuk is essentially the same as that in the book of Jeremiah. The prophets for two hundred years, from the prophet Joel to the prophet Jeremiah, had warned Israel of its idolatry and wickedness, and of judgment to come.

All this is in the background of Habakkuk's book. The writer, a contemporary of Jeremiah, is facing the same questions Jeremiah faced. And his book is written in the same period in which many of the prophecies of Jeremiah were produced. Specifically, Habakkuk's work appears to have been written shortly before 605 B.C., the year when Nebuchadnezzar king of Babylon (called *Chaldeans* in the book) defeated Pharaoh Necho of Egypt in the famous battle at Carchemish, and came south to invade Judah.

The approach of the Chaldeans, as well as the current corruption and violence in Jerusalem and Judah, causes the prophet Habakkuk to pose a number of questions.

One of these questions is, Why does the Lord permit so much evil and injustice to continue in the land?

---

[1] J. R. Dummelow (Editor), *A Commentary on the Holy Bible*, p. 587 (1936).

Another question is, Why is God using the Chaldeans, a heathen nation more corrupt and brutal, to punish Judah?

And another, What is God's final purpose in all this? And what is man's role in all this mystery?

It is the purpose and theme of the book to answer these questions. The answer is not an easy one. A sober reading of the book will reveal that Habakkuk, like Job, was struggling with the twofold mystery of evil in the world, and human suffering. And the ways of God to man.

2. THE STYLE AND COMPOSITION OF THE BOOK

(1) The book of Habakkuk, like the book of Joel, is a single, complete, and unified composition. And like Joel, too, there is no evidence that it was delivered orally as a prophetic discourse, on some previous occasion, and then reduced to writing, as so many of the books of prophecy appear to have been written.

(2) In the second place, the reader will note that Habakkuk's book is classified as "The oracle of God which Habakkuk the prophet *saw.*" That is to say, the book is the type of the *Vision,* which we find illustrated also in the books of Isaiah, Nahum, Obadiah, Ezekiel, and Malachi.

In this type of Scriptural composition, the writer in the Vision *sees* things that are to come to pass, as if they had already happened and were an accomplished fact. This is important for the reader to keep in mind in interpreting the book of Habakkuk.

(3) The reader will note also that the poet Habakkuk advances his *argument,* that is his theme, by means of the rhetorical question.[2] Not that he does not know the answer; for in the "Vision" the prophet through inspiration has "seen" the answer, and knows the outcome. The question therefore is put as a method of presenting ideas and as a way of composition. The author chooses the form of dialogue — the question is put by the prophet, and the answer given by the Lord.

Many readers have been misled by the rhetorical question and answer, and have made the mistake of thinking that the writer is arraigning, not Israel, but God because of the state of violence and wickedness in the nation. In short, Habakkuk is making use of the *panel discussion* so much in use in the modern forum.

(4) Finally, for the reader the situation in the book can be stated briefly. Here is a disobedient and wicked nation, Judah, on the eve of invasion and impending disaster. The Chaldeans (Babylonians), although a barbarous and ruthless people, are the instrument of God's

---

[2]The reader is asked to make a personal experiment in interpretation. After reading this section, "The Style and Composition of the Book," then read two or three of the brief interpretations of Habakkuk listed at the end of the chapter. Now go back and re-read the Bible text of Habakkuk. What is your conclusion as to the meaning of the book?

judgment and punishment of His people. The author's *conclusion* to the situation is that it takes *time* and *faith* while God executes His plan.

This is the whole thought of the book. The rest is *poetic setting*. And from this poetic setting, we get the larger picture, the emotional meaning and content of the book. The author was probably a musician, as well as a poet. Chapter 3 is a psalm with musical directions, and was evidently meant to encourage God's people in their time of adversity. It closes with a beautiful passage on faith.

SELECTED REFERENCES
HABAKKUK

Albright, William Foxwell: *Studies in Old Testament Prophecy,* pp. 1-18 (1950).

*Anderson, Bernhard W.: "Habakkuk's Watchtower of Faith," *Understanding the Old Testament,* pp. 322-323.

Calkins, Raymond: *The Modern Message of the Minor Prophets.*

Gailey, James H.: *The Books of Micah, Nahum, Habakkuk, Zephaniah, Haggai, Zechariah, and Malachi.*

*Stephens-Hodge, L. E. H.: "Habakkuk," *The New Bible Commentary,* pp. 732-735.

*Smith, George Adam: *The Book of Twelve Prophets.*

*Young, Edward J.: "Habakkuk," *An Introduction to the Old Testament,* pp. 287-290.

Right: Conical tower over Ezekiel's Tomb in Kifl, Babylonia. © *Matson Photo Service.*

Below, a fragment of the Habakkuk Commentary from the Dead Sea Scrolls. © *Shrine of the Book,* Jerusalem; *Matson Photo Service*

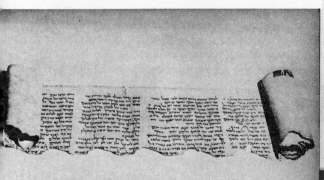

III. BOOKS BY THE PROPHETS OF THE THIRD PERIOD: THE PROPHETS IN EXILE, 605-538 B.C. (The Period of the Babylonian Empire, 612-538 B.C.)

Chapter 12

EZEKIEL

1. EZEKIEL AND THE PROPHETS IN EXILE

Ezekiel was pre-eminently a prophet of the Babylonian Captivity, and the first of the prophets in what we have called the Third Period. The others of this period are Daniel, Jeremiah (Lamentations), and Obadiah.

Ezekiel, a young priest and son of Burzi, was carried away to Babylon with King Jehoiachin and his household, and with large numbers of others of the *second captivity*, in 597 B.C. (see p. 187). With these Jewish exiles, he was settled "by the river Chebar," near a place called Tel-abib, southeast of the city of Babylon. Chebar was the Grand Canal, leading off from the Euphrates River above Babylon and running through Nippur to the Tigris River, and used for inland commerce and irrigation.

In the fifth year of his exile, 593 B.C., as he tells us in the opening paragraph of his book, Ezekiel had a vision of God and received a call to become a prophet among his people. His prophetic ministry thus begun, it was carried on for the next twenty-three years at least, perhaps longer. The latest date in the book is the twenty-seventh year of the Captivity, 570 B.C.

Thus, the book of Ezekiel was written in exile, by an exile, almost a thousand miles away from his native land. The five years in exile, before the call came to become a prophet, would afford ample time for an impressionable young priest such as Ezekiel to think of many things. For example, the major question on his mind would be the meaning of exile for himself and for his people. And, too, there was the great prophet Jeremiah and his prophetic preaching, still in Jerusalem.

Ezekiel and Jeremiah were contemporary prophets, though Jeremiah was much the older of the two. Before his hurried departure from Jerusalem as a captive, he surely would have heard Jeremiah on many occasions. Although neither prophet mentions the other, the book of Ezekiel contains evident traces of Jeremiah's messages and influence. For their prophecies are similar at many points.

2. Ezekiel's Method of Composition

Often Ezekiel is referred to as an artist and poet, and his book as a work of rare literary merit. Indeed, his prophecies have a peculiar style and character, and these qualities of style are due in large part to the author's powerful imagination. In a special way, this book shows the Hebrew's love of symbols and imaginative figures.

Modern readers are all familiar with the method of composition used in such well known *allegories* as John Bunyan's *Pilgrim's Progress* and Jonathan Swift's *Gulliver's Travels;* and doubtless many readers are also familiar with other allegories, not so well known, such as Dante's *Inferno* and Edmund Spenser's *Faerie Queene.*

It will be helpful to readers of the book of Ezekiel, if they remember these other familiar allegories and their method of composition when they approach the reading of our present book of prophecy.

(1) Ezekiel's book records, not one but many *visions.* In fact, it would be almost true to say that the entire series of prophecies is but a chain of visions, the book itself being a unified and artistic composition of these visions.[1]

Too, it should be said again at this point, that the *prophet's* primary function in these visions is not to *foretell* or predict the future, as is the popular notion. But to *reveal* and to interpret the *inspiration* which has come to him.

In the experience of other prophets, there usually came *one* vision, and that only on the occasion of their call to the prophetic office, and appeared no more. But the Divine Glory in which Ezekiel received his call reappeared to him again and again, at many critical points in his ministry.

The vision is the artistic, as well as the religious, motive of the book of Ezekiel as a whole, and is its framework. Now let us take a look at some of the details of the literary method.

(2) Ezekiel, the prophetic teacher, proceeds to instruct his audience by means of a series of object lessons — symbols, if we may use an old word.

The situation was essentially this. The prophet had moved from his location by the river Chebar, to the nearby city of Tel-abib. Here the Elders of the colony of Jewish exiles, and perhaps other representatives of the people, appeared before the prophet almost daily to hear a word from the Lord.

This appears somewhat strange, inasmuch as the general body of Jewish exiles believed the false prophets rather than Ezekiel, that is, they believed that the restoration to their homeland would come soon; whereas Ezekiel, like Jeremiah, prophesied the complete destruc-

---

[1]On the unity of Ezekiel, see Edward J. Young, *An Introduction to the Old Testament,* pp. 256-265; H. H. Rowley, *The Book of Ezekiel in Modern Study.* (1953.)

tion of Jerusalem and a long exile for all Israel. Jeremiah said that the exile would last for *seventy years.*

So Ezekiel taught the Elders of the people, and others who came to him, by symbols. Indeed, his first act was a symbolic one. When he arrived at his post of duty, the enormity of his task overwhelmed him and, like the patriarch Job, he staged a *dumb show* of silence for seven days (3:15).

Like Jeremiah, Ezekiel wished to bring home to his audience the impending destruction and doom of Jerusalem and Judah. And so he takes a *brick* (perhaps a slab of clay tile such as the Babylonians used for inscriptions) and with it demonstrates Jerusalem's siege and captivity (4:1-3).

How long will the siege of Jerusalem last before the city falls, and how many years will the Jewish people remain in captivity? They get their answer. For the prophet is directed, symbolically, to lie so many days on his *left side* and so many days on his *right side,* to demonstrate to his audience the Lord's answer to these questions (4:4-8).

The length of the famine, brought on by the siege of the city, is likewise symbolized (4:9-17). And so on, throughout the book, symbol after symbol, the teaching prophet illustrates his *visions* and Divine *revelations.*

Before we close this section, two favorite allegories deserve special mention. Perhaps the most famous allegory in the book of Ezekiel is that of the Good Shepherd of Israel, recorded in chapter 34. Israel's selfish and unfaithful rulers, careless of what became of the "sheep," were responsible for their being scattered in exile among the nations. Ezekiel prophesies that God, through the family line of David, will set up a Good Shepherd (the Messiah) to feed His sheep.

Another famous symbolic vision of the book is the allegory of the Valley of Dry Bones, chapter 37. This is a most graphic picture and symbol of the revival, reunion, and restoration of the scattered Twelve Tribes of Israel.

3. EZEKIEL AND THE NEW TESTAMENT

The symbol of the shepherd to represent Divine care is a favorite idea in Scripture. David, a shepherd himself, wrote the Twenty-Third Psalm, the most popular of all the Psalms, on that theme.

The comparison of the spiritual leader with the good shepherd was a favorite theme with Jesus, who used it often in conversation and in His teaching.

Chapter 34 in the book of Ezekiel is famous because it is the basis of our Lord's parables of the Lost Sheep (Matthew 18:12-14; Luke 15:3-7), and the Good Shepherd (John 10:1-18). In the latter parable, Jesus proudly calls Himself the Good Shepherd.

The writer of the book of Hebrews repeats the figure of Christ as the Good Shepherd, in his famous benediction at the close of that letter, in these words: "Now may the God of peace who brought again from the dead our Lord Jesus, the great Shepherd of the Sheep . . ."

The Apostle Peter was also familiar with the theme and used it in I Peter to the Christians in the five Roman provinces of Asia Minor: "For you were straying like sheep, but have now returned to the *Shepherd* and Guardian of your souls" (I Peter 2:25).

And the Apostle John, writing in the book of Revelation, says, "For the Lamb in the midst of the throne will be *their Shepherd,* and he will guide them to springs of living water" (7:17).

Perhaps it is no accident that the standard word in modern church usage for minister is the Latin word *pastor,* meaning *shepherd.*

But above all else, the literary forms of the book of Ezekiel were made famous by the Apostle John, in his book of Revelation, in the composition of which he borrowed the language, imagery, and symbols freely from both the books of Ezekiel and Daniel.

4. THE CONTENTS OF THE BOOK OF EZEKIEL

The contents of the book of Ezekiel fall naturally into these three main divisions:

(1) Prophecies delivered *before* the capture and destruction of Jerusalem by Nebuchadrezzar in 586 B.C., chapters 1-24;

(2) Prophecies *after* the destruction of Jerusalem and dealing with God's judgments upon the surrounding Gentile nations, chapters 25 to 32;

(3) And the later prophecies predicting and describing the Restoration of Israel and the establishment of the Ideal Kingdom, chapters 33 to 48.

The big theme of the book is *the Education of the Jewish Exiles* and the perpetuation of the line of David. This education consisted mainly of two things. First, they must repent and accept Jehovah as the One and only God. Second, they must rid themselves of idolatry. "Then they will know that I am the Lord" is another phrase characteristic of Ezekiel, which he uses no less than sixty-three times in the book. It means that God's *revelation* of Himself and His character will finally be accepted.

The Redeemed Remnant, who became the Restoration in the homeland, apparently met these two basic conditions. For there is little or no evidence of idolatry in Israel after the Return to Jerusalem, in 538 B.C.

(1) *Prophecies Delivered Before the Destruction of Jerusalem, in 586 B.C.,* Chapters 1 to 24

1. THE VISION OF GOD'S GLORY. Like other prophets, Ezekiel's call to the office was accompanied by a vision of God. In chapter 1, Ezekiel gives a complete picture of the vision and the circumstances under which it came to him. It should be compared with Isaiah's vision as revealed in chapter 6 of his book. For both prophets it was

an unforgettable experience which motivated the ministries of each for a lifetime.

2. EZEKIEL'S CALL AND COMMISSION. In chapters 2 and 3, Ezekiel reveals the three stages in his call and commission. (1) God has assigned to him a mission as prophet to Israel in exile. Here is Ezekiel's personal statement of his mission, after the call:

> And the Lord said to me, "Son of man, I send you to the people of Israel, to a nation of rebels, who have rebelled against me . . . The people also are impudent and stubborn . . . I have made you a watchman for the house of Israel" (2 to 3:13).

(2) The second aspect of the mission is Ezekiel's responsibility for the fate of his people, a responsibility which is set forth in the title "Watchman" (3:14-21). (3) The third aspect of the call was the mission of Silence, or intermittent speech and silence, as the Lord directed for dealing with a "rebellious people" (3:22-27). He began this mission with silence, thus:

> And I came to the Exiles at Tel-abib, who dwell by the river Chebar. And I sat there overwhelmed among them seven days.

3. BY THE WATERS OF BABYLON. Here we have the beginning of the book proper, chapters 1 to 3 being an introduction to the prophecies that follow and the book as a whole.

It was an overwhelming experience for the population of a great nation to be captured and deported a thousand miles from their native land. It is no wonder that they were "stubborn and rebellious," even if they had not been so before they left Jerusalem. It was Ezekiel's monumental task to reconcile them and teach them. The extent of the bitterness of these exiles is indicated by Psalm 137, which evidently was written by one of them.

The message which is uppermost in Ezekiel's prophecies, and the one which he repeated most often, is the same as Jeremiah's great sermon: Israel must repent in great humility and return to the Lord and His righteousness, and receive His forgiveness, or be destroyed from the face of the earth. Meanwhile, chapters 4 to 6 portray the siege of Jerusalem, in a series of acted symbols, for the purpose of instructing the exiles on the necessity of the destruction of Jerusalem. The chief sin of Judah is still idolatry.

4. "THE END HAS COME." Like Jeremiah the senior prophet, Ezekiel in his book comes quickly to the prophecies of Israel's imminent doom. Addressing the prophet Ezekiel as "the Son of Man," an epithet which occurs some ninety-two times in the book, the Lord places the burden upon him as "Watchman" to declare to the land of Israel that "the end has come."

> Then you will know that I am the Lord. (Chapter 7.)

> The end has come upon the four corners of the land. Now the end is upon you, and I will let loose my anger upon you, and will judge you according to your ways . . . Because the land is full of bloody crimes and the city is full of violence. . . .

5. THE VISION OF ABOMINATIONS IN JERUSALEM. In chapters 8 to 11, Ezekiel portrays the unspeakable crimes in Jerusalem, which came to him in a vision in his house while he sat with the Elders of the exiles. Then he told the exiles all things the Lord had shown him. This vision of sin and doom is usually placed in August-September, 591 B.C., less than two years after Ezekiel's call.

6. THE PROMISE OF A NEW BEGINNING. In chapter 11:16-20, Ezekiel pauses in his stern messages of doom to offer hope for the house of Israel. The Lord will not only gather His scattered peoples and restore them; but He will "put a new spirit within them." This is Jeremiah's new interpretation of religion (see Jeremiah 31:31-34).

7. SYMBOLS, AND MORE SYMBOLS. In chapters 12-19, Ezekiel presents a series of miscellaneous prophecies of Israel's guilt and approaching destruction. These prophecies are remarkably similar in purpose to the messages of Jeremiah, but in method strikingly different. They are composed in Ezekielan symbols. They are dated between August-September, 591 B.C., and July-August, 590 B.C., or about four years before the fall of Jerusalem.

8. HISTORY IS REPEATING ITSELF. It was customary for the Elders of the exiles to come to Ezekiel every so often to learn the answer of the Lord on some question. Chapter 20 tells the story of such an occasion. But there was no answer, because the exiles had engaged in idolatry. So Ezekiel used the occasion, and their insincerity, to review the whole history of Israel regarding their sin of idolatry. They are no better than their forefathers in Egypt! Chapters 20 to 24 contain a final series of prophecies on the necessity of Israel's punishment, and of the destruction of Jerusalem. They are dated in 590 B.C., except chapter 24, which is dated on the day on which the siege of Jerusalem began, January-February, 587 B.C.

(2) PROPHECIES DEALING WITH GOD'S JUDGMENTS UPON THE
SURROUNDING GENTILE NATIONS, Chapters 25-32

The prophecies of chapters 25-32 come between those which deal with the overthrow of the Old Israel (chapters 1-24), and those which foretell the establishment of the New Israel (chapters 33-48).

The significance of these in-between prophecies is suggested in chapter 28:24-26. The destruction of Jerusalem seemed to these heathen nations to be a victory of heathendom, over the people of the true God. Their exultation and contempt for fallen Judah was clear evidence of that. It was necessary for Jehovah to show that this was not so: "Then they will know that I am the Lord God."

1. AMMON, MOAB, EDOM, AND PHILISTIA. In chapter 25, Ezekiel deals respectively with these nations on the east, southeast, and southwest of the territory of Israel. Some had exulted in the fall of Jerusalem, others had participated in it. None of them recognized

Jehovah, and all were idolatrous. They must be eliminated and the way made clear for the New Israel after the Restoration.

2. TYRE AND SIDON. In chapters 26-28 we have prophecies which set the score for the mightiest sea-trader and sea-power of the ancient world, Tyre, the capital of Phoenicia. It joined in the league against Nebuchadrezzar and was besieged by him for thirteen years and destroyed (597-584 B.C.). The destruction of Sidon, a younger rival of Tyre, is predicted to fall also by Ezekiel (28:20-26).

3. EGYPT. Egypt, the most ancient of the rivals, had been both strong and weak for thousands of years. Whenever a crisis came for Israel, Egypt could never be depended upon to come to her rescue, notwithstanding her many alliances. Isaiah had made this clear a hundred years earlier; so had Jeremiah; and now Ezekiel, in chapters 29-32, foretells the destruction of Egypt and gives reasons why, in an unforgettable passage which modern Egyptians would do well to remember, chapter 29:12-16.

(3) PROPHECIES PREDICTING AND DESCRIBING THE ESTABLISHMENT OF THE NEW ISRAEL AND THE IDEAL KINGDOM, Chapters 33-48

Ezekiel's prophecies of chapters 1-24 dealt almost exclusively with Israel's sins and with the necessity of its overthrow. But God's punishment of Israel was not the end of His dealings with His people. The punishment of the Old Israel would be followed by the establishment of the New Israel, and a perfect Kingdom of God. The destruction of the foreign nations, dealt with in chapters 25-32, would prepare the way for the restoration of the exiles in the homeland. The last section of the book of Ezekiel, chapters 33-48, deals with the new conditions of worship and fellowship with God by the New Israel.

1. "SON OF MAN, SPEAK TO YOUR PEOPLE." The prophet Ezekiel has reached the turning point in his ministry. He has proved to be a faithful "Watchman" on duty, and the great event for which he has waited seven years has taken place. A messenger comes from Jerusalem with the news: "The city has fallen."

On its face, such a message would appear to be bad news. But apparently Ezekiel was relieved that the end had come. Now he would be free to devote himself to "the ministry of building up instead of pulling down." In fact, in earlier messages he had already hinted at Israel's future (16:60-63; 17:22-24). Thus, chapter 33 embarks upon the ministry and message of Hope. The Lord speaks,

> As I live, says the Lord, I have no pleasure in the death of the wicked, but that the wicked turn from his way and live; turn back, turn back from your evil ways; for why will you die, O house of Israel?

2. THE GOOD SHEPHERD. The selfish shepherds of Israel (rulers), who have failed the people, in the allegory are contrasted with the Good Shepherd who is promised from the line of David — "and he

shall feed them." This chapter 34 is also the source of our Lord's parables of the Lost Sheep (Matthew 18:12-13; Luke 15:3-6) and the Good Shepherd (John 10:1-16); and the parable of the Sheep and Goats (Matthew 25:31ff) may have been suggested by verse 17 of this chapter.

3. "THEN THEY WILL KNOW THAT I AM THE LORD." After the destruction of Jerusalem and the deportation of the people, Edom and the other Gentile nations moved in to occupy the unoccupied land of Israel, taking it as a sign of God's inability to save His people. Then the Lord visited judgment upon the nations, to vindicate His position, and to prepare the way for the restoration of the exiles, that they may know that He is the Lord. Thus, in chapters 35-36, the prophet Ezekiel looks to the land of Israel and its future.

4. ISRAEL'S RESURRECTION. In a spectacular and wildly beautiful vision, Ezekiel in chapter 37, pictures the dispersed and discouraged exiles suddenly coming to life.

In the vision, the prophet is transported to a valley filled with dry bones. And the Spirit said to him, "Son of Man, can these bones live?" Then breath came into them, and they lived, and stood upon their feet, an exceeding great host. This is an allegory of the revival, restoration, and reunion of the scattered Twelve Tribes of Israel. This dramatic method was used by the prophet to instill courage and hope in his people.

5. GOG AND MAGOG. The king and the land. Here we have another intriguing prophecy. Who is Gog, and where is Magog? Ezekiel alone among the prophets expects another crisis after the restoration. Many think that this is a prophecy against the Scythian hordes from the far north and their threat to Israel.

Others take a different view. The whole prophecy, as related in chapters 38-39, is surrounded with mystery and Ezekiel's love of symbols. For one thing, we have already seen how Jehovah humbled the surrounding nations that undertook to possess the land of Israel after the captivity and exile. Here, however, Ezekiel seems to be portraying a wider extension of God's kingdom and glory, than in the other prophecies. In short, is there something here more than an anticipated invasion of barbarous and cruel hordes from the far north, who will be destroyed by God without any fighting on Israel's part?

The answer could be yes, for the writer of the book of Revelation (20:7-10) presents the same idea, namely; that what seems the triumph of God's kingdom may be followed by a final battle between the forces of evil and the forces of righteousness, in which the forces of evil will be overthrown at last.

6. THE NEW TEMPLE. In chapters 40-48, Ezekiel presents prophecies dealing with the New Temple for Jerusalem, the restoration of

the Temple worship, and the division of the land and the plan of the city. This concluding section of the book is dated in the twenty-fifth year of Ezekiel's exile from Jerusalem, and the fourteenth year after the fall of Jerusalem, 572 B.C.

SELECTED READINGS: PROPHETS OF THE THIRD PERIOD

Bible Readings: The books of Ezekiel, Daniel, Jeremiah (Lamentations), and Obadiah. *The Revised Standard Version;* or *The King James Version,* preferably in modern reader's format.

EZEKIEL

*Anderson, Bernhard W.: "Ezekiel the Priest," *Understanding the Old Testament,* pp. 359-375.

Burrows, Millar: *The Literary Relations of Ezekiel.* (Philadelphia, 1925.)

Hartford, John Battersby: *Studies in the Book of Ezekiel.* (Cambridge, 1935.)

Howie, C. G.: *The Date and Composition of Ezekiel.*

James, Fleming: "The Priestly Writers," *Personalities of the Old Testament.*

May, H. G.: "Ezekiel," *The Interpreter's Bible,* Vol. VI, pp. 41-66.

Moulton, Richard G.: "Ezekiel," *The Modern Reader's Bible,* pp. 610-664, and 1402-1414.

Paterson, John: *The Goodly Fellowship of the Prophets,* pp. 160-178.

*Robinson, H. Wheeler: *Two Hebrew Prophets — Studies in Hosea and Ezekiel.*

*Rowley, H. H.: *The Book of Ezekiel in Modern Study.*

Smith, James: *The Book of the Prophet Ezekiel — A New Interpretation.*

*Young, Edward J.: "Ezekiel," *An Introduction to the Old Testament,* pp. 256-265.

Chapter 13

DANIEL

1. DANIEL'S OWN STORY

The book of Daniel, like the book of Ezekiel, is a product of the exile.

As a youth, Daniel was carried off with the other captives from Jerusalem to Babylon by Nebuchadrezzar in the *first captivity,* 605 B.C. At the palace in the city of Babylon, Daniel was selected because of his princely birth and handsome physique, with other young captives of good birth, to be educated for service at the court.

Daniel's story, much of it told in the first person, reads like the success story of Joseph in Egypt, or a modern success story in the western world. After his special education to serve in the king's palace, he rose from one promotion to another until, because of his many years of faithfulness, he had won the high office of ruler over the province of Babylon and head over its wise men.

In this office, he was honored with the distinction of serving two great Empires — the Babylonian Empire until its fall in 538 B.C., and then the Empire of the Medes and Persians. The story makes it clear that only by the grace of God was he able to remain uncompromisingly faithful to his religion and to himself as a Jewish exile, even when he was brought face to face with death.

Three other young Jewish exiles— Hananiah, Mishael, and Azariah — are associated with Daniel in his trials and successes, although they play supporting roles in this court drama.

Daniel remained in the courts of Babylon and of the Medes and Persians from 605 B.C., the year of his captivity, until about 533 B.C. In all these 72 years he was one of God's most loyal, most faithful servants and witnesses.

Daniel's personal narratives are presented to the reader in the form of an autobiography, and there is no good reason to believe other than that he wrote the book himself, perhaps near the close of his ministry.[1] It is written partly in the third person, and partly

[1] The wide diversity of critical opinion on the authorship and interpretation of the book of Daniel is summarized briefly in Young's *Introduction to the Old Testament,* pp. 380-399 (1958), and more at length in the same author's *The Prophecy of Daniel* (1949). An ultra-liberal view is presented in Anderson's *Understanding the Old Testament,* pp. 515-530. Modifications of opposing views may be found in other works in the reference lists.

in the first, with extensive quotations as if the prophet were quoting himself.

2. The Theme and Purpose of the Book

Taking the autobiographical narrative at its face value, we have a personal success story of unusual charm, made more appealing because of the humility and devotion to principle of the hero. That is, the human incidents within themselves make the book an attractive episode.

But there is a larger meaning. For the writer makes it abundantly clear throughout his composition that the Creator is in charge of the destinies of both men and nations. In short, the book teaches that even though the people of God are in bondage now to a heathen nation, that God Himself is the sovereign ruler and will determine the destinies of both Babylonians and Jews, as outlined in the visions of His servant Daniel.

The purpose of the book is well stated by Professor J. R. Dummelow of Cambridge University, in these words:[2]

> Beneath its artificial literary form we can read the great lessons that God presides over the history of the world; that the Gentile nations as well as the Jews have always been under His control; that the succession of human empires is ordained by Him; that He permits the pride and fury of oppressors for a time, but humbles them in the end, and saves His own; that His kingdom will come at length, and will endure for ever; that faithfulness and constancy to Him lead to a life beyond death, and to an eternal reward of glory.

3. The Literary Composition of the Book

The book of Daniel belongs to a special literary type, described as an *apocalypse*, a *revelation* or unveiling of things heretofore unknown.

In this type of composition the writer makes free use of figures and symbolic images, including *visions* and *dreams,* such as the reader meets with in the books of Ezekiel and Daniel of the Old Testament, and the book of Revelation in the New Testament, which is perhaps the best illustration of the apocalyptic type in our Bible.

In the book of Daniel, the reader meets with a series of "dreams" and "visions," and the correct interpretation of these is likely to cause him difficulty — except in a few instances in which the author explains his own symbols.

For example, chapter 2 relates King Nebuchadrezzar's dream of the Great Image, and gives Daniel's interpretation. The Image has a head of gold, breast and arms of silver, belly and thighs of bronze, and legs and feet of iron and clay.

These images are said, according to traditional and conservative opinion, to represent four successive worldly kingdoms, as follows: The head of gold is Nebuchadrezzar's Babylonian kingdom (612-539

---

[2] *A Commentary on the Holy Bible* (Editor), pp. 531-532. (Macmillan. 1936.)

B.C.); the breast and arms of silver stand for the empire of the Medes and Persians (539-336 B.C.); the bronze belly and thighs is symbolic of the Greek Empire under Alexander the Great and his successors (336-146 B.C.); and the legs and feet of iron and clay represent the Roman Empire (146 B.C.-476 A.D.).

The *Stone,* "cut out by no human hand," represents the Messiah and the Messianic kingdom, a kingdom described as set up by the God of heaven, and which shall never be destroyed, in contrast with the human and temporal empires of the Great Image.

As has been pointed out by Edward J. Young and others,[3] this is the only interpretation which explains verse 2:44 correctly, a verse which clearly states that the Messianic kingdom will be erected in the days of the kingdoms which the writer mentioned.

As we now know, the Messiah came and "set up" His kingdom during the Roman Empire, the fourth and last mentioned in the revelation by means of the Great Image.

These dreams and visions which Daniel saw, therefore, are not to be thought of as ordinary dreams, but as revelations of God, *of things to come.*

For a continuation of this revelation, let us now go directly to chapter 7, the subject of which is the same as that of chapter 2. This time the vision of the Four Beasts is substituted for the dream of the Great Image.

The Four Beasts are four kings who will "rise out of the earth," and are the same four kings and kingdoms described in chapter 2.

The narratives and symbols of the fiery furnace (chapter 3), the madness of Nebuchadrezzar (chapter 4), Belshazzar's feast and the handwriting on the wall (chapter 5), and the den of lions (chapter 6) should present little difficulty to the reader, since the writer explains his own figures.

In chapter 8, however, the writer introduces a new series of symbols, some of which he explains, and some he does not — the allegory of the ram, the he-goat, and the Little Horn.

A vision appeared to the prophet Daniel, and in the vision he was taken to Susa, the Persian capital. He saw a ram with two horns, the two horns being the two kings of Media and Persia.

While he was contemplating the great power of the Ram, both "westward and northward and southward," behold a he-goat came charging from the west, and destroyed the Ram. The he-goat, with "the conspicuous horn," was the first king, Alexander the Great.

But Alexander the Great died suddenly, in 323 B.C., and the "four kingdoms" which arose from his Empire are the four divisions mentioned — Macedonia, Thrace, Syria, and Egypt. The "Little Horn" that came out of them was the cruel and unspeakable Antiochus

[3]"Daniel," *The New Bible Commentary,* pp. 671-672 (1954).

Epiphanes, king of Syria (176-164 B.C.), who persecuted the Jews with great severity because of their resistance to his attempts to introduce heathen religious observances among them.

In chapter 9, the vision of the Seventy Weeks deals with the time of the exile and punishment of Judah for her sin and disobedience. Jeremiah said that it would be seventy years — that is, from the fourth year of Jehoiakim's reign (605 B.C.) to Cyrus' conquest of Babylon (538 B.C.).

But the passage appears to have another interpretation. The traditional and conservative view is that the passage from Jeremiah means, not *seventy years,* but "seventy sevens," or 490 years.

According to this view, the time of redemption of Israel refers, therefore, not so much to the return to Jerusalem in 538 B.C., as it does to the coming of the Messiah and the Messianic salvation, which would require the "seventy sevens" or the 490 years or so to complete. Daniel's prayer for his people, and for himself, and the angel Gabriel's reply would also seem to bear out this interpretation (9: 20-27).

Moreover, this remarkable vision of the Seventy Weeks also hints at the Crucifixion, the destruction of Jerusalem in A.D. 70 by the Roman commander Titus (later Emperor), and closes with the forward-looking view of the End of Time (vv. 26-27).

Chapters 10-12 present Daniel's final vision and revelation of things to come, and should be read together as one connected whole.

What the prophet saw in this vision was a picture of universal history: the coming conflict between Persia and Greece, and especially the struggle between two divisions of Alexander the Great's Empire after his death, Syria and Egypt, the "north" and the "south" kingdoms in the vision.

The climax of these struggles between the north and the south kingdoms came in the reign of Antiochus Epiphanes, and with his extreme persecution of the Jews. In the last chapter, the writer also hints at the Future and further tribulations . . . "but at that time your people shall be delivered, every one whose name shall be found written in the Book."

The prophet's aim in this vision, as elsewhere in his book, is not to deal with political history as such, but to give a picture of coming conflicts in world history in relation to the kingdom of God, and the ultimate victory and triumph of the forces of righteousness, against the forces of evil.

4. The Book of Daniel and the New Testament

The measure of the influence of the book of Daniel is seen in the use made of it by the writers and makers of the New Testament.

Many of the sayings of our Lord are based on the language of the book of Daniel, including the description of the great tree in the

Parable of the Mustard Seed (Matthew 13:32; Mark 4:32; Luke 13: 19), the pictures of the Son of Man coming in the clouds of heaven (Matthew 24:30; 26:64; Mark 13:26; 14:62), and other expressions in the great discourse on the Last Things (Matthew 24; Mark 13; Luke 21).

The most notable parallels to be seen, however, are those between the apocalyptic visions of the book of Daniel and those of the Apostle John's Revelation. The Beast which John saw coming up out of the sea (Revelation 13:1) is a make-up of the Four Beasts which Daniel saw lifting their heads from the sea (Daniel 7:3-7). Daniel saw a lion with eagle's wings, a bear, a leopard with four wings and four heads, and a beast with ten horns. John combines the features of these four beasts into one animal.

Daniel is the only book of the Old Testament to give names to angels — Gabriel and Michael. In Daniel, Michael is the guardian angel of the Jews; in Revelation, he is the leader among the angels, or *archangel*, as in the letter of Jude (verse 9).

For other parallels, compare these passages: Daniel 7:7 with Revelation 12:1-6; 7:13 with 1:7; 7:19 with 1:14; 7:7, 20 with 5:5-7; 7:9, 22 with 20:4; 8:10 with 12:4; 12:4, 10 with 22:10-15.

Both writers compare the four kingdoms of this world in their opposition to the kingdom of our Lord. Both treat Satan as a beast. The visions of the Future, the conflict of the "last days," and the final Victory, are all remarkably similar and suggestive of each other, as are also many images and symbols in both books.

Daniel's apocalypse does not end, however, with the temporal kingdoms and struggles referred to, but envisions other conflicts and "abominations" to the End of Time, between the evil powers of this world and the kingdom of righteousness.

Thus, this last vision of Daniel's suggests at once to us two other famous visions of the Future Time, both of them in the New Testament. Jesus, as reported in Matthew 24, prophesied the signs which would take place before the End, and His Second Coming, and quoted from the prophet Daniel (24:15).

The other famous vision of the approaching End of Time is given in the book of Revelation, the vision of the Seven Seals, chapters 4 to 8:5.

SELECTED REFERENCES
DANIEL

Anderson, Bernhard W.: "The Apocalypse of Daniel," *Understanding the Old Testament*, pp. 515-530.

Howie, Carl G.: *The Books of Ezekiel and Daniel.*

*Leopold, H. C.: *Exposition of Daniel.*

The Lion Monument in the ruins of Babylon, supposedly marking the site of Daniel's den of lions. © *Matson Photo Service*

*Rowley, H. H.: *Darius the Mede and the Four World Empires in the Book of Daniel.*

Welch, Adam C.: *Visions of the End.*

Wilson, Robert Dick: *Studies in the Book of Daniel.*

*Young, Edward J.: *An Introduction to the Old Testament*, pp. 380-399.

*Young, Edward J.: "Daniel," *The New Bible Commentary*, pp. 668-681.

*Young, Edward J.: *The Prophecy of Daniel.*

Chapter 14

LAMENTATIONS

1. JEREMIAH'S ELEGY

The prophet Jeremiah's second book, Lamentations, is the only complete elegy in the Hebrew Scriptures. To the ancient Hebrews, the book was known by its opening word *Ekhah*, meaning *How*. It was called *Threnoi* in the Greek by the Septuagint translators.

Threnoi means *dirges*, which is a much stronger word than our English *elegy*, or grief poem. St. Jerome, in his Latin translation *The Vulgate* (390-405 A.D.), called it *Lamentari*, or *Lamentations* in English.

An elegy is usually written on the death of some person or persons, such as Thomas Gray's *Elegy*, or Alfred Tennyson's *In Memoriam*, or John Milton's *Lycidas*, and others. But in the example of Jeremiah, the poem was written shortly after the destruction and passing of a great city, Jerusalem (586 B.C.), which to the prophet represented a personal, as well as a national loss.

In the original Hebrew the book is anonymous. But a well established early tradition ascribed the authorship to Jeremiah. This tradition first appears in the title of the *Septuagint Version* of *Lamentations* by the Greek translators (between 285-150 B.C.), and reads as follows:

> And it came to pass, after Israel had been carried away captive,
> and Jerusalem had become desolate, that Jeremiah sat weeping,
> and lamented this lamentation over Jerusalem and said . . .

The tradition of Jeremiah's authorship was continued by Jerome in *The Vulgate,* and others, until modern times. Many present day critical scholars have sought to place the date later than Jeremiah, and have looked for a later candidate for the authorship.[1]

The best conservative opinion is that the poem was very likely written during the three months or so between the burning of Jerusalem, July, 586 B.C., and Jeremiah's exile in Egypt, forced by a band of rebels who murdered Gedaliah, Nebuchadrezzar's governor of Judah, and who compelled Jeremiah to accompany them to Egypt, in the late autumn of that year.

2. THE READER AND JEREMIAH'S POEM

Jeremiah, incorrectly, has been called the prophet of doom, and the Weeping Prophet among prophets. This aspect of Jeremiah has

---

[1]For a discussion of the authorship and the date, see Young *An Introduction to the Old Testament,* pp. 362-366 (1958); Stephens-Hodge, "Lamentations," *The New Bible Commentary,* pp. 640-644 (2nd ed., 1954).

been overstressed. An actor who comes upon the stage in the last act of a tragedy must perform the part of tragedy. Such a part fell to the lot of Jeremiah.

In our study of I and II Samuel and I and II Kings, we compared the rise and fall of the Hebrew nation to a great drama. We said that the prophet Samuel "set the stage" for the drama of Israel and introduced the First Act. King Saul and King David, in their struggles for the kingship, staged the "rising action" and conflict, in Act Two. In the Third Act, with a dramatic flourish, Solomon brought the action to a "climax and crisis," and before his act closed, the stage was set for the rapid decline and fall. Jeremiah was one of the main players cast to perform in the fifth and last act of the tragedy, and was on the stage when the curtain fell.

Jeremiah, then, was not necessarily a tragic poet. What he did as prophet was to play the role assigned him. And may we ask, Was he any more a prophet of doom than was Isaiah? Or any more a weeping prophet than was Isaiah before him? The occasion called for a *tragic message* of doom and disaster, and Jeremiah delivered that kind of message.

We come now to a consideration of the composition itself. We have here an elegy or dirge in five parts, each part corresponding exactly to each of the five chapter divisions of the poem.

Also, each of the five dirges contains twenty-two verses, except that the third and middle dirge contains three times as many verses as each of the others, or sixty-six verses.

In turn, each of the verses has three parts, or are in the form of triplets, except in dirges three-to-five many of the verses are in two parts, or are in the form of couplets.

- *The Revised Standard Version* of our Bible (1952) groups these verses into poetic stanzas, and otherwise in verse forms, which makes the reading of the poem more understandable and more enjoyable.

More important, however, than the mechanics of the poem, and its division into five separate but closely related dirges, is its Divine message of Love and Hope.

The reader, as he begins his perusal of the poem, sees a picture of the old prophet sitting on the ruins of a great city, himself overcome with sorrow and grief. After a long silence, he slowly begins his dirge . . .

> How lonely sits the city
> that was full of people!
> How like a widow has she become,
> she that was great among the nations!

The poet then reviews step by step the cause of Zion's sorrows, the people's disobedience and sin and the Lord's anger, until finally he comes to the great passage, the central theme of the poem, which is the hope of God's everlasting love and mercy:

The steadfast love of the Lord
never ceases,
His mercies never come to an end . . .

The Lord is good to those who wait
for Him,
To the soul that seeks Him . . .

3. THE CONTENTS OF THE BOOK OF LAMENTATIONS

The contents of the book may be grouped conveniently under the five chapter divisions corresponding to the five poems, as follows:

(1) The fires of Nebuchadrezzar dispelled the last enchantment of the Holy City. Hence the prophet Jeremiah, disconsolate and sorrowful, sits on the ruins of Jerusalem and writes this national dirge of the people — himself no less lonely than the empty city, the loss of which he mourns.

(2) Zion's sorrows, described in this death-in-life dirge, are due to the Lord's anger, whose doings have humiliated and punished his people.

(3) Zion's hope is in God's love and mercy:

The steadfast love of the Lord
never ceases,
His mercies never come to an end.

(4) Zion's former glory is contrasted with her present misery and humiliation, especially during the last stages of the Babylonian siege.

(5) For a concluding theme, Jeremiah leads Zion's earnest prayer for deliverance, from their present miseries, and for a renewal of their place with the Lord, as in the days of old.

Why dost thou forget us for ever,
Why dost thou so long forsake us?
Restore us to thyself, O Lord, that
we may be restored!
Renew our days as of old!

In this chain of dirges, Jeremiah is much more than a mourner for a lost city. He becomes the spokesman for the sorrowful, and for the disconsolate of all time and all ages, and points to the love and mercy of God as the only hope of any people.

SELECTED REFERENCES

LAMENTATIONS

Halley, Henry H.: "Lamentations," *Halley's Bible Handbook*, pp. 286-287.

Kuist, Howard T.: *The Books of Jeremiah and Lamentations.*

Stephens-Hodge, L. E. H.: "Lamentations," *The New Bible Commentary*, pp. 640-644.

*Young, Edward J.: "Lamentations," *An Introduction to the Old Testament*, pp. 362-366.

(See also the reading list under *Jeremiah*, p. 324 and 325.)

Chapter 15

OBADIAH

1. AUTHORSHIP, DATE, AND OCCASION

Here we have the shortest book in the Old Testament, and yet it is a genuine book of prophecy. The little we know about the prophet Obadiah, we gather from the book itself.

The title of the book is "the vision of Obadiah," and the vision is "concerning Edom." Edom is the rocky, mountainous and desert-like country south of the Dead Sea and east of the valley of the Arabah, and was inhabited by the descendants of Esau.

Obadiah, like the prophets Amos, Isaiah, Micah, and Habakkuk, uses the word *vision* to describe the contents of his prophecy, and the circumstances under which he received his message. Obadiah is a true prophet and thus a spokesman for the Lord, who gives him a message concerning Edom.

The best opinion is that the message must be dated shortly after the destruction of Jerusalem by Nebuchadrezzar, 586 B.C., for verses 11-14 almost surely refer to Judah's recent ruin and the part that Edom played in it.

2. THE MEANING OF OBADIAH'S PROPHECY

What was Obadiah's prophecy "concerning Edom"? In the long, drawn-out siege of Jerusalem by the Babylonian king Nebuchadrezzar, Edom was guilty of taking sides with the Babylonians and against Judah.

Historically, Jacob the ancestor of Judah, and Esau the ancestor of Edom, were twin-brothers and sons of Isaac. But Esau sold his birthright to Jacob, and the two men parted, Esau finally settling in the region south of the Dead Sea and east of the Arabah.

The descendants of Esau, like their first ancestor, never developed a sense of mutual responsibility or loyalty to their brother Judah. The Herods in the time of Jesus were Edomites (Greek, *Idumeans*), and true to type. Thus, Obadiah's prophecy is in consequence of the failure of the Edomites of his day:

> For the violence done to your
> brother Jacob,
> Shame shall come over you,
> And you shall be cut off for ever.

For word has come to the prophet that Edom is to be punished. Indeed, it is about to be driven out of the land by a confederacy of neighboring nations. Specifically, Edom's sin is in aiding the Babylonians in the capture of Judah, in looting Jerusalem, and in gloating over its disaster.

For all these crimes, the Day of the Lord is near, which is the day of judgment for all the enemy nations of God's people, Edom in particular. But Zion shall be saved:

> But in Mount Zion there shall be
> those that escape,
> and it shall be holy.

3. The Main Message of Obadiah

In short, Judah is to be vindicated against her enemies. But this is not the main message of the prophet Obadiah. But is it not in this, that the everlasting hope of men is in the love and mercy of the Lord, and in the knowledge that He will overcome every foe of His rule, and that His kingdom shall endure for ever?

Selected References

Obadiah

Anderson, Bernhard W.: "Obadiah's Denunciation of Edom," *Understanding the Old Testament*, p. 447.

Myers, Jacob M.: *The Books of Hosea, Joel, Amos, Obadiah, and Jonah.*

Oesterley and Robinson: *An Introduction to the Books of the Old Testament.*

*Peckham, George A.: *An Introduction to the Study of Obadiah.*

*Robinson, D. W. B.: "Obadiah," *The New Bible Commentary*, pp. 710-713.

*Young, Edward J.: *An Introduction to the Old Testament*, pp. 276-277.

(See also the special articles in the Bible dictionaries and encyclopedias.)

IV. BOOKS BY THE PROPHETS OF THE FOURTH PERIOD: THE PROPHETS OF THE RETURN AND RESTORATION, 538-432 B.C. (The Period of the Persian Empire, 538-336 B.C.)

Chapter 16

HAGGAI

1. AUTHORSHIP, DATE, AND OCCASION OF THE BOOK

The prophet Haggai was the first of the prophets of the Fourth Period — the Return from Exile and the Restoration.

The reader will recall that Jerusalem and Judah were captured by the Babylonian king Nebuchadnezzar in three main installments — the captivities of 605 B.C., 597 B.C., and 586 B.C., when Jerusalem was captured, looted and burned. The land was stripped of nearly all its inhabitants, who were taken into Babylonian exile.

In 539 B.C., Cyrus, king of Persia, with the aid of the Medes, captured the city of Babylon and took possession of the Babylonian Empire. Almost immediately afterward, Cyrus issued a decree granting the Jews in the Babylonian captivity permission to return to Jerusalem and re-build the Temple and the city. (See the book of Ezra.)

Some 50,000 Jewish exiles took advantage of the decree of Cyrus and returned to their homeland, arriving there within the next year or two for the work of re-building.

Haggai, and his contemporary and colleague, the prophet Zechariah, belong to the period of this first return of exiles from Babylon under the leadership of Zerubbabel, the first governor of Judah, and Joshua his high priest.

The little we know about Haggai is gathered from the messages he delivered and recorded in this short book.[1] Some scholars have taken his reference to the first Temple, verse 2:3, to mean that Haggai was an old man at the time of these prophecies; one who probably had seen Solomon's Temple and had outlived the Babylonian exile. Others think that it is more likely that he was born in the land of captivity, and that his question here is rhetorical and not intended to

---

[1]For a discussion of the authorship and the message of the book of Haggai, see J. McIlmoyle of Belfast, in "Haggai," *The New Bible Commentary*, pp. 743-747 (2nd ed., 1954). See also the book of Ezra, which should be read at this point for its story of the Return.

compare the present sorry state of the second Temple with that of the glory of the first or Solomon's Temple.

Actually, work on the second Temple was begun shortly after the exiles' arrival at Jerusalem, as early as the spring of 535 B.C.; but for various reasons the work was stopped.

So, for sixteen long years the people and their leaders had postponed the re-building of the Lord's house,[2] and it is now September 1, 520 B.C., when Haggai delivered his first message and urgent call to build the house, without further delay.

Since the author gives us the exact month and day of each discourse, it is possible to date his messages with the greatest accuracy, something most unusual in books of Scripture, or in most other ancient books. The first message, as we have noted, was delivered on September 1, 520 B.C.; the second, October 21; the third and fourth, December 24.

Thus, Haggai's four discourses were delivered within the short space of four months.

The purpose of the messages was both to prod the people and to encourage them in building the Lord's house with dispatch and without delay.

The sermons of Haggai and of his colleague Zechariah must have been effective. For the Temple was declared finished on March 3, 516 B.C., about three and one-half years after Haggai's first message.

2. THE CONTENTS AND THE MESSAGE OF THE BOOK OF HAGGAI

The two short chapters of the book of Haggai appear to be a condensed summary or abridgment of four important, and probably much longer discourses.

(1) The prophet reprimands the Jews for spending all their time on their own private homes and businesses, and thus delaying for sixteen years the building the Lord's house. He exhorts them to begin on the Temple now! (Chapter 1.)

(2) The prophet as spokesman for the Lord, addresses Zerubbabel the governor, Joshua the high priest, and the people, as follows: Do not belittle your Temple and its prospects, because it does not compare in your eyes with the glories of Solomon's Temple. For "my Spirit abides with you," says the Lord, "and in a little while, with the treasuries of all nations, I will fill this house with splendor" (chapter 2:1-9).

(3) The prophet, speaking to the priests through a parable on cleanness and uncleanness, teaches Judah a lesson on the seriousness of neglecting the Lord's work. He also explains why their crops and businesses have failed and promises renewed blessings for their obedience (chapter 2:10-19).

---

[2]For a realistic appraisal of Restoration days and the background of the book of Haggai, see John Bright, *The Kingdom of God*, pp. 158-167 (1953).

(4) In his last message, the prophet addresses the governor on the future of Israel, when it will have freedom and an opportunity to realize its spiritual hopes.

The book of Haggai is a book of encouragement and hope. As one writer put it, Haggai may not have added much to the sum total of prophecy in an era when so many authoritative voices had spoken, such as Isaiah, Jeremiah, and others. But the little that he contributed was of great value. Israel was at a critical moment in its history; and what the prophet said, and did, was both timely and vigorous, and held before the Jewish people the great Ideal.

Selected References on the Prophets of the Fourth Period

Bible Readings: The Books of Haggai, Zechariah, and Malachi. Text: *The Revised Standard Version;* or *The King James Version,* preferably in the modern reader's format.

Haggai

*Bright, John: *The Kingdom of God,* pp. 158-167.

Calkins, Raymond: *The Modern Message of the Minor Prophets.*

Gailey, James H.: *The Books of Micah, Nahum, Habakkuk, Zephaniah, Haggai, Zechariah, and Malachi.*

*McIlmoyle, J.: "Haggai," *The New Bible Commentary,* pp. 743-747.

*Smith, George Adam: *The Books of the Twelve Prophets.*

Chapter 17

ZECHARIAH

1. AUTHORSHIP, DATE, AND OCCASION OF THE BOOK

The prophet Zechariah was a contemporary and colleague of the prophet Haggai.

Zechariah, like Haggai, belongs to the period of the first return of the exiles from Babylon under the first governor, Zerubbabel, and the building of the second Temple, 538-516 B.C.

But unlike Haggai, who was a layman, Zechariah was a priest of the tribe of Levi, the grandson of Iddo, a famous priest and head of one of the priestly families that returned with the exiles under Zerubbabel. Moreover, Zechariah, the grandson, must have been a young man, and born in the Babylonian exile (2:4). Thus, like Jeremiah and Ezekiel, Zechariah was a priest as well as a prophet.

The time of Zechariah's prophesying is specifically stated in his book. The reader will recall that one of the first things the returned exiles did was to begin to lay the foundation of the Temple. But, because of their feuds with the Samaritans and other surrounding enemies, and because they were more interested in building and re-establishing their own homes and businesses, they neglected and postponed the building of the house of the Lord, until the latter half of 520 B.C.

Uniting his efforts with Haggai's in exhorting the leaders of the Jewish colony to resume work on the house of God, Zechariah delivered the messages which are recorded in his book.[1]

Zechariah's first discourse was delivered to the people in November, 520 B.C., some two months after Haggai delivered his first prophecy (1:1-6). Following this opening address, Zechariah, three months later, on February 24, 519 B.C., delivered his first series of *Visions* (1:7 to 6). The final series was delivered on December 4, 518 B.C. (Chapters 7 to 14).

2. ZECHARIAH'S STYLE OF COMPOSITION

Although the purpose of the book of Zechariah is essentially the same as that of the book of Haggai, namely, to encourage the people to go forward without further delay and re-build the Temple, the methods of the two prophets are strikingly different.

---

[1]For a realistic appraisal of the difficulties of the Restoration, see John Bright, *The Kingdom of God*, pp. 156-186.

They both agreed that the Temple was the center and symbol of their Return and Restoration from exile, and of God's over-ruling and protecting presence. They both agreed also on the necessity of re-building the Temple *now*. But here their similarity ends.

Haggai, apparently an old man, wrote a plain, simple though vigorous message. It was direct and brief, and with no poetic flights of fancy such as is common among the Hebrew prophets.

Zechariah, on the contrary, was a young man, with a poetic and highly imaginative temperament. Zechariah composed a poetic prophecy, patterned somewhat after the manner of the great poet and prophet Isaiah.

But the prophet Zechariah went far beyond Isaiah in his use of figures and symbols to present his prophecies. His book definitely belongs to the *apocalyptic* type of literature, such as we found in our study of the books of Ezekiel and Daniel, and as we may see illustrated also in the New Testament by the Apostle John's book of Revelation.

The body of Zechariah's book consists of two series of *Visions*.[2] The Visions recorded in chapters 1 to 8 are concerned primarily with *contemporary events*, especially with the re-building of the Temple. The Visions of the second half of the book deal chiefly with the *Future*, with special emphasis upon the coming of the Messiah and the glory of His reign. According to the author, the two series of Visions were separated roughly by a period of two years.

A *vision* is something *seen*. An apocalyptic vision is a revelation or unveiling of something hitherto unknown. The veil between heaven and earth is lifted, so to speak, and God's prophetic servant is permitted to see what is not commonly seen by ordinary men.

3. THE CONTENTS OF THE BOOK OF ZECHARIAH

The contents of the book of Zechariah, as we have seen, fall naturally into two main divisions. The first deals with events during the time of Zerubbabel, the governor of Judah, and especially with the re-building of the Temple (chapters 1-8). The second section records prophecies dealing with the future of Zion, including her struggles in the Greek wars, but with special emphasis upon the coming of the Messiah and the glory of His reign and kingdom (chapters 9-14).

(1) *The Re-building of the Temple*, Chapters 1-8

1. RETURN TO THE LORD. In his first six verses, the prophet exhorts the returned exiles to live and work for Israel's glorious future, and not to imitate the ways of their disobedient forefathers.

2. THE VISION OF THE HORSES. Zechariah, like Ezekiel, teaches in symbols. The vision here is interpreted to mean that the whole world

---

[2]See G. N. M. Collins, *New Bible Commentary*, pp. 748-763.

is at peace under the influence of the Persian Empire, which was favorably disposed toward the Jews. Hence the time is ready for the re-building of the Temple. G. N. M. Collins of Edinburgh is of the opinion that the rider of the red horse in the vision is clearly more than an angel. "He is the divine Mediator, the Lord Jesus Christ, appearing in the scene as the Protector of His people"[3] (chapter 1:7-17).

3. THE FOUR HORNS AND THE FOUR SMITHS. In these figures (1: 18-21), the Four Horns seem to refer to the nations that had destroyed Israel and Judah — Egypt, Assyria, Babylon, and Medo-Persia. The Four Smiths are God's destroyers of the enemies of Israel and Judah, signifying God's might and will to deal with earthly rulers.

4. THE MEASURING LINE. This vision, like the vision in chapter 37 of the book of Ezekiel, is noted for the grandeur of its poetic picture. Jerusalem, overflowing with population, peace and prosperity, will beckon to the nations of the earth to join her under the protecting care of the Lord. So great will it be that no human measuring line can encompass this "Jerusalem" of the future (chapter 2).

5. THE HIGH PRIEST, SATAN, AND THE REDEEMER. In chapter 3, Zechariah presents a gracious allegory in which is pictured the Atonement of Christ, five hundred years before the event.

> Behold, I will bring my servant the Branch . . . and I will remove
> the guilt of this land in a single day.

The High Priest, in "filthy garments," represents symbolically the sinful people. Satan, whose name is first mentioned here in the Old Testament (but see Job 2), and pictured as trying to induce God to forsake His people because of their sinfulness, is here defeated. Zechariah prophesies the Atonement as God's way.

6. THE GOLDEN CANDLESTICK AND THE TWO OLIVE TREES. The promised prosperity to Jerusalem in the former visions was conditioned upon moral and spiritual reforms of the people. In chapter 4, the prophet stresses this theme again, when for the moment he makes Zerubbabel represent "the line of David," and Joshua the High Priest symbolize the High Priesthood of God's Anointed, the Messiah. The candlestick represents the light-bearing qualities and function of God's house, and the two olive trees are Joshua and Zerubbabel the governor.

7. THE FLYING SCROLL AND THE FLYING EPHAH. These visions represent "iniquity" and "wickedness" in the land, which must be banished if the promised blessings of the other visions are to be realized.

8. THE FOUR WAR CHARIOTS. In chapter 6:1-8, Zechariah presents the four war chariots as the messengers of God, who guard Israel from her enemies. Very likely Zechariah intended this vision to have

---

[3]*The New Bible Commentary*, p. 749 (1954).

a more universal application, and that his four armored messengers were to be champions of righteousness against evil "to the four winds of heaven."

9. THE SYMBOLIC CORONATION. In chapter 6:9-15, Zechariah presents a beautiful symbol of the crowning of Joshua the High Priest. Using the gold and silver recently received from Babylon, the artisans make Joshua a crown which will more fully represent the type of the One to come, who is both Priest and King of His people.

10. FAST DAYS, AND THE FUTURE. Fast days as such have no meaning; the true fast is to abstain from sin and listen to the voice of God. In chapters 7-8, Zechariah stresses the theme that God has come to dwell with His people, the Messianic Age is at hand, and the nations of the earth will join Israel for the era of prosperity and happiness for Jerusalem.

(2) *The Coming of the Messianic Age and Israel's Glorious Future,* Chapters 9-14

The last half of the book of Zechariah contains prophecies dealing primarily with the coming of the Messiah and with Israel's future in the Messianic Age.[4]

1. THE MESSIANIC KING. Chapter 9, like so many chapters in the book of Isaiah, contains two distinct but related kinds of material: that which relates to *contemporary* events and that which deals with the *future*. In the opening passage, the prophet records that judgment is about to fall upon the traditional enemies of Israel — Syria, Tyre and Sidon, Philistia, and others — although a remnant from these pagan nations will acknowledge God and share in the glory of the Messianic Age, in which all the daughters of Zion are called upon to rejoice.

In former times the prophets, *seeing* the future and what was to come, predicted that Assyria, and then Babylon, would be the official punisher of the disobedient and wicked nations. Here Zechariah, looking into the future some two hundred years before his time, seems to hint that the Greek Empire under Alexander the Great and his successors will next be the scourge of these recalcitrant nations.

The main theme of the chapter, however, is the coming of the Messianic King and is presented in verses 9-17. This passage is noted for its beautiful prophetic description of the "triumphant and victorious" entry of the Messiah into Jerusalem (Mark 11:7-10; Matthew 21:1-9):

> Lo, your King comes to you . . .
> humble and riding on an ass,
> on a colt the foal of an ass.

The symbol of the ass was not one of lowliness, but of *peace,* as the horse was a symbol of war.

---

[4]Scholars differ among themselves as to the unity of the book of Zechariah and the authorship of chapters 9-14. For a brief summary of critical opinion, see Young, *An Introduction to the Old Testament,* pp. 294-301 (1958).

2. Israel Restored. In chapter 10, the prophet sees how Jehovah will redeem and restore His scattered people from among the nations. The present is only a token of the exiles who are to return.

3. The Parable of the Shepherds. In chapter 11, the prophet is looking far into the future again. Although Israel is being restored to Jerusalem, Zechariah envisions the time when "false shepherds" will arise among them, to betray and reject the Good Shepherd (12-13). This passage must be connected with the betrayal of Christ by Judas, since it is so quoted in the New Testament (Matthew 26:15; 27:9-10; Mark 14:10-11).

In chapter 10 we see Israel restored and prospering under divine blessing. In chapter 11, however, we see that nation deteriorating and on the brink of spiritual and national ruin, because it has forfeited divine guidance. There is a hint also that the Romans, the counterpart of the "worthless shepherd," will punish Israel for her rejection of the Good Shepherd (verses 15-17).

4. Israel Vindicated at Last. Chapters 9, 10, 11, may be said to deal with the "problems" or struggles connected with Israel's return to Jerusalem, in relation to the nations. Chapters 12, 13, 14, *foresee* the "rewards" of Israel in the world of nations, in the era of the Universal Reign of God.

Chapter 12 specifically deals with the deliverance of Jerusalem from its enemies, who will be severely punished by the Lord because of their ruthless treatment of His people. That is, although Israel was rejected because of her rejection of the Good Shepherd, she was yet to be delivered from her punishers and oppressors. This prophecy takes the reader into the Christian Era, far beyond the Roman Empire.

Chapter 13 presents the purification of Jerusalem. As the reader has already observed, *Jerusalem* in these passages means much more than a Jewish city; but as a symbol it represents God's people in the coming age. The "purification of Jerusalem" is pictured in terms of —

A fountain opened for the house of David and the inhabitants of
Jerusalem to cleanse them from sin and uncleanness . . .

Here the prophet foresees *the atoning death* and the great doctrines of the Gospel.

5. The Universal Reign of God. Zechariah reaches the culmination of his many symbolic prophecies in his last chapter. Like the Apostle John in the book of Revelation, he closes his book with the last battle and victory of the Shepherd-King:

And the Lord will become king
over all the earth;
On that day the Lord will be one,
and His name one.

God's universal, eternal religion shall cover all the earth. All mankind will worship Him.

Selected References
Zechariah
Anderson, Bernhard W.: "A Kingdom of Priests," *Understanding the Old Testament,* pp. 430-463.

*Bright, John: "Holy Commonwealth and Apocalyptic Kingdom," *The Kingdom of God,* pp. 156-186.

*Calkins, Raymond: *The Modern Message of the Minor Prophets.*

*Collins, G. N. M.: "Zechariah," *The New Bible Commentary,* pp. 748-763.

Gailey, James H.: *The Books of Micah, Nahum, Habakkuk, Zephaniah, Haggai, Zechariah, and Malachi.*

Robinson, George L.: *The Prophecies of Zechariah.*

*Smith, George Adam: *The Book of the Twelve Prophets.*

*Young, Edward J.: "Zechariah," *An Introduction to the Old Testament,* pp. 294-301.

Chapter 18

MALACHI

1. AUTHORSHIP, DATE, AND OCCASION OF THE BOOK

The book of Malachi is the last of the books of prophecy on the Return and Restoration of Israel at Jerusalem, and also the last book of Old Testament Scripture. All we know of the prophet Malachi is what we gather from the reading of his book. His name means *My Messenger*. He was sent by the Lord to Israel at a moment of great need.[1]

The reader will recall that one of the first acts of King Cyrus of Persia, after his defeat of Babylon and the conquest of the Babylonian Empire, was to issue an edict (538 B.C.) granting permission to Jewish exiles in Babylon to return to Jerusalem, to re-build their Temple, and to establish their homes in Judah.

There was great enthusiasm on the part of the remnant 50,000 or so who returned. That first year after their arrival, in 536 B.C., they built the foundation of the Temple, and then suddenly stopped their work on the house of the Lord. According to the prophet Haggai, who chides Israel for postponing the Lord's work, it was because the people became more interested in building their own homes, farms, and businesses. Moreover, as time passed their initial enthusiasm waned. For the high hopes of the early days were not fulfilled. They suffered from drought and bad crops and famine, as Haggai in his book tells us. It was not until 520-516 B.C., under the leadership of Haggai and Zechariah, that they had re-built the Temple.

Sixty years later, in 457 B.C., Ezra had come from Babylon to Jerusalem, to help reorganize and to teach the people. Finally, thirteen years still later, in 444 B.C., Nehemiah came to re-build the Wall. Nehemiah found that his pagan neighbors, especially the mongrel race who now called themselves *Samaritans*, plagued him and interfered with the plans for re-building.

---

[1]For the background and message of the book of Malachi, see J.T.H. Adamson of Glasgow, in "Malachi," *The New Bible Commentary*, pp. 764-767 (2nd ed., 1954). Anderson, in "A Kingdom of Priests," *Understanding the Old Testament*, pp. 430-463, has a very good analysis of the background of the books of Haggai and Zechariah, as well as Malachi. However, Anderson's dating of Malachi (as also the prophet Joel) is unusual. (See chapter on Joel in this volume, as well as the present chapter.)

Although we have no way of knowing the exact date of the book of Malachi, scholars are generally agreed that it belongs in the period between 460 and 400 B.C., which would make Malachi a contemporary of Ezra and Nehemiah. Some hold to the earlier date within these limits, and some to the later. In general this date is confirmed by the content of the book, which appears to be directed against the same evils that Ezra and Nehemiah tried to reform.

By the time of Malachi, about one hundred years after the first arrival of exiles under Zerubbabel, the people and their leaders had not only lost much of their initial enthusiasm for re-building Jerusalem and Judah, but also they had become lukewarm in their faith. They began to question the love of God and the justice of His rule. They saw evil-doers prospering in the sight of the Lord. So there seemed to be no profit in trying to keep His commandments. Even the priests were lax in the performance of their duties, and permitted the people to corrupt the Lord's worship.

A custom and tradition of great sanctity regarding marriage was often violated. Jewish men divorced the wives of their youth in order to marry foreign and pagan wives; and even officials of high rank were equally guilty of this practice along with the common people. It was at such a time as this that the prophet Malachi, God's Messenger, was sent to Israel with a bold message.

This background picture is also revealed in the two historical books, Ezra and Nehemiah, which should be read with Malachi.

2. The Contents and Message of the Book of Malachi

The contents of the book of Malachi may be grouped conveniently into four divisions corresponding to its four short chapters:

(1) The Lord's Love for Israel Has Not Been Returned. The Lord still loves Israel; but this love is not returned by Israel, for he neither honors nor reverences the Lord in his worship and social conduct. But, by contrast, the name of the Lord is great among the Gentile nations (chapter 1).

(2) The Degeneracy of the Priesthood. The priests, the descendants of Levi, have become degenerate and no longer represent the true covenant "of life and peace," and no longer give "true instruction" to the people as was originally ordained for the Levitical priesthood.

Priests and people alike have forgotten the fatherhood of God:

> Have we not all one father?
> Has not one God created us?
> Why then are we faithless to one another,
> profaning the covenant of our fathers?

(3) The Lord's Swift Punishment of the Guilty. The Lord will bring swift punishment against all evil-doers: first against the sons of Levi, the priests; against the sorcerers; against the adulterers;

against those who swear falsely; against those who oppress the hireling in his wages, the widow and the orphan; against those who rob God by withholding tithes; and, finally, against those who divorce the wives of their youth to marry pagan women, non-Jews.

The Lord has not changed, neither have His standards of conduct for His people. This section closes with the beautiful passage (3:16) in which the prophet pictures the faithful few, in an age of disloyalty and disaffection, encouraging one another, and the Lord recording their names in a "book of remembrance."

(4) THE NEW ELIJAH. The prophet Malachi, like Isaiah and Zechariah and many of the other prophets, produced a Messianic prophecy in the ordinary meaning of the word. Being a true prophet, Malachi condemned the people's sins and boldly summoned them to repentance, in a style that is both simple and direct. He exhorted them to remember the Law of Moses and to come back to the national and personal God of their salvation.

In his last two chapters Malachi is forward-looking in his references to Elijah, who in his day was already being regarded as a type of prophet that would come, and who would herald the coming of the greater One. John the Baptist, as we know, was such an Elijah and prophet. Our Lord quotes from Malachi (Matthew 11:10, 14) and identifies Elijah with John the Baptist. Also, the writer of the book of Matthew quotes our Lord, and identifies this *new* Elijah with John the Baptist. (Jesus quotes Malachi 3:1; see also Malachi 4:5). The full significance of chapters 3 and 4 is frequently overlooked.

Thus, as the curtain falls on the Old Testament, the last prophet before John the Baptist indicates the part both the Law and the Prophets played in preparing the way for the coming of the Lord. (See also Luke 24:44; Mark 9:4). Luke, in the passage 1:67-69, makes the connection between the Old Testament and the New, in which he describes the coming of the Saviour and the role John the Baptist played as the herald and forerunner.

SELECTED REFERENCES

MALACHI

*Adamson, J. T. H.: "Malachi," *The New Bible Commentary*, pp. 764-767.

Anderson, Bernhard W.: "A Kingdom of Priests," *Understanding the Old Testament*, pp. 430-463.

*Bright, John: *The Kingdom of God*, pp. 156-186.

Calkins, Raymond: *The Modern Message of the Minor Prophets*.

*Gailey, James H.: *The Books of Micah, Nahum, Habakkuk, Zephaniah, Haggai, Zechariah, and Malachi*.

*Smith, George Adam: *The Book of the Twelve Prophets*.

*Young, Edward J.: *An Introduction to the Old Testament*, pp. 301-303.

PART SIX

THE FOUR GOSPELS

GREAT

SEA

PHOENICIA

Berytus
Lycus River

Sidon

Sarepta

Tyre
Kanah

Tyrian
Ladder
Achzib
(Ekdippa)
Acco
(Ptolemais)

Sykaminos

Dora

Caesarea

Apollonia

Joppa

Jamnia
Ekron
Azotus
Ascalon

Anthedon
(Agrippias)
Gaza

Raphia

Beersheba

Elusa

Nessana
('Auja el Hafir)

Kurnub

LEBANON MTS.
River Litani

ANTI-LEBANON MTS.

ABILENE

ITURAEA

Abila
Damascus

Kokaba

Caesarea Philippi

MT. HERMON

AURANITIS

TRACHONITIS

LEJA

BATANAEA

GAULANITIS

Raphana

Kanatha
ASALMANUS MTS.

JEBEL
HAURAN

Bozrah

Salecah
(Salkhad)

Gerasa

A R A B I A

Rabbath Ammon
(Philadelphia)

MOABITIS

NABATAEANS

SAMARIA

DECAPOLIS

PEREA

JUDAEA

IDUMAEA

Jerusalem

Bethlehem

Hebron

Jericho

Dead
Sea

PALESTINE
IN THE TIME OF JESUS
(28 A.D.)

Abilene
(Lysanias)

Samaria
(Roman Procurator)

Judaea
(Roman Procurator)

Galilee Peraea
(Herod Antipas)

Livia

Decapolis

Phoenicia
(Syria)

Gaulanitis
(Philip)

Roads

Indefinite   Kokab   Arabic names
Boundaries   underlined

Scale   0   10   20   30 Miles

Copyright by Rand McNally & Company

THE FOUR GOSPELS

Chapter 1

INTRODUCTION

The prophets of the Old Testament from the beginning had predicted the coming of the Messiah. He was to be an Ideal King. He would establish an earthly kingdom, deliver His people from all their enemies, and build for them a glorious future.

But when the Messiah came, He was greater than their understanding of what the prophets had prophesied. He was none other than the Son of God. And the government He came to establish was a spiritual, not an earthly kingdom.

The writer of the book of Hebrews, which was written some years after the Crucifixion and the Resurrection, links up the message of the Old Testament with the message of the New, with these opening words of his book:

> In many and various ways God spoke of old to our fathers by the prophets; but in these last days he has spoken to us by a Son, whom he appointed the heir of all things, through whom also he created the world. He reflects the glory of God and bears the very stamp of his nature, upholding the universe by his word of power.

What was this Gospel? The English word, *gospel,* is derived from the Old English *gōdspel,* from *gōd* good, plus *spell* tidings, or good tidings, and means the good tidings of salvation as preached by our Lord, and by the Apostles and other Christian followers.

Indeed, this Gospel is the Son of God Himself, as stated clearly by the Apostle Paul in the opening verses of his letter to the Romans, thus:

> From Paul, servant of Christ Jesus, apostle by God's call, set apart for the service of the Gospel.
> This gospel God announced beforehand in sacred Scriptures through his prophets. It is about His Son: on the human level he was born of David's stock, but on the level of the spirit — the Holy Spirit — he was declared Son of God by a mighty act in that he rose from the dead: it is about Jesus Christ our Lord.
> *(The New English Bible.)*

Early in the second century A.D., apparently, the word Gospel came to mean also a written biography of Christ, one of the Four Gospels, which by this time were already accepted by the Church as inspired and authoritative documents, and as containing the apostolic testimony to the life and teaching of our Lord.

One thing the reader will do well to keep in mind is that, although the four writers are writing the same biography and inspired message, each is writing as an individual, each differing in background and experience, and with somewhat different viewpoints and audiences in mind. "Each of our Gospels," says Professor F. F. Bruce of the University of Manchester, "is an individual work of literature, with an ethos and genius all its own."[1]

The author of the gospel of Matthew, for instance, was a Jew and a tax-gatherer by profession, and was writing primarily for Jews. He was aware that Jewish civilization and thinking was built largely around the Old Testament Scriptures; and so as a writer he appeals to Jews and quotes widely from their Scriptures.

John Mark, although a Jew, was in Rome at the time of the writing of his famous book, and associated with the Apostle Peter and Peter's preaching. When he wrote therefore he had in mind the Gentiles, principally Greeks and Romans, and the main outline of Jesus' life and ministry as the Apostle Peter developed it in his many sermons. Some are of the opinion also that Mark's emphasis on what Jesus *did*, rather than on what He *said*, may well have been influenced by Roman interest in Imperial power and authority, and so in his story of Jesus, Mark stressed the miracles and Jesus' super-human power, rather than the great sermons and parables.

Luke probably was a Greek by birth, and a physician by profession, and the only non-Jewish author in the New Testament. His gospel, beginning with a classical introduction after the manner of Greek and Latin writers, proceeds in an orderly manner, with wonderful detail and completeness, longer than any of the others, and containing many parables and other materials not found in any of the other Gospels.

Moreover, it is clear that Luke is writing for Gentiles, and especially for Greeks, who loved order and proportion, truth and goodness and beauty, as represented in their literature, science, and philosophy. In what has been described as "the most beautiful book ever written," Luke presents the biography of Jesus the Saviour as the Great Humanitarian, the Perfect, the Universal Man.

The Apostle John was a close relative of Jesus, being the son of Salome, the sister of Mary. John was a fisherman by trade. He was "the disciple whom Jesus loved" most of all, probably because he understood Jesus and His message better than any of the others.

Years after the other gospels were written, and at a time when there was growing skepticism and heresy in certain parts regarding the Divinity of Jesus, John wrote his book to testify as an eye-witness

---

[1]"The Fourfold Gospel," *The New Bible Commentary*, Rev. Ed., 1954, p. 62.

to the fact that Jesus was God, and that He "became flesh and dwelt among us."

According to historians, there were some twenty-odd other biographies written on the life of Jesus; but only these four have been preserved and handed down to us. Each is different from the others, as we have noted, and each is a marvelous masterpiece in its own way and in its own right.

Suggestions for Additional Reading

I. Books on the New Testament As a Whole[2]

*Bright, John: "The Kingdom at Hand," *The Kingdom of God,* Chapters 7-9.

*Bruce, F. F.: *The Spreading Flame — The Rise and Progress of Christianity.*

Buttrick, G. A. and Others, General Editors: *The Interpreter's Bible.* The New Testament, Vol. VII, pp. 1-227.

*Davidson, Francis, A. M. Stibbs, and E. F. Kevan, Editors: *The New Bible Commentary,* Part Three, The New Testament, pp. 769-1199.

Filson, Floyd V.: *Opening the New Testament.*

Goodspeed, Edgar J.: *An Introduction to the New Testament.*

*Hunter, Archibald M.: *Introducing the New Testament.*

*Kee, Howard Clark and Franklin W. Young: *Understanding the New Testament.*

Levison, Nahum: *The Jewish Background of Christianity.*

McNeile, A. H.: *An Introduction to the Study of the New Testament.*

Moffatt, James: *An Introduction to the Literature of the New Testament.*

Orr, James, and Others: *The International Standard Bible Encyclopedia.* 5 Vols.

Richardson, Alan: *An Introduction to the Theology of the New Testament.*

*Tenney, Merrill C.: *The New Testament, an Historical and Analytic Survey.*

* * *

II. Books on the Four Gospels

Bible Readings: The Gospels of Matthew, Mark, Luke, and John. The Text: *The Revised Standard Version;* or *The New English Bible;* or *The King James Version,* preferably in modern reader's format.

---

[2]The student should also be familiar with the important tools of efficient study, such as Bible dictionaries and encyclopedias, atlases, concordances, Bible handbooks, the standard English versions of the Bible, and the outstanding commentaries in sets. These and other useful books are listed in the General Bibliography at the end of the book. Finally, the student must not overlook the fact that his main task as a student is to read and master the *content* of the Bible itself, and that all his other reading is contributary to this end.

Bowman, John Wick: *The Intention of Jesus.*

*Bruce, F. F.: "The Fourfold Gospel," *The New Bible Commentary,* pp. 58-63.

Burton, E. D. and W. A. Stevens: *A Harmony of the Gospels for Historical Study.* Third Edition, Revised.

Guignebert, C.: *The Jewish World in the Time of Jesus.*

*Hunter, A. M.: *The Work and Words of Jesus.*

*Kee, Howard Clark and Franklin W. Young: *Understanding the New Testament,* Chapters 1-5, pp. 1-175.

*Kraeling, Carl H.: *John the Baptist.*

Love, Julian Price: *The Gospel and the Gospels.*

Manson, T. W.: *The Teaching of Jesus.*

*Scroggie, W. Graham: *A Guide to the Gospels.*

Stewart, James S.: *The Life and Teaching of Jesus Christ.*

Streeter, B. H.: *The Four Gospels.*

Taylor, Vincent: *The Life and Ministry of Jesus.*

*Tenney, Merrill C.: *The New Testament, an Historical and Analytic Survey,* Chapters 1-12, pp. 21-237.

Wieand, Albert Cassell: *A New Harmony of the Gospels.* Text: *The Revised Standard Version.*

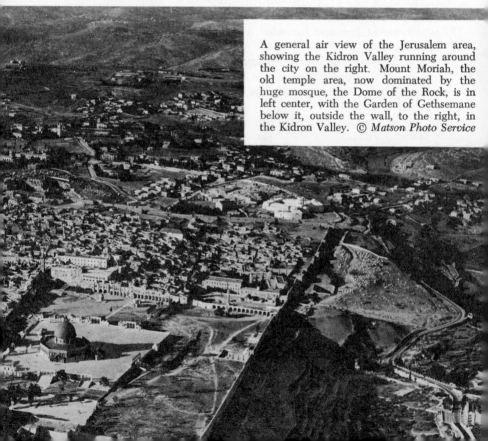

A general air view of the Jerusalem area, showing the Kidron Valley running around the city on the right. Mount Moriah, the old temple area, now dominated by the huge mosque, the Dome of the Rock, is in left center, with the Garden of Gethsemane below it, outside the wall, to the right, in the Kidron Valley. © *Matson Photo Service*

Chapter 2

THE GOSPEL OF MATTHEW

1. THE APOSTLE MATTHEW AND THE FIRST GOSPEL

(1) BIOGRAPHY. The Apostle Matthew was a Jew, and before his call to become an apostle he was a tax-gatherer by profession. More specifically, he was a customs house officer, whose business it was to collect the tolls levied on the merchandise that passed through the two districts of Herod Antipas, Galilee and Perea.

He was called a *publican* because his office related to the public revenues. A publican usually was a social outcast and classified with "sinners" and other irreligious persons, because of the flagrant abuses connected with the tax-collecting job. A publican was scorned also because he was in the employ of the hated Romans and their princes, the Herods, who were Idumaeans (Edom) and not Romans, but who were no better than the Romans in the eyes of the Jews. Matthew performed his task directly under Herod Antipas.

Matthew's office and headquarters were at Capernaum on the Sea of Galilee, on the important caravan route from Egypt and leading to Damascus and the Mesopotamian Valley to the north. Capernaum, moreover, was the station for a detachment of the Roman army.

Capernaum was the home also of others who were to become famous. Zebedee and his two famous sons, James and John, were fishermen there. Andrew and his brother Simon, whom Jesus nick-named "Peter," moved from their native place at nearby Bethsaida and formed a fishing partnership with the sons of Zebedee. Jesus, during the two years of His ministry in Galilee, made His home also at Capernaum.

One day Jesus came by where Matthew sat at the tax office and said to him, "Follow me." It required courage of Jesus to choose as one of His inner circle of disciples a despised publican. Why did He? And it also cost Matthew a pretty penny "to forsake all," and to give up this handsome job with Herod, and come and follow Jesus.

Before the call came, Matthew was probably already a follower of John the Baptist, as was true of some of the other Apostles. But with the call, Matthew felt complimented and grateful and wished to give a feast to celebrate the occasion. His original name was Levi; now it would be Matthew, the name by which he was hereafter to be known in Christian circles.

Jesus was the chief guest at the feast, to which Matthew had also invited many of his fellow tax collectors, publicans and "sinners" all. They all sat down with Jesus and His disciples. This was a memorable beginning for Matthew, and the most important event in his whole life. But because He thus ate with tax collectors and sinners, Jesus was severely criticized by the Pharisees.

Not much is known of the life of the Apostle Matthew after the close of Jesus' ministry on earth. According to the oldest tradition, he preached some fifteen years in Palestine and then visited Ethiopia, Persia, Media, and Parthia. Tradition states also that he wrote his gospel originally in Hebrew for Hebrews, meaning doubtless Aramaic, the spoken language of his day.

(2) THE COMPOSITION OF THE GOSPEL OF MATTHEW. Every author has his characteristic way of presenting his ideas and materials in finished form. One of the features of the gospel of Matthew is the marvelous manner in which the author organizes and arranges his material, which is according to subject matter or large topics, and not chronologically as Luke, for example, arranged his book.

In this way, ideas and materials of the same or similar kind are collected and presented for their accumulative effect upon the reader. Here, for example, are some of the more impressive collected materials and "sermons" in the book:

1. The sermon on the Mount, chapters 5 to 7. This is the most striking and comprehensive statement of Christian ethics ever made.

2. The Great Group of Miracles, chapters 8 to 9. These Miracles immediately follow the Sermon and are intended to illustrate and reinforce its teachings.

3. Instructions to the Twelve Apostles on How to Preach the Gospel, chapter 10. This group of Instructions apparently includes sayings delivered on different occasions.

4. The Group of Unforgettable Parables on the Growth of the Kingdom, chapter 13.

5. The Sermon on Humility and Forgiveness, chapter 18.

6. Jesus' Historical Denunciation of the Hypocrisies of the Scribes and Pharisees and the Sevenfold Woes pronounced upon them, and the Jerusalem they had built, chapter 23.

7. Sayings and Parables in which Jesus foretells the Destruction of Jerusalem and the End of the World, chapters 24 and 25.

The second of the main features of the composition of the book of Matthew is found in the abundance and the length of the *direct quotations* from the Discourses of Jesus.

"The great glory of this gospel," says Professor J. R. Dummelow of Cambridge University, "is the discourses. These are from the pen of the Apostle Matthew himself, who evidently had a special gift of remembering and recording accurately the very words of the Master."[1]

---

[1] J. R. Dummelow, Editor, *A Commentary on the Holy Bible,* p. 620 (1936).

One way of appreciating this excellence of Matthew's reporting is to compare his version of the Sermon on the Mount, with that in Luke's Gospel (Luke's biography in many other respects is more complete than Matthew's). Wherever there is a difference in the versions, Matthew's in almost every instance is more complete than Luke's. For example, compare the two versions of the Lord's Prayer, or the Beatitudes. Also, the whole Sermon on the Mount is greatly abridged in Luke.

This is another way of saying that the excellence of the phraseology and form of the Sermon, the story telling of the Miracles, the Parables, and the other narrative materials, is due to what Professor Dummelow calls "the unapproachable majesty and splendor of Christ's utterances." These apparently Matthew recorded more fully than did any of the other writers.

(3) WRITTEN PRIMARILY FOR JEWISH READERS. The gospel of Matthew appears to have been written primarily for Jewish readers, although not exclusively so, and reflects the view and tone of the early Church in Jerusalem, before it was fully realized that the ceremonial Law in large part had been abolished in favor of the New Gospel. It was very popular and must have had wide circulation among the Jews in Palestine, Antioch, and in other Jewish centers.

Although Matthew's sympathies are predominantly Jewish-Christian, he is a perfectly true witness in that he never attempts to suppress facts or sayings which may be in praise of Gentiles, or a broader view than that of his own race.

This is indicated in his inclusion of the stories of the non-Jewish Wise Men and first worshipers of the infant Jesus, the story of the worthy Roman Centurion, and other similar incidents.

His major concern is how the Old Testament prophecies are brought to fulfillment in Christ, who said openly again and again that He had not come to *destroy* but to *fulfill* the Law.

Also, as a writer of a gospel, Matthew was well aware that Jewish culture and faith were built largely around the Hebrew Scriptures. And so it was natural for him to quote from the Scriptures freely, and for his book to contain almost a hundred direct or indirect quotations from the Old Testament. In fact, his book contains about as many quotations as all the other gospel writers put together.

But when this is said, we must also say, that in no other gospel, not even in Luke's, which is also one of the world's great favorites, are the "unapproachable majesty and splendor of Christ's utterances" so apparent and so attractively presented, for readers of all time as well as for the author's immediate audience of Jewish readers.

2. AUTHORSHIP AND DATE

Although the gospel of Matthew, in common with the other three gospels, is anonymous, the name of the Apostle Matthew has been traditionally connected with it since at least the second century A.D.

In his church history, *Historia Ecclesiastica,* Bishop Eusebius (264-340 A.D.) quotes from Papias, a second century bishop and a disciple of the Apostle John; from Irenaeus, the second century bishop of Lyons; and from Origen, the great Christian scholar of the third century — all testifying to the fact that the first gospel was written by Matthew for Hebrew Christians in Hebrew.[2] Also, Eusebius, the author, adds his own testimony to the same effect.

However, as strong as this testimony appears to be, no trace of this so-called first edition of Matthew's work has survived. Moreover, the earliest quotations from the first gospel are in Greek, and according to Basil Atkinson of the Cambridge University Library Staff, "No scholar today doubts that the Gospel in Greek in its present form was in existence in the second half of the first century."[3]

There has never been any good reason for doubting Matthew's authorship of the gospel that bears his name. In the words of Dean Merrill C. Tenney, "As a publican he must have been literate and accustomed to taking notes as a part of his business activity."[4] William Barclay, another New Testament authority, takes the same view. "But there was one gift which Matthew would possess," says Dr. Barclay. "Most of the disciples were fishermen. They would have little skill and little practice in putting words together on paper; but Matthew would be an expert at that. When Jesus called Matthew, as he sat at the receipt of custom, Matthew rose up and followed Him and left everything behind him except one thing — his pen. And Matthew nobly used his literary skill to become the first man ever to compile an account of the teaching of Jesus."[5]

It is easy to see that the gospel of Matthew is one, unified composition, the work of a single writer. It is a marvelous welding together of many elements, as we have noted elsewhere, chief of which is the longer discourses such as the Sermon on the Mount. In this book, the writer shows himself to be a most extraordinary personality, both devout and competent as a writer, and one who wrote under unmistakable Divine guidance. The book has always been a great favorite with readers.

The outside date for the writing of the gospel of Matthew can be safely placed at about 70 A.D., when the commanding Roman general Titus (later Emperor) destroyed Jerusalem. The author's quotation of Jesus' remarks regarding the destruction of the city indicates that this event had not taken place when the book was completed.

Most conservative scholars place the date of Matthew's gospel not too long before the death of the Apostle Peter and the Apostle Paul at Rome, which is thought to be about 67 or 68 A.D. Luke's gos-

---

[2]Basil F. C. Atkinson, *The New Bible Commentary,* p. 771 (1954).
[3]*Op cit.,* 771.
[4]*New Testament Survey,* Rev. Ed., 1961.
[5]*The Gospel of Matthew,* Vol. 1, Sec. Ed., 1958, pp. xxi-xxii.

pel appeared about 60 or 61 A.D. Since both Matthew and Luke borrowed from Mark's gospel, Mark's work was written still earlier, probably between 50 and 60 A.D.

3. THE CONTENTS OF THE BOOK OF MATTHEW
THE ANALYSIS

Here is a brief analysis of the book for readers who prefer an outline:

1. The genealogy of the Messiah; birth; the worship by the Wise Men; Herod and the flight to Egypt during infancy; return to Nazareth. Chapters 1 and 2.

Note that, although Matthew traces the genealogy of Jesus to Abraham, he stresses the royal descent from David; whereas Luke takes the family line of Jesus all the way back to Adam and to God.

2. Introduction to the public ministry of Jesus, including the preparatory work of John the Baptist, the Baptism and Temptation, and adoption of Capernaum on the Sea of Galilee as headquarters during the two years of the Galilean ministry, which was according to Isaiah's prophecy (Isaiah 9:1). Chapters 3 to 4:16.

3. The Galilean ministry of Jesus, covering approximately two years; the calling of the Twelve Apostles; the Sermon on the Mount, which includes the Beatitudes, the Lord's Prayer, and the Golden Rule; the Great Group of Miracles. Chapters 4:17 to 9:34.

4. The Mission of the Twelve Apostles, and instructions on how to preach. This Mission began with a short sermon, stressing the great need for laborers in the Kingdom, the Master's compassion for a shepherdless people, and how the Apostles were to meet that need. Chapters 9:35 to 10.

Note that Matthew in his narrative presents the Twelve, a Jewish number, and with these instructions: "Go nowhere among the Gentiles, and enter no town of the Samaritans, but go rather to the lost sheep of the house of Israel." Luke, on the contrary, introduces the Seventy, a Gentile number, and with these instructions, with no restrictions as to Jew or Gentile: "Go your way . . . He who hears you hears me, and he who rejects you rejects me, and he who rejects me rejects him who sent me."

5. The Growing Opposition to our Lord's Public Ministry; the months of misunderstanding, conflict, and disappointment in Galilee. Chapters 11-18.

In those cities in which Jesus did most of His mighty works, the people did not repent. The Scribes and Pharisees,·who from the beginning had sought in every way to trip Him, now were openly plotting how to destroy Him. Companies of Scribes and Pharisees from Jerusalem came down to Galilee to join His enemies there. These Jesus rebuked, calling them "blind guides" and "hypocrites"!

Jesus' mother and brothers, not understanding His work and mission, or why He remained away from home, visited Him while He was preaching and healing on the shores of the Sea of Galilee, to urge Him to come with them. But because of the crowds, apparently they returned without seeing Him (12:46-50). Later, on His second visit to His home town of Nazareth, He was rejected by the people and the rulers of the synagogue, and again misunderstood by His own family (13:53-58).

Even John the Baptist sent a committee to interview Jesus, and to inquire if he were the One, or should they look for Another? And at times the slowness of His disciples to comprehend His mission disappointed Jesus. But apparently Jesus was never really discouraged. For He filled His days performing miracles, teaching by parables, feeding thousands, and showing such love and compassion for the multitudes, that He lived more by a sense of mission and eternity than by any feeling of temporary defeat.

During this period Jesus delivered His great sermon and Parables on the Growth of the Kingdom (chapter 13); the sermon on Humility and Forgiveness (chapter 18); and as a climax to the Galilean Ministry, the Transfiguration, which apparently took place on Mount Hermon on the occasion of the visit to Caesarea Philippi, and marked the departure from Galilee.

6. Jesus ends the Galilean Ministry, leaves Capernaum, and begins what is known as the Perean Ministry. Chapters 19 and 20.

The time seems to have been in the summer or early autumn of 29 A.D., or some six months before the trial and Crucifixion. The Perean ministry took place in the territory of Perea "beyond" or east of the Jordan, a district extending from the Sea of Galilee on the north to the Dead Sea on the south. It included also some visits to Jerusalem, one on the occasion of the Feast of the Tabernacles (September), another to the Feast of Dedication (December), and the Mission of the Seventy, which apparently was in Judea rather than in Perea, and is told only by Luke.

The reader will observe that the great events of this period are told very briefly by Matthew and Mark, somewhat more fully by John, but at length by Luke, in chapters 9:51 to 19:28 of his book.

7. The Last Week of Christ's Ministry. Chapters 21 to 28. The main events of the Last Week as related by Matthew:

The Triumphal Entry into Jerusalem; the cleansing of the Temple; the deputation of Pharisees and Sadducees from the Sanhedrin; woes pronounced upon the Scribes and Pharisees; our Lord foretells the destruction of Jerusalem and the End of the World; a group of parables to illustrate His teachings; the Last Supper; the scene in Gethsemane; the arrest and trial of Jesus; the Crucifixion and burial;

the Resurrection and meetings with His disciples, and final commission to go and make disciples of all nations.

The reader will note also that almost half of the gospel of John is devoted to the events of the Last Week.

4. Passages Found Only in Matthew

(1) The following ten parables are found only in Matthew's gospel: The Parable of the Tares (13:24-30); the Hidden Treasure (13:44); the Pearl Merchant (13:45-46); the Net (13:47-51); the Laborers in the Vineyard (20:1-16); the Two Sons (21:28-32); the Wedding Garment (22:1-14); the Ten Virgins (25:1-13); the Talents (25:14-30); the Sheep and the Goats (25:31-46).

(2) Other information found only in the book of Matthew: The genealogy of Jesus (1:1; 17); the Nativity (1:18-25); worship by the Wise Men from the East, and Herod's massacre of children (2:1-18); the flight to Egypt (2:19-23); much of the Sermon on the Mount, including the longer versions of the Beatitudes and the Lord's Prayer (5, 6, 7); part of the charge to the Twelve (10); Peter walks on the water (14:28-33).

(3) Certain well known expressions: "The Kingdom of Heaven" appears 32 times, in place of the Kingdom of God; "That it might be fulfilled which was spoken by the prophet . . ." appears many times and in nearly every part of the Gospel; and "I was sent only to the lost sheep of the house of Israel" (15:22-28).

(4) Incidents during the Last Week: Astonishment of Jerusalem at the Triumphal Entry (21:10-11); woes pronounced on the Scribes and the Pharisees (23); suicide and burial of Judas (27:5-10); Pilate's wife (27:19); Pilate washes his hands (27:24-25); earthquake, opening of tombs, and resurrection of saints (27:51-33); the tomb sealed and a watch set (27:62-66); a great earthquake; an angel "like lightning, and his raiment white as snow," rolls away the stone, and terrifies the guard (28:2-4); Jesus meets the women as they go to deliver the angel's message to the disciples (28:9); bribery of the guards (28:11-15); appearance of Jesus on a mountain in Galilee (28:16-20).

Suggestions for Additional Reading on the Gospel of Matthew

*Atkinson, Basil F. C.: "The Gospel According to Matthew," *The New Bible Commentary*, pp. 771-805.
*Barclay, William: *The Gospel of Matthew*. Second Ed., 2 Vols.
Broadus, John A.: *Commentary on the Gospel of Matthew*.
Dietrich, Suzanne de: *The Gospel According to Matthew*.
Green, F. W.: *The Gospel According to St. Matthew*.
Johnson, Sherman E.: "The Gospel According to Matthew," *The Interpreter's Bible*, Vol. VII, pp. 229-250.

Lange, John Peter: *The Gospel According to Matthew*. Tr. from the Third German Edition by Philip Schaff. Sixth Edition.

McNeile, A. H.: *The Gospel According to St. Matthew*.

Robertson, A. T.: *The Gospel According to Matthew*.

*Stonehouse, Ned B.: *Commentary on Matthew*.

*Tenney, Merrill C.: *The New Testament — A Survey*, Chapters 6-7, pp. 147-161.

Matthew was a tax collector at Capernaum. Drawing by Wilbur G. Adam from *Life and Customs in Jesus' Time*, by Joseph L. Gift. © 1957 Standard Publishing Foundation, Cincinnati, Ohio.

Chapter 3

THE GOSPEL OF MARK

1. MARK AND HIS GOSPEL

Of the Four Gospels, it is now universally agreed that the book of Mark was the first to be written, in the form in which we now have the four biographies of Jesus. For both Matthew and Luke borrowed substantially from Mark's gospel in the composition of their books, and John wrote his gospel some twenty to thirty years after Luke and Matthew wrote theirs.

(1) *The Biography of Mark*

John Mark was the son of Mary, known as "Mary of Jerusalem," to distinguish her from the other four Marys. His surname was *Mark*, and according to Luke his full name was "John Mark" (Acts 12:12; 15:27). Both Paul and Peter referred to him by his Latin or Roman name *Marcus* (Colossians 4:10; Philemon 24; I Peter 5:13).

Mark's mother was evidently in comfortable circumstances, occupying her own house and employing one or more servants or slaves. Chiefly, she used her place as a church or one of the principal meeting places of the early Jerusalem Christians (Acts 12:12-17). There is a likely possibility too that the Last Supper was held in the Upper Room of her house.

The young man referred to in Mark's gospel (14:51), and not found in any of the other Gospels, is generally thought to be Mark himself. If so, the story suggests that he was only a youth at the time of Jesus' arrest and trial. However, since his mother was a devout follower herself, and her house formed an important Christian center, young Mark would be acquainted with the leading disciples, and perhaps Jesus Himself. So, on hearing the shouts from the crowd, he was aroused at midnight and got up hastily, in his night clothes, and ran out to learn the fate of the One in whom the family was interested.

No one knows when John Mark became a disciple. Peter, Paul, and Barnabas were friends of the family, as doubtless were many others. It is likely that the Apostle Peter lodged at Mary's house, and there is an early tradition that Mark was a convert of Peter's. At any rate, Peter afterwards spoke of him as "Mark my son," meaning as many think that he was Peter's convert (I Peter 5:13).

Mark as a young man soon joined the group of apostles and

evangelists, who went out from the mother church at Jerusalem, to the churches in Judea and Samaria, to Antioch in Syria, and eventually westward to Ephesus in Asia Minor, and to Rome.

We first see Mark, about 44 A.D., in the company of his cousin, Barnabas, and Saul, who had been sent by the church at Antioch with contributions for their brethren at Jerusalem, to relieve their suffering from famine. After fulfilling their mission to Jerusalem, Barnabas and Saul returned to Antioch, bringing with them John Mark.

These evangelists continued their preaching for some months at Antioch, and with great success, until one day the Spirit prompted them to begin immediately the missionary work for which they had been specially called. So, after ceremonies appropriate to the occasion, the two greatest leaders of the Antioch Church, Barnabas and Saul, began their First Missionary Journey westward, taking with them as their assistant and "minister" John Mark, about 45 A.D.

They sailed for the island of Cyprus, and from there to the mainland of Asia Minor, in the districts of Pamphylia and Galatia. But at the town of Perga, Mark became dissatisfied, withdrew from the mission, and returned to Jerusalem.

Mark's reason for quitting the party could have been a matter of doctrine, or something more personal. Some scholars feel that Mark, like his cousin Barnabas, belonged to the more conservative party of Christian-Jews, and disliked Paul's treatment of uncircumcised Gentiles as the equals of circumcised Jews. Others feel that Mark's dissatisfaction was more personal, that he resented the growing leadership of Paul over his cousin Barnabas, who about this time began to be known by his Roman name, *Paul,* instead of the Hebrew name *Saul.*

Whatever the reason for Mark's conduct, Paul disapproved it; and a few years later, about 50 A.D., when the time came to begin the Second Missionary Journey, Paul opposed Barnabas' suggestion that they take Mark with them. After some heated words between Paul and Barnabas, the latter disassociated himself from Paul and returned to the island of Cyprus, with John Mark as his companion. Paul chose another companion, a distinguished member of the Apostolic Church at Jerusalem by the name of Silas, who labored with Paul throughout the Second journey, and later.

The island of Cyprus was the birthplace of Barnabas and it appears that he and Mark continued their missionary work here for some time. At any rate, at this point Mark disappears from the history for the next twelve years or so. We hear of him again in two letters by Paul, and affectionately, showing that whatever differences there had been between Mark and the Apostle Paul, now they were forgiven and forgotten (Colossians 4:10; Philemon 24).

In his letter to Philemon, written from his prison at Rome about 61 A.D., Paul refers to Mark as his companion and fellow-laborer. In some of the later letters we learn that Mark is not with him but is in the East, possibly engaged in evangelistic work in Asia Minor or farther East. In the other references Mark is in Rome. Indeed, there can be little doubt that Mark was in Rome, and with both Paul and Peter.

But the tradition of the early Church at Rome associates Mark with the Apostle Peter and his preaching in Rome, rather than with Paul. In I Peter, Peter confirms this relationship (5:13). And according to an unnamed "presbyter" who lived in the Apostolic Age, Mark became the "interpreter" of the Apostle Peter.[1] Some think that this came after the release of the Apostle Paul from his first imprisonment, about 63 A.D.

It is generally believed that the Apostle Peter was not a good Greek or Latin scholar, and that preaching in his native Aramaic, the vernacular or speech-language of the Jews of Palestine, he required the services of an interpreter to translate his sermons, sentence by sentence, into the language of his Greek-speaking and Latin-speaking Gentile audience. Mark is supposed to have performed this service for Peter.

After the martyrdom of the Apostle Peter, around 67 A.D., little is known of the life of Mark. There was a tradition in the early Church that Mark became the founder and first bishop of the important church in Alexandria, Egypt, the second largest city in the world of his day.

The main thing for the reader to remember is that Mark, although not himself an eye-witness, both in his early life at Jerusalem, and in his later association and companionship with the chief of the Apostles, was fitted to become the author of an authentic gospel.

(2) The Purpose of Mark's Gospel

According to the best authorities, Mark wrote his gospel while at Rome, and primarily for Gentile readers in Rome and the Roman Empire.

According to the testimony of both the Apostle Paul and the Apostle Peter, Mark was the companion and fellow-laborer of both, and evidently had spent some years at Rome. And Papias, a disciple of the Apostle John, quotes an apostolic presbyter as saying that Mark was Peter's interpreter, an opinion which others shared.

The Apostle Paul came to Rome as a Roman prisoner about A.D. 61; the Apostle Peter probably came some years earlier. So it was at this time, and in the environment of Rome, that Mark wrote his gospel.

Everywhere Mark gives his reader the impression of a *native* writing for *foreigners*, and he has to explain how John the Baptist was dressed (1:6); the meaning of the word *Bo-anerges* which Jesus used to describe the brothers James and John (3:17); and the Aramaic

---

[1]See Merrill C. Tenney, *The New Testament*, pp. 166-169.

words *Talitha cumi,* used by Jesus and quoted in his sermon by Peter (5:41). The reader has met with other explanations of Palestinian places and Jewish customs and terms in such other passages as Mark 7:3, 4, 11, 34; 12:42; 14:12; 15:22, 42, and others.

There must have been considerable pressure from the Gentile Christians of Rome to have in writing the gospel story and message which the Apostle Peter and the other apostles preached. Indeed, the scope of the gospel appears to parallel the main outlines of Peter's preaching, as is evident from both external and internal evidence.

Mark's Jesus, as has often been observed, is the Jesus of Galilee and Capernaum, the home of Peter. Mark begins his gospel with the baptism of Jesus by John the Baptist, at age thirty, when Peter first knew Him and became His disciple. And more than half of his book is devoted to the Galilean ministry.

The vividness and detail of the narrative suggest how much Mark owed to the eye-witness testimony and preaching of Peter. And the emphasis is on what Jesus *did,* and not so much on what Jesus *said,* just as Peter must have preached to his Roman audiences. For example, only four full parables and one of our Lord's longer discourses are given, as compared with the nineteen miracles which his gospel·reports. Thus, Mark's special emphasis is on the superhuman power of Jesus, and on the miracles as a demonstration that He was the Son of God.

Mark's ultimate purpose in writing his gospel was the same as that of all the evangelists, which was to portray the Personality and Mission of our Lord as the Saviour of all mankind. This he did in a brief but compelling story which has fascinated readers of all time. Its value in part lies in the fact that it was the first authentic gospel story to be written, and that such a large portion of it was borrowed and incorporated in the gospels by both the author of the gospel of Matthew and by Luke.

2. AUTHORSHIP AND DATE

There is little doubt that Mark wrote the book which bears his name.

This is the view the Church has held from earliest traditions, and even modern scholarship gives him credit for writing the book at least in its essentials, if not in the finished form in which we now have it.

Bishop Papias of Hierapolis, a disciple and pupil of the Apostle John, writing about 130 A.D., quotes an earlier and unnamed "apostolic presbyter" as giving this important testimony:[2]

> Mark, having become the interpreter of Peter, wrote down accurate-
> ly, though not in order, as many as he remembered of the things

---

[2]As quoted by Eusebius, 264-340 A.D., Bishop of Caesarea, *Historia Ecclesiae,* III, 39.

said or done by the Lord. For he neither had heard the Lord nor followed Him, but at a later time, as I said, he attached himself to Peter, who delivered his instructions according to the needs of the occasion, but not with a view to giving a systematic account of the Lord's sayings. So that Mark made no mistake, thus writing down some things as he remembered them; for of one thing he took forethought, not to leave out any one of the things he had heard or to state falsely anything in them.

Also, the presbyter's statement that Mark's gospel depended largely on Peter and Peter's sermons is confirmed by certain internal evidence. For example, three important events may be cited: The raising of Jairus' daughter, the Transfiguration, and the Gethsemane scene — at which only Peter, James, and John were present. James was soon martyred by Herod (Acts 12:2); years later the Apostle John wrote an independent Gospel; and so Peter alone remained as Mark's authority for these events.

Other details in the gospel of Mark point in the direction of Peter's influence: Jesus' praise of Peter for his declaration that Jesus was "the Christ, the Son of the living God" (8:29), Peter walking on the water, and other incidents which tend to present Peter in a favorable light, are all omitted; whereas others less favorable, such as Jesus' rebuke, "Get thee behind me, Satan" (8:33), and Peter's denial of his Lord the night before the Crucifixion, are related with some detail.

Although the principal source of Mark's gospel was the preaching and teaching of the Apostle Peter, there is every reason to believe that Mark gathered many incidents and details of his narrative from other eye-witnesses. For example, he certainly had an opportunity to secure first hand information from Mary his mother, from Barnabas his cousin, and from other disciples of Jesus, both at Jerusalem and among the Gentile Christians abroad.

The date of the writing of Mark's gospel is usually placed between 50 and 60 A.D., or slightly earlier.

Both Matthew and Luke appear to have borrowed substantially from the Gospel of Mark. The Gospel of Luke is thought to have been written, either just before the Apostle Paul and Luke left Caesarea on their historic voyage to Rome, or soon after their arrival at Rome, that is, about 60 or 61 A.D. The writing of the gospel of Matthew in the form in which we now have it is usually placed about 67 A.D., or a few years earlier.

So the time of Mark's work is generally placed *before* 60 A.D.

3. THE CONTENTS OF THE GOSPEL OF MARK

Unlike the gospels of Matthew and Luke, the gospel of Mark has no introduction.

Mark begins his story somewhat abruptly with John the Baptist and the baptism of Jesus, omitting all those precious incidents and scenes revealing the birth and infancy of our Lord, and the people connected with them, which Luke and Matthew have made so much of in their first two chapters. Luke, in particular, gives us our best Christmas story.

However, the important thing to note regarding Mark and his gospel is that he was the *first* to compose a connected narrative of our Lord's ministry, and that what he accomplished in his book was so excellent, although brief and incomplete at certain points, that it served as an example and pattern for the other gospel writers who followed him, and who borrowed from and enlarged upon his important work.

The reader will notice that the scenes and narratives in Mark proceed in a more chronological order than in the books of Matthew and Luke.

The Analysis

A brief analysis and outline of the contents may be given as follows:

(1) The beginning of Jesus' public ministry, including the preaching of John the Baptist as Forerunner; the Baptism and Temptation of Jesus. Chapter 1:1-13.

(2) The opening of the Galilean ministry, with headquarters at Capernaum on the Sea of Galilee; the call of the Apostles; the preaching and miraculous healing in the vicinity of Capernaum; rising opposition. Chapters 1:14 to 4:34.

(3) The enlarged Galilean ministry: On both sides of the Sea of Galilee; journeys in the neighborhood of Tyre and Sidon; again on the east side of Galilee, and north, including Bethsaida, Caesarea Philippi, and the Transfiguration, covering two years of intensive preaching, teaching, and miracles; critical opposition. Departure from Galilee. Chapters 4:35 to 9.

(4) The six months' ministry in Perea, and Judea, briefly sketched in Mark's account. Chapter 10.

(5) The Last Week. The Triumphal Entry into Jerusalem (chapter 11); the money-changers driven from the Temple (11); clash with the Pharisees and Sadducees (12); the Second Coming predicted (13); the Passover and the Last Supper (14); the Gethsemane scene (14); the betrayal, arrest and trial (14); the Crucifixion (15). Chapters 11 to 15.

(6) The Resurrection, and the Forty Days before the Ascension. Chapter 16.

Conservative scholars are of the opinion that the last 12 verses of chapter 16 were not written by Mark.[3]

The most common presumption is that the book of Mark, through

---

[3]See Merrill C. Tenney, *op. cit.*, p. 175; C. E. Graham Swift, *The New Bible Commentary*, p. 839.

Fishermen mending their nets at early dawn on the shores of the Sea of Galilee. © *Matson Photo Service* much use or otherwise, had lost its last page. And so a fitting conclusion or summary was added by another writer, presumably one of the early Church fathers.

The reader has noticed that verses 9-20 are written more like a catalogue of facts or summary of events as related elsewhere, and not in the manner of Mark's usual vivid detail.

4. Passages Found Only in Mark

Since approximately 90 per cent of the gospel of Mark is reproduced by either Matthew or Luke, or both, the amount of matter found only in Mark must of necessity be small. In fact, only about 30 verses are peculiar to Mark.

These passages include the parable of the Seed Growing Secretly (4:26-29); the miracle of the Blind Man Healed at Bethsaida (8:22-26); and the story of the Young Man who followed Jesus after the crowd had fled, and whom commentators are strongly inclined to think was Mark himself (14:43-52).

Suggestions for Additional Reading on the Book of Mark

*Barclay, William: *The Gospel of Mark.*
Branscomb, B. H.: *The Gospel of Mark.*
Grant, Frederick C.: "The Gospel According to St. Mark," *The Interpreter's Bible*, pp. 627-647.
*Groenewald, E. P.: *Commentary on Mark.*
Minear, Paul S.: *The Gospel According to Mark.*
Rawlinson, A. E. J.: *St. Mark.*
*Swift, C. E. Graham: "The Gospel According to Mark," *The New Bible Commentary*, pp. 806-839.
Taylor, Vincent: *The Gospel According to St. Mark.*
*Tenney, Merrill C.: *The New Testament — An Historical and Analytic Survey*, pp. 163-177.

Chapter 4

THE GOSPEL OF LUKE

1. THE BIOGRAPHY OF LUKE

So far as we know, Luke is the only non-Jewish author in the Bible. From both internal and external evidence, we infer that he was a Greek by birth.

The Apostle Paul refers to Luke in at least three of his letters, and in these gives the reader some information about him. In the letter to the Colossians (4:14), Paul refers to him as "Luke the beloved physician," which suggests a person of some culture and education.

Moreover, as revealed in his two famous books, the gospel of Luke and the book of Acts, Luke appears not only as a highly educated person, but also as a careful historian and writer, a man of experience, with broad understanding and sympathies. Also, his literary culture appears in the classical introduction to the gospel (1:1-4), in which he followed the manner of the Greek historians.

In two other letters, Paul refers to Luke in affectionate terms as a "fellow worker," friend and companion (Philemon 24; II Timothy 4:11). In one of the references, Colossians 4:10, 11, Luke is not included in the list of those named as "men of the circumcision," and so we infer that he was a Gentile. Too, there might be some significance in the name to whom the book is addressed, Theophilus, which is a Greek name.

According to early tradition, Luke became a Christian at Antioch, in Syria, where he followed the profession of a physician. Before Peter, or Barnabas or Paul or Mark came to Antioch, there were Jewish-Christians who "traveled as far as Phoenicia and Cyprus and Antioch, speaking the word to none except Jews. But there were some of them, men of Cyprus and Cyrene, who on coming to Antioch spoke to the Greeks also, preaching the Lord Jesus" (Acts 11:19-21).

It is likely therefore that Luke was a convert of these Gentile Christians who came first to Antioch, and that he was not a convert of the Apostle Paul.

The reader, however, first meets Luke in the author's story of Paul's Second Missionary Journey, at Troas (Acts 16:10-15), at the beginning of the "we" and "us" passages in his story, indicating that at this point Luke joined Paul's missionary party, perhaps for the first time. So, if he had formerly lived at Antioch, he seems now not to have been stationed there, but instead at Troas or across the Aegean Sea at Philippi, the capital of Macedonia.

Sir W. M. Ramsay is of the opinion that "the man of Macedonia" who appeared to Paul in a vision at night, and who was "beseeching him and saying, 'Come over to Macedonia and help us,'" was none other than Luke himself.[1] This may or may not be so. If so, this would suggest that Luke may well have been a citizen of the Greek district of Macedonia in Europe.

At any rate, Paul obeyed the vision, crossed the Aegean, and made his way straight to the great city of Philippi, the capital of the district, where Paul and company remained and preached for some six months.

For the remainder of his story of the Second Missionary Journey, Luke changes the person of his narrative from the "we" passages to "they," indicating that he probably did not accompany Paul and the others on the rest of the journey, but instead remained and carried on his Christian mission at Philippi.

About six years later, when on his Third Missionary Journey, Paul returned to Philippi, where he was rejoined by Luke, who accompanied Paul on an important mission back to Jerusalem. But when Paul's Jewish enemies learned that he was to come to Jerusalem, they had a trap set to murder him. However, under the protection of the Roman guard, and barely escaping with his life, Paul was hurried away at night to Caesarea, the Roman capital of Judea, where he was safely delivered to Felix the governor. Luke accompanied him and was an eye-witness of these harrowing adventures.

Felix ordered that Paul be placed, and guarded, in Herod's palace, although with considerable freedom. For two long years, while his Jewish enemies in Jerusalem made every effort to carry out their plot against the life of Paul, and during which time Porcius Festus succeeded Felix as governor of the district of Judea, Paul waited for justice and his freedom. One delay followed another, until finally Paul elected to make his appeal to Caesar, which was his right as a Roman citizen.

Meanwhile, Luke, Paul's personal companion and physician, had the freedom of the palace where Paul was being guarded, came and went as his services and presence were required by Paul.

These were momentous years, not only for Paul whose very life hung in the balance, but also for Luke, who at this time was planning, collecting materials, and getting ready to write the two books for which he is world-famous.

Judging by the large amount of original material in his book, there

[1]See Introduction by Professor E. F. Kevan of London Bible College, *The New Bible Commentary*, p. 840.

is good reason to believe that Luke spent the greater part of the two years, while Paul was in prison at Caesarea, interviewing important disciples and eye-witnesses throughout Palestine. Philip and his four daughters and prophetesses were living at Caesarea. The Apostle John and possibly Mary, in whose care Jesus left his mother, were living at Jerusalem or Capernaum. Many other "eye-witnesses" were still living at such important centers as Jerusalem, Bethlehem, Nazareth, Capernaum, and in other towns and villages.

After two years of waiting at Caesarea, and a stormy voyage on the Mediterranean, which Luke describes in some detail (Acts 27, 28), Paul and Luke reached Rome in early spring of 61 A.D. Although under the watch of a Roman soldier, Paul in "prison" for the next two years was allowed the utmost freedom, to rent his own house, and to receive his friends, including Luke his physician and companion, who presumably lodged with Paul.

There is no evidence that the Apostle Paul and his companion and fellow laborer were separated during the next five or six years, until Paul's martyrdom about 67 A.D. Three letters of Paul which mention Luke, from which we have already quoted, all indicate that the two men were laboring together as a team.

The general opinion is that Paul was tried and acquitted, about 63 or 64 A.D.; and that he returned to his missionary work in Greece and Asia Minor, but that he was later re-arrested at the instigation of his enemies, and taken back to Rome for a second imprisonment. Luke was his sole companion in this second and last imprisonment, as Paul reveals in his II Timothy letter (4:11), "Luke alone is with me." This letter was written shortly before Paul's death.

There is no certain information of Luke's later years, or of the time and manner of his death. However, there is a tradition related by a third-century authority that Luke spent his last days as an evangelist in Bithynia, a province to the north of Asia Minor, where he died at age 74, "filled with the Holy Ghost."

In connection with this tradition, it is interesting to remember that, when the Roman author, Pliny the Younger, arrived in Bithynia in 109 A.D., after his appointment as governor of the Province, he found a great many Christians there, "persons of all ranks and ages, and even both sexes," as he wrote to Emperor Trajan two years later. Who knows but that they were Luke's disciples?

2. AUTHORSHIP AND DATE

Although Luke's name is not specifically mentioned in either the gospel of Luke or the book of Acts, it is universally agreed that he was the author of both.

Indeed, in the opening sentence of the book of Acts, Luke refers to his gospel as the "first book"; and of course both books are addressed to or dedicated to the same person, Theophilus, a Greek name of a person of some prominence, and very possibly a convert of Luke's.

Moreover, the introduction to the second book summarizes in a few words what the author covered in his first book, showing that he is beginning his second book where he left off with the first. That is, the second book is a sequel to the first.

The date of the writing of Luke's gospel is usually placed about 60 or 61 A.D., either in the weeks and months before Paul was transferred from Caesarea, the Roman capital of the district of Judea, or soon after his arrival at the imperial capital of Rome.

3. LUKE'S PURPOSE IN WRITING HIS GOSPEL

In the introduction to his gospel, Luke reveals his over-all purpose in writing his book.

He states that a number of written accounts of our Lord's life and ministry were already in existence. But he is ambitious to write another, which shall be more complete, and different in certain important respects from the others.

> It seemed good to me also, having followed all things closely for some time past, to write *an orderly account* for you, most excellent Theophilus, *that you may know the truth* concerning the things of which you have been informed.

It is in this ambition of Luke's as a Great-Hearted Christian, and as a true historian, that the secret of the greatness of the book lies. For apparently he most diligently made use of all the resources available to him to make this the kind of book that he thought it should be.

For one thing, Luke secured materials for his gospel from many different sources. One of these was the Gospel of Mark, nearly all of which, with significant editorial changes, was incorporated in the body of the Gospel of Luke.

And we may suppose that a diligent scholar and historian such as Luke would make use of the many former "narratives," to which he refers in his introduction; at least of such of these works as were authentic and dependable, and none of which have come down to us.

From the nature of the gospel of Luke, however, we infer that he collected much of his material also from oral and direct sources. That is, Luke evidently talked with Apostles and evangelists, such as Paul and Peter and Matthew and Mark and Philip and John, and many other disciples and "eye-witnesses," from whom he secured much information which he could not have secured from any other source.

And the most precious of all his interviews, must have been Luke's visit to Mary herself. For how else could he have learned of those intimate conversations between Mary and her cousin Elizabeth, the visit of the angel Gabriel, the beautiful songs that passed between the two women, and the other private and *personal* details?

And where else, except from Mary herself, did Luke learn of the infancy and boyhood of Mary's Son? Indeed, Luke says that no one but Mary had this information: "And his mother kept all these things in her heart." And these priceless stories are found only in the first two chapters of Luke's gospel.

Indeed, Luke made good use of the two years while Paul, in prison at Caesarea, waited for his case to be acted upon. We can see him now, as he says farewell to Paul and starts on his journey up and down Palestine, going to such likely places as Jerusalem, where Mary still lived with her nephew, the Apostle John, before he moved his headquarters to Ephesus some ten years later; or to Nazareth in Galilee, to talk with Mary's oldest neighbors and friends about her Son.

And no doubt, too, Luke went to the old town of Bethlehem, five miles south of Jerusalem, where Jesus was born under most unusual circumstances. Did Luke get eye-witness stories from the very keeper of the inn, where there was no room for Joseph and Mary? And did he talk also to the older shepherds, the very ones who *saw* and *heard* so many strange things from the heavens on that wonderful night?

Yes, that is precisely what Luke did! "Just as they were delivered to us by those who from the beginning were eye-witnesses and ministers of the word," he informs us in the opening sentence of his gospel. What would a modern reader not give to have a complete list of all the people Luke interviewed in getting material for his gospel story!

Thus, fortunately for the modern reader, and Providentially we may believe, Luke's diligent researches supply us with much invaluable material which otherwise would be missing from the gospel story. And so, he gives us not only the longest, but the most complete story of the Four Gospels.

If we should select a single passage as the key to the message of the book, and to Luke's purpose in writing it, we would unhesitatingly name the quotation from the prophet Isaiah, which Jesus Himself chose for His text and sermon, in the synagogue that Sabbath Day in Nazareth:

> The spirit of the Lord is upon me,
> Because he has anointed me to preach
> the Good News to the poor.
> He has sent me to proclaim release
> to the captives,
> And recovering of sight to the blind;
> To set at liberty those who are
> oppressed,
> To proclaim the acceptable year
> of the Lord (Isaiah 61:1-2).

This passage, as the reader has observed, summarizes the whole message and mission of the Saviour, and emphasizes the great humanitarian character of the Messiah as Luke only has presented Him.

4. "The Most Beautiful Book Ever Written"

Luke's gospel has been called the most beautiful book ever written. What is it about the book to cause readers to give it this high rating?

In the first place, the book is written not for a particular race or people, as for example the Jews, from whom the author of the gospel of Matthew primarily wrote his book; but it is written as if for the whole human family, and for all time.

Luke writes with historical perspective. He records the coming and going of Roman Emperors, governors of Judea, their dates, all in the frame of universal history, as if Something greater than emperors and governors is shaping history and the destiny of peoples. In short, the story he is writing is about One who is able to *make* and *unmake* earthly rulers, and to transcend the dates to which they belong.

Thus, Luke's book is more than a biography of our Lord, although it is that, too. It is a *history* of our Lord: "That which *was, is,* and *ever more shall be.*" In this particular, Luke writes like the Apostle Paul, with whom he was associated the greater portion of his active years; that is, Luke like Paul stresses the universal character of Christianity as embodied in the Person of its Founder.

Matthew, for example, traces the genealogy of Jesus back to Abraham; Luke goes all the way back to Adam and God, thus embracing all mankind. Jesus is presented as the Ideal Man of mankind, and as the Saviour.

If we may so phrase it, the book is written in the "key" of the Lord Jesus at the same time that it narrates His story. Jesus showed the greatest compassion for the masses, the poor, because they were sheep without a shepherd. So Luke, to be true to his Hero, must write an all-encompassing book. Although his work was designed and written for the Gentiles, there is nowhere expressed any prejudice against the Jews, or any other race.

Too, in Luke's day women were underrated and discriminated against. It is thus important to note that in Luke's gospel women are important people and are given a prominence not found in the other gospels.

In temperament Luke was also an artist. For instance, in the interview with Mary, Luke was careful to record Mary's memory of those outbursts of song between herself and her cousin Elizabeth, which one day would be the great hymns of Christianity: *Ave Maria,* the *Benedictus,* the *Magnificat,* and the *Gloria in Excelsis.*

In short, a sensitivity for what is true, and good, and universally lovely, is everywhere present in Luke's narrative. The work as a composition is written in the classic manner, full of simplicity, and in the Messianic grace which the author understood and embodied in his book.

5. The Contents of the Gospel of Luke

An outline of Luke's narrative may be given briefly as follows:

(1) The preface, in which the author explains how his book came to be written. Chapter 1:1-4.

(2) The infancy and boyhood of Jesus, including the annunciations and births of John the Baptist and Jesus, the personal accounts of Mary and Elizabeth, and the hymns of praise. Chapters 1:5 to 2:52.

(3) The preparation for the ministry of Jesus, including the ministry of John the Baptist, the baptism of Jesus, His genealogy and temptation. Chapters 3 to 4:13.

(4) Jesus' Galilean ministry. After some days of preliminary teaching and healing in a tour of parts of Galilee, Jesus came to Nazareth, where He was rejected. Then He went down to Capernaum on the Sea of Galilee, which became His adopted home and headquarters for the ministry of the next two years.

At first His teaching and healing was in the vicinity of Capernaum; but gradually it extended to include all the cities around the Sea of Galilee, and the territory beyond, mainly on three sides of the Sea — north, east, and west. These missions were of the nature of tours with His Twelve Apostles, whom He early appointed, and other followers. Occasionally He went on special journeys outside of Galilee, as far as Tyre or Sidon, or even into Judea. . . . "I must preach the good news of the kingdom of God to the other cities also; for I was sent for this purpose."

For the narrative of the Galilean ministry, Luke follows mainly the same order as that in Mark's gospel, from which he evidently secured the main outline of his Galilean story. But Luke records more of the teaching of Jesus than Mark, and in this respect his gospel reminds us of Matthew's.

But Luke's handling of the sayings and discourses of Jesus is different from that of Matthew. Matthew organizes them into large groups or topics, whereas Luke separates them and relates each of the teachings to the particular occasion which produced it. For example, compare Matthew's Sermon on the Mount, chapters 5, 6, and 7, with Luke's version of the Sermon, chapter 6:17-49, and the succeeding chapters in which part of the Sermon material is also recorded.

Also, in this section, Luke presents some new material found only in his gospel. He records carefully three prayers of Jesus on three special occasions: After cleansing the leper (5:16); before calling the Twelve Apostles (6:12); and at His Transfiguration (9:29). And, too, there are parables and miracles found only in his gospel. Chapters 4:14 to 9:50.

(5) The Perean ministry. Jesus' tours and teachings on the east side of the Jordan river, in the district of Perea, together with certain special journeys to Jerusalem. In all, about six months before the Passion Week — from the fall of 29 A.D. to the spring of 30 A.D.

This section of the book is the most original of Luke's work, and in substance and arrangement seems to have borrowed little from the gospel of Mark. Indeed, large portions of it are composed of matter found only in Luke. The new materials consist of several of the great parables, including the parable of the Good Samaritan, the Prodigal Son, the Rich Man and Lazarus, and many others.

Here also we have the Mission of the Seventy; the two Great Commandments, and Jesus' definition of a neighbor; instruction on how to pray; Jesus' prediction of the End of the World; teachings and discourses on the character and universal nature of the Kingdom of God; on His last journey to Jerusalem, as they approached Jericho, Jesus foretold the manner of His death, and the Resurrection, as prophesied by the prophets. Chapters 9:50 to 19:28.

(6) The Last Week. The Triumphal Entry into Jerusalem; the final teachings of Jesus, in the Temple and to His disciples; the Last Supper; the Mount of Olives; His betrayal, arrest, trials, crucifixion, and burial. Chapters 19:29 to 23:56.

(7) The Resurrection and the Ascension, including Luke's recording of three appearances to His disciples, His interpretation of the Scriptures to them, and His last directions to those who are to be His witnesses. Chapter 24.

6. Passages Found Only in Luke

Evidence of Luke's diligence in collecting materials is that about half of his gospel consists of matter found only in his book.

(1) This new material includes the whole of the first two chapters of his work, and almost the whole of the long section, chapters 9:51 to 19:27, both of which are described in the analyses above.

(2) Of the twenty-three parables recorded by Luke, the following *eighteen* are found only in his book: The Two Debtors (7:41-43); the Good Samaritan (10:25-37); the Friend at Midnight (11:5-8); the Foolish Rich Man (12:16-21); the Watchful Servants (12:35-48); the Barren Fig Tree (13:6-9); the Chief Seats (14:7-11); the Great Banquet (14:15-24); the Rash Builder (14:28-30); the Rash King (14:31-32); the Lost Coin (15:8-10); the Prodigal Son (15:11-32); the Dishonest Steward (16:1-13); the Rich Man and Lazarus (16:19-31); the Unprofitable Servants (17:7-10); the Unrighteous Judge (18:1-8); the Pharisee and the Publican (18:9-14); and the Pounds (19:11-27).

(3) Of the twenty-one miracles in Luke, *seven* of them are found only in his Gospel: The Miraculous Draft of Fishes (5:4-11); the Raising of the Widow's Son at Nain (7:11-17); the Woman with a Spirit of Infirmity (13:10-17); the Dropsical Man (14:1-6); the Cleansing of the Ten Lepers (17:11-19); the Healing of Malchus' Ear (22:50-51); and the Saving of the Thief on the Cross (23:39-43).

(4) Luke is careful to record Jesus' prayers. In particular he

alone records that our Lord prayed on *six* memorable occasions, as follows: At the time of His baptism (3:21-22); after cleansing the Leper (5:12-16); all night before calling the Twelve Apostles (6:12-16); at His Transfiguration (9:28-36); on the cross for His murderers (23:33-34); His last utterance on the cross (23:46).

(5) Other matter found only in Luke include the following: Certain questions put to John the Baptist by the people concerning salvation (3:10-14); the conversation at the Transfiguration (9:28-36); the choice and Mission of the Seventy (10:1-16); the story of Zacchaeus and his conversion (19:1-10); the scene of Jesus weeping over Jerusalem (19:41-44); Jesus' promise to Peter that his faith shall not fail (22:31-32); the bloody sweat in the Garden (22:44); the trial before Herod (23:1-12).

(6) Also, there are the words addressed to the women of Jerusalem (23:27-31); the incident of the penitent thief (23:39-43); the words on the cross, "Father, forgive them; for they know not what they do," and His last words, "Father, into thy hands I commit my spirit!" (23:34, 46); the whole beautiful story of the journey to Emmaus (24:31-35); most of the details of our Lord's appearance on the evening of Easter Day (24:36-43); and the special summary of His teachings concerning the Scriptures during the Forty Days, in relation to His Commission to the disciples (24:44-48).

SUGGESTIONS FOR ADDITIONAL READING ON THE GOSPEL OF LUKE

*Barclay, William: *The Gospel of Luke.*

Cadbury, H. J.: *The Making of Luke-Acts*

*Geldenhuys, Norval: *Commentary on Luke.*

Gilmour, S. MacLean: "The Gospel According to St. Luke," *The Interpreter's Bible,* Vol. VIII, pp. 1-26.

*Kevan, E. F.: "The Gospel According to Luke," *The New Bible Commentary,* pp. 840-864.

*Miller, Donald G.: *The Gospel According to Luke.*

Ragg, Lonsdale: *St. Luke.*

Robertson, A. T.: *Luke the Historian in the Light of Research.*

*Stonehouse, Ned B.: *The Witness of Luke to Christ.*

Tittle, E. F.: *The Gospel According to Luke.*

Chapter 5

The Gospel of John

1. Biography of the Author

The Apostle John lived to a great age, perhaps to be a hundred or more years old, the last of the original Twelve to pass from the scene of the Apostolic Age.

His gospel, too, was written a generation or more after the other three gospels were produced and placed in circulation. John's *purpose* in writing was also different from that of the writers of the other three books.

John and his brother James, who also became an apostle, were sons of Zebedee and Salome, who appears to have been a sister of Mary, the mother of Jesus.

When we first meet John in the gospels of Matthew, Mark, and Luke, he was a businessman of some means, one of five partners with his father in a fishing establishment, prosperous enough to employ "hired servants." Simon Peter and his brother Andrew, whose native home was at nearby Bethsaida, came over and joined them, because Capernaum on the northwest shore of the Sea of Galilee was the site of a Roman military post, a tax collector's seat, and a center of considerable business activity on the important caravan route leading to Damascus.

When we first meet John in the gospel of John, however, he and Andrew are with John the Baptist, on the east side of the Jordan in the vicinity of Bethany where John the Baptist was baptizing. On that very day Jesus passed by, and John the Baptist, recognizing him as the Messiah, introduced him to John and Andrew in this manner, "Behold, the Lamb of God!"

This was a surprise to John, who had known his cousin all these years, but not as the Messiah. But Jesus had changed since His baptism; and apparently John had not seen Him since He began His Messiahship. There was now an appealing magnetism about His personality. John and Andrew had a desire to follow Him immediately. It was about ten o'clock in the forenoon, and they spent the remainder of the day with Him, where He was staying. Andrew was eager for his brother Simon to meet Jesus, too, and so he went and found him. And when Jesus looked Simon over, He said, "So you are Simon, the son of John? You shall be called *Cephas*," which means *Peter* (a stone), the Greek word for Peter's Aramaic name.

Events happened fast. On one day they were with John the Baptist, on the east side of the Jordan opposite Judah. On the next Jesus decided to go to Galilee. On the way He found Philip, who was a friend of Andrew and Simon's, and like them, a native of Bethsaida. And then Philip found his friend Nathanael (the other gospel writers call him Bartholomew), who lived at Cana of Galilee, where the marriage was held the following day, to which Jesus and His disciples were invited as special guests, including the Apostle John, although he characteristically avoids giving his own name.

After the marriage festivities at Cana, Jesus went down to Capernaum with His mother and His brothers and His disciples. And John adds, "And there they stayed for a few days." This is one of the rare occasions, perhaps the only one, when a gospel writer records that Jesus went on a journey with the members of His immediate family. According to Matthew (13:53-56), there were four brothers, James and Joseph and Simon and Judas (or Jude), and at least three sisters, not named.

This would be the first visit of Jesus and the family to John's own home at Capernaum since Jesus assumed His Messiahship and the change had taken place in His personality.

Up to this point, John and the other disciples named in the story had followed Jesus in the role of *learners*, and did not leave their homes and occupations. Not many weeks afterward, however, when they were convinced that He was really the Messiah, Jesus called them and they left everything and followed Him.

John was one of the first four named — Peter and Andrew, James and John; and each was called while at work and engaged with his occupation on the Sea of Galilee near Capernaum. Mark says that Jesus gave John and his brother James a nickname in Greek, *Boanerges,* which means "sons of thunder," because of their impulsive and violent temperaments.

For instance, on one occasion when their Master was rejected in a Samaritan village, they were ready to call down fire from heaven on the inhabitants. But soon their tempest-like natures were refined, and they were equally ready to face death for Him.

John was proud to refer to himself as "the disciple whom Jesus loved," a remark which he repeats five times in his book. John appears to have been about the same age of Jesus, who began his ministry, according to Luke, at age *thirty.*

Jesus and John became the closest of personal and spiritual companions. If Jesus loved John more than He loved His other disciples, it must be because John was the one who knew and understood Jesus, and His message, better than any of the others. Many think that they were rarely, if ever, separated from each other during their three wonderful years as Master and disciple.

Jesus chose John to be with Him at the raising of Jairus' daughter, at the Transfiguration, and at the scene of agony in Gethsemane. At the Last Supper, John occupied the place of honor on the right next to Jesus (13:23); and John alone gives a full-length account of Jesus' Farewell Message to His disciples (chapters 13, 14, 15, 16, and 17).

John followed Jesus from Gethsemane into the palace of the high priest, to Pilate's praetorium, and to the place of Crucifixion. And on the cross, Jesus commended His mother Mary to John's loving care, and John accepted the trust and took her that day to his own home in Jerusalem (19:27). For by this time, or earlier, John seems to have had a home in the capital city as well as at his native city, Capernaum.

When the tomb of Jesus was reported to him empty, by Mary Magdalene, John ran with Peter to investigate, and saw that the Christ had risen (20:1-10). With the other disciples he saw the risen Christ, the same evening, and again a week later (20:19-30). And like the other disciples, John went to Galilee, as Jesus had directed them, and again saw the Lord (21:1-7).

After the Ascension, John was with the other ten Apostles in the Upper Room in Jerusalem (Acts 1:13). And after Pentecost, John became Peter's colleague in active missionary work, in and out of Jerusalem during the persecutions that threatened to undermine the infant Church. Peter and John were still in Jerusalem when the Apostle Paul returned from his First Missionary Journey, about 50 A.D., the occasion being the Conference at Jerusalem to determine whether circumcision should be required of Gentile Christians and converts of Paul and Barnabas, and other Gentile evangelists (Acts 15:6; Galatians 2:9).

According to tradition, John made Jerusalem his headquarters for many years after the Conference at Jerusalem, and continued to care for Mary the mother of Jesus until her death. Whether they spent all their time at Jerusalem, or part of it at Capernaum, his other home, is not known. However, there were two good reasons why he felt compelled to leave Jerusalem about 70 A.D., or perhaps a little earlier.

One of these reasons was the destruction of Jerusalem by the Roman commander Titus (later Emperor) in 70 A.D. The other reason was that the great city of Ephesus in Asia Minor, after Antioch in Syria, had by the close of the Apostolic generation become the center of the Christian population of the West. Paul and his evangelists had done much to make it so.

But Paul closed his Third Missionary Journey and evangelistic work in Asia Minor by the spring of 58 A.D., and had started on his historic journey back to Jerusalem, which ended in imprisonment at Caesarea, and at Rome. Before he left Asia Minor, however, Paul had stationed his disciple Timothy at Ephesus, with specific instructions to keep the Christian faith and teaching pure (I Timothy 1:3-4).

After Paul was released from his first imprisonment at Rome, about 63 or 64 A.D., it appears that among other places he visited Ephesus and joined Timothy for a time. But at the instigation of his tireless enemies, Paul was re-arrested and placed in the Roman prison again. In a second letter, about 66 or 67 A.D., Paul urges Timothy to come to Rome, indicating that his execution and martyrdom was close at hand (II Timothy 4:21).

It was at such a time as this, and under these circumstances, that the Apostle John came to Ephesus. Although John's home and head-quarters was at Ephesus, his mission included the whole of the Roman province of Asia Minor.

He lived and labored here under the extreme persecution of the Roman government, and the confusion produced by the Gnostics and other false teachers, as well as the treachery and double-dealing of the *unbelieving Jews*, who fought the spread of Christianity among the Gentiles every step of the way.

The Apostle became the head of the Church and pastor extraordinary of the "Seven Churches of Asia," and all the province, for the next quarter of a century. Some time in the latter part of the reign of the Roman Emperor Domitian (81-96 A.D.), about 95 A.D., John was exiled to the Isle of Patmos, in the Mediterranean, some sixty miles southwest of Ephesus. He was banished for preaching the Word of God, and for testifying concerning Jesus (Revelation 1:9).

Domitian's successor, Nerva, is said to have freed the Apostle and permitted his return to Ephesus, about 96 A.D., where he composed the book of Revelation, according to the vision he had on Patmos. Bishop Irenaeus of the second century states that the Apostle John continued to reside at Ephesus until his death, in the reign of Trajan (98-117 A.D.). Assuming the accuracy of this statement, the Apostle at the time of his death would have been in excess of one hundred years of age.

During his later years, and presumably at Ephesus, John wrote the five important works that bear his name: The gospel of John, I John, II John, III John, and the book of Revelation. All of them were written in the form of letters.

2. AUTHORSHIP AND DATE

A well established early tradition, including such widely known pupils of the Apostle John as Polycarp, Papias, and Ignatius, states that the fourth gospel was the work of John.[1] Likewise, Christian opinion over the centuries, uniformly, has ascribed the authorship to him.

Moreover, a careful reading of the gospel reveals that the book was written by an eye-witness and one of the Apostles. Indeed, John mentions himself five times as "the disciple whom Jesus loved," and then in the close of his book, he says that "this is the disciple who is bearing witness to these things, and who has written these things" (21:24).

Also, the book is written not only by an eye-witness, but by a writer who has lived in personal contact with Jesus; and who at all times speaks of this personal relationship with the utmost detail and authority (see the Prologue, 1:1-18; the marriage at Cana, 2:1-11; 4:6-14; the Last Supper, chapters 13, 14, 15, 16, 17).

Then, too, the style and thought of the gospel reveal an author who has absorbed both the teaching and the phraseology of his Lord, as the result of his daily, intimate association. Jesus was the Messiah of Love to His disciples; John writes a gospel of *love*.

At this point, if the reader will turn to I John and read this Letter he will see how thoroughly the Apostle John has identified himself with the heart and mind of the Christ. In this manner, the reader can make up his own mind whether any one other than John could qualify for the authorship of the book.

According to ancient authorities, John wrote this gospel in his old age, at Ephesus. The date of the writing is usually placed at about 90 A.D., or a little earlier.

Mark's gospel appeared around 50-55 A.D.; Luke's about 60 or 61 A.D.; and Matthew's about 66 or 67 A.D. These three earlier gospels had been in circulation for a number of years before John's appeared, and most of the churches doubtless had copies of them.

John's purpose in writing a gospel was somewhat different from that of the other three writers, and so his book does not follow the biographical pattern set by the other three books. For this reason John omitted a great deal of the material included in the other books; and for the same reason he includes many valuable sayings and discourses, such as Jesus' Farewell Message at the Last Supper, which are not in the others.

3. The Purpose of John's Gospel

When the Apostle John left the predominantly Jewish community of Jerusalem and Palestine, shortly before 70 A.D., and traveled as far West as Ephesus, one of the first things to impress him was the strange religious ideas and customs among Gentiles, and even among Gentile Christians.

---

[1] See F. F. Bruce, *Are the New Testament Documents Reliable?* H. P. V. Nunn, *The Fourth Gospel.* Against the Apostle's authorship, see Kee and Young, *Understanding the New Testament*, pp. 383-414.

(1) One of these strange ideas or heresies, the particular one which John undertakes to combat in his gospel, is what was known as *Gnosticism*, the word being derived from a Greek word meaning *to know*.

The *Gnostics*, literally the *knowing ones*, speculated about the relation of finite man to infinite God, and how to reconcile the two. How can *physical* man reach *spiritual* God? The reader will recall that this was one of Job's problems. And this is the problem also that lies at the foundation of all ancient religions. How are matter and spirit related? What is *good*, and what is *evil*? How did evil enter the world?

Early thinkers, we are told, were driven by these questions into some form of Dualism. They felt that there must be two Powers in conflict. Inasmuch as *spirit* is higher, *matter* must be evil. The Gnostics held the central doctrine that emancipation came through knowledge, *gnosis*, the possession of which saved its followers from the clutch of matter.

In Ephesus there were two schools of gnostic thought, both confusing and misleading to the Gentile Christians. At the head of one of the schools or cults was a man named Cerinthus, who held that Jesus, as the son of Joseph and Mary, was, like other men, heir to the flesh as well as of the Spirit. Jesus therefore, according to Cerinthus, contained this dualism in His own person.

The other school, the Docetists, denied the fleshly or "evil" nature of Jesus, and held that Jesus had no real human nature, but only a spiritual one. This produced a dualism of another sort, they thought, because of the failure of the different elements in Jesus to constitute a unity.

What these doctrines added up to was a denial of the Incarnation of Jesus, and of the Apostle John's most precious belief and faith, that Jesus was the Son of God.

Thus, to the Apostle the problem was a real one. For the true Message of the Gospel was in danger because of this basic misunderstanding of the Person and work of Jesus Christ. So John's main answer to the gnostics was his gospel. Also, in two of his letters, I John and II John, written shortly after his gospel, he refers to them with such strong language as "false prophets" and "the Deceiver and the Anti-Christ."

The Prologue, and John's gospel as a whole, will have a new meaning if read in the light of these heresies.

(2) Another result of the teaching of the "false prophets" was the *moral lag* between the professions of the Gentile Christians and their daily conduct. Since the spirit and the body are two separate things, in the eyes of the Gnostics, the spirit could enjoy its religious raptures, while the body engaged in its immoral and sensual practices.

The Apostle Paul, as revealed in his letters to the Corinthians, found the same lag in moral conduct among his converts at Corinth and at other centers, a decade or more before the Apostle John came to Ephesus. Paul found it necessary to discipline the converts of his day, just as the Apostle John now sought to combat the false teaching in the Seven Churches in Asia.

(3) Another constant threat to the evangelistic mission of John in the "Seven Churches of Asia" was the antagonism of the *unbelieving Jews*. They had dogged the footsteps of Paul in almost every city he entered, on his missionary journeys — making false charges, stirring up riots, inciting mobs, calling out Roman officials, everything, and every sort of treachery, to obstruct and to defeat the spread of Christianity among the Gentiles.

These same Jews and their fellows were there in John's day. But John used a different tactic. Instead of fighting it out with them, and often going to jail, as Paul did, John wrote a triumphant story, showing Jesus' Sonship and final victory over all His enemies, the Jews included. And, reading between the lines, we may be sure that this is the kind of sermon John preached, in the face of his real and would-be enemies.

No one can state the over-all purpose of John's gospel better than John himself. At the close of his great and persuasive composition, he summarizes his purpose briefly in these memorable words:

> Now Jesus did many other signs in the presence of the disciples, which are not written in this book; but these are written that you may believe that Jesus is the Christ, the Son of God, and that believing you may have life in his name.

4. The Contents of John's Gospel

John's purpose, as we have seen, is to present Jesus, not merely as the Messiah as men thought He would be, but as the Son of God, so that all men might believe on Him and have eternal life.

In order to carry out this purpose, the author selects his materials. The book therefore emphasizes the acts, discourses and conversations which reveal Jesus as the Christ, the Son of God. At the same time the book omits large portions of the narrative, and the acts, found in the other three gospels, as not serving directly the author's purpose. The book also includes much new material not found in the other three books.

Indeed, the book is largely a *personal testimony* by a leading Apostle and eye-witness, "the disciple whom Jesus loved."

The Analysis

A brief outline analysis of the Gospel of John may be stated as follows:

(1) The Introduction. Chapter 1:1-18. In this sublime opening passage, which reminds us of the beginning words of the book of

Genesis, the author expressly states that Jesus was in the *beginning*, that He was one with God, and that He was the Creator of everything that was created.

And John testifies that this Deity, our God, "became flesh and dwelt among us." And "we" beheld His glory, meaning that John and the other eye-witnessing Apostles and disciples *saw* with their own eyes that "The Word" was God revealing Himself to them. The purpose of this testimony, and this book, is to share this experience with all mankind.

(2) John the Baptist's testimony concerning Jesus as the Christ, and the Son of God, before the Committee of Jerusalem Jews sent by the Sanhedrin. Chapter 1:19-34.

(3) Jesus' own testimony to His disciples, Andrew and John and Simon and Philip and Nathanael, a short time before they were made Apostles. Chapter 1:35-51.

(4) Jesus' revelation of Himself in a long series of Acts, Discourses, and Conversations.

They include the first miracle, at the marriage in Cana (chapter 2); the first instance of driving the money-changers from the Temple during the passover feast (chapter 2);[2] the interview with Nicodemus (chapter 3); further testimony of John the Baptist (chapter 3); the conversation at Jacob's Well with the Samaritan woman on the subject of "Living Water" (chapter 4); the remainder of the seven special miracles recorded in this gospel, including the seventh and greatest, the Raising of Lazarus (chapters 5-11); the famous allegories on Living Water (4), the Bread of Life (6), the Light of the World (8), and the Good Shepherd (10). Chapters 2 to 11.

(5) Jesus' fuller revelation of Himself as the Son of God, and the Saviour, as set forth in the events of the Last Week, including His Death and Resurrection.

These events include the Triumphal Entry into Jerusalem (12); Jesus' interview with certain Greeks, indicating His interest in the Gentiles and the universal nature of His Gospel (12); Jesus' last public discourse, the victory message over Satan (12:27-36); Jesus' priceless Farewell Message to the Twelve (13-17); the scene in Gethsemane, the arrest and trial, and the Crucifixion, in which Jesus bore witness, particularly before Pilate, to His Person and Mission in the world (18 and 19); the Resurrection and the testimonies connected with it (20).

The author's book is brought to a definite close, the contents briefly reviewed, and the purpose restated in the end of chapter 20. However, a little later John must have felt that his story needed the

---

[2]The Gospel of John differs from the Synoptic Gospels in placing the Cleansing of the Temple after the Miracle at Cana. For a complete discussion, see James Moffatt, *An Introduction to the Literature of the New Testament*, pp. 550ff (1911).

supplementary material which he subsequently added, in chapter 21. All the manuscripts and versions contain it, indicating that the supplement was written soon afterward, before the gospel had been extensively copied and circulated.

5. Passages Found Only in John's Gospel

(1) The sublime opening passage (1:1-18), which is a strong declaration of the central theme, the Incarnation of the Son of God.

(2) The significant interview with Nicodemus on the New Birth (3:1-21).

(3) The eventful conversation of Jesus with the Samaritan woman at Jacob's Well, and its consequences (4:1-42).

(4) The Last Supper. John only includes the ceremony of feet-washing; the incident of the sop; the details about John himself as the beloved disciple; and most of all, the marvelous discourses recorded in chapters 13 to 17, and closing with Jesus' prayer for Himself, the Apostles, and the world.

(5) These five miracles: Water changed into Wine (2:1-11); the Healing of the Nobleman's Son (4:46-54); the Man Healed at the Pool of Bethesda (5:1-16); Healing on the Sabbath the Man Born Blind (9:1-12); the Raising of Lazarus from the dead (11:1-44).

(6) These special parables: The Parable of the Living Water (4:1-15); the Bread of Life (6:25-51); the Light of the World (8:1-20); and the Good Shepherd (10:1-21).

(7) The incident on the cross in which Jesus commends His mother to the care of the beloved disciple, John (19:25-27).

(8) Here is a list of the titles and epithets recorded by John to describe Jesus as the Son of God: The Word (1:1, 14); the Light of Men (1:4); the Only Son (1:14; 3:16); the Christ (1:20, 24; 3:28; 4:29); the Lamb of God (1:29, 36); the Son of God (1:34, 49; 3:18; 5:25); the Messiah (1:41); the Son of Man (1:51; 13:31); the Saviour of the World (4:42); the Bread of Life (6:35); the Holy One of God (6:69); the Light of the World (8:12; 9:5); the Door (10:7); the Good Shepherd (10:11, 14); the Resurrection and the Life (11:25); the Way, the Truth, and the Life (14:6); the True Vine (15:1).

Suggestions for Additional Readings on the Gospel of John

*Barclay, William: *The Gospel of John.* 2 Vols.

*Bruce, F. F.: *Are the New Testament Documents Reliable?*

Dodd, C. H.: *The Interpretation of the Fourth Gospel.*

Filson, Floyd V.: *The Gospel According to John.*

Howard, Wilbert F.: *Christianity According to St. John.*

*Kee, Howard Clark and Franklin W. Young: *Understanding the New Testament,* Chapter 13, pp. 383-414.

*Luther, Martin: *Sermon Commentaries on John.* 3 Vols.

*Macleod, A. J.: "The Gospel According to John," *The New Bible Commentary*, pp. 865-896.

Nunn, H. P. V.: *The Son of Zebedee and the Fourth Gospel.*

Robertson, A. T.: *Epochs in the Life of the Apostle John.*

Tenney, Merrill C.: *John, the Gospel of Belief.*

*Tenney, Merrill C.: *The New Testament — an Historical and Analytic Survey.*

*Westcott, B. F.: *Commentary on John.*

A peaceful view of the Jordan, near the traditional site where John the Baptist carried on his ministry. © *Matson Photo Service.*

PART SEVEN

THE ACTS OF THE APOSTLES

Chapter 1

THE ACTS

1. AUTHORSHIP AND DATE[1]

The book of Acts is the sequel to the gospel of Luke, and continues the early history of Christianity where the gospel story leaves off. The book begins by referring to "the former treatise" or first book, and is addressed to the same person to whom the other work is addressed, Theophilus, presumably a Roman or Greek officer, but with a Greek name. He is addressed with the title "most excellent," from which he appears to have been a person of some distinction (Luke 1:3).

Although the book of Acts as it stands is anonymous, like the gospel of Luke, the name of Luke was associated with both at an early date, and this uninterrupted tradition of authorship is universally accepted today. The internal evidence, as revealed in the subject matter and composition of both books, points in the direction of Luke as its author. Certain passages (Acts 16:10-17; 20:5-15; 21:1-18; 27:1 to 28) are written in the *first person* plural, and are called the "we-sections," as indicating that the author was present and an eye-witness of the events which he records.

Also, the author and eye-witness shifts from the *third person* to the *first person* at verse 10 of chapter 16, at the city of Troas in the narrative, the point at which Luke is thought to have joined Paul and his company of evangelists. And the other "we-sections" correspond to Luke's further presence as Paul's companion and associate on the other journeys. (For the complete story of Luke, see the chapter on the Gospel of Luke.)

The most natural date to assign to the composition of the book of Acts is about the close of the Apostle Paul's first Roman imprisonment, and this is the date which is generally accepted. Paul and Luke, and the remainder of the party, arrived at Rome early in 61 A.D. Luke closes his narrative with a statement of the "two whole years" of that first imprisonment, thus:

> And he lived there two whole years at his own expense, and welcomed all who came to him, preaching the kingdom of God and teaching about the Lord Jesus Christ quite openly and unhindered.

---

[1]See F. F. Bruce, Introduction, *The Book of Acts*, pp. 15-27 (1954).

This would place the date of the book at about 63 A.D., which coincides with Paul's last visit to Jerusalem, after the Third Missionary Journey, and his two years' imprisonment at Caesarea, before he and Luke came to Rome.

A later date is unlikely. For the Great Fire at Rome took place in 64 A.D., followed by the frightful persecution of Christians by the Emperor Nero. Also, the Jewish Rebellion against Rome began in 66 A.D., and culminated in the destruction of the Temple and all Jerusalem by the Romans, under their commander Titus, in 70 A.D.

It is inconceivable that Luke would have ended his book of Acts, in an atmosphere of gospel preaching and success, if these momentous events had recently occurred, without making any mention of them. Also, from tradition as well as from Paul's later letters, it is generally supposed that Paul was tried before the Emperor Nero, and acquitted, about 63 A.D., not long after the writing of the book of Acts.

2. THE PURPOSE OF LUKE'S BOOK OF ACTS

Luke's purpose in writing the book of Acts is the same as his purpose in writing the former book, the gospel of Luke. And his introduction to the gospel may very well be his introduction also to the book of Acts.[2] In the first book, Luke's ambition as stated in the introduction was to write a complete and orderly account of the gospel story as revealed in the life and ministry of our Lord.

Connecting the two works, the author begins his second book with this significant remark:

> In the first book, O Theophilus, I have dealt with all that Jesus began to do and teach, until the day when he was taken up.

The phrase, "all that Jesus *began* to do and teach," implies that the Lord Jesus is continuing His work, after the Ascension, and the writer's second book is to continue that story through the "Acts" of the Apostles.

The writer's purpose is further evident when he quotes the Lord's Great Command before His departure, in these words:

> And you shall be my witnesses in Jerusalem and in all Judea and Samaria and to the end of the earth.

And these words may be taken as the key to the book of Acts. For it is precisely the story of these witnesses, in the three respective areas mentioned, with which the book of Acts deals.

As an evangelist, Luke may not have had the eloquence of the Apostle Paul, or Barnabas, or Apollos; but as a storyteller and historian of their "Acts," he had no equal. Indeed, no parallel story to his of this period, if ever written, has come down to us. The book of Acts therefore is of the greatest value to the present day reader, because it is the only authentic record which we have of the first thirty-three years of the history of the Christian Church.

---

[2]F. F. Bruce, *op. cit.*, p. 18ff.

Luke's further purpose is revealed in his *interpretation* of the early history of the Christian movement. Just as Mark was the companion and interpreter of the Apostle Peter, and a disciple of Peter's preaching and approach to the gospel story; so was Luke a disciple of the Apostle Paul. Paul and Luke were the top team of Apostles to the Gentiles; and they saw eye-to-eye on the universality of the Gospel, and on the Person of Christ as the All-Sufficient Saviour. Other Jewish Christians might hold to circumcision and the observance of the Jewish ceremonial law. But not these two!

So Luke's main mission and purpose, both as a follower and a historian, was to tell the story of the growth and expansion of the early Christian Church, from "a Jewish sect into a world-wide religion."

Apparently Luke never named his book "The Acts of the Apostles." However, by the second century this title was being used, and it has remained ever since, although the book deals largely with the Acts of two of the apostles, Peter and Paul. The Apostle Peter is the central figure in chapters 1 to 12, and the Apostle Paul in chapters 13 to 28.

3. THE COMPOSITION OF THE BOOK OF ACTS

In the composition of the book of Acts, Luke shows himself the true historian. On every hand there is evidence of painstaking effort to secure the true facts, and to organize and to report them convincingly to the reader, as we saw in the composition of the gospel of Luke.

As he said in his introduction to the gospel, Luke undertook to trace the course of all things accurately from the very first. During the two years while the Apostle Paul was in prison at Caesarea, 58-60 A.D., Luke seems to have been busy interviewing eye-witnesses throughout Palestine, gathering and setting in order materials for the full historical narrative, as recorded in sequence in his two books.

For an important part of the story, he had the authority of no less a person than the Apostle Paul. Also, the Apostle John was still at Jerusalem, as was James, our Lord's brother and head of the Jerusalem Church. And Philip the evangelist, with his four prophesying daughters, was at Caesarea. In Rome, Luke had access to both the Apostle Peter and John Mark, not to mention many other unnamed eye-witnesses.

And, of course, for an important part of the narrative, Luke himself was present and an eye-witness, as may be seen beginning with his report at chapter 16:10, the "we-sections."

One of the characteristics of the work of Luke is that it has stood the test of time for historical accuracy. "Unlike the other historical writers of the New Testament," says Professor F. F. Bruce of the

University of Manchester, "Luke sets his history in the framework of contemporary imperial events. He is the only New Testament writer who so much as mentions a Roman Emperor's name."[3]

And, as the reader has noticed, Luke's pages are full of the names of Roman governors and other officials, including their correct official titles. In all this, Luke has never been criticized for inaccuracies. Indeed, Sir William Ramsay, who devoted many years to intensive archaeological research in Asia Minor, testified to Luke's accuracy, in these words: "Luke's history is unsurpassed in respect to its trustworthiness."[4]

Luke's plan for the composition of Acts, as we have seen, is to group his narrative materials around a central figure, such as the Apostle Peter in chapters 1 to 12, and the Apostle Paul in chapters 13 to 28. In smaller units, the author has followed the same method. For instance, he singles out some one individual's striking story to represent the whole. Philip and the Ethiopian is such a story. Another example is the choice of Peter's most important convert in the early period, Cornelius, the Roman Centurion. In another part of his narrative, Luke points up the family of the young man Timothy, his mother Eunice and grandmother Lois. The reader will be interested to see how this method is developed throughout the book.

Another feature of the book of Acts is the number of speeches which the author reproduces. The first is Peter's great sermon on the Day of Pentecost, 2:14-41; the evangelist Stephen's defense of himself, 7:2-53; Paul's speech before the Areopagus Forum, Athens, 17:22-31. Paul delivered at least five speeches while under arrest or in prison, at Jerusalem and Caesarea, 21:37 to 26:29. Luke records many others, some of which are summarized briefly, while others are given at more length.[5]

But the larger plan of the book, as we have seen, is to tell the story of the expansion of the early Christian Church into a world-wide religion, from the viewpoint of the three areas named in the commission of our risen Lord: (1) In Jerusalem, (2) in all Judea and Samaria, and (3) to the end of the earth. In Acts, Luke has written another beautiful book. Not primarily because of its pleasing rhetoric, although it has that; but chiefly because of its simple truth in presenting sympathetically and comprehensively one of the world's most heroic epochs.

---

[3]"The Acts of the Apostles," *The New Bible Commentary*, p. 898 (1954).
[4]*The Bearing of Recent Discovery on the Trustworthiness of the New Testament*, pp. 81, 222 (1915).
[5]For a discussion of the authenticity of these speeches, see F. J. Foakes-Jackson, *Acts of the Apostles*, pp. xv-xvi (1931); see also Kee and Young, *Understanding the New Testament*, pp. 52-53, and more at length in chapters 7 and 8, pp. 207-267 (1957).

An ancient Roman paved road near Antioch. © *Matson Photo Service*

SUGGESTIONS FOR ADDITIONAL READINGS ON THE BOOK OF ACTS

Bible Readings: The Acts of the Apostles. Text: *The Revised Standard Version;* or *The New English Bible;* or *The King James Version,* preferably in modern reader's format.

*Barclay, William: *The Acts of the Apostles.*

*Bruce, F. F.: "The Acts of the Apostles," *The New Bible Commentary,* pp. 897-938.

Bruce, F. F.: *The Book of Acts.* English Text.

Clark, George W.: *Harmony of the Acts of the Apostles.* New and Revised Ed.

Dodd, C. H.: *The Apostolic Preaching and Its Developments.*

Filson, Floyd V.: *Jesus Christ the Risen Lord.*

Foakes-Jackson, F. J.: *The Acts of the Apostles.*

Hayes, Doremus A.: *The Synoptic Gospels and the Book of Acts.*

*Kee, Howard Clark and Franklin W. Young: *Understanding the New Testament,* Chapters 6-10, pp. 176-322.

Lietzmann, H.: *The Beginnings of the Christian Church.*

MacGregor, G. H. C.: "The Acts of the Apostles," *The Interpreter's Bible,* Vol. IX, pp. 1-23.

*Rackham, Richard B.: *The Acts of the Apostles.*

Scroggie, W. Graham: *The Acts of the Apostles.*

Chapter 2

THE ACTS (Continued)

4. THE CONTENTS OF THE BOOK OF ACTS

The book is called the Acts of the Apostles, although Luke apparently never used the title. Some students, for the sake of convenience, have divided the book into two parts and have assigned the first twelve chapters to Peter and the remaining sixteen chapters to Paul. On the other hand, Dr. A. T. Pierson wrote a book which he called *The Acts of the Holy Spirit,* since the Spirit is the overall controlling influence in the growth and spread of the early Christian Church.

Luke, however, in his planning and writing of the composition seems to have had in mind the threefold commission of our Lord when He said, "You shall be my witnesses in Jerusalem, and in all Judea and Samaria, and to the end of the earth." He quotes this commission near the beginning of his book. And so an analysis of the book may group the contents into three divisions, thus: (1) The Church in Jerusalem, chapters 1 to 8:3; (2) the Church in Judea and Samaria, chapters 8:4 to 11:18; and (3) the Church beyond Palestine, or the World-Wide Church, chapters 11:19 to 28.

(1) *The Church in Jerusalem,* Chapters 1 to 8:3

The main events of the first stage of the early history of the Church may be briefly stated as follows:

1. THE FORTY DAYS. The appearance of Jesus to His disciples during the Forty Days, after the Resurrection and before the Ascension.

Although Jesus, during His ministry, had told His disciples many, many times that His "kingdom was not of this world," nonetheless they still expected Him to set up an earthly kingdom. One purpose of the Forty Days was to convince them, beyond a doubt, that His Kingdom was a Spiritual Kingdom.

Another purpose of the Forty Days was to charge His disciples with the Great Commission to be His witnesses in Jerusalem, in Judea and Samaria, and to the end of the earth.

The third purpose of the Forty Days was to give anew the promise of the Father, to send His Holy Spirit, for their power and guidance.

2. THE PRESENCE OF THE HOLY SPIRIT. The Church began on the Day of Pentecost, with the outpouring of the Holy Spirit as prophesied by the prophet Joel (Joel 2:28-29), as promised by the risen

Lord, and as interpreted by Peter in his great sermon, resulting in the conversion of the first 3,000.

They had no building or church house; but as a Christian community they met daily in various homes to break bread, or met publicly in Solomon's portico of the Temple. Soon their number reached 5,000, to which others were added daily.

3. PETER PERFORMS MIRACLES. The lame man healed by Peter was selected by Luke as typical of the multitude of "signs and wonders done by the Apostles," and as further evidence of the power of the Spirit. This miracle caused the arrest of Peter and John by the Sadducees, the leading faction of the Jewish priesthood.

4. SEVEN DEACONS. The organization of the Jerusalem Church began with the appointment of *seven deacons*, though Luke does not use the term yet, to take over the task of distributing food and other necessities to the poor of the Church community, so that the Twelve Apostles could spend their time preaching. Stephen, "a man full of faith and of the Holy Spirit," was named first of the seven to head up this work.

5. THE MARTYRDOM OF STEPHEN. On trial for his life, and facing his judges, the members of the Jewish Sanhedrin, Stephen delivered a soul-searching speech in defense of himself, which closed with a denunciation of the Jewish Council. The name Stephen is Greek (*Stephanos*), and it is probable that he, like Luke the author, was Greek, or at least a Greek-speaking Jewish Christian who probably had come from outside of Palestine to Jerusalem.

As a result of his speech, Stephen was seized by the Council, carried outside the city, and stoned to death. The witnesses of the stoning left their garments in the care of a young Jew by the name of Saul, who some thirty years later as the great Christian evangelist to the Gentiles must have related the details of this story to Luke.

This dramatic incident was the signal for the wholesale persecution of the Christians of the Jerusalem Church, the details of which are not related by the author. Thus, following the stoning of Stephen, large numbers of believers in Jerusalem were scattered throughout Judea and Samaria, and beyond the borders of Palestine as far as Antioch in Syria. But the Apostles bravely remained in Jerusalem.

There was a tradition that the gospel of Matthew was written for the Jerusalem Jews, and for the twofold purpose of reconciling, in their minds, the doctrine of the Old Testament and the Gospel of the New, and of winning these Jewish readers over to the faith and fellowship of the Jerusalem Church. The author of Matthew quotes more from the Old Testament than the writers of the other three gospels combined.

6. MATTHIAS, THE TWELFTH APOSTLE. At the outset, the Eleven Apostles, after asking God's guidance in their choice, named Matthias as their twelfth to take the place of Judas, the traitor who destroyed himself. Since the foundations of the Church were being laid, it was

necessary thus to complete their number. Unfortunately we have no further information about Matthias.

(2) *The Church in Judea and Samaria,* Chapters 8:4 to 11:18

The stoning of Stephen, as we have seen, and the great persecution that followed it, caused a large community of believers in Jerusalem to become scattered throughout Palestine, and even beyond its borders.

1. THE PREACHING OF PHILIP. Philip, who like Stephen was one of the seven deacons, went down to Samaria and preached, and large numbers believed.

Through an angel as messenger, Philip received another commission. This time he was to overtake an Ethiopian on the road from Jerusalem to the Philistine town of Gaza. When Philip arrived, the Ethiopian was reading from the Fifty-Third chapter of Isaiah, and was having difficulty interpreting what he read. Philip explained the passage, baptized the Ethiopian, and the two men went on their separate ways, rejoicing.

2. THE CONVERSION OF SAUL. The conversion of Saul of Tarsus is the most important event related in this second stage of the history of the early Church community. Indeed, except for the mission of our Lord, and the gift of the Holy Spirit on the Day of Pentecost, the conversion of Saul is the most important event related in the New Testament (9:1-31).

3. PETER PREACHES ALSO TO THE GENTILES. After the conversion of Saul, there was peace in Judea and Galilee and Samaria, and the Church multiplied and prospered, "walking in the fear of the Lord and in the comfort of the Holy Spirit."

Their leader in this period was the Apostle Peter, who went among the saints in their cities, and performed many miracles in the name of the Lord, and prevailed with many to believe on His name. For a time Peter had headquarters at the old city of Joppa, and from here he visited the many churches in the towns and cities in the thickly populated coastal country.

Luke's method of telling the story of the early Church, as we have seen, is to single out some individual's striking story to represent the whole. Here Luke makes a special point of telling the story of Peter's most important convert during this evangelistic campaign, that of Cornelius, the Roman centurion.

Thus far, the Gospel had been preached to the Jews only. Now the time had come to take it also to the Gentiles. The conversion of Cornelius, and Philip's baptism of the Ethiopian eunuch, was the beginning of the spread of Christianity to "all the world."

(3) *The World-wide Church,* Chapters 11:19 to 28

1. THE CHURCH AT ANTIOCH. The first big event in the spread of Christianity beyond Palestine was the founding of the great Gentile

Church at Antioch, in Syria, 42 A.D. This became the center, instead of Jerusalem, for the spread of the Christian movement westward.

Antioch was the capital of the Roman province of Syria. About 300 B.C. it was named by Seleucus for his father *Antiochus,* of the Macedonian Greek dynasty. With a population of more than 500,000 in Apostolic days, Antioch was the third largest city in the Roman Empire, Alexandria (Egypt) being second and Rome first. Antioch was beautifully situated on the Orantes river, between the mountains on both south and west, some fifteen miles from the Mediterranean seaport of Seleucia.

Here the disciples were first called *Christians;* and here for the first time Christians came into contact with a high degree of Greek and Roman civilization. Although the bulk of the population of this great cosmopolitan trading center was Syrian, there were also many Greeks, Jews, Romans, and other nationalities. The Roman governor of the province resided at Antioch, and here, too, was a detachment of the Roman army.

2. THE GOSPEL PREACHED TO GENTILES. It was not the Apostles, but men from the island of Cyprus, and Cyrene, who had been at Jerusalem and who first introduced the Gospel to the Gentiles at Antioch. For the first wave of missionaries, who went out from Jerusalem because of the persecution that arose over Stephen, preached to none except the Jews. "But there were some of them," says Luke, "men of Cyprus and Cyrene, who on coming to Antioch spoke to the Greeks also, preaching the Lord Jesus" (11:20). According to tradition, Luke was living at Antioch at the time and it is very likely that he was one of these early Greek converts.

Gentiles in large numbers believed and turned to the Lord. When news of these conversions came to the ears of the church at Jerusalem, they sent Barnabas to Antioch to investigate. When Barnabas came and saw the success of the Gospel with Gentiles as well as Jews, he was glad and remained a whole year to help with the work.

3. SAUL COMES TO ANTIOCH. By far the most important service Barnabas performed for the church at Antioch, however, was to go up to Tarsus in Cilicia and to persuade Saul to come to Antioch. For as an evangelist Paul was to become the greatest of them all.

Saul was converted about 35 A.D.,[1] approximately five years after

<hr>

[1]Some scholars prefer to date Paul's conversion a little earlier, about 33 or 32 A.D. See F. F. Bruce, *The Book of Acts,* p. 205 (1954); Kee and Young, *Understanding the New Testament,* pp. 215ff (1957). Those who favor an early date for the writing of Galatians, that is before A.D. 50 and the Conference at Jerusalem, usually prefer an earlier date for Paul's conversion. The late Professor J. R. Dummelow of Cambridge preferred the date A.D. 53, or even later, for Galatians, and therefore a later date for the conversion (see "The Acts," and "Galatians," *A Commentary on the Holy Bible,* 1936). John Knox, *Chapters in a Life of Paul,* prefers A.D. 35 for the conversion. See also the present writer's chapter on Galatians.

the Resurrection of our Lord and the founding of the Jerusalem Church, 30 A.D. Before his conversion, Saul had been a student of the University of Tarsus, a member of a distinguished family of means there, and a citizen of Rome. At Jerusalem he was a pupil of the famous Rabbi and teacher, Gamaliel, a doctor of the Law, a Pharisee, and an older member of the Jewish Council called the Sanhedrin.

Paul became a Pharisee and a younger member of the Sanhedrin, and chief among the persecutors of the first Christians, in and outside of Jerusalem. He was stricken blind on the highway to Damascus while carrying out his mission of persecution. This led to his conversion.

After his conversion, Paul lived in Damascus and the desert of Arabia about three years (Galatians 1:15-18). Late in 37 A.D. he came to Jerusalem for fifteen days, principally to see the Apostle Peter. Then he returned to his birthplace at Tarsus, in Cilicia, where he remained and, presumably, preached in the surrounding area, until the great moment when, about 43 or 44 A.D., Barnabas invited him to join the evangelists at Antioch.

Under the leadership of Barnabas and Saul, large numbers of the people were taught and became converts. The impact of all this, as we have seen, was that the disciples were first called "Christians" at Antioch.

4. DEEDS OF MERCY FOR THE POOR. One of the early acts of the Antioch Church was to perform deeds of mercy. There was a great famine in Judea; and so the disciples, every one according to his ability, sent relief to their brethren in the mother Church at Jerusalem, choosing Barnabas and Saul to go on this mission for them. This was Saul's second visit to Jerusalem since his conversion.

5. HEROD AGRIPPA I AND HIS PERSECUTION OF THE CHURCH. Another episode which Luke relates, and which took place about this time (44 A.D.), was the persecution of the Church at Jerusalem by Herod Agrippa I, son of the Herod who beheaded John the Baptist. Included in Herod's many crimes was the murdering of the Apostle James, the son of Zebedee and brother of John, and one of the three inner circle of friends of Jesus.

When Herod Agrippa saw that it pleased the Jews, he arrested Peter and bound him in chains in prison, with a view to putting him to death also. But the miraculous escape of Peter (chapter 12) not only defeated Agrippa's plans, but caused him to leave Jerusalem for his capital at Caesarea, where soon afterward "an angel of the Lord smote him," and he died.[2]

In spite of Herod, the work of the Lord prospered. Barnabas and Saul returned from Jerusalem to Antioch, when they had fulfilled their mission, bringing with them Barnabas' cousin John Mark, who later was to write the gospel of Mark.

---

[2]For an independent account, see Josephus, *Antiquities*, Book XIX, 7-8.

Paul's First Missionary Journey, 45-48 A.D.

6. WESTWARD: SAUL BECOMES PAUL. On their return to Antioch, Barnabas and Saul, together with other outstanding teachers and prophets, continued to minister to the Church at that important center. But the Spirit of Jesus had other work for the Antioch Church, which was to set apart Barnabas and Saul, the two ablest evangelists among them, for the special missionary work to which they had been called.

So Barnabas and Saul, taking with them as their minister and helper, John Mark, started on their first momentous journey westward, to extend the gospel message to the Gentiles.[3] No two evangelists were ever more under the direct call and guidance of the Holy Spirit than were Barnabas and Saul. They felt His directing presence daily and were made bold to declare the Gospel in the face of all danger and opposition.

They arrived at the port of Seleucia, and from there sailed to the island of Cyprus, the birthplace of Barnabas. They landed at Salamis, the principal city of the island, and proclaimed the Word of God in the synagogue of the Jews. From here they went through the whole island as far as Paphos, where was the seat of government. Luke records the striking incident of the conversion of Sergius Paulus, the Roman proconsul, in consequence of the miracle of the blinding of the Jewish magician and false prophet.

At this point, since his contacts from now on were to be with Romans and the Gentile world, Saul dropped his Hebrew name *Saul*, for the well known Roman name *Paulus* (Paul). We may note too that from this point on Paul became a more prominent figure than Barnabas, his name hereafter being given first by Luke whenever the two are mentioned together.

7. JOHN MARK. From Paphos, Paul and his company set sail and came to Perga in Pamphylia, a stretch of coastland in southern Asia Minor. Here John Mark, their associate and "minister," left them and returned to Jerusalem. Luke gives no reason for Mark's quitting their company. Some scholars feel that Mark, like his cousin Barnabas, belonged to the more conservative party of Christian Jews, and disliked Paul's acceptance of uncircumcised Gentiles as the equals of circumcised Jews. Others think that Mark's dissatisfaction was more personal, that he resented the growing leadership of Paul over his cousin Barnabas. However, Mark appears with Paul again later in Luke's story, indicating that the difference between them had been reconciled.

8. ANTIOCH, ICONIUM, LYSTRA, AND DERBE. So Paul and Barnabas, without Mark, extended their journey northward to Antioch in Pisidia. Here Paul preached his great sermon on the Resurrection, and on the following Sabbath almost the whole city gathered to hear him again.

[3]See map, the Journeys of Paul, p. 402.

When the local Jews saw the multitudes following Paul, they became jealous and drove the evangelists out of the district.

They next turned east to the town of Iconium. Here Paul changed his tactics. A great company believed, both Jews and Greeks; but as usual the *unbelieving Jews* stirred up the Gentiles. But Paul and Barnabas, instead of leaving town, decided with the help of the Lord, to battle it out with the Jews. They remained "a long time" and spoke boldly the message of the Lord.

Finally, they decided to leave for nearby Lystra and Derbe. However, the Jews of Antioch and Iconium followed them, and with the help of their fellows at Lystra, they stoned Paul and dragged him out of the city and left him for dead. Next day he and his companions went on to Derbe, where they made many disciples.

All these cities — Antioch in Pisidia, Iconium, Lystra, and Derbe, and possibly others not mentioned by Luke — were situated in the southern part of the Roman province of Galatia. It is now generally supposed that Paul's letter to the Galatians was addressed to the churches in these cities.

After their work was ended at Derbe, the evangelists decided to retrace their steps, and complete church organizations in the several cities in which they had made converts. They appointed and ordained *elders* to be teachers and preachers, and other officials, and exhorted the new converts to continue in the faith.

When they arrived at Antioch, in Syria, after almost three years absence, they reported to the mother church all the wonderful things the Lord had done with them, and how He had opened the door of faith to the Gentiles wherever they preached. They were commended by the church for their work and remained much of the time for the next two or three years at Antioch, before beginning the Second Journey.

The Council Meeting at Jerusalem, 50 A.D.

9. THE QUESTION OF "CIRCUMCISION." After Paul's return from his First Missionary Journey, there continued to be much controversy in the Church at Jerusalem on the question of "circumcision."

The baptism of Gentiles by Paul on this journey, without requiring them to be circumcised or to keep the ceremonial law, was strongly criticized at Jerusalem by the Pharisaic party within the church. In fact, some of them had gone to Antioch and other Gentile centers, teaching and preaching that "except that you be circumcised after the manner of Moses, you cannot be saved."

After dissension arose, Paul and Barnabas were appointed to go to Jerusalem, to submit the question to the authority of the Twelve Apostles.

At the Council meeting in Jerusalem, after Peter had spoken, and after Paul and Barnabas had reported on the work of the Spirit among the Gentiles, then James, the brother of our Lord and head of the Jerusalem Church, urged the Apostles and Elders not to place the burden of circumcision on the Gentile Christians. The vote was unanimous.

A committee was named to accompany Paul and Barnabas back to Antioch, and with them they carried a letter from the Jerusalem Church clarifying the circumcision issue. Paul was pleased with this victory for the Gentile Christians, and on his subsequent missionary journeys he explained to his disciples wherever he went that this decision of the Council granted them "liberty in Christ Jesus."

Paul's Second Missionary Journey, 50-53 A.D.

10. WESTWARD, AGAIN. With the same deep sense of mission, and guidance by the Spirit, Paul and Barnabas were ready by the fall of A.D. 50, or early spring of 51 A.D., to start on another missionary journey West.

Paul had in mind to visit the brethren in the cities where they had preached on their First Journey. But as we shall see, this journey took Paul far beyond the cities of their first tour into Asia Minor, and included also for the first time some of the great cities of Europe — in Macedonia and Greece.

11. PAUL AND SILAS. Barnabas wished to take his cousin John Mark with them again. Paul opposed the suggestion, apparently on the grounds that Mark had deserted them on the first mission. After some heated words between them, Barnabas dissociated himself from Paul and returned to the island of Cyprus, taking with him Mark as his companion.

Paul then chose as his companion on the Second Journey a distinguished member of the Apostolic Church at Jerusalem by the name of Silas, who had come down from Jerusalem with Paul to Antioch. Like Paul, he had two names. Besides his Hebrew or Aramaic name *Silas,* he was also called by his Roman name *Silvanus;* and like Paul, he was a Roman citizen. He became one of Paul's chief helpers, and his name appears again and again in this story and in Paul's letters.

Going this time overland through Syria and Cilicia, Paul and Silas first re-visited the churches founded on the First Journey, strengthening their faith, and their church organization, and adding new converts to their numbers.

12. THE YOUNG MAN TIMOTHY. At Lystra, Paul saw again the young man Timothy, son of Eunice and grandson of Lois, two leading women in the church there. Although Luke does not say so, the whole family had been converted at the time of Paul's first visit.

Paul was so pleased with Timothy, and his spiritual growth as a young convert, that he invited him to join the evangelists. Before they left Lystra, Paul had him circumcised to avoid the criticism of the unbelieving Jews in the cities where they were to go. Timothy, like

Luke, was to be another faithful friend and companion of Paul's until the end.

Paul's next goal was to go into the Roman province of "Asia," which we call Asia Minor proper, and especially to the great city of Ephesus, the metropolis of Asia Minor. But Luke says that they were forbidden by the Spirit. Next, Paul undertook to pass through Asia Minor, going north into the province of Bithynia. Luke again says, "But the Spirit of Jesus did not allow them."

13. PAUL CARRIES THE GOSPEL INTO EUROPE. So, being hindered by Divine direction in both of these plans, Paul next turned to the ancient city of Troas, a seaport on the western extremity of Asia Minor, and overlooking the Aegean Sea, which divides Europe and Asia.

Troas was the site of ancient Troy and the Trojan War, about which the Greek classic poet Homer wrote in his famous book, *The Iliad,* more than a thousand years before. Here at Troas a most important thing happened. A vision appeared to Paul in the night. A man of Macedonia was standing beseeching him, and saying, "Come over to Macedonia and help us."

Macedonia was another Roman province, on the west side of the Aegean Sea, in Europe. This is Luke's way of saying that God's plan for Paul's Second Journey was to bring the Gospel to the great cities of Eastern Europe.

14. THE AUTHOR ENTERS HIS OWN STORY. Some readers are of the opinion that the "man" in the vision may have been Luke himself, now a citizen of Macedonia and probably stationed at the important city of Philippi, and that it was God's plan to have Luke and Paul meet at Troas.

At any rate, Luke seems to have joined Paul at this point, for he changes from the *third person* in his narrative to the *first,* indicating that he now was present and an eye-witness to the events of which he writes.

15. PAUL AT PHILIPPI. So, with Luke as their guide and host, so to speak, the evangelists set sail westward across the Aegean, coming first to the seaport city of Neapolis, and finally to Philippi. Philippi was one of the two leading cities of Macedonia, and founded by Philip, the father of Alexander the Great.

It lay on the great Ignatian Highway, the Roman road which connected the Aegean Sea and the Adriatic, and thus united Italy and Rome with the great trade routes of the East. It was therefore a trading center for merchants and travelers, and of great commercial importance.

Here at this strategic center Paul organized his first European church. In his brief account, Luke states that the evangelists remained in Philippi "some days," an expression meaning long enough to establish a church with many converts, in all about six months.

Luke was left in charge of the church at Philippi, which very likely was his home now, until about six years later, when he rejoined Paul at Troas, near the close of the Third Missionary Journey. The church at Philippi always remained dear to Paul's heart, because it was one of the most faithful, and so far as we know, the only one from which he received pay for the expense of his ministry (Philippians 4:14-17).

16. PAUL AT THESSALONICA. From Philippi the missionaries passed through the cities of Amphipolis and Apollonia on their way to Thessalonica, the capital and second largest city of Macedonia, more than a hundred miles west of Philippi. Thessalonica, like Philippi, lay on the Egnatian Highway which united Italy and Asia; and like Philippi, it was of great commercial importance.

It is evident that Paul's missionary strategy was first to evangelize the commercial centers and seats of governments, knowing that if Christianity was once established in these centers it would spread throughout the Roman Empire. In this he was not mistaken; for within a few generations, in spite of the extreme persecution of its followers, the Gospel had taken over, and the new Church had become the dominant influence.

At Thessalonica, unlike Philippi, there was a Jewish synagogue in which Paul first preached, as was his custom, "and for three weeks he argued with them from the Scriptures," as Luke reports. But evidently Paul was disappointed with the Jews, for most of his converts in these first weeks were Greek men and women. So, for the remainder of his three or four months at Thessalonica, Paul turned to the Gentiles, and with gratifying results.

For in Thessalonica Paul created a great stir. His enemies, as reported by Luke, accused him of "turning the world upside down!" (17:6). These same enemies, unbelieving Jews, hired professional rabble-rousers to "set the city in an uproar," so that they could have Paul and Silas arrested and sent out of the city, on the pretext that they were breaking Roman law and disturbing the peace.

They succeeded, at least temporarily, in their plot. Luke tells briefly the story of how they maneuvered, and how also they followed and heckled the evangelists at their next stop, at Berea, some fifty miles west of Thessalonica, "stirring up and inciting the crowds" in that city (17:4-15).

To avoid a plot against his life, some of Paul's friends took him out of the city secretly and brought him "as far as Athens," to whom Paul gave instructions for Silas and Timothy, who remained in Berea, to follow him as soon as possible. They started for Athens as instructed, but before they arrived Paul had changed his mind. Being filled with anxiety for the recently established churches in Macedonia, Paul now bade Silas and Timothy return to the brethren of these churches. They were to remain some time, exhorting the new converts to remain faithful, and to bring back with them first-hand information (I Thessalonians 3:1-2).

Timothy went to Thessalonica, and it appears that Silas returned as far as Philippi, to visit Luke and the work there.

17. PAUL AT ATHENS. Meanwhile, Paul had finally come to Athens, the greatest city of the world. For a thousand years, from 500 B.C. to 500 A.D., Athens was the center of art, architecture, philosophy, science, and literature.

Athens, too, was the cradle of democracy; and here the great words *democracy, economics, science, politics, poetics,* and hundreds of others used to describe the arts and sciences, were first created. Athens was the home of Pericles, Socrates, Plato, and Aristotle, Phidias, Sophocles, and Demosthenes, and many others of the world's great.

Paul found Athens full of philosophical and religious ideas; a city crowded with temples and altars; a people devoted to religious ceremonies and mysteries. And yet, while he waited for the return of Silas and Timothy to Athens, as Luke reports, Paul's "spirit was provoked within him" as he saw that the city was full of idols, and the masses of the people given to idolatry.

He argued in the synagogue with the Jews, and on the streets, in the market place, with anyone who happened to be there. Like a second Socrates, Paul asked questions, preached, and discoursed daily to such as would hear him. Some of the Epicurean and Stoic philosophers, the two leading schools of the day, met and talked with him.

When Paul was in Athens, *Epicureanism* was the philosophy of the frivolous and irreligious; those who held that *pleasure,* especially the physical pleasures of eating, drinking, and sensual, luxurious living, should be the chief end of life. Their motto was: "Eat, drink, and be merry today; for tomorrow you die!"

Stoicism was the philosophy of the serious-minded, although Stoics for the most part were fatalistic and pagan. Insofar as their thinking affected their daily living, they lived a life indifferent alike to pleasure, pain, or suffering. In a vague, ineffectual sort of way, they believed in many gods and in the conformity of the individual to his destiny. Their faith, such as it was, leaned heavily on a system of idols and idolatry.

These Epicureans and Stoics, like all the other curious ones in Athens, both Athenians and foreigners, in the words of Luke, "spent their time in nothing except telling or hearing something new." So, hoping to hear something different, they took hold of Paul and brought him before the Court of the Areopagus, that famous body of judges and administrators of the affairs of the city, and set him up to speak.

Unfortunately, Luke gives only a brief resume of Paul's speech. After his tactful introductory remarks, Paul preached the Christian doctrine of Creation, the kinship that all men have with the Creator as His offspring, and the need that all men have to "seek God" and His salvation, and His eternal life through the Resurrection by "a man whom he had appointed." Thus, idols, whether of gold or silver or stone, such as were seen everywhere in Athens, could never be a likeness of God, who is immortal and immaterial like men's souls.

Luke records the impression Paul's speech made on his Athenian audience, especially the effect of his doctrine of the Resurrection: "Some mocked; but others said, 'We will hear you again about this . . . But some men joined him and believed.'" Dionysius, a member of the Court of Areopagus, was one of those who believed.

But Paul felt that his visit to Athens was a failure, and to remain longer was a waste of time. He was saddened by the sight of so much idolatry, and the indifference of men to true religion. And there is no evidence that Paul ever organized a church in the great city, or of a letter which he might have written to the few converts he made there.

18. PAUL AT CORINTH. So, without waiting longer in Athens for the arrival of Silas and Timothy, Paul went over to Corinth, some sixty miles west across Gulf Lepanto from Athens. Corinth was the capital of the Roman province of Achaia, the fourth largest city of the Roman Empire, after Rome and Alexandria and Antioch of Syria, with a population of about 400,000. Situated on the Corinthian isthmus, it had two large ports, through which much of the trade between Italy and Asia passed. It was a wealthy commercial and trading center.

Here at Corinth Paul stayed a year and a half, and established one of his strongest churches. Later it was the occasion of his writing two of his most important letters (I and II Corinthians), and two or three others which are referred to but which have not come down to us.

At first, as was his custom, Paul preached in the Jewish synagogue every Sabbath, arguing and persuading both Jews and Greeks. When Timothy and Silas finally arrived from Macedonia, Paul was in the midst of this work. Although Crispus the ruler of the synagogue believed in the Lord, the majority of the Jews opposed and persecuted Paul, who washed his hands of the lot of them, in these heated words:

> Your blood be upon your heads! I am innocent. From now on I will go to the Gentiles.

19. FIRST AND SECOND THESSALONIANS. The reports which Timothy and Silas brought from the young churches in Macedonia were highly gratifying to Paul. Timothy reported that the converts at Thessalonica were keeping the faith and bearing up bravely against severe persecution. But some of them had questions concerning Christ's Second Coming, indicating that Paul had given it some emphasis in his preaching at Thessalonica. Others wished to know the fate of those Christians who died before the Lord's Coming.

So Paul dispatched a letter, I Thessalonians, to them immediately, in which he praised them for their steadfastness in faith and love, and assured them that those Christians who "had fallen asleep" before the Lord's Coming would be at no disadvantage. This church was established about 51 A.D., and the letter was forwarded to them in the autumn of the same year.

Paul's first letter did not entirely satisfy the Thessalonian Christians. So, a few weeks or months after the first, while he was still in Corinth, Paul wrote them another letter, II Thessalonians. Both letters should be read at this time, and as part of the study of the Second Journey.

There was no "problems" in Silas's report of his visit to the church at Philippi. On the contrary, the Philippian Christians sent Paul "gifts," a sum of money, to be used for Paul's expenses, so that his time could be devoted to preaching. The church at Philippi appears to have been the only one which aided him financially in his work. All Jews, however wealthy, were taught a trade. Paul was a leather-worker and tent-maker. On these missionary journeys, Paul took pride in being able to maintain himself at his trade, and was in no way a burden to his young churches (II Corinthians 11:9; Philippians 4:14-18).

20. PAUL RETURNS TO JERUSALEM AND ANTIOCH. Paul had labored successfully at Corinth for eighteen months and had founded a great Christian church. Every reader wishes that Luke had given a more complete account of it. For a supplementary account, including some of the many problems that arose in the Corinthian church, the reader must turn to Paul's two letters, I and II Corinthians, which were written three or four years later while Paul was in the midst of his Third Missionary Journey at Ephesus.

It was now early spring of A.D. 53, and Paul wished to go to Jerusalem for the Passover in April of that year, and for a short visit with the Apostles Peter and John, and the other leaders in the Church there. He must also go to Antioch, in Syria, and report all things that had been accomplished during the Second Journey.

Moreover, Paul was already planning another important evangelistic campaign. His next great mission was to be at Ephesus, the strategic capital of the Roman province of Asia Minor. His heart had been set on going at the beginning of his Second Journey; but the Spirit of Jesus, disapproving, had directed that he go into Macedonia and Greece, instead. Now apparently that prohibition had been removed, and the Spirit was ready for Paul to go to Ephesus.

Taking leave of his friends at Corinth, Paul set sail for Jerusalem and Antioch, bringing with him his friends Priscilla and Aquila as far as Ephesus, where he left them to prepare the way for his return within a few months.

Although Luke does not say so, it is presumed that Timothy and Silas accompanied Paul back to Palestine on this trip.

Paul's Third Missionary Journey, 54-58 A.D.

21. THE THIRD AND LAST OF THE GREAT JOURNEYS WEST. After their visit to the Church at Jerusalem, Paul and his party went down to Antioch, in Syria, where according to Luke, they spent "some time" reporting the things they had accomplished in the name of the Lord Jesus, and making plans for their next mission.

This was to be the last and the greatest of the three missionary journeys — the climax so to speak, to all of Paul's evangelistic work in the great cities, which were the cultural and commercial centers of the West.

Paul and his men this time would be gone approximately four years. They would visit and preach and "strengthen" the disciples in the churches which they had previously founded. They would cover new territory and found new churches. Also, during these four years, Paul would write four of his greatest Christian discourses, in the form of letters (Epistles): to the Galatians, to the Corinthians, and to the Christians at Rome, whom he had never seen.

Finally, it was time to start, probably in the early spring of A.D. 54. As in the Second Journey, Paul and his fellow evangelists again went by way of the overland route, north from Antioch, through the Cilician Gates of the Taurus Mountains, and visited the churches in southern Galatia, and Phrygia, the same churches which he and Barnabas organized on the First Journey, and which he and Silas re-visited in the early part of the Second Journey.

22. PAUL AT EPHESUS. Apparently Paul and his company arrived at Ephesus in the autumn of A.D. 54, and settled there for about three years, using Ephesus as headquarters, and all Asia Minor as his parish. There probably never was another evangelistic campaign, before or since, like the one Paul and his co-workers conducted in Ephesus and the surrounding territory. For here, as one writer puts it, Paul did the most marvelous work in all his marvelous life. And Luke, our author, who is known for his brevity and understatement, says simply, "And God did extraordinary miracles by the hand of Paul."

The reader will recall that Paul had a "vision" one night, near the close of his Second Journey while at Corinth. The Lord appeared to him and challenged him to be bolder and more outspoken in his preaching, and not to be afraid of any harm that would come to him. From the context, there is every reason to believe that he turned Ephesus, as well as Corinth, "upside down" in an intensified campaign against both *pagans* and *unbelieving Jews*. As helpers and co-workers, in addition to Timothy and Silas, Paul had his good friends Aquila and Priscilla, the eloquent Apollos from Alexandria, and others.

23. LUKE'S SUMMARY OF THE EPHESUS MISSION. Paul preached in the Jewish synagogue for three months, "speaking boldly, arguing and pleading about the Kingdom of God." But certain stubborn and unbelieving Jews spoke evil of the Gospel, openly before the congre-

gation, so much so that Paul withdrew from the synagogue, taking his Christian disciples with him.

A teacher named Tyrannus, probably a Gentile, made his living by keeping a "school" of philosophy at Ephesus. Paul arranged to use his lecture hall, according to one text, "from the fifth hour to the tenth," which in Roman time would be from 11 A.M. to 4 P.M., or during Tyrannus' midday recess, when he himself did not use the lecture room.

Luke summarizes briefly the results of Paul's daily preaching in this hall, in these words: "This continued for two years, so that all the residents of Asia (meaning the Roman province of Asia, or west part of Asia Minor) heard the word of the Lord, both Jews and Greeks" (19:10). This is another way of saying that the preaching of Paul extended beyond the capital city of Ephesus, to include the Roman province itself. For to the ministry of these years belongs the founding of the Seven Churches of Asia, named in John's Revelation (1:11): Ephesus, Smyrna, Pergamum, Thyatira, Sardis, Philadelphia, and Laodicea; and also at least three others which Paul founded, Colossae, Hierapolis, and Troas.

Wherever Paul went things happened. At Ephesus his powerful sermons against idolatry and the idol-makers' craft destroyed much of the industry and produced a riot, in which many thousands took part, and in which Paul nearly lost his life.

The white marble Temple of the great goddess Artemis, called "Diana of the Ephesians" in the King James Version, was the center of pagan worship in Ephesus and in Asia Minor. So large and so magnificent was it, that it was rated one of the Seven Wonders of the ancient world!

At the time of Paul's visit to the city, a man named Demetrius, a silversmith, and his fellow craftsmen of the city, made silver shrines and images of Artemis for the people. When their business was endangered by the preaching of Paul, Demetrius called together the image craftsmen and workmen, and delivered to them this speech, as reported by Luke:

> Men, you know that from this business we have our wealth. And you see and hear that not only at Ephesus but almost throughout all Asia this Paul has persuaded and turned away a considerable company of people, saying that gods made with hands are not gods. And there is danger not only that this trade of ours may come into disrepute but also that the Temple of the great goddess Artemis may count for nothing, and that she may even be deposed from her magnificence, she whom all Asia and the world worship.

The indignation of Demetrius spread to the people, as was intended; and the public demonstration and riot followed as planned, in the 24,000-capacity theater of the city, from which Paul's friends dragged him before the mob could lay hands on him.

This episode, as well as others, indicates how successful Paul's mission to Ephesus and Asia Minor had been.

24. PAUL RE-VISITS EUROPE, INCLUDING NEW TERRITORY. Toward the close of his third year at Ephesus, Paul began making plans for his future course. Three missions had taken shape in his mind: (1) To pay a visit to the churches he had formerly founded on his Second Journey, in Macedonia and in Greece (Achaia); (2) to go to Jerusalem; and (3) to go to Rome, and perhaps to Spain and elsewhere in the Far West.

It appears that Paul left Ephesus on the first of his three missions in June, A.D. 57 (I Corinthians 16:8), going directly to Macedonia. Timothy had returned from Corinth, and now accompanied Paul to Macedonia and Philippi, where they rejoined Luke, from whom Paul had been separated since the founding of the church at Philippi, some six years earlier.

From Philippi, they traveled across the northwest border of Macedonia into Illyricum (modern Albania and Yugoslavia), and took the Gospel into new territory, about which Paul proudly writes a few months later in the book of Romans (15:19-21).

After leaving Macedonia, Paul and his party came to Greece, to Corinth, where they remained for three months during the mid-winter of A.D. 57-58 (Acts 20:2-3; I Corinthians 16:5-7).

There were many reasons why Paul wished to re-visit Corinth, and to spend some time there before he closed his Third Journey and returned to Jerusalem. For one thing, it was a great city of nearly a half million population, the capital of the Roman province of Achaia, and one of the richest and most important commercially in the Roman Empire.

Also, being disappointed in the classic city of Athens, Paul therefore turned to Corinth as a strategic center for establishing a great Christian church in Greece. To this end, he had spent eighteen months of his Second Journey founding the Corinthian church.

25. FIRST AND SECOND CORINTHIANS, AND ROMANS. But, just as the church at Philippi had brought him more joy than any other, so the church at Corinth had caused him more grief and headaches than any other. During his ministry at Ephesus, news came to Paul that the disciples at Corinth were engaging in party quarrels, and that many of them had lapsed into immoral conduct and habits not becoming to Christians.

Some months before coming to Corinth, Paul wrote a letter, now lost (I Corinthians 4:9), scolding the Corinthians for their misconduct. In fact, he probably wrote as many as four letters, including I Corinthians and II Corinthians, in an extreme effort to straighten out the difficult situations which had grown up in the Corinthian church.

Paul and his party arrived at Corinth a few months after Titus delivered the last of the series of letters, II Corinthians, in the late fall of A.D. 57. This letter should be read at this point, as indicating what Paul and his evangelists hoped to accomplish by their further stay of three months at Corinth.

The three months at Corinth passed quickly. During these busy weeks Paul found time to think about his plans for the trip to Jerusalem and finally the voyage to Rome. But lately he had had intimations that he might not get to see Rome. So he took time out to write the greatest of all his leters, the letter to the Romans, as a substitute for a personal visit, in the event that he was prevented from going.

26. PAUL'S MOMENTOUS TRIP TO JERUSALEM. Early spring of A.D 58 soon arrived, and with it time to start on the Jerusalem mission. Paul's original plan was to set sail from Corinth and go directly to Syria, taking with him the delegates and gifts from the several churches contributing to the collection for the "poor saints at Jerusalem."

But a plot by the unbelieving Jews to kill Paul on board the ship, in which he and his friends had taken passage, was discovered. So, to elude the trap set by his conspirators, Paul changed his plans and returned north by way of Macedonia and Philippi, going some 600 miles out of his way, and met the other members of his party at Troas, instead, from which he sailed East. But the same band of conspirators followed Paul all the way to Jerusalem, where they joined in the plot of others there to destroy him.

Paul had planned to reach Jerusalem in June, A.D. 58, in time for the Day of Pentecost (Acts 20:16). Luke, Timothy, and others, including the delegates from the Gentile churches bearing their separate church gifts, would be with him.

27. PAUL AT JERUSALEM AND CAESAREA, 58-60 A.D. Thus, Paul's final visit to Jerusalem was surrounded by an air of mystery and tragedy. Luke records that at every city at which they stopped, Paul was warned that danger and "afflictions" awaited him (20:23). And when their ship finally landed at Tyre, the disciples there warned Paul again not to go to Jerusalem!

From Tyre, they went coastwise down to Caesarea, where Philip the evangelist, and the old prophet Agabus, and all the disciples, warned Paul. In the words of Luke, "We and the people there begged him not to go up to Jerusalem."

Why did Paul thus feel impelled to rush into the mouth of danger, against the advice of all his friends?

For one thing, Paul had spent more than a year gathering a great offering among his Gentile churches for the poor Christians of Jerusalem. Also, the churches had sent their personal delegates with their gifts. In Paul's view, this would be both a realistic and symbolic demonstration of the love, and the Unity, of Gentile and Jewish Christians.

In particular, since the day of his conversion, Paul had had a deep sense of mission. He felt that his whole life was a demonstration too of the Gospel, of the salvation of the Lord Jesus. "For me to live is Christ," he was in the habit of saying. He had been a witness to the Gentiles, "to the end of the earth." Now he would be a witness at Jerusalem also. So, contrary to the opinion of his friends, Paul thought that it was the will of God that he face the dangers of this mission, as he had faced the dangers of his Gentile mission.

The vision that came to Paul at night in the Roman barracks, and which Luke quotes as follows, seems to bear out this view:

> The following night the Lord stood by him and said, "Take courage, for as you have testified about me at Jerusalem, so you must bear witness also at Rome" (23:11).

How Paul was rescued from the mob and his enemies by the Roman tribune, and transferred under heavy guard at night to Caesarea, where he spent the next two years in the care of the Roman governor of the province — all this, and more, is reported briefly by Luke, in chapters 21 to 26.

28. THE LONG VOYAGE TO ROME. After two long years of waiting for his freedom, Paul and his two close friends, Luke and Timothy, and perhaps others, set sail for Rome. For Paul finally had appealed his case to Caesar, as was his right as a Roman citizen.

For one reason and another, their passage was delayed until late autumn, in A.D. 60, when the winter storms on the Mediterranean are ordinarily avoided by prudent travelers. Paul left Caesarea as a prisoner, with other prisoners, bound for Rome and a hearing before the Emperor. Before they had completed their voyage, Paul was virtually captain of the ship in which there were a total of 276 passengens, and other cargo. Taking advantage of every opportunity, Paul preached Christ to both officers and men, and many believed and took courage for their safety. Luke gives a most vivid account of the voyage (chapters 27-28).

29. TWO YEARS WITH PAUL AT ROME: THE FIRST IMPRISONMENT, A.D. 61-63. At Rome, as at Caesarea, Paul as a "prisoner" was allowed much liberty. He was permitted to live in his own house, at his own expense, with only one soldier as guard. He virtually kept an open house and carried on his ministry with the greatest freedom.

The last chapter of Acts is characteristic of the book as a whole, in that it pin-points again the two main themes of the book. The first is occasioned by Paul's final interview with the Jews, this time the Roman Jews, in which once more, and finally insofar as this book is concerned, they reject the Gospel. Paul's reaction to their rejection of the Kingdom of God was most devastating, when he quoted from the Sixth Chapter of Isaiah (6:9-10):

> Go to this people, and say,
> You shall indeed *hear* but never understand,
> And you shall indeed *see* but never perceive.

The other main theme of the book is related in the closing words, in which the reader is given a picture of the chief Apostle to the Gentiles, at Rome and in the center of the Gentile world, "preaching the Kingdom of God and teaching the story of the Lord Jesus without let or hindrance." Paul thanked God, and for him it was one of the great moments in his life.

30. PAUL'S LETTERS. During these two years of waiting in Rome, if his busy life can be called waiting, Paul wrote several important letters. We have said that he wrote I and II Thessalonians, from the city of Corinth, during the last half of his Second Missionary Journey; and that while on his Third Journey, he wrote the great discourses in the form of letters which we call Galatians, I and II Corinthians, and the greatest of them all, the letter to the Romans.

During these two years of the first imprisonment at Rome, Paul wrote these five letters: Colossians, Ephesians, Philemon, Philippians, and very likely Hebrews. For inspiration, and sheer Christian zeal, no letters have ever surpassed Paul's superlative compositions.

Luke's history stops at this point; and for the remaining four or five years of Paul's ministry, until his martyrdom about 67 or 68 A.D., the reader must piece together his story from the letters and other sources. The letters, I Timothy, Titus, and II Timothy, were written during this last period.

The Mamertine Prison, in Rome, where both Paul and Peter were imprisoned. At right, a tablet in Latin marking the site of these events. *Photo courtesy of Dr. John F. Walvoord*

Part Eight

THE LETTERS OF PAUL

At the house of Ananias, near Straight Street, in Damascus, where Paul went shortly after his encounter with the Lord on the road (Acts 9:11). © *Matson Photo Service.* Inset: A tablet on Mars Hill, Athens, commemorating Paul's sermon there. *Photo courtesy Mrs. Lowell Orth*

Chapter 1

INTRODUCTION

1. THE LETTERS OF PAUL

The Apostle Paul was a native of Tarsus, the chief city of Cilicia, one of the intellectual centers of the East and the seat of a famous school of learning. He was born *Saul*, the son of a prominent Jewish family with Roman citizenship. Saul's Hebrew name was changed to the Roman Paulus or *Paul* during his first missionary journey.

Paul was sent to Jerusalem as a youth to be educated in the Law, and had for his teacher one of the most learned and distinguished rabbis of the day, Gamaliel. At Jerusalem he early became a member of the Pharisee party, and from his prominence at the time of Stephen's death and the persecution of the Christians subsequently, he apparently already was a member of the Council of the Sanhedrin.

Shortly after his conversion, about 35 A.D., Paul received the unique commission to become "the witness" of the Lord Jesus Christ to the Gentiles, to the utmost parts of the earth. By the beginning of his Second Missionary Journey, late 50 or early 51 A.D., Paul's leadership as the Apostle to the Gentiles was already established. It was during this Journey that the first of the letters were written, I and II Thessalonians.

Luke, as the official historian of the early Christian Church in his book, the Acts of the Apostles, recognized Paul's place in his story by devoting the last sixteen chapters to the leadership of the Apostle Paul. Moreover, we may inquire as to the nature of this leadership as interpreted by Luke. The last book of our Bible is called the Revelation. If we may consider the sixty-six books from the viewpoint of their *content* and *purpose*, each one is seen as a "revelation" of God's overall plan and purpose through the work of the Holy Spirit. Luke, in telling Paul's story, makes this abundantly clear in every incident or episode — from Paul's conversion at the outset to the latest event, to the writing of II Timothy, before his martyrdom. The reader who understands Paul's letters best, will be the first to see this constant guiding influence of the Spirit.

Practically speaking, as the foremost Christian missionary, Paul used letter writing as an important aid in conducting his evangelistic program. He established so many churches on his missionary journeys that it soon became impossible, humanly speaking, to give each of them the personal attention they required. So he wrote them letters as substitutes for his personal visits.

Although his letters were composed to meet the specific needs of particular churches and congregations founded by him, and were thus timely and occasional in nature, they were nonetheless on divinely inspired themes of such universal religious importance, that they have also been of profound interest to readers of every age. Moreover, they were early quoted as part of the Scriptures, and soon found their rightful place in the New Testament canon as inspired writings (II Peter 3:15-17).

Indeed, throughout the centuries since they were first written, no other letters have had anything like the influence that these letters of Paul have had on the millions who have read them.

The purpose of the following short chapters is to introduce each of these letters, briefly, so that the reader may read and enjoy them for himself. Also, the reader is urged to read the two preceding chapters on the book of Acts and the book of Acts itself, as a general introduction to Paul and his letters.

In the older versions of our Bible, these letters are called *Epistles,* after the Greek word *epistolē,* Latin *epistola;* in modern English they are called simply, *Letters,* as written in the way of ordinary correspondence.

Paul seems to have had some difficulty with his eyesight, and so ordinarily he employed a secretary or copyist to write his letters from dictation (Romans 16:22). Then he would add the salutation in his own "large hand," as a "token" of every letter, so that there could be no forgery (I Corinthians 16:21; Colossians 4:18; II Thessalonians 3:17). In the case of the Galatians, however, Paul departed from his usual custom and wrote the entire letter with his own hand (Galatians 6:11).

2. THE CHRONOLOGY OF PAUL'S LETTERS

To simplify the reading and understanding of Paul's letters, they are arranged chronologically, as they were written, as follows:[1]

1. Letters written during Paul's Second Missionary Journey, about 50-53 A.D.: I Thessalonians; II Thessalonians.
2. Letters written during the Third Missionary Journey, about 54-58 A.D.: Galatians; I Corinthians, II Corinthians; Romans.
3. Letters written during Paul's First Imprisonment at Rome, about 61-63 A.D.: Colossians; Ephesians; Philemon; Philippians; Hebrews (?).
4. Letters written after release from the First and during Paul's Second Imprisonment at Rome, about 64-67 A.D.: I Timothy; Titus; II Timothy.

---

[1]For the chronology of Paul's letters, see Alexander Ross, "The Pauline Epistles," *The New Bible Commentary,* pp. 68-71 (1954); John Knox, *Chapters in the Life of Paul* (1950); see also Foakes-Jackson, Lake, and Cadbury, *The Beginnings of Christianity,* Part I, Vol. 5, for a full discussion of Paul's chronology. For the place of Galatians, see the present writer's chapter and footnotes on that book.

SUGGESTED READINGS ON PAUL AND HIS LETTERS[2]

Bible Readings: I and II Thessalonians, Galatians, I and II Corinthians, Romans, Colossians, Ephesians, Philemon, Philippians, Hebrews, I Timothy, Titus, II Timothy.

Text: *The Revised Standard Version;* or *The New English Bible;* or *The King James Version,* preferably in the modern reader's format.

*Conybeare, W. J. and J. S. Howson: *The Life and Letters of St. Paul.*

Davies, W. D.: *Paul and Rabbinic Judaism.*

Deissmann, A.: *Paul, A Study in Social and Religious History.*

Dodd, C. H.: *The Meaning of Paul for Today.*

*Foakes-Jackson, F. J.: *The Life of St. Paul.*

Goodspeed, Edgar J.: *Paul.*

Knox, John: *Chapters in the Life of Paul.*

Knox, W. L.: *St. Paul and the Church at Jerusalem.*

Mackay, John: *God's Order.*

Nock, A. D.: *St. Paul.*

*Ramsay, Sir William: *St. Paul the Traveller and the Roman Citizen.* Fourteenth Edition.

Robertson, A. T.: *Paul, the Interpreter of Christ.*

*Ross, Alexander: "The Pauline Epistles," *The New Bible Commentary,* pp. 68-71.

Stalker, James: *The Life of St. Paul.* A New Edition.

*Stewart, James S.: *A Man in Christ.*

*Tenney, Merrill C.: *The New Testament, A Survey,* pp. 289-355.

Wood, C. T.: *The Life, Letters, and Religion of St. Paul.*

---

[2]For a more complete list of readings on St. Paul, see the bibliography on the book of Acts, and the Books on the Life and Work of Paul in the General Bibliography at the end of this volume.

I. THE LETTERS OF PAUL WRITTEN DURING THE FIRST PERIOD, ABOUT 50-53 A.D.

Chapter 2

I THESSALONIANS

1. THE OCCASION AND DATE OF THE LETTER

Paul wrote the first letter of our collection, I Thessalonians, from Corinth about 51 A.D., a few months after the Thessalonian church was founded, about the middle of his Second Missionary Journey.

The Apostle Paul's main objective on his Second Journey, as we saw in our study of the book of Acts, was to go to the great city of Ephesus in Asia Minor; but being hindered by the Spirit of Jesus, he went across the Aegean Sea into Macedonia, to Philippi. After five or six months here, Paul and his party went on to Thessalonica, the capital and second largest city of Macedonia, where they spent three or four months and established the important church there. Before he reached Corinth in Greece, Paul had sent his two chief co-laborers, Timothy and Silas, back to visit the newly founded church at Thessalonica, to urge them to remain in the faith, and to report back to him.

Timothy brought back good news from the Thessalonian Christians. They were holding up bravely against persecutions of the unbelieving Jews. But they had certain questions which were bothering them. In the letter before us, Paul undertook to answer their questions, and to repeat the gospel message which he delivered to them, when he was formerly in their midst.

2. THE CONTENTS OF THE LETTER

In this letter, I Thessalonians, and the other that soon followed it to the same church, the Apostle Paul's approach is brief, simple, and practical, with little discussion of doctrine. The main ideas in the letter may be described briefly, as follows:

1. Love for one another has always been a prime characteristic of true Christians.

So Paul, both following and helping to establish the tradition, spends much of this first letter in informal, friendly greetings, with much show of appreciation and affection for these new disciples. He wants them to know that they are important — important to himself, Paul, and to the other evangelists, and especially important to God, who by His grace has seen fit to call them. His vocabulary is heavy with the word "brethren."

2. The question which was uppermost in their minds was regarding Christ's Second Coming.

Paul must have given this topic some emphasis in his preaching at the time of his original visit at Thessalonica.

Others, as Timothy reported their questions, wished to know the fate of those Christians who died before the Lord's Coming.

The reader will recall that Jesus Himself said much about His Coming and how it would be sudden and unexpected. So there grew up a feeling among early Christians that this Second Coming would be *soon*. Evidently Paul was speaking from this early tradition in the Christian Church.

So, immediately after receiving Timothy's report, Paul directed this letter to them, praising their steadfastness in faith and love, and assuring them that those Christians who "*had fallen asleep*" before the Lord's Coming would be at no disadvantage.

As to the time of His Coming, the best security, he warned them, was to be both watchful and ready, for "the Lord will come like a thief in the night."

3. Paul's final word of exhortation deals with their relation to one another as a Christian community. In particular he urges the disciples to be respectful and generous toward their new leaders, whether pastors or elders or teachers — "those who labor among you and are over you in the Lord and admonish you."

3. What the Letter Reveals of the Writer, and of the Persons Addressed

This letter was written about twenty-one years after the Ascension of Christ, and is important to students of the Bible for what it reveals of early Christian faith and life.

In this short letter, Jesus is called "the Lord Jesus Christ" five times, "Christ Jesus" or "Lord Jesus" eight times, and "Christ" or "Lord" or "Son" fifteen times.

We learn also that Jesus lived in Judea, and was killed by the Jews (2:14-15); that He rose from the dead and is now in heaven, where He delivers us from the wrath to come (1:10); and that He shall come to judge the world (4:14-18). He is Redeemer and Deliverer (5:9-10).

The Holy Spirit is given to Christians (1:5, 6; 4:8; 5:19).

The Church is already organized, and has a ministry (5:12-13); and the local Church at Thessalonica appears to be affiliated in brotherhood and fellowship with other Churches (1:8; 2:14; 4:10). Prayer is extolled as a main Christian virtue (4:17-18).

The Thessalonian Christians are exhorted to refrain from immorality, including more than one wife, adultery, lust, and all other forms of uncleanness (4:1-8).

Paul, in this and other letters, always addresses himself as *Paul*, using his Roman name instead of the Hebrew *Saul*, as he began doing on the Second Missionary Journey. Likewise, he addresses Silas as *Silvanus*, using his Roman rather than the Hebrew name *Silas*, which is always used by Luke.

Paul closes this, his first letter, with a solemn oath or command, "I *adjure* you by the Lord that this letter be read to all the brethren."

In this connection, it is important to note that, with one or two possible exceptions, all the letters of the New Testament were written to be read aloud in the churches and congregations to which they were addressed.

SELECTED READINGS ON I AND II THESSALONIANS

*Bruce, F. F.: "The Epistles to the Thessalonians," *The New Bible Commentary*, pp. 1052-1062.

Davis, John D.: "Thessalonians," *The Westminster Dictionary of the Bible*, pp. 601-602.

*Milligan, George: *St. Paul's Epistles to the Thessalonians*.

*Morris, Leon: *Paul's Epistles to the Thessalonians*.

Neil, W.: *The Epistles of Paul to the Thessalonians*.

Rolston, Holmes: *Paul's I and II Thessalonians, I and II Timothy, Titus, and Philemon*.

*Tenney, Merrill C.: "The Thessalonian Letters," *New Testament Survey*, pp. 295-300.

Chapter 3

II Thessalonians[1]

1. The Occasion and Date of the Letter

This letter, II Thessalonians, apparently was written in late 51 or early 52 A.D., a few months after I Thessalonians, and from the city of Corinth, like its predecessor.

The occasion for the writing of II Thessalonians in general is about the same as that of the first letter, and so the reader should review the introduction to that letter.

It appears that the Thessalonian Christians had received much encouragement from Paul's first letter, in their Christian living, and in their relations to one another as a Christian community. However, they were still disturbed over the question of the Lord's Second Coming, partly because Paul's explanation in the first letter was misunderstood, and partly as Paul thought because of some teaching they had received from another source — perhaps from false or ignorant teachers.

And so, Paul's second letter undertakes further to set at ease the minds of his Thessalonian disciples on this and related questions.

2. The Contents of the Letter

In his second letter, as in the first, Paul's approach is brief, simple, and practical. And although he must explain a difficult question such as Christ's Coming, he deals with it simply and with little discussion of doctrine.

The main ideas of the Letter may be stated briefly, as follows:

1. In this Letter, as in the former letter to the same church, Paul devotes a liberal portion of his message to greetings and salutations, and to an expression of his joy and thanks, "for your steadfastness and faith in all your persecutions." In fact, their growth in grace has already led him to boast of them to his new disciples at Corinth. As in the former letter, he says much to make them feel important as young Christians.

2. The question which is still uppermost in their minds has to do with the Lord's Coming, notwithstanding Paul's previous answer to their question. This time Paul faces the question directly.

---

[1]The reading references on II Thessalonians are given at the end of the preceding chapter on I Thessalonians.

The walls of ancient Thessalonica. *Georgios*
Lykides Photo Agency

In Paul's absence, someone had suggested to the Thessalonians that it was just possible that the Lord had already "come." Paul assures them that this could not be so and begs them *not to be quickly shaken in mind or excited.*

Jesus Himself had said that the end would not come until the Antichrist appeared, "proclaiming himself to be God," and leading the Great Apostasy. No such event has taken place yet, Paul assures them.

Meanwhile, he exhorts them to continue in the faith and to establish themselves "in every good work."

To give his words practical meaning and application, he proceeds to name things for them to do. For one thing, there had developed *idleness* among them, doubtless because many thought that Christ's Coming would be *soon;* and if so, there would be no need for labor!

They were admonished to separate themselves from such idlers. And, too, they were to discipline anyone who would not work, by seeing that he did not eat.

At the very moment the letter was being written, Paul and his co-laborers were in the midst of their ministry at Corinth, and the Gospel was having tough going in that wicked city, where Satan had held sway for so long. So Paul called on his friends and brethren at Thessalonica to do one more practical thing — to pray that the Word of the Lord may speed on and triumph at Corinth, "as it did among you."

3. WHAT THE LETTER REVEALS

In the first place, it is of interest to note how nearly this second letter is a duplication of the religious faith and practice revealed in the first letter to the Thessalonians. A brief check and comparison of the two letters will show this.

There is one topic, however, which Paul treats more at length in the second letter — and that is how important it is in any society that everyone be willing to work, and to earn his own keep.

Paul uses himself as an extreme example. In both letters (I Thessalonians 1:9; II Thessalonians 3:7-8), he reminds the disciples at Thessalonica that, while he preached in their midst, he worked at his trade night and day that he might earn his own way and not be a burden to any one.

Regardless of his wealth or station in life, every Jew was taught a trade. Even rabbis were expected to earn their living by manual labor, and not to make the teaching of the Law a means of gain. Not here, but in later letters, Paul tells us that he earned his living by tentmaking, or more strictly speaking, by working in leather.

It was Paul's custom, as we have noted, to dictate his letters to a secretary or copyist. At the close of II Thessalonians, he calls atten-

The Arch of Galerius at Thessalonica
Georgios Lykides Photo Agency

tion to the fact that all his letters are authenticated by some word in his own handwriting, *in large letters,* along with his signature.

Each letter opens with a formal introduction of himself, with associates, as author, and the persons to whom the letter is addressed. Each letter closes with a benediction. Notice the similarity of these greetings and benedictions in the different letters.

II. THE LETTERS OF PAUL WRITTEN DURING THE SECOND PERIOD, ABOUT 54-58 A.D.

Chapter 4

GALATIANS

1. WHO WERE THE GALATIANS?

The Gauls, originally from north of the Black Sea, migrated westward into Macedonia and Greece, and eventually as far west as what is now France. However, the Galatians of Paul's story were a branch of the Gaul's split off from the main migration, who settled in central Asia Minor in the early part of the third century B.C. The Gauls were commonly called *Galatai* by the Greeks, whence their name *Galatians*.

This Galatia, which is the name given originally to the territory in north central Asia Minor, was taken over by Augustus Caesar in 25 B.C. To the old Galatia as a nucleus, Augustus added part of Pontus on the northeast, part of Phrygia on the southwest, and most of Lyconia on the south to form the much larger Roman province of Galatia of Paul's day, extending almost to the Mediterranean. These southern and southwestern districts were more highly populated as evidenced by the Roman roads and the cities in them, and were politically and commercially far more important.

Thus, Paul and Barnabas on their First Missionary Journey about 45-48 A.D., founded churches in this important region, at Antioch of Pisidia, Iconium, Lystra, and Derbe, and perhaps elsewhere, all of which came within the comparatively new and larger Roman province of Galatia (Acts 13, 14).

Although the Gauls or Galatians settled originally in the central part of the province, near the modern city of Ankara, capital of Turkey, by Paul's day it appears that they had migrated further south into the region of Paul's churches.[1] They were, like their modern counterparts, impulsive and changeable, ready to worship Paul and Barnabas as gods one moment, and to stone them the next. As heathen Gentiles, many of them accepted the Christianity of Paul gladly. But when Paul was gone, they also listened to the persuasive talk of the Judaizers, who although professed Christians themselves, were Phari-

---

[1]In his letter to the Galatians, did Paul address the churches in old Galatia, or the new Galatia as organized by Augustus? For a summary of the different views, see Merrill C. Tenney, *New Testament Survey*, pp. 279-284; Kee and Young, *Understanding the New Testament*, pp. 231-236.

sees in origin. These Jewish Christians were unsettling the minds of the Gentile Christians by teaching that to be a Christian, Gentiles must be circumcised and observe the Jewish law.

2. The Occasion and Date of the Letter

At Antioch in Syria, at the close of their First Missionary Journey, Paul and Barnabas were able to report the conversion of large numbers of Gentiles and some Jews, all of whom had been received into the church without the rite of circumcision and without requiring them to observe the Jewish ceremonial law.

The outstanding success of their ministry was unmistakable evidence that it had the approval of the Spirit of Jesus, whom all of them had received after baptism. But the strict Jewish Christians, in Judea and elsewhere, challenged Paul's practice of accepting Gentiles into the Church without requiring them to observe Jewish law (Acts 15:1).

Now the Church at Antioch itself, which had already become larger and more influential than the mother Church at Jerusalem, contained both Jews and Gentiles united in fellowship. So the Antioch Church's very existence, and the future of Paul's mission to the Gentiles, were both threatened.

So the issue was taken to Jerusalem, in A.D. 50[2]. Paul and Barnabas and others (Paul names Titus, Galatians 2:1) were appointed by the Church at Antioch to go before the Apostles and Elders at Jerusalem for a decision in this important matter.

After much debate, and special speeches by the Apostle Peter, Paul and Barnabas, and James the brother of Jesus, the Council at Jerusalem decided not to require Gentile converts to observe Jewish ceremonial law, including the rite of circumcision. The Council also drew up a letter to this effect, and named Barsabbas and Silas to accompany Paul and Barnabas back to Antioch with the Council's letter. Both Luke (Acts 14, 15) and Paul (Galatians 1, 2) give the main outlines of this episode, including the disagreements between Paul and Peter after the return to Antioch, although the two accounts are not exactly parallel.

The date of the letter to the Galatians is important because of its bearing on the interpretation of Paul's message, and the course of his journeys. Not all scholars agree on its date, some preferring to date the letter immediately after the return of Paul and Barnabas from the First Journey, and *before* the Council meeting at Jerusalem in A.D. 50;[3] others, reading the context of Galatians closely, and noting the maturity of its message, associate the letter with the Second or Third

---

[2]See chapter 2 on the book of Acts, p. 408ff.
[3]Merrill C. Tenney favors the early date, although he is extremely careful to point out the difficulties of the view, in *New Testament Survey*, pp. 279-284. See also Professors Kee and Young, *Understanding the New Testament*, pp. 235-236, as typical.

Journey, and not too far removed from the date of the letter to the Romans, which it resembles in many respects.[4]

In the opinion of many present day scholars, there need not be any serious question about the geographical location of Galatia or the Galatians, inasmuch as the Emperor Augustus organized the Roman province of Galatia in 25 B.C. to include the cities visited by Paul on the First Journey and named by Luke (Acts 13, 14). And from the context of Luke's narrative, there can hardly be any doubt that Paul visited the same cities on his Second (Acts 16:1-5) and Third Journeys (Acts 18:23). Also, since these cities were generally on the Roman highways, usually traveled by Paul, it is unlikely that Paul traveled or established any churches in north Galatia.

When was the letter to the Galatians written? Again, although there are difficulties, it appears from the context that the letter was written *after* A.D. 50 and the meeting of the Council at Jerusalem. In Galatians 1:11 to 2:10, Paul relates his own biography as something in the past and not near the present, including his conversion, his "three years" in Arabia after conversion, after which he went to Jerusalem, and "Then after *fourteen* years I went up again to Jerusalem with Barnabas, taking Titus along with me." This last reference would almost surely have to relate to the Council meeting of A.D. 50, for he is talking about *circumcision* and the disagreement over the observance of Jewish law, and not about the "famine visit," as some scholars believe.

Thus, the context seems to require the reading of *three* years plus *fourteen* years, or seventeen years from the date of his conversion, which generally is thought to have been about 35 A.D., although some suggest moving the date back to 32 or even 31 A.D. If the conversion date is placed at 35, the date of Galatians would be later than A.D. 50 and the date of the Council meeting. Moreover, as stated above, Luke refers to three visits to the Galatian cities and in no case does he refer to any difficulties Paul had with the churches or the *Judaizing* teachers within them. Indeed, in his narrative of the Second Journey, Luke, speaking for Paul and his company, reports on the decision of the Council meeting in these words: "As they went on their way through the cities, they delivered to them for observance the decisions which had been reached by the Apostles and Elders who were at Jerusalem" (Acts 16:4). And still there is no reference to trouble of any sort, and so we may conclude that the difficulties of which Paul writes with some heat in Galatians took place during the latter part of the Second, or perhaps some time during the Third Journey.

---

[4]The late Professor John D. Davis of Princeton preferred a later date to coincide with the known facts, and is inclined to place it about 55 or 56 A.D., or perhaps a little closer to the date of Romans (5-8), in *The Westminster Dictionary of the Bible*, Fifth Edition, pp. 190-192. See also Sir William Ramsay, *A Historical Commentary on St. Paul's Epistle to the Galatians.*

Moreover, some scholars see in Galatians evidence of a method or pattern which they have observed in many of Paul's letters, namely, that of writing a letter on a special occasion or theme, and then following it soon with a fuller development of the same theme. For example, I and II Thessalonians are thus closely associated; Colossians and Ephesians were written at the same time and delivered by the same messenger, the latter developing more fully the theme of the former. And these scholars see in Galatians the first letter on a theme which, presumably, he developed much more fully not too long afterward in Romans.

If, as seems likely, Paul made his third and last visit to these churches (Acts 18:23) at the beginning of his Third Journey (54-58 B.C.), and at the time no upheaval had taken place worthy of being noted by Luke in his narrative, it appears plausible that these troubles developed afterwards, perhaps while Paul was at Ephesus.

In his absence, at whatever time, news came to Paul that certain influential Judaizing teachers were unsettling the minds of Gentile Christians concerning their obligation to observe Jewish law. In fact, a crisis had arisen. Thus, he writes this letter to correct in their minds this vital doctrine.

Indeed, Paul was thrown into a fit of righteous fury. For it was the glory of the Gospel of the Lord Jesus that it was all-sufficient for salvation, and that it was in no way dependent upon circumcision and the Jewish ceremonial law. In fact, he was so eager to compose his message to the churches of Galatia that he wrote it with his own hand, contrary to his usual method of dictating it to others (6:11).

3. THE CONTENTS OF THE LETTER

In his first two letters, I and II Thessalonians, Paul devoted a third to a half of his message to complimenting the Thessalonian Christians for the trueness of their faith, and for the excellence of their behavior as a Christian community.

But not so in this letter to the Galatian Christians. For there are no "bouquets" in this message.

On the contrary, in the opening greeting itself (1:1-5), the author begins with an *answer* to the two main charges which were made against him and his preaching, in his absence, namely: (1) that he was not an authentic Apostle, and (2) that the Gospel of the Lord Jesus which he preached must be supplemented and supported by Jewish law.

The main contents of the letter may be stated, briefly, as follows:

1. Paul's defense of the validity of his Apostleship. Chapters 1 and 2.

These first two chapters are highly autobiographical, and are especially valuable to students of the Bible for this reason, as both verifying and supplementing the story of Paul in the book of Acts.

In these chapters Paul shows that his call was directly from Christ, and that he was completely independent of the other Apostles — in his call to the Apostleship, in his commission by the Lord Jesus Himself, and in his teaching and preaching to the Gentiles and the Gentile world.

2. Paul's exposition of the doctrine of salvation by faith in Jesus Christ and His plan of salvation. Chapters 3 to 5:12.

In this section, Paul is discussing a profound subject in vital theology, and his somewhat abstruse style is not always too clear. However, the translators of the new *Revised Standard Version* of our New Testament have done a good job of simplifying his diction somewhat, as compared with the *King James Version*.

3. Paul's *exhortation* to the Churches in Galatia, in which he applies the great truths which he sets forth in the preceding passages, and in which he also explains how they as Christians may attain this "freedom in Christ," of which he speaks. Chapters 5:13 to 6.

Paul closes the letter with this cryptic comment: "Henceforth let no man trouble me; for I bear on my body the marks of Jesus," to which he adds a brief benediction.

4. PAUL'S DECLARATION OF RELIGIOUS FREEDOM[5]

Paul's letter to the Galatians has been called the Magna Charta of Christian liberty.

The Judaizing teachers who followed in the wake of his missionary journeys, and who were unsettling the minds of his disciples, had thus challenged Paul to a defense of the revolutionary Gospel which he preached.

This letter is his defense, which, to quote his own phrase, is his call to "freedom in Christ," an expression which is found only in Paul in the New Testament.

What is freedom in Christ?

A brief analysis of the role of the Old Testament will throw light on the meaning of Paul's letter. For the Old Testament developed the doctrine of the Law, which for Israel was a tutor or schoolmaster, which was eventually to bring us all to the true revelation — to Christ the universal Saviour.

Thus, the Law was never intended to *save;* on the contrary, its purpose was to educate and to discipline mankind for the coming of the perfect revelation. Therefore Judaism as a method of salvation was a misrepresentation even of the Old Testament. In the words of Paul, "The Law was our custodian until Christ came."

This is another way of saying that the Law did not bring with it a principle of life. The Gospel of Christ, on the other hand, did supply that principle. That principle is *Faith.* In the words of Paul

---

[5]See Merrill C. Tenney, *Galatians: The Charter of Christian Liberty.*

once more, "A man is not justified by *works* of the Law, but through *faith* in Jesus Christ."

This declaration of religious freedom in Christ, which Paul first stated in this letter, and which he gave more at length in the much longer letter to the Romans, established Christianity as a world religion instead of a Jewish sect.

SELECTED READINGS ON THE LETTER TO THE GALATIANS

Davis, John D.: *The Westminster Dictionary of the Bible,* pp 190-192.

Hunter, Archibald M.: *The Letters of Paul to the Galatians, Ephesians, Philippians, and I and II Corinthians.*

*Luther, Martin: *Commentary on Galatians.* A New Edition.

Ramsay, Sir William: *A Historical Commentary on St. Paul's Epistle to the Galatians.*

*Ridderbos, Herman N.: *The Epistle of Paul to the Churches of Galatia.*

Ropes, J. H.: *The Singular Problem of the Epistle to the Galatians.*

*Ross, Alexander: "The Epistle to the Galatians," *The New Bible Commentary,* pp. 1001-1014.

*Tenney, Merrill C.: *Galatians — The Charter of Christian Liberty.*

Chapter 5

I Corinthians

1. The City of Corinth in Paul's Day

The great Greek city of Corinth was destroyed in 146 B.C. by the conquering Romans; but it was rebuilt of pure white marble, in the grand style, by Julius Caesar just one hundred years later, in 46 B.C.

When Paul reached the city for the first time in the autumn of A.D. 51, it was a thriving commercial city of some 400,000 people, the metropolis of Greece, and the fourth in size in the Roman Empire, being surpassed only by Rome, Alexandria, and Antioch.

Corinth was situated on the Isthmus of Corinth, the narrow neck of land connecting northern and southern Greece, and on the principal trade route of the Roman Empire from East to West. Thus, through its natural harbors flowed the commerce of the world.

The population was largely Greek, with mixed minorities of Romans, Jews, and other nationalities. Besides their trade and commerce, the people gave themselves over largely to pleasure, entertainment, and vices of many sorts. Thus, they earned for themselves the doubtful distinction of being "a renowned and voluptuous city, where the vices of the East and West met."

In religion, they were pagan polytheists and idolators; and, like the inhabitants Paul met on his famous visit to Athens, they had an idol for every god, and a god for every department of life.

On the mountain side, high above the city, was an imposing and magnificent temple of white marble, adorned with dozens of marble columns in the famous "Corinthian" style of architecture. This temple was dedicated to the goddess of the city, Aphrodite (Af'-ro-dí-te), the goddess of love and beauty, identified by the Romans with Venus.

The priestesses of Aphrodite — professional courtesans, 1000 of them in attendance on ordinary occasions, and 1500 for special festivals — were famed for their great accomplishments and beauty, and for the high price which they set on their charms. Hence the old proverb: "It isn't every one that can afford to go to Corinth."

This is the city to which Paul came, and which "he turned upside down" with his preaching of the Gospel; and to which three or four years later he wrote I and II Corinthians.

2. The Occasion and Date of the Letter[1]

On his Second Missionary Journey, A.D. 50-53, Paul and his companions went into Macedonia and Greece(Achaia), founding churches in the great cities of Philippi, Thessalonica, and Corinth. For eighteen months, or about half of the time of the Second Journey, Paul preached and labored at Corinth, and founded one of his greatest churches in that city.

In early spring of A.D. 53, Paul took leave of his Corinthian disciples and sailed for Jerusalem and Antioch, in Syria, for visits with the leaders of the Church at Jerusalem, and for a report to the brethren at Antioch of the great success of his latest mission in the West.

Next year, A.D. 54, Paul set out from Antioch on his Third Journey west, visiting again the churches in Galatia, and finally reaching the capital city of Ephesus in Asia Minor, which was to be the center of his preaching and the founding of Churches for the next three years. From Ephesus, Corinth was only some 200 miles west across the Aegean Sea, with which communication was easy and frequent.

It was in the midst of his long sojourn at Ephesus that "persons of the household of Chloe" (I Corinthians 1:11) came from Corinth to report to Paul the disorders in the church there. It appears that Paul wrote a hurried letter, which is now lost (I Corinthians 5:9), in which he scolded the Corinthians for their misconduct (II Corinthians 2:3, 4, 9), and sent it to Corinth by the hand of Chloe's people who reported the disorders.[2]

Paul had already sent Timothy to Corinth by way of Macedonia, but so far he had not heard from him. Meanwhile, another delegation came from Corinth to confer with Paul, this one led by Stephanas with Fortunatus and Achaicus (I Corinthians 16:17). From them and from a letter (7:1), perhaps brought by Stephanas, Paul was able to get the intimate knowledge which I Corinthians, and a little later II Corinthians, reveal. Some scholars are of the opinion that Paul made a personal visit to Corinth during the period of heated controversy, *before* he wrote I Corinthians (II Corinthians 2:1; 12:14).

Whether Paul went to Corinth for the purpose of exercising further discipline in the church there, I Corinthians itself was certainly written for that purpose, and likely early in 57 A.D. It warns against party factions; deals with questions involving immorality, marriage and divorce, lawsuits, eating meat offered to idols, abuses of the Lord's Supper, the part of women in the church, etc.

It appears that Titus was sent to Corinth as bearer of I Corin-

[1]See W. C. G. Proctor of Dublin, "The Epistles to the Corinthians," *The New Bible Commentary*, pp. 967-970 (1954).
[2]For the problems in the Corinthian church and how Paul met them, see Merrill C. Tenney, *New Testament Survey*, pp. 307-315; Kee and Young, *Understanding the New Testament*, pp. 254-266.

thians or that it was carried by the hand of another, and that Titus was dispatched there by Paul soon after it was delivered, to assist in correcting some of the abuses in the church to which the letter refers.

The letter itself reveals unmistakable evidence of a refusal by the Corinthians to accept Paul's authority, the opposition to him apparently being led by his Jewish enemies (II Corinthians 11:12-23). It would take a firm hand such as Titus's to deal with the crisis and threatened revolt.

3. THE CONTENTS OF THE LETTER

This letter is a combination of two kinds of teaching.

The first — and this embraces much of the letter — consists of practical, elementary correction and discipline of Paul's disciples at Corinth, whom he addresses "as men of flesh, as babes in Christ." This part of the letter is informal, a sort of first-aid to teach Christians their duties as Christians. In other words, "I fed you with milk, not solid food." And much of the present letter is a continuation of the same diet.

The second kind of teaching in I Corinthians consists of those great, fundamental passages on the Sacrament of the Lord's Supper (11:17-34); Love (13); the Resurrection and Immortality (15).

The letter should be read as a most earnest gospel message to a newly established Christian church, struggling to be Christian but against a background of vice, immorality, and paganism.

THE ANALYSIS

Here is a brief topical statement of the main contents of the letter:

1. Introduction. The letter opens with greetings and praise of the Corinthian Christians for their calling, and for what they have attained in the grace of the Lord Jesus Christ (1:1-9).

2. Problems in the Corinthian church suggested by the personal report brought to Paul by Chloe's people (1:11); the evils of parties and party spirit in the church; the misconception of the mission of the Apostles; the wisdom of God as contrasted with the wisdom of the world (1:10 to 4).

3. Two other problems suggested by the report of Chloe's people: First, the evil example reported of a man living with his father's wife, and the fact that the Corinthian church had done nothing to discipline him; second, the un-Christian practice of brethren having lawsuits with one another, before a heathen judge (5 and 6).

4. Further problems submitted in the letter from the Corinthian church (7:1): Marriage and divorce (7); eating food offered to idols (8); Paul's own example of self-denial, and some historical illustrations (9-10); disorders in worship, including the Sacrament of the Lord's Supper (11), and spiritual gifts (12-14).

5. Love (13).

6. The Resurrection and Immortality (15).

7. The gathering of contributions for the poor saints at Jerusalem; personal messages, conclusion, and benediction (16).

Selected Readings on I and II Corinthians

*Barclay, William: *The Letters to the Corinthians.*

Craig, Clarence Tucker: "The First Epistle to the Corinthians," *The Interpreter's Bible,* Vol. 10, pp. 1-13.

Filson, Floyd V.: "The Second Epistle to the Corinthians," *The Interpreter's Bible,* Vol. 10, pp. 263-276.

*Grosheide, F. W.: *Commentary on the First Epistle to the Corinthians.*

*Hughes, Philip E.: *Commentary on the Second Epistle to the Corinthians.*

*Kee, Howard Clark and Franklin W. Young: *Understanding the New Testament,* pp. 254-267, and 276-284.

Kennedy, James H.: *The Second and Third Epistles of St. Paul to the Corinthians.*

Moffat, James: *The First Epistle of Paul to the Corinthians.*

*Proctor, W. C. G.: "The Epistles to the Corinthians," *The New Bible Commentary,* pp 967-1000.

Strachan, R. H.: *The Second Epistle of Paul to the Corinthians.*

Tenney, Merrill C.: "The Corinthian Correspondence," *New Testament Survey,* pp. 307-315.

Canal across the Isthmus of Corinth, Greece. Right: Ruins of Lechaeum Road Corinth. *Photos courtesy Dr. John F. Voord*

Chapter 6

II Corinthians

1. The Occasion and Date of the Letter[1]

For some time Paul had planned to visit the church at Corinth
again, in person. He wrote to that effect in I Corinthians (16:5-8).

Now he had spent the greater part of three years at Ephesus
and the surrounding territory of western Asia Minor. He would remain in Ephesus until Pentecost, he said, which would be in June,
A.D. 57. From there he would go to Corinth, but by way of Macedonia first, and from there on into Greece, and Corinth, by late
autumn.

Meanwhile, Timothy, who had been sent on a mission in Macedonia, and possibly Corinth, had returned to Ephesus and was ready
to accompany Paul. And Titus, too, returning from his special mission
to Corinth, was to join them at Troas. But Paul and Timothy went on
from Troas to Philippi, in Macedonia, in order to meet Titus at the
earliest moment. For they were eager to learn from Titus the present
state of affairs among the Corinthian brethren, and how Paul and his
companions would be received at Corinth.

As Paul had hoped, Titus brought good news from the Corinthian
Christians. He was overjoyed that his disciples at Corinth had changed
their opinion favorably regarding him personally, as well as toward
the leading offenders in the church. Perhaps, the special visits to
Corinth and his letters had been helpful in healing the breach that
the crisis had brought about (see II Corinthians 7:5-8).

So Paul wrote immediately, from Philippi, the letter we call
II Corinthians, and sent Titus back with it, together with two other
brethren (II Corinthians 8:16-24). They delivered the letter and also
had charge of completing the collection for the poor saints at Jerusalem, which had been under way in the different churches for more
than a year. Thus, the date of the letter should be placed some time
in the summer of A.D. 57, a few months after the writing of I Corinthians.

2. The Contents of the Letter

To use the words of one writer, II Corinthians is the least
methodical and most personal of Paul's Letters.

---

[1]For reading references on II Corinthians, see the suggested list at the end of
the preceding chapter on I Corinthians.

It is certainly highly autobiographical, revealing as it does much of Paul's past life as an evangelist, his successes and hardships, as well as his part in the present struggle to evangelize the city of Corinth.

The contents of the letter fall easily into these two main divisions: Chapters 1-9 and 10-13. But there is such a distinct change in *tone*, and *time*, between chapters 1 to 9 and chapters 10 to 13, that many readers are of the opinion that we have here two letters, or parts of two letters, instead of one.

In chapters 1 to 9, the breach between Paul and the Corinthian church, which at one point virtually amounted to open revolt, appears now to be completely healed, and with a peaceful and happy outcome for our Apostle. Moreover, the verses of this section are written in the *past tense*.

In chapters 10 to 13, on the other hand, it is evident that the differences between Paul and his Corinthian brethren have *not* been resolved, and that Paul is still answering charges and defending his Apostleship. Also, the verses here are written in the *present* or *future tense*.[2]

However, it is suggested that we read the letter as a unit, keeping in mind that the material of the last four chapters probably belongs to an earlier period in the controversy between the evangelists and the disciples at Corinth, than that represented by the first nine chapters of the letter.

THE ANALYSIS

The following is a brief outline analysis of the letter:

CHAPTERS 1-9

1. The letter opens with Paul's usual salutation and thanksgiving; but here we have also an expression of *comfort* that comes to those who have been delivered from *affliction* and *suffering*, suggesting welcome relief from the recent crisis in their relations.

2. Paul's sincerity of purpose in all his relations with the church at Corinth, and elsewhere, especially his intention to visit Corinth again is revealed. Chapters 1:12 to 2:2.

3. Thoughts suggested by the purpose and results of a certain "severe letter" which he had written them earlier, and which is now lost. Chapter 2:3-17.

4. Paul's grand defense of his ministry, in spite of its hardships, in terms of its glory, peculiar joy and comfort, as well as inspiration to live and labor nobly for the kingdom of God. Chapters 3 to 5.

5. The Apostle's final appeal to the Corinthian Christians to

---

[2]For a discussion of the problem of the "lost letter" to the Corinthians, and the possible re-arrangement of Paul's II Corinthians, see Kee and Young, *Understanding the New Testament*, pp. 265-267, including footnote (1957).

cleanse themselves "from every defilement of body and spirit," and to live the good life for which they were called. Chapters 6 and 7.

6. Paul's message on the collection for the poor at Jerusalem, and his discourse on the principles of Christian giving. Chapters 8 and 9.

CHAPTERS 10-13

The last four chapters of the letter present Paul's defense of his ministry and appear to have been written earlier than the first part of the letter, and at the time of the *crisis* between the Apostle and his disciples at Corinth.

1. Paul's defense of himself against false charges, with particular reference to his methods. Chapter 10.

2. The Apostle compares himself, and the Gospel he preaches, with that of his enemies in Corinth, "false prophets" he calls them, who are leading the fight against him, and who evidently are Jews. Chapter 11.

3. Paul's main defense is in his life and work, part of which he recalls in the course of his argument. Chapter 12.

4. The author's announcement of his coming visit to Corinth, which is his third, with the added warning that any further charges against him must be sustained by evidence, and that he as God's Apostle will not spare any found in their sins when he comes. He then closes with an exhortation and benediction.

Chapter 7

Romans

1. Paul's Masterpiece

In an impressive list of great letters, Paul's letter to the Romans stands out as his most important work. Indeed, some have even called it the most important book in our Bible, next to the Four Gospels.

It is the author's supreme effort to explain God's plan of salvation, as glorified in the life, death, and Resurrection of Jesus Christ, the perfect revelation.

Paul is the preacher's preacher. For one has only to examine Christian theology to see how largely the ideas of Paul are the ideas of modern, organized Christian theology. And nowhere is the hand of Paul more evident than in the influence of this grand message, which we call the letter to the Romans. Just think what a master mind was his, to so dominate Christian thinking for two thousand years!

Conversely, laymen have always had difficulty *understanding* Paul. And so there has been a tendency to avoid reading his letters.

Part of the difficulty has been Paul's *style*.

And part of it is Paul's preoccupation with a real, live problem in his day, but which to us is no problem at all, namely — whether a Gentile could be a Christian without becoming a convert to Judaism, including the rite of circumcision and the observance of Jewish ceremonial law.

But the heart of Paul's message *is* the same as it *was*, and is as modern for us today as it was for Paul's readers: *How anyone may become a Christian,* and know that he is a Christian.

As for Paul's *style,* the problem here is no longer as difficult as it was. As a first aid, the modern reader is advised to read the letter to the Romans, and the other letters of Paul, in the *Revised Standard Version* of 1952.

Here he will find both the *diction* and the *sentence construction* of Paul greatly simplified, without changing the essential truth of his message. And what is more, the letters will become more easily understood and more enjoyable.

In this connection, it may be said that many have found the reading of Paul in other modern translations extremely helpful. These include such favorites as James Moffatt's *A New Translation of the*

Ruins of the Roman Forum, the Arch of Titus visible in the center background.
Courtesy Dr. John F. Walvoord

Bible; J. B. Phillips' *New Testament in Modern English,* which is noted for its simplicity and clarity of style; or *The New English Bible.*

2. THE CHRISTIAN CHURCH AT ROME[1]

Who were the people addressed in the letter to the Romans?

They included all the Christian converts then living in the great capital city. . . . *To all God's beloved in Rome,* Paul greets them.

The Roman Christian Church in the winter of 57-58 A.D., when Paul sat down in Corinth to compose this letter, certainly included both Jews and Gentiles. However, Paul always referred to himself as the Apostle to the Gentiles, and there is every reason to believe that Gentile readers would form the majority of the Christian community at Rome.

In fact, Paul addresses his Gentile readers in the opening chapter of his letter (1:8-15). Again, in chapter 11:13-14, he declares, "Now I am speaking to you Gentiles. . . . Inasmuch as I am an Apostle to the Gentiles. . . ."

And near the close of the letter, chapter 16, it is significant that of the persons mentioned for special greetings, nearly all have either Greek or Roman names.

And yet, the Jewish minority in Paul's audience of readers must have been a significant minority. For a good portion of the letter deals with the same problem which is the chief theme of the letter to the Galatians, namely, the self-sufficiency of Christianity as compared with Judaism.

Although there were Jewish synagogues in Rome at the time of Paul's writing, yet because of the hostility to the Christians, there were apparently no public church buildings or central Christian organization at Rome. Instead, household groups or small congregations met privately in certain homes.

Five such groups are mentioned in chapter 16, with the leaders in each, as follows: (1) Priscilla and Aquila and "the Church in their house"; (2) Aristobulus and his "family"; (3) those "who belong to the family of Narcissus"; (4) Asyncritus and his brethren, who possibly assembled in the house of Hermes; (5) Philologus and his group, and "all the saints who are with them." It is certain that there was a Christian group also in the Imperial Palace, although Paul does not mention it here.

Where did these "Roman" Christian converts come from?

It had been just 28 years since the Resurrection and Ascension. The Christian disciples were scattered abroad from Jerusalem and Palestine, especially after the stoning of the evangelist Stephen. Many went to Antioch in Syria, or to Cyprus or Alexandria or Ephesus, or elsewhere westward.

---

[1]For a discussion of the Church at Rome, see also A. C. Mackinnon, *The Rome of St. Paul,* p. 73ff.

Not a few were converts of Paul. Some were the disciples of Barnabas or Peter or the other evangelists, who went West. Travel between the large cities in the Roman Empire was common, and sooner or later large numbers found themselves in the Imperial capital of Rome.

3. THE DATE, PLACE, AND OCCASION OF WRITING

Near the close of his Third Missionary Journey, and of his three years' mission at Ephesus, Paul thought much about two personal plans of his. One was to go to Jerusalem, the other to see Rome. . . . "After I have been there," he said in a conversation with Luke, "I must also see Rome" (Acts 19:21).

Paul planned to leave Ephesus after Pentecost, in June of 57 A.D. But before going to Jerusalem, he wished to visit again the churches in Macedonia and Greece. In both I and II Corinthians, Paul expressed the wish to spend the winter of 57-58 A.D. with his Christian friends at Corinth, as the concluding event of his Third Missionary Journey.

Paul carried out this wish of his and spent three months with the Christian disciples at Corinth, from late autumn of 57 to early spring of 58 A.D. It was during these three months that he composed the letter to the Romans, and sent it to Rome by Phoebe, a prominent deaconess of the church at Cenchreae, a suburb and the port of Corinth (16:1-2). She was an active Christian helper, a woman of quality and means, and one that Paul trusted for the safe delivery of this, his most important letter.

Why did Paul write such a long letter, and such a thorough exposition of Christian doctrine, at this time?

Some have said that Paul wrote to the Christians at Rome to announce to them his coming, and the visit he had long promised his friends in the Roman capital.

But there was a much more important reason than that. Lately, Paul had had intimations of the danger to him personally of the trip to Jerusalem. The unbelieving Jews were active with their plot to murder him. All his friends had warned him, and even advised against this trip.

So Paul had come to feel that he might meet his death on this last mission. And if so, there would be no Rome for him! He thought it was his duty to go to Jerusalem; but the Lord had not yet spoken of his safety.

It was in this atmosphere, and with this anxiety regarding the great mission to Rome, that Paul wrote his great, final defense of Christianity, which, if the worst happened, would be his substitute for his personal presence and preaching there.

It was thus fitting that the chief letter of the Apostle to the Gentiles should be a letter to the church in the capital of the Gentile world.

4. The Contents of the Letter

In this letter, Paul's problem was twofold. Although it is addressed to the Christians at Rome, Paul's audience and outlook in the letter is the Roman Empire.

His first problem was with the heathen Gentiles. In Rome as in the other cities of the Roman Empire, the population was chiefly Gentile — Greeks and Romans principally, but with many Jews, and some Asiatics also. These Gentiles were brought up in a pagan environment. And insofar as they had a religion at all, they were idolators and worshiped many gods, in addition to the worship of the Roman Emperor, which was required by Roman law.

Paul's other main problem was with the third main element in the population — the Jews. Percentagewise, only a few Jews were Christians. The overwhelming majority were Jewish proselytes, or converts to Judaism. And Jewish proselytes held that a Gentile could not become a Christian without becoming a Jewish proselyte.

The reader will recall that this is the same problem Paul faced when he wrote the letter to the Galatians. Here, in the letter to the Romans, Paul goes into the matter more at length. Here he renews his declaration of religious liberty in the Gospel of Jesus Christ, and freedom from Judaism, and with greater emphasis. And as the chief Apostle to the Gentiles, he established Christianity in the eyes of the world as a world religion, and not as a Jewish sect.

1. The Preamble, Chapter 1:1-17

Paul opens his letter with a personal introduction of himself, with greetings to the Christians in Rome and thanksgiving for their faith, and with an announcement of his intention to visit Rome and preach to the Romans.

He closes his Preamble with a statement of the main theme of the letter:

> . . . For I am not ashamed of the Gospel: it is the power of God for salvation to every one who has faith . . . For in it the righteousness of God is revealed through faith for faith . . . He who through faith is righteous shall live.

2. The Universal Need of Salvation Through the Gospel,[2]

Chapters 1:18 to 3

From the days of Adam on, men did not see fit to acknowledge God, but instead forgot their Creator, and descended to the low levels of depravity:

---

[2]Two references which will give the student a very satisfactory introduction to the study of Romans are Kee and Young's "The Message for Gentiles — The Letter to the Romans," *Understanding the New Testament,* Chapter 9, pp. 268-291 (1957); and Thomson and Davidson's "The Epistle to the Romans," *The New Bible Commentary,* pp. 939-966 (1954). See the reference list at the end of the chapter for other suggested readings.

. . . They were filled with all manner of wickedness, evil, covetous-
ness, malice. Full of envy, murder, strife, deceit, malignity, they
are gossips, slanderers, haters of God, insolent, haughty, boastful,
inventors of evil, disobedient to parents, foolish, faithless, heartless,
ruthless.

This picture of internal conditions of Rome was evidently
furnished Paul by Priscilla and Aquila and other personal friends, who
had recently lived there.

God shows no partiality. For the Jews, no less than the rest of
mankind, have sinned and fallen short of the glory of God. If they
would avail themselves of the righteousness of God, they also must do
so through faith in Jesus Christ (3:21-25).

3. The Historic Case of Abraham and Salvation Through Faith,
Chapter 4

Abraham's claim to God's righteousness was not through works
under the law, but through faith. . . . "Abraham believed God, and it
was reckoned to him as righteousness."

Moreover, in the words of Paul, this blessing to Abraham was not
reckoned because of *circumcision.* Indeed, it was reckoned *before* he
was circumcised. . . .

He received circumcision as a sign or seal of the righteousness
which he had by faith while he was still uncircumcised. The purpose was to make him the father of all who *believe* without being
circumcised and who thus have righteousness reckoned to them,
and likewise the father of the circumcised who are not merely
circumcised but also follow the example of the *faith* which our
father Abraham had before he was circumcised.
. . . It will be reckoned to *us* who believe in him that raised from
the dead Jesus our Lord, who was put to death for our trespasses
and raised for our justification.

4. The Doctrine of Adam and the Human Family *Versus* Jesus
Christ and Salvation Through Faith, Chapters 5 and 6

Adam sinned, and his sin is the cause of the entrance of sin into
the world!

As sin came into the world through one man, Adam, and death
through sin, so death spread to all men, because all men sinned. . . .[3]

But the free gift of the grace of God, in the Man Jesus Christ,
became the justification for all mankind. . . . That is, our inheritance
from Christ more than satisfied the ruin caused by the *Fall* of Adam.

. . . Then as one man's trespass led to condemnation for all men,
so one Man's Act of righteousness leads to acquittal and life for all
men. For as by one man's disobedience many were made sinners,
so by one Man's Obedience many were made righteous.

5. The Inadequacy of the Law to Save, Chapter 7

The purpose of the law, as developed in the Old Testament, was
to *teach* and to *educate,* the Jews first and through them all mankind.

---

[3]For a treatment of Paul's language of salvation, see C. H. Dodd's *Epistle to the
Romans,* pp. 48-61 (1932).

It was forward-looking and preparatory to the coming of the Saviour, and thus *Faith in Things to Come* was its main idea. That is to say, the law was never intended to *save*.

Law is divine in its character and beneficent in its work, but unable to free men from the power of sin.

6. FREEDOM FROM THE LAW OF SIN AND DEATH THROUGH HEIRSHIP AND UNION WITH CHRIST, Chapter 8

It is not enough for the Christian to be delivered from the *guilt* of sin, that is, by *justification* through faith in Christ. But he must be delivered also from the *power* of sin, which is Paul's doctrine of *sanctification*.

The purpose of the death of Christ, if we may so paraphrase Paul, was not only to win pardon for man, but also to produce in him *the right character and conduct*, so that he will have no desire to sin.

The presence of the Spirit in the life of a Christian, not only *frees* him from the power of sin, but reassures him of his kinship with God and makes him willing to endure persecution and suffering in anticipation of "the glory that is to be revealed" to him.

> . . . For I am sure that neither death, nor life, nor angels, nor principalities, nor things present, nor things to come, nor powers, nor height, nor depth, nor anything else in all creation, will be able to separate us from the love of God in Christ Jesus our Lord.

7. THE PROBLEM OF THE OLD TESTAMENT PROMISE AND JEWISH UNBELIEF, Chapters 9, 10, 11

The Apostle Paul is sorrowful because his kinsmen, the Israelites, have been cut off from Christ, in that they have sought to establish their own righteousness, through the Law, in place of the righteousness of God.

But this must not be taken to mean that the Word of God has failed. ". . . . For not all who are descended from Israel belong to Israel, and not all are children of Abraham because they are his descendants."

In Paul's day it was increasingly evident that the Church of Christ was coming to be largely a Gentile Church, and that the Jews as a whole were refusing to accept Jesus as their Messiah and Saviour. Such was the failure of Judaism.

This led the Jews to argue that Christ could not be the promised Messiah, and that Christianity could not be true. If so, the Jews were shut out from the Messianic kingdom, and God's promises to the Jews in the Old Testament would have been broken, a view which no one was willing to entertain.

Paul's classic answer to this argument is that Israel has been *rejected* because of Israel's *lack of faith*, and he quotes both Moses and Isaiah to substantiate his view (chapter 10).

But Paul does not wish his readers to conclude that Israel's rejection is final. *The Day of Grace* has not been closed. For example, Paul himself, "an Israelite, a descendant of Abraham, a member of the tribe of Benjamin," and chief among sinners, was saved by Grace!

8. THE FRUITS OF A CONSECRATED LIFE, OR CHRISTIANITY IN PRACTICE, Chapters 13, 14, 15

Paul has now completed the doctrinal part of his letter. In the remainder of his message he deals with the practical applications, and closes, as is his custom in all the letters, with an earnest exhortation to Christian disciples to live in conformity with their great profession as followers of the Lord Jesus.

In the earlier chapters, Paul has explained how the free gift of God's grace has made believers what they are and not they themselves by their good works.

Now the big question is, What shall the Christian do in return for, or as an expression of, God's mercy, and this free gift of His grace? In the classic words of the Prophet Micah,

> . . . And what doth the Lord require
> of thee,
> But to do justly, and to love mercy,
> And to walk humbly with thy God?

Paul gives his list of the fruits of a consecrated life. Having gifts that differ according to the grace given to us, he says, let us use them:

> . . . Let love be genuine; hate what is evil, hold fast to what is good; love one another with brotherly affection; outdo one another in showing honor. Never flag in zeal, be aglow with the Spirit, serve the Lord. Rejoice in your hope, be patient in tribulation, be constant in prayer. Contribute to the needs of the saints, practice hospitality.
> . . . Bless those who persecute you; bless and do not curse them. Rejoice with those who rejoice, weep with those who weep. Live in harmony with one another . . . Do not be overcome by evil, but overcome evil with good.

9. THE CONCLUSION, Chapters 15 and 16

Paul has now come to the conclusion of his extraordinary message to the Christians at Rome, which is also his defense of Christianity to the Gentile world.

Addressing the Romans, he says, "I myself am satisfied about you, my brethren, that you yourselves are full of goodness, filled with all knowledge, and able to instruct one another.

". . . In Christ, then, I have reason to be proud of my work for God. For I will not venture to speak of anything except what Christ has wrought through me to win obedience from the Gentiles, by word and deed, by the power of signs and wonders, by the power of the Holy Spirit, so that from Jerusalem and as far round as Illyricum I have fully preached the Gospel of Christ."

The remainder of the letter is more personal. After the proposed journey to Jerusalem, he hopes to visit Rome, and from there, to proceed as far as Spain, "thus making it my ambition to preach the Gospel, not where Christ has already been named, lest I build on another's foundation, but as it is written:

"They shall see who have never been told of him,
And they shall understand who have never heard of him."

The last chapter, 16, is given over to extended greetings and salutations to many friends, brothers and sisters in Christ, and reciprocal greetings from the church at Corinth, to which is added the Apostle's longest and most impressive benediction.

One incidental but human touch is that Tertius, who transcribes Paul's dictation of the letter, sends greetings in his own right (16:22).

SELECTED READINGS ON THE LETTER TO THE ROMANS

*Barclay, William: *The Letter to the Romans.*

Barth, K.: *A Shorter Commentary on Romans.*

*Calvin, John: *The Epistle of St. Paul to the Romans.*

Dodd, C. H.: *The Epistle to the Romans.*

Foreman, Kenneth J.: *The Epistle of Paul to the Romans, and I and II Corinthians.*

*Hodge, Charles: *Paul's Epistle to the Romans.*

*Kee, Howard Clark and Franklin W. Young: "The Message for Gentiles: The Letter to the Romans," *Understanding the New Testament,* pp. 268-291.

Knox, John: "The Epistle to the Romans," *The Interpreter's Bible,* Vol. IX, pp. 353-372.

Moule, Handley G. G.: *The Epistle of St. Paul to the Romans* (Expositor's Bible).

*Murray, John: *Paul's Epistle to the Romans.*

Thomas, W. H. Griffith: *Romans I-XVI, A Devotional Commentary.*

*Thomson, G. T. and Francis Davidson: "The Epistle to the Romans," *The New Bible Commentary,* pp. 939-966.

III. THE LETTERS OF PAUL WRITTEN DURING THE THIRD PERIOD, ABOUT 61-63 A.D.

Chapter 8

COLOSSIANS

1. THE FOUR LETTERS WRITTEN DURING THE FIRST ROMAN IMPRISONMENT

During his first imprisonment at Rome, Paul wrote four letters (perhaps more) which have come down to us: Colossians, Ephesians, Philemon, and Philippians. The complete story of how he came to be imprisoned at Rome is told in the book of Acts, and for the details of that story the reader is referred to the chapter on Acts.[1]

Of these four letters, the three first named were written at the same time and delivered by the same messengers, to Ephesus and the other churches of the Roman province of Asia, which was the western half of Asia Minor.

Which of the three letters preceded which, in the order of composition, is an academic question, for it little matters. However, since the theme of the letter to the Colossians is developed more at length in the letter to the Ephesians, it is often presumed that the writing of Colossians preceded that of Ephesians.

The letter to Philemon, on the other hand, is a private, personal letter, and was conveniently written and delivered at the same time of the other two letters, since Philemon also lived in the city of Colossae and was a member of the church at Colossae, to which one of the letters was addressed.

The circumstances connected with the writing of the letter to the Philippians indicate that it was written later than the others, that is, toward the middle or latter part of the first imprisonment at Rome. It is also likely that Paul wrote the letter to the *Hebrews* at this time.

2. THE OCCASION AND DATE OF THE LETTER TO THE COLOSSIANS

The immediate occasion for the writing of the letter was a visit made to Paul in the prison at Rome by Epaphras, who apparently had founded the church at Colossae, or at least had assisted in its establishment.

One of Epaphras' reasons for coming to Paul appears to have

---

[1]For a summary of the background of Colossians and the other three letters of this group, see Tenney, *The New Testament*, pp. 325-340 (1953).

Present-day site of ancient Colossae in Phrygia (Asia Minor). *Photo courtesy Dr. S. H. Horn, Andrews University* been to report in person a serious heresy which threatened the faith of the Colossian Church.

From Paul's statement in 2:1, we infer that Paul himself had never preached at Colossae. So it is likely that Epaphras was a convert of Paul's, and that the church at Colossae was established while Paul was laboring some three years at Ephesus, on the occasion of the Third Missionary Journey. Colossae was some 100 miles east of Ephesus, and two other nearby churches, at Laodicea and at Hierapolis, to whom also the letter was to be read.

The present letter, and Ephesians and Philemon, were taken from the hand of Paul by Tychicus, who as messenger was accompanied by Onesimus, Philemon's runaway slave, but now a converted Christian whom Paul is sending back to Colossae for reconciliation with his master.

The general opinion is that the letter was written in the first year of Paul's imprisonment at Rome, that is, in A.D. 61.

3. The Dangerous Heresies Referred to in Colossians

Some six years earlier, Paul had written the letter to the Galatians to combat the false teaching of certain *Judaizers*, who were unsettling the minds of Gentile Christians by teaching that it was necessary also for them to be circumcised and to observe the Jewish ceremonial law.

From Paul's statement in verses 2:11, and 16, it appears that the false teachers alluded to in the present letter were again primarily Jews, engaged in their old vicious practice of unsettling the minds of Gentile Christians. Also, to the observance of Jewish ceremonial law, now they had added the importance of the sacred seasons, such as the sabbath, the new moon, the feast day; and had laid down certain restrictions as to meats and drinks.

The heresy, however, is the same as that described in Galatians, namely, that it nullified the doctrine of the All-sufficient Saviour, by holding that the Gospel of Christ must be supplemented by Jewish law.

Another heresy referred to by Paul was the doctrine of "self-abasement and worship of angels" (2:18). In another verse he calls it philosophy:

> See to it that no one makes a prey of you by philosophy and empty deceit, according to human tradition, according to the elemental spirits of the universe, and not according to Christ (2:8).

The religious cult referred to here was not Jewish, but Greek in origin and character. It had wide currency in the Roman province in Asia and elsewhere in the West after Paul's time, as the doctrine of *Gnosticism.* The basic heresy of this doctrine, as we found in our study of the gospel of John, is a denial that Jesus Christ is the Son of God.

The reader will recall that the Apostle John succeeded Paul, shortly after the latter's death, as the Apostle to the Church at Ephesus and the other churches of "Asia"; and that some 25 or 30 years after Paul wrote the letter to the Colossians, John wrote his gospel mainly to combat the heresy of Gnosticism, which in John's day was opposing the divinity of Christ and confusing the minds of Gentile Christians. (For a brief description of Gnosticism, see "The Purpose of John's Gospel," page 395ff.)

4. The Contents of the Letter

Here we have in this relatively short letter, as we have in all of Paul's letters, an expression of great sincerity and earnestness on Paul's one great theme: An exhortation to hold fast to Christ, the All-sufficient Saviour.

Although the letter to the Colossians is informal as a familiar letter should be, the ideas may be grouped generally as follows:

(1) Salutation, chapter 1:1-2. Paul always identifies himself as the writer at the outset of his letters, and more often than not, names one or more of his closest friends and co-laborers as if they were actually assisting with the composition of the letter. In the present letter he names Timothy.

(2) Thanksgiving and praise, with which is combined doctrinal explanation and instruction, chapters 1:3 to 2:7. Paul's letters are noted for their somewhat elaborate praise and commendation of fellow Christians, "saints" he calls them, for their faith and steadfastness. He wants them to know that they are important as individuals, and to the kingdom of God.

He can afford to praise them, perhaps beyond what they have actually attained, because he wished for them to *become* what he describes as "mature in Christ." And while he is on the subject of praise and maturity, he proceeds to instruct them on his favorite theme: The Gospel of Christ, and how He became the All-sufficient Saviour. The heart of this instruction and message of the letter is the great passage, verses 1:15-20.

(3) The doctrinal passage proper: Paul's warning against false teachers and his further answers to their false teachings, chapter 2:8-23.

(4) Exhortation, chapters 3 to 4:6. After setting forth the new life in Christ, Paul next appeals to his "saints" to undertake the *duties of the new life.* He offers himself as an example of one who has paid the price of keeping the faith, of "declaring the mystery of Christ, on account of which I am in prison."

(5) The concluding salutations and personal messages, chapter 4:7-18.

Selected Readings on the Letter to the Colossians

*Hunter, Archibald M.: *The Letters of Paul to the Galatians, Ephesians, Philippians, and Colossians.*

*Jones, J. Ithel: "The Epistle to the Colossians," *The New Bible Commentary*, pp. 1043-1051.

Lightfoot, J. B.: *The Epistles of Paul to the Colossians and Philemon.*

*Radford, Lewis B.: *The Epistle to the Colossians and the Epistle to Philemon.*

Robertson, A. T.: *Paul and the Intellectuals.*

Scott, E. F.: *The Epistles of Paul to the Colossians, to Philemon and to the Ephesians.*

*Simpson, E. K.: *Commentary on the Epistles to the Ephesians and the Colossians.*

*Westcott, B. F.: *A Letter to Asia.*

Chapter 9

EPHESIANS

1. THE OCCASION AND DATE OF THE LETTER

The letter to the Ephesians is the second of three letters which Paul wrote during the early part of his first Roman imprisonment and dispatched at the same time by his special messanger, Tychicus, with whom also was Onesimus, Philemon's runaway slave. The first of these letters, as we have seen, was written to the Colossians.

The occasion for writing the present letter appears to have been the general situation which existed among the churches in the Roman province of Asia.[1] Many Christians in these churches had allowed themselves to be led astray by the clever arguments of certain false teachers and false doctrines. Of this tendency, the church at Colossae, as we have seen, was a specific example.

The reader may be reminded also that the Apostle John some years later wrote his Gospel, I, II and III John, and the book of Revelation which is also a letter, to combat the evil influence of certain false teachers and doctrines in this same province of Asia.

To whom was the present letter addressed?[2]

In certain ancient manuscripts the letter is addressed "to the saints which are at Ephesus, and to the faithful in Christ Jesus." This address is repeated in the *King James Version* of 1611. But in some of the very oldest manuscripts, and discovered since 1611, the words "at Ephesus" are omitted. So present day opinion is that the letter was addressed, not to Ephesians alone, but to other churches of the province of Asia also. Moreover, it is likely that Tychicus had instructions from Paul himself to take the letter first to Ephesus, and then to the other churches, of which the church at Laodicea was one.

There appears to be a reference to the letter to the Ephesians in the closing paragraph of the letter to the Colossians (4:16), in which Paul enjoins the Colossians to read both letters:

> And when this letter has been read among you, have it read also in the church of the Laodiceans; and see that you read the letter from Laodicea.

---

[1]For special studies on Paul's imprisonment and these letters, see Kee and Young, *Understanding the New Testament*, pp. 302-307; G. S. Duncan, *St. Paul's Ephesian Ministry* (1930); M. S. Enslin, *Christian Beginnings*, pp. 273-275.
[2]See Edgar J. Goodspeed, *The Meaning of the Ephesians* (1933).

Remains of the great marble street of the Arkadiane at Ephesus, which ran from theater to harbor. © *Matson Photo Service*

This letter "from Laodicea" was probably the letter to the Ephesians.

Many think that these churches of the province of Asia included the same "Seven Churches of Asia" named by the Apostle John, in the first chapter of Revelation, and to whom he addressed that letter: Ephesus, Smyrna, Pergamum, Thyatira, Sardis, Philadelphia, and Laodicea. To this list should be added at least three others, which Paul himself or his disciples founded: Colossae, Hierapolis, and Troas. As a matter of fact, Paul himself founded, or was instrumental in founding, the seven churches named by John.

Except for Troas, all ten of these cities were situated within a radius of 50 to 100 miles from the capital city of Ephesus.

This letter was written at the same time as the letter to the Colossians, that is, about 61 A.D.

2. The Contents of the Letter to the Ephesians

The letter to the Colossians and the letter to the Ephesians should be read together.

Colossians deals with the doctrine of the all-sufficiency of Christ as the Saviour, the relationship He as the Son has had with God the Father from the *beginning*, both as the Creator of all things, and as the Incarnate presence of God and His will for mankind.

Thus, as the perfect Revelation of God, the Son comes with both the grace and the power of God the Father, and His salvation therefore needs no Jewish law or other condition for its completeness.

The letter to the Ephesians, written for a somewhat different but likely for some of the same audience, repeats much of the letter to the Colossians. In addition, it enlarges on the former letter and adds comprehensiveness to the doctrine of salvation and redemption.

In short, in the letter to the Ephesians, addressed as it is to the larger audience like his earlier letter to the Romans, Paul gives his complete statement of the whole purpose of God in human history.

The Analysis

The plan of the letter is similar to that of Colossians and may be briefly outlined as follows:

(1) The Salutation (1:1-2).

(2) Thanksgiving and Praise (1:3-23). In these verses Paul expresses his gratitude, not merely for the faith and love of the "saints" who are in the various churches in the province of Asia, as is his usual practice in these letters; but he is grateful especially to God for His mercy in revealing His purpose in the mission of His Son.

(3) Here we have Paul's special instruction in doctrine (2 and 3). According to God's purpose in the mission of His Son, Gentiles and Jews the world over are *one* in the New Life in Christ.

At the time of the writing of these letters, Paul's audience consisted of a mixed population of Greeks, Jews, Romans, Scythians, and others. The Jews claimed *priority* with God, because they were His "chosen" people, and because of the "promise" to Abraham.

In this matter of priority, Paul in these letters is trying to do two things. The first is to give the Jews, and all who read the Scriptures, a *new* interpretation of the Old Testament. The promise to Abraham, he is saying in effect, was *conditional*. It was conditioned on *faith* in something. Faith in what? Faith in God's *promise* and *plan*, which would culminate in the promised Messiah, whose identity and mission God, through His prophets, would reveal. The trouble with most of the Jews, Paul discovered, was that they did not have this faith!

The second thing Paul is trying to show in these letters is that the grace which the Messiah and Saviour brought, was for the Gentiles of the whole human family, as well as for the Jews. Thus, the Old Testament is a means of *education* and not of *grace* and *salvation*.

(4) This section of the letter contains another one of Paul's many exhortations to his disciples to walk worthily in the high calling to the New Life in Christ Jesus (4, 5, 6).

(5) The concluding Salutation and Benediction (6:21-24). Special reference is made to Paul's friend and messenger, Tychicus, who bears the letter, and who will supplement it with personal information about the writer and his life in the prison at Rome.

An important part of the message of Tychicus was to give this further personal information, as the letter reveals: "I have sent him to you for this very purpose." Thus, it appears that Tychicus visited each of the churches in the province of Asia, in person, and gave both the written and oral messages to the assembled body of Christians.

SELECTED READINGS ON THE LETTER TO THE EPHESIANS[3]

Findlay, G. C.: *The Epistle to the Ephesians.*

Goodspeed, Edgar J.: *The Meaning of Ephesians.*

*Hodge, Charles: *Commentary on the Epistle to the Ephesians.*

*Martin, W. G. M.: "The Epistle to the Ephesians," *The New Bible Commentary,* pp. 1015-1030.

Miller, H. S.: *The Book of Ephesians.*

*Simpson, E. K.: *Commentary on the Epistles to the Ephesians and the Colossians.*

---

[3]For other references, see Archibald M. Hunter, E. F. Scott, and others with chapters on Ephesians, at the end of the chapter on Colossians, pages 461 and 462.

Chapter 10

PHILEMON

1. THE OCCASION AND DATE OF THE LETTER TO PHILEMON

Paul's letter to Philemon is the last of the three letters which he wrote and dispatched at the same time during the early part of his first Roman imprisonment, probably in 61 A.D.

The letter was carried and delivered in person by Philemon's runaway slave, Onesimus, who in the meantime had been converted under Paul's preaching and was now being sent back to his master at Colossae, in the Roman province of Asia. Onesimus accompanied Tychicus, Paul's messenger, who brought with him the letter to the Colossians (4:7-9) and the letter to the Ephesians (6:21-22).

Philemon was a resident of Colossae. He was a convert of Paul, having perhaps heard the Gospel on some visit to Ephesus during the three years of Paul's stay there, on the occasion of the Third Missionary Journey.

Philemon became a leader in the church at Colossae, his house being a meeting place of a group of Colossian Christians. Paul refers to him as "our beloved fellow worker." Being a devoted follower and a person of some wealth, he evidently had acquired a reputation also for outstanding deeds of charity. The intimate, fine feeling expressed in the letter reveals Paul's friendship for him.

Paul had enjoyed the attentive services of Onesimus, who out of love and gratitude had attached himself to Paul. But Paul felt that it was right and proper that he should first return to his master for reconciliation. So when Tychicus went to the province of Asia on his mission, Paul took advantage of the opportunity to send back Onesimus, with this letter of special commendation and intercession to Philemon.

2. WHAT THE LETTER REVEALS

The letter to Philemon is the only surviving example of many private letters which Paul must have written, and which are now lost. This one is all the more valuable, therefore, for what it reveals of the writer's character and personality.

The salutation, and the words of praise and thanksgiving for the good life which his friend is living in Christ, are in Paul's usual manner, though most graciously said here on this occasion.

Paul's fine ethical sense and humor, are at play when he approaches the main "business" of the letter, which is to make a plea for Philemon's runaway slave, Onesimus, who probably took with him some of his master's money when he ran away. But as the Lord would have it, he fell into Paul's evangelistic trap and was converted.

The reader will note the humor with which Paul makes his appeal to his friend Philemon:

> Though I am bold enough in Christ to *command* you to do what is required, yet for love's sake I prefer to *appeal* to you . . . I appeal to you for my child, Onesimus, whose father I have become in my imprisonment . . . I am sending him back to you, sending my very heart.

This latter expression seems an exaggeration, but perhaps it was meant to be!

The reader will note with what fine sense of honor and delicacy of feeling also the remainder of the letter is phrased, and how it gives us a rare glimpse into the Apostle's private life.

The people Paul mentions in his letters are always of interest. At the head of the letter, verse 2, "Apphia our sister" is probably the wife of Philemon, and "Archippus our fellow soldier" is likely their son, who now may be a minister.

The next group of people, verses 23 and 24, are those who, with Paul, send greetings to the Philemon household. The first is Paul's devoted evangelistic helper, Epaphras, who was first to come to Paul to report the heresies of the false teachers at Colossae, and who was still at Rome taking his turn at ministering to Paul in prison.

Two other names are of special interest to us. The first is Mark, the same John Mark who dropped from sight almost a dozen years ago, and who left Paul and Barnabas in the middle of the First Missionary Journey and went home, and over whom Paul and Barnabas separated when Barnabas proposed that Mark join them on the Second Journey. But it was like Paul to forgive Barnabas and Mark. So, after all these years, here is Mark with Paul, and sending greetings to Philemon at Colossae.

But Paul does not mention the big news regarding Mark. For he had recently written his gospel, the first of the four gospels to be published! It is generally agreed that it appeared between 50 and 60 A.D., and many are of the opinion that it was written shortly before A.D. 60. The letter to Philemon was probably composed in late A.D. 61.

Luke, another one of Paul's "fellow workers" who sends greetings to Philemon, and who like Timothy, was the constant companion of Paul, is supposed to have completed his gospel that very year, A.D. 61. And Luke's pockets must have been bulging with notes, from which to write his other volume, the book of Acts, which he composed the next year or the year following, 62 or 63 A.D. Of course, none of these important matters would be mentioned in this particular letter to Philemon.

SELECTED READINGS ON THE LETTER TO PHILEMON

Knox, John: *Philemon Among the Letters of Paul.*

*Radford, Lewis B.: *The Epistle to the Colossians and the Epistle to Philemon.*

*Robertson, T. E.: "The Epistle to Philemon," *The New Bible Commentary*, pp. 1084-1087.

Scott, E. F.: *The Epistles of Paul to the Colossians, to Philemon, and to Ephesians.*

Chapter 11

PHILIPPIANS

1. THE OCCASION, PLACE, AND DATE OF THE LETTER

The letter to the Philippians is the fourth in the series written by Paul during his first Roman imprisonment, about 61-63 A.D. (Colossians 4:18; Ephesians 3:1; 4:1; 6:20; Philemon 9; Philippians 1:7, 13, 14).[1]

Philippi was dear to Paul, because it was the first European city to be evangelized by him and his associates on his Second Missionary Journey, and because of his cordial reception by the people and the wonderful church he was able to establish there (Acts 16). Of all his churches, the one at Philippi caused him the least pain and the most joy.

The city lay on the great Egnatian Highway (Via Egnatia), the Roman road which connected the Aegean Sea and the Adriatic, and thus united Italy and Rome with the great routes of the East. It was, therefore, a large and strategic trading center, the second in size in Macedonia.

Paul had always taken pride in the fact that, by his trade as tentmaker and worker in leather, he was able to support himself and not to be a burden to any of his churches. In spite of this, however, the church at Philippi on different occasions had sent him money, twice while he was in Thessalonica (Philippians 4:16), also while he was at Corinth (II Corinthians 11:9), and now while he is a prisoner at Rome (Philippians 4:18).

The immediate occasion of this letter, therefore, was to acknowledge this latest gift in money which the Philippian Christians had sent by the hand of one of their members, Epaphroditus. Epaphroditus has been with Paul some time as brother and fellow worker, and is now returning and taking with him the letter to the Philippians. Meanwhile, he has been serving Paul, and has fallen ill, but is now somewhat recovered:

> I have thought it necessary to send to you Epaphroditus my brother and fellow worker and fellow soldier, and your messenger and minister to my need, for he has been longing for you all, and has been distressed because you heard that he was ill . . . (2:25-30).

---

[1]For the place and chronology of the letters in this group, see references in the footnote, p. 431; also Merrill C. Tenney, *New Testament Survey*, pp. 336-340 (1953); J. B. Lightfoot, *St. Paul's Epistle to the Philippians* (Eighth Edition, 1888).

Ruins of ancient Philippi. *Photo courtesy Dr. John F. Walvoord*

The reference to Timothy, and the plans of both Paul and Timothy to visit the Philippians soon (2:19-24), suggests that Paul thought his case before Emperor Nero was about to be disposed of and his imprisonment about to end . . . "I hope therefore to send him just as soon as I see how it will go with me; and I trust in the Lord that shortly I myself shall come also."

Thus, for several reasons, the date of the letter is usually placed toward the end of Paul's first Roman imprisonment, about 62 or 63 A.D.

2. THE CONTENTS OF THE LETTER

This is the happiest of all Paul's letters. It is a letter of Christian friendship and fellowship, "full of affection, confidence, good counsel and good cheer."

Like the short letter to Philemon, this letter is one of self-revelation of Paul at his spiritual best. Indeed, it is a classic of religious autobiography.

THE ANALYSIS

The contents of the letter may be informally outlined as follows:

1. The salutation (1:1-2). In sending greetings, Paul joins with himself Timothy, who on this as well as on many other occasions, served as Paul's amanuensis and copied Paul's dictation. And only in this letter did Paul include church officers in his greeting, in this case "bishops and deacons."

2. With verse 3, the letter proceeds on its joyous note. In fact, *joy* is the keynote of this entire letter.

The writer is thankful to God for the Philippian Christians, and every prayer for them is said with *joy* . . . . "I am thankful for your partnership in the Gospel from the first day until now. . . ." By their gifts, and by their remembrance of him, the Philippians had become sharers in his work, and in the Kingdom.

Paul is thankful too that even his imprisonment in Rome has resulted in advantage for the Gospel:

It has become known throughout the whole praetorian guard and to all the rest that my imprisonment is for Christ.

And Paul rejoiced because of Timothy. . . . "I have no one like him."

3. No letter of Paul's, however brief and informal, is complete without its usual *exhortation*. He rejoices in the Lord, and again and again he urges the Philippians to rejoice in the Lord, "Finally, my brethren, rejoice in the Lord."

The letter served another purpose — to warn against the *Judaizers*. For, as Epaphroditus had reported, they were a constant threat to the Philippians, as they were in all the cities where Paul founded churches. "Look out for the dogs, look out for the evil-workers," he warns.

The older Paul became, the more real heaven became to him:

"I press on toward the goal for the prize . . . Brethren, join in imitating me," he exhorts.

And near the end of the letter, as if to make sure that he had not omitted anything, he lists these virtues:

> Finally, brethren, whatever is true, whatever is honorable, whatever is just, whatever is pure, whatever is lovely, whatever is gracious, if there is any excellence, if there is anything worthy of praise, think about these things.

Paul was deeply touched and profoundly grateful for the money the Philippians had sent, and especially their concern for him while a prisoner, and so he returns to that subject in two final paragraphs before the close.

Selected Readings on the Letter to the Philippians

*Davidson, Francis: "The Epistle to the Philippians," *The New Bible Commentary*, pp. 1031-1042.

Hunter, Archibald M.: *The Letter of Paul to the Galatians, Ephesians, Philippians, and Colossians.*

*Martin, R. P.: *The Epistle to the Philippians.*

Michael, J. H.: *The Epistle of Paul to the Philippians.*

*Muller, Jac. J.: *Commentary on Philippians and Philemon.*

Robertson, A. T.: *Paul's Joy in Christ.*

Chapter 12

Hebrews

1. The Authorship of Hebrews

No one knows for certain who wrote the letter to the Hebrews. The Eastern Church accepted Paul's authorship as a matter of course from the beginning. The Western Church, however, did not accept it as the work of Paul until the fourth century A.D.

Following in this well established tradition, the *King James Version* of 1611 called it "The Epistle of Paul the Apostle to the Hebrews." Likewise, the *English Revised Version* of 1885 ascribed it to Paul.

But the *American Standard Version* of 1901, following the earliest manuscripts, discovered since the King James translation of 1611 was made, and in which the author of Hebrews is not named, calls it simply "The Epistle to the Hebrews."

The earliest evidence as to the authorship of Hebrews comes from Clement of Alexandria, near the end of the second century A.D. Bishop Eusebius, in his famous *Church History*, VI, 14, quotes Clement as saying,

> That the Epistle is Paul's, and that it was written to Hebrews in the Hebrew language, and that Luke translated it with zealous care and published it to the Greeks; whence it is that the same complexion of style is found in the translation of this Epistle as in the Acts; that the "Paul an Apostle" was not placed at the head of the Epistle for good reason; for, he says, in writing to Hebrews who had formed a prejudice against him and viewed him with suspicion, he was wise not to repel them at the beginning by setting his name there.

About fifty years later, Origen, the most learned man of the early Church and a voluminous writer, says of the authorship:

> . . . If I were to express my opinion I should say that the thoughts are the thoughts of the Apostle, but the language and composition that of one who recalled from memory, and, as it were, made notes of what was said by his master. . . . It was not without reason that the men of old time have handed it down as Paul's. But who wrote the Epistle, God only knows certainly.

Moreover, the reference to Timothy at the end of the letter, and the manner of that reference, is strong circumstantial evidence of Paul's authorship of Hebrews.

It is well known that Timothy, during the last few years of Paul's ministry, was one of Paul's two closest friends and associates. Luke was the other. Timothy spent much of his time in companionship with Paul. Timothy is named in the salutations of three of the four letters written to the Churches in the province of Asia during the first Roman imprisonment, 61-63 A.D.: Colossians, Philemon, Philippians.

Finally, the last paragraphs, verses 18-25, in which the writer is giving his final messages and benediction, and in which for the first time he speaks of himself in the first person singular — all these appear to have been phrased by Paul, personally, and written in his own hand.

On the whole, therefore, Paul still remains the best candidate for the authorship of the letter, whether originally written in one language or another.[1]

2. The Occasion, the Persons Addressed, and the Date

If Paul wrote the letter, it is highly likely that he wrote it during his first Roman imprisonment, A.D. 61-63. That is, as a sequel to his unsatisfactory experience in the ill-starred visit to Jerusalem.

In his concluding salutation, the writer says, "They of Italy salute you," or in Moffatt's translation, "The Italians salute you." The most likely meaning is that the Christians in Rome are sending greetings to the Hebrews, that is, Jewish Christians at Jerusalem and in Palestine. For, from the context, it is strongly evident that the letter is written to Jewish Christians, in a Jewish environment and with a background of Jewish traditions.

The nature and purpose of the letter to the Hebrews is to take care of *unfinished business*. During the last weeks and months of his Third Missionary Journey, Paul had thought much of his forthcoming trip to Jerusalem, and how it should serve to bring about a better understanding between Gentile Christians and Jewish Christians. In short, he thought the time had come to make an appeal for greater unity among all Christians, under the banner of the All-Sufficient Christ. The bringing of gifts from the Gentile Churches of the west to the poor and needy Christians at Jerusalem was evidently his approach to a delicate question.

But his visit to Jerusalem was a complete flop! The plot against him was already formed before his arrival. He never had a chance to

---

[1]This is the view generally held by conservative scholars. However, many do not accept Paul's authorship, the objections being based mainly on what is thought to be a difference in "language and style," and in interpretation of the priesthood and the Law, of Paul and the hypothetical author of Hebrews. For a more liberal discussion of the problems in Hebrews, see Kee and Young, and Purdy and Cotton, both listed in the references at the end of the chapter. For a more conservative approach, see Tenney and Stibbs, also listed in the references. Many students of Hebrews still regard Paul tentatively as the author, directly or indirectly, and are of the opinion that the objections so far have been largely subjective in nature, and that the later objectors have followed somewhat uniformly a pattern set by older critical writers.

make his plea for a better understanding. Within the first week of his appearance, he was seized and dragged from the Temple, and only the Roman tribune, Claudius Lysias, and his guards saved Paul from death at the hands of his Jewish enemies.

Three years have passed and Paul, now in prison at Rome, feels the necessity of accomplishing by this letter what he was unable to do in person.

The letter to the Romans had presented at length his interpretation of the Gospel of Jesus Christ for the Gentile world and the universal scene. Now the letter to the Hebrews is to set Jerusalem and the world of Jewish thought straight on this same Gospel of Jesus Christ. Indeed, this should work for unity in the Church, if it must be done by a different approach.

Since there was so much prejudice against him and his name in Jewish centers, Paul's message of necessity must arrive in an indirect way, and without his name being attached, and perhaps through the "translation" of another.

After his conversion, Paul began his New Life with a sense of destiny. Although his mission was primarily to the Gentiles, he could never free himself of the burden of the salvation of the Jewish race. This letter to the Hebrews might well be his last and final effort to "sell" Jewish Christians, and all Jews, on the full and complete meaning of the Gospel as compared with Judaism. For at the moment even the Jewish Christians were in danger of returning to Judaism.

3. The Contents of the Letter to the Hebrews

The central theme and purpose of the letter to the Hebrews is to warn the Jewish Christians, under persecution, against the danger of falling away from their faith and of drifting back into Judaism.

The letter is a masterful discussion of Christian values as embodied in the Life and Death of Jesus Christ, as compared with the limitations of Judaism. And it has every right to be, if it is as we believe, the joint work of the incomparable team of Paul, who furnished the ideas and much of the phraseology, and of Luke, the master of organization and classical Biblical style.

The Analysis

The following brief analysis indicates the main ideas and arguments of the letter:

1. The Preamble (1:1-3). The two methods of revelation, that of the Old Testament and that of the New, are contrasted in order to point up the perfect revelation of God through His Son. The reader's special attention is called to this opening paragraph of the letter, which for sheer grandeur and power compares favorably with the opening passages of the book of Genesis and John's Gospel.

2. The superiority of the revelation and salvation given by God in His Son Jesus Christ, as compared with that of angels, prophets, high

priests, and other leaders of the Old Testament, whose revelation was imperfect and provisional; whereas the revelation of Christ was perfect and eternal, as being that of the Son of God (1:4 to 4:13).

3. The next section presents the *value* of Christ and His High Priestly Office, in terms of the true heavenly and eternal character of the rewards thus fully offered through faith. This appears to be the end of the historical survey, brought down from the Creation, through Moses, Joshua, and the other appointed leaders. Thus, the superiority of Christ's priesthood, as typified in Melchizedek, to the Levitical and temporal, is again demonstrated in the all-sufficiency of Christ (4:14 to 7).

4. Christ having placed the New Covenant in the minds and hearts of His people, and having offered for all time a single sacrifice for their sins, sat down at the right hand of God as the High Priest and mediator of the New Covenant, so that all those who are called may receive the promised eternal inheritance (8 to 10:18).

5. Having completed his statement of the great truths as set forth in the preceding chapters, the writer now *urges* and *exhorts* his Jewish friends to show the same steadfastness under present trials and persecution, as they had shown in a previous time of affliction, by an enduring faith.

To reinforce his exhortation, the writer composes an essay on Faith, chapter 11, in which he illustrates his theme by naming many men and women heroes of faith of the past (10:19 to 12).

6. The writer concludes his exhortations with a catalogue of specific items, which may be labeled "The Fruits of Faith" (13:1-18).

7. The concluding salutation and benediction (13:20-25). The reader will note that the writer, beginning with verse 18, changes from the *third person*, in which he has written the body of the letter, to the *first person* singular for the last eight verses.

SELECTED REFERENCES ON THE LETTER TO THE HEBREWS

*Barclay, William: *The Letter to the Hebrews.*
Bowman, John Wick: *The Letters of Hebrews, James, and I and II Peter.*
Bruce, A. B.: *The Epistle to the Hebrews.*
*Bruce, F. F.: *The Commentary on Hebrews.*
Davidson, A. B.: *Hebrews.*
Kee, Howard Clark and Franklin W. Young: "The Community Seeks a Religious Philosophy — The Epistle to the Hebrews," *Understanding the New Testament,* Chapter 14, pp. 415-432.
Manson, William: *The Epistle to the Hebrews.*
*Murray, Andrew: *The Holiest of All.*
Purdy, Alexander C. and J. Harry Cotton: "The Epistle to the Hebrews," *The Interpreter's Bible,* Vol. XI, pp. 577-594.

Scott, E. F.: *The Epistle to the Hebrews.*

*Stibbs, A. M.: "The Epistle to the Hebrews," *The New Bible Commentary,* pp. 1088-1117.

*Tenney, Merrill C.: "The Break from Judaism — Hebrews," *New Testament Survey,* pp. 371-379.

*Westcott, B. F.: *The Epistle to the Hebrews.* Second Edition.

Beginning of the Epistle to the Hebrews (with ending of Romans) on a leaf from the Michigan Papyri (Beatty-Michigan MS.). *Courtesy University of Michigan Library*

IV. THE LETTERS OF PAUL WRITTEN DURING THE FOURTH PERIOD, ABOUT 64-67 A.D.

Chapter 13

I TIMOTHY

1. PAUL IS RELEASED FROM THE ROMAN PRISON

The best opinion among biblical scholars is that Paul, after two years of waiting, finally had his trial before the court of Emperor Nero, to whom he had appealed his case from the Jerusalem Jews. Evidently he was found "not guilty" of the charges which his Jewish enemies had lodged against him.

At any rate, Paul was soon thereafter set at liberty, about 63 A.D., and for a while allowed to engage in travel and active missionary work, before he was again arrested and brought back to Rome, where he met martyrdom about 67 or 68 A.D.

The inevitable question is, where did he go from here, and how did he spend his time during these few brief years out of prison?

The record is incomplete. If he visited Spain, as he had hoped before all his troubles and imprisonment at both Caesarea and Rome, it must have been immediately after his release.

The first certain information we have of Paul, however, is that he has re-visited the churches of his earlier labors in Macedonia and possibly Ephesus (I Timothy 1:3).[1] From another letter, Titus 1:5, we learn that, with one of his chief fellow workers, Titus, he had visited the important island of Crete.

So, in one way and another, Paul was going forward with his evangelistic work, before time for him should run out. If we had more of his letters during this period, instead of only I Timothy and Titus, we should know more of his story during these important years.

2. THE OCCASION AND DATE OF I TIMOTHY

Timothy, as we know, was a native of Lystra, in the province of Galatia, son and grandson respectively of two well known church women, Eunice and Lois; his father was a Greek. Timothy was one of Paul's converts on the First Missionary Journey, and as a very

---

[1]For a different and liberal view of the authorship and other problems of I Timothy and the other letters in this group, see Kee and Young, *Understanding the New Testament*, pp. 67ff (1957); see also P. N. Harrison, *The Problems of the Pastorals*.

promising young man, joined Paul as a helper on the Second Journey, and again on the Third Journey.

At the close of the Third Journey, Timothy may have gone with Paul to Jerusalem, in the spring of A.D. 58, or he may have remained at Ephesus. The best opinion is that he went to Jerusalem, although his name is not mentioned in most of the story.

At any rate, he was present at Rome with Paul during the first imprisonment when the five letters, Colossians, Ephesians, Philemon, Philippians, and possibly Hebrews, were written, A.D. 61-63. Timothy and Luke were Paul's two closest friends and associates. Writing to the Philippians, Paul said of Timothy: "I hope in the Lord Jesus to send Timothy to you soon. . . I have no one like him, who will be genuinely anxious for your welfare."

When Paul wrote I Timothy, Timothy had been in Ephesus for some time. The Apostle had asked him to remain at Ephesus for a longer period, possibly on his journey to Macedonia by way of the island of Crete, where he left Titus for a work similar to that Timothy was engaged in at Ephesus. Paul wrote the letter from Macedonia to Timothy in Ephesus, perhaps in 65 or 66 A.D.

The immediate occasion for the writing of I Timothy was to give Timothy further instructions on how to perform the work of his mission, both as Christian evangelist and as an overseer of other ministers and helpers of the great church at Ephesus, and possibly of the province of Asia. Paul lays great stress on the quality and qualifications of the people who are to help and are to become leaders in the Church.

3. The Contents of the Letter

This letter is informal and personal, and written by the Apostle Paul to one of the most trusted and useful of his fellow workers and associates. For this reason the moods and tones of the letter are such that no analysis or outline can adequately represent its message.

The following brief outline will suggest the organization of the letter:

(1) The formal greeting (1:1-2).

(2) Paul's instructions concerning the Church, including warnings against false teachers, the place of women in the church, instructions on proper methods of worship, the choosing of ministers and other officials, and how the truth and dignity of the Church can be maintained through good ministers of Christ (1:3 to 3).

(3) Advice for Timothy's own personal guidance (4-6).

(4) As compared with Paul's other letters, this one closes almost abruptly.

Suggested Readings on I Timothy, Titus, and II Timothy

Bible Readings: I Timothy, Titus, II Timothy.

Text: *The Revised Standard Version;* or *The New English Bible;* or *The King James Version,* preferably in modern reader's format.

*Easton, B. S.: *The Pastoral Epistles.*

Falconer, Sir Robert: *The Pastoral Epistles.*

Gealy, F. H.: "The Epistles I and II Timothy and Titus," *The Interpreter's Bible,* Vol. XI, pp. 350-360.

*Guthrie, Donald: *The Pastoral Epistles.*

*Hendriksen, W.: *New Testament Commentary* (Vol. on I and II Timothy and Titus).

Parry, R. St. John: *The Pastoral Epistles.*

Scott, E. F.: *The Pastoral Epistles.*

Simpson, E. K.: *The Pastoral Epistles.*

*Stibbs, A. M.: "The Epistles to Timothy and Titus," *The New Bible Commentary,* pp. 1063-1083.

Chapter 14

TITUS

1. THE OCCASION AND DATE OF THE LETTER

The Apostle Paul wrote two letters between his release from his first imprisonment at Rome (about 63 A.D.) and his second imprisonment (about 67 A.D.). The first of these letters, as we have seen, I Timothy, was written about 65 A.D. The second, written about the same time or shortly afterward, was the letter to Titus.

The name Titus first appears in the Christian story as one of the delegates who attended the Council meeting at Jerusalem (50 A.D.), not named by Luke in Acts but listed by Paul in his letter to the Galatians (2:3-5). Titus was a Greek, probably a native of Antioch in Syria, and one of Paul's early converts (1:4).

At the time of the Third Missionary Journey, A.D. 54-58, Titus appears with Paul at Ephesus. He was sent to Corinth by Paul to look after certain improprieties and abuses in the church there. As messenger and deputy apostle, he rendered valuable service to the Apostle Paul during the crisis and threatened open rebellion in the church at Corinth.

The next we hear of Titus is in this letter, about A.D. 65 or 66, some seven years after the former events at Ephesus and Corinth. In the letter Paul says, "This is why I left you in Crete" (1:5), implying that he himself had been in Crete, probably on his way to Macedonia by way of Ephesus, where he would stop by to confer with Timothy also.

The letter also informs us why Titus was "left in Crete." It was for Titus to superintend the organization of the churches in the island, especially to choose suitable officers and ministers for the different churches. In Paul's absence the position of Titus in the island of Crete seems to have been, like that of Timothy at Ephesus, that of an apostolic deputy.

Paul's immediate occasion for writing the letter therefore was to give Titus further and detailed instructions on how to perform his duties. The instructions, though briefer, are remarkably similar to those given to Timothy in I Timothy, which presumably was written about the same time.

2. THE CONTENTS OF THE LETTER

Here, as in I Timothy, we have another personal letter, written by the Apostle Paul to one of his most intimate fellow-workers, Titus.

THE ANALYSIS

This brief outline analysis will suggest the main contents of the letter, although no outline can adequately reproduce the moods and tones of a private letter written to a personal friend:

1. The formal greeting (1:1-4). It may appear amusing to the modern reader to find such a lengthy, formal salutation, and loaded with such weighty matter, in a short letter to a familiar friend. But to the Apostle we may surmise, the beginning was of the utmost importance. It was describing the dignity and purpose of the apostolic message.

2. The Apostle Paul comes to the point at once and tells Titus why he was left in Crete: "That you might amend what was defective, and appoint Elders in every town as I directed you. . . ."

By *elders* (or *bishops,* as he called them also in I Timothy) he means preachers, pastors or ministers, we should call them today; men who were *overseers* and organizers as well as ministers (1:5-9).

3. Paul warns against "the circumcision party," the Judaizers in the island, as they were everywhere else Paul and his evangelists went. To the argument of circumcision, these same Jews had other false doctrines described here as "Jewish myths" or fables, apparently the same as our Lord condemned in the Pharisees as recorded in Matthew 15 and 23 (1:10-16).

4. Advice for Titus's own personal guidance, on how to instruct, train, and discipline the various classes of people in the church (2).

5. Instructions concerning the duty of Christians to society, as an example to others in good deeds (3:1-11).

6. The personal message and concluding salutation (3:12-15).

The personal message at the end of the letter reveals the Apostle Paul's plan to have Artemas or Tychicus, two other fellow workers, take over Titus's duties in the island, as soon as that could be arranged, and to have Titus come and spend the winter with him at Nicopolis, which was in western Greece overlooking the Adriatic Sea.

The last reference we have to Titus is in Paul's II Timothy 4:10, in which the Apostle relates that Titus had gone to Dalmatia, which was a part of the Roman province of Illyricum, and which was the farthest point west reached by Paul in his Second Journey (Romans 15:19-20).

Evidently, after their winter together at Nicopolis, Paul was arrested and taken back to Rome, Titus accompanying him. Titus left Rome for Dalmatia, perhaps to plant the Gospel among its wild inhabitants, whom the Romans under Augustus Caesar had subdued in A.D. 9. In all probability, then, this further missionary project for Titus was decided upon by Paul and Titus during their winter together at Nicopolis, and that may well be the reason Paul sent for Titus.[1]

---

[1]For suggested reading references on Titus, see the list at the end of the chapter on I Timothy.

Chapter 15

II TIMOTHY

1. THE OCCASION AND DATE OF THE LETTER

The letter we call II Timothy is the last of the letters of Paul that have come down to us, and is very likely the last he ever wrote. The best opinion is that it was written about 67 A.D., shortly before his final trial and execution. So that for modern readers it may be regarded as Paul's farewell message.

The reader will recall that at the end of the letter to Titus, the Apostle Paul had requested that Titus, as soon as he could arrange for Artemas or Tychicus to take over his duties in the island of Crete, come and join him at the seaport town of Nicopolis for the winter, which probably was the winter of 66-67 A.D.

Evidently, after their winter together at Nicopolis, Paul was arrested (some think at Troas, II Timothy 4:13) and taken back to Rome, Titus probably accompanying him. But Titus, as this letter reveals, had gone to Dalmatia; and Paul's other friends and fellow workers had also left him, except one. "Luke alone is with me," Paul plaintively writes.

From the letter we also learn that a crisis has been reached in Paul's trial for life, and that he wants his closest friends with him. "At my first defense," he says, "no one took my part; all deserted me. . . . But the Lord stood by me. . . . So I was rescued from the Lion's mouth."

The purpose of this letter, and the immediate occasion for writing it, then, was to urge Timothy to come to him at once at Rome, and to bring Mark with him if this were possible. By letter or messenger, Paul had already instructed Tychicus to go to Ephesus to take over Timothy's work there (4:12).

That Paul realized the end for him was rapidly approaching, is indicated also by his instructions to Timothy to bring with him Paul's personal things, such as his winter cloak, his books, and especially his parchments (4:13).

Suddenly the curtain falls on the tragic scene, as we have no record of how soon the end came, or whether Timothy and John Mark were able to be there in time, to add their aid and comfort to that of Luke.

2. The Contents of II Timothy

This letter has brought hope and encouragement to many Christians. For it contains not only the Apostle Paul's last words and farewell to those who knew and loved him personally. But more than that, it sings out the words of triumph and victory of an indomitable spirit, one of God's rarest noblemen; one who had fought and won the good fight, and who charges all Christians, no less than Timothy, to keep the faith and win the great fight!

The Analysis

Here is a brief outline analysis of the letter:

1. The formal greeting (1:1-2). Paul's opening salutations, whether to his closest friends and associates, or to a general audience such as that in the letter to the Romans, are remarkably similar in their formality and in their Christian tone. They are in keeping with the dignity of the apostolic message.

2. This section is most personal. The writer recalls the intimate associations of the two men, how they met, Timothy's conversion and "sincere faith," his noble mother and grandmother . . . and all the years since. And now, "I thank God, when I remember you constantly in my prayers . . . and long day and night to see you . . ." (1:3-18).

This expression of affection leads the Apostle to his final appeal to his young friend, whom by necessity he is about to leave, to be courageous and steadfast in the faith which they both share, regardless of the trials and persecutions of this life.

3. In chapter 2, Paul lays down some rules for God's ministers: "Be strong in the grace that is in Christ Jesus . . . and take your share of suffering as a good soldier of Christ Jesus . . . Do your best to present yourself to God as one approved, a workman who has no need to be ashamed, rightly handling the word of truth . . ."

4. He next warns Timothy of coming apostasy and describes the vices of evil men in an unforgettably modern passage, which begins,

> For men will be lovers of self, lovers of money, proud, arrogant, abusive, disobedient to their parents, ungrateful, unholy, inhuman, implacable, slanderers, profligates, fierce, haters of good, treacherous, reckless, swollen with conceit, lovers of pleasure rather than lovers of God . . .

The Apostle would have Timothy keep in mind what he has learned and what he has believed: "My teaching, my conduct, my aim in life, my faith, my patience, my love, my steadfastness, my persecutions, my sufferings . . . Indeed, all who desire to live a godly life in Christ Jesus will be persecuted" (3).

5. The Apostle Paul's final charge to Timothy is to *preach!* "Preach the word, be urgent in season and out of season, convince, rebuke, and exhort, be unfailing in patience and in teaching . . . For the time is coming when people will not endure sound teaching."

And then the Apostle concludes this section with the famous passage, "For I am already on the point of being sacrificed; the time of my departure has come . . ." (4:1-8).

6. The personal message to Timothy, with late news and directions (4:9-18).

7. The concluding salutation and benediction (4:19-22).[1]

---

[1]For suggested readings, see list for I Timothy.

PART NINE

THE LETTERS OF THE APOSTLES JAMES, PETER, JUDE, AND JOHN

The courtyard of the house of Caiaphas, where a monk looks at a plaque representing a cock crowing, in remembrance of Peter's denial of his Lord. © *Matson Photo Service*

Chapter 1

INTRODUCTION

Although the letters of the Apostle Paul have had priority with readers generally, nonetheless the letters of the other Apostles have had an important place in the history of the Christian Church.

Those Apostolic letters that have survived the vicissitudes of time, and have come down to us by the Spirit's guidance, include one letter by the Apostle James, two by the Apostle Peter, one by Jude, and three short letters and a long one, the apocalyptic Revelation, by the Apostle John.

There were doubtless many other letters by these and other Apostles that we do not have, just as the Apostle Paul wrote other letters which were not preserved and handed down to us. Although the modern reader would no doubt find some of these lost letters invaluable, he is grateful for the marvelous ones he has and accepts them as adequate for the essential Christian story.

Five of the letters of this group were called "General Epistles" in the titles prefixed to them in the Authorized or *King James Version* of 1611: James, I and II Peter, I John and Jude. The term *General* usually means that the letters were encyclical in nature, that is, intended for wide or general circulation. Paul's letters were usually addressed to a particular church or individual, although he requested that certain of his epistles be read by others than those addressed (see Colossians 4:16).

From the beginning, so far as the Roman government was concerned, the Christian movement grew up within Judaism, and there was little conflict between it and the Roman authorities. However, early in the sixth decade, or near the close of Paul's career, the situation began to change rapidly. More and more — in fact, and in the eyes of Rome — the Christians had separated themselves from Judaism. This no doubt accounts for the martyrdom of both Paul and Peter in the late sixties, as many scholars agree. The reader should keep this change in mind when he approaches the study of the letters of this group.[1]

---

[1]For a summary discussion of this background, see Merrill C. Tenney, *The New Testament: A Survey*, pp. 359-362 (1953). See also the selected reading list at the end of this chapter.

These letters and their introductions have been arranged chrono-logically on the following pages.

SUGGESTED READINGS ON THE LETTERS BY THE APOSTLES JAMES, PETER, JUDE, AND JOHN AS A GROUP IN RELATION TO THE HISTORIC PERIOD:

*Burleigh, J. H. S.: "The Primitive Church," *The New Bible Commentary,* pp. 64-67.

*Goguel, M.: *The Birth of Christianity.*

Harnack, A.: *The Mission and Expansion of Christianity in the First Three Centuries;* trans. by James Moffatt.

Kee, Howard Clark and Franklin W. Young: *Understanding the New Testament,* Chapters 11 to 15, pp. 325-472.

*Knox, John: *The Early Church and the Coming Great Church.*

Lietzmann, H.: *The Beginnings of the Christian Church.*

Moffatt, James: *The General Epistles.*

Streeter, B. H.: *The Primitive Church.*

Chapter 2

JAMES

1. The Biography of the Apostle James

There are four persons with the name *James* mentioned in the New Testament. They are James the son of Zebedee, James the son of Alphaeus, James the brother of Jesus, and James the father or brother of the Apostle Jude (or Judas).

The general opinion among scholars is that this letter was written by James, the brother of our Lord, the early head of the Jerusalem Church. What is the story of this Apostle James? In Matthew's and Mark's lists of the brothers of Jesus, James's name stands first, and it is likely that he was the oldest (Matthew 13:55; Mark 6:3).[1]

Like so many others, including his own brothers, it appears that James was one of those who was unable to accept Jesus as the Messiah during His earthly life (John 7:5). But after the Resurrection, Christ appeared to him in a special interview and James believed (I Corinthians 15:7).

From the first organization of the Church in Jerusalem, James seems to have been its leader and head (Acts 12:17; 15:13; 21:18; Galatians 1:19; 2:9, 12). All the leading Apostles, including Peter and Paul, when they were in Jerusalem felt that they must report to James.

In A.D. 50, on the occasion of the famous meeting of the Council at Jerusalem on the question whether circumcision should be required of Gentile Christians, it was the Apostle James who, after all the others had spoken, arose and announced this decision: "Therefore my judgment is that we should not trouble those of the Gentiles who turn to God . . ." (Acts 15). And this judgment of James seemed good also to the apostles and elders.

The final reference to James in Luke's account has to do with Paul's last visit to Jerusalem (Acts 21:18-25). It was James who advised Paul that he take the Nazarite vow to placate his enemies, the unbelieving Jews, before he went to the Temple.

---

[1] For a discussion of authorship, as well as James's relationship to our Lord, see A. T. Robertson, *Practical and Social Aspects of Christianity,* Second Edition; Andrew McNab, "The General Epistle of James," *The New Bible Commentary,* pp. 1118-1128 (1954); and for a more liberal view, see Kee and Young, *Understanding the New Testament,* pp. 318-320 (1957); M. Goguel, *The Birth of Christianity,* Part IV, chapter 6 (1954).

From these and other references, it is evident that James held a position of leadership and authority in the mother church at Jerusalem, presiding over assemblies, speaking the final and authoritative word on important issues, and receiving reports from the activities of others.

According to the Jewish historian Josephus, the Apostle James was martyred in a popular uprising of the Jews in the interim between the death of the Roman governor Festus and the arrival of the new governor, Albinus, in A.D. 62.

According to this story, Ananias, the High Priest and a Sadducee, brought James before the Sanhedrin and demanded that he declare publicly that Jesus was not the Messiah. This Ananias did apparently to frighten the people who were embracing Christianity in such large numbers. When James refused, the High Priest, taking advantage of the absence of a Roman governor, caused James to be put to death by stoning, in spite of the pleas of many of his fellow countrymen.

2. The Date, Audience, and Purpose of the Letter

Some scholars place the date of James as early as 45 to 49 A.D., which is about the date of Paul's earliest letters; others prefer to assign the letter to about 55 A.D. or a little later. At any rate, it was written somewhat early, when the Jerusalem Church was still regarded as the center and head of the Christian community.

James, who was the accepted leader and head of the mother church at Jerusalem after the withdrawal of Peter from Palestine, thus wrote his letter from the Jewish capital. His message is addressed to "the twelve tribes in the dispersion." That is, to Jewish Christians scattered over various parts of the Roman Empire, beyond the homeland of Palestine. He did not mean the Twelve Tribes of Israel, for as such it did not exist at the time James was writing.

To state it another way, James's address indicates that his special interest and concern was his fellow Jews, who in recent years had become professed followers of Christ, and who were in need of practical instruction in the ethics and art of Christian living. He wished for them to become good Christians, as well as good Jews.

3. The Contents of the Letter

In his perusal of this letter, the reader need not feel, as some readers of the past apparently have thought, that the Apostle James is writing a reply to the Apostle Paul, who stressed the doctrine of Faith in his letters. In fact, it is likely that James's letter was written before Paul's, or at least before any except Paul's very earliest letters.

The *principles* of Christianity are based on faith in the Lord Jesus as the All-Sufficient Saviour. This view the letter of James takes for granted, as is evident from this and other pertinent statements:

> My brethren, show no partiality as you hold to the faith of our Lord Jesus Christ, the Lord of glory (2:1).

What this letter stresses, on the contrary, is the *application* of Christian principles, in what the writer calls *works* . . . "Show me *your faith* apart from your works, and I by my works will show you *my faith.*"

To state it another way, in scientific research the terms *pure science* and the *applications of science* are used. So in religion. James's letter, not excluding faith, specialized in the *applications of faith,* which he keenly felt needed to be stressed to his fellow Jewish converts, wherever they happened to be at the time of his letter.

As someone has aptly said, we are not told so much about *how to become Christians,* as *how to live as Christians.* The letter is a great sermon, and a great favorite with modern readers.

THE ANALYSIS

Here is a brief outline analysis of the contents of the letter:

1. The greeting to Christian Jews (1:1). This is a short and direct greeting, which simply identifies the writer and the audience.

2. BE DOERS OF THE WORD (1:2-27). The writer shows himself to be a true Hebrew, in that his discussion, like that of Ecclesiastes and other Hebrew writers, moves in waves and circles instead of a straight line. For example, in chapter 1 he mentions almost every topic he later discusses in the complete letter: The Jewish dispersion, the trials of Christians, patience, wisdom, prayer, faith, the lowly and the rich, the vanity of riches, endurance of trials, the tongue, the doers of the word, sin, pure religion, and others.

Trials and hardships are means of testing faith, and of producing steadfastness. Wisdom is necessary in meeting the problems of life; and he who lacks wisdom, let him ask of God, provided he asks for it with a singleness and sincerity of purpose. The rich man and the poor man are on the same footing with God. And blessed is the man who endures trial and wins the victory. Indeed, the test of a person's faith is his works: "Be doers of the word, and not hearers only, deceiving yourselves."

3. FAITH AND WORKS (2). Beware of looking *up* to one man, and *down* at another. For the rich as compared with the poor, has no advantage with God. Therefore, "My brethren, show no partiality as you hold the faith of our Lord Jesus Christ."

In short, if you really want to fulfill the Royal Law, according to the Scripture, "You shall love your neighbor as yourself."

All this means that a Christian inevitably shows his faith by his works: "So faith of itself, if it has no works, is dead."

4. ON BRIDLING THE TONGUE (3). Be not unduly eager to teach, for teaching carries great responsibility; rather strive for understanding, and for example, self-control in bridling the tongue. "Who is wise and understanding among you? By his good faith let him show his works in the meekness of wisdom."

5. DRAW NEAR TO GOD (4). What causes wars, and why do men commit crimes? Is it not because men covet, and desire to have what

belongs to another? Therefore, to withstand temptation and all forms of worldly-mindedness, "Draw near to God and he will draw near to you."

You forget, in your grasping and selfish planning, how uncertain the tomorrow is! "For you are a mist that appears for a little time and then vanishes."

6. THE COMING OF THE LORD (5). Begin to weep now, you grasping rich, for the miseries that are sure to come upon you. For you have laid up treasures that are already rotten, and "your gold and silver have rusted, and their rust will be evidence against you."

On the contrary, make ready for the Coming of the Lord: "Establish your hearts, for the coming of the Lord is at hand . . . Behold, we call those happy who were steadfast."

If any one among you is suffering, let him pray: "The effectual fervent prayer of a righteous man availeth much."

Finally, if any one brings back a sinner from the error of his way, let him know that he has saved a soul from death and has covered a multitude of sin.

SPECIAL READINGS ON THE LETTER BY JAMES

Bible Reading: The Letter by James.

Goguel, M.: *The Birth of Christianity*, Part IV, Chapter 6.

Knowling, R. J.: *The Epistle of St. James.*

Mayor, J. B., *The Epistle of St. James.* Third Edition.

*McNab, Andrew: *The New Bible Commentary*, pp. 1118-1128.

*Moffatt, James: *The General Epistles.*

Robertson, A. T.: *Practical and Social Aspects of Christianity,* Second Ed.

Ross, Alexander: *Commentary on the Epistles of James and John.*

*Tasker, R. V. G.: *The Epistle of James.*

Chapter 3

I Peter

1. The Apostle Peter

Although from time to time the authorship of I Peter has been questioned, scholars generally agree that the letter is authentic and was written by the Apostle Peter.

The Apostle Peter, following a common custom in the first century may have employed one of his associates as scribe to copy his dictation of the letter, perhaps Silas or John Mark, both of whom are mentioned at the close of the message. Verse 5:12 suggests Silas. This might account for the quality of the language and style in the Greek of its composition.

A brief account of Peter's life may serve to bring into better focus the two letters of Peter we are about to read.

We first meet Simon and his brother Andrew at Bethany beyond the river Jordan where John the Baptist was baptizing. Here we have also our first recorded meeting of Jesus and Simon, whom Jesus looked over searchingly and nicknamed *Cephas* (in Aramaic) or *Peter* (in Greek), both of which mean *rock*, the main feature of Peter's character in later years.

In this letter the writer introduces himself as "Peter," using his Greek name, by which the world in turn has preferred to call him. Peter was a fisherman of Bethsaida, with his brother Andrew; they moved over to Capernaum and became fishing partners with Zebedee's sons James and John, on the northwest shore of the Sea of Galilee.

One day Jesus passed by where they were and Peter was the first to leave everything and follow the call of his Master. Of the Twelve Apostles, Peter was the first to be named.

Peter was present and heard the Sermon on the Mount. He was one of the three Apostles present at the Transfiguration. It was Peter who was first to recognize and confess that Jesus is the Christ.

Although Peter denied his Lord three times the night before the Crucifixion, shortly afterward he wept bitterly and repented, and Jesus forgave him and promised Peter his faith should not fail.

It was Peter who preached the first Christian sermon, the great sermon at Pentecost, at which time three thousand were converted.

It was Peter who preached to the Roman Centurion, his first Gentile convert, and thereafter became overseer and bishop of the

Gentile Churches throughout the Roman Empire, as well as leader of the Twelve Apostles.

At the Council meeting in Jerusalem in 50 A.D., on whether circumcision should be required of Gentile Christians, it was Peter's speech which swayed the opinion of the delegates in favor of not placing this added burden on the Gentiles.

It was Peter, in later years in his preaching at Rome, who largely influenced Mark, who was Peter's secretary and interpreter, in his writing of the second gospel.

It is a distinct loss to the story of early Christianity that the Apostle Peter did not have an effective "press agent," such as Paul had in the person of Luke, to present fully Peter's great work for the Church during his middle and later years.

The Apostle lived to an advanced age, before his martyrdom, and the wisdom and authority of these many years are stated briefly in his two Letters.

2. THE OCCASION AND PURPOSE OF THE LETTER

Peter writes the letter from Rome.[1] The expression in the close of the letter, "She who is at Babylon, who is likewise chosen, sends you greetings," most surely refers to Rome, and the Christian Church there.

For security and symbolic reasons, the name Babylon was often used for Rome. The Apostle John, in his long letter, the Revelation, calls Rome "Babylon" (chapters 17 and 18). So Peter, in this letter, because Rome of his day resembled ancient Babylon in its wealth, luxury, and wickedness, calls it Babylon.

The date of the letter is usually placed between the date of Paul's letter to the Ephesians (about A.D. 62), from which it apparently indirectly quotes, and the death of Peter, which usually is set about 67 A.D. It is likely that it was written about 64 A.D., or perhaps a little later.

In 64 A.D., Emperor Nero set fire to the city of Rome. He was ambitious to build a new and grander Rome, and his first step was to get rid of the old Rome. But the people became so disturbed over the city's destruction that Nero found it necessary to seek a scapegoat. So he accused the Christians publicly and began their persecution, which was much more severe than it had been before.

From the Apostle Peter's letter, it appears that the new outbreak of persecution had not actually taken place; or if so, it was only in its beginning in Rome, and had not yet reached the Roman provinces to which the letter is addressed. But the news had spread, and it is evident from the tone of the message that both writer and reader

---

[1]Against Peter's authorship of I Peter are Kee and Young, *Understanding the New Testament,* pp. 432-435 (1957); F. W. Beare, *The First Epistle of St. Peter,* pp. 1-41 (1947). One of the best defenses of Peter's authorship is that of E. G. Selwyn, *The First Epistle of St. Peter,* pp. 7-38 (1952). See also McNab, Stibbs, and others in the selected reading list at the end of this chapter.

were expecting a severe persecution: "Beloved, do not be surprised at the fiery ordeal which comes upon you to prove you" (4:12).

The letter is addressed "to the exiles of the dispersion in Pontus, Galatia, Cappadocia, Asia, and Bithynia." That is, to the whole body of Christians now living in the five Roman provinces of Asia Minor, who were largely Gentiles. These churches were founded and watched over mainly by the Apostle Paul, and to them Paul earlier had written his letter to the Galatians, and more recently the letters to the Ephesians and the Colossians. Paul also had re-visited them on occasions, during his Second and Third Journeys. Peter's letter indicates that these Gentile Christians owed their conversion to others than himself, and he appears to be writing to them in his capacity as overseer or bishop.

Some two or three decades later, the Apostle John wrote his famous letters to many of these same churches. He was then living at Ephesus, the chief city and center of Asia Minor.

Peter's letter has been called "pre-eminently the Epistle of Hope." The Christian's hope. For in it the primary purpose of the Apostle was to instill hope in his readers, against the "fiery ordeal" which was about to come upon them.

3. The Contents of the Letter

If the reader has often wished to know more about what the great Apostle Peter preached, especially during his last years, he can learn much from this letter and the one which immediately follows it, II Peter. For the outline and content of Peter's earlier sermons, the student should examine closely Mark's gospel, which is supposed to have been largely influenced by Peter's preaching, and the sermons quoted by Luke in the book of Acts.

The Analysis

This brief outline analysis will suggest the contents of I Peter:

1. The formal salutation and opening of the letter, like those of the Apostle Paul's, is in keeping with the dignity of the Apostolic message (1:1-2).

2. The Imperishable Gospel of Hope. In the first chapter of the letter God is praised for the ineffable blessings of His Gospel of salvation; and those Christians addressed are urged and exhorted to walk worthily of this salvation. It is an occasion for them to rejoice, although for a little while they may have to suffer fiery trials, which have for their purpose the testing of the genuineness of their faith.

3. The Earthly Pilgrimage of God's Own People. In chapters 2 to 4:6, the Apostle continues with a series of exhortations on how to live worthily as Christians, in a world of evil and trials, and quotes Scripture to reinforce his teaching (Isaiah 40:6; 28:16; 43:21; 8:14f; 53; Psalm 34; etc.). This is the way of life for believers, he is saying: "Even if you do suffer for righteousness' sake, you will be blessed . . .

Since therefore Christ suffered in the flesh, arm yourselves with the same thought."

4. THE END OF ALL THINGS IS AT HAND. Verses 4:7-19 contain the famous warning of impending persecution and death:

> Beloved, do not be surprised at the fiery ordeal which comes upon you to prove you. . . . But rejoice in so far as you share Christ's sufferings, that you may also rejoice and be glad when his glory is revealed.

According to trustworthy tradition, the Emperor Nero chose the Christians as the pretext for the burning of Rome. So, at the moment, his soldiers were already on the march. Thus, these strong words of warning and hope.

5. In verses 5:1-11, we have the Apostle's exhortation to the elders, *pastors* or *ministers* we should call them, to tend their flocks diligently against the day when the Great Shepherd comes. Likewise, he charges the flocks to make themselves subject to their elders, and living in all humility, to cast all their anxieties upon the Lord.

6. In verses 5:12-14, we have the concluding salutation and benediction. Regarding the part that Silas may have had in the composition of the letter, one noted commentator offers this free translation of the meaning of verse 5:12: "I have used Silvanus as my secretary; he has, I am sure, given my thoughts faithfully, though he has written them out in his own language."[2] Note the informality of Peter's benedictions, as compared with Paul's.

SUGGESTED ADDITIONAL READINGS ON I PETER, II PETER, AND JUDE

Bible Readings: The Letters of I Peter, II Peter, and Jude.

Beare, F. W.: *The First Epistle of St. Peter.*

Foakes-Jackson, F. J.: *Peter, Prince of Apostles.*

Mayor, J. B.: *The Epistle of St. Jude and the Second Epistle of St. Peter.*

*McNab, Andrew: *The New Bible Commentary*, pp. 1129-1150.

Robertson, A. T.: *Epochs in the Life of Simon Peter.*

*Selwyn, E. G.: *The First Epistle of St. Peter.*

*Skilton, John H.: *The Epistles of Peter and Jude.*

*Stibbs, A. M.: *The First Epistle of Peter.*

*Tenney, Merrill C.: *New Testament Survey*, pp. 359-367; 383-392 (1953).

Thomas, W. H. Griffith: *The Apostle Peter.*

Wand, J. W. C.: *The General Epistles of St. Peter and St. Jude.*

---

[2] J. R. Dummelow, *A Commentary on the Holy Bible*, p. 1040 (Third Edition).

Chapter 4

II PETER

1. AUTHORSHIP, DATE, AND AUDIENCE OF THE LETTER

This is the second of two letters written by the Apostle Peter.

Although some think that the difference in style and language is great enough to suggest a different author, the more conservative opinion is that it is the work of the same Apostle.[1]

However, there is reason to believe that Silas, referred to in I Peter as having a connection with that letter, perhaps as scribe or amanuensis, had no such connection with the writing of II Peter, and that Peter may have composed it himself independently, in his own natural style.

The important fact for the modern reader is that the letter itself, in a forthright and authoritative manner, claims to be by "Simon Peter, a servant and Apostle of Jesus Christ," and that the conservative Church Fathers ascribed it to him and included it in the Canon as apostolic.

In verse 1:14, the writer speaks as if he expected his death soon. The best opinion is that Peter's martyrdom came about A.D. 67 or 68, about the same time or perhaps shortly after that of the Apostle Paul. And so the date of this letter should be placed at about 67 A.D.

Unlike I Peter, this letter does not name the churches to which it is addressed. However, in verse 3:1, the writer says, "This is now the second letter that I have written to you." Assuming that he refers to I Peter, and not to another letter perhaps now lost, we may conclude that this letter is also addressed to the Churches in the five Roman provinces of Asia Minor — Pontus, Galatia, Cappadocia, Asia, and Bithynia — the same which he mentioned in the opening verse of the other letter.

We may assume also that the letter, like I Peter, was written from Rome.

---

[1]The opinion of modern scholars on the authorship and date of II Peter is sharply divided. Kee and Young favor a much later date than the Apostle Peter, in *Understanding the New Testament*, pp. 342, and 464ff (1957). For a brief summary of opinion on both sides, but favoring the Apostle's authorship, see Andrew McNab, "II Peter," *The New Bible Commentary*, pp. 1143-1150; see also Merrill C. Tenney, *New Testament Survey*, pp. 384-386.

2. The Occasion and Purpose of the Letter

The immediate occasion for the writing of II Peter is stated in chapter two of the letter. News had reached the Apostle Peter of the iniquitous doctrines of certain false teachers within the Church itself.

These false teachers were accused of "secretly bringing in destructive heresies, even denying the Master" who had redeemed them with His own blood. This was downright apostasy and appears to have been the work of Judaizers, such as the Apostle Paul had dealt with in his letters to the Galatians, the Colossians, and elsewhere.

The further descriptive details in the same chapter make us feel that another heresy of a different sort is also referred to, the false beliefs of the Gnostics.

In their analysis of *spirit* and *matter,* the Gnostics denied that Jesus is the Son of God. A heresy is always a denial of Christ's work and authority.

Also, since spirit is good and matter bad, God could have nothing to do with the material universe. A person could lead two lives, or have a dual existence, they taught — a life of the spirit and a life of the flesh, and with no connection one with the other. Hence a person could debauch himself and live a life of gluttony and licentiousness in the body, without affecting his spirit!

The Apostle says of them,

> They count it pleasure to revel in the daytime. They are blots and blemishes, reveling in their dissipation, carousing with you. They have eyes full of adultery, insatiable for sin. They entice unsteady souls. They have hearts trained in greed.

The purpose of the letter is to warn against the insidious heresies here described, and to exhort all believers to remain steadfast in the faith and practice of the Gospel of the Lord Jesus.

> This is the second letter that I have written to you, beloved, and in both of them I have aroused your sincere mind by way of reminder; that you should remember the predictions of the holy prophets and the commandment of the Lord and Saviour through your apostles.

What the Apostle is saying is that the coming of false teachers is spoken of again and again in the Scriptures, and that the Lord Himself warned against them and of the necessity of remaining steadfast in the faith.

3. The Contents of the Letter

1. After the brief greeting, verses 1-2, there is the usual reminder of what God has done for us, in that He has granted us all things that pertain to life and godliness, even to becoming partakers of the divine nature.

This gift and inheritance entails the Christian's growth in grace and love, which Peter states after the manner of Paul in a formula, thus:

For this very reason make every effort to supplement your *faith* with *virtue,* and virtue with *knowledge,* and knowledge with *self-control,* and self-control with *steadfastness,* and steadfastness with *godliness,* and godliness with *brotherly affection,* and brotherly affection with *love* (chapter 1:3-11).

2. Since the Apostle must depart this life soon, he intends to use his final message as a reminder of the things he has always spoken. There is a hint here that Peter was conscious that somehow his "reminder" was spoken not merely for the present generation of Christians, but for Christians of all time to come.

Moreover, the Apostle would have his readers believe that his message was authoritative, because he is an eye-witness and an Apostle, and one who was singularly honored by being present at his Lord's Transfiguration. And then, with a touch of poetry, he adds, "You will do well to pay attention to this as to a lamp shining in a dark place, until the day dawns and the morning star rises in your hearts" (chapter 1:12-21).

3. Warnings against false teachers, as mentioned above (Chapter 2).

4. The author calls his readers' attention to the fact that this is the second letter he has written to them, reminding them to be on guard against false teachers, and to see to it that their lives be holy and godly while they wait for Christ's Coming.

To reinforce his message, the author refers to the letters of the Apostle Paul (see Galatians, Colossians, Ephesians, etc.), which they have received, and in which Paul reminds them of the same things. From his two letters, and from this reference, the Apostle shows that he, too, has read Paul's letters.

5. The letter closes with a brief benediction, verse 3:18.

Chapter 5

JUDE

1. THE AUTHOR, DATE, and OCCASION OF THE LETTER

The writer of this letter describes himself simply as "Jude, a servant of Jesus Christ and brother of James."

Several men by the name of *Judas* (Latin) or *Jude* (English) are mentioned in the New Testament. Two of the Twelve Apostles were of this name: Judas Iscariot, the betrayer of Jesus, and the other Judas named by Luke (Luke 6:16, Acts 1:13), but called Thaddaeus by Matthew and Mark.

Tradition, however, has ascribed this letter to still another Jude, the younger brother of James, and Jesus, of the household of Joseph and Mary (Matthew 13:55).[1] This James later became leader of the Jerusalem Church, and this fact may explain why his younger brother Jude did not think it necessary to identify himself further than to say simply that he was the "brother of James." His readers would understand.

It is generally agreed that the immediate occasion for the writing of Jude is the same as Peter's for the writing of II Peter. That is, to give stern warning against certain destructive heresies and to exhort all believers to remain steadfast in the faith of the Lord Jesus.

Peter states that his first letter is addressed to the Churches in the five Roman provinces of Pontus, Galatia, Cappadocia, Asia, and Bithynia. It appears that II Peter is also addressed to one or all of these same churches, although he does not say so in the letter. Was the letter of Jude, although the writer does not name his church or churches, written also to these same Churches of Asia Minor? It would seem quite likely.

The fact that II Peter and Jude are on the same general theme, and are remarkably similar in many details, has led some scholars to think that Peter, as general supervisor or bishop of the Gentile Churches, took alarm at the growing dangers and conferred with several leaders. He may have, according to this view, even sent a copy of his letter to Jude or otherwise revealed his message to Jude, so that the latter sent a similar message to these churches.

---

[1]On the authorship and date, see Robert Robertson, *The New Bible Commentary*, pp. 1161-1167 (1954); Tenney, *New Testament Survey*, pp. 388-390; Kee and Young, *Understanding the New Testament*, p. 342.

500

Thus, from the similarity of the situation in both letters, it appears likely that they were both addressed to the same churches, and at about the same time. It is suggested also that Jude's letter followed II Peter, and both probably about A.D. 67, not long before the martyrdom of Peter and Paul at Rome.

2. The Contents of the Letter

As compared with II Peter, the letter of Jude is more direct and more vigorous in its denunciation of the "ungodly persons" in the church to which his letter is addressed.

1. The formal greeting, conforming to the manner and pattern of the apostolic letter (1:1-2).

2. Jude's short letter is filled with terrible epithets, pointed not to evil men of the world, but to certain vicious imposters and would-be leaders within the Church itself:

> Ungodly persons who pervert the grace of our God into licentiousness and deny our only Master and Lord, Jesus Christ . . . These men in their dreaming defile the flesh, reject authority, and revile the glorious ones . . . They walk in the way of Cain, and abandon themselves for the sake of gain . . .
> These are grumblers, malcontents, following their own passions, loud-mouthed boasters, flattering people to gain advantage . . . scoffers, following their own ungodly passions . . . It is these who set up divisions, worldly people, devoid of the spirit . . . (verses 3-19).

3. In verses 20-23, the scene changes, and the writer has these beautiful words of commendation and exhortation to the men of faith:

> But you, beloved, build yourselves up in your most holy faith; pray in the Holy Spirit; keep yourselves in the love of God; wait for the mercy of our Lord Jesus Christ unto eternal life.

4. A feature of this short letter is the Benediction with which Jude closes it, verses 24-25. It is one of the famous benedictions of the Bible, and is better known than the letter of Jude itself. The reader will note that it is an expansion of the Apostle Peter's farewell blessing at the close of II Peter.

Chapter 6

I JOHN

1. THE APOSTLE JOHN AND HIS LETTERS FROM EPHESUS

We begin now the reading of the last group of letters in the New Testament, the four letters by the Apostle John: I John, II John, III John, and Revelation.

Several men by the name *John* are mentioned in the New Testament, three of whom were very prominent in connection with the gospel story: John the Baptist, the Apostle John and son of Zebedee, and John Mark the author of the second gospel.

Both tradition and internal evidence are so strongly in favor of the Apostle John's authorship of I John that few scholars have ever seriously questioned it. In thought and ideas, as well as in style and language, this letter is remarkably similar to John's gospel, which scarcely any one doubts is the work of the Apostle John.[1]

In the letter, as in the gospel, the author writes as an Apostle, with the authority of one who was present and an eye-witness of the gospel story and message of which he writes:

> That which was from the beginning, which we have heard, which
> we have seen with our eyes, which we have looked upon and
> touched with our hands, concerning the word of life . . . the life
> was made manifest, and we saw it . . .

John, with his intimate and daily companionship with Jesus as "the disciple whom Jesus loved," could speak with authority as no one else could.

Where was John when he wrote, and to whom did he address his message? Answers to these questions, as well as the date of the writing, cannot be given exactly, since we have no direct evidence.

However, John is said to have written his gospel between 80 and 90 A.D., perhaps near the end of that decade. And I John, which often has been closely associated with the gospel in point of time and ideas, many believe may have been written shortly after the gospel, and from Ephesus.

John's readers are not specifically named or located, just as the

---

[1] The Apostle John's authorship is stoutly defended by these scholars: Merrill C. Tenney, *The New Testament Survey*, pp. 393-398 (1953); Drummond and Morris, "The Epistles of John," *The New Bible Commentary*, pp. 1151-1160. For a liberal view, see Kee and Young, *Understanding the New Testament*, pp. 67, 342; M. S. Enslin, *Christian Beginnings*, pp. 447-451 (1938).

name of the writer is not given. Perhaps these details were not necessary, since those who received the letter would know. But it is strongly inferred that the letter was a pastoral or circular letter, addressed to the Churches in the province of Asia, doubtless the same as those addressed in the much longer letter, the Revelation, which was presumably written some five or ten years later. Revelation is addressed to the "Seven Churches in Asia."

The Apostle Paul and his associates, as we have seen, organized these churches during the Third Missionary Journey, 54-58 A.D. It is commonly believed that the Apostle John left Jerusalem and took up his residence and ministry at Ephesus, about A.D. 70, when the commander Titus (later Emperor) destroyed Jerusalem, and shortly after the martyrdom of the Apostles Peter and Paul at Rome.

2. The Occasion and Purpose of I John

The occasion and purpose of I John are essentially the same as they were when John wrote his gospel: "That you may believe that Jesus is the Christ, the Son of God, and that believing you may have life in his name" (John 20:31).

However, in I John the emphasis is shifted from *becoming a Christian,* to *continuing* in the faith, as if I John was a sequel to the gospel. Thus, the letter being addressed primarily to those who had already become Christians, was intended to give assurance of their possession of lifegiving faith in Jesus Christ, and to give them further instructions in the truths of that faith: "I write this to you who believe in the name of the Son of God, that you may know that you have eternal life" (5:13).

The immediate occasion for the writing of I John was to combat certain false teaching which had made its appearance, undermining the faith of Christian converts, and insidiously subverting the meaning of the Gospel.

Opposition to the Gospel of Christ, at Jerusalem and at Antioch and elsewhere in the first generation of the Apostolic age, had come mainly from unbelieving Jews. Soon, however, as the Church spread westward to Ephesus and the great centers of European Macedonia and Greece, Christianity found itself in conflict with other ideas, especially with the philosophy and the religious ideas of pagan Greece. The new Church had now been in the world some sixty years, and had grown rapidly in numbers, power, and influence in many parts of the Roman Empire. Thus, it is not surprising that it should be challenged by the older ideas of religion and ways of life.

One of these ideas was what is known as Gnosticism.[2] What this false doctrine amounted to was a denial of the Incarnation and Jesus as the Son of God. These ideas gained considerable headway among the Churches under John's care. He wrote his gospel and the three

---

[2]For a discussion of Gnosticism, see chapter on John's gospel, p. 391.

letters, as the testimony of an Apostle and a personal witness, that Jesus *is* the Son of God. And we may be sure that these wonderful messages did much to refute and to defeat these and other heresies and false teaching in his time.

3. THE CONTENTS OF THE LETTER

Here is a brief outline analysis of the contents of the letter:

(1) The Prologue (1:1-4). The Apostle John usually begins his compositions with a significant *prologue*. For instance, the reader will recall the sublime prologue with which he introduces his gospel (1:1-18), and the special pronouncement in the prologue to the book of Revelation (1:1-8).

Here we have in this opening passage of I John a resume of John's whole life and ministry, from the beginning of his apostleship and intimate, personal relationship with our Lord, to the time of the writing of this letter, about 90 A.D.

(2) The conditions of fellowship with the Father and the Son (1:5 to 2:6). God is light, and in him there is no darkness. This was revealed by the Son. Therefore those who would have fellowship with Him, in their inward and outward life, must walk in that light.

(3) The place of Christian love as a "new commandment" in this fellowship, and a statement of the conflict between the love of the world and the love of the Father (2:7-17).

(4) While the Apostle urges his readers to love one another, and warns against loving the world and the things in the world, he also warns them against false teachers and the Antichrist, a term which John alone uses in the New Testament (2:18-29). The Gnostics are here called *Antichrists*, those who deny that Jesus is the Christ. All this is of special importance, because Christ's Coming is at hand.

(5) The duties and privileges of the children of God (3). The commandment is always the same: "And this is his commandment, that we should believe in the name of his Son Jesus Christ and love one another." This is the sure test of true discipleship.

(6) The test of true fellowship with God is further illustrated in chapter 4, by comparing it with the false teaching of "false prophets" to whom John's disciples were subjected.

(7) The witness of the Spirit is the true evidence of salvation and discipleship (5:12).

(8) The summary and conclusion of the discussion of true discipleship of Christ (5:13-21). The purpose of the letter is thus summarized: "I write this to you who believe in the name of the Son of God, that you may know that you have eternal life" (verse 13).

SUGGESTED ADDITIONAL READINGS ON I JOHN, II JOHN, III JOHN

Bible Readings: I John, II John, and III John.

*Drummond, R. J. and Leon Morris: "The Epistles of John," *The New Bible Commentary*, pp. 1151-1160.

Robertson, A. T.: *Epochs in the Life of the Apostle John.*

Ross, Alexander: *Commentary on the Epistles of James and John.*

Thomas, W. H. Griffith: *The Apostle John — His Life and Writings.*

*Westcott, B. F.: *The Epistles of John.* Third Edition.

(See also readings on the Gospel of John, pages 399, 400, the special articles in the dictionaries, and standard sets.)

Chapter 7

II JOHN

1. THE WRITER AND THE PURPOSE OF HIS LETTER

The Apostle John introduces himself as the Elder (or *Presbyter* in the Greek), in a manner similar to that of the Apostle Peter in I Peter 5:1, and addresses his letter to "the elect lady and her children."

Scholars are of the opinion that John is writing simply as the *pastor* or minister to a certain church and its members. The letter could have a further connotation, that of a message from an elder Churchman, the last surviving Apostle writing years after all the others had died or suffered martyrdom. For John, supposed to be about the same age as Jesus, would now be an old, old man, probably no less than ninety years of age, and likely older.

No mention is made of the place from which he writes, nor the name of the writer, nor the church to which the letter is addressed, since in a private letter such as this one all these circumstances would be understood.

The purpose of the letter is to convey a message of love and Christian fellowship, and especially to warn the Church against certain false teachers and their deceptive doctrines, the same as he described in I John.[1] This short letter could have been another in a series, and addressed to a different church from that of I John.

2. THE CONTENTS OF THE LETTER

The contents of the letter center around the twofold purpose mentioned in the paragraph above. However, the keynote of this letter, as in all of John's letters, is Christian love and fellowship.

But in the background of this letter, as in I John, is the Apostle's reference to false teachers and doctrines, and his warning against them.

John also makes much of the word Truth, which as he uses it has about the same meaning as used by Jesus: "I am the Truth, the Way, and the Life. . . . The Truth shall make you free. . . . For this purpose came I into the world. . . ." Truth in this sense is synonymous with the Christ and His Gospel.

---

[1]See the selected reading references on I John.

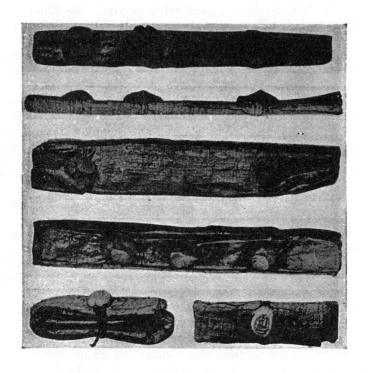

Sealed letters, or epistles, sheets of papyrus
rolled, tied and sealed, to be delivered by
messenger. Photo courtesy J. H. Kok, publishers: *De Antieke Wereld en Het Nieuwe
Testament*, by A. Sizoo; Kampen, Holland

Chapter 8

III JOHN

1. THE APOSTLE JOHN AND HIS THIRD LETTER

In III John we have a personal letter from "the Elder," pastor or minister we should say in modern usage, to the Apostle John's good friend Gaius, whom he greets warmly. In its personal nature, the letter reminds us of Paul's letter to his good friend Philemon. The Apostle congratulates Gaius for his Christian faith, and for his hospitality to others, especially to visiting brethren from other churches.

The letter is one of a series by the Apostle John, written presumably from Ephesus and about A.D. 90. Many others doubtless were written but have not come down to us. This letter, like I John and II John, is commonly dated *before* A.D. 96, when Emperor Domitian intensified his persecution of the Christians. Gaius likely was a member of one of "the Seven Churches" in the Roman province of Asia.

The letter is remarkably similar in ideas, language, and in style to I John and II John, and all three are similar in these respects to John's gospel.[1]

It has been said that the Apostle John understood Jesus and His message better than any other Apostle or disciple. One evidence of this relationship is seen in John's interpretation of the Gospel, his words, and even his phraseology, which are often almost identical with those of Jesus, as reported in the gospels, and especially in Matthew.

2. THE CONTENTS AND PURPOSE OF THE LETTER

The purpose of the letter is to commend Gaius for his good deeds as a member of the Christian community: "No greater joy can I have than this, than to hear that my children follow the Truth."

Reports have come to the writer that Gaius is not only a follower of Christ, "the Truth" as he calls it, but he has also entertained the visiting brethren from other churches, and in other respects has been conducting himself as a worthy member of the fellowship of Christ. He is presented in the letter as an example of noble Christian living.

But not all Christians are like Gaius, as the letter bears evidence. For a certain Diotrephes, presumably an officer in the church, "likes to put himself first," even to the point of not acknowledging the

[1]See footnote and references on I John, p. 502.

508

distinguished Apostle's authority. John has written the church about this (in a letter we do not have). And so, when he visits the church, he proposes to have Diotrephes face his open criticism of the Apostle.

Also, Diotrephes refuses himself to welcome the visiting brethren from other churches, and even undertakes to prevent others from entertaining the visitors!

John urges Gaius not to follow the bad example of Diotrephes. On the contrary, he commends a certain Demetrius for his loyalty to the Truth. Could this be the Demetrius, head of the silversmith's union at Ephesus, and who caused Paul so much trouble at an earlier date?

The writer closes his short letter with the hope that he shall be able shortly to come to see his friend in person, and with an exchange of kindly messages from mutual friends.

Chapter 9

THE REVELATION

1. HOW THE LETTER CAME TO BE WRITTEN

Here we have the last of the Apostle John's letters, and the last book of the New Testament. It is the vision of prophecy, and is called the Revelation to John.

The word *Revelation,* which is the English translation of the Greek *Apokalypsis* or apocalypse, means the unveiling of something hidden until now. In a word, it is the uncovering of God's Truth concerning divine things previously unknown.

Indeed, John's opening sentence states that the book is "the Revelation of Jesus Christ, which God gave Him to show to his servants what must soon take place." It was delivered by an angel to His servant John.

What are the background circumstances connected with the writing of the book?[1] About A.D. 70, the Apostle John had come from Jerusalem to Ephesus, where he became the Apostolic supervisor and minister-at-large of the churches in the Roman province of Asia, apparently the same churches which the Apostle Paul founded on his Third Missionary Journey, about 54-58 A.D., and subsequently visited and supervised.

For some twenty-five years John had labored in this region and no doubt had accomplished much for the cause of Christianity. Fortunately, after the death of Emperor Nero in 68 A.D., the persecution of the Christians by Rome was somewhat relaxed, at least until the last years of Emperor Domitian's reign (81-96 A.D.), when he became ambitious to be worshiped as a god, had laws passed, and required emperor-worship of everyone under penalty of death.

The Apostle John ignored this Roman law and continued to preach the Gospel of Jesus Christ. In his own words, he states that he was banished to the island of Patmos, "on account of the word of God and the testimony of Jesus." Patmos was a small, rocky and barren

---

[1]Opinion on the authorship and date, as well as on the interpretation of the book of Revelation, differs widely among modern scholars. See the summary discussion, G. R. Beasley-Murray, *The New Bible Commentary,* Part Three, pp. 1168-1199; Merrill C. Tenney, *New Testament Survey,* pp. 401-413. Conservative opinion still strongly favors the Apostle John's authorship.

island about sixty miles southwest of Ephesus. Apparently, the Roman plan was for him to die there. Thus, the Roman officials were determined to eradicate the Christian Church, root and branch.

Emperor Nerva (96-98 A.D.), Domitian's successor, seems to have released the Apostle from his banishment, but not until after the Vision which John describes in the book.

The general opinion is that the date of the work is about A.D. 96, and that it was likely written at Ephesus, after John's return from Patmos and the Revelation which came to him there. In verse 1:9, the writer makes use of the past tense, "*was* on the island," and refers to the place as if he were no longer there.

The message of the letter is of such transcendent importance to the Churches addressed, that the Apostle enjoins the readers and hearers in these strong words:

> Blessed is he who reads aloud the word of the prophecy, and blessed are those who hear, and who keep what is written therein; for the time is near (1:3).

2. THE PURPOSE OF THE LETTER

The main purpose of the book of Revelation is to give courage to the membership in the Seven Churches addressed, and to Christians everywhere, who were undergoing the severest trials and persecutions for their faith.

Although the Apostle John was released personally from his banishment, there is every reason to believe that vigorous persecution of Christians throughout the Empire continued. Emperors Nerva (96-98 A.D.) and Trajan (98-117 A.D.), Domitian's immediate successors, are not listed as cruel emperors; but since Domitian's days, Christianity was regarded as an illegal religion, because it did not sacrifice to Roman gods and because it took no part in emperor-worship. All Roman officials felt the necessity of upholding Roman law.

There is a much larger purpose which the Apostle John had in mind in writing this book.

The great battle of the earth was to be the war between the forces of *good* and *evil*, between the forces of *Christ* and *Antichrist*. In John's day, the struggles of God's people with the tyranny and paganism of Rome, was symbolic of the universal struggle of Christians everywhere against the power of Satan, and the ultimate victory which Christ will bring to all those who persevere.

The purpose of the book, then, is to give a picture of that titanic struggle, and through prophetic visions, to *reveal* the victorious outcome of the last, final battle. The book closes with a vision of the Holy City and the rewards of the faithful, those who have endured all the trials and persecutions of this life and have remained faithful to the Lord, to the end. The letter therefore is primarily a book of prophecy.

3. How to Read the Book of Revelation[2]

The Apostle John had written other letters to "the Seven Churches of Asia," that is, the Roman province of Asia in the western part of Asia Minor. Of these we have read the three that have come down to us, described as I John, II John, and III John.

(1) What would be more natural, then, than to approach the reading of the book of Revelation as another one of these epistolary messages? These churches had been under John's care for many years now; he knew their needs, their strengths and their peculiar weaknesses. In Revelation therefore John writes with a practical, realistic situation in view, namely, the urgent prospect that Caesar-worship would be enforced upon all Christians, in the province of Asia as well as in Rome and elsewhere.

John knew that the severest trials and persecutions would follow. So this letter was written with far greater implications than any of the Apostle's previous letters we know about.

(2) The main difficulty in reading and understanding the book, however, centers around the meaning of the *visions* and the other elaborate symbolic subject matter.

For the book of Revelation belongs to the literary type known as the *apocalypse*. Indeed, it has been called the most mysterious book in all Scripture. It is also one of the most amazing, as well as one of the most fascinating, books ever written. Is it that men are looking for something, and that they are half persuaded they may find it in this most unusual book?

Other apocalyptic books in the Canon include in particular the books of Ezekiel, Daniel, Isaiah, and Zechariah, in the Old Testament, from which John borrowed both ideas and imagery for his composition of Revelation. For a discussion of the symbolic imagery and the apocalyptic features of these books, and their probable influence on the composition of Revelation, see especially the chapters on Ezekiel and Daniel.

(3) The Apostolic letters, such as the letters of the Apostle Paul and the Apostle John and others, were originally written to be read aloud to members of a particular church, or in some cases to be circulated and read to several churches. Because there were no church houses, and because the early Christians were often barred from the Jewish synagogues, they met in private households and other available places, in groups and assemblies apparently never very large. At least seven such churches were known to have been in existence in Rome

---

[2]In addition to the reading references in the footnote at the beginning of this chapter, see also John Bright, Kee and Young, Ned Stonehouse, and others, all listed at the end of this chapter. Over the years, many strange ideas of interpretation of the book of Revelation have been brought forth. These references will acquaint the student with this range of opinion in summary form.

in Paul's day.[3] The same was true of this long letter which we call the Revelation.

What then, for the modern reader, would be more natural than to view the book of Revelation, as the reader and audience must have done to whom it was first addressed?

Return to the book of Daniel, an Old Testament book of prophecy, for instance, from which the book of Revelation borrowed most. The writer of Daniel was concerned primarily with two things: first, the present life and existence of his people the Jews, in exile in Babylon; second, their hopes and prospects of deliverance from the conqueror, and their future as a people. No Hebrew had any difficulty understanding Daniel's autobiography and the realistic life of his fellow countrymen as they lived it in Captivity, although he may have had trouble interpreting some of its symbolic imagery and prophecy.

But what of the book of Revelation, a New Testament book of prophecy which has borrowed so much from Old Testament prophecy and its method of composition? Indeed, we are not surprised to find that the Apostle John is dealing with *his* audience's *present* in terms of their future, and their future in terms of their present, much as the writer of the book of Daniel did in his book in his day.

4. THE CONTENTS OF THE LETTER

The contents of Revelation consists of *seven* main divisions, with a brief introduction and a brief conclusion to each. The seven divisions are actually seven *visions*, or series of visions, and are themselves subdivided usually into seven parts.

THE PROLOGUE: A preview of the glory that is to come (1:1-8).

The writer introduces (vv. 1-3) the book as an *Apocalypse*, the Greek word meaning *unveiling* or *revelation;* a divine message dictated by Jesus Christ Himself, which in turn was given Him by the Father. Elsewhere John speaks of it as a prophecy (1:3; 22:7, 10, 18), and of himself as a *prophet* (10:11; 22:9).

The Apostle gives the salutation of the letter to the Seven Churches of Asia (vv. 4-8) and sounds the keynote of the book: the eternal character of God, and the redeeming Lordship of Christ, who will return and overthrow all His enemies.

I. THE VISION OF THE SON OF MAN and his commission to the Apostle to write what he saw, in a book, and to send it to the Seven Churches (1:9 to 3).

In the Hebrew tradition *seven* is the number which signifies *completeness*. Since seven is the perfect number, the Seven Churches would represent all the Churches of the province of Asia. Moreover, these Seven Churches in the vision symbolize also the whole Church of Christ, regardless of place or time.

The Seven Churches in Asia mentioned by name, and which

---

[3]See chapter on the book of Romans, p. 451ff.

represent the whole Church, are Ephesus, Smyrna, Pergamum, Thyatira, Sardis, Philadelphia, and Laodicea.

Ephesus was the capital and great commercial center of the
province and famous for its Temple to Diana (Artemis). The Apostle
Paul used the city as his headquarters and center of his evangelistic
campaign during the Third Missionary Journey (54-58 A.D.). Timothy,
in Paul's absence, led the mission at Ephesus, and was followed
shortly by the Apostle John, who also resided there until his death
about the end of the century.

The Church at Ephesus is praised for its work for Christ, for its
faithfulness and steadfastness in the face of trials and persecutions;
but it is blamed chiefly because its former love has cooled. "I have
this against you, you have abandoned the love you had at first. . . ."

Each of the other churches is characterized briefly and, like
Ephesus, each is exhorted to hold fast to the faith, and thus be able to
endure the further trials and persecutions, which are expected soon.

A look at the map of the western part of Asia Minor will locate
each of the seven cities, in which the Seven Churches were situated,
and indicate that they were all within a radius of fifty to one hundred
miles of one another, and all connected by a great triangular highway.

II. THE VISION OF THE SEVEN SEALS, chapters 4 to 8:5.

At this point, the scene of the Apostle John's Vision changes from
earth, and its earthly realism, to heaven and its tumultuous glory, and
remains there until Chapter 10, after which the point of view continually alternates from heaven to earth, and from earth to heaven.

For an introduction to this scene, John records the vision of God
upon His throne — an indescribable picture of the heavenly worship,
and the majesty and the glory of God (ch. 4).

Also, John records the vision of Christ seated upon the throne,
and with the roll of a book covered with writings on both sides, signifying the full contents of God's purposes for the future.

The Apostle is told that the Victory which Christ has won, as the
Lamb who was slain, has qualified Him to take and open the Seven
Seals of the book or roll of destiny. The Lamb opens the Seven Seals,
thus:

THE SEVEN SEALS

(1) The Vision of the White Horse and its rider, the conqueror,
signifying *triumphant militarism;*

(2) The Vision of the Red Horse and its rider, symbolizing *war*
that "takes peace from the earth";

(3) The Vision of the Black Horse and its rider, representing
famine;

(4) The Vision of the Pale Horse and its rider, signifying *death;*

(5) The Vision of the Souls of Martyrs;

(6) The Vision of universal earthquakes and other cosmic dis-

turbances, symbolizing the End, "The great Day of His Wrath is come. . . ."

At this point, there is an interlude between the Sixth and Seventh seals, chapter 7, in which a picture is given of Christian souls standing before the throne, and their present status, while the judgments described in the book are being executed.

(7) The Vision of silence in heaven, in order to hear the prayers of the saints.

INTERPRETATION

Jesus Himself is our best interpretor of the meaning of the Seven Seals.

Indeed, the key to these visions appears to be His prophecy, recorded in Chapter Twenty-Four of Matthew's Gospel, in which Jesus foretells the *signs* preceding the destruction of Jerusalem, the destruction of the city itself, and especially those signs which will precede the Second Coming of Christ.

III. THE VISION OF THE SEVEN TRUMPETS, chapters 8:6 to 11.

This is the vision of seven angels who stood before God, and who were ready to blow their trumpets to herald God's visitation of judgment upon the sinful world.

The first four trumpets announce the wrath of God, as evidenced by the convulsions of nature, the earth, the sea, the rivers, and the heavenly bodies.

The fifth and sixth trumpets herald the punishment sent upon men themselves, the unrepentant world, to the extent of a third of mankind.

At this point, we have another interlude, as between the sixth and seventh Seals, which again emphasizes God's care of His redeemed.

The Seventh trumpet announces the establishment of the eternal Kingdom of God . . . "the mystery of God, as he announced to His servants the prophets, should be fulfilled . . . The Kingdom of the world has become the Kingdom of our Lord and of His Christ, and He shall reign for ever and ever."

IV. THE VISION OF THE WOMAN AND HER STRUGGLE WITH THE DRAGON AND THE TWO BEASTS, chapters 12 to 14.

As the reader of the book of Revelation is well aware, the Apostle John found it necessary, to avoid persecution of himself and others, to use figures and symbolic representations for men and things in his prophetic message to the Seven Churches.

For instance, in these chapters the Woman is the Church of the covenants of both the Old and New Testaments, which bore a manchild, the Messiah and the Christ, the Saviour of the world.

The Dragon, Satan, is waiting to destroy Him at birth. The contest is taken up into heaven where Satan, defeated by the forces of the

Almighty, is thrown out of heaven upon the earth, where he continues his fight to destroy the Woman, the Church.

Satan's two most powerful allies and agents on earth are Two Beasts, usually thought to symbolize the Roman Empire and the Roman religion, especially the official fight by Rome to establish emperor-worship, and at the same time to destroy its opposition by the Christians.

The Beast rising out of the sea (Aegean) "with ten horns and seven heads" refers to the city of Rome, built on seven hills, and to the ten Roman Emperors since, and including, Augustus Caesar (27 B.C.-14 A.D.), Tiberious (14-37 A.D.), Caligula (37-41), Claudius (41-54), Nero (54-68), Galba (68-69), Otho and Vitellius (69), Vespasian (69-79), Titus (79-81).

The writer of the book of Daniel used the term "horn" to represent kings, and apparently John borrowed the term for his Roman Emperors.

Since Domitian's reign (81-96) appears to be omitted from the count, the plan of the book may have been made before the Emperor's actual death, in 96 A.D.

This section closes with the prophecy of the fall of the wicked city of Babylon, which is Rome in the allegory, and the victory of the Lamb, Christ, and His redeemed.

V. The Vision of the Seven Bowls of God's Wrath, chapters 15 and 16.

The crisis of Revelation, as recorded in the Apostle's book, is drawing near. With this dreadful vision, the wrath of God is ended.

The enemies of Christ and His Church — Satan, and his chief agents, the Roman Empire and the tyranny of the Roman religion — in previous chapters have been shown in their power and cruelty.

In chapter 15, there is a pause of suspense, in which is described the approach of the judgments of wrath which are about to fall upon the Roman Empire and upon the heathen and unrepentant world.

In chapter 16, the suspense is ended, and the angels pour out from the figurative Seven Bowls God's wrath upon the earth, in a series of dreadful and destructive plagues, reminding the reader of the plagues of Egypt recorded in the book of Exodus. There are plagues of the earth, the sea, the rivers, the sun, and air, and Rome.

These plagues, unlike those pictured in the vision of the Seven Trumpets, cover not a third, but the whole of mankind, and fall principally upon the heathen world of the Roman Empire.

And signs are made of the approaching *Armageddon*, apparently a symbolic term to represent the Last Battle of the wicked kings of the earth against the Lamb. This Battle is to be Satan's Waterloo!

VI. THE VISION OF THE HARLOT CITY OF BABYLON (ROME), AND THE VICTORY OF CHRIST OVER HER, AND THE ENEMIES IN LEAGUE WITH HER, chapters 17 to 19.

In chapter 17, the destruction of Rome, which had been announced before, is given in vivid detail.

The Beast, earlier in the book identified with the Roman Empire, is here personified as the Emperor Nero, who as the embodiment of all evil during his lifetime, is to ascend from the bottomless Pit for a little while, and join those who will make war on the Lamb. But the Lamb (Christ) will conquer them . . . "for he is Lord of lords and King of kings."

In chapter 18, the angel appears with the proclamation of the Fall of Rome. The greatness of the doom of Babylon (Rome) is indicated by the lamentations of the kings of the earth, and the merchants, and all those who have been wanton with her; and by the songs of thanksgiving by the angels of heaven.

In chapter 19, judgment having been visited upon the Harlot City, the marriage of the Lamb (Christ) with His Bride (the Church) is announced. But before the marriage can take place, the Lamb's enemies must be overcome, the Beast, his prophet, and his armies.

And so the final battle proceeds. In the vision, the Apostle John sees the riding Conqueror, Christ, coming forth upon His White Horse, with His armies, and engaging the Beast and the kings of the earth with their armies gathered to make war against Him. This is the promised battle of Armageddon.

The Beast was captured and his false prophet, and the two were thrown into the lake of fire. The rest were slain by the sword of Him who sits upon the horse.

VII. THE VISION OF THE LAST JUDGMENT, AND THE ETERNAL HOME OF THE REDEEMED, chapters 20 to 22:5.

The Apostle John, in chapter 20, describes the vision of how Satan, having already been defeated, was seized by the angel and cast into the bottomless Pit for *a thousand years*, that he should deceive the nations no more.

The scene then changes to the thrones of heaven and a vision of the saints, of the first resurrection, and of those who were to reign with Christ for a thousand years. After this, Satan was to be released for a little while, and the contest for the souls of men was to be continued until the Last Judgment.

The final judgment scene is of God and His Great White Throne. The books of the deeds of men and the Book of Life were opened, and men were judged by what was written in the books, by what they had done. All the dead were there, and all were judged. If any one's name was not found written in the Book of Life, he was thrown in the lake of fire.

In chapters 21-22:5, the writer gives his blissful vision of the eternal home in the Holy City. The enemies of Christ have been conquered. The Judgment is over. In the words of the Psalmist, the righteous shall dwell in the House of the Lord for ever.

THE EPILOGUE (22:6-21). The conclusion of the book is that now the *Revelation* is complete. Those who will not now turn and repent because of the Revelation which our Lord has completed, will not!

So the book closes with the master thought and refrain, the same as the first chapter of the book of Genesis: "I AM THE ALPHA AND THE OMEGA, THE FIRST AND THE LAST, THE BEGINNING AND THE END."

As G. R. Beasley-Murray of London has pointed out,[4] John's conclusion, which must be taken to be the words of our Lord, stresses three themes: the *authenticity* of the visions narrated in the book (verses 6, 7, 16, 18, 19), the *imminence* of our Lord's Second Coming (verses 6, 7, 10-12, 20), and the necessity for *holiness* in view of the impending consummation (versus 10-15).

The *time* of Christ's coming has bothered many people. The Angel said, "Do not seal up the words of the prophecy of this book, for the time is near."

And the Lord Jesus, who gave the commission to John to write His Revelation in this book, said, "Surely I am coming soon."

How soon is *soon?* The Hebrew language (even when it comes by way of the Greek) is highly figurative and symbolic. The *millenium* literally means a thousand years, and by association it has come to mean a long period of time, during which there will be *peace*.

A thousand years, like the number *seven*, also means perfection or completeness; a round number representing the time necessary for completing something. As, a thousand years with God is but a day! (Psalm 90:4).

So the terms *soon* and *a thousand years* may have much the same meaning. And both mean the time necessary for accomplishing great and beneficent ends, in the Providence of God.

The epilogue also closes with a re-affirmation that the Apocalypse *is the Word of God*, and warns the reader and the hearer of its importance. He opened his book with, "Blessed is he who reads aloud the words of the prophecy" (1:3), and closed it with, "Blessed is he who keeps the words of the prophecy of this book" (22:7).

ADDITIONAL READINGS ON THE BOOK OF THE REVELATION

Bible Readings: The Book of the Revelation.

Baldinger, A. H.: *Preaching from Revelation.*

*Beasley-Murray, G. R.: "The Revelation," *The New Bible Commentary*, pp. 1168-1199.

Beckwith, Isbon T.: *The Apocalypse of John.*

---

[4] *The New Bible Commentary*, Part Three, p. 1198 (1954).

*Bright, John: "Even to the End of the Age," *The Kingdom of God,* pp. 244-274.

Case, Shirley Jackson: *The Revelation of John.*

Guy, H. A.: *The New Testament Doctrine of the Last Things.*

*Hendriksen, William: *More Than Conquerors.*

Kee, Howard Clark and Franklin W. Young: "The Hope of the Community," *Understanding the New Testament,* pp. 445-462.

Kiddle, M.: *The Revelation of St. John.*

Lang, G. H.: *The Revelation of Jesus Christ.*

Ramsay, Sir William: *The Letters to the Seven Churches.*

*Stonehouse, Ned B.: *Commentary on the Revelation.*

Tenney, Merrill C.: "The Expectant Church: Revelation," *New Testament Survey,* pp. 401-413.

Wilder, A. N.: *Eschatology and Ethics in the Teaching of Jesus* (Revised Edition, 1950).

On the Island of Patmos, a view from the monastery. It was while in exile here that John wrote the Revelation. © *Radio Times Hulton Picture Library, British Broadcasting Corporation, London*

BIBLIOGRAPHY

Suggestions for Additional Reading

Part One: General Books

I. ARCHAEOLOGY

Albright, William Foxwell: *Archaeology and the Religion of Israel.* Revised Edition. Baltimore: John Hopkins Press, 1946.

*Albright, William Foxwell: *The Archaeology of Palestine and the Bible.* Baltimore: Johns Hopkins Press, 1949. For a long time Professor Albright has been leader of the American Schools of Oriental Research, and an acknowledged authority in the field. Of his many books, these two are his best for the general reader.

*Burrows, Millar: *The Dead Sea Scrolls.* New York: Viking Press, 1955. The author gives the story of the Dead Sea Scrolls and translates many of them into English.

Cross, Frank: *The Ancient Library of Qumran and Modern Bible Study.* Garden City: Doubleday & Co., 1958. One of the best and most recent in this field.

Free, J. P.: *Archaeology and Bible History.* Wheaton (Ill.): Van Kampen Press, 1950.

*Garstang, John: *The Foundations of Bible History — Joshua-Judges.* London: Constable and Co., 1931. A basic work in establishing the foundations of early Hebrew Chronology.

Keller, Werner: *The Bible as History.* Translated from the German by William Neil. New York: William Morrow & Co., 1956. The findings of modern archaeology related to the historical truth of the Bible story. Popularly written; and a best seller.

*Pritchard, James B.: *Ancient Near Eastern Texts Relating to the Old Testament.* Second Edition. Princeton: University of Princeton Press, 1956. Translations of inscriptions, ancient documents, letters, and other written archaeological findings, invaluable to the student.

Pritchard, James B.: *The Ancient Near East in Pictures Relating to the Old Testament.* Princeton: Princeton University Press, 1954. Companion volume to the above.

*Wright, G. Ernest: *Biblical Archaeology.* Philadelphia: Westminster Press, 1957. A beautifully illustrated introduction to the field of archaeology.

II. BIBLE DICTIONARIES

Dictionary of the Bible. James Hastings, Editor. 5 Vols. New York: Charles Scribner's Sons, 1904. The classic work in this field; very complete and scholarly.

Dictionary of the Bible. James Hastings, Editor. One-volume Edition. Completely revised, by the same Editor, 1937.

Harper's Bible Dictionary. Madeleine S. Miller and J. Lane Miller, Editors. New York: Harper & Brothers, 1954.

International Standard Bible Encyclopedia. James Orr and Others, Editors. 5 Vols. Grand Rapids: Wm. B. Eerdmans Publishing Co., 1952.

New Bible Dictionary, J. D. Douglas, General Editor. Grand Rapids: Wm. B. Eerdmans Publishing Co., 1962.

Zondervan Pictorial Bible Dictionary, Merrill C. Tenney, General Editor. Grand Rapids: Zondervan Publishing House, 1963.

Interpreter's Dictionary of the Bible. 4 Vols. New York: Abingdon Press, 1960.

Westminster Dictionary of the Bible. John D. Davis, Editor. Revised and Rewritten by Henry Snyder Gehman, Fifth Edition. Philadelphia: Westminster Press, 1944. Perhaps the best one-volume Bible dictionary in English.

III. ENGLISH VERSIONS OF THE BIBLE[1]

Authorized or King James Version; work of 54 translators appointed by the King, including both Anglican Churchmen and Puritans, 1611.

English Revised Version, 1881-1885; translated and revised by 65 English scholars chosen from the Church of England, and 34 American scholars.

American Standard Version, 1901; a continuation of the work of the *English Revised Version,* by American scholars, incorporating changes not endorsed by the English but favored by the American Committee.

Revised Standard Version, 1946-1952; translated and revised by a Committee of 34 American scholars, assisted by an Advisory Board of 50 representatives from Canada and the United States, being the Cooperating Church Denominations. New York: Thomas Nelson & Sons, 1952.

New English Bible 1961——; translated by a large group of scholars and literary advisers of Great Britain, and sponsored by the major religious bodies (other than the Roman Catholic) of the British Isles. New Testament, March 1961; date of complete Bible to be announced; Cambridge University Press and Oxford University Press, jointly.

Modern Reader's Bible. Richard G. Moulton, New York: The Macmillan Co., 1895. Professor Moulton of the University of Chicago was a pioneer in arranging and publishing an edition of the Bible for modern readers according to literary form and content. His text was the *English Revised Version* of 1881-1885. Still an important source book.

A New Translation of the Bible. James Moffatt. New York: Harper & Brothers, Revised Edition, 1935.

The Bible, An American Translation. J. M. Powis Smith and Edgar J. Goodspeed. Chicago: The University of Chicago Press, 1939.

The New Testament in Modern English. Translated by J. B. Phillips, an English scholar and clergyman. New York: The Macmillan Co., 1958. Noted for its simplicity and clarity of style.

The Berkeley Holy Bible in Modern English. Gerrit Verkuyl, Editor, assisted by a staff of 20 eminent scholars. Grand Rapids: Zondervan, 1959.

The Amplified Bible. By twelve scholars. Grand Rapids: Zondervan, 1958, 1962.

The Simplified New Testament. Olaf M. Norlie. Especially good for new Christians and young people. Zondervan, 1961.

IV. GEOGRAPHY

Barnett, Lincoln: *The Universe and Dr. Einstein.* Second Revised Edition. New York: William Stone Associates, 1957.

*Kahn, Fritz: *Design of the Universe — The Heavens and the Earth.* New York: Crown Publishers, Inc., 1954. An amazing story, "A magnificent adventure"; non-technical.

*Kraeling, Emil G.: *Bible Atlas.* New York: Rand McNally & Co., 1956.

Smith, George Adam: *The Historical Geography of the Holy Land.* New York: Armstrong, 1895. A classic work in this field in spite of its age.

*Wright, G. Ernest, and Floyd V. Filson: *The Westminster Historical Atlas to the Bible.* Revised Edition. Philadelphia: Westminster Press, 1956. Incorporates recent archaeological discoveries in Bible lands. Noted for its excellent plates and maps.

---

[1]For a description of each of these versions, see the General Introduction, Chapter 4, p. 40ff.

Part Two: Works on the Bible as a Whole

I. COMMENTARIES

Abingdon Bible Commentary. Frederick Carl Eiselen and Others, General Editors. New York and Nashville: Abingdon-Cokesbury Press, 1952.

**The Biblical Expositor.* Carl F. H. Henry, Editor. Philadelphia: A. J. Holman Co., 1960. 3 Vols. Old Testament, Vols. 1 and 2.

*Calvin, John: *Commentaries.* New Edition, 45 Vols. Grand Rapids: Eerdmans, 1949-1959.

Cambridge Bible for Schools and Colleges. J. J. S. Perowne, General Editor. Cambridge: Cambridge University Press, 1886——. In spite of its age, it is still very good, especially on the Old Testament.

**Commentary on the Holy Bible.* J. R. Dummelow, General Editor. New York: The Macmillan Co., 1936. Pp. 1092. Some 43 distinguished contributors named in the Preface, but the articles are unsigned, lessening somewhat the value of the work for the student.

**International Critical Commentary.* S. R. Driver, A. Plummer, C. A. Briggs, General Editors. Edinburgh: T. & T. Clark Co.; New York: Charles Scribner's Sons, 1895. The most scholarly work in the English language. All students should be acquainted with this work.

Interpreter's Bible. George Arthur Buttrick and Others, General Editors. 12 Vols. New York: Abingdon Press, 1952. The writers cover a wide range of liberal and conservative viewpoints.

**Layman's Bible Commentary.* Balmar H. Kelly and Others, Editors. 25 Vols. Richmond: John Knox Press, 1959-1964. More conservative than *The Interpreter's Bible.*

**New Bible Commentary.* Francis Davidson, A. M. Stibbs, E. F. Kevan, General Editors. Grand Rapids: Wm. B. Eerdmans Pub. Co., Revised Edition, 1954. Produced by 50 scholars representing the best scholarship in England, Europe, and America today, and in the tradition of historic Protestantism. Also, containing as it does a surprising amount of detail, it is probably the best one-volume commentary in English today.

**Westminster Commentaries.* Walter Lock and D. C. Simpson, General Editors. London: Methen & Co., 1934. More conservative than *The Interpreter's Bible.*

II. OTHER BOOKS ON THE BIBLE AS A WHOLE

Anderson, Bernhard W.: *Rediscovering the Bible.* New York: Association Press, 1951. This work and C. H. Dodd's *The Bible Today* listed below are on the Biblical faith of Israel.

*Bright, John: *The Kingdom of God.* New York: Abingdon Press, 1953. The book stresses the essential continuity of Scripture and the unity of the Bible, around the Kingdom concept.

Broomall, W.: *Biblical Criticism.* Grand Rapids: Zondervan Publishing House, 1957.

*Bruce, F. F.: *The English Bible: A History of Translations.* New York: Oxford University Press, 1961.

Burrows, Millar: *An Outline of Biblical Theology.* Philadelphia: Westminster Press, 1946.

Dodd, C. H.: *The Bible Today.* New York: The Macmillan Co., 1947.

Filson, Floyd V.: *Which Books Belong to the Bible.* Philadelphia: Westminster Press, 1956.

*Foreman, Kenneth J., Balmar H. Kelly, Arnold B. Rhodes, Bruce Metzger, and Donald Miller: *Introduction to the Bible.* The Layman's Bible Commentary, Vol. I. Richmond: John Knox Press, 1959.

*Halley, Henry H.: *Halley's Bible Handbook.* Grand Rapids: Zondervan, 23rd Edition, 1962.

Harris, R. L.: *Inspiration and Canonicity of the Bible*, Grand Rapids: Zondervan, 1957.

*Manley, G. T.: *The New Bible Handbook*. London: Inter-Varsity Fellowship, 1948. Excellent for reference.

Miller, Alexander: *The Renewal of Man*. Garden City: Doubleday & Co., 1955.

Miller, H. S.: *General Biblical Introduction*. Houghton (N.Y.): The Word-Bearer Press, 1937. A good treatment of the origins of the Bible.

*Paterson, John: *The Book That Is Alive*. New York: Charles Scribner's Sons, 1954. Emphasizes the vitality and variety of the Bible.

Price, Ira M.: *The Ancestry of Our English Bible*. Third Revised Edition by William A. Irwin and Allen P. Wikgren. New York: Harper & Brothers, 1956.

Rowley, H. H.: *The Faith of Israel*. Philadelphia: Westminster Press, 1957.

*Rowley, H. H.: *The Unity of the Bible*. London: Oxford University Press, 1953.

Westminster Introduction to the Books of the Bible. Philadelphia: Westminster Press, 1958.

Part Three: Books on the Old Testament

I. HISTORICAL BOOKS OF THE OLD TESTAMENT

Albright, William Foxwell: *The Biblical Period*. Pittsburgh: Biblical Colloquim, 1950. Reprinted from *The Jews: Their History, Culture and Religion*. New York: Harper & Brothers, 1949.

*Albright, William Foxwell: *From Stone Age to Christianity*. Baltimore: Johns Hopkins Press, 1940.

Alleman, H. C. and E. E. Flack, Editors: *Old Testament Commentary*. Philadelphia: Muhlenberg Press, 1949.

*Allis, Oswald T.: *The Five Books of Moses*. Second Edition. Philadelphia: The Presbyterian and Reformed Publishing Co., 1949.

Anderson, Bernhard W.: *Understanding the Old Testament*. Englewood Cliffs (N.J.): Prentice-Hall, Inc., 1957. Liberal.

Bentzen, Aage: *Introduction to the Old Testament*. Second Edition. 2 Vols. Copenhagen: G. H. C. Gads, 1948.

Bewer, J. A.: *The Literature of the Old Testament in Its Historical Development*. Second Edition. New York: Columbia University Press, 1933.

Bright, John: *The History of Israel*. Philadelphia: Westminster Press, 1950.

Burney, C. E.: *The Book of Judges*. London: Rivingtons, 1930.

Chapman, A. T.: *An Introduction to the Pentateuch*. Cambridge: University Press, 1911.

Driver, S. R.: *Introduction to the Literature of the Old Testament*. Revised Edition. New York: Charles Scribner's Sons, 1913.

*Edersheim, Alfred: *Old Testament Bible History*. 2 Vols. Grand Rapids: Wm. B. Eerdmans Publishing Co., 1949 Edition.

*Edersheim, Alfred: *The Temple — Its Ministry and Service*. Revised Edition. Grand Rapids: Wm. B. Eerdmans Publishing Co., 1950.

Finegan, Jack: *Light From the Ancient Past*. Princeton: University Press, 1946.

Francisco, Clyde T.: *Introducing the Old Testament*. Nashville: The Broadman Press, 1950.

*Garstang, John: *The Foundations of Bible History; Joshua and Judges*. London: Constable & Co., 1931.

Good, Edwin M.: *You Shall Be My People*. Philadelphia: Westminster Press, 1959.

Green, William Henry: *The Unity of the Book of Genesis*. New York: 1910.

Gray, G. Buchanan: *Sacrifice in the Old Testament*. Oxford: Clarendon Press, 1925.

Jacob, Edmond: *Theology of the Old Testament*. New York: Harper & Brothers, 1958.

*James, Fleming: *Personalities of the Old Testament*. New York: Charles Scribner's Sons, 1939.

Leslie, E. A.: *Old Testament Religion in the Light of Its Canaanite Background*. New York: Abingdon Press, 1936.

*Leupold, Herbert C.: *Exposition of Genesis*. Columbus: Wartburg Press, 1942.

*Manley, G. T.: *The Book of the Law — Deuteronomy*. Grand Rapids: Wm. B. Eerdmans Publishing Co., 1957.

McNeile, A. H.: *Deuteronomy, Its Place in Revelation*. New York: Longmans, Green & Co., 1912.

Napier, B. Davie: *From Faith to Faith*. New York: Harper & Brothers, 1955.

Oesterley, W. O. E. and T. H. Robinson: *Hebrew Religion, Its Origin and Development*. Oxford: University Press, 1937.

Orlinsky, H. M.: *Ancient Israel*. Ithica: Cornell University Press, 1954.

Pedersen, Johannes: *Israel, Its Life and Culture*. London: Oxford University Press, Vols. I-II, 1926; Vols. III-IV, 1940.

Rowley, H. H.: *The Rediscovery of the Old Testament*. Philadelphia: The Westminster Press, 1946.

Rowley, H. H.: *The Growth of the Old Testament*. London: Hutchinson's University Library, 1950.

*Rowley, H. H.: *From Joseph to Joshua*. London: Oxford University Press, 1950.

Rowley, H. H. (Editor): *The Old Testament and Modern Study*. Oxford: Clarendon Press, 1951.

*Simon, J. J.: *Jerusalem in the Old Testament*. London: E. J. Brill, 1952.

Smith, J. M. Powis: *The Origin and History of Hebrew Law*. Chicago: The University of Chicago Press, 1931.

*Snaith, Norman H.: *The Distinctive Ideas of the Old Testament*. Philadelphia: The Westminster Press, 1946.

Von Rad, Gerhard: *Studies in Deuteronomy*. Chicago: Henry Regnery Co., 1953.

Welch, Adam C.: *The Code of Deuteronomy*. London: James Clark & Co., 1924.

Welch, Adam C.: *Post-Exilic Judaism*. London: William Blackwood & Sons, 1935.

*Welch, Adam C.: *The Work of the Chronicler*. London: British Academy, 1939.

*Wright, G. Ernest: *The Old Testament Against Its Environment*. Chicago: Henry Regnery Co., 1950.

*Young, Edward J.: *An Introduction to the Old Testament*. Grand Rapids: Wm. B. Eerdmans Publishing Co., Revised Edition, 1958.

II. The Psalms

Alexander, J. A.: *The Psalms*. Grand Rapids: Zondervan, 1955.

James, Fleming: *Thirty Psalmists*. New York: G. P. Putnam's Sons, 1938.

Leslie, E. A.: *The Psalms*. New York: Abingdon Press, 1949.

*Leupold, Herbert C.: *Exposition of the Psalms*. Columbus: The Wartburg Press, 1959. 1010 pp.

Oesterley, W. O. E.: *The Psalms*. London: SPCK, 1955.

*Paterson, John: *The Praises of Israel*. New York: Charles Scribner's Sons, 1950.

*Rhodes, Arnold B.: *The Book of Psalms*. Richmond: John Knox Press, 1960.

Robinson, T. H.: *The Poetry of the Old Testament*. 1947.

*Terrien, Samuel: *The Psalms and Their Meaning for Today*. Indianapolis: Bobbs-Merrill Co., 1952.

III. Books by the Wise Men of Israel

Bradley, G. C.: *Lectures on the Book of Job*. Oxford: Clarendon Press, 1887.

Genung, John F.: *The Epic of the Inner Life*. New York: Houghton, Mifflin and Co., 1891.

Gordis, Robert: *The Wisdom of Ecclesiastes*. New York: 1945.

Jastrow, M.: *The Book of Job*. Philadelphia and London: 1920.

*Leupold, Herbert C.: *Exposition of Ecclesiastes*. Columbus: Wartburg Press, 1953.

Macdonald, Duncan B.: *The Hebrew Literary Genius*. Princeton: Princeton University Press, 1933.

McNeile, A. H.: *An Introduction to Ecclesiastes*. Cambridge: University Press, 1904.

*Oesterley, W. O. E.: *The Wisdom of Egypt and the Old Testament*. New York: The Macmillan Co., 1927. Very useful background material.

Oesterley, W. O. E.: *The Book of Proverbs*. The Westminster Commentaries. London: Methuen & Co., 1929.

*Paterson, John: *The Book That Is Alive*. New York: Charles Scribner's Sons, 1954. One of the best brief discussions of Wisdom Literature.

Peake, A. S.: *The Problem of Suffering in the Old Testament*. London: 1904.

*Rankin, O. S.: *Israel's Wisdom Literature — Its Bearing on Theology and the History of Religion*. Edinburgh: T. & T. Clark, 1936. A standard work on the Wisdom Literature of Israel.

Ranston, Harry: *Ecclesiastes and the Early Greek Wisdom Literature*. London: 1925.

*Ranston, Harry: *The Old Testament Wisdom Books and Their Teaching*. London: Epworth Press, 1930.

Robinson, H. Wheeler: *Suffering Human and Divine*. London: 1940.

*Rylaarsdam, J. Coert: *Revelation in Jewish Wisdom Literature*. Chicago: University of Chicago Press, 1946.

Stevenson, W. B.: *The Poem of Job*. London: 1947.

Strahan, James: *The Book of Job*. Revised Edition. Edinburgh: 1914.

*Terrien, Samuel: *Job, The Poet of Existence*. Indianapolis: Bobbs-Merrill Co., 1957.

Waterway, Leroy: *The Song of Songs*. Ann Arbor: 1948.

Williams, A. L.: *Ecclesiastes*. Cambridge Bible Series. Cambridge: 1927.

IV. BOOKS BY THE PROPHETS

*Allis, Oswald T.: *The Unity of Isaiah*.

Burrows, Millar: *The Literary Relations of Ezekiel*. Philadelphia: 1925.

Calkins, Raymond: *The Modern Message of the Minor Prophets*. New York: Harper & Brothers, 1947.

*Calvin, John: *The Prophet Isaiah*. 4 Vols. New Edition. Grand Rapids: Wm. B. Eerdmans Publishing Co., 1947. The student will welcome this opportunity to investigate a classic authority in one of his best commentaries.

Gailey, James H.: *The Books of Micah, Nahum, Habakkuk, Haggai, Zechariah, and Malachi*. The Layman's Bible Commentary, Vol. 15. Richmond: The John Knox Press, 1962.

Gordon, T. Crouther: *The Rebel Prophet — Studies in the Personality of Jeremiah*. London: 1931.

Kuist, Howard T.: *The Books of Jeremiah and Lamentations*. The Layman's Bible Commentary, Vol. 12. Richmond: The John Knox Press, 1961.

Hartford, John B.: *Studies in the Book of Ezekiel*. Cambridge: 1935.

Henderson: *Commentary on the Minor Prophets*.

Howie, C. G.: *The Date of the Composition of Ezekiel*. Philadelphia: Society of Biblical Literature, 1950.

*Hyatt, J. Philip: *Jeremiah, Prophet of Courage and Hope*. New York: Abingdon Press, 1958.

Hyatt, J. Philip: *Prophetic Religion*. New York: Abingdon Press, 1947.

Knight, Harold: *The Hebrew Prophetic Consciousness*. London: Lutterworth Press, 1947.

Leupold, Herbert C.: *Exposition of Daniel.* Columbus: Wartburg Press, 1946.

Lofthouse, W. F.: *Jeremiah and the New Covenant.* London: 1925.

Myers, Jacob M.: *The Books of Hosea, Joel, Amos, Obadiah, and Jonah.* The Layman's Bible Commentary, Vol. 14. Richmond: John Knox Press, 1959.

North, C. R.: *The Suffering Servant in Deutro-Isaiah.* London: Oxford University Press, 1948.

Paterson, John: *The Goodly Fellowship of the Prophets.* New York: Charles Scribner's Sons, 1948.

Peckham, Ccorge A.: *An Introduction to the Study of Obadiah.* Chicago: 1910.

Pilcher, C. V.: *Three Hebrew Prophets and the Passing of Empires.* London: 1931.

Prince, J. D.: *A Critical Commentary on the Book of Daniel.* Leipzig: J. C. Hinrich's, 1899.

Robinson, George L.: *The Twelve Minor Prophets.*

°Robinson, George L.: *The Prophecies of Zechariah.* Chicago: 1896.

Robinson, H. Wheeler: *Two Hebrew Prophets; Studies in Hosea and Ezekiel.*

°Rowley, H. H.: *Darius the Mede and the Four World Empires in the Book of Daniel.* Cardiff: University of Wales Press Board, 1935.

°Rowley, H. H.: *The Relevance of the Apocalyptic.* London: Lutterworth Press, 1944.

Scott, R. B. Y.: *The Relevance of the Prophets.* New York: The Macmillan Co., 1947.

Skinner, John: *Prophecy and Religion — Studies in the Life of Jeremiah.* Cambridge: University Press, 1936.

°Smith, George Adam: *The Book of Isaiah.* Revised Edition. London: Hodden and Stoughton, 1927.

°Smith, George Adam: *The Book of the Twelve Prophets.* New York: Harper & Brothers, 1928.

Smith, James: *The Book of the Prophet Ezekiel, A New Interpretation.* London: 1931.

Smith, J. M. Powis: *The Prophets and Their Times.* Second Edition by W. A. Irwin. Chicago: University Press, 1941.

°Snaith, Norman H.: *Amos, Hosea, and Micah.* The Preacher's Commentaries. London: The Epworth Press, 1928.

Welch, Adam C.: *Jeremiah, His Time and His Work.* Oxford: University Press, 1928.

°Wright, G. Ernest: *God Who Acts.* Chicago: Henry Regnery Co., 1952.

Wright, G. Ernest: *The Book of Isaiah.* The Layman's Bible Commentary. Richmond: The John Knox Press, 1964.

°Young, Edward J.: *Studies in Isaiah.* Grand Rapids: Wm. B. Eerdmans Publishing Co., 1945.

°Young, Edward J.: *The Prophecy of Daniel — A Commentary.* Grand Rapids: Wm. B. Eerdmans Publishing Co., 1949.

°Young, Edward J.: *My Servants the Prophets.* Grand Rapids: Wm. B. Eerdmans Publishing Co., 1952.

Part Four: Books on the New Testament as a Whole

I. COMMENTARIES

American Commentary on the New Testament. Alvah Hovey, Editor. Philadelphia: American Baptist Publications Society, 1881——. Covers completely the New Testament.

°*The Biblical Expositor.* Carl F. H. Henry, Editor. Philadelphia: A. J. Holman Co., 1960. 3 Vols. New Testament, Vol. 3.

°*Daily Study Bible Series.* William Barclay, Editor and Author. Philadelphia: Westminster Press, 1953-1960. The complete New Testament, 17 Vols. Dr.

Barclay is a skilled writer who combines scholarship and popular appeal to a remarkable degree.

Erdman New Testament Commentaries. Philadelphia: Westminster Press, 1916-1936. Charles R. Erdman, Author. New Testament complete from *Matthew* to *Revelation.* Widely recommended.

Harper's New Testament Commentaries. New York: Harper & Brothers, 1958——. Now in process of publication; Gospel of *Luke, Acts, Romans,* etc., issued first. Comparable in quality to the James Moffatt Series of commentaries.

Interpreter's Bible. New Testament, Vols. VII-XII. George Arthur Buttrick and Others, General Editors. New York: Abingdon Press, 1952. The writers cover a wide range of liberal and conservative viewpoints.

°*Layman's Bible Commentary.* Balmar H. Kelly and Others, General Editors. Richmond: John Knox Press, 1959-1964. 25 Vols. Volumes 16-25 on the New Testament. Although generally conservative, some writers are liberal in viewpoint. The early volumes generally have been well received.

°*Lenski New Testament Commentaries.* Richard Charles Lenski, Author and Editor. 12 Vols. Columbus (Ohio): Wartburg Press, 1932-1946. Widely recommended.

Moffatt New Testament Commentary. New York: Harper & Brothers, 1927-1950. 17 Vols. Moffatt's commentaries follow the text of Moffatt's translation of the New Testament in his famous work, *A New Translation of the Bible,* Revised Edition, 1935. Both the translation and the commentaries are widely read.

°*New Bible Commentary.* New Testament, Part Three, pp. 769-1199. Francis Davidson, A. M. Stibbs, and E. F. Kevan, General Editors. Grand Rapids: Eerdmans, Second Edition, 1954. Written by 50 men representing the best scholarship in England, Europe, and America today. Probably the best one-volume commentary in English today.

°*New International Commentary on the New Testament.* Ned B. Stonehouse, Editor. 17 volumes when completed; more than half have been issued. Grand Rapids: Eerdmans, 1950——. The volumes issued so far are of high quality.

New Testament Commentary. H. C. Alleman, Editor. Philadelphia: Muhlenberg Press, 1944.

°*Tyndale New Testament Commentaries.* R. V. G. Tasker of the University of London, General Editor. Grand Rapids: Eerdmans, 1957——. Ten volumes in this Series have appeared, all of which are of high quality. Generally briefer than the titles in *The New International Commentary.*

Westminster Commentaries. Walter Lock and D. C. Simpson, Editors. London: Methuen & Co., 1912-1934. Generally more conservative than *The Interpreter's Bible.*

II. OTHER BOOKS ON THE NEW TESTAMENT

Bright, John: *The Kingdom of God.* New Testament, Chapters 7-9. New York: Abingdon Press, 1953.

°Edersheim, Alfred: *The Life and Times of Jesus the Messiah.* 2 Vols. Eighth Revised Edition. Grand Rapids: Eerdmans, 1953. The work of a lifetime, and an outstanding contribution.

Filson, Floyd V.: *Opening the New Testament.* Philadelphia: Westminster Press, 1952.

Goodspeed, Edgar J.: *An Introduction to the New Testament.* Chicago: University of Chicago Press, 1937.

Heard, Richard: *An Introduction to the New Testament.* London: A. & C. Black Co., 1950.

°Hunter, Archibald M.: *Introducing the New Testament.* Philadelphia: Westminster Press, Revised and Enlarged Edition, 1958.

Josephus, Flavius: *The Antiquities of the Jews; The Wars of the Jews.* Translated by H. St. John Thackeray and Ralph Marcus. In the Loeb Library Translation, 8 Vols. London: William Heinemann, 1926——. A classic reference work, often referred to and quoted by scholars.

*Kee, Howard Clark and Franklin W. Young: *Understanding the New Testament.* Englewood Cliffs (N.J.): Prentice-Hall, Inc., 1957. A companion volume to Bernhard W. Anderson's *Understanding the Old Testament,* and with a similar approach to its subject matter. An outstanding contribution to New Testament interpretation, although in general liberal.

Kent, Charles Foster: *A History of the Jewish People During the Babylonian, Persian, and Greek Periods.* Fifth Edition. New York: Charles Scribner's Sons, 1902. A good reference book, although written from the liberal viewpoint.

*Levison, Nahum: *The Jewish Background of Christianity.* Edinburgh: T. & T. Clark, 1932.

*Machen, J. Gresham: *Christianity and Liberalism.* New York: Macmillan (now Grand Rapids: Eerdmans), 1923. The author is a conservative.

*McGregor, G. H. C.: *Jew and Greek, Tutors Unto Christ.* New York: Charles Scribner's Sons, 1936. The Jewish and Hellenistic background of the New Testament.

McNeile, A. H.: *An Introduction to the Study of the New Testament.* Revised by C. S. C. Williams. Oxford: Clarendon Press, 1953.

Milligan, George: *The New Testament Documents — Their Origin and Early History.* London: Macmillan Co., Ltd., 1913.

*Palmer, E. H.: *The Holy Spirit.* Grand Rapids: Baker Book House, 1958.

Richardson, Alan: *An Introduction to the Theology of the New Testament.* New York: Harper & Brothers, 1958.

*Swete, Henry B.: *The Holy Spirit in the New Testament.* London: Macmillan Co., 1910.

*Tenney, Merrill C.: *New Testament Survey.* Grand Rapids: Eerdmans, Second Revised Ed., 1961.

Thiessen, Henry C.: *Introduction to the New Testament.* Grand Rapids: Eerdmans, 1951.

Zahn, Theodor B.: *Introduction to the New Testament.* Translated and edited by J. M. Trout and Others, from the Third German Edition. 3 Vols. Edinburgh: T. & T. Clark, 1909. Grand Rapids: Kregel Publications, 1953. Very thorough and scholarly.

Part Five: Books on the Four Gospels

I. Jesus and the Four Gospels

Bowman, J. W.: *The Intention of Jesus.* Philadelphia: The Westminster Press, 1943.

Burkitt, F. C.: *The Gospel History and Its Transmission.* Edinburgh: T. & T. Clark Co., 1907.

Cadoux, C. J.: *The Historic Mission of Jesus.* New York: Harper & Brothers, 1943.

Colwell, E. C.: *An Approach to the Teaching of Jesus.* Nashville and New York: Abingdon-Cokesbury Press, 1947.

Dodd, C. H.: *Parables of the Kingdom.* New York: Charles Scribner's Sons, 1936.

*Edersheim, Alfred: *In the Days of Christ.* Chicago: Fleming H. Revell Co.

Fahling, Adam: *The Life of Christ.*

*Guignebert, C.: *The Jewish World in the Time of Jesus.* London: Routledge and Kegan Paul, 1939. One of the best studies of Judaism of the first century A.D.

Goguel, M.: *The Life of Jesus*. Translated by Olive Wyon. New York: The Macmillan Co., 1944. Deals with the form and method of Jesus' teaching.

*Hunter, Archibald M.: *The Work and Words of Jesus*. Philadelphia: The Westminster Press, 1951.

Jeremias, J.: *The Parables of Jesus*. Translated by S. H. Hooke. New York: Charles Scribner's Sons, 1956.

Knox, John: *The Man Christ Jesus*. Chicago: Willett, Clark & Co., 1941.

*Knox, John: *Christ the Lord*. Chicago: Willett, Clark & Co., 1945.

*Kraeling, Carl H.: *John the Baptist*. New York: Charles Scribner's Sons, 1951.

Love, J. P.: *The Gospel and the Gospels*. Nashville and New York: Abingdon-Cokesbury Press, 1953.

McCasland, S. Vernon: *By the Finger of God*. New York: The Macmillan Co., 1951.

Major, H. D. A., T. W. Manson, and J. C. Wright: *The Mission and Message of Jesus*. New York: E. P. Dutton and Co., 1938.

Manson, T. W.: *Jesus the Messiah*. Philadelphia: The Westminster Press, 1946.

*Manson, T. W.: *The Teaching of Jesus*. Cambridge: The University Press, 1948. A serious study of the teachings of Jesus.

Marshall, L. H.: *The Challenge of New Testament Ethics*. London: Macmillan & Co., 1950. A systematic treatment of the ethics of Jesus.

Moorhead, William G.: *Studies in the Four Gospels*. Westminster Handbooks. Philadelphia: The Westminster Press, 1900.

Robertson, A. T.: *The Pharisees and Jesus*. New York: Charles Scribner's Sons, 1920.

*Scroggie, W. Graham: *A Guide to the Gospels*. London: Pickering & Inglis, 1948. One of the best modern introductions to the content of the Gospels.

*Stewart, James S.: *The Life and Teaching of Jesus Christ*. Edinburgh: Church of Scotland Committee on Youth, 1954.

Streeter, B. H.: *The Four Gospels*. New York: The Macmillan Co., 1951.

Taylor, Vincent: *The Life and Ministry of Jesus*. Nashville and New York: Abingdon-Cokesbury Press, 1955.

*Tenney, Merrill C.: *The Genius of the Gospels*. Grand Rapids: Wm. B. Eerdmans Publishing Co., 1951.

*Wieand, Albert Cassel: *A New Harmony of the Gospels*. Text: *The Revised Standard Version*. Grand Rapids: Eerdmans, 1953. An important reference book for the *Revised Standard Version*, including useful diagrams and maps.

Wilder, A.: *Eschatology and the Ethics in the Teaching of Jesus*. New York: Harper & Brothers, Revised Edition, 1950.

Windisch, H.: *The Meaning of the Sermon on the Mount*. Translated by S. M. Gilmour. Philadelphia: The Westminster Press, 1951.

II. The Gospel of Matthew

*Barclay, William: *The Gospel of Matthew*. 2 Vols. Second Edition. Philadelphia: Westminster Press, 1958. Noted for his combination of scholarship and popular appeal.

Broadus, John A.: *The Gospel of Matthew*. American Commentary on the New Testament Series. Philadelphia: American Baptist Publication Society, 1886. Although it is old, it is still very good.

Dietrich, Suzanne de: *The Gospel According to Matthew*. Richmond: John Knox Press, 1964. Vol. 16 in the Layman's Bible Commentary. Series.

Green, F. W.: *The Gospel According to Matthew*. Oxford: Clarendon Press, 1945.

Lange, John Peter: *The Gospel According to Matthew*. Translated from the Third German Edition by Philip Schaff. Sixth Ed. New York: Charles Scribner's Sons, 1867. Still recommended.

McNeile, A. H.: *The Gospel According to Matthew*. London: Macmillan & Co., 1915.

Plummer, Alfred: *An Exegetical Commentary on the Gospel According to St. Mathew*. Grand Rapids: Eerdmans, 1953.

*Robertson, A. T.: *Commentary on the Gospel According to Matthew*. New York: Macmillan Co., 1911.

*Stonehouse, Ned B.: *Commentary on Matthew*. The New International Commentary on the New Testament Series. Grand Rapids: Eerdmans, 1955.

III. THE GOSPEL OF MARK

Alexander, Joseph Addison: *Commentary on the Gospel of Mark*. Grand Rapids: Zondervan, 1956.

*Barclay, William: *The Gospel of Mark*. *Second Edition*. Philadelphia: Westminster Press, 1956. Attractively written and scholarly.

Branscomb, B. H.: *The Gospel of Mark*. New York: Harper & Brothers, 1937.

*Cole, Alan: *The Gospel of Mark*. Grand Rapids: Eerdmans, 1960. The Tyndale New Testament Commentary Series.

*Groenewald, E. P.: *Commentary on Mark*. Grand Rapids: Eerdmans, 1956. The New International Commentary on the New Testament Series.

Lindsay, Thomas: *The Gospel According to St. Mark*. Edinburgh: T. & T. Clark, n.d. Handbooks for Bible Classes Series.

*Rawlinson, A. E. J.: *St. Mark*. London: Methuen & Co., 1934. The Westminster Commentaries Series.

Robertson, A. T.: *Studies in Mark's Gospel*. New York: The Macmillan Co., 1910. Lectures on certain aspects of Mark.

Swete, H. B.: *The Gospel According to St. Mark*. Third Ed. Grand Rapids: Eerdmans, 1951. One of the best advanced studies on Mark. Greek text.

Taylor, Vincent: *The Gospel According to St. Mark*. New York: Macmillan Co., 1953.

IV. THE GOSPEL OF LUKE

*Barclay, William: *The Gospel of Luke*. Second Edition. Philadelphia: Westminster Press, 1956. Dr. Barclay writes with a rich background of scholarship and understanding.

*Cadbury, H. J.: *The Making of Luke-Acts*. New York: Macmillan Co., 1927. Contains much useful background material. See the larger and fuller work of the period, *The Beginning of Christianity*, the five-volume study of Acts by F. J. Foakes-Jackson, K. Lake, and H. J. Cadbury, and others, under bibliography for the book of Acts.

Creed, J. M.: *The Gospel According to St. Luke*. London: Macmillan & Co., 1942.

*Geldenhuys, Norval: *Commentary on Luke*. The New International Commentary on the New Testament Series. Grand Rapids: Eerdmans, 1951. Probably the best modern commentary on Luke.

Godet, F.: *A Commentary on the Gospel of Luke*. Translated from the Second French Edition by E. W. Shalders and M. D. Cusin. Third Edition. New York: Funk and Wagnalls, 1887. Reprint: Grand Rapids, Zondervan, n.d. 2 Vols.

Lindsay, Thomas M.: *The Gospel According to St. Luke*. The Handbooks for Bible Classes Series. 2 Vols. Edinburgh: T. & T. Clark, n.d.

MacLachlan, H.: *St. Luke, The Man and His Work*. London: Longmans, Green & Co., 1920. Contains material on Luke's biographical and literary background.

*Miller, Donald G.: *The Gospel According to Luke*. Richmond: Layman's Bible Commentary Series, Vol. 18, John Knox Press, 1959. An excellent shorter interpretation.

Plummer, Alfred: *A Critical and Exegetical Commentary on Luke.* Fourth Ed. Edinburgh: T. & T. Clark, 1906.

*Ragg, Lonsdale: *St. Luke.* The Westminster Commentary Series. London: Methuen & Co., 1922. One of the better commentaries on Luke.

Robertson, A. T.: *Luke the Historian in the Light of Research.* New York: Charles Scribner's Sons, 1923.

*Stonehouse, Ned B.: *The Witness of Matthew and Mark (and of Luke) to Christ.* Grand Rapids: Eerdmans, 1958. 2 Vols.

Tittle, E. F.: *The Gospel According to Luke.* New York: Harper & Brothers, 1951.

V. THE GOSPEL OF JOHN

*Barclay, William: *The Gospel of John.* 2 Vols. Second Ed. Philadelphia: Westminster Press, 1958. The longest and perhaps the author's best commentary in the Daily Study Bible Series.

Dodd, C. H.: *The Interpretation of the Fourth Gospel.* Cambridge: University Press, 1958. Advanced, scholarly, Greek text.

Filson, Floyd V.: *The Gospel According to John.* Richmond: John Knox Press, 1960. The Layman's Bible Commentary Series, Vol. 19.

*Godet, Frederic: *Commentary on the Gospel of John.* 2 Vols. (Reprint) Grand Rapids: Zondervan, 1955.

Griffith-Thomas, W. H.: *The Apostle John, His Life and Writings.* Grand Rapids: Eerdmans, 1948.

Hendriksen, William: *The Gospel of John.* Grand Rapids: Baker Book House.

*Howard, W. F.: *Christianity According to St. John.* Philadelphia: Westminster Press, 1946.

Howard, W. F.: *The Fourth Gospel in Recent Criticism and Interpretation.* Third Edition. London: Epworth Press, 1945.

Nunn, H. P. V.: *The Son of Zebedee and the Fourth Gospel.* London: The Society for Promoting Christian Knowledge, 1927.

Robertson, A. T.: *Epochs in the Life of the Apostle John.* New York: Fleming H. Revell Co., 1935.

*Tenney, Merrill C.: *John, The Gospel of Belief.* Grand Rapids: Eerdmans, 1951.

Westcott, B. F.: *The Gospel According to John.* 2 Vols. London: John Murray, 1908. Very scholarly and thorough. Greek text.

*Westcott, B. F.: *The Gospel According to St. John.* Grand Rapids: Eerdmans, 1954.

Part Six: Books on the Acts of the Apostles

*Barclay, William: *The Acts of the Apostles.* Second Edition. Philadelphia: Westminster Press, 1956. Recommended especially for introductory students.

Blaiklock, E. M.: *The Acts of the Apostles.* Grand Rapids: Eerdmans, 1958. The Tyndale New Testament Commentaries.

*Bruce, F. F.: *The Spreading Flame — The Rise and Progress of Christianity.* Grand Rapids: Eerdmans, 1953. This volume combines the trilogy on the rise and progress of Christianity: *The Dawn of Christianity, The Growing Day,* and *Light in the West,* by the same author.

*Bruce, F. F.: *The Book of Acts.* Grand Rapids: Eerdmans, 1954. One of the best commentaries on the book of Acts. The New International Commentary on the New Testament Series.

Bruce, F. F.: *The Acts of the Apostles.* Grand Rapids: Eerdmans, 1952. Advanced; Greek text. An outstanding piece of scholarship.

Cadbury, H. J.: *The Making of Luke-Acts.* New York: Macmillan Co., 1927.

Clark, George W.: *Harmony of the Acts of the Apostles.* A New and Revised Edition. Philadelphia: American Baptist Publication Society, 1897. Still a useful work.

*Dodd, C. H.: *The Apostolic Preaching and Its Developments*. New York: Harper & Brothers, 1951. In this important work, Dr. Dodd deals with the primitive Christian message commonly referred to by its Greek name *kerygma*, or "the gospel behind the Gospels."

Enslin, M. S.: *Christian Beginnings*. New York: Harper & Brothers, 1938.

*Foakes-Jackson, F. J., K. Lake, H. J. Cadbury and others: *The Beginnings of Christianity*. 5 Vols. London: Macmillan & Co., 1920-1933. The fullest study in print on the book of Acts in relation to the origins of Christianity. It includes a thorough treatment of the historical backgrounds, the commentary on the text of Acts, and the various problems relating to the beginning of the Christian Church.

*Foakes-Jackson, F. J.: *The Acts of the Apostles*. New York: Harper & Brothers, 1931. Though much briefer than the five-volume work referred to above, this single volume is better for the non-technical reader.

Knox, John: *The Early Church and the Coming Great Church*. New York: The Abingdon Press, 1955.

Knox, W. L.: *The Acts of the Apostles*. Cambridge: University Press, 1948.

Lietzmann, H.: *The Beginnings of the Christian Church*. Translated by B. L. Woolf. New York: Charles Scribner's Sons, 1952. The history of the first century Church.

*Rackham, Richard B.: *The Acts of the Apostles*. Fourteenth Edition. London: Methuen & Co., 1951. The Westminster Commentaries Series. One of the finest commentaries on the book of Acts.

*Streeter, B. H.: *The Primitive Church*. New York: Macmillan Co., 1929. On the origins of the Christian ministry.

Willoughby, H. R.: *Pagan Regeneration*. Chicago: University of Chicago Press, 1929. A detailed description of the religions of the Graeco-Roman world.

Part Seven: Books on the Life and Letters of Paul

I. BOOKS ON THE LIFE AND WORK OF ST. PAUL

Bultmann, Rudolph: *Theology of the New Testament*, Vol. I. Translated by Kendrick Grobel. New York: Charles Scribner's Sons, 1951. A highly technical analysis of Paul's thought.

Conybeare, W. J. and J. S. Howson: *The Life and Epistles of St. Paul*. New Edition. Grand Rapids: Eerdmans, 1949. 850 pp.

*Davies, W. D.: *Paul and Rabbinic Judaism*. London: SPCK, 1948. An analysis of Paul's thinking against the background of first century rabbinic teaching.

Deissmann, A.: *Paul, A Study in Social and Religious History*. Translated by W. E. Wilson. New York: George H. Doran, 1926. A study in Paul's social and religious background.

*Dibelius, M. and W. G. Kuemmel: *Paul*. Philadelphia: Westminster Press, 1953. An attempt to reconstruct the life and thought of Paul.

*Dodd, C. H.: *The Meaning of Paul for Today*. New York: Meridian Books, 1957. A contribution to present day Christian thinking.

*Foakes-Jackson, F. J.: *The Life of St. Paul*. London: 1927.

Goguel, M.: *The Birth of Christianity*. New York: Macmillan Co., 1954. A favorite theme of this work is Paul's break with "Jewish Christianity."

Goodspeed, Edgar J.: *Paul*. New York: Abingdon Press, 1947.

Knox, John: *Chapters in a Life of Paul*. New York: Abingdon Press, 1950.

Knox, W. L.: *St. Paul and the Church at Jerusalem*. Cambridge: University Press, 1925. An analysis of the issues and relationships between Paul and the Jerusalem Christians.

*Machen, J. Gresham: *The Origin of Paul's Religion*. New York: Macmillan Co., 1923 (now Grand Rapids: Eerdmans).

Mackay, John: *God's Order*. New York: The Macmillan Co., 1953.

Nock, A. D.: *St. Paul.* New York: Harper & Brothers, 1938.

Ramsay, Sir William: *The Cities of St. Paul.* New York: Armstrong, 1908.

*Ramsay, Sir William: *St. Paul the Traveller and the Roman Citizen.* New York: G. P. Putnam's Sons, 1896. Contains much useful background information.

Robertson, A. T.: *Epochs in the Life of Paul.* New York: Charles Scribner's Sons, 1909.

*Robertson, A. T.: *Paul, The Interpreter of Christ.* New York: G. H. Doran Co., 1921.

Schweitzer, Albert: *Paul and His Interpreters.* Translated from the German by W. Montgomery. London: A. & C. Black Co., 1912.

Smith, David: *The Life and Letters of St. Paul.* New York: G. H. Doran Co., 1920.

*Stewart, James S.: *A Man in Christ.* New York: Harper & Brothers, 1935. A conservative and constructive treatment of Paul's thought, in terms of his religious experience.

Wood, C. T.: *The Life, Letters, and Religion of St. Paul.* Edinburgh: T. & T. Clark, 1946. A somewhat comprehensive treatment of the whole of Paul.

II. Letters of the First Period: Written During the Second Missionary Journey, 50-53 a.d.

I and II THESSALONIANS

Hendriksen, William: *I and II Thessalonians.* Grand Rapids: Baker Book House.

Milligan, George: *St. Paul's Epistles to the Thessalonians.* Grand Rapids: Eerdmans, 1952. This work is based on the Greek text; very thorough.

*Morris, Leon: *The Epistles of Paul to the Thessalonians.* Grand Rapids: Eerdmans, 1957. The Tyndale New Testament Commentaries.

*Neil, W.: *The Epistles of Paul to the Thessalonians.* New York: Harper & Brothers, 1950. The Moffatt New Testament Commentary Series.

Rolston, Holmes: *Paul's I and II Thessalonians, I and II Timothy, Titus, and Philemon.* Richmond: John Knox Press, 1963. The Layman's Bible Commentary Series, Vol. 23.

III. Letters of the Second Period: Written During the Third Missionary Journey, 54-58 a.d.

GALATIANS

Findlay, George G.: *The Epistle to the Galatians.* New York: Armstrong & Co., n.d. The Expositor's Bible.

*Hunter, Archibald M.: *The Letters of Paul to the Galatians, Ephesians, Philippians, and Colossians.* John Knox Press, 1959. The Layman's Bible Commentary, Vol. 22. A very good brief introduction and commentary.

Lightfoot, J. B.: *St. Paul's Epistle to the Galatians.* London: Macmillan & Co., 1921. Scholarly; Greek text.

*Luther, Martin: *Commentary on Galatians.* A New Edition. Grand Rapids: Eerdmans, 1930. 536 pp. Here the student has an opportunity to become acquainted with a great classic.

*Machen, J. Gresham: *The Origin of Paul's Religion,* Chapter 3. Grand Rapids: Eerdmans, 1947. Widely recommended.

Ramsay, Sir William: *A Historical Commentary on St. Paul's Epistle to the Galatians.* New York: G. P. Putnam's Sons, 1900.

*Ridderbos, Herman H.: *Commentary on Galatians.* Grand Rapids: Eerdmans, 1953. The New International Commentary on the New Testament Series. One of the best commentaries on Galatians.

Ropes, J. H.: *The Singular Problem of the Epistle to the Galatians.* Cambridge: Harvard University Press, 1929.

*Tenney, Merrill C.: *Galatians, The Charter of Christian Liberty.* Grand Rapids: Eerdmans, 1951.

I and II CORINTHIANS

*Barclay, William: *The Letters to the Corinthians.* Second Edition. Philadelphia: Westminster Press, 1956. The Daily Study Bible Series.

Foreman, Kenneth J.: *Paul's Letters to the Romans and Corinthians.* Richmond: John Knox Press, 1962. The Layman's Bible Commentary, Vol. 21.

Godet, F.: *Commentary on St. Paul's First Epistle to the Corinthians.* Translated from the French by A. Cusin. 2 Vols. Edinburgh: T. & T. Clark Co., 1889. (Now Grand Rapids: Zondervan, 1957.)

*Grosheide, F. W.: *Commentary on the First Epistle to the Corinthians.* Grand Rapids: Eerdmans, 1953. New International Commentary on the New Testament Series.

Hodge, Charles: *An Exposition of the First and Second Epistles to the Corinthians.* 2 Vols. Grand Rapids: Eerdmans, 1950.

*Hughes, Philip E.: *Commentary on the Second Epistle to the Corinthians.* Grand Rapids: Eerdmans, 1952. New International Commentary on the New Testament Series.

Kennedy, James H.: *The Second and Third Epistles of Paul to the Corinthians.* London: Methuen & Co., 1900.

McFadyen, John E.: *The Epistles to the Corinthians.* Hodder & Stoughton, 1911.

Moffatt, James: *The First Epistle of Paul to the Corinthians.* New York: Harper & Brothers, 1938. The Moffatt New Testament Series.

*Morris, Leon: *Paul's First Corinthians.* Grand Rapids: Eerdmans, 1958. The Tyndale New Testament Commentaries Series.

Strachan, R. H.: *The Second Epistle of Paul to the Corinthians.* New York: Harper & Brothers, 1938. The Moffatt New Testament Commentary Series.

*Tasker, R. V. G.: *Paul's Second Corinthians.* Grand Rapids: Eerdmans, 1958. The Tyndale New Testament Commentaries Series.

ROMANS

*Barclay, William: *The Letter to the Romans.* Philadelphia: Westminster Press, 1957. Second Edition. The Daily Study Bible Series.

Barth, Karl: *A Shorter Commentary on Romans.* Richmond: John Knox Press, 1959.

*Calvin, John: *The Epistle of St. Paul to the Romans.* A New Edition. Grand Rapids: Eerdmans, 1947. Here the introductory student has an opportunity to become acquainted with another great classic. Calvin's commentaries are surprisingly modern and relevant.

*Dodd, C. H.: *The Epistle to the Romans.* New York: Harper & Brothers, 1932. The Moffatt New Testament Commentary Series. The English text.

Foreman, Kenneth J.: *Paul's Letter to the Romans* and *I and II Corinthians.* Richmond: John Knox Press, 1962. The Layman's Bible Commentary Series, Vol. 21.

Godet, Frederic: *Commentary on the Epistle to the Romans.* Grand Rapids: Zondervan, 1956. (Reprint.)

*Hodge, Charles: *Commentary on the Epistle to the Romans.* New Edition, Revised. Grand Rapids: Eerdmans, 1951. Theological.

*Murray, John: *Commentary on Romans.* Grand Rapids: Eerdmans, 1958. New International Commentary on the New Testament Series.

Moule, Handley: *The Epistle of St. Paul to the Romans.* New York: A. C. Armstrong & Son, 1894. The Expositor's Bible. Still useful.

McQuilkin, Robert C.: *The Message of Romans*. Grand Rapids: Zondervan Publishing House, 1947.

Thomas, W. H. Griffith: *Romans I-XVI, A Devotional Commentary*. Grand Rapids: Eerdmans, 1953.

IV. LETTERS OF THE THIRD PERIOD: WRITTEN DURING PAUL'S FIRST IMPRISONMENT AT ROME, 61-63 A.D.

COLOSSIANS, EPHESIANS, PHILEMON

Findlay, G. C.: *The Epistle to the Ephesians*. Grand Rapids: Eerdmans, 1947. The Expositor's Bible.

Goodspeed, Edgar J.: *The Meaning of Ephesians*. Chicago: University of Chicago Press, 1933.

Hodge, Charles: *Commentary on the Epistle to the Ephesians*. Grand Rapids: Eerdmans, 1950.

*Hunter, Archibald M.: *The Letters of Paul to Galatians, Ephesians, Philippians, and Colossians*. Richmond: John Knox Press, 1959. The Layman's Bible Commentary.

Knox, John: *Philemon Among the Letters of Paul*. Chicago: University of Chicago Press, 1935.

Lightfoot, J. B.: *The Epistle of Paul to Colossians and Philemon*. London: Macmillan & Co., 1892. Scholarly; Greek text.

Miller, H. S.: *The Book of Ephesians*. Houghton (N.Y.): The Word-Bearer Press, 1931.

*Radford, Lewis B.: *The Epistle to the Colossians and the Epistle to Philemon*. London: Methuen & Co., 1931. The Westminster Commentaries.

Robertson, A. T.: *Paul and the Intellectuals*. Garden City: Doubleday, Doran & Co., 1928.

Scott, E. F.: *The Epistles of St. Paul to the Colossians, to Philemon, and to the Ephesians*. London: Macmillan Co., 1906.

*Simpson, E. K. and F. F. Bruce: *Commentary on the Epistles to the Ephesians and the Colossians*. Grand Rapids: Eerdmans, 1958. The New International Commentary on the New Testament Series. An excellent commentary.

Westcott, B. F.: *A Letter to Asia*. London: Macmillan & Co., 1914.

PHILIPPIANS

Lightfoot, J. B.: *St. Paul's Epistle to the Philippians*. Eighth Edition. London: Macmillan & Co., 1888. Advanced; Greek text.

*Martin, R. P.: *The Epistle to the Philippians*. Grand Rapids: Eerdmans, 1958. The Tyndale Commentaries.

Michael, J. H.: *The Epistle of Paul to the Philippians*. London: Hodder & Stoughton Co., 1928.

Moule, H. G. C.: *Philippian Studies*. Fifth Edition. London: Hodder & Stoughton Co., 1904.

*Muller, Jac. J.: *Commentary on Philippians and Philemon*. Grand Rapids: Eerdmans, 1955. Revised Edition. The New International Commentary on the New Testament Series.

Robertson, A. T.: *Paul's Joy in Christ*. New York: Fleming H. Revell & Co., 1917.

HEBREWS

*Barclay, William: *The Letter to the Hebrews*. Second Edition. Philadelphia: Westminster Press, 1957. Rich in scholarship and experience; readable.

Bowman, John Wick: *The Letters of Hebrews, James, and I and II Peter*. Richmond: John Knox Press, 1961. The Layman's Bible Commentary Series, Vol. 24.

Bruce, A. B.: *The Epistle to the Hebrews.* New York: Charles Scribner's Sons, 1899.

*Bruce, F. F.: *Commentary on Hebrews.* Grand Rapids: Eerdmans, 1959. New International Commentary on the New Testament Series.

Davidson, A. B.: *Hebrews.* Edinburgh: T. & T. Clark, 1950.

*Hewitt, Thomas: *The Epistle to the Hebrews.* Grand Rapids: Eerdmans, 1960. The Tyndale New Testament Series.

Manson, William: *The Epistle to the Hebrews.* London: Hodder & Stoughton Co., 1951.

*Murray, Andrew: *The Holiest of All.* New York: A. D. F. Randolph & Co., n.d.

Scott, E. F.: *The Epistle to the Hebrews.* London: Hodder & Stoughton Co., 1933. The Moffatt New Testament Commentary Series.

Westcott, B. F.: *The Epistle to the Hebrews.* Second Edition. Grand Rapids: Eerdmans, 1950. Advanced; Greek text. Thorough and scholarly.

V. Letters of the Fourth Period: Written After Paul's Release from First and During Second Imprisonment at Rome, About 64-67 A.D.

I TIMOTHY, TITUS, II TIMOTHY

*Easton, B. S.: *The Pastoral Epistles.* New York: Charles Scribner's Sons, 1947.

Falconer, Sir Robert: *The Pastoral Epistles.* Oxford: Clarendon Press, 1937. Introduction, Translation and Commentary.

*Guthrie, Donald: *The Pastoral Epistles.* Grand Rapids: Eerdmans, 1957. The Tyndale New Testament Commentaries.

Harrison, P. N.: *The Problem of the Pastoral Epistles.* London: Oxford University Press, 1921.

Hendriksen, William: *I and II Timothy and Titus.* Grand Rapids: Baker Book House.

Hillard, A. E.: *The Pastoral Epistles of St. Paul.* London: Rivingtons, 1910. Commentary; Greek text.

James, J. D.: *The Genuineness and Authorship of the Pastoral Epistles.* London: Longmans, Green & Co., 1906.

Parry, R. St. John: *The Pastoral Epistles.* Cambridge: Cambridge University Press, 1920. Text, and Commentary.

Rolston, Holmes: *Paul's I and II Thessalonians, I and II Timothy, Titus, and Philemon.* Richmond: John Knox Press, 1963. The Layman's Bible Commentary Series, Vol. 23.

Scott, E. F.: *The Pastoral Epistles.* New York: Harper & Brothers, 1936. The Moffatt New Testament Commentary Series.

Shaw, R. D.: *The Pauline Epistles.* Edinburgh: T. & T. Clark, 1903.

*Simpson, E. K.: *The Pastoral Epistles.* Grand Rapids: Eerdmans, 1954.

Part Eight: Books on the Letters by the Apostles James, Peter, Jude, and John

I. Books on the General Epistles and Their Background

Cullmann, O.: *The State in the New Testament.* New York: Charles Scribner's Sons, 1956. Deals with the relation of the Church and the Roman government.

*Goguel, M.: *The Birth of Christianity.* New York: Macmillan Co., 1954. Chapters 2 and 3 of Part II give a careful reconstruction of the fall of Jerusalem (70 A.D.) and the end of the Apostolic Age. Pages 393-435 treat the theme of "false teaching" in the early Church.

*Harnack, A.: *The Mission and Expansion of Christianity in the First Three Centuries.* New York: G. P. Putnam's Sons, 1908. Translated by James Moffatt, Vol. I. A thorough study of the development of the Church in relation to its environment.

Knox, John: *The Early Church and the Coming Great Church.* New York: Abingdon Press, 1955. Deals with the development of organization in the early Church.

Lietzmann, H.: *The Beginnings of the Christian Church.* New York: Charles Scribner's Sons, 1952. Translated by B. L. Woolf. A survey of the historical development of the New Testament Church.

*Moffatt, James: *The General Epistles.* New York: Harper & Brothers, 1928. The Moffatt New Testament Commentary Series.

*Streeter, B. H.: *The Primitive Church.* New York: Macmillan Co., 1929. See on the origins of the Christian ministry.

II. Books on the Letter of James

Knowling, R. J.: *The Epistle of St. James.* London: Methuen & Co., 1904. The Westminster Commentary Series.

Mayor, Joseph B.: *The Epistle of St. James.* Third Edition. London: Macmillan & Co., 1910.

*Ross, Alexander: *Commentary on the Epistles of James and John.* Grand Rapids: Eerdmans, 1954. The New International Commentary on the New Testament.

*Tasker, R. V. G.: *The Epistle of James.* Grand Rapids: Eerdmans, 1958. The Tyndale New Testament Commentaries.

(See James Moffatt above, *The General Epistles,* which contains one of the best commentaries on James; also Goguel's *The Birth of Christianity,* chapter 6 of Part IV.)

III. Books on I and II Peter, and Jude

Beare, F. W.: *The First Epistle of St. Peter.* Oxford: Blackwell & Mott Co., 1947.

*Foakes-Jackson, F. J.: *Peter, Prince of Apostles.* London: Macmillan & Co., 1927.

Mayor, Joseph B.: *The Epistle of St. Jude and the Second Epistle of St. Peter.* London: Macmillan & Co., 1907.

*Robertson, A. T.: *Epochs in the Life of St. Peter.* New York: Charles Scribner's Sons, 1933.

Selwyn, E. G.: *The First Epistle of St. Peter.* London: Macmillan & Co., 1946.

*Skilton, John H.: *The Epistles of Peter and Jude.* Grand Rapids: Eerdmans, 1952. The New International Commentary on the New Testament Series.

*Stibbs, A. M.: *The First Epistle of Peter.* Grand Rapids: Eerdmans, 1956. The Tyndale New Testament Commentaries. Highly recommended.

Thomas, W. H. Griffith: *The Apostle Peter.* Grand Rapids: Eerdmans, 1946.

*Wand, J. W. C.: *The General Epistles of St. Peter and St. Jude.* London: Methuen & Co., 1934. The Westminster Commentaries.

IV. Books on I John, II John, and III John

*Love, Julian Price: *The Letters of I John, II John, III John, Jude, and Revelation.* John Knox Press, 1960. The Layman's Bible Commentary, Vol. 25.

Robertson, A. T.: *Epochs in the Life of the Apostle John.* New York: Fleming H. Revell Co., 1935.

*Thomas, W. H. Griffith: *The Apostle John, His Life and Writings.* Grand Rapids: Eerdmans, 1948.

Westcott, B. F.: *The Epistles of John.* Third Edition. Grand Rapids: Eerdmans, 1950. Scholarly; Greek text.

(See also Alexander Ross' volume listed above, *Epistles of James and John;* James Moffatt's *General Epistles;* and other works devoted in part to the Epistles of John.)

V. Books on the Revelation

Baldinger, A. H.: *Sermons on Revelation.* New York: George H. Doran Co., 1924.

Beckwith, Isbon T.: *The Apocalypse of John.* New York: Macmillan Co., 1919.

Case, Shirley Jackson: *The Revelation of John.* Chicago: University of Chicago Press, 1919.

Charles, R. H.: *The Revelation of St. John.* New York: Charles Scribner's Sons, 1920. A complete analysis of Revelation.

Dean, J. T.: *The Book of the Revelation.* Edinburgh: T. & T. Clark, 1915.

Guy, H. A.: *The New Testament Doctrine of the Last Things.* New York: Oxford, 1948.

*Hendriksen, William: *More Than Conquerors.* Grand Rapids: Baker Book House.

*Kiddle, M.: *The Revelation of St. John.* New York: Harper & Brothers, 1940.

Lang, G. H.: *The Revelation of Jesus Christ.* London: Oliphants, Ltd., 1945.

Moorhead, Wm. G.: *Studies in the Book of Revelation.* New York: Fleming H. Revell Co., 1908.

Morris: *The Drama of Christianity.*

*Ramsay, Sir William: *The Letters to the Seven Churches of Asia.* New York: George H. Doran Co., 1905. Deals with the historical and archaeological background of "the Seven Churches."

*Stonehouse, Ned B.: *Commentary on the Revelation.* Grand Rapids: Eerdmans, 1956.

*Swete, Henry B.: *The Apocalypse of St. John.* London: Macmillan & Co., 1911 (now Grand Rapids: Eerdmans, 1951).

*Tenney, Merrill C.: *Interpreting Revelation.* Grand Rapids: Eerdmans, 1957.

INDEX

View of Mount Hermon and the
Sea of Galilee. © Matson Photo Service